Language in the British Isles

THE UNIVERSITY OF
WINCHESTER

The British Isles are home to a vast range of different spoken languages and dialects. Language continues to evolve rapidly, in its diversity, in the number and the backgrounds of its speakers and in the repercussions it has had for political and educational affairs. This book provides a comprehensive survey of the dominant languages and dialects used in the British Isles. Topics covered include the history of English, the relationship between Standard and Non-Standard Englishes, the major non-standard varieties spoken on the islands, the history of multilingualism, and the educational and planning implications of linguistic diversity in the British Isles. Among the many dialects and languages surveyed by the volume are British Black English, Celtic languages, Chinese, Indian, European migrant languages, British Sign Language, and Anglo-Romani. Clear and accessible in its approach, it will be welcomed by students in sociolinguistics, English language and dialectology, as well as anyone interested more generally in language within British society.

David Britain is Senior Lecturer in Linguistics at the University of Essex. His recent publications include the books *Social Dialectology: In Honour of Peter Trudgill* (2003, edited with Jenny Cheshire) and *Linguistics: An Introduction* (1999, with Andrew Radford, Martin Atkinson, Harald Clahsen and Andrew Spencer, published by Cambridge University Press).

Language in the British Isles

Edited by
David Britain

CAMBRIDGE
UNIVERSITY PRESS

CAMBRIDGE UNIVERSITY PRESS
Cambridge, New York, Melbourne, Madrid, Cape Town, Singapore, São Paulo

Cambridge University Press
The Edinburgh Building, Cambridge CB2 8RU, UK

Published in the United States of America by Cambridge University Press,
New York

www.cambridge.org
Information on this title: www.cambridge.org/9780521794886

© Cambridge University Press 2007

First published 2007

Printed in the United Kingdom at the University Press, Cambridge

A catalogue record for this publication is available from the British Library

ISBN 978-0-521-79150-2 hardback
ISBN 978-0-521-79488-6 paperback

Contents

Contents

Figures

Tables

Contributors

Dennis Ager, School of Languages and Social Sciences, Aston University, UK

Peter Bakker, Afdeling for Lingvistik, Institut for Antropologi, Arkæologi og Lingvistik, Aarhus University, Denmark

Martin Ball, Department of Communicative Disorders, University of Louisiana at Lafayette, USA and Centre for Speech and Language Therapy, University of Wales Institute, Cardiff, UK

David Britain, Department of Language and Linguistics, Essex University, UK

Gerard Docherty, School of Education, Communication and Language Sciences, Newcastle University, UK

Paul Foulkes, Department of Language and Linguistic Science, University of York, UK

Penelope Gardner-Chloros, School of Languages, Linguistics and Culture, Birkbeck, University of London, UK

Mark Gibson, School of Healthcare, University of Leeds, UK

Andrew Hamer, Department of English Language and Literature, Liverpool University, UK

Roxy Harris, Centre for Language, Discourse and Communication, King's College London, UK

Raymond Hickey, English Linguistics, Essen University, Germany

Paul A. Johnston, Jr., Department of English, Western Michigan University, USA

Mari C. Jones, Peterhouse and the Department of French, University of Cambridge, UK

Donald Kenrick, Independent Scholar

Paul Kerswill, Department of Linguistics and English Language, Lancaster University, UK

Constant Leung, Centre for Language, Discourse and Communication, King's College London, UK

Li Wei, School of Languages, Linguistics and Culture, Birkbeck, University of London, UK

Kenneth MacKinnon, Department of Celtic, University of Aberdeen, UK

Kevin McCafferty, Department of English, University of Bergen, Norway

James Milroy, Centre for Linguistics and Philology, University of Oxford, UK

Pádraig Ó Riagáin, School of Linguistic, Speech and Communication Sciences, Trinity College, Dublin

Robert Penhallurick, Department of English, School of Arts, Swansea Unversity, UK

Heinrich Ramisch, Englische Sprachwissenschaft und Mediävistik, Otto-Friedrich-Universität Bamberg, Germany

Ben Rampton, Centre for Language, Discourse and Communication, King's College London, UK

Mike Reynolds, MultiLingual City Forum, Sheffield, UK

Paul Russell, Department of Anglo-Saxon, Norse and Celtic, University of Cambridge, UK

Mark Sebba, Department of Linguistics and English Language, Lancaster University, UK

Rachel Sutton-Spence, Centre for Deaf Studies, University of Bristol, UK

Mahendra Verma, Department of Language and Linguistic Science, University of York, UK

Ann Williams, Department of Linguistics & English Language, University of Wales, Bangor Gwynedd, UK

Bencie Woll, Deafness, Cognition and Language Research Centre, Department of Human Communication Science, University College London, UK

Acknowledgements

This volume was a long time in the making – there's been a wedding, a funeral, two births and two moves since this all began. I thank all of the patient and prompt authors who contributed work to this volume, Mark Gibson for stepping in at the last minute, Kate Brett and Andrew Winnard from Cambridge University Press for setting the whole thing off and seeing it through, and Jenny Cheshire and Viv Edwards for advice along the way.

Many thanks to Molly and Ella for their patience while dad was stuck in front of the [kəmpu:ʔə] and to Sue for always being there.

Map of the British Isles

Introduction

David Britain

Over twenty years have passed since Peter Trudgill's first edition of *Language in the British Isles* (Trudgill 1984a). A great deal has happened in those years, both to the British Isles in ways which have had fundamental linguistic consequences, and in terms of the research which has been conducted on issues concerning the way people on these islands use language. This volume attempts to provide a snapshot both of the languages and dialects spoken and signed here, and of some of the implications for education of that linguistic diversity.

At the beginning of the century, almost 60 million people lived in the UK[1] and almost 4 million in the Irish Republic.[2] In the UK, around 4.6 million people claimed an ethnicity other than White[3] (and the White category included a large number of people claiming White Irish ethnicity and 1.3 million people who claimed an 'Other-White' ethnicity, of which only 20% were born in the UK (Gardener & Connolly 2005:7)), or roughly 7.9% of the total, representing an increase of 53% since the previous census in 1991.[4] Since the last British census in 2001, the non-White population has continued to increase. There has been a net inflow of population of at least 100,000 per annum in every year since 1998, and in 2004 the net inflow was 223,000.[5] The Irish Republic didn't ask questions about ethnicity in its 2002 census,[6] but 5.8% of the population had a nationality which was not Irish. These islands are, therefore, increasingly multiethnic. This volume consequently includes chapters which survey the histories and current sociolinguistic status of some of the larger ethnic minority languages of the islands: the Indic languages, Chinese, the

---

[1] http://www.statistics.gov.uk/cci/nugget.asp?id = 6. This, and all other websites listed in this chapter, were last accessed on 11th April 2006.
[2] http://www.cso.ie/census/prelim_press_release.htm
[3] http://www.statistics.gov.uk/cci/nugget.asp?id = 455
[4] http://www.statistics.gov.uk/cci/nugget.asp?id = 273
[5] http://www.statistics.gov.uk/cci/nugget.asp?id = 1311
[6] Though its 2006 census did.

Englishes and creoles of the British Black community and the languages of European immigrants. Perhaps surprisingly, we know especially little about this latter European language group. Many Europeans have the automatic right to travel, live and work in the UK and Ireland because of their home countries' EU membership, but many are classed as 'White' in the census and so headline figures often misleadingly underestimate the size of the non-White British, non-anglophone community. A case in point here is the Portuguese community of the largely rural Norfolk district of Breckland, which most estimates put at around 15,000–20,000 strong (roughly 12–16% of the total population in a district of 124,000). The 2001 census data for the district, however, appear unaware of the Portuguese community[7] there because most of its members claim 'White' ethnicity.

Frustratingly for linguists, and surely for policy makers too, the British and Irish censuses do not collect information about language use (other than use of the indigenous Celtic languages in Wales, Scotland and Ireland), so our understanding of the numbers of speakers of spoken and signed languages other than English and the Celtic languages is actually extremely limited and often based on relatively crude calculations based on the size of the ethnic minority population.[8] Furthermore, and unlike in the USA and New Zealand in particular, we know very little indeed about the varieties of English spoken by the ethnic minority population (apart from that spoken by the British Black community), though a few studies are beginning to appear which address this issue (Fox 2007, A. Khan 2007, Khattab 2002a, 2002b).

The size and linguistic practices of one of Britain's longer resident ethnic groups is perhaps even less well understood. Unlike in Ireland,[9] the British census and the British authorities in general make little serious attempt to put an accurate figure to the traveller/Gypsy community,[10] and it is recognised as being one of the most deprived ethnic groups in the UK on a wide range of measures, such as health indicators and educational achievement, largely because of its invisibility and isolation. Yet in a number of parts of Britain it is claimed to be the largest ethnic minority

[7] http://www.statistics.gov.uk/census2001/profiles/33UB-A.asp
[8] On 8 March 2006, the Office for National Statistics (ONS) in the UK produced a news release saying that a 'strong case' had been made for a language question in the 2011 census to enable equality legislation to be properly monitored and for service provision to ethnic minority groups to be improved – http://www.statistics.gov.uk/pdfdir/cenew0306.pdf
[9] The Irish Census of 2002 finds 23,000 Irish Travellers, and provides detailed coverage of their employment, health and housing status – see http://www.cso.ie/census/documents/vol8_entire.pdf
[10] The Office of the Deputy Prime Minister commissions twice-yearly 'Caravan counts' which, of course, ignore those of Gypsy/traveller ethnicity who are settled.

group, for example, in Cambridgeshire.[11] This lack of information is all the more surprising given that this community has felt the brunt of a swathe of recent government legislation which directly impacts it, such as the Anti-Social Behaviour Act (2003), the Planning and Compulsory Purchase Act (2004) and the Criminal Justice and Public Order Act (1994). Consequently we know very little indeed about their linguistic behaviour, including, for example, whether or not there exists a distinctive traveller/ Gypsy variety of English (see Britain 2003). Included in this volume is a chapter on their ancestral language, Angloromani.

Angloromani as a living language is in a somewhat precarious position. Some languages of the British Isles which did fall into obsolescence are now undergoing attempted revivals (e.g. Cornish – see Sayers 2005). French in the Channel Islands clings on to life. The 2001 census for Jersey, for example, makes the seriousness of the decline of Jérriais quite clear: 'Jersey French was spoken by a total of 2,874 people (3.2% of the population). Of this total, two-thirds were aged 60 and over. The number of Jersey French speakers in 2001 was half the number recorded in 1989' (Etat Civil Committee 2002:23). Of this 2,874, just 113 claimed it as their first language.

In 2003, British Sign Language was recognised by the British government, alongside English and the Celtic languages Welsh, Gaelic and Irish. Woll and Sutton-Spence in this volume put the number of signers at between 30,000 and 60,000. It will be interesting to see what effect recognition has on the status and visibility of signed languages, and how resources and infrastructure will be targeted for a speech community that is not concentrated in clustered geographical locales.

The censuses of 2001 in the UK provided mixed news for the surviving Celtic languages. Overall figures for Welsh show a small increase in the number of speakers, but this hides quite considerable fluctuations. H. Jones (2005:7), comparing the 1991 and 2001 censuses, shows a marked increase by 2001 in the numbers of school-aged children claiming to be able to speak Welsh, but also a decline in the numbers of retired people who speak the language. Worryingly, in comparing the number of 15-year-olds who claimed to be able to speak Welsh in 1991, with the number of 25-year-olds a decade later, who also claimed to speak the language, he found that the number had dropped by a third (2005:5). He proposes a number of reasons for this decline, including inaccurate completion of questionnaires by parents on behalf of the 15-year-olds, and loss of confidence in the language. These comparisons are both useful and important, because they

[11] http://www.cambridgeshire.gov.uk/community/travellers/

show the extent to which educational provision in Welsh is triggering (or not) long-term acquisition and maintenance of the language. The number of people in Scotland claiming to speak Gaelic was down by 11% in 2001 and the only areas showing an increase in speakers were those areas outside the traditional heartlands (Registrar General for Scotland 2005). The Northern Irish Census reports 75,000 people who can read, write and speak Irish, and a further 92,000 with a more limited competence in the language.[12] In the Irish Republic, approximately 40% of the population claimed to be able to speak Irish, but as Ó Riagáin warns in this volume, most of this number have but a moderate command of the language and their 'ability did not typically express itself in active use of Irish in conversation, but in passive, non-reciprocal activities'.

The British Isles also constitute a mobile population. One in every nine people had moved in the year before the 2001 census in the UK,[13] and the gradual population shift out of the large conurbations towards the suburbs and the countryside continues. Of all the English counties in the 2001 census, those which were growing the most were Cambridgeshire, Oxfordshire, Buckinghamshire, Lincolnshire and Wiltshire, all with population increases of over 7% since 1991,[14] with Merseyside, Tyne and Wear, Cleveland and the West Midlands all shrinking in population terms over the same period. This mobility has linguistic repercussions (see, for example, Trudgill 1986) and a number of the chapters on varieties of English in this volume point to mobility-induced linguistic changes such as dialect levelling. The book contains chapters on the Englishes of each of the main states and islands/island groupings of the British Isles, as well as one for standard varieties of English, and these contributions highlight ongoing changes, the social embedding of non-standard varieties, and the consequences, for example, of language contact on the grammars and phonologies of our Englishes.

The volume concludes with three chapters on applied sociolinguistic concerns. Given the rapid demographic change that was mentioned earlier, the final section begins with a chapter on language policy and planning, which tracks how policy makers have addressed the language issues that have arisen from large-scale immigration, commitments under Human Rights and other EU legislation and the call for increased educational provision to meet the needs of a diverse and multicultural population. The final two chapters address educational issues – of English speakers who do not speak Standard English as their first variety – a solid majority of the

---

[12] http://www.nicensus2001.gov.uk/nica/common/home.jsp
[13] http://www.statistics.gov.uk/cci/nugget.asp?id = 1310
[14] http://www.cornwall.gov.uk/index.cfm?articleid = 10605

Anglophones in the British Isles – and of those residents of these islands whose first language is not English.

Language in the British Isles has evolved rapidly since 1984, and continues to do so, in its diversity, in the number and the backgrounds of its speakers and in the repercussions it has had for political and educational affairs. This volume, I hope, provides a brief glimpse at some of the notable landmarks in this ongoing journey.

Part I

English

1   The history of English

James Milroy

Introduction

Typological change

During the past nine centuries, English has undergone more dramatic changes than any other major European language in the same period. Old English was moderately highly inflected for case, number, gender, tense, mood and other grammatical categories. Present English, however, has a vastly simplified inflectional morphology with total loss of inflections in, for example, adjectives and the definite article, and very considerable inflectional losses in other word classes. There have also been many phonological changes, and the lexicon has been altered from mainly Germanic to a mixed Germanic–Romance type. In syntax, a mixed SVO–SOV word order has become mainly SVO, and there have been great changes in the tense, mood and aspect systems of the verb. These changes, taken together, amount to a typological change from mainly synthetic to mainly analytic, and to considerable modification of the Germanic character of English. As a result, OE (Anglo-Saxon) is not immediately accessible to the modern native reader and can be acquired only through intensive study – as though it were a foreign language.

Origins and geographical spread

English is descended from the Germanic branch of the Indo-European family of languages. Within this it is assigned to the West Germanic group, and its nearest relative is Frisian (still spoken by a few thousand people on the coasts and islands of northern Germany and the Netherlands), with which OE shared some common developments (for example, raising of Germanic (Gmc) /a/ to /æ/: 'Anglo-Frisian brightening'). It is also closely related to Dutch and Low German, and slightly less closely to High (standard) German.

The beginnings of English as a distinct language are conventionally placed at AD 449, at which date Angles, Saxons and Jutes from the

9

north-west European continent are reputed to have begun their settlement in Britain. They brought with them a series of related West Germanic dialects, which at this time could hardly have differed significantly from those that remained on the Continent. Thus, this conventional date depends on geography and politics, rather than on internal structural distinctiveness of Anglo-Saxon as a separate language. Those Germanic dialects that were spoken on British soil are retrospectively known as Old English (also as Anglo-Saxon). The first appearance of the name 'English' (*englisc*) for the language is in the late ninth century in King Alfred's writings.

By the seventh century, Anglo-Saxon dialects had been established in the several kingdoms in east and central Britain as far north as Edinburgh, while dialects of Celtic (Cymric) were still in use in the west from Cornwall to Cumbria and Strathclyde. Since then, English has continued to displace the Celtic languages, to the extent that some have disappeared, and there are now probably no monoglot speakers of those that remain.

Chronology

Scholars have traditionally distinguished three periods in the history of English. The OE period lasts from the first Anglo-Saxon settlements in Britain until just after the Norman Conquest, i.e. 1100–1150. The transition from OE to Middle English (ME) appears in the texts to be abrupt, even in the earliest extensive ME text (the final Peterborough continuation of the *Anglo-Saxon Chronicle*, c.1154), although some areas retained more OE features than others. The break between ME and Modern English (ModE) is less clear. The conventional date for the transition (c.1500) is dictated, not by any substantial shift in linguistic form, but by cultural factors such as the introduction of printing in the late fifteenth century.

There is difficulty in assigning precise dates to specific changes. This is because most changes in spoken language occur first in specific speech communities, and not in the entire 'language' as represented by the written form. They may then diffuse more or less widely and may ultimately become changes in 'English' and recorded in writing. Traditionally, historians of English have tended to assign a late date to any attested change – the date at which it is completed in the whole language or well-defined dialect area. Work in sociolinguistics in recent years (see Milroy 1992) suggests that such a date is often the endpoint of the diffusion of a change that may have been completed considerably earlier in some specific speech community or locality. Therefore, many changes detected in written English at some particular date could well have originated much earlier. We shall bear this difficulty in mind.

Old English as a Germanic language

Phonology

OE, like other Germanic languages, usually has its main stress on the root syllable of words. This results from a very early change known as Germanic accent shift, and it has some consequences for the general phonology. A series of Indo-European (IE) vowel-shift rules, known collectively as *ablaut*, are preserved more systematically in Gmc than in other IE languages, particularly in the 'strong verb' system. Thus OE:

Infinitive	Pret. sing.	Pret. pl.	Past part.	
drīfan	*drāf*	*drifon*	*ʒedrifen*	'drive'
singan	*sang*	*sungon*	*ʒesungen*	'sing'

The vowel variations are ascribed to the effects of variable pitch accent and stress accent in IE. In IE the preterite plural/past participle forms had stress on the suffix with a 'zero' vowel in the root syllable; in Germanic the stress was shifted to the root syllable, and a short vowel then appeared in that syllable. Ablaut variation is well represented in the strong verb. It also affected other parts of the lexicon, as in present-day English (PresEng) *ride* (v.), *road* (n.).

In the consonant system, OE shares with other Gmc languages the reflexes of the 'First Consonant Shift', which stipulates that certain series of Gmc obstruents correspond to related series in IE. For example, the IE voiceless stop series: /p, t, k, kw/ (as in Latin *piscis, tres, cornu, quando*) correspond to Gmc /f, þ, x, xw/ (as in PresEng *fish, three, horn, when*). When one of these fricatives, or /s/, had occurred in IE in syllables that did not bear the main stress and in voiced surroundings, they were additionally subject to voicing in Germanic, by the operation of 'Verner's Law'. OE preserves many of the reflexes of this, for example in the accent-shifted preterite plural/past participle of strong verbs such as *weorþan* 'become' (pret. sing. *wearþ*, pret. pl. *wurdon*: the voiced fricative in the latter is presumed to have developed to /d/). Verner's Law alternations have been almost completely levelled out in PresEng, but with occasional residues such as *was/were; seethe/sodden* (< OE *sēoþan* 'boil').

Of the various vowel changes that took effect within the OE period, the most important is i-*umlaut* or 'front mutation'. This operated when, in Gmc, [i] or [j] followed in the succeeding syllable: under these conditions a low or back vowel in the root syllable was raised and/or fronted. The process can be thought of as vowel harmony or anticipatory assimilation in height and/or frontness. It was pre-literary in date and had, amongst other things, the effect of creating new vowel alternations within noun and verb paradigms: thus, OE *mūs* 'mouse', *mȳs* 'mice'; *fōt* 'foot', *fēt* 'feet'. All other extant Gmc languages except Gothic have i-umlaut, but they appear to have implemented it independently.

OE is also affected by common West Gmc changes, for example, consonant gemination before original [j] (cf. OE *sittan* < **sitjan*, but ON *sitja* 'sit'), and rhotacism, whereby [z] > [r]: thus, OE *wǣron* < Gmc **wǣzun* 'were'.

Various specifically OE changes, such as breaking and back mutation, have few consequences at the present day; however, there was a general tendency towards palatalisation of [k, sk, g] (under various conditions) which gives the following contrasts: PresEng *choose, cheese, edge, fish* (OE *cēosan, cīese, ecg, fisc*); cf. Gothic *kiusan*, German *Käse, Ecke*, Danish *fisk*.

Morphology

OE was rather highly inflected with, for example, three genders, four cases (with residues of a fifth – instrumental), inflected determiners and adjectives and many different conjugations of verbs and declensions of nouns.

The Germanic features not shared with other IE languages affect chiefly the adjectives and verbs. OE distinguishes between the 'strong' (definite) and 'weak' (indefinite) declensions of adjectives, the weak declension being used when some definite element (e.g. the definite article or demonstrative) precedes the adjective, and the strong declension otherwise. The distinction was lost at varying dates in ME dialects.

Verbs are divided into two inflectional types, also known traditionally as 'strong' and 'weak'. Strong verbs form their preterite and past participle by undergoing change of the root vowel (by ablaut), whereas weak verbs add a suffix containing a dental (or alveolar) consonant. Whereas the strong verb vowel alternations are descended from IE, the dental preterite weak verbs are peculiar to Gmc. They are of less ancient origin and can often be shown to be derivatives of strong verbs or of other parts of speech. The relation between the following pair, for instance, is causative, and the weak verb is derived in Proto-Gmc from the preterite of the strong:

	Infinitive	Pret. sing.	Pret. pl.	Past part.		
Strong:	*licȝan*	*læȝ*	*lāȝon*	*ȝeleȝen*	'lie'	
Weak:	*lecȝan*	*lēde*	*lēdon*	*ȝelēd*	'lay'	(i.e. 'cause to lie')

The strong and weak verbs remain in PresEng, with some tendency for strong verbs to transfer to the weak system, but with some transfers in the opposite direction. Thus:

	OE	PresEng
help	strong	weak
weep	strong	weak
wear	weak	strong

Some weak verbs like *hide/hid, sell/sold* owe their 'strong' appearance to various conditioned sound changes in pre-OE, OE, ME and Early Modern English (EModE), and not to IE ablaut.

Syntax

Some of the syntactic differences between OE and PresEng reflect the typological difference between a highly inflected and weakly inflected language. Thus, OE had many more surface rules of agreement, concord and government than PresEng has.

OE *word order* was also noticeably different from PresEng (see further Traugott 1972). Although variable, it generally conformed to rules similar to those of modern German. Single main clauses normally had SVO order. Embedded or subordinate clauses had SOV order. VS order occurred in interrogatives and in declaratives introduced by adverbials or object noun phrases. Thus, in the following sentence the italicised noun clause has SOV order:

(1) Ōhthere sǣde his hlāforde ... *þæt hē ealra Norðmanna norðmest būde*
     'Ohthere said to his lord ... *that he of all Northmen northmost lived*'

SOV order is also generally found in OE relative clauses and in subordinate clauses of time, place, result, condition, etc. As the subordinate clause is the object in (1), the sentence as a whole has SVO order. SOV order, however, is also found in a second or subsequent co-ordinate clause, as in:

(2) Hē fōr on Bretanie ... *and wið þā Brettas gefeaht*
     'He went to Britain ... *and against the Britons fought*'

The VS order in negative declaratives is demonstrated in:

(3) Ne con ic nōht singan
     'I cannot sing' (lit. 'Not can I not at all sing')

While the subordinate temporal clause in the following example is SOV, the italicised main clause demonstrates the Gmc 'verb-second rule', which is still usual in Gmc languages (except for English).

(4) Þā ic ðā ðis eall gemunde, *ðā gemunde ic ...*
     'When I then this all remembered, *then remembered I ...*'

The inverted VS order after adverbials is usual in OE, but the order becomes more variable in ME. In EModE it remains mainly in more formal literary styles, especially poetry. In spoken PresEng, the main residues of VS order in statements are after certain negative or quasi-negative adverbs, as in:

(5)   Never have I seen such a thing
      Scarcely had he arrived . . .

Lexicon

It is clear from the above examples that the grammar of OE was that of an older Gmc language. The OE lexicon was also predominantly Gmc, although some everyday words had been borrowed into West Gmc (before the Anglo-Saxon migration to Britain) from Latin (or from Greek through Latin) and are therefore common to West Gmc languages. These include OE *cīēse* 'cheese', *strǣt* 'street', *cyrice* 'church', *biscop* 'bishop' and *cealc* 'chalk'. Borrowing from Latin and Greek in the OE period is often ecclesiastical in type and includes *candel* 'candle', *mynster* 'monastery' and *reogol* 'rule'.

There are few borrowings from the indigenous Celtic: examples are *brat* 'apron' and *brocc* 'badger'. Scandinavian influence on the lexicon was very heavy in many areas in late OE, but does not become evident in surviving texts until after the breakdown of the West Saxon scribal and literary tradition; i.e. after the Norman Conquest.

The Germanic character of the OE lexicon is again clear in its methods of word formation. Abstract, technical and intellectual terms were derived by compounding and affixation from the basic word stock. Examples are: *þrīnes* 'trinity' (lit. 'three-ness'), *rīmcræft* 'arithmetic' (lit. 'rime-craft': skill in numbers), *þrōwung(e)* 'suffering', 'passion' and *ārfæstnesse* 'piety' (lit. 'fastness', i.e. firmness, in reverence). The later English preference for borrowing abstract terms from French, Latin and Greek (and Arabic) came about not because the OE language was incapable of expressing the ideas in its own terms, but because of the sociopolitical and linguistic consequences of the Norman Conquest. These borrowings have displaced most of the OE abstract vocabulary.

Dialectal variation in OE

The Germanic peoples who settled in different parts of Britain appear to have spoken slightly divergent dialects from the beginning, and their approximate geographical distribution is evident in the four main literary dialects. Reputedly, the Angles settled in the Midlands and east between the Thames and the Forth. The main Anglian dialects are conventionally known as Northumbrian (north of the Humber) and Mercian (from the Humber to the Thames). The Jutes settled in Kent and along the south coast to the Isle of Wight: the OE dialect of that area is Kentish. Among the Saxons, the West Saxon dialect proved dominant and was used in the rest of the OE-speaking area to the south and west of the Thames.

After the Viking invasions and wars of the eighth and ninth centuries, most Anglian-speaking areas came under Danish rule (the *Danelaw*). West Saxon, the language of Wessex, which was not in the Danelaw, became the main OE literary language, and, unlike Anglian, it was only trivially influenced by Norse. Fewer records remain of Anglian dialects (Mercian and Northumbrian), but these, and not West Saxon, are the direct forebears of Standard English.

The development of Modern English

Divergence of Middle and Modern English from Old English

It is clear from the above citations from OE, and from the heavily Germanic nature of OE vocabulary and syntax, that it was very different from PresEng. Not only is PresEng a weakly inflected language, it is also a less 'Germanic' language than OE. Other Germanic languages have reduced inflections, but none except Afrikaans has lost grammatical gender, and no other Germanic language is as un-Germanic as English in vocabulary and syntax. The change started early. Already in the twelfth century, we can detect substantial divergence from late eleventh-century written OE. By the mid-thirteenth century, ME texts are beginning to look like 'English' as we know it today. This thirteenth-century lyric is an example (first two lines cited):

> When þe nyhtegale singes þe wodes waxen grene.
> Lef ant gras ant blosme springes in Aueryl, Y wene ...
> [Bennett & Smithers 1966:126]

Conventional histories of English have tended to present the transition from OE to ME as smooth and uninterrupted. This opinion is encouraged by a strong tradition which asserts that English is a very ancient language, and that, despite appearances to the contrary, OE is the 'same' language as PresEng. In the nineteenth century, much of the underlying purpose of this was to give the language a long and glorious history and a noble lineage, as befitted the mighty nation-state in which it had developed. One effect of this ideological stance was to overstate the similarities between OE and PresEng.

These overstatements continue to appear. Kaufman (Thomason & Kaufman 1988:263–331), in a highly eccentric case study, declares that

English has changed more since c.1600 than it did in the years 900–1300 (from OE to ME). This claim is not defensible by any competent internal analysis, and the case study is best regarded as a latter-day attempt by a non-anglicist to support the traditional position. The internal changes between 900 and 1300 are vastly greater than the (admittedly considerable) changes between 1600 and 2000.

The traditional view was that the sharp break between OE and ME is more apparent than real. First, many orthographic changes may be purely scribal, not reflecting phonological changes. For example, the substitution of *a* for OE *æ* does not necessarily indicate lowering and/or retraction of OE /æ/ (ME *sat*, OE *sæt*). Second, the conservative West Saxon scribal tradition may well have concealed the presence of changes already beginning in spoken OE by the tenth century or so. Indeed, some changes are already detectable in our scanty records of Old Northumbrian (Smith 1996:94).

Despite this necessary caution, it is clear that these medieval changes were by any standards considerable. The first substantial ME text, the final Peterborough extension to the *Anglo-Saxon Chronicle* (c.1154), already shows many changes from late OE. As the West Saxon scribal tradition had been disrupted, the orthography is variable, already much influenced by French conventions, and there is French influence on vocabulary. Nielsen's (1998:210) summary of changes mentions 'conspicuous' changes in accented and unaccented vowels, loss of most of the noun stem-classes of OE (with generalisation of the -*as* plural) and simplification of the case and gender systems. OE inflections are drastically reduced and grammatical gender has actually disappeared. Nielsen also notes the loss of the aspectual prefixes of OE: *a-, be-, ȝe-* and *of-*, which has consequences for syntax. Subsequently, texts dating from c.1200–1300 show considerable variation in orthography and dialect, with varying degrees of lexical influence from French and Scandinavian and varying simplification of inflections.

The degree of conservatism in Early ME texts correlates with their geographical provenance. South-west and south-west Midland texts (*Ancrene Wisse*, Caligula MS of Laȝamon's *Brut*) are conservative in that they maintain, among other things, relatively full inflection and grammatical gender. Early texts from counties south of the Thames are also quite conservative. The more innovatory texts (e.g. *Havelok*) tend to be from the east Midlands and East Anglia. There are few northern records of early ME, but the following fragment from York, dated 1272, is well advanced towards modern Scottish and northern English dialects:

> Wel, qwa sal thir hornes blau
> Haly Rod thi day

Nou is he dede and lies law
Was wont to blaw thaim ay

['Alas, who shall blow these horns, Holy Cross (on) thy day? Now is he dead and
lies low, (who) was wont to blow them always'] ([Dickins & Wilson 1951:118])

The traditional view has been that the structural changes between c.900
and c.1300 would have taken place anyway, even if there had been no
contacts with Old Norse and Norman French. However, it is unlikely to be
a coincidence that the 'conservative' texts (those most like OE) are from
areas in which the invaders had little immediate influence, while the
'advanced' texts come from areas where both influences were strong. In
the West Midlands, as Bennett & Smithers (1966:ix) note, 'the saintly
Saxon Wulfstan was left on his episcopal throne', and Norman influence
was slow to penetrate there. The above 'advanced' northern text, on the
other hand, contains a demonstrative, personal pronoun and verb inflection that are all from Scandinavian (*thir* 'these', *thaim* 'them', 3rd sg.
pres. *-es*). Although the traditional view is that the structural differences
between OE and ME were internally triggered, many of them are probably
due to, or accelerated by, language contact.

Some scholars have claimed that language contact was so intimate that
it led to creolisation of the language. C.-J. Bailey (1996) has argued that
ME is so radically altered that it is no longer a Germanic language, but a
mixed language built on a French-based creole. This emphasises the
importance of French. Pat Poussa (1982), on the other hand, has argued
that ME is based on an Anglo-Danish creole that arose in late OE times in
the Danelaw, before the arrival of the Normans. Very little is directly
known about the details of mixing of populations during the Scandinavian
settlements, but the traditional view was that the settlers were numerous
and the two populations roughly equal in social status. Scandinavian
placenames are very numerous in the east Midlands, North Yorkshire
and elsewhere, and many traditional dialects in these regions have a
heavily Scandinavian everyday vocabulary. It is possible, however, that
some Danish settlers formed an aristocracy, as their influence on administrative matters is very clear; thus many Scandinavian borrowings may
have been prestige borrowings. However this may be, the languages were
similar, and the settlers seem to have been rapidly assimilated. Thus, the
contact with Old Norse is more likely than the contact with French to have
triggered in OE spoken usage the kind of structural changes that become
apparent in ME.

It does not necessarily follow, however, that late OE actually went through
a creole stage – unless 'creole' is loosely defined. A number of general
tendencies observed in creoles are also found in bilingual and multilingual

situations, such as those that existed during contact with Norse and Norman French. These include loss of inflections and development of an analytic structure and fixed word order, and these tendencies can result from the need for communication, in times of rapid social change, between speakers who do not have reliable knowledge of each other's languages.

The contact with Norman French differed in important ways from the contact with Norse. The Norman settlers were few in number, but they immediately seized positions of national political power. Contact with Normandy was maintained until 1204, and until that time Anglo-Norman was being spoken and had prestige as a literary language and the language of government. During the thirteenth century, however, Anglo-Norman as a spoken language became sharply recessive. It survived until the later fourteenth century as an official language of administration and law. Laura Wright (1996) has shown how much Anglo-Norman also contributed to the mixed or 'macaronic' written codes that were used in London business dealings in these centuries.

The *structural* effect of these contacts was not, in general, direct borrowing from the grammatical apparatus of Scandinavian and French, although Old Norse did supply some pronouns, determiners and inflections. The structural simplifications did not chiefly result from any particular characteristics of Norse and Norman French, but from the contact situation itself, in which speakers in daily use abandon distinctions that might be considered redundant or inessential to everyday communication. Although OE and Old Norse were related, there were substantial morphological differences, and neither could have been *easily* intelligible to speakers of the other (Milroy 1997). Some 'accommodation' (Trudgill 1986:1–38) was certainly necessary on a large scale, and the structural simplifications in ME could have arisen from these efforts at accommodation.

The development of Standard English

Even though there were several major social upheavals in the centuries after 1300, English in Britain was never again subjected to the cataclysmic effects of invasion followed by bilingualism and language mixing. The language has, however, been subjected to other important influences, chiefly that of Central French from about 1250 to 1500 and the classical languages (Latin and Greek) from 1500 onwards. These effects have come about through formal and literary, rather than everyday spoken, channels and are largely lexical (see pages 31–2). Their importance has been to increase the vocabulary available for formal and technical uses of the language and hence to contribute to the *functional elaboration* (Haugen 1966) that is involved in progress towards a national *standard* language.

Although late West Saxon had developed a near-standard literary form, English after the Conquest was cut off from any immediate possibility of developing into a national standard language. There were many reasons for this, including immense variability in written forms (Smith (1996:68) points out that about 500 spellings of the word *through* are recorded in ME), but the chief reason was that Norman French, rather than English, was used for official and administrative purposes, and so English could not acquire the status associated with official languages. A second reason for the low status of English was that Latin was the language of learning, and this continued to be the case until about 1700. In one sense the history of English since 1200 is one of rising 'respectability' and the gradual acquisition of a wider range of functions, including administrative and learned functions.

From the Middle Ages onward, there is a literature of complaint about the low status and inadequacies of English. Robert of Gloucester (c.1300) complains that a man must know French if he is to be well thought of. In the late fifteenth century Caxton is faced with the problem of devising a normalised language for use in printed books. He is perplexed by the variability of English and complains that the language is like the moon ... 'which is neuer stedfaste/but euer Wauerynge/wexynge one season/and waneth and dycreaseth another season'.

Sixteenth-century writers regard the language as lacking in eloquence and seek to 'improve' it by large-scale lexical borrowing from Latin and Greek (Jones 1953). Seventeenth-century writers can still think of English as ephemeral and unimportant: it is not until the eighteenth century that the status of English is finally assured. Swift in 1712, while continuing the complaint tradition ('I do complain to your lordship ... that our language is extremely imperfect...'), is confident enough of the importance of English to propose that the language should be fixed and standardised ('ascertained') by an academy. However, the task of codifying and standardising was in fact carried out by private persons: the lexicon and orthography are codified in Dr Johnson's Dictionary of 1755, and the grammar is codified in a spate of grammar books, the most influential of which was Bishop Lowth's *Introduction to English Grammar* (1762).

The chief linguistic symptom of a standardised language is *invariance*, which comes about from the suppression of optional variants at all levels of language structure. In this (strict) sense, standardisation has been fully achieved only in the written channel: English speech is still extremely variable, especially in phonology but also in other ways. It is also clear that standardisation has come about as a result of commercial, political and social needs rather than for purely linguistic reasons or through the direct influence of literary works, but it is implemented largely through the written medium. Technological advance, starting with the invention of printing and the commercial need to disseminate printed documents, has been instrumental in diffusing knowledge of standard forms.

Some movements towards a national written standard are retrospectively discernible around 1400. Samuels (1963) distinguishes four types of 'incipient standards', including the London-based language of Chaucer and, especially, the *Chancery Standard* – the language of legal and administrative documents – which showed similarities to Central Midland dialects and is seen by some as the main forerunner of the PresEng written standard. These pre-standards were not invariant, but the variation exhibited was within stricter limits than that of earlier ME documents. Conventional approaches to the rise of the standard have, however, been selective, neglecting early commercial and business writing (Wright 1996:3). It may no longer be as important as it used to be to trace the origin of standard English to any single regional 'dialect'. A standardised language has multiple origins – both linguistic and social, and it is susceptible to deliberate planning.

Phonological change since 1100

Interpreting the evidence

Progressive standardisation of written records from about 1500 has led conventional histories of English to concentrate from that period almost exclusively on the history of Standard English (SE). Thus, Southern British SE sound changes, such as rounding of [a] after labials (as in *swan, quart*), are described in the handbooks as changes in 'English', even though many varieties do not have this rounding. Regional and low-status changes, on the other hand, such as loss of initial [h], are either dismissed or not mentioned, although they are also unquestionably sound changes. The very diverse dialects of PresEng in the British Isles have their own histories, greater knowledge of which would increase our knowledge of the nature and processes of linguistic change.

Our sources for reconstructing EModE pronunciation are: (1) the testimony of sixteenth- and seventeenth-century writers on pronunciation – the 'orthoepists' (Dobson 1968); (2) casual and informal spellings in personal letters and diaries (Wyld 1936); (3) the evidence of rhymes and puns; (4) 'the use of the present to explain the past' – reconstruction of past uses from forms preserved in PresEng dialects. Advances in dialectology in recent years suggest that the fourth type of source has much to offer (Labov 1994, Milroy 1992). Using the findings of the *Survey of English Dialects* (Orton *et al.* 1962–71), Ogura (1990) has thrown light on the geographical diffusion of vowel changes in the history of English. Stockwell & Minkova (1997) have made impressive use of the same source to illuminate the history of the 'Great Vowel Shift' – to which we now turn.

The Great Vowel Shift

If we compare a selected set of OE words with their PresEng equivalents, it is clear that there have been many phonological changes since OE times. Consider OE *īs* [iːs] 'ice', *fēt* [feːt] 'feet', *hām* [hɑːm] 'home', *gōs* [goːs] 'goose' and *hūs* [huːs] 'house'. In these instances, the spelling suggests that the consonants have not changed; however, the vowels certainly have. For example, the long high vowels [iː] and [uː] as in *īs* 'ice'; *hūs* 'house' have become diphthongs with the first element of the diphthong having been lowered in each case to a vowel as low as [a] in many dialects. Thus, we have [ai, ɑʊ] in *ice*, *house*. In general, consonants have not changed as much as vowels, and ME long vowels (as in the forms cited) have changed much more than ME short vowels.

The series of changes that brought about the present reflexes of the earlier long vowels is known collectively as the 'Great Vowel Shift' (GVS). This appears retrospectively as a 'chain shift' in which the low and mid long vowels were each raised one height, and the two high vowels diphthongised. Thus, by about 1600 in the London area, it is likely that ME /aː/ had been raised to /ɛ/, as in [nɛːm] 'name', ME /ɛː/ to /eː/, as in [meːt] 'meat', ME /eː/ to /iː/, as in [miːt] 'meet' and ME /iː/ diphthongised to /ei/, as in [beit] 'bite'. In the back vowel series ME /ɔː/ had been raised to /oː/, as in [hoːm] 'home', ME /oː/ to /uː/, as in [guːs] 'goose' and ME /uː/ diphthongised to /əʊ/, as in [əʊt] 'out'.

There is dispute about how the GVS was implemented (e.g. which vowel moved first), whether it is a unitary phenomenon or not, how far the ME input vowels were monophthongs or diphthongs and what was the EModE pronunciation of the affected vowels. It is usually assumed that in the shift, the vowel contrasts had to be maintained; thus, as one vowel shifted, a second also shifted in order to remain distinct from the first ('push-chain') or to fill a gap left by the first ('drag-chain') – and so on. Some argue that it started with diphthongisation of the two highest vowels /iː/ and /uː/, as prior movement of /eː/ and /oː/ would have brought about merger with the highest vowels; however, some occasional spellings from before 1400 suggest a very early movement of the mid-vowel /oː/ towards a higher vowel (see Lass 1999:75). Therefore, it is also argued that it started with the mid-vowels. It is unlikely that the ME input vowels were all monophthongs, although this is what is usually assumed: the distribution of centring diphthongs (such as [eə] or [ɛə] in, e.g. *gate*) in present-day northern dialects suggests that some were centring diphthongs (see especially Stockwell & Minkova 1997). It is difficult also to see the GVS as a unitary phenomenon, as the dialects of ME were grossly divergent from one another, and the outcomes of the shift differed widely in different places. Furthermore, the vowel changes did not all take place simultaneously (raising of /aː/ in London was noticed much later than raising of /eː/ and /oː/, for example). The EModE pattern described above may represent a coming together of changes originating in different varieties and at different times. It is an idealisation that greatly simplifies a complex situation. Furthermore, conventional descriptions of the GVS apply mainly to what is now viewed as *standard* English.

In southern England, the vowels of 1600 have undergone subsequent changes. In EModE there was much variation between [eː] and [iː] in the *meat* set; this is now effectively merged with the *meet* set. There has been a marked tendency towards development of closing glides – notably EModE /eː/ and /oː/, which are now [ei, əʊ] (as in *name, home*) in RP. The first elements of the EModE diphthongs have been considerably lowered: thus EModE [ei, əʊ] in, e.g. *ice, house* are now (approximately) [ai, aʊ] in RP.

London urban speech, together with other southern and Midland (and southern hemisphere) dialects, has carried the GVS a stage farther than RP has. For example, PresEng /ei/ (< EModE /eː/) has been lowered to [ai]: thus, *mate* becomes almost identical to RP *mite*. The diphthong [ai], as in *pint*, has undergone rounding to [ɔi]. Merger with /ɔi/ is avoided by raising [ɔi] to [oi]; thus, *pint* and *point* remain distinct. If the GVS is regarded as a unitary phenomenon, then it is plainly still in progress in these dialects.

The patterns so far described above apply mainly to the south of England. Other British English dialects have either implemented a similar pattern at different rates or implemented a somewhat different pattern of shift. Dialects in many rural areas or in towns remote from London have implemented the shift more slowly than RP. In some dialects, for example Northumbrian and Ulster English, the diphthong arising from ME /iː/ has not categorically lowered its first element beyond the EModE stage: thus, *ride*, for example, is [reid]. Some dialects, e.g. north-west England, maintain [ɛː] in words of the *name, make* class, and others, notably Irish English, maintain (variably) the EModE distinction between the *meet* class and the *meat* class (/iː/ vs. /eː/).

In dialects derived from Old Northumbrian, the GVS took a different form. The main differences are in the 'original' back vowels, and the results can be seen in Lowland Scots. In these dialects ME /uː/ was not diphthongised, but remained in, e.g. *oot, hoose* 'out, house'. Thus, ME /oː/ could not be raised to /uː/, as in *boot*, without merger. It was fronted to a vowel near /yː/ or slightly lower, and is unrounded in many Scots dialects: thus [bɪt] 'boot'. OE /ɑ:/ in *ham* 'home', was not raised to /ɔ:/ in northern ME, but was front-raised and unrounded; thus, Scots *hame*, *stane* 'home, stone'.

Restructuring and alternations

While the ME long vowels have been massively changed in quality, the short vowels have changed much less. In RP, ME short *i*, *e* and *a* have changed relatively little, although they have probably been subject in the past to fluctuation, sometimes being raised or diphthongised, sometimes lowered or backed. ME short *u* was lowered and unrounded in older Scots, and in southern varieties of English except after labials (cf. *sup/pull*, both from ME *u*). In northern and many Midland dialects, *u* failed to lower and unround; in these *look* and *luck* can be homophones. In southern England ME, *a* and *o* were lengthened before /s, θ, f/, and in some dialects they were also backed: hence RP has a contrast between *pat* ([æ]) and *path* ([ɑ:]) and between *cot* ([ɒ]) and (conservative) *cloth* ([ɔ:]). In many varieties, as noted above, *a* was not rounded after [w]. In these, *wasp*, for example, has [a].

Failure of the short vowels to change dramatically (while the long vowels were subject to raising and diphthongisation) has resulted in a configuration of the vowel system that is very different from OE. In some dialects, e.g. Scots, these changes have led to a large-scale loss of phonemic length. In OE, it is believed, long and short *i*, for example, were distinguished mainly by length. In modern Scots, however, the vowels in *bead* and *bid* are about the same length, but are markedly different in quality. Scots vowel length is usually allophonic and does not distinguish phonemes; thus, /i/ in *seed* is a short vowel, but in *seize* a (very) long one. Most other varieties have a phonemic contrast between long and short vowels, but the lexical distribution of these has been greatly altered since ME.

The ME vowel system presumed as a basis for the GVS already showed phonetic and structural differences from the OE system. OE long and short /y/ had merged, in the east Midlands, with /i:/ and /i/ respectively, and the West Saxon (long and short) diphthongs spelt *io*, *eo* and *ie* were monophthongal in most of ME. New diphthongs /ai, au, oi/ arose in ME from various sources. Short vowels in open syllables were subject to 'open syllable lengthening' (MEOSL), and the products of this (examples are: OE /a, ɛ/ > ME /a:, ɛ:/ > PresEng *make*, *steal*) later participated as long vowels in the GVS. OE /ɑ:/ was raised and rounded to /ɔ:/ quite early in the south and Midlands, and this /ɔ:/ also subsequently participated in the GVS. This example suggests that some tendency towards raising of long vowels was already present around 1200. The GVS may therefore be regarded not as a particular change with a determinate beginning and end, but as a manifestation of a general tendency to raise long vowels, which was accelerated in late ME/EModE, but which may have been in progress long before in some dialects. In this view, it is the acceleration of this tendency during a particular time span that historical linguists must try to explain. Smith (1996) argues that earlier contact with Old Norse was a triggering factor.

The redistribution of long and short vowels referred to above has greatly complicated the outcomes of the GVS. In the history of English there have been a series of lengthenings of original short vowels and shortenings of original long vowels under specified conditions. Original long vowels that have been shortened have from that point failed to participate in the GVS. Not only have lexical items with an original long vowel become short vowel items (as in *foot, deaf*), but also derivationally related pairs in PresEng may now be seen to alternate between the reflexes of the original 'long' and 'short' vowels, as in, e.g. *serene/serenity*.

Alternations generally arise from variation in syllable structure and syllabification. Thus, an alternation such as /iː/ vs. /ɛ/ in *steal/stealth* arises from MEOSL. As ME [ɛ] in *stelen* 'steal' was in an open syllable, it was lengthened, whereas [ɛ] in *stelþe* was not – and could not therefore partic-ipate in the GVS. Alternations such as *keep/kept* and *five/fifty* arise from late OE shortening before consonant clusters (other than sonorant con-sonant + homorganic voiced stop, e.g. [-nd, -ld]) and geminates. Pairs such as *south/southern, sheep/shepherd* arise from late OE/early ME shortening in trisyllabic words (see e.g. Fisiak 1968 for further details). These and other quantitative changes give rise to complex vowel-shift networks in related words in PresEng.

For some later shortenings affecting RP, the phonetic conditioning factors are not always clear, and in these cases different dialects exhibit widely varying patterns. ME [oː] in *flōd, blōd* should give *[fluːd], etc. by the GVS, but these items together with others underwent shortening early enough to participate in the southern English change of short /u/ to /ʌ/ (from about 1550). Other items from the same source, ME /oː/, (e.g. *good, foot*) underwent later shortening in EModE, and their vowel fell together with ME short /u/ when it remained rounded (i.e. after labials, as in *push, full*, etc.). Thus, the RP /ʊ/ class today (*good, foot, full*, etc.) is largely composed of ME /oː/ items that underwent late shortening and ME short /u/ items with initial labials.

Consonants

Changes in the consonant system have been less dramatic. OE had long consonants (as in *sittan* 'sit'), but these were generally lost by 1400. OE did not have a phonemic contrast between voiced and voiceless fricatives: the contrast begins to appear in intervocalic positions in the north-east Midlands around 1200 and is then reinforced in all positions by borrowing from French (e.g. *vertu* 'virtue'; OE had no initial voiced labial fricative). There have been numerous cluster simplifications: OE initial /hl, hr, hn/ were merged with /l, r, n/ in ME; initial /hw/ was merged with /w/ in some ME dialects, but still remains in some present-day dialects; medial and final /xt/, as in OE *riht* 'right', remains in Lowland Scots; but the fricative was lost (with vowel lengthening) in some ME dialects and was probably generally lost in most London and east Midland areas before 1600. Final [b] was lost after [m] in ME (as in *lamb*, *dumb*, etc.), but parallel loss of [g] after [ŋ] (as in *sing*) has been variable: it was lost quite early in Scots and was probably variable in EModE, but the stop remains today in west Midland dialects. Loss of the alveolar stop [d], after [n] seems to have been widespread around 1700: its probable loss is indicated by hyper-correct spellings such as *gownd* 'gown' and the survival of the hypercor-rection *sound* (ME *soun* < Fr *soun*) (see Wyld 1936).

Consonant simplification has proceeded further in regional varieties than in RP. Syllable-initial /h/ is lost in many vernaculars; London English merges /ð, θ/ with /v, f/ except in voiced initial position; loss of final /t/ after other obstruents is very common, so common that in some dialects (Lowland Scots, northern Hiberno-English) the weak verbs *keep*, *sleep*, etc. have the past tenses *kep*, *slep*, etc. and are effectively reanalysed as strong verbs; loss of final [d] after [l] and [n] is also widespread, as in Scots *fin'* 'find'; Ulster [weil] 'wild'. Loss of pre-consonantal [r] (especially) before [s] had already taken place in some south-east Midland varieties by about 1500 and enabled forms like *cuss*, *hoss* and *passel* to be translated to the New World. General loss of non-prevocalic /r/ was probably in pro-gress in the sixteenth century, but could hardly have been complete in 'polite' London English until much later – possibly even the late nineteenth century. Its loss in some dialects has resulted in a division into rhotic and non-rhotic dialects (Wells 1982). In addition to RP, eastern English and Midland varieties are mostly non-rhotic. Rhotic dialects include those of Scotland, Ireland and many in England south and west of a curved line running from rural Kent to North Lancashire.

Syntactic and morphological change

Inflectional loss and simplification

At varying speeds in different dialects, OE inflectional morphology was greatly reduced in ME. Chaucer's English, being more conservative than some northerly dialects, still retained traces of OE adjectival inflection (now simplified to -*e* as in *shoures soote* 'sweet showers'), and rather more variation in noun plural inflections than those dialects that were rapidly generalising the -*es* plural. There was still a distinction in conservative dialects between the singular and plural of the definite article/demonstrative (*þe/þo*), and an indefinite article (unknown in OE) derived from the numeral *ān* came into use. The third person singular present of the verb was inflected in -*eth* in more southerly dialects and in -*s* and -*es* in northerly ones. Northern dialects tended to simplify the strong verb pattern by losing the prefix *ȝe*- and the -*en* inflection on past participles. In Chaucer's English, the Scandinavian *th*- forms of the third person plural pronoun (general in the north in earlier ME) had penetrated only to the nominative form (*they*). The oblique cases were still initial *h*- forms descended from OE. The third person singular feminine *she*, in various spellings (e.g. *scho, sche*) occurs in the east Midlands as early as the Peterborough continuations (c.1154). It is probably a phonetic development from OE *heo* > *hjo* (with stress shifted to *o*) > *ʃo* (Britton 1991). Initial *h*- forms, such as *ho*, have survived until recently in some southern and western varieties.

Shakespeare's inflectional morphology is already virtually that of PresEng. In the strong verb, it is actually simpler, as past participle forms are often identical to the preterite (e.g. *writ, rode, chose* 'written, ridden, chosen'). The third person singular present of the verb now varies between -*eth* and -*(e)s* endings and continues to do so in formal writing into the eighteenth century (and later in poetry). The genitive of the neuter personal pronoun is still *his* in formal style, but a new colloquial genitive *its* has appeared. Nevalainen & Raumolin-Brunberg (1994) have shown how rapidly the modern *its* form displaced the older forms in the course of the seventeenth century. Otherwise, many early ME morphological distinctions are lost in later ME and EModE, e.g. the verb present plural ending (-*en*), the infinitive ending (-*en*) and adjectival inflection; but there are sporadic archaisms, e.g. the *ȝe*- perfective prefix (by now *y*-) in, e.g. *yclept* 'named'.

Some general trends in syntax

As a result of the availability of large corpora (notably the *Helsinki Corpus of English Texts*), there have recently been many advances in the study of historical English morphosyntax. These include pioneering work in the social embedding of change in late ME and EModE (see especially Nevalainen & Raumolin-Brunberg 1996). See also the chapters by Rissanen (1999) and by Dennison (1998) in volumes III and IV of the *Cambridge History of the English Language*. The present account is necessarily brief.

In OE, relative clauses were introduced by the indeclinable particle *þe*, or by forms of the demonstrative pronoun, sometimes with *þe* attached. Place and time clauses used the adverbials *þā* 'then' and *þǣr* 'there' (often as correlatives), while adverbial clauses of reason, cause, purpose, etc. often used prepositions followed by the demonstrative + (variably) *þe*: thus *for-þǣm-þe* 'because' (lit. 'for-that-which'). The OE relativiser system was modified and extended in ME. For example, *þæt*, which in OE was the neuter singular article or demonstrative, appears as a relativiser with non-neuter and even plural antecedents as early as the Peterborough continuations (1154).

The main innovation in ME relative and other subordinate clauses is the use of the OE interrogatives – WH-forms, such as *who, which, when, where*, etc. – as relativisers and subordinators. This change may be attributed partly to a tendency to interpret some subordinate clauses as indirect questions, but the imitation of Latin and French models is clearly important, especially as the WH-forms tend to occur in the more formal styles. Although these uses were well established by 1600, the specialisation of *who/whom* to use with human antecedents and *which* to non-human antecedents postdates 1600 (Hope 1994). Furthermore, WH-relatives are still today much rarer in everyday use than in written and formal English, being largely confined to non-restrictive clauses. Otherwise, *that* or zero is preferred as in *the man that I saw* ... or *the man I saw* ....

In early English, interrogatives were formed as in other Germanic languages – by subject/verb inversion, as in *Go you?* and *When came you?* By 1600, *do*-interrogatives are well established. Shakespeare uses both constructions, as in *think'st thou?* and *dost thou think?* Forms with *do*-support appear in informal contexts, and this strongly suggests that the gradual adoption of *do*-support, which first appears in the fifteenth century, is a 'change from below' (Labov 1994:78). These points apply *mutatis mutandis* to negation also (cf. *he sees not/he does not see*).

From ME onward, with loss of inflections and a growing tendency to expect the subject in initial position, there is gradual loss of impersonal verb constructions. These were common in OE with certain 'private state' verbs (e.g. *think, like*). An OE sequence such as *þām cyninge līcodon peras* is to be interpreted as IO (dative)-V-S, 'to the king – were pleasing – pears' (see further Fischer & van der Leek 1983). By EModE the impersonal verbs (e.g. *like*) have been reinterpreted as personal verbs in an SVO order, and only *methinks* ('it seems to me') survives as a residue.

Tense/mood/aspect

The PresEng tense/mood/aspect system makes greater use of auxiliary verbs than the OE system did. For the passive, OE had lost the Germanic inflected form and now used auxiliaries: the dynamic passive was expressed by the use of *weorþan* 'become': *he wearþ ofslæჳen* ('he was slain'), and the stative passive by *bēon/wesan*: *he wæs ofslæჳen*. But the various aspectual meanings of the verb – stative, habitual, progressive, future – could normally be expressed by the simple present or preterite form. The perfective also was quite likely to be expressed by a simple form, as in *ic syngode* 'I sinned' (Luke 15:21), to translate the Latin perfect *peccavi* 'I have sinned'.

Verb Phrases using the auxiliaries *bēon/wesan* 'be' and *habban* 'have' were quite common in OE, but not necessarily to express progressive and perfective aspects (as in PresEng). Thus, in Orosius 12:35: *sēo ēa biδ flōwende ofer eal Aegypta land*, the verb phrase *biδ flōwende* expresses a general condition rather than a progressive aspect. When constructions with *habban* + past participle occur, they are not usually perfect tenses, as in Present English; *habban* is commonly to be interpreted as a full verb denoting possession, as in *ic hæfde hine gebundenne* 'I had him in-a-state-of-being-bound' (see Traugott 1972, Brinton 1994). Verbs of motion and verbs of becoming formed their perfects with *be* rather than *have* and continued to do so until Early Modern English. Shakespeare, for example, still preferred *be* to *have*, as in *The King himself is rode to view their battle* (*Henry V*, iv.iii.2).

The history of the *do* auxiliary is complicated. By Shakespeare's time it has virtually become a dummy marker of tense, as in *he did go* ('simple' past meaning), replacing the earlier *gin* (from *begin*), favoured by Chaucer. By about 1600, it has become more common in negative statements and questions than in affirmatives. The *be* progressive (as in *I am going*) is uncommon in EModE literary use, but it was almost certainly more common in spoken English.

Modality

In OE, the Gmc preterite-presents, now modal auxiliaries such as *cunnan* 'to know', functioned as full verbs as well as auxiliaries. They had infinitive forms and could take direct objects. The specialisation of *shall* and *will* as future auxiliaries is gradual: in ME *will* was strongly volitional in meaning, with *shall* preferred as a predictive; *shall*, however, could still carry strong connotations of obligation well into Early Modern English. In early varieties of English, *can* (as auxiliary) meant 'know how to' and *may* 'have the ability to'. Thus:

(6)   I can ne I ne mai tellen ... (Peterborough Chronicle, c.1154)
      'I do not know how (to count), nor have I the power to count ...'

By later ModE, forms like *might* and *should* sometimes function in subordinate clauses where earlier English would have used subjunctive inflections, with no auxiliary.

Tense/mood/aspect in different varieties

Dialects of English can differ quite substantially in how they use auxiliaries and in how tense, mood and aspect are expressed. Some dialects use only *will* (not *shall*) for prediction and may lack certain other modals, e.g. *shall* and *may*. Some dialects extend the use of the progressive construction to certain 'private state' verbs, as in *I'm not caring* for *I don't care*. Others avoid the standard perfect tense and use constructions superficially similar to the OE 'possessive' + participle, as in *he has it bought*; in contrast, in Southern British English the perfect construction seems occasionally to be preferred to the simple past, where the latter would be predicted (as in *He's won it last year*). Other dialects retain *do*-support in affirmatives, sometimes with 'habitual' meaning, as in Irish English *He does be coming round now and again* (where no emphasis is intended).

Vocabulary change

Introductory

Whereas OE vocabulary was predominantly Germanic, at least 80% of the PresEng lexicon is estimated to be non-Germanic – borrowed chiefly from French, Latin and Greek sources from ME times onward. These borrowings contribute mostly to formal and literary registers, while, in everyday speech English vocabulary is still quite noticeably Germanic. Often, a borrowed word and a 'native' word exist with the same, or similar, referent. In pairs like *house/mansion, deep/profound, child/infant*, for example, the first item is Germanic and the second French. In most (but not all) such cases, the native word is more appropriate to casual usage, whereas the French word is more formal, technical or 'high-sounding'. The more formal and technical an English text is, the more likely it is to contain many words borrowed from French, Latin and Greek.

German provides a contrast to English in the matter of loanwords. It has been rather resistant to borrowing, and 'new' words in German have tended to be constructed from the native word stock. Thus, German has *freiwillig* (cognate with 'free will') for English *voluntary* (from French) and *Hauptmann* (lit. 'head-man') for English *captain* (from Norman French). Since early ME times, new words in English have not usually been created from native elements (an OE example is the 'loan-translation' *gospel* < OE *god spell* < Gk ευαγγελιον 'good news'), and many that were originally created in this way have been lost. Borrowing was encouraged by the influence of translation from French and classical writings in the Middle Ages and Renaissance, by the need for precise technical terminology in science and philosophy as these branches of learning progressed, and by a general sense of inferiority about the English language – a belief that it lacked eloquence and expressiveness.

Not all of the borrowing into English is due to general literary or cultural influences. Some of it has arisen from direct spoken contact with speakers of other languages. There are sporadic borrowings that were adopted in the course of commerce and colonisation from the late sixteenth century onwards. Items like *yacht* and *schooner* are from Dutch, *bungalow* from Malay and *tobacco* from a Native American language. Much more important than these, however, are the borrowings that came about during prolonged language contact with Scandinavian and Norman French speakers in medieval England.

I have been careful above to speak of the 'Germanic', rather than 'Anglo-Saxon', vocabulary of English. Old Norse was also Germanic, and our everyday vocabulary contains a large Scandinavian element. Most of these loanwords were adopted between c.800 and c.1050, but they do not normally appear in English documents until after the Conquest. They do not call attention to themselves as 'non-native' in the way that classical borrowings do, and that may be partly why Scandinavian influence tends to be understated. In fact, many of the commonest words in the language are Scandinavian loans.

Apart from a few administrative terms surviving from Danish rule (*by-law* 'town-law', *husband* 'householder'), Scandinavian loanwords include common verbs, adjectives and nouns, such as: *get, take, want, scrape, call, flat, ill, awkward, ugly, sky, skill, egg, leg, skirt*. They are particularly numerous in north Midland, northern and Scots dialects, e.g. *brig* 'bridge', *gate* 'way, road' (thus the street name 'Briggate' in Leeds), *laik* 'play', *gar* 'do', *speer* 'ask' and *kist* 'chest'. Many 'grammatical words' are Scandinavian, e.g. the third person plural pronoun: *they, their, them*. Indeed, a very commonly occurring sequence – *they are* – is probably wholly Scandinavian: the OE form was *hie sindon*.

Many Anglo-Saxon and Old Norse words were too similar to each other to be distinguishable historically, and when this is so, the modern form is presumed to be from Anglo-Saxon. Thus, *lamb* and *house*, for example, are taken to be Anglo-Saxon, even though Old Norse would have given identical forms in PresEng (< ON *lambr, hús*). The best basis for explaining the close intertwining of Anglo-Saxon and Norse elements in English is to postulate the existence at some stage of a Norse-English contact language in the Danelaw. Perhaps this contact language, rather than 'pure' Old English, is the immediate ancestor of the modern language.

Many early French (particularly Norman French) borrowings have also become very common words, e.g. *chair, table, just, very, faith, peace, war, catch*. Here again there was everyday contact, but the Normans were politically dominant. Thus, Norman influence is clearest in the legal, military and domestic fields and in terms relating to social organisation, law and administration. Basic vocabulary in these areas is largely Norman: *prison, burglar, attorney, war, captain, sergeant, soldier, beef, boil, duke, baron, bailiff, rent, treasure*. Many literary and religious terms also were adopted from Norman French. Many OE words were displaced by French ones; some disappeared entirely (e.g. OE *friþ* 'peace'), whereas others remained with altered meanings (thus OE *bord* 'table' remains as 'board').

The chief period of French borrowing was between c.1250 and 1400 (see Baugh & Cable 1978), and this came from the Central French dialect, mostly through written channels. After that French influence declined, although English has continued to borrow French words occasionally ever since (e.g. *garage*, c.1900). Often the same word has been borrowed two or three times, first in its Norman French form, then in a later medieval French form and later again either in a Latinised French (or original Latin) form, or in a modern French form. For example, *kennel, cattle, catch* are Norman, whereas *channel, chattel, chase* are the Central French equivalents; *jaunty* is Norman, *gentle* is Central French and *Gentile* a Latinised form; *chief* is early French and *chef* is modern French.

Many bound morphemes (especially suffixes) have been adopted from French, and some, such as *-able, -ity* and *-age*, are still productive. They can be used to form derivatives from Germanic roots as well as French (thus, *likeable, roughage*). Sometimes, the suffixes are ultimately from Greek or Latin, but through the medium of French, and it is not always clear which of these languages was the direct source of a borrowing. Sometimes, Gmc affixes are attached to French or Latin roots: thus, *nationhood, beautiful*.

Although Latin had always had some influence on English (either direct or through Latinised forms in French), the main period of classical borrowing started with the Renaissance in England (from about 1500). Latin and Greek made the chief contributions to what we have called the 'functional elaboration' of English (see page 18); not only did they provide an immense battery of general abstract terms, they were also used as the sources for the entire vocabulary of technical terms that were needed in the developing sciences, e.g. *momentum, equilibrium, apparatus* (from Latin), and *criterion, phenomenon* (from Greek). In sixteenth-century literary circles, there was some resistance to the borrowings that came in through written use, and they were labelled 'inkhorn terms'. Some of these, such as *immorigerous* and *obstupefact* were short-lived, but they were very numerous: even Johnson's Dictionary of 1755 lists many such borrowings that did not survive his own century. Nonetheless, the influence of classical borrowing on the more elaborated styles of written English is extremely strong.

Semantic shift

Just as words can vary in meaning in different dialects, so their meanings also change in the course of time. They may, for example, become wider and more general in their application, or they may become narrower. Some Anglo-Saxon words that have survived alongside loanwords seem to have narrowed in their meanings. Thus, OE *dēor*, *stōl*, *heofon* 'animal, chair, sky' have more restricted meanings ('deer, stool, heaven') in PresEng and are replaced in their old meanings by loanwords. In rarer cases, it is the loanword that has narrowed in meaning: thus, *science* is no longer all kinds of 'knowledge'. Many of the more learned classical borrowings have shifted in meaning as they have been pressed into everyday use. Often, an original literal meaning has become figurative only. The 'extravagant and erring spirit' of Hamlet did not spend lavishly or make mistakes – *extravagant* and *erring* both retained their Latin meanings, approximately 'wandering'. Sometimes, over long periods, meanings have shifted quite radically away from their sources; thus, *cardinal* (now a cleric) is derived from Latin *cardo* 'hinge', and the Greek root of *cynic* meant 'dog-like'. In other cases, the rational connections in meaning are more discernible: thus, the Greek-derived *hygiene* 'health' has come to mean 'cleanliness', pre- sumably because cleanliness was believed to be necessary to good health, whereas Latin *sanus* 'clean' has undergone specialisation: *sane* now means only 'mentally healthy'. During the progress of a semantic shift, the new usages are often considered 'incorrect'; the word *refute*, for example, which meant 'disprove', is now often used to mean only 'reject, disagree with'. Of course there are protests, but they will be in vain. Semantic shift is con- tinuously in progress, and it is the usage of the many, not the complaints of the few, that determines how words are used.

Closing comments

The history of English has been closely researched, and much is known about it (see now the volumes of the *Cambridge History of the English Language*). However, two major traditional characteristics of the subject have tended to bias past research. First, disproportionate attention has been given to OE and its Germanic and IE ancestry, with some neglect of recent centuries. This has been underpinned by the 'genetic' model of language relationship, in which languages are believed to be traceable to a *single* parent language. In the present account, I have attempted to balance the traditional genetic account of English with emphasis on the importance of language mixing and borrowing.

The second traditional characteristic is the emphasis on a variety known as *standard* English. In the present chapter I have been unable to avoid some of this bias. But there has been progress – much of it inspired by social and regional dialectology and a new emphasis on the importance of urban language studies. There has been pioneer work on the social history of English (e.g. Leith 1983), and new methods of accessing the social embedding of historical change are being successfully used by the Helsinki School and others. New developments of this kind promise to bring about further advances in our understanding of the history of English.

2   Standard and non-standard English

Paul Kerswill

'Standard English' and spoken English as opposing norms: a demonstration

The populations of the British Isles have a varied, and often strained relationship with the language with which they have to engage every day in print and in the spoken media. This is the language through which they are (almost) all educated, and which, many of them are persuaded, is both correct and, in an absolute sense, good. Some are at ease with this language, others struggle to master it. A few turn their backs on it. This bald characterisation of the multiple relationships between language users and Standard English is intended to highlight, not only the diversity of the sociolinguistic set-ups throughout the islands, but also the wide range of beliefs, opinions and responses relating to the notion of 'Standard English' on the part of educators, policy makers and professional linguists, as well as, of course, those millions who do not belong to any of these groups. This chapter will address, first, how 'Standard English' and 'Received Pronunciation' (RP) have been conceptualised by those who have an academic, professional or policy-maker's interest in them. Second, the chapter will deal with the nature of the 'variety space' which is said to be bounded by Standard English and RP on one side and by 'non-standard', 'vernacular' speech on the other.

As we shall see later, the standard–non-standard dimension is closely related to the distinction between written and spoken language. But let us begin with an illustration of how norms involving standard/written English interact with norms of spoken or non-standard usage. Sixteen adult non-linguistically trained speakers of British English were asked to perform a task judging the 'use in spoken English' of the following sentences:

1 He and I are going shopping
2 I and he are going shopping
3 Him and me are going shopping
4 Me and him are going shopping

For their judgements, respondents could choose between: 'Normal and natural', 'OK, but perhaps something a bit odd', 'OK, but rather odd', 'Very odd' and 'Virtually impossible'. The rationale for the task was as follows. English insists on nominative forms in subject positions (such as *I*, *he*), and accusative forms in object positions (*me*, *him*). However, it is apparent that, in conjoined subjects, the accusative form may appear, giving such utterances as *Me and him are going shopping*, among speakers who would not dream of using *me* or *him* as single subjects. This discrepancy between the single and conjoined subjects has been explained as the use of the *default accusative* in conjoined subjects, of the same type that gives the answer *Me* to the question, *Who wants ice cream?*[1] There is, thus, a potential conflict between the default accusative subjects and the 'correct' *He and I are going shopping*.

The second area tested here is the 'correct' order of presentation of the other and the self: many children have been taught that it is polite to mention the other person before themselves, so that second and third person pronouns should appear before the first person pronoun. Thus, in the task, judgements about both orders were sought.

In order to allow respondents to choose their own criteria, the question itself was phrased in as bare a form as possible ('Below are four sentences. Please judge their use in spoken English by placing an x in the appropriate column.'). The judgement categories do not refer to correctness, but to usage, in a way that allows respondents to invoke both prescriptive and frequency-of-use criteria. Finally, the implied context (mundane, involving oral production) was chosen to increase the acceptability of default accusatives even in sentences presented in printed form. The results are shown in Table 2.1.

Both the nominative (1 or 2) and the accusative (3 or 4) forms are fairly widely accepted. An inspection of the individual responses shows that there is, however, an overwhelming tendency for respondents to go for *either* the nominative *or* the accusative, only three accepting both by entering a tick in either the first or the second response column.

---

[1] There are technical linguistic explanations for this pattern, and I am grateful to Mark Newson for pointing these out to me. In English, the grammar has difficulty in assigning the nominative case in conjoined subjects, preferring the default form, such as *me* or *him*. Other languages, such as Hungarian or German, do not follow this pattern; this is a parametric difference. The presence of *He and I*, etc., as conjoined subjects is the result of a prescriptive rule, and conflicts with the normal grammar. That this is an imposed rule is suggested by the occasional presence of nominative forms in prepositional phrases or in object positions, such as *between you and I* or *She came over to meet you and I*; these forms originate in hypercorrection. Similarly, the preferred ordering of third and second person subjects before the first person, as in *You and I*, is a prescriptive rule without a basis in the grammar of English.

Table 2.1. *'Use in spoken English' judgements*

	Normal and natural	OK, but perhaps something a bit odd	OK, but rather odd	Very odd	Virtually impossible
1 He and I are going shopping	8	3	1	3	1
2 I and he are going shopping		2	2	6	6
3 Him and me are going shopping		7	3	4	2
4 Me and him are going shopping	5	2	2	4	3

An interpretation of this result would be to say, simply, that there are two grammars at play: some people have the default accusative rule in conjoined subjects, while others don't. However, this would imply a massive difference in the grammars of the two sets of speakers. Given that all but two of these speakers are university graduates (i.e. they have a similarly high involvement with written norms), this seems unlikely – though one would not wish to exclude the possibility. A better explanation is that different people are orienting, more or less consciously, to different norms: either those of 'Standard English', corresponding quite closely to the written language, or those of speech, incorporating both informal and dialectal features. Further support for this interpretation is the fact that, for those who chose the nominative, the prescribed order of third-person-first is strongly preferred (sentence 1), while, for those who selected the accusative, first-person-first is favoured (sentence 4) – corresponding, in all likelihood, to spoken usage. The experiment did not explore whether people felt uncertain in their judgements. It is likely that they did, as witnessed by Trudgill's (1975:42) assertion that some speakers feel uneasy about the utterance *It was him that did it* because it is not 'correct'.

This simple experiment demonstrates the existence, and strength, of the two opposing sets of norms, which we can probably label as 'mainly written/ standard' and 'mainly spoken/non-standard'. If people seem able to choose which set to orient themselves to in this experiment, with its straightforward choices and barely contextualised language, then it is certain that they do so, too, in 'real' instances of language use, but in far more complex ways that involve much more than a single binary selection. So we have to recognise that, in the plethora of overlapping and nested speech communities of the British Isles, there will be a multiplicity of linguistic norms. One of these is Standard English, which as we shall see has a privileged position.

Understanding 'Standard English'

Whose perspective?

So far, I have avoided trying to define 'Standard English'. This is because the way this notion (or lay externalisations of it such as 'correct' or 'good' English) is understood is closely related to the perspective of the particular language user or commentator. A member of the population 'at large' will have a view informed, at the very least, by his or her early socialisation, family history, educational experience, socio-economic class (however defined), social network, participation in the 'linguistic market' at work (Sankoff & Laberge 1978), ethnic (including national) origin and personal, including political, beliefs. Academic commentators (such as the present writer) will claim to perform a rational analysis of the notion of 'Standard English', accountable to the axioms of their academic sub-discipline. For some, this will involve a dissociation from the long list of social factors just given, with the claim that popular beliefs do not have face validity and that a linguistic analysis is required. Others will integrate their analyses with due recognition of the social factors. For a third group of academics, lay beliefs about and behaviours towards Standard English will themselves be the object of research, as will the social, demographic and ideological factors impinging on the status and use of Standard English and other varieties. In the course of this chapter, all these perspectives will crop up in different guises. Finally, it must be realised that policy makers, who are often politicians and not necessarily 'experts', may or may not have the academic's reflective or critical skills – or may choose not to apply them (see Chapter 24). However, because of their huge influence, what they determine affects millions of people in their everyday lives.

Time, place and ideology

Ideas surrounding 'Standard English' depend on the social and economic relationships between sections of the population in a particular time and place – and on the ideologies that are linked to these social conditions. This is most clearly seen in the rise of a belief in a 'standard' pronunciation in Britain. Early and mid-Victorian England saw unprecedented social change, with the emergence of an urban industrial working class. According to L. Milroy (1999:184), rural dialects had become 'revalorised' as 'class dialects', as the population became urbanised under the capitalist system. A discourse of 'class' emerged, reflecting a view of social formation which was 'not necessarily determined by birth' (Mugglestone 1995:74) and, at the same time, one of the main symbols of class became pronunciation. A typical commentator of the time stated that, 'The language of the highest classes . . . is now looked upon as the standard of English pronunciation' (Graham 1869:156, quoted in Mugglestone 1995:70). The intrinsic 'superiority' of RP (as this variety became known) was argued for by Wyld, who called it 'the most pleasing and sonorous form' (1934, quoted in J. Milroy 2000:19), and its basis in upper class usage is explicit in his writings.

Increased social mobility in the second half of the twentieth century has apparently led to the downgrading of the status of this 'standard' pronunciation, RP, in favour of mildly regionally accented varieties such as 'Estuary English' (Rosewarne 1984, Crystal 1995:365, Kerswill 2001). The diminishing status of RP has brought to the surface yet again the class-based 'standard ideology', by which the inherent correctness, even morality, of Standard English and of RP continue to be asserted as being a matter of common sense (L. Milroy 1999:174–5). Commenting on a study of the English of the new town of Milton Keynes (Kerswill 1996b, Kerswill & Williams 2000, 2005), John Osborne wrote:

> It was announced last week that Essex girl has been supplanted by the children of Milton Keynes, who uniformly speak with a previously unidentified and hideously glottal accent . . . Nothing is more depressing than [Milton Keynes], this gleaming gum-boil plonked in the middle of England. And now there is a home-grown accent to match. (*Daily Mail*, 7 August 1994)

– thus making an explicit link between a purportedly disreputable place and this new, degenerate, accent, which was held to be an example of Estuary English. (I return to the Estuary English debate in the last section.)

Few of today's academic commentators espouse this view, and this signals a gulf between the academy on one hand and opinion formers and policy makers on the other (cf. Chapter 23). However, J. Milroy (2000) argues that the prominence of Standard English in English historical linguistics is precisely a result of this 'standard ideology'; arguably this ideology partly lies behind the willingness of today's (socio)linguists to engage with Standard English and RP as entities that can be described, rather than as abstract notions that are constructed discoursally. The remainder of the chapter, however, focuses on the description, rather than the construction, of these entities.

Standard English and Received Pronunciation: the descriptive approach

Accent and dialect

It has long been customary in British dialectology to distinguish between *accent* and *dialect* differences between varieties of English (Abercrombie

1967:19, Trudgill 1975:20, Crystal 1995:298). Minimal definitions are that an accent is 'a particular way of pronouncing a language' (Trask 1997:3), or that 'the term *accent* ... refers solely to differences in pronunciation' (Trudgill 2000:5). These are set against 'dialect', which, according to Hughes & Trudgill (1996:9), refers to 'varieties distinguished from each other by differences of grammar and vocabulary' – such as the verb forms in *I wrote it* and *I writ it*, or the different patterns of negation found in *I don't want any* and *I don't want none*, or the use of the verb *grave* for 'dig' in parts of northern England (Trudgill 1999a:128). There are also various sociolinguistic definitions of the terms in the British and Irish contexts. Britain (2005a) points out that, while 'accent' has not proved particularly controversial, 'dialect' has been subject to a range of definitions. In the 'Anglo-Saxon' world, 'dialect' is used to cover any variety of language that can be delimited linguistically or (more rarely) socially; thus, Standard English is a dialect – a description of it that goes against most lay understandings. For lay speakers, and for many linguists, a dialect is a subset of a language, usually with a geographical restriction on its distribution. By most definitions, dialects are not standardised, and are hence more subject to variability (Britain 2005a). Some commentators claim that non-standard dialects lack 'communicative functionality' (Ammon 1998:197, cited in Britain 2005a), while others oppose this idea, saying that, outside most institutional contexts, they are, in fact, more functional than standard varieties (Britain 2005a). We will have more to say on the definition of Standard English later in this chapter.

Despite apparent agreement, the term 'accent' as used in British dialectology is problematic. For a descriptive linguist, the definitions given above for 'accent' hardly suffice, even if they are adequate pointers for most lay needs. Greater specificity leads to difficulties, as we shall see. Hughes & Trudgill (1996:36) list three types of accent variation:

Type 1   'systemic or inventory variability, when different speakers have different sets (or systems) of phonemes', such as the absence of /ʌ/ in northern England, so that words like STRUT[2] have /u/;

Type 2   'realisational variability [referring] to the ways in which a single phoneme may have different phonetic realisations'; an example would be London [æ] corresponding to Northern [a] in words like TRAP;

Type 3   '"lexical" variability, referring to the use of different series of phonemes for the same word', such as the older south-east English use of /ɔ:/ in words like *off* and *cross* (rhyming with *morph*), rather than /ɒ/ (the first vowel in *toffee*).

Both Francis (1983:28) and Wakelin (1972:84) take fundamentally the same approach.

---

[2] Wells' (1982) mnemonic keywords are shown in small capitals.

However, Wells (1982:2–5) argues for the particular importance of Hughes & Trudgill's third type of accent variation when investigating regional dialect differences – and it is here a difficulty emerges. He notes that many of the differences between a 'traditional-dialect' (as spoken by linguistically conservative, typically rural people) and an accent of what he calls 'General English' (more mainstream varieties) are 'phonological', that is, composed of accent differences that are a matter of 'the lexical incidence of particular phonemes in particular words' (1982:5) – corresponding to Hughes & Trudgill's Type 3. Differences of this kind include the form [brɪg] ('brig') for *bridge* and [rɪad] for *road*, both from the far north of England, and [wɒm] for *home* in the English Midlands. All of these differ in terms of the phonemes present in the 'same' words in other traditional-dialects and in General English. Wells cites extensive accent differences of this kind, particularly in Scotland. In a study of Durham dialect (Kerswill 1987), I informally noted some 120 features of this kind from general conversation, including [θaʊt] for *thought*, and [pʊnd] for *pound*.

This pervasive phonological variation between dialects is 'paradoxical', according to Wells. This calls into question the idea that differences in lexical incidence are 'mere' accent differences. There is, in fact, strong evidence that speakers themselves behave as if this kind of difference is of the same order as more 'deep' (i.e. grammatical) dialect differences as well as lexical (vocabulary) differences. It is apparent that, in rural northern England and rural Scotland, a certain amount of 'dialect switching' occurs (Cheshire & Trudgill 1989:99): speakers switch between two 'codes', one (perhaps) for school, another for use elsewhere. The 'school' variety avoids most of the local phonological forms of words, in addition to not containing dialect vocabulary. A discussion with some older Durham speakers on the subject of dialect made it clear that, when chatting to me (a southern 'Standard English' speaker), they were conscious of avoiding dialect words, such as *beck* for 'stream', as well as dialect phonological forms such as [tak] for *take* or [gan jɛm] for *go home* – which, with me, they would pronounce [goː hoːm], using a locally accented version of 'General English'. Thus, for these speakers, dialect vocabulary and Type 3 accent features went hand-in-hand, and together constituted their overt construction of 'dialect'. That this is so is supported by their scorn for new features entering the dialect, especially /f/ and /v/ for /θ/ and /ð/ in words such as *thing* and *brother*, as well as youth slang, on the grounds that they were neither 'dialect' nor 'good English'.

Traditional and mainstream dialects

A solution to the problem of distinguishing between 'accent' and 'dialect' differences lies in the particular characteristics of 'traditional-dialect' and

'General English'. At this point, we will adopt the more commonly used terms for the same concepts, as elaborated by Trudgill (1999a:5). 'Traditional dialect' (without the hyphen) refers to the speech of some people in rural and peripheral areas. Traditional dialects differ greatly from Standard English and from each other (*ibid.*), and would include such hypothetical utterances as:

[a tɛlt ði   ʔə se: ðu: hazn   ʔə gan jɛm   ðə   nɪit]
ah telt thee to seh thoo hazn't to gan yem the neet

which in Durham corresponds to 'I told you to say you musn't go home tonight'.

The second term is 'mainstream dialect', which refers to the 'Standard English Dialect' and 'Modern Nonstandard Dialects' (Trudgill 1999a:5), characteristic of urban (especially southern) England, most of Wales, younger people in general and the middle class. The term seems to correspond closely to Wells' 'General English'. In Reading in the south of England, utterances such as:

[ʃɪ   kʌm   ʌʔp   ʋedɪn   jestədeɪ]
She   come   up   Reading   yesterday

together with its Standard English equivalent, spoken with a Reading or other accent,

She came to Reading yesterday

are both 'mainstream dialect', as is the 'Standard English' version of the Durham utterance above, spoken with a Durham accent:

[a to:ldʒə tə se: jə mʊsnt? go: ho:m tənaɪt].

The crux of the matter is that these and all other mainstream dialect utterances are phonologically closely related to one another and to utterances in spoken versions of Standard English. This means that the differences between them are mainly of Type 2 in Hughes & Trudgill's taxonomy, with a few Type 1 and Type 3 differences represented. Thus, mainstream dialects in England, Wales and much of Ireland share largely the same phonological system, with similar distributions of phonemes across the vocabulary. In Scotland and those areas of the north of Ireland where the dialects are Scots-derived, the situation is a little different, since most speakers use a radically different vowel system, governed by the Scottish Vowel Length Rule (Wells 1982:400, Scobbie, Hewlett & Turk 1999, see Chapter 5). Despite this, it is possible to draw correspondences across all mainstream, but not traditional, dialects in terms of the phonemes used in particular words, as Table 2.2 shows.

Table 2.2. *Dialect correspondences for* daughter *and* night

	Traditional		Mainstream			
	Scots	Durham	Scots	Durham	London	Received Pronunciation
daughter	[dɒxtər]	[dauʔʒə]	[dɔʔər]	[dɔːtʒə]	[douʔə]	[dǫːtə]
night	[nɛxt]	[nɪːt]	[nɛɪʔ]	[naɪt]	[nɑɪʔ]	[naɪt]

Surprisingly, only two of ten features discussed by Hughes & Trudgill (1996:54–64) are of Type 2 ('Long Mid Diphthonging' in the vowels of FACE and GOAT and the realisation of /t/ as [ʔ] after vowels). Three others concern phonological differences of Type 1 (the absence of /ʌ/ in the north of England, the variable dropping of /h/ and the difference between English and Scottish vowel systems). However, the remainder do not fit into any of the three categories, and include the distribution of /æ/ and /ɑ:/ in words like *path* and *dance* (phonologically patterned distribution with exceptions), the presence/absence of /r/ before consonants in words like *card*, the use of /ɪ/ or /iː/ word-finally in words like *city* and *money* and the use of /ɪŋ/ or /ɪn/ in the suffix *-ing*. The important generalisation about all ten features is that they have a high degree of phonological predictability. This means that, with knowledge of a pronunciation in Dialect A, it is usually possible to determine what it will be in Dialect B, *either* because there is a one-to-one correspondence *or* because a general rule can be applied. For example, if we know that a southern accent has /ɑ:/ in a word containing a following voiceless fricative, as in *bath*, then we can be almost certain that a northern accent will have /æ/ in the same item. Interestingly, the reverse prediction does not hold so well, since we find items like *gas* and *mass* with /æ/ in the south.

On the basis of these observations, we can refine the notion of 'accent difference' to refer to any pronunciation difference where there is a *high degree of predictability in at least one direction*. This has the effect of excluding the large number of Type 3 phonological differences found between traditional dialects and between these and spoken Standard English. Type 3 differences, then, fit in easily with the 'dialect' differences that otherwise pervade traditional dialects – and this is consistent with the way speakers treat them sociolinguistically, as we have seen. It has the advantage, too, of taking into account speakers' own intuitions. As for mainstream dialects, we can say that the differences between them are almost exclusively predictable in the senses just outlined.

Standard English as a discrete set of rules and lexis

A number of linguists have argued strongly that Standard English is easily defined and delimited. Standard English across the world basically shares the same grammar, with only a small number of minor differences. Its vocabulary is less fixed, though it avoids regional, traditional words. While it is the only form of English used in writing, it is also used in speech, and has native speakers throughout the world. Trudgill (1999b) gives perhaps the clearest statement of this position. He argues that Standard English is not a style, a register or an accent, noting that its speakers have access to a full range of informal styles, and can produce it with different accents, while non-standard speakers can discuss technical subjects without switching to Standard English. Standard English is a dialect, defined by the criteria I have discussed. However, because it is standardised and codified, it is not part of a continuum of dialects: either a feature is standard, or it is not (Trudgill 1999b:124). It also does not have a particular pronunciation associated with it. Trudgill lists eight 'idiosyncrasies' of Standard English grammar, four of which (perhaps the most widespread in mainstream dialects) are the following:

1 Standard English does not distinguish between the forms of the auxiliary *do* and its main verb forms. Non-standard varieties normally include the forms *I done it* (main verb), *but did he?* (auxiliary): Standard English has *did* for both functions.
2 Standard English does not permit double negation (negative concord), as in *I don't want none*.
3 Standard English has an irregular formation of the reflexive, with *myself* based on the possessive *my*, and *himself* based on the object form *him*. Non-standard dialects generalise the possessive form, as in *hisself*.
4 Standard English redundantly distinguishes between the preterite and past participle forms of many verbs, as in *I saw – I have seen*, or *I did – I have done*, where dialects have forms such as *seen* or *done* for both.

(adapted from Trudgill 1999b:125)

Another linguist working along similar lines is Hudson (2000b), who lists further Standard English features, including:

5 Standard English adverbs ending in *-ly*, as in *Come quickly!* Most non-standard varieties use the bare form, as in *Come quick!*
6 Standard English relative pronouns *that* or *which*. Non-standard varieties tend to have *what*.

Despite the strength of the Standard norm, there are some areas of variability, such as differing preferences for (spoken) forms such as: *I haven't finished* vs. *I've not finished* (see Hughes & Trudgill 1996:15–21 for a discussion of grammatical variation within Standard English).

Both Trudgill and Hudson give sociolinguistic characterisations of Standard English. For Trudgill it is a 'purely social dialect' (1999b:124). He estimates that it is spoken natively by 12–15 percent of the population, concentrated at the top of the social class scale. It was selected because it was the variety of the most influential social groups. Subsequently, according to Trudgill, its 'social character' was reinforced through its use in an 'education to which pupils ... have had differential access depending on their social-class background' (1999b:124). Hudson takes a slightly different approach, focusing more on the written form and literacy. He states (2000b) that Standard English is '(1) written in published work, (2) spoken in situations where published writing is influential, especially in education ..., [and] (3) spoken natively by people who are most influenced by published writing ...'. These ideas mesh with the notion of the 'linguistic market' referred to above (Sankoff & Laberge 1978).

Pushing at the boundaries: the grammar of spoken Standard English

It is clear that a spoken Standard English norm firmly based on written norms was not fully established until the latter part of the nineteenth century. Thomas Hughes, while using Standard English for his narrative in *Tom Brown's Schooldays* (1857), gives the privileged (but not upper-class) Rugby School pupils dialogue including: 'It ain't such good fun now', 'It don't hurt unless you fall on the floor', and (with a zero subject relative) 'There's no other boy in the house would have done it for me'. By the end of the century, popular publications on polite behaviour and etiquette began to appear, dispensing advice about 'good' spoken usage to a receptive aspiring middle-class audience. Most dealt with both pronunciation and lexical and grammatical choices. On the latter, we find statements such as: 'Don't speak ungrammatically. Study books of grammar, and the writings of the best authors' ('Censor' n.d. (c. 1880):61). Later, we find: 'Whether or not we are aware of doing so, we do note how people use words; and we may find that educated people agree in the manner. They say "you were" and not "you was". They say "He and I are a pair" and not "Him and me is a pair." Now, a rule of grammar is simply a statement of the agreement among educated people ...' (Weston n.d. (c. 1945):15). Clearly, 'Censor' considers good writing to be the best model for speech, a view which we explore further below. Weston, too, is specific about models for good speech – educated people's usage – though he does not refer the reader to grammar books. Yet even educated upper-class speakers in the mid-twentieth century could use non-standard forms, in a country still with rigid class boundaries. An example is the former

Prime Minister Harold Macmillan's use of *it don't* (Wardhaugh 1999:149), continuing the non-standard, but privileged norm we saw in *Tom Brown's Schooldays*.

More recent definitions of Standard English intended for a popular market maintain the idea that it can be defined with reference to speech; thus: 'Standard English is that form of the English language which is spoken by the generality of cultured people in Great Britain' (Phythian 1993:180, quoting the *Shorter Oxford Dictionary*). For Phythian, a distinction should be made between 'Standard English' and 'colloquialism', which he defines as 'informal Standard English, [consisting] of a vocabulary and, occasionally, a syntax ... which are appropriate to familiar conversation ... Colloquialisms, in time, may be promoted to the status of Standard English ...' (Phythian 1993:180). Phythian clearly singles out features of spoken grammar (though he does not give any examples) as being distinct from Standard English, though still acceptable since they are future candidates for inclusion. Ayto (1995), however, accepts that there is both written and spoken Standard English, and cites the use of *bust* for 'broken' as appropriate in speech but probably not in writing (p. 279). He also accepts *I didn't use to like eggs* as the spoken alternative to *I used not to like eggs*, which he recommends for written usage (pp. 279–80). Ayto's features of 'spoken Standard English' closely correspond to Phythian's 'colloquialisms'.

Ayto's view is very close to that of Trudgill (1999b:120), who accepts as Standard English informal usages such as *The old man was bloody knackered after his long trip*. However, Trudgill expands the definition by accommodating constructions which are typical of oral production, as in *There was this man, and he'd got this gun ...* (p. 121). He argues that the use of *this* as an indefinite is to be seen as a feature of colloquial style, not related to the standard–non-standard dimension. A counter-argument to Trudgill is that indefinite *this* is probably not widely used by Standard English speakers, though here we see a conflict between spoken norms and a 'standard language ideology' based on writing – to which we turn now.

Cheshire explores the specific and complex relationship between the grammars of written and spoken Standard English in detail (1999b, Cheshire & Stein 1997). In her 1999 article, she appears to make two overarching claims in relation to spoken Standard English. The first is that much descriptive and theoretical work on Standard English is based on intuitions that are more firmly grounded in written norms than in speech. This is so for three reasons. First, academic linguists have intense contact with Standard English, particularly in its written form (p. 131). Second, until recently corpora of authentic speech have been derived from conversations among academics (p. 130). And third, it appears that very many speakers' access to intuitions about typically spoken or non-standard constructions is very shaky. Cheshire states that, even among educated people, forms such as *There's lots of museums* are much more frequent than the 'correct' *There are lots of museums*, which shows concord between verb and postverbal subject. Despite the preponderance of the former construction, people's intuitions usually lead them to accept only the latter (Cheshire 1999b:131, quoting Meechan & Foley 1994). This is closely tied to the notion of Standard English as an ideology, an idea I explore below.

Cheshire's second claim is concerned with the actual properties of spoken Standard English. She concludes that we have to look outside generative grammar to find explanations for some of the phenomena observed. Following Sundby, Bjørge & Haugland (1991) and Meechan & Foley, Cheshire discusses concord (subject–verb agreement) as an area where codification has influenced judgements and usage. She argues that the preference in speech for the singular in the 'existential *there*' construction, as in *There's lots of museums*, may be related to the function of *there's*. Spoken language shows a preference for the presentation of new information at the end of a clause, with light elements at the beginning. These are supplied by *there's*, which contains both a light subject and an empty verb. It is also likely that the form *there's* is stored, economically, as a prefabricated phrase. It is functionally identical to the invariant *il y a* in French and *es gibt* in German, both used to present new information in discourse (Cheshire 1999b:138). Meechan & Foley find that a generative explanation for the prescribed plural is complex; Cheshire claims that, since the singular is preferred in discourse, there is simply no plural to be explained (p. 136).

This kind of argumentation allows us to see more clearly the nature of the conflicting judgements revealed in the 'default accusative' experiment. As with existential *there*, there was a choice between two alternatives, one prescriptively 'correct' according to the codified norms of Standard English, the other in line with spoken usage. There is a difference, however. In the case of the default accusative, there are strong internal arguments for the grammaticality of *Me and him went shopping*, in a way that is unrelated to discourse function. Cheshire's argument seems to be that the grammaticality (or, rather, acceptability established through use) of *There's lots of museums* is directly related to its discourse function, and need not (or, perhaps, cannot) be 'explained' through generative grammar.

We turn briefly to the way policy makers have dealt with issues of spoken grammar. As we have seen, grammar, prescription and discourse function clearly all interact in an unsuspectedly complex way. Given this, it is perhaps not surprising (though still unfortunate) that the compilers of the *National Literacy Strategy* for England and Wales (Department for Education and Employment 1998) fail to grasp basic functional distinctions between speech and writing when they state:

Writers and speakers may use ellipsis for purposes of economy or style. For instance in the exchange: 'Where are you going?' 'To town', the second speaker has missed out 'I am going'. She/he assumes that the reader will understand the omission; this saves boring repetition. (DfEE 1998:79)

Sealey (1999) points out the confusion in the passage between speakers and writers – this is clearly a dialogue. More importantly, 'the notion of an "omission" here is quite misplaced: when speakers share a context for their talk, they do not set about modifying a written script, judiciously missing out details so as to "save boring details"' (Sealey 1999:6). This is very much akin to Cheshire's argument that we must not interpret, still less judge, spoken grammar by the criteria of the grammar of written language.

RP as a 'variety'

We turn now to 'Received Pronunciation', or 'RP'[3] – an abbreviation which has been claimed to be part of the institutionalisation of this variety (Macaulay 1997:42). The idea that there is, or should be, a standard or correct spoken form of English goes back at least to Puttenham (1936 [1589]), Thomas Sheridan being an important eighteenth-century proponent (1999 [1762]). In purely descriptive (rather than socio-political or ideological) terms, the salient fact about RP is its non-regional nature. Even though RP is phonologically a south-eastern accent, in that it possesses /ʌ/ in STRUT, uses /ɑː/ in BATH and is non-rhotic (i.e. it lacks non-prevocalic /r/ in words such as *bird*), it is in principle impossible to tell the provenance of an RP speaker. There is uncertainty about when such a non-regional accent first emerged. Despite the interest aroused by Sheridan and other writers, there is no evidence that any kind of non-regional pronunciation was in widespread use until the last quarter of the nineteenth century. Honey (1989, cited in L. Milroy 1999:185) argues that it was not until after 1870 that British people with a privileged education began to have a standard accent, a position implicitly endorsed by Macaulay (1997), who quotes Ellis as writing: 'At present there is *no* standard of pronunciation. There are many ways of pronouncing English *correctly* . . .' (1869:630, cited in Macaulay 1997:36). Although Crystal dates the emergence of RP to slightly earlier in the nineteenth century (1995:365), it is clear that, by the end of the century, RP had become a dominant feature of the fee-paying public schools, students and

---

[3] See Crystal (1995:365) and McArthur (1992) for information on the origin of the term.

academics at Oxford and Cambridge universities, the colonial service, teachers, the Anglican Church and the officer class of the Army (L. Milroy 1999:186).

The privileged social position of the users of RP meant, and still means, that discussion of it can be sensitive, and that nuances make a difference: Trudgill claims that, since RP is an implicitly codified variety, 'it only takes one non-RP feature for a speaker not to be a speaker of RP' (2002b:174). Trudgill's view, however, causes difficulties, since RP, unlike Standard English, appears to be changing quite rapidly. This leads to problems of finding criteria for determining what are changes and/or permissible variations within RP, and what are features which make a person's speech non-RP. Trudgill's own criterion is simply to say that, for inclusion as part of RP, a feature must not be a regional feature (2002b:175). The difficulty, I think, with this is that almost all of the 'new' RP features, such as the glottalling of /t/ before another consonant (as in *let me*) or the fronting of /uː/ (as in GOOSE) to [ʉː], are already widespread across regional accents. RP is following wider trends, perhaps a step or two behind. This convergence, or in some cases shared change (as with the fronting of /uː/ – see Kerswill & Williams 2005) involving RP and other varieties means that there is an attrition of *distinctively* RP features. Other features must remain to distinguish RP, even though they will be fewer in number. For the time being, however, there is no danger of *all* the distinguishing features of RP disappearing (Trudgill 2002b:177).

The approach to RP taken by a number of linguists is to name different varieties defined according to various non-linguistic criteria, and then to list the phonetic characteristics of each. The classifications vary, and do not completely match. Gimson (1970:88) distinguishes between: 'the *conservative* RP forms used by the older generation and, traditionally, by certain professions or social groups; the *general* RP forms most commonly in use and typified by the pronunciation adopted by the BBC; and the *advanced* RP forms mainly used by young people of exclusive social groups ...' (emphases in original). Wells (1982:279) refers to a 'central tendency', which he calls *mainstream* RP, corresponding to Gimson's general RP. This contrasts with *U*-RP (upper class RP) and with *adoptive* RP (spoken by those who did not speak RP as children). Wells (1997) suggests a more explicit set of social criteria, involving a strictly sociolinguistic approach: we identify people who we might expect to speak RP, and observe their speech. He does not develop the idea. Finally, Cruttenden (2001b), in his revision of Gimson's work, lists *general* RP, *refined* RP (upper class and associated with certain professions which traditionally recruit from the upper class) and *regional* RP (RP with a small number of regional features, such as vocalised /l/ in *milk*, or /æ/ for /ɑː/ in *path*). Wells (1982:280) identifies problems with Gimson's implicit age dimension – and these are

Table 2.3. *Eight changes in RP*

Change	Comment
1 Fronting of the vowel of GOAT from [oʊ] to [əʊ] or [əʉ].	'Advanced' RP in 1970; now almost complete; supersedes earlier hyper-fronting to [ɛʊ].
2 Final /ɪ/ replaced by /iː/ in *happy*.	Well established.
3 r-intrusion, giving *idea* [r] *of*.	A long-completed change, but avoided by some in adoptive RP.
4 Lowering of /æ/ in TRAP from [æ] to [a].	Nearing completion.
5 Use of /ɔː/ for /ʊə/ in *sure, poor*, etc.	Well established.
6 t-glottalling (use of [ʔ] for word-final /t/).	Well established before a consonant, as in *let me*; incipient before a vowel across a boundary as in *quite easy*.
7 Split of allophones of /əʊ/ before syllable-final /l/ and elsewhere.	Well established; a consequence of (1). Leads to [əʊ] in GOAT, [ɒʊ] in GOAL.
8 Fronting of /uː/ as in GOOSE to [ʉː] or [ʏː].	Well established.

removed by Cruttenden. However, Cruttenden now allows for some regional differentiation, something which Trudgill (2002b:177) excludes as a possibility for RP.

Between them, these three authors establish four intersecting criteria for differentiation within RP: age, social class, acquisition and regionality. Rather than trying to disentangle the minimum of sixteen potential sub-types this gives rise to, I shall briefly summarise some changes in RP, as given in the works cited in the previous paragraph (see Table 2.3). I base myself particularly on Wells (1982:279–301), who is so far the only author to attempt a detailed description of the sub-types of RP.

I have already mentioned (and largely rejected) the convergence between RP and other varieties as a possible source of the disappearance of RP. A further, more substantial argument in support of the 'disappearance' hypothesis is the rise of what has become known as 'Estuary English', as a popular variety of spoken Standard English with phonetic features placing it between RP and broad London Cockney. Before we can judge the matter, we must look at the evidence for Estuary English, and set it in the context of dialect levelling.

Dialect levelling, social mobility and 'Estuary English'

Since the mid-1990s, a number of studies have reported *dialect levelling* – by which differences between local accents/dialects are reduced, features which make them distinctive disappear and new features develop and are adopted by speakers over a wide area (see Chapter 3; chapters in Foulkes & Docherty 1999, Stuart-Smith & Tweedie 2000, Watt 2002, Kerswill 2003). Levelling is thought to centre on large urban areas, such as Tyneside or London, from which new features diffuse, and within whose reach high degrees of contact and mobility may lead to linguistic homogenisation. Estuary English is the only regional levelling process to receive a name and to become the subject of public debate. First described by Rosewarne (1984), it was characterised by him as follows:

Estuary English is a variety of modified regional speech. It is a mixture of non-regional and local south-eastern English pronunciation and intonation. If one imagines a continuum with RP and popular London speech at either end, Estuary English speakers are to be found grouped in the middle ground. They are 'between Cockney and the Queen', in the words of *The Sunday Times*. (Rosewarne 1994:3)

For Rosewarne, with its combination of parts of Cockney pronunciation with Standard English grammar, it is the speech of the upwardly mobile, as well as being a target for some RP speakers who feel that RP may arouse hostility (1984). Wells (1994a, b) has even suggested a standardised transcription for Estuary English – perhaps reinforcing the 'standard ideology' concept. Trudgill (2002b) contests Rosewarne's claims that Estuary English is new and that it is replacing RP. Instead, it is, simply, a south-eastern lower-middle-class accent which has become more prominent as RP is being adopted by fewer people (a development already noted by Barber 1964:26), while its phonetic features (e.g. l-vocalisation, as in 'miwk' for *milk*) are spreading individually from London. Meanwhile, RP is still spoken natively by many pupils at public schools, albeit with features (notably glottal stop for /t/ before consonants) which are spreading throughout Britain and are therefore non-regional.

What is not in dispute is that Estuary English spans a very wide range of accents, from near-Cockney (the variety vilified in the press as a sloppy replacement of 'real' dialect and 'good' English in general – cf. L. Milroy 1999:181–2) to near-RP. This being so, it is difficult to call it a 'variety', and this is emphatically confirmed by the findings of Haenni (1999), Przedlacka (2002) and Altendorf (2003).

A far more realistic approach to Estuary English is to see it, instead, as referring to a set of levelled (relatively homogenised) regional – as opposed to local – accents or dialects spoken in the south-east of England. These varieties, and their counterparts throughout the British Isles, are a result of greatly heightened mobility since the period just after the Second World War, coupled with a change in ideology allowing non-RP users to occupy a range of occupations, especially in broadcasting, from which they were formerly effectively barred. Britain (2002b) sees the loss of local dialects in the east of England as resulting from greater short- and long-term mobility, the replacement of primary and secondary by tertiary industries, labour market flexibility and family ties over greater geographical distances. The resulting contacts between people speaking different varieties of English lead to the attrition of strongly local forms. The working-class dialect of the new town of Milton Keynes represents, perhaps, an extreme version of this type of levelled variety, having no single distinguishing feature (Kerswill & Williams 2000); in this context, it is easy to see the reason for its castigation at the hands of the press.

Mobility does not guarantee ideological change. In Kerswill (2001), I suggested that the social changes that have allowed non-RP accents to be used in new contexts should be seen in the context of the ideology, first emerging in the 1960s, of gender and racial equality and the legalisation of contraception, abortion and homosexuality – coupled with a generally greater access to education. Set against this 'liberal' change is the rapid development, since the 1980s, of a meritocratic ideology, by which a traditional education and 'breeding' are of lesser consequence than the ability of the individual to make economic progress. These opposing ideological trends – the democratic/liberal and the meritocratic – have similar consequences for dialect change: in both cases, the old upper-class based 'standard ideology' is challenged. The demographic changes over the same period have led to the development of new, levelled regional accents which, to a great extent, coincide linguistically to lower-middle-class accents. It is precisely this type of accent that is in the ascendancy *both* geographically (across Britain) *and* in the occupations once reserved for RP speakers. It is in the reaction of parts of the press that we see the ideological conflict being played out.

3 Phonological variation in England

Paul Foulkes and Gerard Docherty

> *... though the people of London are erroneous in the pronunciation of many words, the inhabitants of every other place are erroneous in many more*
> John Walker (1791)

Introduction

The long history of English dialectology has furnished a wealth of information on variation in the language. The most extensive record concerns the geographical distribution of segmental variables. More recently, the pioneering work of investigators such as Labov (1966, 1994, 2001), Trudgill (1974, 2002a), L. Milroy (1987), J. Milroy (1992) and Eckert (2000) has revealed the social constraints on variation. Instrumental methods have further enhanced our understanding of the fine-grained and gradient nature of variation.

It is not possible in the space available in this chapter to provide a comprehensive descriptive survey of phonological variation in English. Instead, our aim is to provide a critical summary of work from the last twenty years or so, since the first edition of this book was in preparation. While our focus is on the English of England, we also draw comparisons with other varieties of English, and indeed other languages, where it is pertinent to do so.

We begin by outlining key developments in methodology and analysis. We then summarise the findings of descriptive work at the segmental and suprasegmental levels, drawing attention to theoretical issues which have emerged from this work.

For their help during the preparation of this chapter we are grateful to Will Allen, David Britain, Judy Dyer, Bronwen Evans, Matthew Gordon, Esther Grabe, Barry Heselwood, Patrick Honeybone, Ghada Khattab, Helen Lawrence, Carmen Llamas, Inger Mees, Lesley Milroy, Catherine Sangster, Graham Shorrocks, Ishtla Singh, Jane Stuart-Smith, Ros Temple, Erik Thomas, Jenny Tillotson and Dominic Watt.

Recent advances in methods and analysis

Research into phonological variation in English underwent something of a revolution during the latter half of the twentieth century. The principal interest from the nineteenth century to the late 1960s was in the geographical distribution of lexical forms and pronunciations. The main products of such work were dialect dictionaries and grammars (e.g. Wright 1905) and linguistic maps (Orton, Sanderson & Widdowson 1962–71). Emphasis was mainly on the forms used in rural areas, with dialectologists collecting material designed to reveal conservative, 'pure dialect' forms. The subjects whose speech was recorded were mainly non-mobile older rural males (NORMs). The findings from such studies continue to be analysed (e.g. Klemola & Jones 1999), providing extremely valuable historical material for comparison with data collected in current research.

Work within this 'traditional dialectology' framework has been criticised, however, on a number of counts (see Chambers & Trudgill 1998, Milroy & Gordon 2003). Most important, perhaps, is that the methods permit little insight into variability within the speech of an individual or a community, since it was generally one speaker in each location who was recorded, in interview with a fieldworker. Since the 1960s variationist sociolinguistics has shifted the focus to within- and across-speaker variation, investigating urban as well as rural settings, and with a view to identifying and explaining the trajectories of change over space and time (Labov 1994, 2001).

A methodological consequence of these interests has been the collection in a range of locations of large samples of speech from a broad and socially heterogeneous population of speakers. From the earliest studies in the USA (e.g. Labov 1966, Labov, Yaeger & Steiner 1972) the dimensions of class, sex, age, ethnicity and style have been shown to influence pronunciation. Much work has gone into refining our understanding of the effects of these influences. Sociolinguistic and dialectological work has also become increasingly entwined with research in other areas of linguistics, including phonetics and phonology. We turn now to a brief discussion of advances in understanding variation, bearing in mind the apposite comment by Hodge & Kress (1993:vii) that 'disciplines, unlike cows, yield least when most contented'.

Class and network

Socioeconomic background, abbreviated as 'class', has a particularly strong influence on linguistic behaviour. Class is rather problematic to define and quantify, however (Ash 2002, Milroy & Gordon 2003). Most studies therefore handle class in an informal way, for example contrasting neighbourhoods with markedly different types of housing (e.g. Docherty & Foulkes 1999, Watt & Milroy 1999).

Social network and sociometric analysis have enhanced our understanding of the role of social differences, particularly in settings where social class is relatively homogeneous (Milroy & Milroy 1985, L. Milroy 1987). These studies have shown that patterns of behaviour are closely dependent on a person's degree of entrenchment in any social group. The more tightly knit the network structure, and the more integrated an individual is into the group, the stronger the impetus to adhere to the group's accepted norms of behaviour. In Western societies strong, tight-knit networks can be found in traditional 'working-class' communities. People tend to live, work and socialise in a compact setting. More middle-class communities tend to be characterised by looser network structures, with greater mobility for work, leisure and housing. Strong networks promote the maintenance of local linguistic features, while looser networks are conduits for linguistic change (Milroy & Milroy 1985). Change is facilitated by face-to-face interaction, in which interlocutors typically accommodate to one another. Accommodation involves selecting linguistic alternatives to establish solidarity with (or distance from) the interlocutor (Giles & Coupland 1991). Accommodation normally promotes *convergence*. That is, speakers avoid linguistic features which are restricted in currency in favour of those which mark the common ground with the interlocutor. In prolonged contact situations speakers with differing dialects may converge with each other to such an extent that long-term change ensues (Trudgill 1986). Loose networks act as a catalyst for change through accommodation since they increase an individual's range of contacts.

Britain (1997a) refines the network hypothesis, drawing on Giddens' (1984, 1989) theory of *routinisation* as a factor in the perpetuation and maintenance of social structures. Routine activities serve to promote the maintenance of patterns of behaviour, including language use. Norm enforcement is achieved by the perpetuation of routines. Social and political changes may cause breaks in routine, which may therefore open windows for changes in behaviour. Typical middle-class communities are distinguished by relatively weak cycles of routine, since factors such as travel for leisure or work provide breaks in routine. Over recent years major social upheavals have been felt in British society which have come to cause major disruption to patterns of routine. There has been a dramatic decline of many traditional industries and a fragmentation of the communities which they supported, a marked increase in leisure opportunities and a huge expansion of the communication media. Concomitant with these events has been a rise in geographical and social mobility. These factors together have contributed to the disruption of routines, the weakening of networks and hence the promotion of rapid linguistic change through more widespread contact between speakers of different varieties.

The principal linguistic effect of these social changes is homogenisation. Sociolinguists have described some homogenisation processes as dialect (or accent) *levelling* (e.g. Watt & Milroy 1999, Williams & Kerswill 1999, Dyer 2002, Watt 2002). Levelling emanates mainly from the loss of minority and regionally restricted forms in favour of variants shared by the majority of speakers who are in contact (Trudgill 1986, Kingston 2000). Levelling is not a new phenomenon, as witnessed for instance by research into linguistic change in the Fens from the seventeenth century onwards (Britain 1997a, b, 2001). It does, however, seem to be increasing rapidly. There is abundant evidence pointing to the erosion of the traditional dialects found in small geographical regions, and the development of new regional varieties (sometimes referred to as regional standards). The latter comprise phonological (as well as lexical and grammatical) features which cover large areas (Trudgill 2002a). Regional varieties appear to be developing around several major cities, including London ('Estuary English'; see Przedlacka 2002, Altendorf 2003 and John Wells' website: www.phon.ucl.ac.uk/home/estuary/home.htm), and Newcastle (Watt & Milroy 1999). Homogenisation may also be achieved by the *diffusion* of features as well as contact-induced levelling. Ongoing changes such as the spread of glottal stops and the use of [f, v] for (θ, ð) have been analysed as diffusing from the south-east (Kerswill 2003).

Trudgill (2002a) claims that (contrary to popular perceptions) the phonologies of these regional standards are mainly diverging, not converging, since there are numerous examples of change being promoted within the boundaries of a particular dialect. For example, several ongoing changes in Norwich have no obvious external motivation (Trudgill 1999c).

Sex and gender

Although sociolinguists often refer to the effects of speaker sex (e.g. Labov 1990), Eckert (1989, 2000) has shown that the social construct of gender offers a more accountable explanation of linguistic variation than the binary category of biological sex. In a study of teenagers in Detroit, Eckert found that some of the linguistic differences between groups of schoolgirls were greater than those found between girls and boys. Eckert (2000:122ff) concludes that 'the primary importance of gender lies not in differences between male and female across the board, but in differences within gender groups ... a general constraint against competition across gender lines leads people to compete, hence evaluate themselves, within their gender group'.

Numerous studies have shown that males and females within a community exploit phonological resources differently. It has been argued, in fact, that gender should be seen as prior to class in its influence on linguistic variability, since in many communities the distinction between gender roles is greater than that between social classes (e.g. Milroy, Milroy & Hartley 1994).

Early studies (e.g. Trudgill 1974) showed that men produce more vernacular forms than women, and explained the results by identifying women's speech as more influenced by the norms of the standard language. More recent work, however, suggests a more complex picture. Milroy & Milroy (1985), for instance, argue that reference to a local/supralocal dimension is more revealing than the vernacular/standard continuum. Men are typically more oriented to local norms, while women show more extensive usage of forms with supralocal currency, whether or not these are aligned with the standard language. Such a hypothesis receives support from studies where gender-correlated variability involves forms which cannot be associated with the standard language (e.g. Watt & Milroy 1999, Mathisen 1999).

Gender-based distinctions have been explained with reference to the different type of network ties typical of men and women. A particularly clear case is that of Ballymacarrett, Belfast (L. Milroy 1987). Men in Ballymacarrett rarely leave the neighbourhood, since they work and socialise locally, and their movements are greatly constrained by the city's territorial boundaries, drawn on ethnic lines. Their social networks are therefore particularly dense. Women do not face such restrictions, enjoying greater mobility. Women therefore also construct looser networks, with weaker ties than men to the Ballymacarrett community.

Age

Eckert (1997) deconstructs the apparently innocuous dimension of age, showing that culturally determined *life stages* are more important than a speaker's biologically determined age. In the context of the USA Eckert identifies three key life stages (childhood, adolescence and adulthood) which form the focus of much of our understanding of the relationship between age and language use. She notes that the analysis of life stages should probably be more fine-grained than this, pointing, for example, to our very poor understanding of the effect of ageing on language use (a factor which is ripe for further investigation in light of the rapid expansion of the elderly population).

Like Eckert, Cheshire (1982a) and Kerswill & Williams (2000) identify the importance of the adolescent peer group in the transmission of vernacular forms. Adolescence is a time at which conformity to peer group norms becomes especially important. The vernacular takes on a special role: its use becomes symbolic of the construction of identity, a means by which adolescents can align themselves with some speaker groups and differentiate themselves from others. As a result, usage of vernacular forms tends to accelerate beyond those of the previous generation, a phenomenon which emerges most clearly where the parents' generation has different regional dialects from the adolescents, as in Milton Keynes.

A consequence of such work has been to show that it is often adolescents who display the greatest use of vernacular forms. This finding therefore calls into question the assumption of early dialectological work that older men are the 'best' source of local linguistic forms (Milroy & Gordon 2003:18). Furthermore, the common hypothesis that language patterns are fixed through adulthood has been brought into question by *real-time* studies, which have shown that individuals may change linguistic performance as they get older and their social circumstances change (e.g. Harrington, Palethorpe & Watson 2005).

The acquisition of variable forms in childhood is less well understood, although recent work shows that complex patterns of variation are acquired from the earliest stages (Roberts 2002, Foulkes, Docherty & Watt 2001, Docherty, Foulkes, Tillotson & Watt 2006). Work on bilingual acquisition has also shown that children learn specific rules of articulatory timing and perceptual categorisation, even where the phonological systems of their two languages apparently overlap (Khattab 2002a).

Ethnicity

Another major social development of the late twentieth century in Britain has been the huge rise in immigration, and the establishment of large ethnic communities in many cities. In the 2001 census, 13% of the population of England registered their ethnicity as other than White British (www. statistics.gov.uk/census2001). The figure is far greater in cities such as Bradford, where over 50% of the residents in some suburbs are of Pakistani origin (Bradford Education 1996), and Leicester, where in 1998 over 35% of the city's state school pupils spoke English as an additional language (OFSTED 1998). Some recent research has investigated phonological changes in British Panjabi (Heselwood & McChrystal 1999). However, there is strikingly little work on the phonetics and phonology of the English spoken in ethnic sub-communities. The few readily available sources include the studies of Caribbean immigrants by Wells (1973), Sutcliffe (1982) and Sebba (1987), and Fox's (2007) thesis on Bangladeshis in Tower Hamlets. Heselwood & McChrystal (2000) present a preliminary study of the accent features of Bradford Panjabi–English bilinguals. Intriguingly, their results suggest that young males in Bradford employ much more marked features than do females, for example using more noticeable retroflexion in stop articulations.

Focussing on ethnicity based on religious rather than racial criteria, L. Milroy (1987) and McCafferty (1999, 2001) provide detailed discussions of Protestant/Catholic differences in Belfast and (London)Derry respectively.

Speaking style

All individuals, even young children, are capable of modifying their speech in relation to different styles of speaking. So much so, in fact, that one of the thorniest problems in dialectology has been obtaining speech samples which are *not* modified, but representative of the speaker's habitual vernacular (the *Observer's Paradox*: Labov 1972:209). In early sociolinguistics style was viewed as a continuum along which a speaker could vary. At one pole lay the vernacular, defined by Labov (1972:208) as the style in which a speaker pays minimal attention to speech. The remainder of the continuum was punctuated by various degrees of formality, defined in terms of self-monitoring and elicited in fieldwork by different types of interview method, including reading tasks. It has generally – but not always – been found that in more self-conscious styles speakers modify their speech increasingly towards the standard language (or at least their perceptions of it).

Analysis of style has been revised somewhat over time. Reading tasks have been criticised since they may present quite discrete speaking challenges for speakers of dialects which are particularly distinct from the standard (Milroy & Gordon 2003:201ff.). Rather than inducing gradual shifts in articulatory performance, reading tasks can cause individuals to enter a different mode of speaking, not unlike the kind of shift associated with bilinguals. In Belfast, for example, the vernacular form of *brother* may be [bɹɔəɹ]. In reading style the presence of *th* in the orthographic form causes most people to make a categorical shift to the standard form with [ð].

It has also been shown that speech is modified for reasons other than self-consciousness. Adjustments can be made in order to express solidarity with, or distance from, an interlocutor. A clear example of this was encountered by Trudgill (1986:8) in Norwich, who found his own use of [ʔ] varied in correlation with the proportion of glottals used by his interviewees. Bell (1984) has termed this effect *audience design*. In a similar vein, Lindblom (1986, 1990) has suggested that speakers operate along a continuum from *hyper-* to *hypo-speech* in accordance with the perceived interactional needs of the interlocutor. More elaborated (hyper) articulations can be used where a speaking situation demands 'listener-oriented' speech, such as giving instructions or speaking in noisy conditions. On the other hand, articulatory control in interactions such as informal conversations may be more 'speaker-oriented', permitting a greater degree of underarticulation (hypo-speech).

The work of Bell and Lindblom further intersects with findings from conversation analysis, which reveal that phonetic cues may be manipulated for pragmatic purposes such as delimiting speaking turns. Phonetic cues therefore take on a role particular to the participants in a specific interaction (see for example Local, Wells & Sebba 1985, Local, Kelly & Wells 1986, Local 2003).

Geography

As we noted earlier, academic study of the geographical distribution of linguistic forms has a long history, dating back to the 1800s. Britain (2002a) refines the sociolinguist's understanding of geographical space, concluding that space has usually been viewed as 'a blank stage on which sociolinguistic processes are enacted' (p. 603). He argues that it is not just *Euclidean* (geographical or objective) space which acts as a force in the maintenance or change of linguistic forms. There may also be contributions from *social* space – the distance between individuals derived from socio-economic and political distinctions and through human communication; and *perceived* space – a psychological correlate of the physical and social space dimensions. Britain shows that the Fens are less affected than the neighbouring city of Peterborough by various changes diffusing from London. While the physical distance to London is similar, Peterborough is much closer to London in social terms, for example via high-speed commuter rail links. The Fens are further removed from Peterborough, and thus from the influence of London, both in social and perceived space. Contact between Fenlanders and residents of Peterborough takes place mainly in the social amenities of the city, which are served by relatively poor transport links from the Fens. Attitudinal factors serve to further increase the distance between the two populations, with a strong negative perception of the Fenlanders as "country bumpkins". Watt & Ingham (2000), in their discussion of changes in progress in Berwick, similarly note the effect of the 'psychological border' between English and Scottish identity as well as the geographical boundary dividing England from Scotland.

Analytic techniques

Recently research in phonological variation has benefited greatly from technological advances. Fieldwork has been facilitated by the development of high quality but cheap and portable recording equipment (Ladefoged 2003). Fieldwork techniques themselves have undergone various refinements in light of the advancements in our understanding of the social constraints on language use. Llamas (1999), for instance, has developed a very useful method for eliciting comparable data on the phonological, lexical and grammatical levels simultaneously. Instrumental analysis has also become far easier, faster and cheaper with the development of computer-based acoustic analysis software.[1] Acoustic analysis has always been central to Labov's work in the USA, where extensive vowel formant analysis has formed the basis of the chain shift model of change (Labov 1994). Formant analysis has played a less prominent role in work on British English, although it is exemplified by a number of studies on RP (Henton 1983, Deterding 1997, Fabricius 2002b, Hawkins & Midgley 2005), and also by Watt & Tillotson (2001, with data from Bradford), Torgersen & Kerswill (2004: Ashford), and Nevalainen & Aulanko (1996: Somerset). Harrington, Palethorpe & Watson (2005) use acoustic analysis to show that Queen Elizabeth II's vowels have changed during the course of her adult life. Vowel duration rather than quality has been analysed by Scobbie, Hewlett & Turk (1999) and Watt & Ingham (2000) (see below).

Acoustic analysis of consonants, while virtually absent in North American work, has proved revealing in recent British work. Docherty & Foulkes (1999, 2005) show that patterns of stop realisation in Derby and Newcastle vary with respect to fine-grained aspects of inter-gestural timing, and that these patterns correlate with the social characteristics of the speaker. Similar findings emerge in Foulkes & Docherty (2000) on prevocalic (r) and Lawson & Stuart-Smith's (1999) work on (ʍ) and (x) in Glasgow.

There has been relatively little articulatory analysis of consonantal variation, but see Wright (1989) and Hardcastle & Barry (1989) for electro-palatographic investigations of (l) vocalisation. Newer articulatory techniques such as MRI and ultrasound are also being applied to large speaker samples (e.g. Zhang, Boyce, Espy-Wilson & Tiede 2003).

Technological advances are furthermore facilitating new insights into the way in which listeners show sensitivity to variable features in speech perception. For example, Strand (1999) shows that gender stereotypes influence listeners' categorisation of tokens on a nine-step [s]–[ʃ] continuum,

---

[1] Free acoustic analysis software systems can be downloaded via the Internet. The SFS system (from www.phon.ucl.ac.uk), Wavesurfer (www.speech.kth.se/wavesurfer) and Speech Analyzer (www.sil.org/computing/speechtools/speechanalyzer.htm) offer spectrographic and spectral analysis, while Praat (www.praat.org) is a more sophisticated package which also includes functions for statistics and speech synthesis.

suggesting that 'higher-level relatively complex social expectations might have an influence on such low-level basic processes as phonological categorisation of the speech signal' (p. 93). Such work has intriguing implications for theories of phonological representation and acquisition which have tended to assume that one of the key tasks in speech perception was to filter out the variable features of the signal. We expect the role of variability in speech perception to be an area of increasing interest to researchers in speech perception in the coming years (see further Hawkins & Smith 2001, Hawkins 2003).

This sketch of the research methods of dialectal variability is by necessity very brief (see further Chambers 2003, Milroy & Gordon 2003). But it serves, we hope, to identify the complex set of factors which influence pronunciation, and also to explain why there is unevenness in the extent of knowledge we have about particular accents and variable features. In the next two sections we discuss aspects of segmental and prosodic variation in the light of these influences, combining descriptions of geographical distributions with what is known about social and stylistic constraints.

Segmental variation

Following Wells (1982) we employ a set of keywords such as GOAT, FACE and START, to illustrate classes of words which contain a particular phonological vowel. /l/, /h/ and /θ, ð/ and other consonantal variables are given in standard sociolinguistic notation, e.g. (h).

Stops

Probably the most widely studied variable in English phonology is (t), in particular with reference to its realisation as a glottal (for a thorough survey see Fabricius 2000, 2002a). We hesitate to say glottal *stop*, since acoustic analysis shows that sounds perceived as [ʔ] or an oral plosive with glottal reinforcement in fact tend not to contain a glottal stop closure (e.g. Grice & Barry 1991). Our work in Newcastle revealed that 70% of audibly glottal(ised) segments were fully voiced, with the glottal percept being cued by creaky phonation (Docherty & Foulkes 1999, 2005).

Glottal forms of (t) are increasing in frequency across much of the British Isles. Indeed it is becoming rare to hear word-final pre-consonantal (t), as in *get ready*, articulated as a plain oral stop. Collins & Mees (1996) demonstrate, in fact, that RP speakers born as long ago as 1848 used pre-consonantal glottals. For younger RP speakers (t) may be deleted altogether in some contexts (Fabricius 2000:85). In word-final prevocalic position (e.g. *get off*) glottals are less common, but now well established even for RP speakers (Fabricius 2000, 2002a). Most varieties tolerate glottals before syllabic nasals and/or laterals, and also in turn-final position (Newcastle provides an exception on the latter score: Docherty, Foulkes, Milroy, Milroy & Walshaw 1997). It is really in intervocalic position, e.g. *water*, where the ongoing spread is most noticeable. In Derby, for example, older speakers produced only 4 medial glottals in almost 1,000 tokens in unscripted conversation. By contrast, younger speakers produced 22% glottals (Docherty & Foulkes 1999). The use of glottals remains a stigmatised feature for many self-appointed guardians of the language (e.g. Norman 2001), although the stigma is undoubtedly waning fast and is probably now restricted to intervocalic positions. Today's undergraduates fail to see what any of the fuss is about. Glottals can also be heard, but much less frequently, as realisations of (p) and (k) and occasionally for fricatives and (d) (e.g. Sullivan 1992, Tollfree 1999, Trudgill 1999c). Glottal realisations of the definite article can be found across many northern regions, although these are probably retreating in the face of standardisation (Shorrocks 1991, 1998, Jones 2002).

Deletion of (t) and (d) in word-final consonant clusters (e.g. *last piece*) is the norm in many dialects, particularly in faster and more casual speech styles. This phenomenon has been investigated in many US dialects (e.g. Guy 1980), but so far few in the UK. However, Tagliamonte & Temple (2005) show that patterns of deletion in York differ from those found in North American studies.

A range of voiced variants of intervocalic (t) can be found across varieties, including [ɹ] and [ɾ]. The former is restricted to a small set of lexical items, mostly in final position, e.g. *get off*, *what if*, *that is*, but also medially in *better* and *getting*. This variant is mainly found in northern areas, is often stigmatised and seems to be receding in currency. This is true at least in Newcastle (Watt & Milroy 1999:29) and Derby (Docherty & Foulkes 1999:51). The distribution of [ɾ] and voiced stop variants is less clear. Mathisen (1999:110) reports [ɾ] to be mainly a feature of older male speech in Sandwell. On the other hand, it appears to be on the increase in Newcastle (cf. Watt & Milroy 1999:29). Docherty & Foulkes (1999) discuss innovative pre-aspirated variants in Newcastle, which mainly affect pre-pausal (t) and are strongly associated with young women. See also Sangster (2001), Honeybone (2001) and Watson (2002) for discussions of fricated stops in Liverpool English.

Variation in voice onset time is discussed by Heselwood & McChrystal (2000), who report deaspiration of voiceless stops for some Bradford Asians. Variable deaspiration is also mentioned by Lodge (1966, 1978) for Stockport and by Wells (1982:370) for North Lancashire (see also Scobbie 2006). Another source of variation, at least at an individual level, is whether or not vocal cord vibration is present within the closure phase of voiced stops (Docherty 1992, Khattab 2002a). Some speakers in Manchester and London employ audible affrication, yielding for instance a [tˢ] quality for (t), which Tollfree (1999:170) associates with confident, affected or emphatic speech styles.

While realisational differences have received the most attention, it has also been shown that dialects may differ in the connected speech processes they permit. Nolan & Kerswill (1990) found variable assimilation effects for schoolchildren in Cambridge. Kerswill & Wright (1990) showed that place assimilations common in standard varieties, such as *red car* [ɹɛg kɑː], appear not to occur in Durham. Durham, by contrast, permits regressive voicing assimilation which is not found for RP. Thus *like bairns* may be pronounced with a final [g] in the first word. Parts of West Yorkshire, notably Bradford, follow a similar pattern with voiceless assimilation, thus *Hyde Park* may be [haɪt̚ pɑːk] (or [haɪʔ pɑːk] via glottalling).

Fricatives

Two particularly striking changes are affecting the fricative system of English. The first concerns the realisation of (h). Although (h) dropping is cited by Wells (1982:60) as 'perhaps the single most powerful socio-linguistic shibboleth in England', it appears from recent work that the spread of H-loss has been halted or even reversed. Tollfree (1999:173) suggests that the feature has stabilised in London. In Hull younger and older speakers use roughly the same proportion of [h], while in Milton Keynes and Reading, children have a strong tendency to pronounce [h] in interview style (Williams & Kerswill 1999:157–8).

The second change concerns labiodental realisations of the dental frica-tives (θ, ð). Use of [f, v] in e.g. *think*, *mother* is spreading as rapidly and widely as any feature bar glottalling (J. Milroy 1996, Kerswill 2003). Speakers can, however, usually differentiate dentals and labiodentals in careful speech (Wells 1982:328). Initial (ð) in function words (*the*, *this*, *they*, etc.) is rarely affected but instead may be articulated as a dental or alveolar stop.

The [ʍ] pronunciation in words such as *which* has all but disappeared from accents in England, having merged with [w] (or [h] preceding the GOOSE vowel, e.g. *who*). Exceptions include conservative RP and parts of rural Northumberland (Wells 1982:228ff.).

Subtler or more restricted variations in fricative production may also be found, although they have received less attention. Word-initial (f, s, ʃ, θ) may be voiced in the south-west, including Somerset, Devon and Cornwall, although these are yielding rapidly under the influence of standard English and are virtually extinct for young urban speakers (e.g. Wakelin 1986:17, 29). In contrast, devoicing of (z) is cited as a shibboleth to identify speakers of Welsh origin in the border town of Oswestry (Elmes 2000:112).

Dialects may also differ in the relative sibilance typical of (s) and (z). Some older speakers in Derby, for example, tend to use a retracted lingual articulation for these fricatives, resulting in an audibly lower frequency (Docherty & Foulkes 1999:51).

Nasals

Several studies have investigated variability in the realisation of (ŋ). It is well known that the [n] realisation tends to outweigh [ŋ] in colloquial speech, and is usually most closely associated with male speakers from lower socioeconomic groups (e.g. Trudgill 1974). Tagliamonte (2004) discusses language-internal constraints on variation in (ŋ) in York, showing that the most significant factor was the grammatical category of word: verbs favour [n] while nouns and adjectives favour [ŋ].

The variant [ŋg] is common in many parts of the north and middle west (e.g. Knowles 1978, Heath 1980, Shorrocks 1998, Mathisen 1999, Newbrook 1999, Docherty & Foulkes 1999). In fact it appears to be emerging as a local prestige form in some of these areas. In Sandwell, for example, it is commonest for women, is increasing in currency for younger speakers and occurs more frequently for all speakers in more careful styles (Mathisen 1999:120).

Liquids and approximants

The phonetic quality and phonotactic distribution of (r) are both variable. The most widespread form used is the alveolar approximant [ɹ] (e.g. Gimson 1980:204ff.). Several other variants can be found which are restricted to particular phonological positions, regional dialects and/or certain speech styles. These include [ɾ], which is common in northern varieties (e.g. Shorrocks 1998) and conservative RP, especially in inter-vocalic position; [r], which seems restricted to affected or theatrical styles; [ʀ], on the verge of extinction but which can still be heard in rural Northumberland and parts of Cumbria; and [ɻ], in the south-west (Wakelin 1986). A labial or labiodental variant, usually transcribed [ʋ], has also long been recognised but has usually been dismissed as a feature of immature, defective or affected speech (e.g. Gimson 1980:207). In recent years, however, [ʋ] has become firmly established as an acceptable mature variant in many urban dialects, and appears to be diffusing from south to north (Foulkes & Docherty 2000). Acoustic analysis of labial variants suggests in fact that a range of phonetic forms are in currency, and [ʋ] should be understood as a convenient cover label rather than a precise transcription (Docherty & Foulkes 2001).

Variability in phonotactic distribution primarily concerns whether or not (r) is articulated in postvocalic positions, a division encapsulated in the descriptive labels *rhotic* vs. *non-rhotic*. While rhoticity is socially prestigious in North America, Ireland and Scotland, the reverse is true for England. Speakers of rhotic varieties are often subject to ridicule (note, for instance, the comments made to Cornish speakers recorded by Elmes 2000:59, 62). In the face of such stigma, it is no surprise to find that non-rhoticity is encroaching on traditionally rhotic areas such as Berkshire (Williams & Kerswill 1999:147), Exeter (Sullivan 1992) and Bolton (Shorrocks 1998:388–9), especially in urban areas. On the other hand, Vivian (2000) shows rhoticity to be very well maintained in a sample of lower-class speakers in Accrington and Blackburn, and slightly less well in Burnley.

Most non-rhotic dialects have a contextualised alternation between [r] (of any phonetic form) and Ø. This is referred to as linking (r), where a rhotic consonant may be pronounced only if a vowel follows, as in (1).

(1)   dollar [Ø]   dollar [Ø] bill   dolla[r] or two

The alternation is usually an automatic phonological process with little social variation, although in Newcastle it was found to be significantly less common in the speech of the working-class group and the young (Foulkes 1997).

In most non-rhotic dialects (and occasionally in rhotic ones) this alternation is extended to words which did not historically contain (r) (as in 2).

(2)   Tessa [Ø]   Tessa [Ø] Smith   Tessa[r] O'Brien

The pattern illustrated in (2), called intrusive (r), has traditionally been stigmatised and speakers tend to avoid pronouncing intrusive [r] in conscious styles. Newcastle is again an exception (Foulkes 1997).

Variation in (l) centres on phonetic quality. While RP is traditionally described as having 'clear' (alveolar) [l] in syllable onsets and 'dark' (velarised or pharyngealised) [ɫ] in codas, the distinction does not always hold in other varieties. Clear (l) is found in all positions in the north-east (Watt & Milroy 1999:31) and also in Bradford Asian speech (Heselwood & McChrystal 2000). By contrast (l) appears universally dark in the southwest (Wakelin 1986:31), and variably dark in all positions in Leeds (Khattab 2002b). An intermediate quality tends to obtain in other parts of the north (Wells 1982:370). Where coda (l) is dark, delateralisation may occur, resulting in a variety of vowel sounds (Wells 1982:258ff., Wright

1989, Tollfree 1999, Altendorf 2003). In Hardcastle & Barry's (1989) study, vocalisation was more prevalent in the context of a preceding front vowel and/or a following palato-alveolar or velar consonant. Vocalisation seems to be spreading even though it is usually thought to be stigmatised. It is found in Peterborough (Britain 1997a:42) and the West Midlands (Mathisen 1999:111), but not yet Norwich (Trudgill 1999c:140). It is also increasing in Derby, although historical records show it to have a considerable time-depth in the surrounding region (Pegge 1896, Hulme 1941). There are signs, too, that the perceived stigma is disappearing. Johnson (2001) found no significant difference in rate of vocalisation in casual speech vs. word-list reading for Derby informants.

It furthermore appears from phonological research that the degree of darkness in (l) may be linked to the quality of (r) that is used in the dialect. Kelly (1995) and Carter (2003) show that clear (l) entails dark (r) and vice versa, although these findings are yet to be tested on large speaker samples.

The approximant (j) is variably deleted in consonant clusters in most accents (Wells 1982:206ff.), although it is often categorically absent in Norfolk and the East Midlands (Trudgill 1999c:133). Among many young speakers over a wide area alveolar stop + (j) sequences are assimilating into affricates [tʃ] and [dʒ], thus *tune* is frequently [tʃʉːn]. Likewise, in triconsonantal clusters initial (s) may also palatalise through assimilation: *stupid* and *strong* can be heard as [ʃtʃʉːpɪd] and [ʃtɹɒŋ].

Vowels

It is widely recognised that vowels carry the bulk of responsibility for differentiating English accents from one another (Wells 1982:178). The vowels with perhaps the greatest sociolinguistic significance in England are STRUT and BATH. The main alternants, [ʊ] *versus* [ʌ] and [a] *versus* [ɑː] respectively, divide the linguistic north and south. The *Survey of English Dialects* (*SED*) data yield famous isoglosses for both from the Severn to the Wash (Upton & Widdowson 1996:6–14). Britain (2001) investigates the performance of speakers who live close to these isoglosses, in the Fens. His findings show that almost all individual speakers vary in their pronunciations for STRUT and BATH, but the patterns for younger and older speakers differ. For STRUT the older speakers show a gradual transition across the Fens, with [ʊ] dominant in the north and giving way gradually to [ʌ] further south. For younger speakers, however, the transition is much sharper, and an interdialectal 'fudged' form [ɤ] has emerged as the main variant for speakers living in the centre of the area. The north to south gradation also applies to BATH, although in the central area speakers tend to use either [a] or [ɑː], with no intermediate phonetic forms, but with the alternative variant cropping up in occasional lexical items. Fabricius (2000:35) suggests that northern [a] may be spreading by lexical diffusion into southern varieties.

A study of vowels in Newcastle reveals substantial ongoing change with respect to FACE, GOAT and NURSE (Watt & Milroy 1999, Watt 2000). The traditional local forms of FACE and GOAT, [ɪə] and [ʊə], are becoming restricted to older males, and are virtually absent in the speech of women. Younger speakers are opting instead for monophthongal variants [eː] and [oː], which have a wide distribution over much of the north of England (see also Kerswill 1984). The traditional variant of NURSE, [ɔː], is also shown to be highly recessive. The standard-like [əː] is more frequent, but younger women show a distinct preference for a front rounded [øː]. Gender is overall the most important social constraint on the distributional patterns for these three vowels. Coupled with the shift away from traditional forms, and the relatively small number of standard variants found, Watt & Milroy argue that these patterns are indicative of accent levelling. Watt (2000) furthermore suggests that the apparent parallelism of the FACE and GOAT developments is best analysed with reference to their social connotations rather than as a system-internal development, as predicted by the chain shift model (Labov 1994).

Levelling is also the principal theme of research centred on Milton Keynes (Kerswill 1996a, Williams & Kerswill 1999, Kerswill & Williams 2000). Several vowel variables have shown levelling to be underway as children reduce the wide variety of forms used by their elders, both long-term residents and in-migrants to the town from various other locations.

Levelling to various degrees is found in other new towns, Telford (Britain & Simpson 2007) and Corby (Dyer 2002). In Telford, young speakers display focussing to an interdialectal form [ʌi] in PRICE words (compare the traditional Shropshire form [ai] and urban Birmingham [ɔi]), although variants of GOAT remain highly variable. Corby is particularly interesting for its large population of in-migrant steel workers from Glasgow, who moved to the town in the 1960s. Some imported Scottish forms are being eradicated by the younger generation, such as the merger between the LOT and THOUGHT sets (which render cot and caught homophonous, [kɔt]). Others, however, are being maintained, but with new social evaluations. For GOAT, the Scottish monophthongal form [oː] is winning out over English diphthongs, especially in the speech of young men. By referring to overt linguistic and sociological comments by her informants, Dyer shows that speakers' ideologies have changed, and so too have the social connotations associated with linguistic variants. Monophthongal GOAT variants are emblematic, for older speakers, of ethnic affiliation to Scotland. For younger speakers the ethnic division has been erased. For them [oː] has become a marker of locality, differentiating Corby from neighbouring towns such as Kettering.

Britain's study of the Fens (1997a, b, 2001) furthermore shows that in dialect contact situations competing forms can be reallocated to allophonic status with different contextual constraints from those found in the contributing dialects. In the Fens, PRICE vowels with an open onset typical of the areas to the west, [ɑi, ɑː], have entered into contact with eastern variants containing a more central first element, [əi]. Among younger Fenlanders the latter variants have become restricted to positions before voiceless consonants, as in *night*.

Vowel fronting (sometimes coupled with unrounding), especially of GOAT, STRUT and GOOSE, has been in progress in RP for some time (e.g. Gimson 1984, Altendorf 2003). It seems to be spreading to parts of the Midlands (Docherty & Foulkes 1999). Fronting patterns with a different outcome, [əː] or [øː], have been found for GOAT in an acoustic study of Bradford English (Watt & Tillotson 2001) as well as Hull (Williams & Kerswill 1999). Watt & Tillotson suggest it is an innovatory form diffusing across Yorkshire and Teesside from a Humberside source.

Competing vowel length is the subject of an acoustic study of Berwick English undertaken by Watt & Ingham (2000). Berwick lies three miles from the Scottish border, and shares many linguistic features with both rural Northumbrian English and also dialects of Scotland, including the Scottish Vowel Length Rule (SVLR; see further Scobbie *et al.* 1999). Watt & Ingram show that SVLR is present in Berwick, but it is becoming less consistent among younger speakers. This change is discussed as a diagnostic of individual affiliation to a Scottish vs. English identity. J. Milroy (1995) also shows SVLR to be present, at least for PRICE, in Newcastle.

Finally, Wells (1982:257ff.) discusses an innovation in the happy class, where the final vowel is shifting from [ɪ] to [iː]. The shift appears complete in London (Tollfree 1999:169) and Norwich (Trudgill 1999c:139), and nearly so in the Wirral (Newbrook 1999:97). More open qualities, approaching [ɛ], can be found in some northern dialects (e.g. Stoddart, Upton & Widdowson 1999), while Local (1990) shows that length and quality are variable in Newcastle, and subject to harmony with the preceding vowel.

Suprasegmentals

Suprasegmentals are aspects of speech which extend over domains larger than single segments. They include intonation, rhythm and vocal setting. Such features may vary across speakers and speaker groups, just as consonant and vowel realisations do. Nevertheless, there has been relatively little formal study of suprasegmental variation, particularly in varieties other than RP. In part this is due to the considerable methodological problems associated with suprasegmental analysis. First, it is often difficult to identify the phonetic correlates of suprasegmental features, even with instrumental analysis. Compared, for example, with quantifying the number of glottal versus alveolar stops a speaker produces, it can be problematic to make a reliable judgement of a feature such as velarised voice quality. Second, quantitative analytic frameworks are in many cases quite complex and require considerable training to use reliably. Furthermore, the *form–function problem* faced by those investigating grammatical variation (e.g. Cheshire 1999a) is also acute in suprasegmental analysis. Comparison of any type of linguistic variation is grounded on the hypothesis that a linguistic unit may be realised in a variety of different physical forms. In examinations of segmental variation the issue is generally uncontroversial. We can be confident, for example, that the pronunciations [wɔːtə] and [wɔːʔə] are equivalent in their linguistic function. We can therefore analyse a body of data to quantify how often a speaker uses one form or the other and draw meaningful comparisons across speakers or dialects. In suprasegmental analysis, however, it is often open to debate whether two formally different expressions are semantically equivalent.

O'Connor & Arnold (1973) and Cruttenden (1997, 2001a) offer detailed discussions of the problems in identifying the meanings of particular intonation patterns. Cruttenden argues that intonational meanings are composed of at least three strands, derived from (i) the grammatical structure of the utterance, (ii) the speaker's attitude, and (iii) the pragmatic or discourse function of the utterance (see also Pierrehumbert & Hirschberg 1990). Moreover, the degree of importance of these three levels may vary from token to token. It is therefore often difficult to isolate groups of functionally equivalent utterances, and in turn problematic to make quantitative analyses of the suprasegmental features they contain.

In spite of such methodological problems, recent studies have significantly advanced our understanding of the phonetic, phonological and sociolinguistic patterns of suprasegmental variation.

Vocal setting and voice quality

Vocal setting is defined by Laver (1994:396) as the 'tendency underlying the production of the chain of segments in speech towards maintaining a particular configuration or state of the vocal apparatus'. Speakers who tend to keep the velum lowered, for instance, will possess a habitually nasal voice quality. Extensive studies of the phonetic correlates of vocal settings can be found in Laver (1980) and Nolan (1983).

As already noted, there has been little formal study of the social or stylistic correlations of vocal settings, although impressionistic comments on voice (phonation) quality are more widespread than those on supralaryngeal settings. Creaky phonation as a general dialect feature is associated with RP and many regional forms of US and Australian English (e.g. Laver 1980:4, Henton & Bladon 1988). In many dialects creak performs pragmatic functions, in particular marking turn-endings. Honikman (1964) suggests that RP is also characterised by a slightly retroflex tongue setting, and an overall lax articulatory setting.

Knowles (1978) comments on the velarised voice quality and raised larynx setting used in Liverpool, while Trudgill (1974) describes Norwich voice quality in some detail. Typical features here include nasalisation, creak and raised larynx.

The most detailed studies, however, have been carried out on varieties of English spoken in Scotland. Esling (1978) found class differences in voice qualities used by Edinburgh speakers. For example, the working-class subjects tended to display protruded jaw and harsh phonation. Stuart-Smith's (1999) study of thirty-two Glasgow speakers stands as a model for future studies in a variationist framework, revealing significant differences correlated with class, age and gender.

Rhythm

The rhythmic pattern of speech is a perceptual effect 'produced by the interaction in time of the relative prominence of stressed and unstressed syllables' (Laver 1994:152). Languages are said to be either *syllable-timed* or *stress-timed*, although in practice these constitute two poles of a continuum. In syllable-timed languages (e.g. French), syllables tend to be more regular in duration than in stress-timed languages (e.g. English). In the latter the time from each stressed syllable to the next is roughly equal, while unstressed syllables are compressed in between.

This difference in rhythmic organisation may also occur across different dialects of a language. Welsh English is generally said to be syllable-timed, but Cardiff rhythm is more like the stress-timed pattern of Standard English (Mees & Collins 1999:194). Syllable timing is also suggested as a feature of Bradford Panjabi English (Heselwood & McChrystal 2000) and Jamaican Creole (Sebba 1987). Trudgill (1999c:124) notes the characteristic rhythm of Norwich and Norfolk speech, involving very long stressed syllables and very short unstressed ones. Nolan & Kerswill (1990) make comparable comments for local Cambridge speakers.

As with vocal setting, there have been few cross-dialectal studies of rhythm. However, recent work in phonetics has yielded a useful framework, the Pairwise Variability Index (PVI), which allows us to quantify and compare rhythmic features (Grabe & Low 2002).

Stress and intonation

Although word stress in English is not wholly fixed (Fudge 1984), dialects seem to differ relatively little in the location of main stress placement. This is true both for word stress and sentence stress. Thus, words like *acquisition, deliver, telephone* will almost invariably take stress on the indicated syllable, no matter what the dialect or style of speech. Counter-examples can be found, which as often as not appear to reflect differences between British and North American usage. North American dialects tend to opt for initial word- and phrase-stress (*ice* cream, *cigarette*, *inquiry*, *The English Patient*), some of which have filtered into British usage (as has *kilometre*). However, the traffic is not one-way, with the British pattern for *controversy* replacing the initial-stressed pattern in the USA (Wells 1995). Nolan (2002) shows furthermore that speakers vary in the precise location of peak pitch alignment within a stressed syllable.

Differences may occur in the type of pitch pattern used to represent the main stress within a sentence. In order to circumvent form–function and methodological problems, Cruttenden (2001a:57) identifies two basic and largely universal phonological categories which are signalled by contrasting intonation patterns. *Open* tones, which may be used in yes/no question constructions, parenthetic comments and requests, indicate a 'continuative' meaning. They signal, for example, that the speaker has not completed the speaking turn, and that there is 'more to come'. These contrast with *Closed* tones, which offer no indication of any continuing speech. These are typically used in statements, exclamations and commands.

All languages and dialects appear to contrast these two categories, although their realisations may vary phonetically. RP, for instance, tends to use a falling pitch pattern to signal Closed category meanings, with a pitch rise for Open category meanings. Cruttenden (1997:128) further notes that use of low-rise and fall-rise patterns in Open tones are typical of more formal speech styles in English. Cruttenden (2001a) presents data from four women from Salford, showing that the commonest patterns they use are rise-slump in the Closed category, and fall-level in the Open category. ('Slump' is defined as a fall from a relatively high pitch to a relatively medium pitch within a speaker's overall range; 'fall' strictly involves a pitch drop to the speaker's base line.) The Salford study is intended as a preliminary attempt to describe the intonation of a non-standard dialect, and as such its focus is mainly a comparison with RP.

What also emerges, however, is the degree of variability within the data sample. The two principal patterns only account for 27% and 32% of the data in the Closed and Open categories respectively.

The use of rising patterns in Closed tones in many northern cities is cited by Cruttenden (1997:133) as the most noticeable cross-dialectal variation in English intonation. Rises are traditionally associated with Birmingham, Liverpool and Newcastle (as well as much of Wales, Ireland and urban Scotland, but not Edinburgh). Cruttenden further points out that there are actually four different varieties of tone involved in these 'rises'. See further Knowles (1978), Bilton (1982), Local, Kelly & Wells (1986), Cruttenden (1997:128–38) and Grabe (2004).

Intonational differences have also been reported for London Jamaican (Local, Wells & Sebba 1985, Sebba 1987). Unlike most other varieties of English, nuclear syllables are not marked by pitch movement, which is used only to signal conversational turn-endings. Moreover, the phonetic cue for turn-delimitation in London Jamaican occurs on the final syllable of a speaking turn, whereas in RP and Tyneside it is centred on the final foot (Local, Kelly & Wells 1986). One way by which syllables bearing information focus can be highlighted in London Jamaican is through lengthening initial fricatives, as in (3) (Sebba 1987:64):

(3)   You could be getting [s:]ixty pounds a week and I get thirty pounds a week.

One of the most noticeable innovations in recent years has been the development of rising intonation in the Closed tone category in dialects which traditionally use falls. This has been found in the USA, Australia and New Zealand as well as Great Britain, and has been variously labelled *high rising tone* (HRT), *Australian Question(ing) Intonation* (AQI) and *uptalk* (see Cruttenden 1995, 1997:129–31, Fletcher, Grabe & Warren 2005). The pattern is associated with the upwardly mobile ('yuppies') in England (Cruttenden 1997:130), but lower class and/or female speech elsewhere.

Because of its perceptual salience, HRT has been the subject of much comment by non-linguists, including the mass media. Some of these comments are highly speculative and empirically untested, for example, that Australian soap operas are responsible for the spread of HRT (Bathurst 1996, Lawson 1998). Others, taking up the mantle of John Walker and others in lamenting change of any kind, identify HRT as a sign of unstoppable decay in modern English (e.g. Bradbury 1996, Norman 2001). Still others draw a logical but naive conclusion, based on comparison with standard English, that rises indicate questions, and thus the use of rises in declaratives reflects a psychological state of uncertainty. The voice coach Patsy Rodenburg, for example, is quoted by Kennedy (1996) as claiming 'that rising inflection is about being unsure . . . you make a question rather than a statement because you are scared'. Such statements are ill-founded in that they equate a particular intonation pattern with a single linguistic function. They thereby fail to take account of issues raised earlier: the form–function problem; the fact that intonational meaning is derived from a complex set of sources; and that social and linguistic evaluation of features may vary from speaker to speaker. It is obvious from examination of intonation patterns in dialects such as Newcastle and Liverpool that rises may be employed in the Closed category without any indication of interrogative meaning or uncertainty. Furthermore, linguists who have analysed HRT have identified its positive discourse functions. It has been shown that HRT serves to track the listener's comprehension and attention, especially when the speaker is presenting new information. Listeners perceive HRT to be deferential but friendly (Guy & Vonwiller 1984). It also acts as a turn-holding mechanism in narratives (e.g. Warren & Britain 1999).

Finally, recent work has shown that dialects differ not only in the type of pitch patterns used for Open and Closed tones, but also in the way these patterns are executed in different phonological environments (Grabe, Post, Nolan & Farrar 2000). When voiced material is reduced, for example by reducing the number of syllables upon which a particular intonation contour is overlaid, pitch patterns can either be *compressed* or *truncated*. In compression, the speed at which an intonational change is articulated varies, so that a roughly equal change in fundamental frequency is achieved no matter how much voiced material is available. Grabe *et al.* found this pattern to dominate in RP and Newcastle. In truncation, the rate of change in fundamental frequency stays roughly constant, so that in shorter contexts the change is not as great as in longer contexts. Speakers from Leeds and Belfast tended to use this pattern.

Outlook

Our review of recent studies reveals, we hope, that research into phonological variability is increasingly multiplex and dynamic, thanks to advances in methodology, technology and improved understanding of the social and linguistic factors which affect language use. The findings of such work are being exploited for an ever-widening range of purposes. Within academic linguistics, empirical data are used to inform theoretical issues, discussion of phonological representation and organisation, linguistic change and first language acquisition, while empirical studies are in turn shaped by theoretical developments.

Descriptive and theoretical linguistic work are furthermore vital for the development of automated speech recognition systems and speech synthesisers, for speech and language therapy and for reference in forensic analysis of recorded speech central to crimes. Understanding how accents are evaluated, positively or negatively, is important also for industries which are speech-oriented, such as telephone sales and call centres.

Evaluation is of undoubted relevance in everyday situations, too. People's accents are indexical of their social backgrounds and emblems of group allegiances. Linguistic differences have always been the subject of comment and opinion and always will be. However, as Lippi-Green (1997) demonstrates, language differences and uninformed opinions about those differences can make a tangible difference to people's lives. Jobs are won or lost on the basis of traits of speech. People are informed that their speech is good or bad. They may be persuaded to change their speech, which may covertly entail a change in the social allegiances they signal through their speech. Linguistic prejudice can be used as a proxy for other kinds of prejudice.

The most important role of all, perhaps, for work in understanding linguistic variability and its social values, is that it raises awareness of these issues, and promotes acceptance of difference.

4   Grammatical variation in England

David Britain

Introduction

There have been rather fewer studies of grammatical as opposed to phonological variation in the English of England, and fewer have provided quantitative analyses to highlight relative distributions of grammatical forms (and the social and linguistic factors which affect them) across the country. This situation has perhaps been due to the fact that larger corpora are usually needed to analyse grammatical phenomena statistically because of their less frequent occurrence in spoken language than the segmental phonological features that have tended to dominate the literature on sound variation. The collection of larger corpora has facilitated studies of grammatical variation, however, and we are now fortunate to have, for some non-standard features at least, a number of systematic analyses of an appropriate empirical depth to begin to piece together a more sensitive picture of variation in England.

Our knowledge, though, is still patchy. This chapter reviews the literature on grammatical variation in the non-standard dialects of England since the mid-1980s, when *Language in the British Isles* was first published, and, as the review shows, some of the detail about non-standard features still comes from relatively informal observation, with little known about regional distribution, nor about just how robustly some of the features are still used. One example of this is the reflexive pronoun system. Many non-standard dialects of England have a regularised paradigm, adding the reflexive suffix *-self* to the relevant possessive pronoun, hence: *myself*, *yourself*, *hisself*, *herself*, *ourselves*, *theirselves*. This pattern is widely reported in general descriptions of non-standard varieties both across the country and across particular regions (Anderwald 2004b, Beal 1993, 2004a, Cheshire, Edwards & Whittle 1989, 1993, Edwards 1993, Hudson & Holmes 1995, Hughes & Trudgill 1979, Trudgill 1999a, 2003, Wagner 2004), as well as in specific locality studies which provide a whistle-stop tour of grammatical non-standardness as part of the investigation (e.g. Shorrocks 1999, Stenström, Andersen & Hasund 2002, Watts 2006). But who uses it – is there social stratification in its use? Where exactly – is its use geographically restricted, is it spreading or contracting? What are the linguistic constraints on its use? We simply don't know the answers to these questions for this and many other non-standard grammatical features mentioned in the literature. Alternatively, what we do know is based on evidence from scanning the orally administered traditional dialectological questionnaires of the *Survey of English Dialects* which sampled non-mobile old rural men (Chambers & Trudgill 1998) back in the 1950s and 1960s, people born well over a century ago, with nothing more recent to update our knowledge. Systematic studies of the following are required, therefore: secondary contraction of negated contracted forms; variation in the present tense of *BE*; participle forms; past tense verb forms; the use of modal verbs; imperatives, adverbs, plurality marking on nouns; possessive and reflexive pronouns, demonstratives, comparison forms and article allomorphy.[1] Many of these features, of course, occur extremely rarely in everyday speech and consequently analyses need to be based on large corpora of appropriately collected data if we are to find out more about their social, geographical and linguistic distribution. Large corpora are also extremely important for the identification of grammatical innovations, and locating the social, geographical and linguistic contexts in which these new features began. So, for example, our understanding of relatively recent innovations such as quotative *BE like* and the invariant tag *innit* have come from careful analyses of large datasets of informal conversation (see, for example, Buchstaller 2004, 2005, 2006 and Stenström *et al.* 2002, respectively). Finally, of course, large corpora are useful for enabling comparative studies of different dialects across the country. The work of Tagliamonte and her colleagues in amassing databases from a wide range of locations across England[2] have vastly improved our understanding of, for example, forms of contraction of copula and auxiliary *BE* and auxiliary *HAVE* and relative pronoun choice in the south-west and the north (e.g. Tagliamonte & Smith 2002, Tagliamonte 2002b, Tagliamonte, Smith & Lawrence 2005). In addition, the collection of the Freiburg English Dialect (FRED) corpus at the University of Freiburg – from oral history collections across the country and from relevant subsections of the British National Corpus (BNC) – has led to

---

[1] Cheshire *et al.* (1989, 1993) sent questionnaires to a large number of schools across the country in order to ascertain whether schoolchildren recognised a wide range of non-standard grammatical features as being present in their neighbourhoods. These studies provide valuable information, therefore, on the continued existence of some features, and some indication of their geographical distribution, but as the authors themselves admit, such a data collection technique is not without problems.

[2] And beyond, though these non-English studies fall outside the scope of this chapter.

significant comparative work on negation (Anderwald 2002), relativisation (Herrmann 2003, 2005), pronominal gender (Wagner 2003, 2005) and verbal concord (Pietsch 2005a, 2005b).

Research on the social embedding of grammatical variation is less well advanced. Cheshire's (1982a) landmark study of Reading is now a classic, examining the use of a range of non-standard forms in the speech of adolescents at a recreation ground and showing the relationship between non-standardness, gender and central/peripheral membership of the group. Moore's (2003) research on Bolton is an analysis of language and identity among adolescent females, using a community of practice approach. In this study she examines, in particular, forms of the past tense of *BE* (see also Pichler & Watt 2006 for an identity-based study of grammatical variation). Some studies using Labovian variationist techniques have examined grosser social categories such as class, age, gender, educational level and so on to enable them to broadly identify significant intra-community variation and changes in progress (e.g. Ito & Tagliamonte 2003, Kingston 2000, Levey 2006, Petyt 1985, Spurling 2004, Stenström *et al.* 2002, Tagliamonte 1998, Trudgill 1974).

In the following section, I briefly discuss a number of recurrent themes in the study of grammatical variation, before, in the final section, providing a summary assessment of what we know about individual non-standard grammatical features in England.

Current trends in the analysis of non-standard grammatical variability in England

The common core of non-standardness and dialect levelling

Back in 1974, Peter Trudgill claimed that only 12% of the population spoke Standard English (for a discussion of how he came to propose this figure, see Trudgill 2002a:171). Few have 'tested' this claim, but the nearest we have to a contemporary figure is a 1995 study of schoolchildren by Hudson & Holmes. They wrote a report on non-standard grammatical features found among schoolchildren in four locations across the country (the south-west, London, Merseyside and Tyneside) deliberately targeting the collection of a more formal style of speech. Their data were collected 'in school situations likely to have inclined pupils more towards the use of standard than to non-standard forms ... speaking in the presence of an unfamiliar adult whom they knew to be a teacher, and they were carrying out specific spoken language tasks' (Hudson & Holmes 1995:5). Collecting only five to ten minutes of speech from each child they surveyed, they found that 61% of the 11-year-olds and 77% of the 15-year-olds used non-standard forms at some point (1995:10). Given the formal context in which the data were being collected, Trudgill's 1974 claim does not seem to be too unrealistic even today. Cheshire *et al.*'s Survey of British Dialect Grammar (1989, 1993), also focussed on schoolchildren, found a large number of non-standard forms to be reported in more than four out of every five questionnaires. Their findings, those of Hudson & Holmes and others have strengthened claims that there is perhaps a common core of non-standard forms that are used by a majority of people in the country, and which don't appear to be regionally circumscribed (see, for example, Hughes & Trudgill 1979.)[3] This common core appears to include the following:[4] *them* as a demonstrative; absence of plural marking on nouns of measurement; *never* as a past tense negator; regularised reflexive pronouns; *there's/there was* with notional plural subjects; present participles using the preterite rather than continuous forms; adverbs without *-ly*; *ain't/in't*; non-standard *was*. Cheshire *et al.*'s (1989, 1993) survey was also useful in finding that some forms, assumed to be common across the country, were, in fact, restricted to certain areas, or found in much higher proportions in some areas than others – this set includes, perhaps surprisingly, multiple negation, which was reported at much lower levels in the north than in the south.

This existence of a common core of features used robustly across the country led researchers to investigate whether some other non-standard forms were actually being levelled away, either in favour of other more common non-standard forms, or of standard forms (see, for example, Britain, in press, Cheshire *et al.* 1989, 1993, Kingston 2000). Cheshire *et al.* (1989:209) show, for example, that non-standard positive *were* as in (1) was being less commonly reported in urban Birmingham than in the surrounding areas of the Midlands and that the demonstratives *this here* and *that there* were undergoing attrition in urban Manchester faster than in surrounding parts of the north-west (1989:212).

(1)   I were singing

Other individual studies, as we shall see, have reported attrition and levelling of other non-standard features. Kingston (2000) and Spurling (2004) both report quite dramatic attrition of verbal third person singular present tense Ø marking in rural and urban Suffolk, and Tagliamonte & Ito (2002:249) report a decline in the use of adverbs without *-ly* in York.

---

[3] Chambers (2004) discusses the extent to which some of these features might represent 'vernacular universals' of English.

[4] These features are all discussed in greater detail in the final section of the chapter.

The origins of overseas Englishes and the diffusion of innovations to Britain from North America

Increased interest in the past twenty years in the origins of varieties of English outside England, and beyond the British Isles, has led a number of researchers of grammatical variation to perform comparative analyses of British dialects with contemporary non-British varieties. Most notable here is the research of Tagliamonte and her colleagues analysing connections between mostly relatively isolated, rural varieties in Britain on the one hand, and varieties in North America (such as AAVE and a number of African-American and White varieties of Canada) and the Caribbean (for example, Samaná), on the other (see, for example, Godfrey & Tagliamonte 1999, Jones & Tagliamonte 2004, Poplack 2000, Tagliamonte 2002a).[5] This research poses strict criteria for the establishment of linguistic connections between Britain and North America, such as similar hierarchies of linguistic constraints on non-standard variation, and a by-product of this research has been that we understand variation in Britain a great deal better as a result.[6] Other researchers who have investigated linguistic links between England and North America include Clarke (1997, 1999, 2004), Pargman (2004), Trudgill (1997) and Viereck (1985). Clarke (e.g. 1997, 2004) questions the extent to which such strict criteria are always necessary to establish trans-Atlantic relationships, given that in some cases, when direct demographic connections between Britain and North America are well established, the dialects in the latter show relatively more regularised systems than the source dialects in the former suggesting that 'dialect contact may well have produced a type of koineisation, in which variation ... among the source dialects has undergone some degree of levelling or simplification ... to result in an innovative system' (Clarke 1997:290).

Some researchers are now noting that North America appears to be diffusing grammatical innovations *to* England. The work of Buchstaller (2004, 2005, 2006) and Tagliamonte & Hudson (1999) has shown that the use of quotative *BE like* appears to be an Americanism that has somehow

---

[5] Much of this research, given the demographic histories of Anglophone settlement of North America, has concentrated on grammatical forms shared between *Scotland and Ireland* on the one hand, and North America and the Caribbean on the other, but a discussion of the connections are beyond the scope of this chapter – see the papers in Hickey (2004a) for a detailed overview.

[6] It's noteworthy that relatively little comparative grammatical research has investigated connections between Britain and the Anglophone communities of the southern hemisphere in the same way, with the notable exception of Schreier's research on Tristan da Cunha (see, for example, Schreier 2003).

reached English shores.[7] Buchstaller's research clearly shows that *BE like* was reported earlier in the US than in England (2006:10) yet the social differentiation and stereotypes attached to its use in England differ quite markedly from those in the US. In the latter, *BE like* is both used by and stereotyped as being associated with young women. In England, it is actually used slightly more by *men* in Buchstaller's study (2005:64) and of all the social variables only age significantly accounts for the distribution of the data. Furthermore, usage and attitude are at one – she finds that British speakers only stereotype *BE like* as being associated with young people and not with a particular gender or social class (2005:65–6) and more than half of the people she asked in a social attitudes questionnaire had 'no idea' about which place *BE like* came from (2005:70), leading her to conclude that 'British speakers have not borrowed the social attitudes attached to *like* along with the surface item' (2005:73) and that just as linguistic forms can be reallocated in the process of linguistic diffusion (Britain 2005b, Britain & Trudgill 2005), so too can social stereotypes (see also Meyerhoff & Niedzielski 2003).

Interactions with syntactic theory

Despite early attempts by American variationists to find connections with Chomskyan approaches to theoretical syntax in the 1960s and early 1970s through 'variable rules', sociolinguistic and psycholinguistic approaches to analysing syntax have tended on the whole to steer well clear of each other, and given that grammatical non-standardness has tended to be the domain of the sociolinguist, little theoretical syntactic work on non-standard grammatical features, let alone on variability in general, has been carried out. This is changing. From the late 1990s, interaction between the two sides has flourished, in terms of the analysis both of non-standard forms and variability in general (see, for example, Adger & Smith 2005, Börjars & Chapman 1998, Bresnan & Deo 2001, Britain, Rupp, Bray, Fox, Baker & Spurling 2007, Chapman 1998, Cornips & Corrigan 2005a, 2005b, 2005c, Henry 2002, 2005, Hudson 1999, Pietsch 2005a, 2005b, Rupp 2005, Rupp & Britain forthcoming, Wilson & Henry 1998). What is more, these collaborations have triggered the evolution of new methodologies in data analysis, combining the sociolinguist's insistence on coming to terms with inherent

---

[7] That 'somehow', of course, is an interesting question in itself. The speed at which *BE like* has diffused across the English-speaking world has prompted the claim that this innovation may well have been transmitted via the media. Traditionally the idea of media-driven phonological or grammatical change has been played down by sociolinguists (see, for example, Trudgill 1986, Chambers 1998).

variability in sensitively collected informal conversational data with the syntactician's 'technical apparatus ... [for] analysing very closely related grammatical systems' (Cornips & Corrigan 2005b:7) and their carefully constructed intuition tasks. The papers in Cornips & Corrigan's (2005a) edited collection provide a representative sample of state-of-the-art research in this rapprochement. In terms of non-standard grammatical variability in England, this interaction between syntax and sociolinguistics has proved to be fruitful in the analysis, especially, of subject–verb concord (e.g. Börjars & Chapman 1998, Bresnan & Deo 2001, Britain, Rupp, Bray, Fox, Baker & Spurling 2007, Chapman 1998, Hudson 1999, Pietsch 2005a, 2005b, Rupp 2005).

Grammatical variation and the nature of spoken language

Traditional sociolinguistic analyses of linguistic variability have tended to assume that the relationship between language variation on the one hand and the social significance of that language variation on the other, is the same, whatever level of language we are observing. Consequently, the 'linguistic variable' as a theoretical tool has been applied to a wide range of levels of language – lexical, phonetic, phonological, morphological, syntactic and even discourse and pragmatic features. Some linguists have not been convinced by this straightforward application of the linguistic variable to every level of language and have set out to demonstrate that the social embedding of syntactic variation is often more complex and indirect than that of phonology 'because speakers use syntactic forms in the construction of discourse including, crucially, the conveying and construction of propositional and attitudinal meaning' (Cheshire 2005b:479), and consequently 'syntactic forms can be involved in distinguishing social groups and in the construction of social identities, but ... [t]hey do not necessarily achieve their social function in the same way as phonological forms do' (2005b:481).

Cheshire's approach (see, for example, 1989, 1998a, 1998b, 2003, 2005a, 2005b) is both innovative and important because it clearly demonstrates that the notion of the linguistic variable applied to syntactic variation – looking at semantically equivalent items that vary only in form – is problematic. In order to demonstrate this, Cheshire (e.g. 2005b) investigated a feature that has been subject to countless quantitative investigations using the linguistic variable as the analytical tool, variation in existential *there's* forms as in (2).

(2)   There's a new Top Shop opened next to the post office

Such existentials are often used by speakers to introduce new information into their conversation, and Cheshire's analysis then led her to identify other ways speakers in her dataset performed a similar function in discourse, including left dislocation, *have (got)* constructions and *it-* constructions, forms known to explicitly create inter-speaker involvement (see, for example, Cheshire 1989 – such as the use of set marking tags such as *and stuff like that*, pragmatic particles such as *you know*, high-rising terminals and the use of indefinite *this*), immediate expansions of previously uttered noun phrases and the use of non-restrictive relative clauses. Across these different ways of performing the same function, she found no consistent sociolinguistic patterning. Over 40% of the discourse-new items in her database, however, had no overt marking at all, and it was here that significant social indexing of variation was found. These bare noun phrases carrying new information showed significant gender (female) and class (working) associations with the same patterns holding in three very different urban centres in England – Reading, Milton Keynes and Hull. So the social meaning of this example of grammatical variation was both indirect and buried deep in the system by which speakers perform something as fundamental to communication as presenting new information in the flow of talk. Cheshire concludes, therefore, that 'in order not to overlook the social embedding of syntactic constructions, it may be necessary to ... [take] as the starting point of an analysis the function of a specific syntactic construction rather than the form, and then explore the full range of other linguistic forms that speakers use to fulfil the same function' (2005b:500). This groundbreaking research should lead scholars of language variation to begin to 'stretch' this sort of analysis, applying it to studies across real or apparent time, across languages and across different types of social context.

Grammatical variability: individual features

This chapter surveys research carried out since the first edition of *Language in the British Isles* in the mid-1980s. Fortunately, a nationwide summary of research on grammatical variation was published roughly at the same time (Edwards, Trudgill & Weltens 1984). The summary that follows, therefore, updates the research noted in that summary, and follows the same framework for ordering and classifying grammatical variation.

Negation

Multiple negation

The use of two or more negatives in a clause (as in 3) where Standard English requires just one is such a frequently occurring feature of the world's Englishes that Chambers (2004) labels it a vernacular universal.

(3)   I didn't make no mess nowhere

It is reported in studies from across England (Anderwald 2002, 2004b, Beal 2004a, Beal & Corrigan 2005, Cheshire 1982a, Cheshire, Kerswill & Williams 2005, Edwards 1993, Hughes & Trudgill 1996, Milroy & Milroy 1993, Moore 2003, Shorrocks 1999, Stenström et al. 2002, Trudgill 1999a, 2004, Wagner 2004). Cheshire et al. (1989:205) found, in their Survey of British Dialect Grammar, that multiple negation was reported more in the south than in the north of England. Anderwald (2002:105, 2004b:187), on the basis of an analysis of data from the BNC, finds that multiple negation is highest in the south Midlands, London, East Anglia and the north-east, though Beal & Corrigan (2005) report that multiple negation in Tyneside is restricted to working-class males.

Negation of auxiliaries and modals

Perhaps surprisingly, this is one of the more substantially studied features of the dialect grammar of England. Here we will briefly mention the following: whether negation triggers the auxiliary to be contracted ('auxiliary (AUX) contraction'), as in (4), or the negator itself ('negator (NEG) contraction'), as in (5); regional variation in the negated form as in (6) and (7), types of 'secondary contraction' as in (8) and (9), and variation between *doesn't* and *don't* (10):[8]

(4)   he's not been feeling very well

(5)   she isn't feeling very well

(6)   they canna walk any further

(7)   he diven't do it

(8)   she ain't gonna come

(9)   he in't gonna come either

(10) it don't seem to matter

A number of studies (Cheshire 1982a, Tagliamonte & Smith 2002) of AUX versus NEG contraction of *BE* and *HAVE* have drawn attention to Hughes & Trudgill's (1979) claim that AUX contraction, as in (4) above, is more common 'the further north one goes' (1979:20). Hughes & Trudgill's claim (1979:21), however, referred solely to speakers of *Standard English*, and did not include negation of *BE* (for which they claim southern speakers actually use AUX contraction). For negated *BE*, Cheshire

---

[8] Negated forms of the past tense of *BE* will be discussed below alongside past *BE* in general.

(1982a:52) found that AUX contraction was dominant in Reading, Tagliamonte & Smith (2002:270) find AUX contraction of *BE* extremely high in Cumbria and the north-east, very high also in the south-east, and used somewhat more than half the time in Yorkshire and the south-west, and Anderwald (2002:76) finds nowhere with less than 80% AUX contraction (thereby confirming rather than contradicting Hughes & Trudgill's (1979:21) finding that the south, like the north, uses high levels of AUX contraction for negated *BE*).[9] Tagliamonte & Smith (2002:272), considering data from Ironbridge in the Midlands, find much lower levels of AUX contraction of *BE*, suggesting that perhaps the Midlands form a buffer zone of lower levels of AUX contraction between regions to the north and south with much higher levels. Anderwald's (2002:78) research supports this, showing higher levels of NEG contraction in the Midlands than anywhere else in England. Breaking down *BE* into auxiliary and copula forms, Cheshire (1982a:52) found auxiliary *BE* to favour AUX contraction over copula *BE*, as did Tagliamonte & Smith (2002:275). The latter also found that phonological environment played an important role, with preceding vowels favouring AUX contraction over preceding consonants (2002:275).

For negated *HAVE*, Tagliamonte & Smith (2002:268) show extremely low levels of AUX contraction across England, and for negated *WILL*, AUX contraction is either negligible, or, in their fieldwork site near Durham, very high, approaching levels found in southern Scotland and Northern Ireland (2002:268).

A number of regional negated forms have been reported, such as *-na*, from parts of the west and north-west Midlands (e.g. Viereck 1997:761, 763), Scottish-type *-nae* forms such as *dinnae* (for *don't*) and *cannae* (for *can't*) reported for Berwick-upon-Tweed in the far north-east (Pichler & Watt 2006) and *divvent* (for *don't*) reported across the north-east (Beal 2004a, Crinson & Williamson 2004, Jones 1985, Pichler & Watt 2006, Rowe, forthcoming). Anderwald (2004a:55) reports *amn't* for first person singular negated *BE* (see also Francis 1985, Hudson 2000a) in parts of the north-west Midlands in the *Survey of English Dialects* (*SED*) data, but it is not clear whether it is still extant there.

Secondary contraction of negative contracted forms to some form of *ain't* is widely reported (e.g. Anderwald 2002, 2003, 2004b, Beal 2004a, Cheshire 1982a, Cheshire *et al.* 1989, 1993, Edwards 1993, Hudson & Holmes 1995, Ojanen 1982, Petyt 1985, Shorrocks 1999, Stenström *et al.*

---

[9] Anderwald (2002:76) actually shows, on the basis of BNC data, that east–west divisions better account for her findings, with East Anglia showing the lowest levels of AUX contraction for *BE*.

2002, Trudgill 2004, Viereck 1997), though Tagliamonte & Smith find very few examples in their data from a number of sites in both northern and southern England (2002:262). *Ain't* can be used to negate copula *BE* (as in (11)), auxiliary *BE* (as in (12)) and auxiliary *HAVE* (as in (13)).

(11)   It ain't my book

(12)   We ain't coming yet

(13)   They ain't seen him for ages

Cheshire finds it most for AUX *HAVE* and least for AUX *BE* (1982a:51). Anderwald finds an AUX *HAVE* > AUX *BE* > copula *BE* hierarchy (2002:138). She shows that *ain't* for negated *BE* in general is most common in the south-west, East Anglia, the Midlands, Yorkshire, Lincolnshire and Cumbria (2002:127) and for negated *HAVE* in the south-west, the Midlands, London, East Anglia, Yorkshire and the north-east (2002:129).

Few studies distinguish between different forms of *ain't*. Anderwald (esp. 2002) considers this in some detail, showing that *in't* [ɪnt] (as opposed to ain't, e.g. [æɪnt]) is concentrated in Lancashire, London, the central and north-west Midlands and the central north of England. She reports *in't* being absent in East Anglia (2002:130, 131) in both main clauses and tags, yet Trudgill (2004) claims this to be the dominant East Anglian form, and it is the dominant form in the Fens, too. Viereck (1997:251) reports *hain't* for East Anglian negated auxiliary *HAVE* and Ojanen (1982) reports *een't* [iːnt] for southern Cambridgeshire – a form also found further north in the Fens. Cheshire (1981) shows evidence of a functional distinction between *ain't* and *in't* in Reading, with *in't* being the form of choice in tag questions, especially what she calls 'aggressive tags', which demonstrate some sort of hostility or divergence by the speaker towards the hearer.

Don't for third person singular *doesn't* is widely reported (e.g. Anderwald 2003, 2004b, Cheshire 1982a, Cheshire *et al.* 1989, 1993, 2005, Hudson & Holmes 1995, Ojanen 1982, Stenström *et al.* 2002). Anderwald (2003) compares the geographical distribution of *don't* in the *SED* data and the BNC. In the *SED*, she finds *don't* largely restricted to the area south of a line running from the Wash to the Mersey. In the much more recent BNC, however, she states that *don't* is 'present in practically every dialect area throughout Great Britain' and has been 'spreading from the south over the last few decades' (2003:515). She finds *don't* is used most in the south Midlands and East Anglia (in over 60% of possible cases), and least (<10%) in the north-west Midlands, Merseyside and Humberside (2003:525). She also shows that *don't* is favoured when the subject of the verb is human rather than inanimate (2002:162). Kingston (2000:56) finds that whilst *don't* is the dominant form among older and middle-aged people in rural Suffolk, it is being replaced by *doesn't* among younger, especially female speakers.

Never *as a negator*

A number of studies report *never* being used as a negator with definite time reference, as in (14) (Anderwald 2004b, Beal 2004a, Cheshire 1982a, 1989, 1998a, Cheshire *et al.* 1989, 1993, Edwards 1993, Hudson & Holmes 1995, Stenström *et al.* 2002, Viereck 1997):

(14)   I saw him yesterday and he never told me!

Cheshire (1989:54) reports that *never* in these contexts acts to foreground the event being negated.

Present-tense verbs

The dialects of England vary with respect to how and whether they mark present tense verbs. Perhaps the most commonly found non-standard feature is a wider use of *-s* beyond third person singular (e.g. Cheshire 1982a, Cheshire & Ouhalla 1997, Edwards 1993, Godfrey & Tagliamonte 1999, Ihalainen 1985, Peitsara 2002b, Pietsch 2005a, 2005b, Poplack & Tagliamonte 2001, Shorrocks 1999) as in (15):

(15)   They kicks the ball into the river

This feature is reported in the south and south-west of England and the north, and appears to have two linguistic constraints associated with its use. The first is the so-called Northern Subject Rule, whereby *-s* is favoured following noun phrases and non-adjacent pronouns, but disfavoured after adjacent pronouns. This is reported as being an active constraint in the south and south-west (Cheshire 1982a, Godfrey & Tagliamonte 1999:106, Peitsara 2002b) and the north (Beal 2004a, Shorrocks 1999:110, 114). The second is the 'following clause constraint' reported by Cheshire & Ouhalla (1997). Despite high levels of *-s* marking throughout the paradigm, if a) the subject is not third person singular and b) the complement of the verb is a clause or a very long and heavy NP, *-s* is not found – see the main verbs in (16) and (17) below:

(16)   I bet the wife enjoys it

(17)   they think you're a bloody hippy

Across the paradigm *-s* marking in these varieties is perhaps declining. Godfrey & Tagliamonte in their study from the late 1990s report lower levels of -*s* marking than Cheshire did in the early 1980s. They also report that -*s* marking is lowest in second person contexts and highest in third singular (1999:100), and that it is favoured after preceding vowels (1999:106). They find conflicting evidence with respect to the aspectual marking of -*s* in the south-western variety they study. -*s* marking in third singular contexts favours habitual marking whereas in first person it favours punctual (1999:106).

Traditionally in East Anglia present tense verbs are not marked at all, even in third person singular contexts (Kingston 2000, Peitsara 1996, Spurling 2004, Trudgill 1974, 1996, 1998, 1999a, 2004, Viereck 1985), as in (18):

(18)   She love going up the city

This third person zero, however, appears to be undergoing attrition. Kingston (2000) and Spurling (2004) all find zero on the decline across apparent time in rural and urban Suffolk, though, perhaps surprisingly, it seems to be on the wane more rapidly in rural areas than in urban Ipswich. Kingston also finds that zero marking is retained more in main clauses than in subordinate ones and when the sound at the end of the verb stem is voiceless or labial or fricative and when the following sound is coronal (2000:50–1). Zero forms are also found for the verbs *DO* and *HAVE*, with *DO* more resistant to incoming -*s* than *HAVE* (2000:56 7). The encroaching of verbal -*s* in third person contexts in East Anglia has enabled researchers to investigate whether the Northern Subject Rule is arriving in East Anglia along with -*s*. It appears the reverse is happening, with -*s* marking *more common* after adjacent pronouns than after NPs (Britain, Rupp, Bray, Fox, Baker & Spurling 2007, Kingston 2000) in both rural and urban East Anglia. Since -*s* marking is variable across the paradigm in the south-west of England, zero marking is also occasionally found in third person singular contexts there (Godfrey & Tagliamonte 1999, Williamson & Hardman 1997a).

Tagliamonte (2003) discusses competition between *HAVE* and *HAVE got* for possessive *HAVE*. She finds regional variation within the north of England, with Wheatley Hill near Durham favouring *HAVE got* far more than York (2003:537), and that *HAVE got* is on the increase across apparent time (2003:548). Interestingly, however, she notes that *HAVE* is becoming specialised to certain contexts, namely generic and especially abstract full noun phrase subjects (2003:550).

Present tense of BE

Edwards *et al.* (1984:19) reported that 'virtually all dialects simplify the conjugation of *to be*', but beyond a wealth of discussion about the use of singular forms in plural existential contexts (see below), there have been very few reports of other forms of simplification, and no quantitative studies. Ihalainen (1985:65) reports the use of cliticised *'m* in Somerset, but notes that these forms can only be attached to pronoun subjects and not full NPs, as does Wagner (2004). Britain (2002c:25–6) reports the use of *bes* in the Fens signalling habitual durative aspect, as in (19) and (20):

(19)   Stephen says she bes in the Wisbech Arms a lot

(20)   You know that John Virgo what bes on 'Big Break'

The use of *is*, or much more usually *'s*, in plural existentials is an extremely widely reported phenomenon (e.g. Anderwald 2004b, Beal 2004a, Cheshire 1982a, Cheshire et al. 1989, Hudson & Holmes 1995 (who report it as the most used non-standard grammatical form in their survey), Ojanen 1982, Peitsara 1988, Petyt 1985, Rupp 2005), as in:

(21)   there's crumbs all over the floor

Periphrastic do/did

In the south-west of England, an unstressed periphrastic *do/did* is found as in (22) and (23) below (Ihalainen 1976, 1991a, 1994, Megan Jones 2002, Jones & Tagliamonte 2004, Klemola 1994, 1996, Kortmann 2002, Trudgill 1999a, Wagner 2004, Wakelin 1986):

(22)   In autumn, cider becomes too strong and that do wake 'ee up a bit (Megan Jones 2002:120)

(23)   I did see him every time I was there

Klemola (1994, 1996) shows, on the basis of an analysis of the *SED* and its fieldworker notebooks, that periphrastic *do* was found in west Cornwall, Somerset, Dorset, west Hampshire, Wiltshire, Gloucestershire, Herefordshire, Worcestershire, and even into Shropshire and Berkshire. Periphrastic *did* was more geographically restricted (e.g. few examples found in Cornwall). Contrary to some claims, he also shows that only periphrastic *did* marked habituality (1996:123–4). Megan Jones (2002, Jones & Tagliamonte 2004) conducted a Varbrul analysis of obsolescing periphrastic *do* in contemporary rural Somerset and confirms Klemola's claims about habituality applying solely to *did* (2002:121). Her analysis revealed that *do* was found more frequently before verbs the tense of which is ambiguous from the verb stem itself (e.g. PUT – *I put, I put, I've put*) (2002:126), before transitive verbs, and before verbs in subordinate clauses. For periphrastic *did* she finds that it is favoured: a) with the verb *say* along with the ambiguous verbs mentioned above (2002:123); b) when a preverbal adverb, such as *always* is present (2002:123); and c), like *do*, in subordinate clauses. Furthermore, Jones & Tagliamonte (2004) found parallel processing played an effect, such that periphrastic *did* was found more often when it had previously occurred in the same utterance (2004:112) and with non-stative anterior verbs (2004:115).

Participle forms

A small number of studies (Hudson & Holmes 1995:20, Trudgill 1999a) report the use of the preterite rather than the progressive in present participles, as in (24):

(24)   I'm *sat* at a desk all day and I don't even have a window

Hughes & Trudgill (1979) and Beal (2004a) also point to the regional variation in the use of participle forms after the verbs *need* and *want*. Hughes & Trudgill report the progressive after *need* in the south of England and after both *need* and *want* in the Midlands and the north (1979:21), but Beal reports the preterite after *need* and *want* in the northeast (2004a:135).

Past tense verbs

General descriptions of regional varieties of English in England always point to the great differences between the past tense systems used in the dialects and that used in the Standard (Anderwald 2004b:179–81, 183–4, Beal 2004a, Cheshire 1982a, Cheshire *et al*. 1989, 1993, 2005, Crinson & Williamson 2004, Edwards 1993, Hardie & McEnery 2003, Hudson & Holmes 1995, Hughes & Trudgill 1979, Hughes, Trudgill & Watt 2005, Ojanen 1982, Petyt 1985, Poplack & Tagliamonte 2001, Shorrocks 1999:130–49, Stenström *et al*. 2002, Tagliamonte 2001, Trudgill 1999a, 2003, 2004, Wagner 2004, Watts 2006). No single system appears to account for the wide range of different non-standard past tense paradigms, but we can point to the following as being relatively common:

a) Past participle = preterite (e.g. *I do, I done, I've done; I draw, I drawed, I've drawed; I write, I writ, I've writ; I fall, I fell, I've fell; I take, I took, I've took, I begin, I begun, I've begun*);

b) Present = preterite = past participle (e.g. *I (be)come, I (be)come, I've (be)come*);

c) Strong non-standard preterite forms that are weak in the standard (e.g. East Anglian *owe, snow* becoming /u:/ and /snu:/ (Trudgill 2003:52–3));

d) Weak non-standard forms that are strong in the standard (e.g. *I grow*, *I growed*, *I've growed*).

Tagliamonte (2001) conducted a systematic sociolinguistic analysis of the social and linguistic conditioning of the past tense of *come*, finding that non-standard *come* is most common among less educated men over the age of 70 or under the age of 30, reminiscent, consequently, of an age-graded pattern.

A number of studies (Hughes & Trudgill 1979, Cheshire 1982a, Cheshire *et al.* 1989) point to the difference in non-standard varieties between the past tense of full verb and auxiliary *do*, as in (25):

(25)   You done it, did you?

Past tense BE

Non-standard paradigms of past *BE* are well reported in England (Anderwald 2001, 2002, 2003, 2004a, Beal 2004a, Britain 2002c, Britain *et al.* 2007, Cheshire 1982a, Cheshire *et al.* 1989, 1993, 2005, Hudson & Holmes 1995, Ihalainen 1985, Levey 2005, Moore 2003, Ojanen 1982, Pietsch 2005a, 2005b, Shorrocks 1999, Stenström *et al.* 2002; Tagliamonte 1998, 2002a, Trudgill 1999a, 2003, 2004, Watts 2006).

In varieties of English outside England, the dominant pattern of past *BE* marking appears to be a levelled system pivoting around *was* across the paradigm (Britain 2002c, Chambers 2004), both positive and negative as in (26) and (27):

(26)   You was never gonna get there in time

(27)   The women wasn't prepared to stay any longer

The empirical studies which have been conducted in England, however, have largely found a system which levels to *was* in the positive paradigm and *weren't* in the negative (Anderwald 2001, 2002, 2003, Britain 2002c, Cheshire 1982a, Levey 2005, Tagliamonte 1998), a pattern reported less widely outside England, apart from in the well-known studies of the Mid-Atlantic coast of the US (e.g. Schilling-Estes & Wolfram 1994, Wolfram & Schilling-Estes 2003), as in (28) and (29):

(28)   he weren't really ready for it, was he?

(29)   the old men was drinking cider, weren't they?

A number of these studies from the south of England (e.g. Britain 2002c, Levey 2005) find levelling to *weren't* at higher levels than levelling to *was*. Anderwald's nationwide survey on the basis of BNC data shows both *was* and *weren't* levelling highest in East Anglia and parts of the south-west

(2002:174, 178), with *weren't* levelling also high in London and the Midlands (2002:178). Tagliamonte (1998) and Anderwald (2001, 2002) both find that *weren't* levelling seems to be more common in tags than in main clauses.

Some studies, however, find evidence of levelling to *were* in positive contexts (Anderwald 2001, 2002, 2003, Beal 2004a:122, Britain 2002c, Moore 2003, Petyt 1985, Pietsch 2005a, 2005b, Shorrocks 1999). Many of these show that levelled *were* is found in an area concentrated in the north-west (parts of southern and western Yorkshire, Derbyshire, the north-west Midlands and southern Lancashire). Both Ojanen (1982) and Britain (2002c) find *were* levelling among older speakers in Cambridgeshire and the Fens, though it is now becoming much rarer.

As for the present tense of verbs other than *BE*, past *BE* is often found to adhere to the conditions of the Northern Subject Rule, with *was* less likely after adjacent pronouns than after NPs or non-adjacent pronouns. This pattern is found in Devon (Tagliamonte 2002a), York (Tagliamonte 1998:180), parts of the north of England (Pietsch 2005a, 2005b) and among older speakers in southern Lincolnshire and north-west Cambridgeshire (Britain 2002c:35–6). As with the present tense, however, the Northern Subject Rule is overturned in East Anglia. Britain (2002c) and Britain *et al.* (2007) show that across that region, from the Fens in the north-west to Basildon and Brentwood in the south-east, in both middle-class and working-class speech, *was* is favoured after third person plural pronouns in contrast to third plural noun phrases. Given the robustness of this pattern across East Anglia and in both past *BE* and present tense verb forms, they label this the East Anglian Subject Rule.

Levelling of past *BE* after plural existentials, as in (30), is reported widely (Britain 2002c, Cheshire *et al.* 1989, 1993, Ihalainen 1985, Ojanen 1982, Peitsara 1988, Tagliamonte 1998):

(30)   there was loads of things to do

In a detailed analysis, Tagliamonte (1998:170–1) shows that *was* in existentials is favoured where the determiner on the plural noun is *no* as in (31), and found least where the noun has no determination (32), or a quantifier or numeral (33) and (34). She also finds that *was* is used most by educated females, in her York study (1998:183).

(31)   there was no crisps left so I got peanuts

(32)   there was papers scattered everywhere

(33)   there was a few sandwiches, a few cocktail sausages, not much really

(34)   there was seven when I last looked

Perfective aspect

Standard English uses forms of the verb *have* as the auxiliary in the construction of the perfect tense, as in (35):

(35)   they've heard all sorts of rumours about him

In the East Midlands and western parts of East Anglia, it is still possible to hear forms of *BE* used as the auxiliary instead[10] (see Britain 2003:205, Ojanen 1982:118–9, 143, 164, Peitsara & Vasko 2002, Viereck 1985:250), as in (36) and (37):

(36)   I'm been strawberrying at Wisbech

(37)   I'm seen straw on the floor in the Rose and Crown

Modal verbs

The little research here on non-standard varieties concerns either the distribution of double modals (usually in the form of reports rather than detailed empirical investigations – e.g. Beal 1993, 2004a, Milroy & Milroy 1993, Trudgill 1999a) or comparisons between the functions of the modals in different varieties. Trousdale's (2003) fine discussion of the differences between the Tyneside and Standard modal systems stands out here (see also McDonald & Beal 1987). He demonstrates that since Tyneside English rarely uses *may* or *shall* or uncliticised *will*, this has repercussions for the means by which certain modalities can be expressed in that variety. He shows that in Tyneside English, unlike Standard English, each modal verb tends to be monosemous, carrying either epistemic modality or root modality but not both. So, for example, epistemic possibility is expressed with *might* and root possibility and permission with *can* (2003:275). *Must* tends to carry epistemic modality in Tyneside rather than root necessity, for which *have got to* or *should* are used.

Quotative verbs

Given the speed at which *BE like* (as in (38)) has spread with quotative function across the English-speaking world, a small number of recent studies have investigated the quotative system in England (Buchstaller 2004, 2005, 2006, Stenström *et al.* 2002, Tagliamonte & Hudson 1999).

---

[10]   This feature is also reported in the Shetlands (Melchers 1992, Pavlenko 1996).

(38)   and she was like 'no way, get out of here!'

Stenström *et al.* (2002), on the basis of the COLT corpus of London teenage speech collected in the early and mid 1990s, find very low levels of *BE like* (accounting for less than 1% of their quotatives), with *go* and *say* ((39) and (40) below) much more frequent (together accounting for over half of the quotatives), and zero quotatives (41) common when speakers are mimicking other varieties.

(39)   and Helen went 'aaaaarrrgh'

(40)   and then I says 'yeah whatever'

(41)   and then there was Milo 'it would be awfully kind of you to let us in'

They found that *go* was associated largely with working-class, ethnic minority adolescents in their data.

Tagliamonte & Hudson find, in their York data, that *go* is associated with the reporting of non-lexicalised sounds and direct speech, especially in first person contexts, *say* with third person contexts in direct speech and *BE like* with first person contexts, the reporting of non-lexicalised sounds and internal dialogue, with *BE like* being found more among women than men. They concluded that *BE like* was still 'highly localised' in their data (1999:166). Buchstaller (2004, 2005, 2006) finds low levels of *BE like* in her analysis of data from Newcastle and Derby (also collected in the mid-90s), but finds it is used most in the 14–19-year-old age group (2006:9), as is *go* (2006:12). *Go* is also found to be used more by women and by middle-class speakers (2005:64).

Imperatives

Few studies report variation in imperative forms. Trudgill (2003, 2004) and Peitsara (1996) note that in East Anglia, the second person pronoun is usually explicit in imperative forms (see (42) below), even when strengthened by the verb *do* (43):

(42)   Shut you up!

(43)   Do you sit down!

Adverbs

Many varieties of English in England show variation with respect to whether adverbs append the inflection *-ly* or not (Hughes & Trudgill 1979, Trudgill 1999a). Inflectionless forms, as in (44) and (45) below, are reported in the south of England (Anderwald 2004b, Cheshire 1982a,

Cheshire *et al.* 1989, 1993, Edwards 1993, Hudson & Holmes 1995, Ojanen 1982, Stenström *et al.* 2002, Wagner 2004) and the north (Beal 2004a, Shorrocks 1999, Tagliamonte & Ito 2002, Watts 2006).

(44)   Come quick!

(45)   It happened real fast

Tagliamonte & Ito (2002), in the most detailed empirical investigation of this phenomenon, show a sharp decline in York English in the use of inflectionless forms across apparent time, but this decline is almost totally accounted for by the decline in the use of adverbial *real* as opposed to *really* in intensifiers. In their corpus, forms of *real(ly)* accounted for two-thirds of all their examples of adverbs (2002:249). The use of zero marked adverbs otherwise showed a much shallower decline in apparent time, though for both *real* and other zero marked forms there was a strong association with, especially, male speakers with lower levels of educational achievement (2002:252–3) and with concrete objective meanings (such as (46)) rather than abstract, subjective ones, as in (47) (2002:255–6).

(46)   he deliberately walked really *slow*

(47)   come on, do it *properly*

A number of researchers have investigated adverbial intensification of the kind that Tagliamonte & Ito noted for *real* (Hudson & Holmes 1995, Ito & Tagliamonte 2003, Stenström *et al.* 2002). Hudson & Holmes (1995:14) note that the use of the adverb *dead* as an intensifier was one of the few grammatical features found predominantly on Merseyside in their survey. Stenström *et al.* (2002:151) show that *real* as an intensifier, as in (45) above, is used most by *middle*-class speakers in their London corpus – showing a radically different social stratification of the feature than in York. They also show that intensifiers *right* as in (48) and *well* as in (49) were also predominantly middle-class forms, with *fucking* showing no particular class preferences.

(48)   I was *right* pissed off with that

(49)   And I thought she was *well* hard, sticking up for herself like that

Ito & Tagliamonte, in their York data show that *very* and *real(ly)* dominate, with the only other intensifier accounting for more than 10% of the total being *so*. Across apparent time, they find that *very* is declining and *really* increasing (2003:267) except among less educated men (2003:276). Furthemore, the scope of *really* as an intensifier is expanding into the realms of adjectives of physical property (*cold*, *tight*, *hard*, etc.), and, among the young, *very* is only common as an intensifier of adjectives of position (such as *close*, *far*, *near*, etc.) (2003:270).

Prepositions

Shorrocks (1999) reports a wide range of non-standard prepositional usages in his analysis of Bolton, and Vasko (2005) presents a splendid monograph-long treatment of prepositional usage in Cambridgeshire. Cheshire et al. (1993) report that the use of a simple preposition where Standard English has a complex one (as in (50)) and the use of a complex preposition where Standard English has a simple one (as in (51)) both tend to be features of southern varieties of English (1993:77, see also Edwards 1993:233):

(50)   I'm going up my friend's house

(51)   He knocked his hat off of his head

Watts (2006:322) discusses variation in the omission and reduction of *to* in Cheshire and southern Lancashire, contrasting Cheshire, where *to* is often completely omitted by working-class speakers, as in (52), with neighbouring Lancashire and Greater Manchester where it is reduced to some form of glottal stricture or devoicing of the final consonant of the preceding word (Shorrocks 1990, 1999).

(52)   my dad needs to go the opticians (Watts 2006:323)

Despite historical evidence that it was once more grammatically wide-spread, Watts only finds omission after the verb *GO* in her Wilmslow data. In other contexts, reduction or assimilation is found. Ojanen/ Vasko (Ojanen 1982:252, Vasko 2005:168–74) finds similar deletion in southern Cambridgeshire.

Plurality

A wide range of studies mention the failure of some varieties to overtly mark plurality on a subset of (especially measurement) nouns (Anderwald 2004b, Beal 2004a, Cheshire *et al.* 1989, 1993, Crinson & Williamson 2004, Edwards 1993, Hughes & Trudgill 1979, Ojanen 1982, Peitsara 1996, Petyt 1985, Shorrocks 1999, Trudgill 2003, Wagner 2004, Watts 2006), as in (53), (54) and (55) below:

(53)   that's three mile away from here

(54)   I need four foot of polythene sheet

(55)   two pound of plums, please!

Pronouns

Personal pronouns

A number of non-standard forms are considered here: the use of distinct
second person plural subject pronouns, as in (56); the use of 'gendered
pronouns' as in (57); 'pronoun exchange' as in (58) and (59); and the use of
dummy *that* instead of *it* as in (60):

(56)   Yous'll have plenty of time for that

(57)   He have been a good watch

(58)   I did give she a hand and she did give I a hand (Wagner 2004:157)

(59)   Us don't think naught about things like that (Wagner 2004:158)

(60)   Come in quick – that's raining

A few studies report the use of *youse* as a plural form of *you* in some
varieties. Beal notes its presence in Tyneside, Liverpool and Manchester
(2004a:118) (see also Cheshire *et al.* 1993:81), and Stenström *et al.* (2002)
find it in London. Beal discusses the possibility that this form may have
its origins in Ireland. Beal also discusses the continued existence in the
traditional dialects of many parts of northern England (with the exception
of Liverpool and Tyneside) of *thou* and *thee* (see also Cave 2001). Trudgill
(1999a, 2003) shows that in East Anglia, *you . . . together* can be used as the
plural form of the second person, as in (61):

(61)   Hurry you up together!

Dialectologists of the south-west of England have long recognised
the existence there of 'pronoun exchange', whereby subject personal
pronouns are used in non-subject positions and the reverse (see
Ihalainen 1991b, 1994, Wagner 2004) (see (58) above). Wagner, following
an analysis of the *SED* data, shows that subject forms are used more in
non-subject slots than vice versa, and that the geographical areas where
subject forms are used in non-subject slots – Devon, north-east Cornwall
and the very west of Dorset and Somerset – barely overlap with the areas
that place non-subject pronouns in subject slots – Wiltshire, east Somerset,
south Dorset and west Cornwall (2004:157–9). She also claims, on the
basis of more recently collected data, that 'with a frequency of occurrence
of about 1% ... pronoun exchange seems to be all but dead in its
former heartlands' (2004:159). In addition, the use of the subject pronoun in non-subject position was once found in Essex (Trudgill 2003,
2004), and is still found in Tyneside (Beal 2004a:117–18, Crinson &
Williamson 2004).

Gendered pronouns are 'instances of pronouns which are marked for masculine or feminine gender but which refer to inanimate count nouns' (Wagner 2004:159; see also Ihalainen 1984, 1991b, 1994, Paddock 1991, Wagner 2003, 2005) as in (57) above. Ihalainen's study (e.g. 1984) shows a number of phonetic forms for these pronouns – *he, er, em* (found before labials/labiodentals) and *en* found in non-labial/labiodental contexts. Wagner's research (2003, 2004, 2005) represents the most substantial analysis of this feature. She compares gendered pronouns in the *SED* with those found in a wide range of oral history recordings of speakers born in the first two decades of the twentieth century from the south-west. The *SED* data show extremely robust use of these forms, ranging from areas of near categorical use of gendered forms in Cornwall, west Devon, and parts of Dorset, Hampshire, Wiltshire and Gloucestershire, and other areas such as Somerset and the rest of Devon and Dorset still showing significant levels of use (2004:161). The oral history recordings show Cornwall and Somerset to be the areas with greatest use of the gendered pronouns, with Devon and Dorset showing considerably fewer examples (2005:337). But this very healthy picture holds only for these very much older speakers. Wagner (2004) claims these forms are now 'rare', but 'by no means dead' (2004:163).

In East Anglia and the south Midlands, *that* is often found in place of Standard English *it* as in (60) above (Peitsara 1996, Trudgill 2003, 2004), a feature that is still robustly in evidence across the social and age spectrum.

Possessive pronouns

One obsolescing non-standard form reported in some varieties is the use of -*(e)n* forms, such as *hisn, hern, ourn* and *yourn*. Trudgill (1999a:90–1) reports that these seem to be most common in the Midlands and the south and south-east (excluding the south-west and East Anglia).

In East Anglia, possessive pronouns alone can be used to refer to someone's house (Peitsara 1996:293, Trudgill 2003:61) as in (62):

(62)   Do you want to come round mine later?

Petyt (1985:190) reports the use of *us* as a possessive pronoun in West Yorkshire (see also Beal 2004a), as in (63):

(63)   We all take us cars to work nowadays

Reflexive pronouns

Non-standard varieties of English in England often solely use possessive pronouns to form reflexive ones, unlike the Standard system which uses both object and possessive pronouns. Consequently, we find (64) and (65) in a number of dialects.

(64)   he bought hisself one of them iPods

(65)   they really shot theirselves in the foot by doing that

This is reported by, for example, Anderwald (2004b), Beal (2004a), Edwards (1993), Hudson & Holmes (1995), Hughes & Trudgill (1979), Shorrocks (1999), Stenström et al. (2002), Trudgill (1999a, 2003), Wagner (2004) and Watts (2006). Cheshire et al. (1993:77) find these forms to be common right across the country.

Relative pronouns

Variation is endemic in the relativisation system in English. The range of relative pronouns used in Standard English overlaps with those used in the non-standard varieties of England (e.g. *who, which, that, Ø*) but both have forms not used in the other (e.g. *whom, what, as*), and the forms they share often differ from each other, and differ across the non-standard varieties, in terms of their relative frequency in different syntactic environments. General descriptions of non-standard dialects have naturally focussed on those relativisers that are not shared by Standard English, such as *what* and *as* (see, for example, Anderwald 2004b, Beal 1993, 2004a, Cheshire et al. 1989, 1993, Edwards 1993, Hughes & Trudgill 1979:17–18, Ihalainen 1985, Shorrocks 1999, Stenström et al. 2002, Trudgill 1999a, 2003, 2004, Wagner 2004, Watts 2006).

A number of studies have looked in more detail at the relativisation strategies in local dialects of English in England. Table 4.1 shows the dominant relativisers in a number of varieties, looking at two syntactic contexts: whether the antecedent noun plays a subject (66) or object role (67) in the relative clause and whether the gender of the antecedent is human, animate, or non-human or inanimate.

(66)   Gemma screamed at the man what crashed into our car

(67)   That's the cat what he picked from the sanctuary

As the table makes clear, not every researcher investigates the same syntactic constraints on relativisation in their studies and this limits comparability in some cases. Differing types of speakers in the different databases used for analysis cause another problem of comparability – Cheshire (1982a) and Levey (2006) are investigating adolescent and pre-adolescent children respectively, whilst others (Herrmann 2003, Kekäläinen 1985, Ojanen 1982, Peitsara 2002a, Poussa 1994, Van den Eynden Morpeth 2002)

Table 4.1. *Restrictive relative pronoun choice in subject and object positions in a number of dialects of English in England (In the table a relativiser in* **bold** *signifies it accounts for more than 33% of the total, in italics between 20% and 33% and normal print between 10% and 20%. Relativisers which account for less than 10% of the total are not shown.)*

Location of study	Hierarchy of common relativisers in SUBJECT position in the relative clause	Hierarchy of common relativisers in OBJECT position in the relative clause
Central south-west (Dorset, Somerset, Wiltshire, Avon, Oxon) (Herrmann 2003:107)	Ø > **that** > what (no distinction between subject and object functions noted)	
Devon (Tagliamonte 2002b)	**that** > *who* > Ø (human antecedent) **that** > Ø (non-human antecedent)	**that** > Ø (human antecedent) Ø > **that** (non-human antecedent)
Somerset (Tagliamonte 2002b)	**that** > *who* > Ø (human antecedent) **that** > Ø > which (non-human antecedent)	Ø > **that** > who (human antecedent) Ø > **that** (non-human antecedent)
Dorset (Van den Eynden Morpeth 2002; see also Van den Eynden 1996)	**that** > **wh-** > Ø (no distinction between subject and object functions noted)	
Reading (Cheshire 1982a)	**who** > that > Ø > what (animate antecedent) **that** > **what** (inanimate antecedent)	Ø > *that* = *what* = *who* (animate antecedent) Ø > *what* > that > which (inanimate antecedent)
London (Levey 2006)	**that** > **who**	Ø > *that* > what
East Anglia (Norfolk and Suffolk) (Herrmann 2003:107)	Ø = *that* > who > what (no distinction between subject and object functions noted)	
Cambridgeshire (Ojanen 1982)	**what** > Ø (human antecedent) **what** > Ø (non-human antecedent)	Ø > *what* (human antecedent) **what** > Ø (non-human antecedent)
Suffolk (Peitsara 2002a; see also Kekäläinen 1985:354)	*that* > Ø > *which* > what	Ø > *what* > that
Norfolk (Poussa 1994; see also 2001)	**who** > Ø (human antecedent) **what** = **which** > Ø > that (non-human antecedent)	Ø > **who** > which (human antecedent) Ø > **what** > which (non-human antecedent)

Table 4.1. (*cont.*)

Location of study	Hierarchy of common relativisers in SUBJECT position in the relative clause	Hierarchy of common relativisers in OBJECT position in the relative clause
Central Midlands (Nottinghamshire) (Herrmann 2003:107)	**that** > *Ø* > who (no distinction between subject and object functions noted)	
York (Tagliamonte 2002b)	**who** > **that** (human antecedent) **that** (non-human antecedent)	*Ø* > **that** > who (human antecedent) *Ø* > **that** (non-human antecedent)
Wheatley Hill, Durham (Tagliamonte 2002b)	**that** > *who* > *Ø* (human antecedent) **that** > *which* > *Ø* (non-human antecedent)	*Ø* > **that** (human antecedent) *Ø* > *that* (non-human antecedent)
Tyneside (Beal & Corrigan 2002)	**who** > **that** > *Ø* (animate antecedent) **that** > *which* (inanimate antecedent)	*Ø* > *who* > *that* (animate antecedent) **that** > *Ø* (inanimate antecedent)
Central north (Cumbria) (Herrmann 2003:107)	**that** > *Ø* (no distinction between subject and object functions noted)	
Maryport, Cumbria (Tagliamonte 2002b)	**that** > *Ø* (human antecedent) **that** > *Ø* (non-human antecedent)	*Ø* > **that** (human antecedent) *Ø* > **that** (non-human antecedent)
Standard English (Quirk 1957)	**who** (animate antecedent) **that** > **which** (inanimate antecedent)	**who** = *Ø* > *that* (animate antecedent) *Ø* > **that** > *which* (inanimate antecedent)

are explicitly using data from non-mobile older rural speakers (Chambers & Trudgill 1998). Herrmann (2003, 2005) uses data drawn from a number of oral history sources and also from the BNC.

In subject position, *that* is the dominant form across the country, except perhaps in northern East Anglia which, overall, prefers *what*. Ø, too, although rarely the most frequently occurring subject relativiser, is common in many of the country's dialects, especially in existentials, such as (68), and clefts, such as (69):

(68)   there's not many people like getting up at stupid o'clock to go to work

(69)   it's a small bungalow they moved to

Ø is the dominant form in object position, regardless of antecedent animacy. *That* is also very common there, except, again, in East Anglia, where it is only a minority form in Peitsara's (2002a) Suffolk data and barely present in any of the other East Anglian studies. Poussa (1994:424) finds very little *that* in Norfolk and speculates about how far the area of '*that*lessness' extends, and whether it is simply an East Anglian phenomenon.

The two relativisers that occur only in non-standard varieties, *what* and *as*, seem to be experiencing somewhat different fates. *As* appears obsolescent. Peitsara (2002a) finds that relativiser *as* is rarely used in her Suffolk data, as does Ojanen (1982) for Cambridgeshire. It seems to be found at its highest levels in the south-west (see Peitsara 2002a:180, Ihalainen 1980). Herrmann (2003), by contrast, found it to be absent in East Anglia and the south-west but did find a few examples in Nottinghamshire and Cumbria. *What* appears to be quite robust, however, from this overview in Table 4.1. It accounts for more than 10% of the relativisers in the south-west and East Anglian corpora in Herrmann's research (2003), as a dominant form in both subject and object position in Reading (Cheshire 1982a), in object position in London, and is used heavily in East Anglia (Ojanen 1982, Peitsara 2002a, Poussa 1994). Further north, however, it is barely used. Tagliamonte notes that '*what* is virtually non-existent' (2002b:154). Herrmann (2003:138) claims, however, that *what* is spreading: 'from its south-eastern (East Anglia including Essex) heartland ... *what* has been radiating out through the adjoining Midlands and the Home Counties, especially London, to the south-west and, eventually, to the north'. She adds, furthermore, that although *what* originated in East Anglia, it is not thriving there now because of stigmatisation, unlike in the urban centres, especially of the south (2003:141).

More generally, comparing her studies from the south-west and the north, Tagliamonte claims that 'the sheer lack of WH-words ... is astounding' (2002b:163). *Wh-* forms were barely used in object positions at all, and *which* (along with *what*) in particular were rare in any environment. An analysis of *who* in subject position across apparent time in her York corpus showed it to be used least among younger (under 35 years) and less well educated speakers, whilst *that* was more common among the young. Given that *wh-* forms had been considered to be steadily *entering* the system, Tagliamonte adds that 'linguistic change in the English relative marker system may be like a pendulum swinging back in the opposite direction' (2002b:164). Van den Eynden Morpeth (2002) does, however, show an increase in *wh-*forms in the south-west of England. She compares her and Ihalainen's (1980, 1985) data from 1980s Dorset and Somerset, with roughly 34% *wh-* words, with Harris' (1967) study of Devon in the 1960s where he found just 8% (Van den Eynden Morpeth 2002:433, 434).

Pronominal word order

Kirk (1985:135) discusses the regional distribution of different word order possibilities in clauses with both a direct and indirect object pronoun. His analysis, based on *SED* data, shows that ordering such as in (70) below,

(70)   Give it to me

was only reported as the vernacular form in the south-west, with (71) being the dominant form in the Midlands, Lancashire and parts of the south-east, and (72) in the north and East Anglia.

(71)   Give it me

(72)   Give me it

Demonstratives

A number of dialects in England have a different demonstrative system to that of Standard English. Well reported is the use of *them* as a distal plural demonstrative (Anderwald 2004b, Cheshire 1982a, Cheshire *et al.* 1989, 1993, Crinson & Williamson 2004, Edwards 1993, Hudson & Holmes 1995, Hughes & Trudgill 1979, Shorrocks 1999, Stenström *et al.* 2002, Trudgill 1999a, Wagner 2004), as in (73):

(73)   fetch me them eggs from the cupboard

Cheshire *et al.* (1989:194) find that *them* is the most well-reported non-standard grammatical feature from across the country, with almost 98% of their respondents claiming its use in their neighbourhood. Hudson & Holmes, similarly, find that *them* is one of the top twelve features used in their survey of the English of schoolchildren, found in over 40% of possible contexts (1995:14). A number of varieties also report *this here*, *these here*, *that there* and *them there* used as demonstratives (e.g. Wagner 2004:164, Harris 1991 for the south-west, Shorrocks 1999:51 for Bolton, Trudgill 2003:62 for Norfolk).

Wagner (2004) reports that *thick(y)* as a demonstrative has 'all but died out' in the south-west (2004:164), and Kortmann (2002) reports *they* used in Somerset as the distal plural form (see also Trudgill 1999a).

Comparison

In Standard English, comparative and superlative forms are created in two ways: either adding *-er* or *-est* to one of a large set of adjectives and adverbs (e.g. *bright, brighter, brightest; soon, sooner, soonest*), or using the analytic marker *more* or *most* before the uninflected adjective or adverb (e.g. *difficult, more difficult, most difficult*). A number of varieties are found to have 'double comparison' and use both the inflectional ending and the analytic marker, as in (74) and (75):

(74) it's a lot more easier than it used to be

(75) the most wonderfulest trip I've ever been on

The use of these forms is widespread, and they are reported, for example, in the south-east (Edwards 1993:231, Stenström *et al.* 2002:134), Merseyside (Hudson & Holmes 1995:20), the north-east (Crinson & Williamson 2004) and Cambridgeshire (Ojanen 1982:211).

Definite and indefinite articles

A well-known phenomenon from across the north of England is so-called Definite Article Reduction, whereby *the* is reduced to [t] or [ʔ] (see Mark Jones 1999 for discussion of regional variation in pronunciation, and also Mark Jones 2002, Ihalainen 1994, Shorrocks 1991, 1999, Rupp & Page-Verhoeff 2005, Petyt 1985), as in (76):

(76) They had a baby, and as soon as *t' baby* arrived he got jealous (from Rupp & Page-Verhoeff 2005)

Fox (2007), in a study of language use among a friendship group of adolescents of White and Bangladeshi ethnicity in the East End of London, finds that allomorphy of both the definite and indefinite articles is being rapidly eroded. Both articles are sensitive, in Standard English, to whether the following sound is a vowel or a consonant, as in (77) and (78). Fox finds, however, that the prevocalic variants are undergoing attrition, as in (79), with *a* being used before vowels in 74% of all possible cases among the Bangladeshi boys in her sample, and [ðə] before vowels in 81% of cases:

(77)   an apple, a pear

(78)   the [ði] apple, the [ðə] pear

(79)   a apple, the [ðə] apple

This phenomenon has been found sporadically in a number of locations (see, for example, Britain 2003:203, Claxton 1968:8, Ojanen 1982:126, Peitsara 1996:288 for East Anglia; Shorrocks 1999:45 for the north-west; Wagner 2004:155 for the south-west), but given that these reports are from areas well away from London, it appears Fox's dramatic findings represent a diffusing innovation, possibly from within the ethnic minority community.[11]

Conjunctions

A small number of studies report the use of non-standard conjunctions (e.g. Shorrocks 1999, Peitsara 1996, Trudgill 1995, 1997, 2003, 2004). The East Anglian research by both Trudgill and Peitsara discuss what the latter labels 'consecutive conjunctions' (1996:300), such as (80) and (81):

(80)   Don't stroke the cat *do* he'll scratch you

(81)   Take the dog for a walk *time* I get tea ready

Question tags

Studies carried out in the south-east of England (Andersen 2001, Stenström & Andersen 1996, Stenström *et al.* 2002, Tandberg 1996; see also Anderwald 2004b, Cheshire *et al.* 2005, Hudson & Holmes 1995) have noted the increasing use of the invariant tag *innit?* as in (82):

(82)   You told mum yesterday, innit? (Stenström *et al.* 2002:169)

Stenström *et al.*'s analysis (2002), based on their corpus of London adolescent speech, looks at *innit?* alongside other tags such as *yeah?* and *right?* They find that *innit?* is largely used by working-class, ethnic minority females (2002:187, 188, 189), with *yeah?* used most by adolescent middle-class males and *right?* (which they found was as popular as *innit?*), like *innit?*, used most by working-class ethnic minority adolescents. They also found regional variation *within* London, with *innit?* and *right?* used most in Hackney and *yeah?* in Camden.

---

[11] The examples of this in the Fens (Britain 2003) were from a speaker of Romani ethnicity.

5   Scottish English and Scots

Paul A. Johnston, Jr.

Introduction

Although Scottish Gaelic from the Highlands and a plenitude of immigrant languages exist, the language ecology of Lowland Scotland has been dominated by the relationship between two closely related daughters of Old and Early Middle English, Scots and Scottish Standard English (SSE). This is one of the most interesting multi-varietal situations in Western Europe, and reveals how the attribution of 'languagehood' is as much of a socio-political judgement as a linguistic one.

Scots

Scots is, more or less, the direct descendant of the Northumbrian form of Old English, planted in south-eastern Scotland between 525 and 633, which eventually spread over the whole Lowland Zone up to Morayshire by the 1200s (Duncan 1975, Nicolaisen 1977, Johnston 1997a:61–2). Later expansion brought it further to Caithness, Orkney and Shetland, where it replaced the Insular Norse language, Norn, and to Galloway and a number of Celtic-speaking areas along the Highland Line, as well as Ulster, where Scots-speaking communities live today in several places settled by Presbyterians. While it functions as the localised dialect of Lowland Scotland, it enjoys a special status due to an important aspect of its history: it is the only Germanic variety in Britain besides Standard English ever to have functioned as a full language within an independent state (the Kingdom of Scotland) and to have been used for all domains that implies, including a good-sized and sometimes brilliant corpus of literature from the early fourteenth to the early seventeenth centuries, exhibiting a range of genres, styles and registers comparable to any Western European national language. It even underwent the early stages of standardisation about the same time as English did, and there is no question that it would have become as independent from English as Portuguese is from Spanish or Dutch from German had not the religious and political turmoil of the sixteenth century changed the course of Scottish history. As it was, the lack of a complete Protestant Bible in Scots and the resultant use of English religious materials, the increasing political ties between Scotland and England and the expanding prestige of London-based Standard English resulted in a gradual decline in the use of Scots as a written tongue outside of self-conscious dialect literature (Murison 1977, Aitken 1984b, Devitt 1989), and the rejection of Scottish nationalism by the urban upper classes in the wake of the Union and the Jacobite failures to gain power in 1715 and 1745, together with the rise of a London-based spoken standard in Britain generally (Jones 1996, 1997, Beal 2004b) paved the way for anglicisation in speech as well, at least among these groups. This left Scots largely with the typical social distribution of a localised vernacular, complete with working-class associations and the stigmatisation that goes with them.

'Largely', however, is the operative word. The association between Scottish national identity and Scots still remains strong, even if nationalist discourse was and is mainly carried on in Standard English (Macafee 1985). The post-1700 Scots literary corpus, which may have set the tone for what dialect literature means in the English-speaking world through authors like Burns and Scott, contains too much diversity and experimentation with language to be narrowly defined in this way. In fact, some writers, like the poet Hugh McDiarmid, who aimed to recreate a modern equivalent to the Older Scots literary language, consciously eschewed any association with a dialect-literary tradition (McClure 1988:41). Only the utilitarian, non-literary prose genres seem denied to Scots, and even here there is recent, increasing experimentation (McClure 1988:25–7), along with proposals to expand the use of Scots within education (Niven & Jackson 1998).

While the bulk of sociolinguistic studies have been done in the urbanised Central Belt (Macaulay & Trevelyan 1977, Reid 1978, Romaine 1978, 1979, Johnston 1983, Macafee 1983, 1994, Pollner 1985, Macaulay 1991), where Scots is the most tied to social class and middle-class members tend primarily to use it 'in quotation marks' (Pattern IV, cf. Johnston 1997b:438–40), there are still large regions within Scotland, notably Caithness and the north-east, including at least one major city, Aberdeen, where people of high social prestige speak Scots on a daily basis, at least to fellow locals in casual situations (Pattern II). Even in rural areas around the periphery of the Central Belt, upwardly mobile middle-class members are not pressured to give up Scots, and they also use it in the same contexts (Pattern III). Middle-class speakers in these areas are capable of prodigious feats of 'clean' code-switching, as they may use 'modified' RP-like types of Standard Scottish English in formal styles

(Johnston 1997b). The Northern Isles exhibit yet another pattern, where the stylistic shifting that goes on results in the substitution of widespread Scots forms for local ones as well as SSE forms for Scots (Pattern I), so that 'pure' SSE is only approached, never attained, even by university graduates and local professionals (Melchers 1985).

Given the historical legacy and synchronic variation patterns, it is no wonder that many Scottish literati and cultural nationalists inspired by McDiarmid's philosophy have claimed that Scots is a true minority language, like Welsh or Gaelic, and the European Union, in 1995, accepted this claim along with those of many other erstwhile European dialect groups. McClure (1988) has laid out their position eloquently. While some of the facets of his argument are probably specious (that Scots cannot be a dialect because it itself has dialects, when most linguists would at least entitle it a dialect *group* within English on the same order as Hiberno-English or American English, cf. McClure 1988:18, Wells 1982, Johnston 1997b), and he does concede the fact that there are no universally agreed-upon criteria for language-hood in cases like this (McClure 1988:17), he is certainly right that Scots has more traits of a full language than other varieties declared independent at the same time, such as Asturianu, Schwäbisch, Limburgs or Venetian. Calling Scots a language may be controversial, but is hardly unreasonable.

A declaration of independence is the easy part, however. Scottish people have got used to written media and public speech in English (Macafee 1985), and have had 250 years of teachers, often in the overt service of union within Britain, calling Scots substandard and inappropriate for serious discourse. Most writing of any type done in Scotland is in Standard English, which also serves as the medium of education and even of Scottish institutions like the courts, the Kirk, and now the Parliament. Nevertheless, with the coming of devolution, the political conditions are not so unfavourable for Scots as they once were. Although authorities seem agreed on the idea of using it in more domains of writing (McClure *et al.* 1980, McClure 1988), and in education (Niven & Jackson 1998), there is a real cultural divide as to what type of Scots should be promoted as a new standard. Some, like Aitken (in McClure *et al.* 1980:43–60) feel the solution lies in doing as little linguistic engineering as possible, and simply promoting the use of any type of Scots, with a broad-based Standard Scots emerging from the resultant variation. Others, like McClure (in McClure *et al.* 1980:11–40) call for a more activist stance, overtly encouraging the use of a Standard Scots – in practice, usually *Lallans*, a synthetic, archaising, and somewhat artificial literary variety developed by McDiarmid and his followers for this purpose – in official documents and as the language of education and the media. If the history of other European standards provides valid parallels, the first course would lead to a strongly Central Belt-flavoured Scots, simply because of the predominance historically of this area's dialects; the fact that Mid Scots is a central rather than a peripheral dialect; and the sheer population and economic influence of this region, which contains all but one of Scotland's major cities. However, Mid Scots is also the dialect that is most regarded as a working-class vernacular (see above), and has suffered the most lexical and phonological erosion and English influence (Macafee 1994). On the other hand, Lallans enthusiasts' passion for linguistic purity, employing distinctively Scottish lexis from any dialect or any period, may assure that it is not narrowly regional, but also ensures its opacity to any ordinary native Scots speaker, who may not know the 'resurrected' vocabulary (such as the nearly stereotypical *leid* for *language*, instead of the idiomatic *tongue*) or the calqued terms (like *yearhunnir* for *century*; cf. German *Jahrhundert*) often found in Lallans prose. The promotion of Lallans may simply perpetuate the stigmatisation of Central Belt Scots, which is native to the majority of speakers, and so work *against* idiomatic Scots (Morgan 1983:195, McClure 1988:13). In addition, the conservative and archaising tendencies of Lallans may suggest a nostalgia for some kind of past, pre-industrial age that may lead people to associate Scots with a culture that is dead and gone. The dispute resembles the Norwegian Bokmål/Nynorsk conflict in part, and has a similar tendency to become regional; many of the prominent Lallans advocates, from McDiarmid and Douglas Young on, either come from or are based in the north-east and the Borders, while those based in Central Belt towns and cities tend to agree more with Aitken.

Scottish Standard English

The other main component of Scottish linguistic ecology is Scottish Standard English (SSE) which sprang up during the seventeenth and eighteenth centuries as a compromise system between London and localised Scots norms.[1] SSE co-exists with Scots in a sort of sociolinguistic equilibrium, and, given easy travel connections and migration between England and Scotland, has evolved into a continuum of types, ranging from a highly-Scotticised ('Basic') version used by working-class speakers

---

[1] Although SSE is a compromise, it may be less of one than usually supposed: such 'Scottish' features as monophthongal /eː oː/, different vowels in *perfect*, *girl* and *turn*, and rhoticity are features shared by at least some eighteenth-century English Standard models (Beal 2004b).

in formal styles, with extensive concessions to Scots in everyday vocabu-lary, such as *wee*, *bairn/wean*, *messages* (= 'groceries'), *lad(die)/lass(ie)*, common syntactic constructions (e.g. *I'll not be going* rather than *I won't be going*), and in phonology, the combination of Scots accent features with Standard-like lexical incidence (e.g. *stone*, *gold* with monophthongal /o/ rather than /e/ in the first and /ʌʉ/ in the second), to outright Standard British English with near-RP pronunciation used by some upper-middle-class members in cities like Edinburgh. Most middle-class speakers use something in between ('mainstream SSE'), and are immediately recognis-able as Scottish. Few native English speakers have problems understand-ing SSE, though the odd word or form might be unfamiliar.

As a general trend, all types of SSE, including mainstream varieties, seem to have become more Scottish-accented since World War II, and the near-RP ('Panloaf') and elocuted, hyper-RP-like types (the so-called 'Morningside/Kelvinside accent' (Johnston 1985a)) are approaching extinc-tion as their last speakers die off. More recently, an 'anti-Morningside' variety has been created by younger upper-middle-class women (Johnston 1985a), with concessions to Scots where Morningside/Kelvinside had hyper-RP features, and English-like forms where it had Scots values; this remains current, though it too may be cartooned as the language of fashion-conscious trendies, the Scottish equivalent of 'Valley Girl'.[2]

SSE also forms the basis of Highland and Hebridean English, spoken in the old Gaelic areas to the north of the Highland Line. Here, it was originally a second language, learned in school and favoured by the edu-cated elites (C. Ó Baoill 1997:565), but it now functions as a first language in many parts of the Highlands. Where Gaelic is still spoken, it has left traces in the phonology and syntax, particularly in Hebridean English (Shuken 1985, D. P. Ó Baoill 1997). Nevertheless, relatively weak Scots influence is present even in these dialects, especially in lexis (Mather & Speitel 1975, 1977), while the vowel system strongly resembles a high-prestige SSE inventory (Johnston 1984, Shuken 1986). Closer to the Highland Line, Highland English contains more Scots accentual features, so that the English of Inveraray resembles a watered-down Glaswegian SSE, and working-class Invernesian has the accent features of the Black Isle.

The polar structure of Scots and Scottish English

The interplay between Scots and SSE is one of the most fascinating things about the linguistic ecology of Lowland Scotland. Since the linguistic

---

[2] One male Morningside informant entitled it the 'Ahctually Ahccent', with the stereotype sentence-introducer [ɑkʃʌɫe].

difference between the two is greater than between any English Standard/vernacular pair, many speakers have a distinct sense of possession of two linguistic codes, each with its own grammar, and they feel they code-switch between the two. In this respect, the pattern resembles obviously bilingual situations. However, writers like Macaulay & Trevelyan (1977; cf. Macafee 1997:520–4), who saw a linguistic continuum between Scots and SSE, were not entirely wrong, as the two grammars are partially interpenetrable. Thus, speakers can code-drift as well as switch in contexts of increased formality, gradually editing out blatantly Scots features. Who drifts and who switches depends on the usual sociolinguistic factors (social class, gender, age, network membership and attitudes towards Scots), as well as what degree of importance class or the ingroup/outgroup distinction has in the specific community. It also seems to be the case that 'dialect' variables (Petyt 1980), which involve lexis, morphology or gross phonological differences (like *hoose/ house, stane/stone* or *dae/do*) involve a polar, 'either/or', choice between Scots and SSE, while accent variables, even if they are quite diagnostic of class membership (as say, /a/ realisations in words like *cat* are) show more of a continuum.

An oft-reprinted, but highly informative schematic diagramming what is counted as Scots and English was formulated by Aitken (1984b:520) and expanded by Macafee (1997:519), and is presented in Table 5.1.

According to this model, one is speaking Scots if one utilises items from Columns 1 to 3, and SSE if one uses words and phrases from Columns 3 to 5 (note that the central column is a common core, so there is always quite a bit of overlap). Columns 2 and 4 are distinctively Scots and English forms of the same word with different underlying phonology, while the outer two columns consist of distinct Scots and English lexical items or phrases for the same concept. These groups of columns could be said to constitute a Scots and an English *pole*, and if we listed and sorted every item known by a given speaker, we could abstract out two related, but distinct, linguistic systems. Code-switching would then be defined as a fairly clean alternation between the two poles. This is the type of variation middle-class members in Pattern II and III communities may illustrate, but clean code-switching is also typical of speakers from the middle part of the social scale, working-class women and men not embedded in typical multiplex social networks, and those well disposed toward the current 'Scots revival'[3] within Pattern IV communities.

---

[3] Middle-class 'clean' code-switchers in whatever type of community may have a stronger knowledge of traditional Scots vocabulary, particularly literary registers, than the usual vernacular speaker (Macaulay & Trevelyan 1977:55, Macafee 1994:69).

Table 5.1. *The bipolar model (after Aitken 1984b:520 and Macafee 1997:519)*

	Scots		English	
1	2	3	4	5
bairn	hame	name	home	child
brae	hale	hole	whole	slope
kirk	mare	before	more	church
ken	puir	soup	poor	know
darg	muin	room	moon	job of work
cuit	yuis n.	miss	use n.	ankle
kenspeckle	yaize v.	raise	use v.	conspicuous
birl	cauld	tie	cold	spin
girn	auld	young	old	whine
mind	coo	row (= fight)	cow	remember
sort	hoose	winter	house	mend
ay	pey	bite	pay	always
gey	wey	tide	way	very
ein	deid	feed	dead	eyes
shuin	dee	see	die	shoes
deave	scart	leave	scratch	deafen, vex
gaed	twa(w)/twae	agree	two	went
ben the hoose	no (= not)	he	not	inside the house
	-na(e)	his	-n't	

Code-drifters, on the other hand, not only select from one or the other pole, but also mix systems, using scattered items from one pole within the overall matrix of another, which they are plainly dominant in and use most often. The attenuated, non-dominant pole appears as only a partial grammar of the other variety. For instance, some lower-middle-class speakers in Type III and IV communities might use the odd Scots item 'outside of quotation marks' in their most casual styles, especially if they grew up in a Scots-speaking environment (Johnston 1983), and have a highly eroded Scots pole, with a large number of originally distinctively English items in their Column 3. They switch between this 'mixed' pole and more-or-less pure SSE. The converse situation might be found among informants of very low social standing, whatever type of community they are found in, who have a similarly attenuated English pole.

In what I have called Pattern I communities, found in the Northern Isles, speakers code-drift in a similar way, in that the 'English' pole is in fact highly attenuated, what SSE word forms are contained in it are highly accented – [stɒn] rather than [sten ~ stin] for *stone*, for instance – and SSE is only approximated, never attained, even by local professionals and college graduates. However, the locals themselves perceive what they do as code-switching, as they edit specifically Insular Scots vocabulary and grammar items and replace them with Scots features of wider distribution (Melchers 1985:91–2, 97).

While this view of the polar structure differs from Aitken's (1984b:520–3), and presents some problems if a linguist wants to account for passive knowledge as well as active use of Scots, it does reflect what the speakers, at least those older than thirty or so (Macafee 1994:207–11) actually feel their active grammar is.

This perception of bipolarity, of *whole* systems, even if one pole is attenuated, distinguishes the Scottish situation from a classic standard-and-dialect dichotomy, even from other divergent-dialect situations as found in northern England or Northern Ireland, where the localised pole is always attenuated and shifting is under much less conscious control. It provides necessary, if not sufficient, evidence for the claim that Scots is a separate language from English, rather than a dialect group within it.

The forms of Scots and Scottish English: consonant phonology

Generally, in the Germanic language group, consonants seem to be more stable over time than vowels, which means dialectal consonant systems across a language resemble each other relatively closely, and the vowels do much of the 'work' of distinguishing varieties phonologically. Scots and Scottish English are no exception to this; they are, indeed, identical to each other in consonant phonemic inventory, if not always in lexical incidence, so that they can largely be treated together.

Most forms of both Scots and SSE include the stops /p t k b d g/, the affricates /tʃ dʒ/, the fricatives /f v θ ð s z ʃ ʒ x h/, the nasals /m n ŋ/, the lateral /l/, the tap or approximant /r/ and the semi-vowels /j w ʍ/. In addition, the consonantal phonetic realisation rules of SSE spoken by habitual Scots speakers are identical to their Scots rules although, since a continuum exists between SSE and RP, socially-tied SSE varieties in the same communities may differ substantially from each other in this respect.

Only /x ʍ/ are not found in RP or similar English dialects. /x/ occurs in SSE in place and personal names from Gaelic (*Auchtermuchty, Lachlan*) and in Scots words without English cognates (*dreich*, meaning 'dreary (of weather)'), while /ʍ/ occurs in words from OE /xw/, spelled < wh-> like *where, whisky, whine.*[4] Traditionally, Scots would have /x/ in all words containing OE or Gaelic /x/, even those with English cognates such as *richt, fecht, eneuch*, and /ʍ/ in all OE /xw/ words, including *wha(e)*, corresponding

---

[4] In the Northern Scots group, this sound is lacking, as it became /f/ in late Older Scots times.

to English *who*. The rest of these phonemes occur in SSE in the same words as they do in other English dialects, although there are a few systematic differences:

1. SSE (and Scots) is generally rhotic, so words like *barn* and *car* generally have some type of /r/: a tap or trill appears at least intervocalically, and often in all positions (Grant *et al.* 1931–75:xxiv, Johnston 1983:26–9), though high-status SSE has [ɹ]. Localised Central Belt Scots dialects, and increasingly others, use a pharyngealised vowel [ʌˤ] for post-vocalic /r/ (Romaine 1978, Macafee 1983:33).
2. /h/ is retained in SSE and all Scots but that of the Black Isle.
3. Most Scots and SSE have a dark [ɫ] in all positions for /l/ where it was not vocalised in Older Scots (in codas after back vowels, except in the sequence /ɑld/; Scots has *aw, baw, gowd, shoother* for *all, ball, gold, shoulder*, but *aul(d), caul(d)* for *old, cold*).
4. The voiceless stops /p t k/ are unaspirated, though this is recessive (Dieth 1932:100–101, Zai 1942:20).
5. Glottalling of /t/ (and often /k/ and /p/ in at least some positions) is frequent, and has spread recently to rural as well as urban varieties. There are usually additional constraints about glottal stops occurring in two consecutive syllables (Macaulay 1991:31).
6. In Scots, but not usually in SSE, there are numerous combinative changes, usually involving lenition or deletion of consonants in clusters. Some of these, like /nd ld/ > /nl/ (*hand > haun*; *old > aul* in Northern Scots), /pt kt/ > /p k/ (*accept > accep*; *act > ack*), and /-NC-/ > /-N-/ (*candle > cannel*; *Campbell > Cammell*; *finger*/ŋg/ > *finger* /ŋ/) have regional English analogues, while others (/θr/ > /hr/; *three > hree~chree*) are mainly Scots. On the other hand, peripheral Northern and/or Insular Scots dialects may retain initial /kn gn/ in *knee, gnaw*, /wr-/ or a /vr-/ derived from it in *write*; and even original postvocalic /w/ (as /v/) after certain vowels (*blow > blyaave*).

In addition, there are consonant differences between Scots and SSE because of different but related etyma for individual items: thus SSE *stitch, church, bridge* from OE, but Scots *steek, kirk, brig* from ON cognates.

Vowel phonology

As for consonants, the Scots and SSE phonemic inventories in a given area are similar, if not identical, and also may resemble each other in fine phonetic detail. However, the lexical incidence of each vowel class differs between the two poles so much that it is necessary to separate the descriptions of SSE and Scots, while using a system of vowel classes that could be used for either variety. For this, I use a system developed by Aitken

Table 5.2. *Vowel classes in Scots/Scottish English*

Aitken Class	Johnston Class	Early Northern Middle English source	Common core words
1S	BITE	/iː/ in short environments	*pipe, bide, wife*
1L	TRY	/iː/ in long environments	*five, prize, tyre*
2	MEET	/eː/	*meet, need, queen, beer*
3	BEAT	/ɛː/	*meat, knead, clean, near*
4	MATE	/aː/	*late, made, plane, hare*
5	COAT	/ɔː/	*coat, code, hole, score*
6	OUT	/uː/	*out, loud, clown, tower*
7	BOOT	/øː/	*root, food, soon, poor*
7a	*FOOT*	/ø/ or /ʊ/	*foot, good, bull*
8	BAIT	/ai/	*bait, braid, rain, hair*
8a	*PAY*	/ai/ word finally/before pal.	*change, may, pay*
9	VOICE	/ɔi/	*Boyd, voice, boy*
10	LOIN	/ʊi/	*join, avoid, oil*
11	——	/ei/	*die, eye, lie, fly*
12	CAUGHT	/au/	*salt, laud, dawn, saw*
13	LOUP	/ɔu/	*loup, -knowe*
14	NEW	/iu/	*new, duty, immune, pure*
14a	DEW	/ɛu/	*dew, few, beauty*
15	BIT	/ɪ/	*bit, lid, sin, fir*
16	BET	/ɛ/	*bet, bed, wren, Kerr*
16a	——	/ɪ/ (ME /ɛ/)	*never, seven, next, earth*
17	CAT	/a/	*rat, lad, pan, jazz*
17a	——	/a/ + voiceless fric., etc.	*pass, bath, grant, far, ah*
18	COT	/ɔ/	*pot, cod, don, north*
19	CUT	/ʊ/	*cut, mud, sun, fur*

(1984a:95–8), modified in some cases by my own system (Johnston 1997b:453), shown in Table 5.2.

Scottish Standard English vocalism is well described as a compromise between London-based and Scots norms. In its 'Basic', most Scottish form it has the following characteristics:

1. Like Scots, it possesses the Scottish Vowel Length Rule (SVLR, also known as Aitken's Law), whereby, except for Vowels 15/16a and 19, which are always short, all vowels are long before voiced fricatives, /r/ and morpheme-finally. In practice, because of later changes, the SVLR holds strictly only for high vowels and Vowels 1S/1L-11, which are distinguished as /əi/::/ae/. There is a tendency for low-mid and low vowels to be at least half-long in much of central and southern Scotland before all voiced sounds, and, in west central Scotland, there is a general

lengthening of all non-high vowels under breath-group stress (the 'Glasgow Drawl' (Macafee 1983, Johnston 1997a:67)[5]).

2. Vowels 2/3, 4/8/8a, 7/7a, 10/11, 12/18, 14/14a, and 17/17a are merged. More 'Modified', RP-like types may distinguish several of the pairs as [a]/[ɑ] (14/14a), [ɔ]/ [ɒ] (12/18) and [ʉ] /[ü] (7/7a) respectively, though the lexical incidence may not match that in RP.

3. Before /r/, most vowels have the same quality as in other positions. Therefore, *north* and *score* (Vowels 12/18 and 5) have different vowels, and so do *perfect*, *girl* and *turn* (Vowels 15, 16, and 19). Some midscale speakers may have a separate 16a in words with RP /ɛ/ but Scots /ɪ/ (the 'Abercrombie vowel'), and if so, *earth* is different from the rest before /r/.

The 'Basic' SSE system therefore has an inventory of /i ɪ e ɛ a ʌ ɔ o u əi[6] ʌʉ oe/, and it is homologous to a Stirlingshire or West Mid Scots system.

Scots systems are far more varied than SSE ones, so that it is not easy to characterise their lexical incidence in a unified manner. However, a number of features are common to most or all Scots:

1. The SVLR operates on Scots as it does on SSE, with the modifications mentioned above. A few peripheral dialects may have length contrasts, some largely lexical in nature (e.g. /iː/ in *weak*, but /i/ in *week*), others involving a more restricted SVLR, with Older Scots /ɛː ɔː ɑː/ not subject to shortening, so that there are length-based 5/18, 12/17 and/ or 4/8 contrasts, as in Insular, Northern, and Fife/Perthshire dialects.

2. Vowel 4 represents the reflex of OE /aː/ and the outcome of /a/ lengthened in open syllables.[7] Thus, *stone, home, bone, toe, more* (and *apple, father, saddle*) go in the same group with *name, face* and so on. The reflex of OE /ar/ like *arm, bairn, heart* also lengthened to merge with Vowel 4.

3. The same development before original /w/ means that *blow, crow, throw* take Vowel 12, not 5 or 13. Words with /alC/, such as *old, cold*, later joined this class.

4. Vowel 7 (and 14 before consonants) represent the reflex of Early Northern ME /oː/, which was fronted early to /øː/, and develops as a front vowel. It is often merged out of existence, especially in long environments, with patterns involving merger with 2 (north-east), 3

---

[5] For other views on the SVLR, see Agutter (1988) and Scobbie *et al.* (1999).

[6] In SSE, as opposed to Scots, [ae] can be taken as an allophone of /əi/ since contrasts like *pie/ pay* do not hinge on this distinction. *Tied/Tide* is not taken as a true minimal pair, as the morphological structure is different, as in *brood/brewed* or *road/rowed*.

[7] Open syllable lengthening in Scots happens to all short vowels and before any open syllable, not just those originally ending in final *-e*, so that *apple, father, summer, city* have their stressed vowels developed as long. In the case of words like *summer*, with Vowel 7 originally, for the most part they have been reshortened or replaced by SSE forms.

and 4 (Dundee, Fife, Perth) or a split pattern (= 15 when short, 4/8 when long in much Mid and Southern Scots) predominating.

5. Vowel 6, from Early Northern ME /uː/, stays monophthongal isolatively, with the vowel in words like *shoulder, coulter* < /ʊlC/ joining this class. It is fronting over most of Scotland now, with only the Northern Isles and part of the north-east retaining /u(ː)/; an independent fronting happened in Caithness. Vowel 13, which includes the vowel of words with old /ɔlC/, like *gold, colt, bolster* is fronting to [əü] in parallel.

6. Vowel 11, from Early Northern ME /ei/ merges with Vowel 2, not Vowel 1L.

7. Vowel 2 is also added to by the lengthening of OE /ɪ/ in open syllables and French loans with short /i/, like *city, pity, minister, decision*, all with Scots /i/.

8. There is always a class of words under Vowel 8a (*may, pay, clay, stay* and more) that merge with 1S, producing minimal pairs with 1L such as *pay/pie*.

9. Scots vowels seem to be sensitive to the gravity of surrounding consonants, with a preceding /w/ having the most effect. All dialects of Scots have /wɪ ~ wɪ / > /wʌ ~ ʍʌ/, particularly if a grave consonant follows (*whip > whup*), and /wɛ/ > /wɑ/ (*west > wast*). Outside the southeast, /waː/ finally > /wɑː/ (to develop with Vowel 12 (*whae, twae, awa(y) > wha(w), twa(w), awa(w)*)). North of the Forth/Clyde line, a preceding /w/ diphthongises Vowels 3 and 4 (*wame > wyme; weaver > wyver*), while in the Scottish north-east, there is a whole row of other vowels affected by /w/ and other grave consonants: *wheel > fyle; good > gweed; coal > quile; wey (way) > wye; claes (clothes) > cleys*.

10. Each major group has a number of special developments not mentioned above. For instance:
    i. Southern Scots has diphthongised Vowels 2/3 and 6 to [ëi] and [ʌu] respectively, has backed Vowel 17 > [ɑ(ː) ~ ɒ(ː)], lowered 16 > [æ(ː)] and 15 > [ë], raised 18 > [o(ː)], merged 12/17, and diphthongised mid vowels before /x/, so that *fecht (fight) > fey(ch)t* and *bocht (bought) > bow(ch)t*. The changes involving Vowels 15 and 17 also are found in the Lothians.
    ii. Mid Scots also tends to raise Vowel 18 and lower 15, but in addition may raise Vowel 12 to [ɔ(ː)], a development shared in words like *hand, land, bar, car* where the /ɑ/ was lengthened before these sonorants; the raising is spreading from west to east. Vowel 7 is often unrounded, so that *poor, do > pair, dae* and *moon, pool > min, pil*, while Vowel 6 fronts to take its place, pulling 13 along with it. In the Central Belt, 2 = 3, 4 = 8 and 5 = 18, but in Galloway and Fife/Perthshire, there tend to be height or length contrasts here.

iii. Besides the developments mentioned above, Northern Scots tends to have long nuclei for 5, 8 and 12, but Vowels 2 and 7 merge as [i(ː)] (*moon, poor* > *meen, peer*). Except in Caithness, /u/-fronting in *down, out* is recent. Vowel 15 is [ë], but often [ɨ] around grave consonants, while BET and MATE may merge in the core of the area. In Caithness and north coastal varieties, high vowels might be slightly diphthongised to [ɪi ʊu ~ ʏy], and Vowels 3 and 4 more strongly to [ɛi], while 18 and 19 are diphthongised before /g ŋ/ (*dug (dog)* > *dowg*; *tongue* > *towng*). Vowel 4 goes to /i/ before /n/, and sometimes /l m/ as well. Aberdeenshire has 2 = 3 and 4 = 8 isolatively.

iv. In Insular Scots, most of the old short vowels have two reflexes, with a vowel shift involving raising of Vowels 16 and 17 to [æ(ː)] and [ei] before voiced sounds, backness switch of 15 and 19 before grave ones, and lowering of 5 and often 12 isolatively to [ɒ(ː)]. Vowels 6, 7 and sometimes 8 are often close to their Older Scots values of [u(ː)], [øː] and [ɛː] respectively, while 1L reflexes may occur before all voiced sounds. Systems tend to be large, with many length contrasts.

Scots morphology and syntax

While dialectologists dealing with Scottish varieties as far back as Murray (1873) and Grant & Main Dixon (1921) have paid some attention to their morphology and syntax, these grammatical levels often fall in between two stools. Traditionally, dialectologists and sociolinguists have shown more interest in phonology, where tokens are plentiful and, in part, less subject to conscious control, while syntacticians of the Chomskyan persuasion have shied away from examining dialects which require empirical methods of study. Furthermore, many syntactic constructions may be confined to specific styles or registers which are not easily recorded, though they may readily occur in literature. It has therefore been only recently that the methods necessary to access speakers' use and knowledge of morphosyntax have been available; works using them like Beal (1997) for morphology, or Macaulay (1991) or Miller (1993) for syntax, have uncovered a great deal of the most important and distinctive Scottish variants. Because of space constraints, I list some of the most salient features here, and point the reader to these sources to discover the rest.

Bar a few irregular verb forms like *gotten* for *got*, SSE morphology *is* Standard English morphology. The Scots morphological system differs from the SSE/English ones in the following ways:

1. Individual, recessive irregular plurals exist, such as *ee/een* 'eye', *shae/ shuin* 'shoe', *oax/owsen* 'ox', *horse/horse* 'horse', *cauf/caur* 'calf', *broo/ breer(s)* 'brow', with the last two confined to the north.

2. As in other dialects, the uninflected form of words of temporal or spatial measurement like *year*, *foot*, *pound* (and *quid*, *bob*, *p.*) or *mile* may appear after numerals, as in *three year ago*, *six/sax fit lang*, *seiven mile fae here*. On the other hand, semi-liquid foods, such as *parritch* 'porridge', *kail*, *broth*, *brose* and so on, are usually treated as plurals (Grant & Main Dixon 1921:80, Beal 1997:344): *Thae kail arenae het eneuch*.

3. The distinction *thou/you*, with all the overtones the equivalent distinction has on the Continent, is highly recessive outside of the Northern Isles; instead, *you/youse* has come in from Ireland, and is associated with areas where Irish influence is strong, like Clydeside (Beal 1997:346).

4. As in many colloquial forms of English, the objective case can serve as a sort of resumptive pronoun, even in subject position (*Me, I had chased't*) and in conjunct structures (as in the Border shibboleth *Yow an mey'll hae some tey, gaun up the hill an pow a pey*).

5. The form *us/is/wis* is often used for the singular, especially in indirect object constructions (*Gie's a pint of special*; Murray 1873:188, Beal 1997:347).

6. The Scots reflexive pronouns end in *-sel*, which also serves for the free-standing *self* for many speakers. Miller (1993:108) reports that hefty phrases may occur between the pronominal element and *sel*.

7. Scots has a three-way demonstrative deictic system, with *this/thir* designating something near the speaker, *that/thae* near the hearer and *yon* or *thon* something remote from both. *These/Those* are well established now in both Scots and SSE contexts, though *(th)is/(th)at* can often be found as a plural in the north (Johnston 1985b, Beal 1997:350), and *thae* survives elsewhere, being used variably along with the incomer *them/thaim* and Standard *those*. *Thir* is now confined to Lallans usage alone.

8. Like northern dialects of English, Scots has two distinct present tense paradigms: one matches the Standard one in broad outline and is used when a personal pronoun immediately precedes in a non-habitual, non-narrative context; in other cases, the other one, with a suffix *-s*, is found (Murray 1873:212, Grant & Main Dixon 1921:112, Macaulay 1991:60).

9. Some peripheral (Insular, Northern and Southern) Scots dialects (and Lallans) still retain a difference between gerundive *-ing* > [-in] and present participial *-an(d)* > [-ʌn ~ -n] (Murray 1873:210–11, Beal 1997:356).

10. The regular Scots past tense/weak past participial marker is *-it*, with allomorphs *-t*, *-(e)d* around sonorants.

11. The number of modals possible has declined. Old modals like *dow*, and even *sall*, so frequent in Older Scots, are now gone, and even

maun is on its last legs, soon to be replaced by *huv tae* and the like. Even in SSE, the modals *must* (cf. *have to/be to*), *may* and *shall* are largely foreign now.

The distinctively Scottish (or sometimes, Scottish plus northern English) syntactic features fall into several different categories: some are found in both SSE and Scots, as in the general preference for *I'll no(t) do/dae that* vs. *I won't/wullnae do/dae that*, and some of the uses of the definite article mentioned below. Others are, if not strictly Scots, at least local and vernacular, like the Glaswegian focussing strategies. Then, there are the usual general non-Standardisms, as we have described for other levels, found more often in a Scots matrix than in SSE only because of class-tying, and not treated here. For syntax, the idea of style or register seems more important than geographical variation, although there are forms that are distinctive to specific dialect areas – particularly Insular or Urban Central Belt Scots ones.

1. Verbs are negated by either the clitic *-nae* or the independent negator *no*, which for the most part parallel SSE *-n't/not*, with the first joining on to auxiliaries and the second following main verbs, including, preferentially, *to be* and the main verb *to have* (Macaulay 1991:53–4). In questions with *do*-support, both Scots and, to a large extent SSE, employ the independent negator rather than the clitic.

2. Both Scots and SSE accept 'benefactive' genitive pronouns, as in *I'm away to **my** bed*, or *We're going home to **our** tea* (Macaulay 1991:71, Miller 1993:129, Beal 1997:363).

3. The definite article appears in a number of contexts where it would be omitted in English varieties, or in some cases, where indefinite *a/an* would be used instead. It appears:

   i. with names of institutions: *The bairns are gaun tae the schuil this year; I always go to the church Sundays.*

   ii. with names of trades/occupations: *He decided to take up the soldiering.*

   iii. with names of games, sports and hobbies: *Jimmy's a yin for goin tae the fitba.*

   iv. with names of languages and school subjects: *She's a whiz at the maths; That family all have the Gaelic.*

   v. with names of diseases: *He has got the cold.*

   vi. with seasons and other 'certain periods of time': *I shall see you in the summer; I shall see you the morn* (= 'tomorrow').

   vii. in the phrase *the noo/the now* = 'immediately': *I cannae think o any the now.*

   viii. in the fixed phrases 'the fifteen', 'the forty-five', referring to the two Jacobite rebellions: *The McLachlans came out in the forty-five.*

4. Double modal constructions have been studied in depth by Miller (1993:119–20 and cf. Beal (1997:369)), who found that many of them – but not all (cf. *You might would like to come with us* Miller (1993:120)) – involve *can* or *could* as a second element. This is significant, as Murray (1873:216) still finds *can* to have characteristics of a main verb, including an infinitive form *to can*, a present participle *cannin/cannan* and a past participle *cuid*. In modern Scots, these constructions have disappeared, but sequences like *may can, might could, will can, would could, used to could* abound. They are negated on the second element: the opposite of *I'll can fix that caur for ye* is *I'll cannae fix that caur for ye*,[8] not **I willnae can* ....

5. Verbs of mental process like *think, doubt* (= 'reckon') can freely take the progressive aspect in both Scots and SSE (Beal 1997:172–3). Other stative verbs too, even in SSE, can take progressives, as in *Where are you staying in Edinburgh?* (= 'Where do you stay...').

6. Where there are two pronoun objects, the indirect object comes first as in *Gie's't (Give us it)* (= 'Give it to me/us').

7. The preposition or conjunction *than* is traditionally absent from Scots comparative constructions, with *nor* or *as* serving instead (Murray 1873:169): *This stick is langer nor that yin.*

8. At present, the usual relative pronoun in speech is *that* (or *at*), as in *That's the man that did it*, used with both inanimate and animate reference, and in both restrictive and non-restrictive clauses. Macaulay (1991:63–4) lists a tendency for WH forms like *who, whose* to be used more when the noun being modified is in subject position, or is human. There tends to be a high tolerance for constructions such as *The man that his father drowned works down the pit* and *The hoose that the end o't fell is aw away noo* (Murray 1873:197). Zero relatives are particularly common after existentials and main verb *have* (Murray 1873:197, Macaulay 1991:64): *It's every house has got a television* from the latter work is roughly parallel to *There's mony yins does that* from the former.

9. Vernacular Scots and working-class SSE have various methods of throwing focus on specific NPs (Macaulay 1991:79–81). These include:
    i. demonstrative focussing: *So that was me on the rope* ...
    ii. *It* clefting: *It was her that got there.*
    iii. NP fronting: *Davie Drummond you called him.*
    iv. right dislocation: *In fact, he offered me a job, Mr Cunningham.* (= 'he')
    v. *See* fronting with coreferential NP: *See you, Jimmy, ye're beginnin tae get up ma wick* ...

[8] *I'll no can* ... is found also (Miller 1993:120).

Some of these are particularly associated with Glaswegian, but only *See* fronting really has a West Mid Scots distribution (Macafee 1983:19). In fact, rules like right dislocation or *It* clefting seem to be general non-standard British features, and these focussing techniques are common concomitants of a working-class narrative style.

Scots lexis

To deal intensively with the lexicon of Scots would triple the length of this chapter. Besides Standard English, no Germanic dialect used in the British Isles has as much vocabulary in as many registers, simply because of the long history and literary tradition Scots has. Furthermore, as stated earlier, many Lallans writers both coin or calque new words and resuscitate obsolete vocabulary, so that, theoretically, any word that ever was used in Scots is potentially still current, at least in literature.

As to 'ordinary' vocabulary, two seminal studies, both based on Central Belt data, give conflicting scenarios. The older, Agutter & Cowan's (1981) study of lexical change and turnover, paints a portrait of a vocabulary in flux, but also in balance, with the loss of traditional vocabulary made up by an increase in new, localised coinages, mostly slang, but which are beginning to constitute a new dialect vocabulary. The other study, Caroline Macafee's (1994) monograph on change in lexis in Glasgow, explored language attitudes in more depth, and gives a much less sanguine scenario than the first, where the rate of creation of new words cannot possibly match the erosion of traditional vocabulary, especially in the present climate of modernisation which devalues what is old as obsolete, or, at best, worth recycling in a very inauthentic, 'antiqued' way, and which tends to equate words which have survived over centuries with slang and even taboo terms as simply 'colourful language'. Her scenario, however, does not signal the death knell for all Scottish lexis. She stresses the unevenness of the decline of Scots, even as individual items retreat from active use to passive knowledge (Macafee 1994:233–4). There may be rather a contraction of the vocabulary to a hard core of commonly used everyday words, which will be retained to form the basis of a new, vital, if less distinctive regional norm.

6   Northern Irish English

Kevin McCafferty

English was established in the north of Ireland by the British colonisation of Ulster from the late sixteenth century onwards. This 'Plantation' brought large numbers of settlers from Great Britain – especially central and southern Scotland and the north, north-west Midlands and south-west of England – but never achieved its goal of replacing the Irish with a British population. This left Ulster with three major vernacular language varieties, Irish Gaelic, Scots and English, with Scottish Gaelic in some areas. Northern Irish English is the outcome of contact between these. Most of its phonology, syntax, morphology and lexicon are shared with other varieties of English, particularly Southern Irish English, but like Southern Irish English, Northern Irish English retains Early Modern English features now defunct or marginal in Great Britain. There is a broad distinction between the more English-influenced dialects of Mid and South Ulster and the more Scottish varieties of eastern and northern coastal areas, but the predominance of Scottish settlers in the Plantation era is seen in Scots influence beyond the core Ulster Scots dialect areas. And the effects of the Gaelic substrate can still be traced, especially where Irish remains an everyday vernacular or has gone out of use relatively recently.[1]

Northern and Southern Irish English

Some lexical and phonological differences between Northern Irish English and Southern Irish English are mapped in P. L. Henry (1958). Distinctive Ulster lexicon is largely shared with Scotland and northern England (P. L. Henry 1964, 1985).[2] Barry (1981) uses 45 phonological features to

Thanks to Anniken Telnes Iversen and John Kirk for commenting on drafts of this chapter, and to Karen Corrigan, Michael Montgomery and Dónall Ó Baoill for copies of their work. Any remaining flaws are the author's responsibility.
[1] Since Harris (1984a), Kirk (1997a) has surveyed work on Northern Irish English (cf. also Corrigan 1990). On Ulster Scots, cf. Montgomery & Gregg (1997). Kirk (2003) discusses the debate on the state and status of Ulster Scots.
[2] The *Concise Ulster Dictionary* (Macafee 1996) is a record of the Ulster lexicon.

Table 6.1. *North–south phonological differences in Ireland (after Barry 1981)*

Consonants	NIE	SIE	Vowels	NIE	SIE
BREA<u>THE</u>	[ð]	[d̪]	P<u>O</u>NY	[o]	[ɔ]
<u>TH</u>IRD	[θ]	[t̪]	G<u>OO</u>SE	[ʉ]	[ʊ]
CA<u>T</u>	[t]	[tˢ]	H<u>OR</u>SE	[ɔː]	[ɑ(ː)]
<u>C</u>AT	[kʲ]	[k]	B<u>OI</u>L	[oi - ɔi]	[ɑi]

map the north–south boundary along a line from Donegal Bay in the west to Carlingford Lough-Dundalk Bay on the east coast. Some of the features used are listed in Table 6.1 (cf. also Barry 1982, Adams, Barry & Tilling 1985). Harris (1985a) locates the boundary according to whether certain vowels have phonemic (Southern Irish English) or phonetic (Northern Irish English) vowel length, i.e. whether or not they apply a variant of the Scottish Vowel Length Rule, which also distinguishes systematically between northern varieties.[3]

Dialects of Northern Irish English

Early attempts at lexical mapping of the Ulster Scots zone failed to distinguish Ulster Scots from Mid Ulster English areas because Scots words had spread beyond the core Ulster Scots areas (Gregg 1985:27), but three major regional varieties of Northern Irish English are distinguished on the basis of vowel phonology.

Ulster Scots dialects are the traditional speech of three coastal areas of Ulster – north and east Down, most of Antrim and north-east Co. (London)Derry, and the Laggan district of north-east Donegal (Gregg 1972, 1985). Rural varieties are described by Gregg (1958, 1959) and Douglas (1975, also Douglas-Cowie 1978), while accounts of urban Ulster Scots exist for Larne (Gregg 1964) and Coleraine (Kingsmore 1995, 1996).

Mid Ulster English is the most widespread variety of Northern Irish English. It is spoken in the largest urban centres, Belfast (J. Milroy 1981, 1992, L. Milroy 1987) and (London)Derry (McCafferty 1998a, 1998b, 1999, 2001), and the smaller town of Lurgan (Pitts 1985, 1986, 1989). Rural Mid Ulster English is treated in Todd's (1984, 1989) work on Tyrone, Fermanagh and Armagh dialects.

South Ulster English occupies an east–west band across Ireland. The best phonological description to date is by Harris (1985a:33–41), whose

---

[3] Kallen (2000) observes an east–west dialect division for some phonological features that distinguish Ulster and Leinster in the east from Connacht and Munster in the west.

Table 6.2. *Ulster Scots (USc), Mid Ulster English (MUE)*
and South Ulster English (SUE)

	Conservative USc	MUE	SUE	Southern Irish English (Wells 1982:419)
KIT	[ǽ]	[ĕ]	[ï]	[ɪ]
FOOT	[ï]	[ʌ - ʉ]	[ʉ]	[ʊ]
GOAT	[oː] (e.g. *foal*)	[o]	[oː]	[oː]
	[eː] (e.g. *home*)			
	[ɔː] (e.g. *snow*)			
MOUTH	[ʉ]	[əʉ]	[əʉ]	[aʊ]

boundary between Mid Ulster English and South Ulster English marks the southern limits of Scots-influenced phonology with the Scottish Vowel Length Rule (SVLR).

Vowel quality

Using Wells' (1982) reference sets, Table 6.2 summarises data from Harris (1984a, 1985a), Gregg (1972, 1985) and Wells (1982) to show some vowel quality distinctions between conservative Ulster Scots, Mid Ulster English (in Belfast) and South Ulster English. Vowel quality in more progressive (urban) Ulster Scots overlaps with the Mid Ulster English system, as does South Ulster English. Conservative Ulster Scots diverges from the others, requiring the GOAT class (and others) to be further differentiated.

Some accounts attribute the Northern Irish English vowel system to Gaelic substrate influence (e.g. Gregg 1972). Gregg (1959, 1964) regards Gaelic as the model for the Ulster Scots of Glenoe and Larne. This is also assumed of the Irish English vowel system generally (D. P. Ó Baoill 1997). However, some historical phonological studies show that features attributed to the Irish substrate may be Early Modern English retentions. Thus, rounded Northern Irish English realisations of the STRUT vowel (*cut* [kɔ̈t]) are traceable to seventeenth-century English English (Harris 1990, 1996), as are front-raised realisations of /a/, giving *bag* [bɛːg] (Harris 1987).

Vowel quantity

Treatment of vowel quantity is the major typological difference between regional varieties of Northern Irish English. Harris (1985a) sets the boundaries between Ulster Scots, Mid Ulster English and South Ulster English on the basis of vowel quantity.

Table 6.3. *Vowel quantity in Northern Irish English (after Harris 1985a)* *(* = does not occur in open syllables)*

		Long	Short
Ulster Scots	/i/	see, breeze, fear, Fiat, died	keen, seed, geese, feet, feel
	/e/	day, daze, rain, fade, face, fate	
	/ɛ/*	Des, pen, dead, mess, pet	
Mid Ulster English	/i/	see, breeze, fear, Fiat, died	keen, seed, geese, feet, feel
	/e/	day, daze, rain, fade	face, fate
	/ɛ/*	Des, pen, dead, mess	pet
South Ulster English	/i/	see, breeze, keen, seed, geese, feet, fear, Fiat, died	
	/e/	day, daze, rain, fade, face, fate	
	/ɛ/*		Des, pen, dead, mess, pet

Ulster Scots has the SVLR, having lost phonemic length distinction for most vowels, so that vowel quantity is determined by phonetic environment. Mid Ulster English is a mixed dialect with a modified Scots vowel length pattern. South Ulster English is transitional between these two and Southern Irish English, having phonemic vowel length (like Southern Irish English and other Englishes) but Northern Irish English vowel quality, as in the FOOT and MOUTH classes (Table 6.2), where South Ulster English has characteristically northern vowels.

Differences between the three varieties can be illustrated by treatments of /i, e, ɛ/ in the FLEECE, FACE and DRESS classes (Table 6.3). In Ulster Scots, FACE and DRESS vowels are long in all environments, while FLEECE is long in SVLR environments, i.e. before /r, v, ð, z/, in hiatus and before a boundary; it is short elsewhere. South Ulster English has long FLEECE and FACE vowels, while DRESS is short, regardless of environment. Mid Ulster English is more complex: FLEECE follows the SVLR; FACE is affected by the SVLR, but is also long before /n/ and /d/ (sonorants and voiced stops); and DRESS is long under the same conditions as FACE, but adds /s/ (voiceless fricatives) to the long environments (Harris 1985a:43).[4]

Northern Irish English consonants

Northern Irish English has /r/ in all positions. Initially, it is an alveolar approximant [ɹʌn] *run*, while post-vocalic /r/ lends the preceding vowel a

---

[4] For Wells, this 'Ulster Lengthening' gives long /e, ɛ, a, ɔ/ in monosyllables closed by any consonant other than /p, t, tʃ, k/ (1982:439).

retroflex quality, e.g. [fɔɹ] *fur*. A dental tap may occur after dental consonants, e.g. [θɾiː] *three*. As in the rest of Ireland, /h/ is generally pronounced in Northern Irish English, even word-initially.

While /t, d, n, l/ can be dental in some varieties of Mid Ulster English and South Ulster English, this is regarded as a rural stereotype in Belfast (Harris 1985a:58). It is characteristic of older males in conservative Belfast and Lurgan vernaculars (Pitts 1982:207f.). Dental realisations are attributed to Irish influence (Adams 1986a:107f., Ó Baoill 1991), though Ó Baoill also suggests a Scottish source.

Northern Irish English has been assumed to have clear /l/ in all environments (Harris 1984a:130). However, dark /ɫ/ has been observed in Belfast (Adams 1986a:109) and (London)Derry (McCafferty 1999:250). In Belfast, this may be an innovation (Harris 1985a:60) that is sensitive to social factors like age, sex and area (J. Milroy 1992:93f.) as well as the ethnoreligious divide (Owens 1977): in formal styles, Belfast Catholics shift towards dark /ɫ/, while Protestants shift to greater use of clear variants. Dark realisations in Coleraine are typical of working-class males, while clear /l/ is favoured by women, the middle-class and speakers with tight-knit rural networks (Kingsmore 1995:135f.). /l/ vocalisation is a feature of Ulster Scots (cf. transcriptions in Gregg 1985).

Cluster simplification is frequent in Belfast and other varieties of Northern Irish English. In conservative speech, it is often categorical in, e.g. [kɛp] *kept*, [hɑːn] *hand*, [əʉl] *old*. In some Ulster Scots varieties, the simplifications in *lamb, sing, hand*, etc. are generalised to medial positions, giving [θɪməl] *thimble*, [fɪŋər] *finger*, [kanəl] *candle* (Harris 1985a:58–9).

Palatalised /k, g, n/, e.g. [kʲaːn] *can*, are common in South Ulster English and Belfast, where it is, however, recessive (e.g. J. Milroy 1992:56f.). It remains robust in (London)Derry (McCafferty 1999:249) and Lurgan (Pitts 1986), especially among women. Gaelic substrate influence has been assumed (e.g. Adams 1986a). However, Harris (1987, 1997) argues that this comes from the superstrate, given its presence in, e.g. earlier metropolitan English and regional varieties of English English.

Tapped intervocalic /t/ – ['reirər] *writer* – is said to be a South Ulster English feature that has entered Belfast (Harris 1984a). It is also present in Lurgan (Pitts 1982:85), Coleraine (Kingsmore 1995:138ff.) and (London)Derry (McCafferty 1999:249). It has spread to Coleraine from Belfast via working-class men with loose-knit social networks who work in Belfast (Kingsmore 1995:233–5, 1996).

A major north–south distinction in Irish English is the realisation of the dental fricatives /ð, θ/, which are dental stops [d̪, t̪] in Southern Irish English and fricatives [ð, θ] in Northern Irish English. D. P. Ó Baoill attributes Southern Irish English stops to Irish and Northern Irish English dental fricatives to strong Scots influence (1997). /θ/ is often lenited to [h] in initial and medial contexts. /ð/ is often dropped intervocalically in Belfast and other places, giving [brɔ́ər] *brother* (Harris 1984a, Adams 1986a). *Th*-dropping is socially significant in Belfast (e.g. L. Milroy 1987) and (London)Derry, where it is also frequent word-initially. In (London)-Derry, /ð/ is also variably realised as [l] (e.g. McCafferty 1999:260ff., 2001), especially among younger Catholic working-class women.

Glottal replacement and glottalisation of non-initial voiceless stops and affricates is said to be an Ulster Scots feature in Belfast vernacular, but is not found in South Ulster English (Harris 1984a). Pitts (1982:85) observes that glottalised /p, t, k/ are entering Lurgan from Ulster Scots, and this is also a feature of (London)Derry English (McCafferty 1999:249). A detailed study of Coleraine (Kingsmore 1995:138ff., 1996) shows women in close-knit networks leading the change towards higher glottalisation rates for intervocalic /t/.

The voiceless velar fricative [x] in e.g. *thought* is diagnostic of Ulster Scots (Gregg 1972:117f.). /x/ is found throughout Ulster in certain names and dialect words, though it is often lenited to [h] or zero, or replaced with /k/, especially word-finally, e.g. [lɑk] *lough* (Adams 1986b:106, Harris 1984a:131). It is recessive in many places, including (London)Derry (McCafferty 1999:249f.).

Northern Irish English intonation

Rising intonation in statements is the normal neutral intonation in Northern Irish English (cf. Jarman & Cruttenden 1976, Harris 1984a, 1985a, McElholm 1986, Cruttenden 1995, Rahilly 1997). However, the rise does have social significance in some areas. In contrast to Douglas-Cowie & Cowie's (1999) conclusion that stylistic variation is not associated with particular intonation patterns in rural Northern Irish English, Lowry (2002) finds that Belfast teenagers overwhelmingly use rising nuclei in informal styles and shift to falling intonation in careful styles. There are also sex differences: in informal speech, neither sex uses many falling nuclei, but girls use much higher proportions of falling nuclei than boys in careful speech.

Northern Irish English syntax

A good survey of Northern Irish English syntax is Harris (1993). Filppula's (1999) book describes Southern Irish English, but the features studied are also relevant to Northern Irish English. A. Henry (1997) comments on social distribution and robustness of features of Northern Irish

English syntax in Belfast, while A. Henry (1995) studies five features from a Principles and Parameters perspective (cf. also A. Henry 1992, 1994, 1996). The syntax of South Armagh English is studied by Corrigan (1993, 2000a, 2000b, forthcoming), applying insights from Universal Grammar, creole linguistics and second language acquisition. Todd (1984:169–76, 1989:346ff.) has studied dialects of Tyrone, Fermanagh and Armagh. The next sections concentrate on constructions that have received detailed treatment in the recent literature.

Perfect aspect

Harris' argument for the underlying syntactic non-identity of Englishes (Harris 1984b, 1985b, 1991) rests largely on evidence that Irish English and Standard English 'perfects' are not identical in form or function. Speakers of vernacular Irish English frequently use the constructions in (1)–(4) to express semantic nuances that are all conveyed in other Englishes by *have* + past participle.

(1) Extended now:
     I know his family all me life

(2) Indefinite anterior:
     I never saw a gun in my life nor never saw a gun fired

(3) Resultative:
     a. I've it pronounced wrong (transitive)
     b. I went back to school and all but I'm not long left (intransitive)

(4) Hot-news:
     A young man's only after getting shot out there (Harris 1991:202)

The non-standard perfects in (1)–(3) are retentions from earlier stages of English, reinforced by the existence of parallel constructions in Irish (Harris 1984b:317, 1985b, 1991:204). The only Irish English perfect that clearly derives from Gaelic is the 'hot-news' perfect (4), which is calqued on an Irish construction referring to situations in the recent past. A Standard English equivalent of (4) is 'A young man's just been shot [. . .]' (cf. also Harris 1993:160ff.).

In varieties of present-day Southern Irish English, the *after*-construction reportedly covers the same range of functions as the Standard English perfect (Kallen 1991, Fieß 2000), rather than being an exclusively hot-news perfect. This does not appear to be the case in Northern Irish English (Harris 1984b, Corrigan 1993, Kirk 1997b). A diachronic study of usage with temporal adverbials in literary texts of the last three hundred years shows that the wider range of perfect uses documented in Southern Irish

English is found from the late sixteenth century onwards (McCafferty 2005c, 2006).[5]

Habitual be(s)

Habitual use of *be(s)* or *do(es) be* in Irish English have also been assumed to derive from the Gaelic substrate (the Irish copula has habitual and punctual paradigms).[6] *Be(s)* is the most prevalent form in Northern Irish English, as opposed to Southern Irish English *do(es) be* (Harris 1986, Kallen 1986, Kirk & Millar 1998). *Be(s)* agrees with its subject, either as in Standard English or in accordance with the Northern Subject Rule (see below).

Harris (1986:188) considers habitual *be(s)/do(es) be* to have its roots in dialects of Britain, where it survived into the nineteenth century at least. Kirk & Millar (1998:83–8) survey historical evidence from Scots and find that *be(s)* expressed semelfactivity and durativity but not habituality. Data from emigrant letters suggest habitual *be* did not arise in Northern Irish English until the mid-nineteenth century – the earliest occurrences being (5) and (6), from Montgomery & Kirk (1996:316):

(5)   When I *be* long getting A letter I have nothing to plie to but the likness. (Sproule Letters, 1860)

(6)   He *bes* up 3 or 4 times a night With Her. (Sproule Letters, 1861)

This suggests an Ulster origin for habitual *be(s)* in the period of language shift that is also supported by literary evidence: habitual *be* is rarer in early nineteenth-century representations of dialect than in the early twentieth century (Montgomery & Kirk 1996:317f., Montgomery & Robinson 1996:423). Further support for this view comes from Corrigan (forthcoming), who concludes that habitual *be(s)* is the outcome of contact between Irish and English/Scots: the Irish substrate, with its grammaticalised habitual aspect, conspires to preserve Early Modern English and Older Scots *be(s)*, and functional extension produces the mainly habitual semantics of present-day Northern Irish English.

---

[5]   McCafferty (2003a, 2003b, 2004a) examines future uses of *be after V-ing* from the seventeenth century to the twenty-first, and McCafferty (2005a) studies variation between future and perfect uses in works by a nineteenth-century Gaelic-English bilingual author.

[6]   Montgomery & Kirk (1996) find *be(s)* across a range of semantic categories. Besides habitual senses, *be* has durative, punctual and conditional meanings, and *bes* also has durative reference. They suggest that a more general category, such as 'extended state', may be required to encompass the full semantic scope of *be(s)/do(es) be*. Kirk & Millar (1998:96ff.) find semelfactive, durative and habitual readings in Northern Irish English; though the habitual predominates, age patterns indicate that other meanings are not dying out.

Modal be to

Corrigan (2000a) examines invariant *be to* in South Armagh English, a variety of South Ulster English. In South Armagh English, *be to* parallels its Standard English counterpart *must* in being invariant as regards person and tense, as in (7)–(8). It cannot, however, be used in negative expressions of either type of modality (while epistemic *must* can be negative), and it requires a marked infinitival complement.

(7)   He be to go down Tom Roverty's Street (deontic use: 'must') (Corrigan 2000a: 34)

(8)   The Plunketts be to have great sway in Louth that time, for they seemed to be able to do what they liked (epistemic use: 'must have had') (Corrigan 2000a:34)

Use of *be to* in epistemic senses like (8) has no direct parallel in either the Irish substrate or the English/Scots superstrate (Corrigan 2000a:50). Corrigan suggests that South Armagh English speakers adopted modal *be to* from the superstrate, but extended its use to epistemic as well as deontic meanings. It is thus an outcome of acquisition strategies in a contact situation.

Subordinating and

Corrigan (2000b) studies the use in South Armagh English of subordinating *and*, as in (9)–(10) (cf. also Harris 1986, 1993, Filppula 1991, 1999). Use of subordinating *and* in South Armagh English (and other varieties of Irish English) differs in too many respects from a similar construction in non-Celtic English vernaculars for British English to be the source.

(9)   What does she do but snip a piece of the linin' – an' him lookin' at her. (Corrigan 2000b:86)

(10)   'How can I lift it', says he, 'and our Paddy swinging down on it'. (Corrigan 2000b:86)

Corrigan shows that the potential Early Modern English and Irish models differ from one another in important respects (2000b:84ff.). In South Armagh English, present participles are the preferred category following the subject, as in (9) and (10), and temporal implications (9) are preferred, with none of the conditional relations or exclamatory functions of the Early Modern English construction. On the other hand, South Armagh English subordinating *and* does express the full range of Irish non-temporal relations: attendant circumstance, causality and concessive relations. And, as in Irish, object pronouns are categorical in the South Armagh English construction (Corrigan 2000b:86ff.). In this instance, South Armagh

English is more heavily influenced by the Irish substrate than the superstrate.

Northern Subject Rule

The Northern Subject Rule (NSR) describes the use of the verbal -s ending with plural subjects under certain conditions. For this feature, we have both synchronic and diachronic evidence from the last four centuries (Montgomery & Robinson 1996:416–21). The NSR can be traced to an Older Scots and northern English system dating back beyond the fourteenth century (Meurman-Solin 1992, Montgomery 1994). The NSR consists of two constraints: (a) the 'subject type constraint', by which -s is used with all third person plural subjects other than the personal pronoun *they* (11); and (b) the 'subject proximity constraint', by which a verb separated from its subject by another sentence element may take verbal -s, regardless of subject person or number (12) (e.g. Montgomery 1995:37f.).

(11)   [. . .] aw Things *grows* here that ever I did see grow in England. (Montgomery 1997a:132)

(12)   They have behaved well in general and is clear of censure (Montgomery 1997a:136)

Scots and northern English dialects are the source of this concord system in early Northern Irish English (cf. also, for example, Montgomery 1997b, 2001, Montgomery & Robinson 1996).[7]

The subject type constraint remains robust in Belfast, where -s can occur with all plural subjects but *they* (Policansky 1982, Finlay 1994, Finlay & McTear 1986). The NSR is found in dialect data from the entire Northern Irish English region, but is more robust in the west than in the east (Pietsch 2003). While A. Henry (1997:96) notes that plural verbal -s is most frequent when subject and verb are adjacent, Policansky (1982) reports it to be more likely when the subject is separated from the verb, as also observed by Finlay (1994) for Belfast children, and Corrigan (forthcoming) for South Armagh. Use of the NSR also varies socially: it is less frequent

---

[7] Studies of nineteenth-century emigrant letters show a robust NSR throughout Ireland (McCafferty 2005b); it was as strong in Mid Ulster English dialects as in Ulster Scots areas (McCafferty 2003c, 2003d), and was present in all Southern Irish English areas for which data were available, and as strong in some Southern Irish English regions as in Ulster (McCafferty 2004a).

among the better educated (Policansky 1982),[8] and one study found that middle-class Belfast children do not use the NSR, while it is quite frequent among the working class, especially boys (Finlay & McTear 1986:177). Meanwhile, Wilson & Henry (1998:11f.) find plural -*s* not only robust among the working class in Belfast, but also spreading to middle-class users. Finally, A. Henry (2002) reports that Belfast children acquire the NSR even when caregivers use it at low rates.

Whenever

Montgomery & Kirk (2001) report that *whenever* is used in Northern Irish English with the same range of senses as *when* in other Englishes, including the punctual meaning in (13), which is current in Scottish and Irish usage and may have been more widespread earlier. They also note an 'extended time *whenever*' (14).

(13)   My mother, whenever she passed away, she had pneumonia. (Montgomery & Kirk 2001)

(14)   *Whenever* my mother was alive, we had so many chores to do before we could get away. (Northern Ireland Transcribed Corpus of Speech) (Montgomery & Kirk 2001)

The punctual use is well attested in Northern Irish English (e.g. Macafee 1996), though it is not documented until the twentieth century. Montgomery & Kirk (2001) note that it is not always easy to distinguish punctual from recurrent uses, so that a hybrid recurrent/punctual meaning must be recognised (15).

(15)   *Whenever* you'd get three or four young fellows there, they would destroy the whole table. (Montgomery & Kirk 2001:240)

Montgomery & Kirk note that overlap of this kind might protect Ulster *whenever* from negative comment and stigmatisation.

For-to *infinitives*

Corrigan (2003) reports on acceptability judgements for *for-to* infinitives in South Armagh English. *For-to* infinitives were initially purposive in older English, like the South Armagh English example in (16). This type

---

[8] A. Henry (1995:16–44) offers a Principle and Parameters analysis of Belfast concord. Corrigan (forthcoming) shows South Armagh English to be subject to the same constraints as Belfast, and suggests that the Northern Irish English pattern is the result of the operation of universal constraints.

remains highly acceptable in South Armagh English and Belfast (cf. also A. Henry 1992, 1995, Finlay 1994). Non-purposive uses like (17) are somewhat less acceptable in these Northern Irish English varieties. Corrigan (2003:334–5) attributes the persistence of both types to contact with Irish, since Irish has a preposition + verbal noun construction with equivalent function and syntactic structure.

(16)   They'd go up be Shankil *for to close* a gap. (Corrigan 2003:328)

(17)   This woman had expected her *for to cure* her. (Corrigan 2003:328)

In Belfast, *for-to* infinitives are frequent in purpose clauses, especially among older speakers (A. Henry 1992, 1995, Finlay 1994). In South Armagh English, men find *for-to* infinitives more acceptable than women (Corrigan 2003:332–3).

Zero relatives

Tagliamonte, Smith & Lawrence's (2005) study of relativisation in northern England, Scotland and Northern Ireland shows WH-relative clause markers (*who, which, what, whom*) to be rare in these varieties. In their Northern Irish English locations, Cullybackey and Portavogie, *that* (65%) and zero (22%), as in (18)–(19), are the most frequent relative markers.

(18)   They were good herring *that* we got. (Tagliamonte *et al.* 2005:76)

(19)   But there were a boy in Ballyclare Ø told me this. (Tagliamonte *et al.* 2005:76)

Zero relatives are most common in existential and cleft constructions, and in simple, short sentences. In subject relative clauses, zero is most likely to occur with indefinite NP antecedents; in non-subject relative clauses, it is more likely with indefinite pronoun and definite NP antecedents (Tagliamonte *et al.* 2005:99–103).

Sociolinguistic studies

Sociolinguistic variation in Northern Irish English is documented in studies from places ranging from tiny Articlave, Co. (London)Derry, to the largest urban centres of Belfast and (London)Derry city. If a general pattern emerges, it is that these studies validate the gravity model of diffusion (Chambers & Trudgill 1998) and the social networks model (J. Milroy & L. Milroy 1985). Features of the Belfast urban vernacular – whether they enjoy overt or covert prestige, whether stigmatised or not – tend to diffuse into other towns and cities and into rural areas. Belfast features tend to progress via loose-knit social networks, while there is plenty of evidence that speakers embedded in close-knit networks – whether in small places like Coleraine or larger ones like (London)Derry city – resist Belfast influence.

Gravity-driven diffusion moderated by the workings of social network patterns is evident within Belfast itself. L. Milroy (1987) and J. Milroy (1981, 1992) show patterns of language change and maintenance in Belfast to correlate with the density and multiplexity of social networks: change in the urban vernacular also appears to originate in the more prestigious inner-city working-class areas of east Belfast and diffuse from there into the west of the city. Extending the Belfast surveys into nearby Lurgan, Pitts (1985, 1986, 1989) finds change to be closely related with ongoing innovation in Belfast: inner- and outer-city neighbourhoods of the city are sources of innovations that have covert and overt prestige, respectively, for Lurgan speakers.

Douglas-Cowie's (1978) work on situational code-switching in Articlave, Co. (London)Derry, is a study of linguistic conflict between rural Ulster Scots and urban (Mid Ulster English) speech in a village that has recently undergone modernisation, coming under stronger urban cultural influence. Use of standard forms correlates more strongly with informants' ideas of one another's 'social ambitions' – they all knew one another – than with their social class status, which were often at odds (Douglas-Cowie 1978:51).

Similarly, one of the aims of Kingsmore's (1995) survey of urban Ulster Scots in Coleraine was to investigate the influence of Belfast English on speakers in a smaller town, caught between urban and rural Ulster Scots norms. Kingsmore (1995) reports that close-knit ties contribute to the maintenance of older (more rural) Ulster Scots forms in Coleraine, while those with looser social ties adopt variants associated with Belfast (and Mid Ulster English).

Finally, McCafferty's survey of (London)Derry English (2001) studies changes originating within and without the local speech community. Changes from the east of Northern Ireland (and Belfast) tend to be adopted first by Protestants, while Catholics lead in using local innovations and older features of (London)Derry speech, the latter often identical with rural Mid Ulster English and even Ulster Scots forms (cf. also McCafferty 1998a, 1998b, 1999). Here too, network strength plays a part in promoting or retarding the spread of change (McCafferty 2001).

7 Southern Irish English

Raymond Hickey

Introduction

The English language was taken to Ireland with the settlers[1] from Britain who arrived in the late twelfth century. Since then the fate of English has been closely linked with that of the Irish language which it came largely to replace in the late modern period. In addition the interaction of existing forms of English with the Scots imported in the early seventeenth century in the north of the country led to a linguistic division arising between Ulster, the most northerly province, on the one hand, and the rest of the country to the south on the other. This state of affairs provides the rationale for two chapters on Ireland within the current volume.

For the many varieties of English on the island of Ireland there are different designations. In the north of the country terms are used which reflect historical origins, e.g. *Ulster Scots* for the English[2] stemming from the initial Lowland Scots settlers, *Mid Ulster English* for geographically central varieties which are largely of northern English provenance. *Contact English* is found occasionally to refer globally to varieties spoken in areas where Irish is also spoken. In general treatments of English in the south of Ireland three main terms are to be found.

1. *Anglo-Irish* is an established term in literature to refer to works written in English by authors born in Ireland. The difficulty with the term is its occurrence in other spheres and the fact that it strictly speaking implies

I would like to thank various colleagues who have taken time and trouble to comment on previous drafts of this chapter, especially Karen Corrigan, Kevin McCafferty, Michael Montgomery and David Britain. Needless to say none of these are to be associated with the shortcomings of the chapter.

[1] This group was actually quite heterogeneous. The Anglo-Normans were the military leaders and the English largely artisans and tradespeople who settled in the towns of the east coast. There may well have been a few Welsh and Flemings among these settlers.

[2] There is much discussion of Ulster Scots as a possible separate language and similarly the status of Scots is debated. A discussion of this issue is, however, well beyond the brief of the current chapter. For further references, see the comprehensive bibliography in Hickey (2002).

an English variety of Irish and not vice versa. Within the context of other varieties – Canadian English, for instance – the term is still used to refer to English in Ireland.

2. *Hiberno-English* is a learned term which is derived from the Latin term *Hibernia* 'Ireland'. The term enjoyed a certain currency in the 1970s and 1980s but in the 1990s many authors ceased to employ it, as it contributes nothing in semantic terms and is unnecessarily obscure, often requiring explanation to a non-Irish audience or readership.[3]

3. *Irish English* is the simplest and most convenient term. It has the advantage that it is parallel to the labels for other varieties, e.g. American, Australian, Welsh English and can be further differentiated where necessary. Throughout the present chapter this term will be used.

A non-linguistic term with a considerable history is *brogue* meaning a clearly recognisable Irish accent, frequently of rural origin. The term comes either from the Irish word for 'shoe' (Murphy 1943) or possibly from an expression meaning something like 'a lump in one's tongue' (Bergin 1943). It is often used in a loose sense to mean the Irish pronunciation of English (Walsh 1926) and the term is also found outside Ireland, e.g. in Ocracoke Brogue on the islands off the coast of North Carolina.

In the current context it is appropriate to mention that *Irish* refers to the Celtic language still spoken on parts of the western seaboard of Ireland. *Gaelic* is a cover term for the Celtic languages in Ireland and Scotland (the latter historically derives from the former); taken together with Manx they form the Q-Celtic languages, the P-Celtic languages comprising Welsh, Cornish and Breton.

Because the interface between Irish and English has been a permanent feature in the history of Irish English the weighting of contact in its genesis is the single most controversial issue in this field. Older authors accorded considerable weight to the contact factor (Bliss 1972) but studies in the 1980s attached much more importance to the retention of archaic or regional features. In recent years the pendulum has swung back somewhat with contact and retention accorded approximately equal weight. An additional third factor, the rise of features typical of the sociolinguistic situation in which the Irish learned English historically – much like that which gives rise to 'foreigner talk' – has been added to the sources put forward to account for the non-standard features of Irish English.

---

[3] Not all authors share this opinion, however; see Dolan (2005 [1998]) who uses the term 'Hiberno-English'.

History

Periodisation of Irish English

The most cursory glance at the history of Irish English reveals that it is divided into two periods. The first period starts in the late twelfth century with the arrival of the first English-speaking settlers and finishes around 1600 when the second period opens. The main event which justifies this periodisation is the renewed and vigorous planting of English in Ireland at the beginning of the seventeenth century. One must understand that during the first period the Old English – as this group is called in the Irish context – came increasingly under the influence of the Irish. The Anglo-Normans who were the military leaders during the initial settlement had been completely absorbed by the Irish by the end of the fifteenth century. The progressive Gaelicisation led the English to attempt planting the Irish countryside in order to reinforce the English presence there (Palmer 2000). This was by and large a failure and it was only with James I that successful planting of (Lowland Scottish and English) settlers in the north of the country tipped the linguistic balance in favour of English in the north. The south of the country was subject to further plantations along with the banishment of the native Irish to the west during the Cromwellian period so that by the end of the seventeenth century Irish was in a weak position from which it was never to recover. During the seventeenth century new forms of English were brought to Ireland: Scots in the north and West/ North Midland varieties in the south (where there had been a predominantly West Midland and south-west input in the first period). The renewed anglicisation in the seventeenth century led to the view, held above all by Alan Bliss (see Bliss 1977, 1984), that the forms of English from the first period were completely supplanted by the varieties introduced at the beginning of the modern period. However, this is not true. On the east coast, in Dublin and other locations down to Waterford in the south-east, there is a definite continuation of south-west English features which stem from the imported varieties of the first period (Hickey 2001).

The medieval period

The documentary record of medieval Irish English is confined for all intents and purposes to the collection of 16 poems of Irish provenance in BM Harley 913 which are known collectively as the *Kildare Poems* (Heuser 1904, Lucas 1995) after one of the poems in which the author identifies himself as from the county of Kildare to the south-west of Dublin. The collection probably dates from the early fourteenth century. The language of these poems is of a general West Midland to southern character. There are many features which can be traced to the influence of Irish phonology (Hickey 1993). Note that it is a moot point whether the *Kildare Poems* were written by native speakers of Irish using English as an H-language in a diglossic situation and whether indeed the set was written by one or more individuals.

The Early Modern period

Apart from the *Kildare Poems* and other minor pieces of verse (see McIntosh & Samuels 1968 for a detailed list) there are attestations of English in the first period among the municipal records of various towns in Ireland (Kallen 1994:150–6), especially along the east coast from Waterford through Dublin and up as far as Carrickfergus in the north. But such documents are not linguistically revealing. However, at the end of the sixteenth century attestations of Irish English begin to appear which are deliberate representations of the variety of the time. These are frequently in the guise of literary parody of the Irish by English authors. The anonymous play *Captain Thomas Stukeley* (1596/1605) is the first in a long line of plays in which the Irish are parodied. Later a figure of fun – the stage Irishman – was to be added, establishing a tradition of literary parody that lasted well into the twentieth century (Bliss 1976, 1979, Sullivan 1980). The value of these written representations of Irish English for reconstructing the language of the time has been much questioned and it is true that little if any detail can be extracted from these sources. In addition most of the satirical pieces were written by Englishmen so that one is dealing with an external perception of Irish English at the time. Nonetheless, this material can be useful in determining what features at the beginning of the Early Modern period were salient and hence picked up by non-Irish writers.

Satirical writings are not the only source of Irish English, however. There are some writers, especially in the nineteenth century, who seriously attempt to indicate colloquial speech of their time. The first of these is probably Maria Edgeworth whose novel *Castle Rackrent* (1801) is generally regarded as the first regional novel in English and much admired by Sir Walter Scott. Other writers one could mention in this context are William Carlton and the Banim brothers (see the collection and discussion in Hickey 2003a).

The language shift

Literary parodies do not reveal anything about the then relationship of Irish to English or the spread of English and the regional input from

England. No censuses before 1851 gave data on speakers of Irish and English (after that date one can draw a reasonably accurate picture of the decline of Irish). Adams (1965) is a useful attempt to nonetheless produce a linguistic cartography of Ireland at the beginning of the Early Modern period. The upshot of this situation is that there are no reliable data on the language shift which began in earnest in the early seventeenth century and which had been all but completed by the late nineteenth century. This has meant that statements about the shift have been about what one assumes must have happened rather than on the facts revealed in historical documents. Nonetheless, the external history of this shift shows what the overall conditions were and allows some general statements in this respect. The first point to note about the shift from Irish to English is that in rural areas there was little or no education for the native Irish, the romanticised hedge schools (Dowling 1968 [1935]) notwithstanding. So it is clear that the Irish learned English from other Irish who already knew some, perhaps through contact with those urban Irish who were English speakers, especially on the east coast and through contact with the English planters and their employees. This latter group plays no recognisable role in the development of Irish English, i.e. there is no planter Irish English, probably because this group was numerically insignificant, despite their importance as a trigger in the language shift process. What one can assume for the seventeenth and eighteenth centuries in rural Ireland is a functional bilingualism in which the Irish learned some English as adults from their dealings with English speakers. By the early nineteenth century (Daly 1990) the importance of English for advancement in social life was being pointed out repeatedly, by no less a figure than Daniel O'Connell, the most important political leader before Charles Parnell.

The fact that the majority of the Irish acquired English in an unguided manner as adults had consequences for the nature of Irish English. Bliss (1977) pointed out that this fact is responsible for both the common malapropisms and the unconventional word stress found in Irish English. However, the stress pattern in verbs with final long vowels, e.g. *distribute* [dɪstrɪˈbjuːt], *educate* [edjuˈkeːt], can also be due to English input, particularly as non-initial stress is only a feature of Southern Irish and so influence due to contact with Irish could only be posited for the south of Ireland.

Another point concerning the language shift in Ireland is that it was relatively long, spanning at least three centuries from 1600 to 1900 for most of the country. The scenario for language shift is one where lexical transfer into English is unlikely, or at least unlikely to become established in any nascent supraregional variety of English in Ireland. After all, English was the prestige language and the use of Irish words would not have been desirable, given the high awareness of the lexicon as an open class. This statement refers to Irish lexical elements in present-day English in Ireland. In some written works, and historically in varieties close to Irish, there were more Irish words and idioms; on the latter, see Odlin (1991).

For phonology and syntax the matter is quite different. Speakers who learn a language as adults retain the pronunciation of their native language and have difficulty with segments which are unknown to them. A simple case of this would be the use of stops (dental or sometimes alveolar, depending on region) in the THIN and THIS lexical sets in Irish English. A more subtle case would be the lenition of stops in Irish English, e.g. *cat* [kæṯ], which while systemically completely different from lenition in Irish could be the result of a phonological directive applied by the Irish learning English to lenite elements in positions of maximal sonority.

In syntax there are many features which either have a single source in Irish or at least have converged with English regional input to produce stable structures in later Irish English. To begin with one must bear in mind that adult speakers learning a second language, especially in an unguided situation, search for equivalents to the grammatical categories they know from their native language. The less they know and use the second language, the more obvious this search is. A case in point would involve the habitual in Irish. This is a prominent aspectual category in the language and generally available by using a special form of the verb 'be' and a non-finite form of the lexical verb in question *Bíonn sí ag léamh (gach maidin)* 'is she at reading (every morning)'. There is no one-to-one correspondence to this in English, formally and semantically, so what appears to have happened (Hickey 1995, 1997) is that the Irish availed of the afunctional *do* of declarative sentences which was still present in English at the time of renewed plantation in the early seventeenth century (especially if one considers that the input was largely from the West Midlands) to produce an equivalent to the habitual in Irish. This use of an English structure in a language contact situation to reach an equivalent to an existing grammatical category in Irish depends crucially on a distinction between the existence of a category and its exponence. The difference in exponence (the actual form used) between the habitual in Irish and Irish English has often led scholars to either dismiss Irish as a source for this in Irish English or to produce unlikely equations to link up the category in both languages formally. But if one separates the presence of a category in a grammar from its exponence then one can recognise more clearly the search for equivalence which the Irish must have undertaken in acquiring English and can understand the process of availing of means in English, present but afunctional, i.e. declarative *do*, to realise an existing category in their native language. This habitual category in Irish English, usually expressed by $do + be +$ V-*ing*, may well have been carried to the anglophone Caribbean by Irish deportees and indentured labourers in the seventeenth century; see the arguments for and against this in Hickey (2004b, c).

Supraregionalisation

It is obvious from English loanwords in Irish that early Irish English had not progressed through the so-called Great Vowel Shift, e.g. Irish *bacús* 'bakehouse' shows unshifted /aː/ and /uː/. The play *Captain Thomas Stukeley*, referred to above, consistently uses <*oo*> for words with /au/ from /uː/ in English, e.g. *toon* for *town*. Furthermore, comments from Thomas Sheridan in the late eighteenth century (Sheridan 1781) show that Middle English /aː/, as in *patron*, still had not shifted, nor had Middle English /ɛː/ as in *meat* /mɛːt, meːt/. But present-day Irish English shows little trace of these unshifted vowels. The reason is not that the shift took place in Irish English some time in the nineteenth century but that the unshifted forms were replaced by mainstream English pronunciations due to a process which I have labelled *supraregionalisation*. The essence of this process is the replacement of salient features of a variety (Hickey 2003b) by more standard ones, frequently from an extranational norm, as with southern British English vis à vis Irish English. The motivation for this move is to render a variety less locally bound, more acceptable to a non-vernacular community, hence the term 'supraregionalisation' (similar to the label 'supralocal'). The process is particularly obvious in Irish English because there are records of features before it set in. In Ireland, and probably in other anglophone countries, supraregionalisation is bound up to education and the formation of a middle class and so it is a process which can be largely located in the nineteenth and early twentieth centuries. For Irish English this has meant that certain features disappeared in the course of the nineteenth century. For instance, the lowering of /e/ before /r/ (historically attested in England in words like *dark*, *barn* and in county names like *Hertfordshire*) was very widespread in Ireland and is recorded at the beginning of the nineteenth century in pronunciations like *serve* /saːrv/. This lowering has been lost entirely in Irish English; significantly the only instances which remain are those which are part of mainstream English.

Vernacularisation

The story of supraregionalisation does not end with the disappearance of strongly local features. There is another pathway which such features can take. This is the relegation to vernacular varieties. Take the instance of

Middle English /eː/ as in *beat* /beːt/. This pronunciation is now confined to strongly local varieties where supraregionalisation has not taken place. Furthermore, non-local speakers can style-shift downwards to achieve a vernacular effect. It is part of the competence of all speakers of Irish English that they know what features can be donned to impart a popular touch to their speech. Another example of this would be the use of *youse* or *yez* for the second person plural (see Hickey 2003c for a full treatment). This is shunned by non-local speakers but can be employed when deliberately switching to a vernacular mode.

The process of vernacularisation has in some instances resulted in a lexical split. Consider the reflex of velarised [ɫ] before [d] in Irish English: this led to the diphthong [au] as in the words *old* [aul] and *bold* [baul] with post-sonorant stop deletion. These forms are available alongside /oːld/ and /boːld/ to non-local speakers but the meanings are somewhat different as the original forms with [au] have gained additional meaning components: [aul] 'old + affectionate attachment', e.g. *His* [aul] *car has finally given up the ghost*, [baul] 'daring + sneaking admiration', e.g. *The* [baul] *Charlie is back on top again*.

Varieties within the south of Ireland

It is obvious that linguistically as well as politically Ireland is divided into two broad sections, the north and the south (see Figure 7.1). The former consists of the six counties within the state of Northern Ireland and of the large county of Donegal which is part of the Republic of Ireland. The north has a complex linguistic landscape of its own with at least two major historical varieties, Ulster Scots, the speech of those directly derived from the original Lowland Scots settlers, and Mid Ulster English, the speech of those descendants of English settlers to central parts of Ulster. In addition there is the sociolinguistically complex capital, Belfast. Co. Donegal by and large goes with the rest of Ulster in sharing key features of English in the province and also in the varieties of Irish used there.

The north of the country is quite distinct from the south, accents of northerners being immediately recognisable to southerners. A dividing line can be drawn roughly from Bundoran in south Co. Donegal to Dundalk on the east coast just below the border with Northern Ireland (Ó Baoill 1991, Barry 1981). North of this line the accents are distinctly Ulster-like. South of this line the northern features rapidly give way to southern values. The term 'line' here might imply a clearly delimited boundary, perhaps 'zone' might be more accurate as border counties such as Monaghan, Cavan or Louth show mixed accents which have adopted features from both northern and southern types.

The transition can be seen clearly moving down the east coast: Dundalk has a northern flavour to its speech but this is lost by the time one reaches

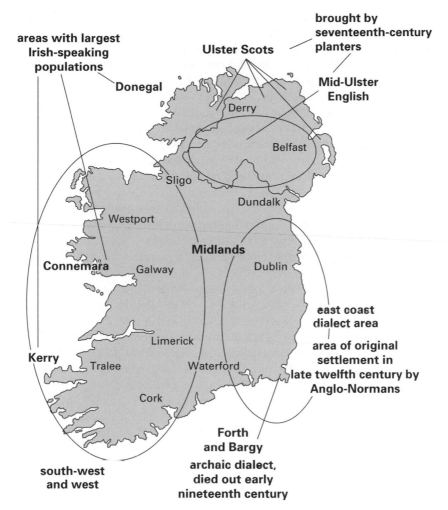

Figure 7.1 Dialect divisions within Ireland

Drogheda travelling southwards. Below is a list of features which are typical of the north. These will not be commented on further as the north is not the subject of this chapter.

Northern features of the transition (from south to north)

- Use of interdental fricatives for dental stops in the south (these can be lost or alternate with laterals, especially in (London)Derry; see McCafferty 2001 for details);

- Use of a fronted allophone of /uː/ and /u/, i.e. [ʉ(ː)], as opposed to [u(ː)] in the south;
- A reduction in the vowel length distinctions found in the south;
- Use of a retroflex [ɻ] in syllable-final position (also found in new pronunciations in the south, see below);
- Greater pitch range between syllables in stressed + unstressed pairs;
- Greater allophony of /æ/ with raised variants in a velar environment *bag* [bɛg] and a retracted realisation in a nasal environment *family* [ˈfɑmli] (these are east Ulster features; for (London)Derry, see McCafferty 1999);
- Recessive occurrence of glides after velars and before front vowels, often used as a stereotype of a northern pronunciation as in *Cavan* [ˈkjævən] (a border county).

There has long been the view that the south of Ireland shows little or no regional differentiation. Compared to the north it shows less variation and there are no identifiable separate input groups such as Scots and English in Ulster. However, to imagine that there is no regional variation in the south is quite mistaken.

The south can be divided into two large areas, the east coast, which includes Dublin, and the south and west. There are historical reasons for this division: the east coast is the area of initial settlement by the English in the late Middle Ages and English there (from Dublin down to Waterford) shows traces of the south-west input to the region (Hickey 2001). The south and west on the other hand are the parts of the country where Irish survived longest and where its influence was greatest.

East band features from Dundalk down to Waterford (including the capital Dublin)

Phonology

- Fortition of dental fricatives to alveolar stops (also in south), e.g. *think* [tɪŋk];
- Lack of low vowel lengthening before voiceless fricatives (not in Dublin), e.g. *path* [pat];
- Front onset of /au/, e.g. *town* [tæʊn], [tɛʊn];
- Centralised onset of /ai/, e.g. *quite* [kwəɪt];
- Breaking of long high vowels (especially in Dublin), e.g. *clean* [klijən];
- Fortition of alveolar sibilants in pre-nasal position, e.g. *isn't* [ɪdn̩t] (south-east);
- No lowering of Early Modern /u/ (only in Dublin), e.g. *done* [dʊn];
- Glottalisation of lenited /t/, e.g. *foot* [fʊt] → [fʊt̞] → [fʊʔ] → [fʊh] (especially Dublin).

Syntax
- Uninflected auxiliaries *do*, *be* and *have*;
- Verb deletion in a range of contexts (as copula, in existential sentences, etc.), e.g.:
  She Ø a teacher in the tech. There Ø no hurry on you;
- Cliticisation of *do* on *be* – as *He* [də'bi] *working late on Fridays* – for habitual aspect;
- Variable use of suffixal -*s* in the present tense (depending on type of subject, number and person), especially with third person plural: *My parents knows the Keenans*.

The south and west from Cork through Limerick up to Galway and Sligo (transition to north)

Phonology
- /ɛ/ to /ɪ/ before nasals;
- Tense, raised articulation of /æ/ (also in east);
- Considerable intonational range (only south, south-west);
- Dental stop realisation in THIN, THIS lexical sets (especially in west);
- Low central onset for /ai/ and /au/, e.g. *quite* [kwaɪt], *town* [taʊn];
- Shift of /tj/ to /k/ in word-internal position, e.g. *fortune* ['fɔrkuːn] (Midlands feature).

Syntax
- Preference for *do* + *be* in habitual aspect constructions.

Ireland as a linguistic area

The above lists do not contain features which readers may think are typical of Irish English, e.g. the epenthesis in words like *film*, *girl*, *arm* or the distinction of short vowels before /r/, e.g. *term* [tɛɹm] and *turn* [tʌrn]. The reason is simply that these are traits of vernacular varieties throughout the entire island. So when treating features of Irish English a holistic view can be useful, that is, rather than stress differences, one could examine the features common to most or all varieties and indeed go a step further and compare these to parallel structures in Irish. This approach is largely typological and sees Ireland (north and south) as a linguistic area (Hickey 1999a). It has actually quite a distinguished pedigree and ante-dates the recent interest in Irish English of the past three decades. In 1959 Heinrich Wagner published a monograph in which he attempted to link up the common structures among the languages of the British Isles. While one can be critical of Wagner's method, his main thesis, that these commonalities (especially in the verbal area: aspectual distinctions and the existence of continuous forms) are not the product of chance but of prolonged contact, has received support from recent areal studies (Vennemann 2000). For the south of Ireland (and in many instances for the north also) one can note the following features shared by all vernacular varieties (not all of these are diagnostic of Ireland as a linguistic area as they are also found in forms of English in Britain). Furthermore, non-existent features can be used as negative definers for Irish English. For instance, *r*-lessness and/or *h*-dropping are definite signs that a speaker is not Irish.

Shared features in vernacular varieties of (southern) Irish English

Phonology
- Lenition of alveolar stops in positions of high sonority, e.g. *city* [sɪt̬i];
- Use of clear [l] in all positions in a word (only in conservative varieties);
- Retention of syllable-final /r/;
- Distinction of short vowels before /r/ (only in conservative varieties);
- Retention of the distinction between /w/ and /ʍ/.

Morphology
- Distinction between second singular and plural personal pronouns;
- Epistemic negative *must*, e.g. *He musn't be Scottish*;
- *Them* as demonstrative, e.g. *Them shoes in the hall*.

Syntax
- Perfective aspect with two sub-types:
  a. Immediate perfective, e.g. *She is after spilling the milk* (She has just spilled the milk);
  b. Resultative perfective, e.g. *She has the housework done* (She has finished the housework). (OV word order);
- Habitual aspect, expressed by *do + be* or *bees* or inflectional *-s* in the first person singular:
  a. *She does be reading books*;
  b. *The boys bees up late at night* (Wexford, south-east);
  c. *I gets awful anxious about the kids when they're away*;
- Reduced number of verb forms, e.g. *seen* and *done* as preterite, *went* as past participle;
- Negative concord, e.g. *He's not interested in no cars*;
- Clefting for topicalisation purposes, e.g. *It's to Glasgow he's going*;
- Greater range of the present tense, e.g. *I know him for more than six years now*;

- *Be* as auxiliary, e.g. *They're finished the work now*;
- *Till* in the sense of 'in order that', e.g. *Come here till I tell you*;
- Singular time reference for *never*, e.g. *She never rang yesterday evening*;
- *For to* infinitives of purpose, e.g. *He went to Dublin for to buy a car*;
- Subordinating *and* (frequently concessive), e.g. *We went for a walk and it raining*;
- Preference for *that* as relative pronoun, e.g. *This is the book that I read*.

Interpreting features of Irish English

In the history of Irish English studies the pendulum of opinion concerning the role of contact in the genesis of these forms of English has swung back and forth. Writers up to the mid-twentieth century assumed that every feature which had a parallel in Irish was of Irish origin. This stance has been labelled the *substratist* position and came under heavy fire in the mid 1980s most noticeably in John Harris' influential article (Harris 1984b). The *retentionist* standpoint saw the input varieties of English in Early Modern Ireland as the source of features hitherto accounted for by contact. This position has been represented by various scholars, notably Roger Lass (e.g. Lass 1990). But in the 1990s the pendulum moved more to the centre with the gradual acceptance of contact as a source of specific features in Irish English (Hickey 1995), not for ideological reasons, as often previously, but from a better understanding of the mechanisms of language transfer and language shift. This was due, not least, to authors on Irish English, such as Markku Filppula, taking on board the ideas of other linguists examining contact in general, expressed most clearly in the seminal monograph of Thomason & Kaufman (1988). Convergence became the new standard wisdom with contact and retention occupying places of equal standing in the history of Irish English. The consideration of other scenarios in the development of English led to a third force entering the discussion, namely pidginisation/creolisation as a possibility during the formative stages of Irish English. Two long articles – Corrigan (1993) and Hickey (1997) – consider the issue but, while rejecting it because there was no break in linguistic continuity in Ireland, maintain that the uncontrolled adult second language acquisition which characterised the language shift in Ireland in the Early Modern period was the historical setting closest to the restructuring of English seen in anglophone creoles, e.g. in the Caribbean. This time it was not due to the creativity of generations without full linguistic antecedents but to substrate interference and the grammatical simplification typical of adult L2 learning during language shift.

Table 7.1. *Suggestions for sources of key features of Southern Irish English*

Phonological features	Possible source
Dental/alveolar stops for fricatives	Transfer of nearest Irish equivalent, coronal stops
Intervocalic and pre-pausal lenition of /t/	Lenition as a phonological directive from Irish
Alveolar /l/ in all positions	Use of non-velar, non-palatal [l] from Irish as well as English input
Retention of [ʍ] for < *wh* >	Convergence of input with Irish /f/ [Φ]
Retention of syllable-final /r/	Convergence of English input and Irish
Distinction of short vowels before /r/	Convergence of English input and Irish
Morphological features	
Distinct pronominal forms for second person singular and plural	Convergence of English input and Irish
Epistemic negative *must*	Generalisation made by Irish based on positive use
Them as demonstrative	English input only
Syntactic features	
Habitual aspect	Convergence with English input in south, possibly with influence from Scots via Ulster; otherwise transfer of category from Irish
Immediate perfective aspect with *after*	Transfer from Irish
Resultative perfective with OV word order	Possible convergence, primarily from Irish
Subordinating *and*	Transfer from Irish
Variant use of suffixal -*s* in present	English input, particularly on east coast
Clefting for topicalisation purposes	Transfer from Irish, with some possible convergence
Greater range of the present tense	Transfer from Irish, with some possible convergence
Negative concord	Convergence of English input and Irish
For to infinitives indicating purpose	Convergence of English input and Irish
Reduced number of verb forms	English input only
Be as auxiliary	English input only
Single time reference for *never*	Transfer from Irish, English input

Apart from the putative source of specifically Irish English features there have been various suggestions concerning the linguistic models to use in interpreting such features. For instance, in the area of aspect there have been attempts to use grammaticalisation models (Kallen 1989, 1990) and prototype theory (Hickey 2000a) to arrive at a satisfactory description of the linguistic facts. Greene (1979) and Ó Sé (1992, 2004) are influential articles describing the verbal systems of Irish.

The lexicon of Irish English

The linguistic level which has been given greatest attention by non-linguists is certainly the lexicon. The tradition of gathering word-lists goes back at least two centuries if one considers the glossaries gathered by Vallancey for the archaic dialect of Forth and Bargy in the south-east corner of Ireland (Vallancey 1788).

Some Irish English words represent archaic or regional usage which has survived in Ireland. For instance, the adjectives *mad* and *bold* retain earlier meanings of 'keen on' and 'misbehaved' respectively. In some cases the words are a mixture of archaism and regionalism, e.g. *cog* 'cheat', *chisler* 'child', *mitch* 'play truant'. There are also semantic extensions and shifts which have taken place in Ireland as with *yoke* with the general meaning of 'a thing/device' or *hames* 'complete mess' (from 'collar on a horse'). An additional feature is the merger of items which are complementary in meaning: *ditch* is used for *dyke*; *bring* and *take*, *rent* and *let*, *borrow* and *lend* are often interchanged and *learn* is used colloquially to mean 'teach' (archaic English usage) as in *That will learn you!*

Although Irish today is spoken natively by less than one percent of the population and although the knowledge of Irish among the majority is, in general, very poor indeed, there is a curious habit of flavouring one's speech by adding a few words from Irish, sometimes condescendingly called using the *cúpla focal* (lit. 'couple of words'). Such words are always alternatives to readily available English terms, e.g. *ciúineas* 'silence', *piseog* 'superstition', *sláinte* 'health' or *plámás* 'flattery'. Such incursions into the lexicon of Irish are brief and superficial. Borrowings can go both ways, e.g. the common term *craic* for 'social enjoyment' is a loan from Irish, itself originally a borrowing from English.

The difficulty with the lexicon of Irish English lies not in finding words which come from Irish or from regional/archaic English but in determining whether these are current in present-day Irish English and, if so, for what sections of the population. There is a great difference in the lexical items available to and used by, say, older rural inhabitants and young urbanites.

Lexicographically, the north of Ireland is well served by Fenton (2001 [1995]), Macafee (1996) and Todd (1990), and the south in recent years has experienced a number of publications in this sphere (with varying degrees of linguistic analysis), for example Ó Muirithe (1996), Share (2003 [1997]) and Dolan (2005 [1998]). Traynor (1953) and Moylan (1996) are regional lexical studies. For more detailed discussions of the Irish English lexicon, see Hickey (2007). Kallen (1996) provides a linguistically interesting examination of the structure of the present-day lexicon. There also exist studies of the vocabulary of individual literary authors, especially James Joyce, e.g. Dent (1994), O'Hehir (1967). Wall (1995) is a general lexicon of literary works.

Sociolinguistic developments

In present-day Ireland the major instance of language change is undoubtedly the shift in pronunciation of Dublin English. To understand the workings of this shift one must realise that in the late 1980s and 1990s the city of Dublin, as the capital of the Republic of Ireland, underwent an unprecedented expansion in population size and in relative prosperity with a great increase in international connections to and from the metropolis. The in-migrants to the city, who arrived there chiefly to avail of the job opportunities resulting from the economic boom formed a group of socially mobile, weak-tie speakers and their section of the city's population has been a key locus for language change. The change which arose in the last two decades of the twentieth century was reactive in nature: fashionable speakers began to move away in their speech from their perception of popular Dublin English, a classic case of dissociation in an urban setting (Hickey 2000b). This dissociation was realised phonetically by a reversal of the unrounding and lowering of vowels typical of Dublin English hitherto. The reversal was systematic in nature with a raising and rounding of low back vowels and the retraction of the /ai/ diphthong and the raising of the /ɔi/ diphthong representing the most salient elements of the change (Hickey 1999b). These changes are displayed in tabular form below.

Summary of the present-day Dublin Vowel Shift

a) retraction of diphthongs with a low or back starting point:

time	[taɪm]	→	[tɑɪm]
toy	[tɒɪ]	→	[tɔɪ], [toɪ]

b) raising of low back vowels:

cot	[kɒ̠t]	→	[kɔ̠t]
caught	[kɒːt]	→	[kɔ̠ːt], [ko̠ːt]

	oɪ		oː
	↑		↑
	ɔɪ	ɔ	ɔː
Raising	↑	↑	↑
	ɒɪ	ɒ	ɒː
Retraction	ai	→	ɑɪ

These changes are progressing by a slow and gradual process which affects all the elements which are potential candidates for the change. In this respect the change is by Neogrammarian advance, i.e. every possible input is affected. But because Dublin is the capital city the change is spreading rapidly throughout the Republic of Ireland (see the many recordings in Hickey 2004d). For some older speakers the spread is by lexical diffusion (Wang 1969) because speakers outside Dublin adopt the change through particularly frequent words they hear with the new Dublin pronunciation and not because of any motivation to dissociate themselves from any group of low-prestige speakers in their surroundings, which is the internal motivation in Dublin (Hickey 1999b).

Non-vernacular speech of the capital acts as a de facto standard when people outside Dublin are seeking a non-local, i.e. supraregional, form of Irish English (Received Pronunciation is obviously not a model in the Irish context). This has meant that the retroflex [ɻ] used by fashionable speakers in Dublin (probably as a reaction to the low-rhoticity of vernacular Dublin English) has spread outside of the capital, especially with younger urban-ites. Five other features, which are part of what one could call the *New Pronunciation* of Irish English (Hickey 2003d), can be mentioned here: (i) a velarised, syllable-final [ɫ], e.g. *meal* [miːəɫ]; (ii) a fronted-onset for the diphthong in the MOUTH lexical set, i.e. [mæut]/[mɛut]; (iii) a fronting (and shortening) of /ɑː/ before /r/, e.g. *part* [pæɻt] (probably a reaction to the dated and snobbish Dublin 4 accent which had retraction here: *part* [pɑːɻt]); (iv) GOAT-diphthongisation as in *home* [əʊ]; and (v) T-flapping as in *water* [wɛɾər].

Conclusion

The history of English in the south of Ireland has provided food for linguistic discussion, and continues to do so, due to the long-term inter-action between Irish and English and due to the different types of regional input. It is a measure of the maturity of the field that recently all sub-areas have been covered by significant publications and that the arguments for various standpoints, especially the relative weight accorded to contact versus retention, are based on strictly linguistic arguments and show a balanced consideration of both sources. Avenues which remain to be explored do exist, most noticeably contemporary urban Irish English and non-native varieties used by immigrants, the most likely locus of linguistic change in years to come.

8 English in Wales

Robert Penhallurick

Introduction

The construction of Offa's Dyke in the late eighth century AD tells us that by that time the English language had advanced westwards in mainland Britain at least to a line corresponding more or less to the modern boundary between England and Wales. However, it was not until the early twelfth century that English made incursions into Welsh territory significant enough to mark the beginnings of the long process of anglicisation. These incursions came in the wake of the Normans, who established strongholds through the north and south of Wales. English speakers arrived in numbers, not only in the eastern border or 'marcher' lordship areas, but also in substantial parts of south Wales – the Vale of Glamorgan, the Gower Peninsula and south Pembrokeshire. It seems that some of these English speakers came to south Wales by sea, across the Bristol Channel, inaugurating south-west-of-England influenced dialects in Pembrokeshire and Gower. The process of anglicisation has involved social pressure as well as the westward advance of English, and by the time the Tudors came to the English throne at the end of the fifteenth century, it had become socially and politically advantageous for the upper classes of Welsh society to be able to speak English. The education system in the late nineteenth century further advanced the cause of English in Wales, but it was the Industrial Revolution which saw huge increases both in the population of Wales, particularly in the south-east, and in the proportion of that population speaking English. Davies (2000:89) points out that, between 1801 and 1891, the number of English monoglots in Wales increased sevenfold, and the number of inhabitants with a knowledge of English increased seventyfold. From the end of the nineteenth century, English can be considered the majority language in Wales. By the 1960s, if not earlier, all adult speakers of Welsh in Wales also spoke English, and three-quarters of the population was monolingual in English.

In this chapter, I use the term *Welsh English*, but it has not been the universal label of choice, and in Wales probably not the preferred option. At the outset of the only national survey of spoken English in Wales,

David Parry chose the term *Anglo-Welsh* for the varieties used by elderly English-speaking Welsh people in rural Wales – hence the Survey of Anglo-Welsh Dialects. In addition, the perception in Wales of the process of anglicisation as one of invasion, subjugation and coercion has led some to shy away from even acknowledging the possibility of a *Welsh English*. If I have a problem with the term, it is that it masks both the considerable diversity of English in Wales, and the connections that some varieties have with dialectal English outside Wales. The oldest connections have already been indicated, between the English of the eastern borders of Wales and that of the neighbouring counties of England, and between the English of Gower and south Pembrokeshire and that of the south-west peninsula of England. That said, it is the traditional regional dialects of the Welsh language which have probably had the greatest influence overall on the special character of English in Wales. There are notable differences between the Welsh dialects of north and south Wales, and these differences are mirrored to a degree in Welsh English, particularly in its pronunciation. It is possible therefore to talk of two main types of Welsh English, one centred in the north-west, the other in the mid-south, in which many non-standard features are derived from Welsh-language influence.

The main but not exclusive focus in the present chapter is on traditional, rural Welsh English as investigated by the above-mentioned Survey of Anglo-Welsh Dialects, or SAWD. Under the directorship of David Parry, material was gathered for SAWD in rural areas of Wales, from the 60-plus age group, between 1968 and 1982. This material is collected, summarised and analysed in Parry's *A Grammar and Glossary of the Conservative Anglo-Welsh Dialects of Rural Wales* (1999). Other major publications in the SAWD project are Parry (1977, 1979) and Penhallurick (1991). Pitkänen's work (such as her essay of 2003), is the first to make use of material collected for SAWD in urban areas of Wales, from all age groups, between 1985 and 1987. Material from the SAWD archives, housed at the Department of English, University of Wales Swansea, also informs Williams (2000). Further information on SAWD and these archives can be accessed via: http://www.swan.ac.uk/english/crew/englishhome.htm

In addition to these publications, the other chief sources for the present chapter are Parry (2003), Penhallurick (1994, 1996), Walters (2003) and Coupland & Thomas (1989).

Phonology

Parry (1999) attempts a general phonemicisation for Welsh English based on the rural data of SAWD, drawn from the 60-plus age group, which I have recast as follows:

Short vowels: /ɪ ɛ a ʌ ɔ ʊ/
Long vowels: /iː eː ɛː œː aː ɔː oː uː/
Diphthongs: /ɪu ai au ɔi oə iə/
Unstressed vowels: /i ~ iː ~ ɪ ə ~ ʌ/
Consonants: /p b t d k g f v θ ð ɬ s z ʃ ʒ x h tʃ dʒ m n ŋ l w j r/

The list below matches the vowel phonemes above against the lexical set used by Wells (1982) and augmented in Foulkes & Docherty (1999). STAY and SNOW are included for comparison with FACE and GOAT respectively, and highlight a tricky area in the phonemicisation. In the list, the vowels for STAY and SNOW are not given phonemic status, in order to remain consistent with the system above – however, I discuss alternative analyses and the status of the vowels in FACE/STAY and GOAT/SNOW later in this section. The following keywords have also been added to the list: ONE, BOAR, POWER, FIRE, EARS, TUESDAY.

KIT	ɪ
DRESS	ɛ
TRAP	a
LOT	ɔ
STRUT	ʌ
ONE	ʌ~ɔ
FOOT	ʊ
BATH	a ~ aː
CLOTH	ɔ
NURSE	œː
FLEECE	iː
FACE	eː
STAY	[ei]
GOAT	oː
SNOW	[ou]
PALM	aː
THOUGHT	ɔː
GOOSE	uː
PRICE	ai
CHOICE	ɔi
MOUTH	au
SQUARE	ɛː
START	aː
NORTH	ɔː
FORCE	ɔː
BOAR	oə
CURE	(ɪ)uwə
POWER	auwə
FIRE	aijə
NEAR	iə
EARS	œː ~ iə

TUESDAY	ɪu
happʏ	iː
lettɛʀ	ə ～ ʌ
horsɛs	ɪ
commᴀ	ə ～ ʌ

In the remainder of this section on phonology, I look in more detail at noteworthy regional and social variants/realisations of the vowel and consonant phonemes above (the chief source being SAWD data, as presented in Parry 1999), and give a brief overview of prosody. I draw on work carried out for Penhallurick (2004a), which has further discussion of phonology. I begin with stressed vowels.

STRUT

In STRUT there is a marked tendency to a vowel raised and centralised compared with RP /ʌ/, even to the extent that [ə] is a common variant. Similarly, in unstressed syllables there is variation between [ʌ] and [ə]. Wells (1982:380) speaks of the 'STRUT-Schwa Merger' in Welsh English, that is to say, the lack of phonemic distinction between /ʌ/ and /ə/. Parry (1999:15) opts for /ʌ/ as the phonemic designation for STRUT vowels (rather than /ə/), which can be justified on grounds of frequency of occurrence, but he adds the rider that [ʌ] in his STRUT group is 'most commonly a raised and centralised Cardinal Vowel 14'. The Welsh language has no /ʌ/ phoneme, but it does have /ə/, and this may be behind both the centralising tendency in STRUT and the blurring or even erasing of distinction between /ʌ/ and /ə/.

Also, [ʊ] can occur in STRUT words, and is recorded in the north-east corner and the south-west corner of Wales. The north-east occurrences can be readily explained by the presence of the well-known northern English [ʊ] in STRUT in neighbouring Cheshire, but the south-west occurrences, mainly in south Pembrokeshire, an area subject to anglicising influences since the twelfth century, are more mysterious. One is tempted to say that they may result from historical connections with south-west England, but as Parry (1999:18) points out, there is only a small amount of evidence of [ʊ] in STRUT words in the traditional accents of Cornwall, Devon and Somerset.

ONE

Wells (1982:362) notes that *one* and other words (for example, *none, nothing*), which have /ʌ/ in RP and an -o- in their spelling, have /ɒ/ as their stressed vowel across a wide band of the mid-north of England. Similarly, in Wales ONE words sometimes fall in with the LOT group, though more frequently they belong with STRUT. ONE with [ɔ ~ ɒ] is associated with the traditional Welsh-speaking areas of north and west Wales, where it may result from Welsh-influenced spelling pronunciation, and also with the north and mid border with England and the long-anglicised areas of south Pembrokeshire and the Gower Peninsula, to where it may have travelled from the accents of the north-west, west and south-west of England.

As with STRUT, [ʊ] can occur in ONE words, though less frequently according to Parry (1999:18).

FOOT

Whilst the usual realisation of FOOT words is [ʊ], there are also instances of 'hypercorrect' [ʌ] recorded in Parry (1999:16) in the north-west, eastern mid Wales, and the south-west. The instances that occur in Welsh-speaking areas, in the north-west and south-west, are all of FOOT words with ortho-graphic -*u*- (*bull*, *butcher*, *put*), and these might be spelling pronunciations. The instances elsewhere (eastern mid Wales, the south-west corner) might in most cases be linked with traditional [ʌ]-forms in west and south-west of England accents.

BATH

Referring to Welsh English in 1982, Wells stated that, 'The situation in the BATH words is not altogether clear' (1982:387), and the same could be said now that SAWD material for the whole of rural Wales has been made avail-able. In BATH words there is competition between the short forms [a ~ æ] and long forms [aː ~ æː ~ ɑː], with [a] the most common realisation, occurring in all regions. Of the long realisations, [aː] is also fairly common, whilst [ɑː] is less so, though it too is not regionally restricted. The general picture (as Wells concluded in 1982:387) seems to be of ´confrontation between a non-standard short /a/ and a standard-influenced long /aː/, with the short vowel more than holding its own. However, whilst it is clearly sensible to differentiate between two phonemes here (a short and a long), this is one of those areas in Welsh English phonology where there is fluidity, as indicated also by the sporadic occurrence of the long vowel in TRAP words. On the other hand, it is likely that variation between the short and long forms can be correlated to some extent with register and social class.

NURSE

A realisation of NURSE identified with the southern region of Welsh English is the long, rounded, centralised-front, half-open [œː]. There is

no ready explanation for this realisation, although it may mark an intermediate stage between Welsh English stressed /ə/ + /r/ and RP long /ɜː/
(the NURSE group is one of several subject to rhoticity in Welsh English).
Parry (1999:21) shows that this realisation is not exclusive to the south, but
occurs throughout Wales. However, its main competitor, /ə/, which is also
widespread, is notably absent from the mid-south-east (that is, the
Rhondda Valleys), the area associated in the public mind with [œː].

FACE/STAY and GOAT/SNOW

The regional patterning of two characteristic sounds of Welsh English, the
long monophthongs [eː] and [oː], is rather complex. They occur in both the
main northern and southern areas in words such as *bacon, break, great, make*
(FACE group) and *coal, road, spoke, toe* (GOAT) respectively, which have
diphthongal /eɪ/ and /əʊ/ ~ oʊ/ in RP. In these cases, the monophthongs
can be regarded as phonemic, but overall their distribution is complicated by
their occurrence also in words such as *clay, drain, weigh, whey* (STAY) and
cold, shoulder, snow (SNOW). In STAY and SNOW, it is difficult to argue that the
monophthongs are phonemic, for in these groups the diphthongs [ei] and [ou]
are more likely. In addition, diphthongal forms can occur in FACE and GOAT.

What lies behind this? Firstly, the Welsh language has no diphthongs of
the /ei/ and /ou/ types, and the Welsh monophthongs /eː/ and /oː/ have
exerted an influence in Welsh English over words which have /eɪ/ and /oʊ/
in RP. Running counter to this are spelling pronunciations affecting STAY
and SNOW, leading to the diphthongal forms, the general rules being:
spellings with *ai, ay, ei, ey* encourage [ei], and spellings with *ou, ow*
encourage [ou] – with *ol* spellings falling in with SNOW rather than GOAT.
Furthermore, there has been influence from neighbouring accents of
English English: [eː] and [oː] have been reinforced in the north of Wales
by the influence of monophthongs occurring in the north-west of England;
[ei] and [ou] have been supported by the diphthongs of the west and south-
west of England, not forgetting of course those also of RP.

For a more detailed breakdown of the regional distribution of monophthongs and diphthongs in these groups see Penhallurick (1993, 2004a).

PALM

There is evidence from SAWD that PALM words are subject to competition
between short [a] and long [aː], like that which occurs in BATH; for example,
Parry's (1999:216) maps for *calf* show an area with the short realisation in
south-western Wales, and another in mid Wales. However, it is likely that
for PALM words as a whole the main contest is between non-standard long,

front [aː] and RP-style long, back [ɑː]. The maps for *calf* show the long, front vowel just about dominating and the long, back vowel scattered across the south-west through to mid Wales and the north-east.

A note here on PALM in the urban accent of Cardiff: in Cardiff English, PALM words typically have a long, front, raised [aː], which Collins & Mees (1989:95) note is 'undoubtedly considered to be the most characteristic vowel of the accent'. It also tends to be nasalised and longer than the RP equivalent. Similarly, raising of front, open [a] and [aː] affects TRAP and BATH words in Cardiff.

GOOSE

The dominant realisation in GOOSE is [uː], although short [ʊ] is also recorded in certain words, especially *tooth*, giving one of the well-known lexical pronunciations of Welsh English. Parry's map of *tooth* (1999:229) shows the short form [ʊ] covering the majority of Wales, with the exception of most of the north and a pocket in the south-west corner. In other GOOSE words used by Parry (*goose, hoof, root, stool*), the short form is more sporadic. See also TUESDAY below.

PRICE, CHOICE, MOUTH

What these three groups have in common is a very close final element in the diphthong: [i] in PRICE and CHOICE, [u] in MOUTH. The first element in PRICE and MOUTH tends also to be very open: [a]. There is, however, a major counter-tendency in PRICE and MOUTH, that is, for a central [ə] to be used as the first element. SAWD data show a pretty clear regional distribution, with [əi] and [əu] restricted to the main southern, especially south-eastern, areas. Tench's (1989:141) view is that this variation in PRICE and MOUTH diphthongs tells us something about the chronology of English-speaking in Wales: diphthongs with central first elements indicate areas of earlier English-speaking, diphthongs with open first elements indicate the more recent arrival of English.

SQUARE, START, NORTH, FORCE, BOAR

The main point of interest in each of these groups is rhoticity, to which all are subject. An outline of types of rhoticity and their regional distribution is given below in the subsection on /r/. However, whilst the situation varies from word to word, overall here it is non-rhotic forms that have the upper hand in terms of frequency of occurrence.

Also worth noting in START is competition between front [aː] forms and back [ɑː] forms (compare BATH and PALM above), with front realisations dominating in SAWD data: Parry's (1999:215) phonetic map for *arm* shows only pockets of back realisations in the mid borders and south-west.

CURE, POWER, FIRE

These groups tend to be firmly disyllabic, with /w/ separating the syllables in CURE and POWER, and /j/ separating them in FIRE. The first syllable in CURE tends towards the /ɪu/ found in TUESDAY (see below); the first syllable in POWER exhibits the variation between [au] and [əu] found in MOUTH; and the first syllable in FIRE falls in with the division between [ai] and [əi] found in PRICE. In their final syllable, all three tend towards an [ʌ] realisation rather than a schwa.

NEAR, EARS

Two points to note here: a sporadic rhoticity (in the form of r-colouring) in both groups in south Pembrokeshire, Gower and the borders; and a strong tendency for EARS to have an initial /j/ followed either by [œː] (as in NURSE, above) or [əː]. This latter feature, especially as [jœː], is prevalent throughout south Wales except for pockets in the west.

TUESDAY

In TUESDAY words we find a Welsh English phoneme which does not occur in RP: /ɪu/. Parry (1999:28) records this phoneme in TUESDAY in the overwhelming majority of SAWD localities. It is found also in the CURE group. As both Parry (1999:28) and Walters (2003:76) note, it is likely that there are two separate sources for this /ɪu/: one is influence from Welsh-language /ɪu/ (represented in ordinary orthography by *iw*), which probably lies behind /ɪu/ in most regions of Welsh English; the other is influence from similar diphthongs occurring in west of England accents, which probably lies behind the forms recorded in the south-east border regions. In Wells (1982), TUESDAY words are subsumed under GOOSE, whereas Welsh English separates out words with *eu, ew, u* and *ue* spellings, thus showing this additional contrast compared with RP, between /uː/ and /ɪu/.

Unstressed vowels

Walters (2003:74), referring to Rhondda Valleys English (south-east Wales), reports that 'the vowel in the final unstressed syllables of *butter*, *sofa*, etc. is characteristically lengthened and with a fuller quality than normally ascribed to schwa', a phenomenon which, along with the 'merging' of [ʌ] and [ə] in STRUT, is 'paralleled in Welsh, which has a single central vowel and in which final unstressed syllables are said never to be reduced to schwa'. The data in Parry (1999:34–5) corroborates this to some extent: [ʌ] is shown as a widespread realisation in the *lettER* group, but occurring in most other parts of Wales as well as in the south-east. Its chief competitors are [ɚ] and [ɛ ~ ɛ·] which occur chiefly in the long-anglicised areas of south Pembrokeshire, Gower and the borders. (Note also [ʌ] in the final syllables of CURE, POWER and FIRE, mentioned above.) However, we should remember that the 'single central vowel' of Welsh is actually schwa, and in the STRUT group above there is a considerable trend towards a central vowel. Thus whilst both STRUT and *lettER* exhibit variation between [ʌ] and [ə] types, in STRUT the movement (compared with RP) is towards schwa, in *lettER* the movement is away from schwa.

Also worth noting is the widespread tendency in *happY* for the final unstressed vowel to be very close and, according to Parry (1999:36), long.

Pharyngealisation

Just as [œː] in NURSE is particularly associated with southern Welsh English in popular opinion, so too is a certain 'throatiness' associated with northern Welsh English. This 'throatiness' is actually *pharyngealisation*, that is, contraction of the pharyngeal arches. It probably arises out of Welsh-language influence. Jones (1984:57) has noted that pharyngealisation affects the articulation of the two high central vowels of northern Welsh, but Penhallurick (1991) records it with many Welsh English vowels in the traditional Welsh-speaking areas of west and central north Wales (Anglesey, Gwynedd, Conwy and Denbighshire). In Penhallurick (1991), the only unaffected northern Welsh English vowels are the most open ones. [ɬ] tends also to be pharyngealised in northern Welsh English – see below.

Next there follows a description of the more notable non-standard consonant realisations of Welsh English.

Strongly aspirated /p t k/

In north Wales, strong aspiration (which sometimes approaches affrication) affects the voiceless plosives /p t k/, particularly in word-initial and word-final positions. This strong aspiration is exceptionally prominent in the north, but Parry (1999:37–8) notes that throughout Wales each voiceless plosive 'normally has strong aspiration in initial stressed position, and often finally before a pause'.

Dental /t d n/

In mid Wales and especially in the north (where they are the norm), dental realisations of /t d n/ occur. In the Welsh language, /t d n/ tend to have dental realisations in northern accents, and presumably Welsh-derived sound-substitution lies behind dental /t d n/ in northern Welsh English. Such dental realisations are infrequent elsewhere in Welsh English.

Unvoicing of /d/ and /z/

Parry (1999:37) records the very occasional use of [t] finally in *cold, second*, which he links to certain English loanwords in Welsh in which final /ld/ becomes /lt/, and final /nd/ becomes /nt/ (for example, *golt* 'gold', *diamwnt* 'diamond').

Also, in traditional Welsh-speaking regions in the north-west and west-to-south-west, there is a considerable tendency to use [s] for RP /z/ in word-medial and word-final positions, for example, in *thousand*, and *cheese*. This again can be explained by influence from the Welsh language, which has no /z/, although the phoneme can occur in loanwords from English.

Should these cases of 'unvoicing' in Welsh English – when compared with RP phonology – be treated as phonemic substitution (/t/ for /d/, and /s/ for /z/), or as variant realisations (of /d/ and /z/)? Given the evident phonotactic constraints, the latter analysis is perhaps tidier. However, the apparent underlying cause (originating in the Welsh language) is phonemic.

Initial Fricative Voicing

Parry (1999:39) records the use of initial /v/ where RP has initial /f/ in *first, four, furrow* in south-eastern Powys, Monmouthshire, south Pembrokeshire and in south Gower. He (1999:40) also records one instance of /ð/ for /θ/ in *third* in west Powys. Such Initial Fricative Voicing, as Wells (1982:343) calls it, is associated with west-country accents of England, where traditionally it can affect /f θ s ʃ/. Penhallurick (1994:145–8) provides evidence of voicing of initial /f s/ in the southern half of the Gower Peninsula from the seventeenth century to the late twentieth century – though by the 1980s it was very much a relic feature in Gower English. Where it occurs, or has occurred, in Welsh English, Initial Fricative Voicing is no doubt due to long-standing influence from west English English.

/ɬ x/

These two fricatives belong to the sound system of the Welsh language, in which they are represented orthographically by -*ll*- and -*ch*- respectively. Excepting placenames, they each have a very limited occurrence in traditional Welsh English, in loans from Welsh, such as *cawellt* 'wicker basket' and *crochon* 'bread-basket'.

/l/

The detail of the distribution of clear [l] and dark [ɬ] in Welsh English is rather intricate, but the data from SAWD permits the following summary. In the south and midlands of Wales, [l] dominates in all phonetic environments. In the north, particularly in Gwynedd, [ɬ] dominates in all positions. The peripheral, historically anglicised regions follow RP, with [l] before a vowel, and [ɬ] before a consonant or pause. This Welsh English pattern is influenced by the Welsh language, in which /l/ is clear in southern Welsh and noticeably dark in northern Welsh, where it is accompanied by strong pharyngealisation. Thus /l/ provides two of the popular diagnostics of Welsh English: clear [l] in all positions for the main southern variety, and dark, pharyngealised [ɬ] in all positions for the main northern variety.

/r/

The Welsh language has two *r* phonemes: a voiced alveolar rolled /r/, which is sometimes realised as a flap [ɾ], and sometimes, particularly in the Bala area, north Wales, as a uvular rolled [ʀ] or uvular fricative [ʁ]; and a voiceless alveolar rolled /r̥/ (*rh* in ordinary orthography). Rolled [r] realisations occur often in the spoken English of north and south Wales, excepting the border areas, the Gower Peninsula and south Pembrokeshire, where an approximant [ɹ] dominates. There is also a high frequency of flapped [ɾ] in Welsh English, particularly in traditional Welsh-speaking areas, compared with RP, and this can be interpreted as further evidence of Welsh influence on Welsh English /r/. Uvular realisations of Welsh English /r/ are confined to the north, where they are rare and possibly usually idiolectal.

Orthographic *r* is always articulated in the Welsh language, in all word positions, and this practice is carried over at times into Welsh English, causing postvocalic /r/ word-medially and word-finally in the north and the south, this rhoticity being centred in the traditional Welsh-speaking areas in the west half of Wales. This Welsh-influenced rhoticity in NURSE, SQUARE, START, NORTH, FORCE, BOAR sometimes leads to a short vowel followed by /r/, such as: /ʌr/ in *first, third, work* (Parry 1999:16) in western mid Wales; /ɛr/ in *heard* (a spelling pronunciation, Parry 1999:14) and in *chair, mare, pears* (Parry 1999:14) in pockets in the west; /ar ~ ɑr/ in *arm, farmer, farthing* (Parry 1999:15) in the west; /ɔr/ in *forks, morning* and in *boar, four* (Parry 1999:17) a few times in north, mid and west Wales. Occasionally the short vowel minus following /r/ is recorded. Rhotic forms with long vowels are common in NURSE, SQUARE, START, NORTH, FORCE, BOAR with the general pattern as follows: long vowel followed by /r/ (that is, forms influenced by the Welsh pronunciation convention of always articulating orthographic *r*), widespread in the western half of Wales; long r-coloured vowel without a following /r/ (that is, forms influenced by west of England accents), occurring in the mid- and south-eastern border areas, and in south Pembrokeshire and the Gower Peninsula.

Lengthened consonants

The following consonants – /p b t d k g v θ s ʃ tʃ m n ŋ l/ – are all recorded by Parry (1999:37–40) as being subject to lengthened duration of pronunciation in Welsh English, when located in word-medial position. Parry records these lengthened forms in most parts of Wales. In the Welsh language, medial consonants tend to be long, especially between vowels when the preceding vowel is stressed. The most likely cause for these lengthened consonants in Welsh English is therefore once again influence from Welsh, even though SAWD data show lengthening affecting medial consonants when followed by a consonant as well as when followed by a vowel. Furthermore, many instances occur in the more anglicised regions of Wales. See also below on prosody.

And finally in this section on phonology, some comments on prosody. In 1982 Wells noted: 'Popular English views about Welsh accents include the claim that they have a "sing-song" or lilting intonation', a characteristic associated particularly with the industrial valleys of south Wales (1982:392). Comparatively little has been published on Welsh English intonation, but studies have been carried out since Wells' *Accents of English*. Tench (1989:138–40) comments on the intonation of the English of Abercrave in the Swansea Valley, Connolly (1989:126) briefly on that of Port Talbot English, south Wales, but the most useful here is the detailed analysis of the suprasegmental phonology of Rhondda Valleys English in Walters (2003:76–84), which shows that the 'sing-song' quality arises out of features which are 'clear and direct transfers from the Welsh language' (p. 76). These include rhythmic features already touched on above, for example, the tendency to lengthen a consonant closing a stressed syllable (and, Walters notes, 'to markedly shorten' (p. 78) the stressed vowel itself), and the tendency towards 'strong' vowels rather than schwa in unstressed syllables. Welsh-language influence in intonation shows up in a striking degree of pitch movement around the stressed syllable, which 'may under-lie the intonation of most Welsh accents of English' (p. 81). Walters concludes (p. 85) that '[f]eatures of stress, rhythm and intonation seem to be substantially the same in Welsh as in the Welsh English dialect studied and to form the strongest "Celtic" imprint on it'.

Lexis

Space restrictions force me to make the briefest comments on lexis here. There are two main sources for the distinctive dialectal vocabulary of Welsh English: the non-standard dialectal vocabulary of the English of the west and south-west of England, and the Welsh language. One might expect that the influence of the former is to be found in the historically anglicised areas of the borders and south of Wales, and the latter in the remaining strongholds of Welsh-speaking in the west and north. This is indeed the case, but borrowings from the dialects of England can occur in the least 'anglicised' dialects of Welsh English (for example, *jangle* 'to gossip', in the Welsh heartlands of the north-west), and borrowings from Welsh remain in the most 'anglicised' Welsh English dialects (for example, *twp* 'foolish, stupid', in the dialects of the south-east).

For detailed listings of Welsh English lexis see Parry (1999, 2003), Penhallurick (1994) and also Lewis (1989).

Morphology and syntax

As with phonology and lexis, the more distinctive features of Welsh English grammar can be subdivided into two main categories: those apparently resulting from Welsh-language influence; and those resulting from the influence of non-standard English English. I will begin this section by looking at two features of Welsh English syntax that have been subject to appreciable attention in the scholarly literature and in which influence from Welsh is a factor. These are, firstly, *predicate fronting* and, secondly, *periphrastic verb phrases* and *periphrastic progressive verb phrases*. Then I will follow this with a summary of other features in the two main categories above.

Writing in 1985, Alan Thomas (p. 215) noted that '[o]ne of the more familiar distinctive features of sentence structure in Welsh English is the fronting of a constituent, when attention is focussed upon it: the fronted constituent is accompanied by emphatic stress'. Examples of this feature in SAWD data are restricted to incidental material (that is, material occurring in incidental conversation, as distinct from responses to items in the SAWD questionnaire), so we are lacking a comprehensive picture of geographical distribution. The eight instances recorded in Parry (1999:119–20), under the heading *sentence-initial emphasis*, come from the west and south of Wales, and include: *A horse, 't was*; *A weed it is*; *Coal they're getting out mostly*; *'Shelving wagons' they were calling them*. Penhallurick (1996:338) notes one further example from mid Wales: *'tundish' they do call them*. Parry (1999:119–20) observes that in the Welsh language 'special sense-emphasis can be imposed upon a word or phrase by placing it at the beginning of the sentence', and Thomas, whilst noting the occurrence of *clefted* and *pseudo-clefted* sentences in other varieties of English (in which clauses are divided into two separated sections), agrees that Welsh English fronting is 'best accounted for as an instance of interference from Welsh' (1985:216). In Welsh, clefting is a simpler, blunter process than in English: any constituent of a sentence can be moved forward in a sentence (fronted) for emphasis. The examples above are thus seen as transfers of this practice from Welsh into Welsh English. Tristram (2002:265–7, 269–70) takes the case for this type of transfer further (that is, beyond Welsh English), arguing that it may have occurred in varieties of present-day English 'in those areas where English has enjoyed long-standing contacts with Late British or Welsh' (2002:265). Although scholars have found it difficult to gauge accurately the frequency and regional distribution of this fronting in Welsh English, there is little doubt that it *is* characteristic of Welsh English and that Welsh-language influence lies behind it. An investigation of some complexity and subtlety into this phenomenon in Welsh English is provided by Malcolm Williams (2000). Williams labels it *predicate fronting*, although he takes exception to the notion of movement suggested by the term 'fronting' when applied to the Welsh language, in which instances of 'fronting' can 'simply represent the neutral, unmarked sequence of a Welsh copular, identificatory sentence' (2000:217). Williams detects two types of predicate fronting in his Welsh English material, which he distinguishes according to their 'pragmatic function', that is, according to the amount of new information contained in the fronted constituent. He argues that predicate fronting as it occurs in the now English-speaking valley communities of south-east Wales 'appears to be distinguished by a relatively small "quantity" of new information appearing in the fronted constituent and consisting mainly of a reformulation of previous, immediately accessible textual material for modal purposes' (p. 226). His other data, however, collected from Welsh-language-first bilinguals in Llandeilo in west Wales, indicates a Welsh English fronting in which '[t]he "fronted" element is textually and situationally new, and there is no modal component' (p. 227), and which is therefore a replica of Welsh syntax. Williams suggests that the first type is the more 'anglicised' kind of Welsh English predicate fronting, in which a modal component has been added to a structure transferred from the Welsh language, where the pragmatic function of the fronted constituent is merely to provide new information. (I'll just add a short coda here: immediately after writing this section and probably being more sensitive than usual to Welsh English fronting, I noticed the following two instances, each from non-Welsh-speaking natives of the Swansea/Neath region of south Wales: *Welsh he was*; *Bryncoch I come from*. According to Williams' classification these are examples of the more Welsh type of predicate fronting – however, both 'informants' are very 'anglicised' Welsh English speakers.)

Turning now to *periphrastic verb phrases* and *periphrastic progressive verb phrases*, we find variation in which there is, though perhaps only to an extent, competition between non-standard constructions arguably caused by dialectal English English influence, non-standard constructions apparently caused by Welsh-language influence and Standard English constructions. The non-standard dialectal-English-influenced constructions are periphrastic (that is, involving the use of separate words rather than inflections) *do* verb phrases, and the non-standard Welsh-influenced constructions are periphrastic progressive *be* verb phrases.

A periphrastic *do* verb phrase in Welsh English consists of: auxiliary unstressed and uninflected *do* + base form of main verb. There is also a corresponding past tense structure: auxiliary unstressed *did* + base form of main verb. Ihalainen (1976) discussed such phrases in traditional East Somerset English, in which they are used to refer to repeated or habitual activity. In some of the academic literature there has been the assumption that, where they occur in Welsh English, these *do* phrases are the result of influence from and contact with the dialects of the west and south-west of England. Juhani Klemola, following on from Ihalainen, has looked at non-standard periphrastic *do* in English English in great detail (as summarised and updated in his essay of 2002), and in the process throws into question the view of Welsh English periphrastic *do* as straightforwardly arising out of dialectal English English influence. I will return to this issue shortly.

Unlike these *do* phrases, periphrastic progressive *be* verb phrases can be found in present-day British Standard English. For example, the present progressive: auxiliary unstressed and inflected *be* + -*ing* form of main verb, which refers to an event or action in progress in present time; and the past progressive: auxiliary unstressed and inflected past tense *be* + -*ing* form of main verb, referring to an event or action in progress in past time. The 'non-standardness' of such constructions in Welsh English arises because they can be used to express different-from-standard meanings, and it seems clear that the explanation for this lies in Welsh-language influence.

Penhallurick (1996) and Pitkänen (2003) focus on this area of Welsh English syntax, but it was Thomas (1984, 1985) who set the template, even though the data available to him at the time were from southern Welsh English only. Thomas identified the following 'parallel occurrences' (1985:214) in the present habitual aspect:

- *He goes to the cinema every week* – inflected present (standard);
- *He do go to the cinema every week* – uninflected *do* (unstressed) + uninflected main verb;
- *He's going to the cinema every week* – inflected *be* (unstressed) + inflected main verb (*-ing* form).

Thomas' view in 1985 (p. 215) was that:

> the *do* pattern is characteristic of dialects [of Welsh English] which have a relatively long historical connection with the English dialects of the West Midlands – i.e. they fit into a dialect subcontinuum which reaches out from neighbouring English counties; and the *be* pattern is characteristic of the speech of those who have a dominant Welsh-language influence, in being either bilingual or first generation monolingual English speakers.

Thomas pointed out (1985:215) that there is a direct correlation of *be* forms with a present habitual construction in the Welsh language, for example: *Mae ef yn mynd i'r sinema bob wythnos*, which translates literally as 'He is going to the cinema every week'. The structure is: *bod* (realised as *mae*) 'be' + subject nominal (*ef* 'he') + linking *yn* + uninflected main verb (*mynd* 'go'). (From which we can see that the truly literal translation is 'Is he in go to the cinema every week'.) Thomas noted also (p. 214) that there was a matching set of past habitual contrasts:

- *He went/used to go to the cinema every week;*
- *He did go to the cinema every week;*
- *He was going to the cinema every week.*

Following the publication of Penhallurick (1991, 1994, 1996) and Parry (1999), the regional distribution of *do* and *be* forms in the traditional rural dialects of Welsh English has become clearer. SAWD data for south Wales, as summarised in Parry (1999:110–12), show *do* forms sporadically across the south – in south Pembrokeshire, the Gower Peninsula, and south-east Wales. The presence of these *do* forms in south-east Wales is in keeping with Thomas' view about their spreading from neighbouring English counties, but their presence in south Pembrokeshire and Gower, on the face of it, implies a link with the dialects of south-west England across the Bristol Channel (and there is plenty of other evidence showing strong historical connections between the old English of Pembroke and Gower on the one hand, and south-west England on the other). Klemola (2002) argues for a heartland of periphrastic *do* in affirmative declarative sentences in south-western English English going back to the Middle English period, so it looks entirely reasonable for *do* forms to turn up in the varieties of Welsh English with old and long-enduring links with these English dialects. However, Klemola also makes a cautious case for the idea that periphrastic *do* arose in English English as a result of Celtic influence: 'the geographical distribution of periphrastic DO supports the conclusion that Celtic, especially Brythonic, contact influence may be a factor in explaining the origin of periphrastic DO in English' (2002:208). Klemola mentions (2002:206) a Welsh construction 'with a verb corresponding to periphrastic DO' attested before the late thirteenth century, and highlights evidence for the persistence of Celtic culture in north-west Wiltshire into the seventh century AD (not to mention of course the more persistent Celtic influence in Cornwall). Pitkänen (2003) adds to the picture by suggesting that auxiliary *gwneud* 'do' in Welsh might have reinforced (rather than caused) the use of periphrastic *do* in Welsh English. To be fair, Thomas summed up the possibilities in his essay for the first edition of the present volume: 'It is not clear whether this construction [periphrastic *do*] derives from Welsh-language interference; Welsh has an exactly parallel construction: inflected verb "do" (+ subject nominal) + uninflected verb – but the construction with "do" occurs also in neighbouring English counties where it might, of course, represent an older Celtic substratum' (Thomas 1984:191–2).

Returning to SAWD data (Parry 1999:110–11), and moving north in Wales, we see *do* forms petering out whilst periphrastic progressive *be* phrases become more common – evidence both for the view that *do* forms entered Welsh English from south-western English English, and for the view that Welsh-language influence gives rise to the *be* forms. The most complete (SAWD) listing of *be* constructions is in Penhallurick (1996), which looks at northern Welsh English, and which gives 110 instances of non-standard periphrastic progressive *be* phrases, plus another 2 of non-standard periphrastic *do* phrases. The overwhelming majority of *be* items were obtained in localities where the first language of the 60-plus age group was Welsh, and indeed all but 3 of the 110 were obtained from Welsh-language-first bilinguals. No *be* forms were found in the two non-Welsh-speaking localities in the north Wales SAWD network, along the border with England; and no *do* forms were found in the Welsh-speaking heartland of the north. Thus, the picture of regional distribution provided by SAWD data suggests little in the way of direct competition between *do* and *be* forms.

The northern Welsh English data exhibit considerable heterogeneity in the *be* forms, with the progressive tendency spreading beyond the habitual aspects (just as there is a present habitual construction in the Welsh language that can be translated into an English progressive construction, so are there similarly susceptible types of construction in Welsh representing the past habitual, the present perfective and the future tense).

Penhallurick (1996) presents a comprehensive classification of the *be* items, making use of a total of fourteen categories.

Pitkänen's work (2003) attempts to update the picture by assessing the frequency of occurrence of non-standard progressive forms in her southwest Wales, north Wales, and urban SAWD corpora compared with rural SAWD. What she finds overall is that use of the progressive forms in their 'basic' non-standard habitual aspect remains pretty consistent throughout her corpora, but also that standard forms are used more in her newer corpora, apparently at the expense of progressive forms in the other semantic categories.

In the remainder of this section, I discuss briefly a small further selection of the particularly distinctive non-standard features of Welsh English, dealing firstly with Welsh-language influence, and then dialectal English English influence. Additional discussion can be found in Penhallurick (2004b), the present section as a whole being informed by this earlier piece. Non-standard forms which exemplify less specific influence – such as double negation and demonstrative *them*, for example – are not treated here, although they may well illustrate a general 'vernacularisation' of Welsh English in progress, as Thomas (1985:219) suggested. For a summary of such 'general' non-standard forms in SAWD data see Parry (1999:105–20).

Generalised *isn't it* as a confirmatory interrogative tag: this third person singular form, used as a confirmatory interrogative tag, applying to the whole of a preceding statement, irrespective of the main verb, is common in Welsh English. Parry (1999:115) states that it is 'fairly widespread' throughout Wales, except for Monmouthshire. Penhallurick (1991:204–5) records fourteen examples in incidental material from the Welsh-speaking heartland of the north, including: *you have to rig him up in his clothes, isn't it*; *I've heard the word, isn't it*; *we say 'clean under the grate', isn't it*; *we saw some the other day, isn't it*; *they had them in their hair, isn't it*. In these examples, pronunciation is frequently truncated to forms of the type [ɪnɪ] or [nɪ]. It is highly likely that this tag in Welsh English is caused by the transfer of the Welsh generalised confirmatory interrogative *ydy fe?* 'isn't it?'; however, it is also entirely possible that its use is reinforced by the widespread occurrence and influence of *innit* tags in English English.

There's + adjective, as an introductory adverbial phrase: Standard English *how* + adjective/adverb as an introductory adverbial phrase is commonly expressed in Welsh English by *there's* + adjective, as in, for example: *there's funny questions*; *there's twp* ('stupid') *I've been*; *there's nice to see you* (all from Parry 1999:120). Although it can occur in the north, this feature is associated more with southern Welsh English. As Thomas (1985:216) and Parry (1999:120) point out, it can be firmly linked with a corresponding formation in the Welsh language: *dyna* 'there is' + adjective.

On, in the phrase *the name/term on*: Penhallurick (1991:207) records several examples of this combination in north Wales (though not in the anglicised border region), such as: *I don't know the English term on that*; *there's a special name on that*; and even, *there's a word on that*. Parry (1999:119) records similar expressions mainly in mid Wales. Almost all of the instances in Parry (1999) and Penhallurick (1991) occur in traditional Welsh-speaking regions, which adds weight to the clear connection with the Welsh syntagm *yr enw ar* 'the name on'.

With regard to non-standard English English influence in Welsh English grammar, material from SAWD and Penhallurick (1994) provides many examples of forms which can be connected with the dialects of the west and south-west of England occurring mainly in those Welsh English dialects diagnosed as 'most anglicised' by Parry (2003).

Pronoun forms include: *thee* – subjective and objective second person singular personal pronoun; *thou* – subjective second person singular personal pronoun; *a* [ə] – subjective third person singular masculine personal pronoun, unstressed; *'en/un/n* – objective third person singular masculine and neuter personal pronoun, unstressed; *thy* – second person singular possessive adjective; *thine* – second person singular possessive pronoun; *yourn* – second person singular possessive pronoun; *ourn* – first person plural possessive pronoun; *theirn* – third person plural possessive pronoun (these examples from Parry 1999:108–10).

Verb forms include the following non-standard instances of *be*, *do* and *have*: *I be/thee art/thee bist/you am/she be/we am/we be/they'm/they be/ them be*, all present tense, unstressed; *he do/he doth*, auxiliary, present tense, stressed; *he hath/he have*, auxiliary, present tense, stressed (all from Parry 1999:114–17). Parry (1999:112–13) also records numerous examples of non-standard inflections of other verbs, though these tend towards connections with a more general English English.

But as for the more specific west and south-west English English influence, it is the traditional Welsh English varieties of the borders, south Pembrokeshire and the Gower Peninsula – that is, areas subject to anglicisation since the twelfth century and the aftermath of the Norman invasion of Wales – that have been especially affected. These are the varieties designated by Parry (2003) as the 'most-anglicised dialects' in the SAWD rural network. What is open to some doubt is the extent to which forms such as those listed above remain current. With the exception of Gower English (see Penhallurick 1994), the erosion (or not) of dialectal English English influence in varieties of Welsh English is a neglected topic of study.

9   English on the Isle of Man

Andrew Hamer

The Isle of Man was included in the *Survey of English Dialects*, which remains the principal published source for our knowledge of Manx English in the late nineteenth and early twentieth centuries (here referred to as traditional Manx English). The nature and size of the Manx population have changed considerably since the time of the *SED*, however. The 1961 census gave the size of the population as 47,166; by 2001, it had grown to 76,315. This growth is entirely due to immigration, the 2001 census revealing that only 48% of the resident population were born on the island; 38.2% of the resident Manx population are immigrants from England, with a further 8.1% from Scotland and the island of Ireland.

It will be apparent that the Isle of Man is potentially an area of accent levelling. Irish and Scots accents may almost certainly be ruled out as contributors to any such levelling, however, to judge from the speech of the school-age children of parents from Ireland or Scotland, who almost without exception do not have Irish or Scottish accents. RP, and accents from north-west England, including that of Liverpool, are the significant current influences on Manx English.

Traditional Manx English phonology

Consonants

The consonant system is as that of RP, with the addition of the voiceless velar fricative /x/, found in loanwords from Manx Gaelic: *chiollagh* [tʃɒləx] 'hearth'; *loghtyn* [lɒxtən] 'the native species of sheep'.

Manx Gaelic has influenced:
1. The realisation of /t/, /θ/ and /ð/.
   a) /t/ is frequently realised as a dental stop [t̪]: *tea, tried, stream, daughter, bit of, shut, not*. Medially after /s/ there is a tendency towards realisation as a dental fricative [θ]: *master, Easter*.
   b) /θ/ is also frequently realised as [t̪]: *thaw, third, thousand, throw, Thursday*. For these speakers, therefore, *tree* and *three* are homophones.

c) /ð/ may also be realised as [t̪] initially in the demonstratives *this*, *that*, *these*.
2. Devoicing of consonants.
   a) In final position, /d/ is frequently devoiced to [d̥], as in *neighbourhood*, *hundred*, *stupid*; /v/ is frequently realised as [f] – *Christmas Eve*, *five* (also recorded as [v̥]); /z/ is frequently realised as [s], common in noun plurals: *stars*, *years*, *boys*, *girls*, *cousins*, *eggs*; also *haze*, *lose*, *these* (with stopping of initial /θ/, as described above, recorded as [t̪iːs]).
   b) Medially, /ð/ may be [θ] in *either*, *further* (also recorded with [d]), *mother*; /z/ is frequently realised as [s], as in *busy*, *cousin*, *Tuesday*, *is it*, *dizzy* (also recorded as [z̥]).

These Gaelic-influenced features are now all disappearing.
   Other features:
1. /r/:
   Non-prevocalic. The *SED* evidence points to a change from rhoticity to non-rhoticity, around the end of the nineteenth century. Examples with the /r/ pronounced include: *first*, *years*, *turn*, *they're not*, *turf*; examples without /r/ include: *thirty*, *Thursday*, *morning*, *farmer*, *work*, *stars*, *on purpose*. Manx English is now non-rhotic.
   Prevocalic. Before stressed vowels, /r/ is usually either an alveolar trill [r] or tap [ɾ], as in *road*, *ruts*; *trench*, *stream*; *break*, *bridge*; *grow*, *ground*. This variant is now becoming restricted to the speech of older adults, particularly males.
2. In traditional Manx English /t/ is realised as a glottal stop only when /n/ is closely proximate, although in this environment it is regular. Examples of [ʔ] following /n/ include: *twenty*, *apprentice*, *winter*; examples before /n/ (with or without intervening schwa) are: *getting* [gɛʔn], *cutting* [kʊʔən], *lightning* [leɪʔnən], *frighten* [freɪʔən], *straighten* [stræɪʔn]. Glottal stopping of /t/ is now spreading in Manx English, probably as part of a growing national trend (Foulkes & Docherty 1999:11), with a current rate of occurrence among children and teenagers of more than 80% of all tokens in some contexts, the lowest rate of occurrence being medially between vowels.
3. Initial /w/ from earlier /hw/, as in *whey*, *whisker*, *wheel*, *white*, is often realised as [kw].
4. The final consonant clusters /nd ld lt st lv/ are regularly simplified. Thus, from the *SED*: *husban'*, *len'*, *poun'*; *chil'*, *gol'*; *faul'*; *breakfas'*, *firs'*, *las'*; *twel'*.

Vowels

Traditional Manx English has the following vowel system: [iː ɪ e æː a ɒ ɔː uː ʊ ə ɜː].

1. An important process is the lengthening of /ɛ a ɒ/ to [ɛː/ɛˑˀ æː ɔː]. The three vowels are not equally affected, but lengthening is so widespread as to affect the speech rhythm. /e/ and /a/ are frequently lengthened before voiceless and voiced stops (*gap; wet; sexton, back; glad; eggs, bag*); voiceless and voiced fricatives (*nephew, after; west, last; seven, haven't*); nasals (*remember, dams; fence, anvil*); approximants (*twelve, pals; buried*). /ɒ/ is lengthened only before voiceless fricatives: *soft; cross, gossiping*. Young adults and children now rarely show vowel lengthening.

2. /ɒ/ is fronted to [a], commonly in *not*, and frequently elsewhere, as in *lot, body, off, bothersome, from, once, holiday*.

3. Traditional Manx English shares with accents of Northern England:
   a) [a] (when not lengthened) in *laugh, ask, aunt*;
   b) [ʊ] in *butter, uncle*;
   c) [uː] before /k/ in some words, and in certain other words: *book, look, cook, took; soot; good, could*.

   Despite considerable numbers of immigrants with RP-like vowels in *laugh, aunt; butter; book, look*, Manx school pupils generally adopt the northern variants, and it seems certain that these forms will continue to characterise Manx English for the foreseeable future. (The vowel in *book, look*, etc. is also now found with a more centralised pronunciation [ʉː].)

4. Where RP has /ɑː/ <ME /a/ + /l/ or /r/ many speakers have a fronted vowel [æː]: *half, arm*.

5. The typical pronunciation of *tea, pleased, steal, stream, clean* is with [eː] or [e̞ɪ]; compare RP /iː/.

Diphthongs

The first elements of the diphthongs in *fine* and *day* are higher than their RP counterparts: [fæɪn], [de̞ɪ], the latter frequently being realised almost as a monophthong [eː].

The first element of the diphthong in *house* (RP /(ɑʊ/) is typically fronted: [hæʊs]. This local variant is still widespread, among all age groups and both sexes.

The (-ing) ending

This is almost always realised in traditional Manx English as [ən] or syllabic [n̩]. Nowadays [ən] is used by men more than women, and by older men most of all. Both sexes, adults and children, have [ɪŋ] as a majority variant, with women scoring noticeably higher than men, and girls somewhat higher than boys. A minority variant in the speech of children of both sexes is [ɪŋg], although it is noted that many of these children have at least one parent from the Midlands or north of England.

Traditional Manx English grammar and morphology

Non-standard grammatical features include some breach of number concord in *we/you was*; non-standard *them*, as in *them days, them ones up by the ...*; the use of *for to* as a complementiser; and some double negation, although this is not common.

Manx Gaelic lies behind non-standard *at*, as in *there's a big house at him* ('he has a big house'), and non-standard (*-ing*) forms, which reflect confusion of the English continuous and habitual verbal aspects: *they were getting a sap of straw* (= 'they usually got a wisp of straw' – Barry 1984:176).

Noun and verb morphology is generally standard, although the *SED* records the plural noun *childer* ('children'). Forms of the copula are standard (though see above for number concord), while standard past tense and past participle verb forms include *break, broke, broken; take, took, taken*. Non-standard forms recorded as minority variants include: present tense *I has; I does*; past tense *he give it me*; past participle *where has he went?*

Traditional Manx English idiom and lexis

Much non-standard idiom and lexis is either translation of or direct borrowing from Manx Gaelic. Knowledge of these items is in decline, although the regular appearance of a number of terms in local radio programmes and newspaper articles may help towards their survival. Such items include *to put a sight on someone* ('to visit someone') and the Gaelic expression *traa dy-liooar* ('there's time enough'), both of which are commonly known.

Manx Gaelic words that are still widely known represent a few semantic areas:

- the supernatural (*yn moddey doo* 'the black dog'; *buggane* 'the hob-goblin'; *mooinjer veggey* 'fairies' (literally 'little people'));
- native topography, flora and fauna (*curragh* 'marshy ground'; *broo* 'low-lying land'; *hibbin* 'ivy'; *brashlag* 'charlock, wild mustard'; *govvag* 'dog-fish', used as a mildly humorous term of abuse);
- the household (*thie* 'house'; *tholtan* 'ruined house'; *chiollagh* 'hearth' (see above for pronunciation); *jouish* 'pair of shears or scissors'));
- people and their interactions (*I'm only moal* 'not very well'; *he's in a jarood* 'in an absent-minded state'; *coosh* 'a chat, natter'; *skeet* 'news, gossip, a gossip'.

Current developments

Scouse features, which are stigmatised, are apparent in the speech of a small minority of younger adults, and a considerably larger minority of teenagers and children; among adults, males show more Liverpool influence than females.

Scouse influence is restricted to a small number of familiar features:

- a velarised voice quality (Knowles, 1978:89), found in the speech of some adults; among children, found in the speech of both sexes;
- the realisation of /t/ and /k/ as affricates [ts], [kx] or, rarely, fricatives [s], [x] (Hughes & Trudgill 1996:93): affrication of /k/ is more common than that of /t/, the latter occurring rarely in the speech of those over thirty years of age; boys affricate /k/ noticeably more than girls; affrication of either consonant seems regularly to co-occur with a velarised voice quality;
- a Scouse-like variant of the diphthong /əu/, with the first element fronted, [ɛu], is found mainly in the speech of young children, and is probably best explained as an example, not of Liverpool influence, but of a tendency among young speakers to front the first elements of diphthongs (O'Connor 1973:167).

th-fronting

Not found in the speech of adults over the age of thirty, this is a significant minority variant in the speech of children and teenagers, especially males. Among children and teenagers, fronting of /θ/ occurs with a frequency of about 20% of all tokens, while fronting of medial /ð/ is much less common (about 5%).

10   English in the Channel Islands

Heinrich Ramisch

In traditional dialectology the Channel Islands (Jersey, Guernsey, Alderney and Sark) are regarded as a French-speaking area, because the original language in the islands is a form of Norman French that has been spoken there for centuries.[1] Yet there can be no doubt that English is the dominant language in the islands today. The number of speakers of Norman French is relatively small and constantly decreasing. Over the last 200 years, English has gained more and more influence and has gradually replaced the local Norman French dialects. Indeed, there are clear indications that they will become extinct within the foreseeable future.[2]

A brief look at a map (see p. 359, this volume) shows that from a geographical point of view, the Channel Islands are much closer to France than to England. Alderney is just 9 miles away from Cap de la Hague in France, while Jersey is only about 15 miles from the French coast but 90 miles south of England. Therefore, it comes as no real surprise that the native language in the Channel Islands is Norman French rather than English. From a political point of view, however, the islands have been connected with England for a long time.[3] Originally, the islands were part of the Duchy of Normandy, but after the Battle of Hastings in 1066, Duke William II of Normandy (William the Conqueror) also became King of England, and the Duchy of Normandy was united with England under one ruler. Thus, 1066 is the date that first associates the Channel Islands with England and the

---

[1] The Channel Islands are included in J. Gilliéron & E. Edmont's *Atlas Linguistique de la France* (1902–10), and also in the regional dialect atlas for Normandy, *Atlas Linguistique et Ethnographique Normand*, by P. Brasseur (1980–84). The European project *Atlas Linguarum Europae* (ALE) likewise regards the Channel Islands as a French-speaking area only (cf. Alinei 1997:XLVIII).
[2] A more detailed account of the sociolinguistic situation in the Channel Islands and their linguistic history can be found in Ramisch (1989:5–62). See also Mari Jones (this volume), Mari Jones (2001), Tomlinson (1981:3–20) and Viereck (1988).
[3] For the history of the Channel Islands see in particular Lemprière (1974), Guillot (1975:24–55) and Syvret & Stevens (1998).

English Crown, and this association has existed ever since.[4] The exceptional
political situation of the Channel Islands really arose after the year 1204,
when King John (Lackland) lost all his territories on the Continent to King
Philippe Auguste of France, but the Channel Islands were *not* conquered by
the French. As a result, they became the only part of the former Duchy of
Normandy to remain in the possession of the English king, who continued
to reign in the islands in his function as Duke of Normandy.

After the separation of the Channel Islands from the Norman mainland,
their political links with England at first had no far-reaching consequences
(cf. Guillot 1975:31–2 and Le Patourel 1937:35). The native inhabitants,
their culture and their language were Norman, keeping them in close contact
with their neighbours on the Norman mainland. At a time when distances
played a far greater role than today, trade with the outside world mainly took
place with Normandy. On the whole, it seems that English influence in the
Channel Islands during the Middle Ages was rather limited. However, the
situation began to change towards the late eighteenth and early nineteenth
centuries, when larger military units from England were brought to the
islands to defend them against the French. It was above all the tradespeople
and the inhabitants of the capital towns St Helier (in Jersey) and St Peter Port
(in Guernsey) who first came into contact with English through the medium
of soldiers stationed in the area. Furthermore, English merchants had also
settled in these towns, which had developed into international trade centres.
But during the first half of the nineteenth century the Channel Islands were
still largely French-speaking. There is an interesting comment from the 1830s
by an Englishman called Henry Inglis. Writing in a guidebook, he comments:

[. . .] there are certain points of interest attached to the Channel Islands, peculiarly
their own [. . .], their native civilized inhabitants, their vicinity to the coast of
France, and the general use of the French language. (Inglis 1844:2)

Talking about Jersey, he makes clear what he means by 'French language':

The universal language is still a barbarous dialect. (Inglis 1844:72)

But Inglis also reports on the beginnings of a process of anglicisation:

Children are now universally taught English; and amongst the young, there is an
evident preference of English. The constant intercourse of the tradespeople with the
English residents; and the considerable sprinkling of English residents in Jersey
society, have also their effect. (Inglis 1844:73)

---

[4] These historical facts form the background of a long-standing joke. When asking local
people whether they think that the Channel Islands belong to England they will tell you that
just the opposite is true. They will point out that after all they were on the winning side in the
Battle of Hastings and it was them who conquered England.

English influence really started to grow after the Napoleonic wars (1815), when a larger number of English immigrants came to live in the Channel Islands. And immigration from Britain continued throughout the nineteenth century. The census figures of 1891 (Census 1891:4) reveal, for instance, that 5,844 people (or 15.49%) of the inhabitants of Guernsey were immigrants from England, Wales, Scotland or Ireland. At the same time, immigration from France had been rather low, comprising only 2.92% of the total population. Other factors that contributed to an increased influence of English are to be seen in the growing trade relations with England, the emergence of tourism and improvements in communication and traffic links. For example, the introduction of steamboats played an important role. From 1824 onwards a regular service between England and the islands was established, which offered new opportunities for commerce and made it much more convenient for British tourists to visit the islands (cf. Tupper 1876:403). Towards the end of the nineteenth century a historian comments:

During the present century the English language has both in Guernsey and Jersey, made vast strides, so that it is difficult now to find a native even in the country parishes who cannot converse fairly well in that tongue. (Nicolle 1893:387)

The influence of English continued to rise during the twentieth century. The mass media, such as radio and television, brought English into practically every home. Tourism greatly increased and became a major industry. Moreover, immigration from Britain has remained remarkably high. The 2001 census figures show that 33.5% of the resident population of Jersey (total: 87,186) were born in the UK and 2.3% in the Republic of Ireland. In Guernsey 27.4% of the population (total: 59,807) originally came from the UK and 0.7% from Ireland.

The decline of the Norman French dialects has rapidly progressed over the last 100 years and it seems certain that they will not survive as a living language. In Alderney, Norman French has already disappeared. The results of the 2001 census show that only 3.2% (2,874 people) of the population in Jersey still claim to be active speakers of Jersey French. About two-thirds of these speakers are in fact aged 60 and above. In Guernsey 1,327 people (2.2% of the total population) stated that they 'speak Guernsey French fluently'. But most of them (934 or 70.4%) are 65 or older. As for Sark (total population: 550) local estimates assume that 50 people still speak Sark French.

In the second part of this chapter I will be concerned with the variation of English in the Channel Islands.[5] First of all, due to the language contact

---

[5] For a detailed description of features to be found in Guernsey and Jersey English see in particular Ramisch (1989:91ff., 1994, 2004) and Barbé (1995).

between English and the local Norman French dialects, there are features in English which can be attributed to an influence from Norman French. Following Clyne (1975), I call these *transference phenomena*. On the syntactic level, for instance, one can notice that the objective forms of the personal pronouns (*me, you*, etc.) occur at the end of a sentence for emphatic purposes.

– *I went to prison for the Germans, me – for a month.*
– *There was a few* [crystal sets]. *My brother-in-law had one. But we didn't have any, us.*

Syntactic structures like these are obviously based on a parallel structure in Norman French where the personal pronouns [mɛ], [tɛ], etc. are also used for emphatic purposes in sentence-final position.

Another transference is the use of the definite article in certain contexts, as for example, in connection with names of languages:
– *Well, my father knew the good French and the English and the patois.*

In this case, the entire phrase *the good French* is indeed a literal translation from [lə bwõ frãse] ('le bon français'). Similarly, the expression *But yes* used as an emphatic form of consent (cf. *Yes, of course* in Standard English) obviously is a direct translation of [mɛ wi] ('mais oui'). On the phonological level, one can notice features of stress and intonation that seem to have been influenced by Norman French. There can be a change in the stress pattern in words such as *grandfather* [ˌgrænd'fɑːðə] or *bankrupt* [ˌbæŋ'krʌpt], or it may be that the difference between stressed and unstressed syllables is less marked as in *English* ['ɪŋˌglɪʃ] or *places* ['pleɪˌsɪz] with secondary stress on the second syllable.

It is particularly noteworthy that transference phenomena may occur not only with speakers of Norman French but also with (younger) people who are monolingual speakers of English. Therefore, it is not appropriate to regard features of this type as merely transitional phenomena in the process of acquiring English. Some of the features can become stable and continue to exist even if the speakers themselves are no longer bilingual.

A further aspect of the variation in Channel Island English is the use of general non-standard features that occur in numerous other varieties of British English.[6] One encounters, for example, instances of multiple negation (*I can't say nothing about Alderney, I've only been there once*) or cases of unmarked plurality (*You get 14 pound a month; two year ago*). On the phonological level, the ending *-ing* may be realised with an alveolar nasal [ɪn]. Some other developments are more recent and can be found especially in the speech of younger people in St Helier (Jersey) and St Peter Port

---

[6] Cf., for example, Hughes and Trudgill (1996:22f., 30, 62f.).

(Guernsey), as for example ᴛ-glottalisation (the glottalling of intervocalic and word-final [t]) or TH-fronting (the use of [f] and [v] instead of [θ] and [ð]). There is no evidence that a transference from Norman French has ever played a role in any of these cases. One can assume that these general non-standard features have arrived in the islands as a result of the close connections with Britain and because of the many British immigrants.[7]

With other features, however, the analysis is more complex because both a transference from Norman French and an influence from other varieties of English seem plausible. To illustrate this, a number of features from different linguistic levels will be analysed in more detail here.

The starting point of the RP diphthong /aɪ/ tends to be further back. Words such as *fight* or *buy* are pronounced [faɪt] and [bɑɪ]. Additionally, the first element of the glide may be rounded, resulting in [fɒɪt] and [bɒɪ]. The realisation of /aɪ/ as [ɑɪ] or [ɒɪ] is certainly not restricted to the Channel Islands, but commonly found in many other accents of English. It is particularly typical of Cockney (London) and of urban areas in the south of England in general (cf. Wells 1982:149, 308). Certain varieties of Irish English equally have [ɑɪ] or [ɒɪ] in place of /aɪ/, which has led to the stereotype view in the United States that speakers of Irish English pronounce *nice time* as 'noice toime' (cf. Wells 1982:425–6). The question of whether the variable pronunciation of /aɪ/ in the Channel Islands may also be due to an influence from Norman French cannot be resolved conclusively. It is not a case of phone substitution, since the diphthong [aɪ] does exist in Channel Island French. But it is noteworthy that the diphthong [ɑɪ] is a typical and frequently occurring sound in the local French dialects. Verbs which end in *-er* in Standard French (StF) have the diphthong [ɑɪ] in the same position in Guernsey French, for example: [dunɑɪ] (StF *donner*). Similarly, the ending [ɑɪ] is used in the second person plural of the present tense [vu dunɑɪ] (StF *vous donnez*), in the imperative plural [dunɑɪ] (StF *donnez!*) and in the past participle forms of verbs [dunɑɪ] (StF *donné*).

The RP vowel /ʌ/ may be pronounced as [ɔ] in Channel Island English. Words such as *sun* or *duck* are locally realised as [sɔn] and [dɔk]. In comparison to the RP vowel, [ɔ] is further back and above all, the vowel is rounded. Parallels to this feature in other varieties are rather difficult to find. In the data of the *SED* (Orton *et al.* 1962–71), [ɒ] is very occasionally used in place of the standard /ʌ/. An influence from Norman French seems more likely in this case. Channel Island French does not have a vowel sound comparable to English /ʌ/. One can therefore assume that a phone substitution takes place in English, replacing /ʌ/ by [ɔ]. This hypothesis is

---

[7] For a discussion of other phonological features, including non-prevocalic /r/ and H-dropping, see Ramisch (2004).

Table 10.1. *Typical vowel realisations in Channel Island English*

KIT	ɪ ~ ï	FLEECE	iː ~ ɪi	NEAR	ɪə ~ iə
DRESS	ɛ ~ ë	FACE	eɪ ~ ẹɪ	SQUARE	ɛə
TRAP	æ	PALM	ɑː ~ ɑ̧ː	START	ɑː ~ ɑ̧ː
LOT	ɒ ~ ö	THOUGHT	ɔː ~ oː	NORTH	ɔː ~ oː
STRUT	ɔ ~ ʌ	GOAT	ɔʊ ~ əʊ	FORCE	ɔː ~ oː
FOOT	ʊ	GOAL	ɔʊ ~ əʊ	CURE	jʊə
BATH	ɑː ~ ɑ̧ː	GOOSE	uː ~ ʉː	happY	i ~ iː
CLOTH	ɒ ~ ö	PRICE	ɒɪ ~ ɑɪ ~ aɪ	lettER	œ ~ ə
NURSE	ɜː ~ əː	CHOICE	ɔɪ ~ oɪ	horsES	ɪ ~ ï
		MOUTH	aʊ	commA	ə

confirmed by the fact that the same phone substitution occurs in English loanwords in Channel Island French. Thus, the word *bus* is pronounced [la bɔs] in the local French dialects.

On the syntactic level, the particle *eh* is frequently used as a tag in Channel Island English. *Eh* is usually realised as a diphthong [eɪ], but it can also be pronounced as a short [e]. From a functional point of view, *eh* induces the hearer to express his opinion on what is said by the speaker.
– *There was no television eh, we had no electric anyway eh*
– *yes a gramophone eh.*
– *You grow your own stuff, eh – eh?*
Eh has indeed become a stereotype. Channel Islanders refer to it when they are asked about typical features of their own variety of English. Although *eh* generally occurs in present-day English (cf., for example, Quirk, Greenbaum, Leech & Svartvik 1985:814), the question is why *eh* occurs with such a high frequency in the Channel Islands. A transference from Norman French immediately suggests itself, because *eh* is equally common in the local French dialects and is also used as a tag as in English.

Another interesting feature is the syntactic structure *there is* or *there was* + plural subject, which is frequently used in Channel Island English (cf. Ramisch 1989:92–103):
– *Well, there's ten parishes and for sure there's seven different ways of speaking the patois in the island.*
– *There was no fridges in those days.*
The construction *there is* + plural subject is common in many varieties of English and characterised by Quirk *et al.* (1985:1405) as 'informal'. Therefore, it is only natural that it occurs in the Channel Islands as well. But there are indications which suggest that a transference from Norman French may have contributed to the frequent use of *there is* + plural subject. One finds examples in which *there is* occurs in combination with

a time reference, something which constitutes a clear parallel to a construction with [ja] in Norman French (*il y a* in StF):

– *I don't smoke now.* [. . .] *There's four years I don't smoke.*
  (cf. Norman French: [ja katr ã kə ʒən fym pɑ] ('Il y a quatre ans que je ne fume pas.')

– [. . .] *after the Norman conquest, there's nearly a thousand years we are British – we are not English we are British.*
  (cf. Norman French: [ja kazi ɛ̃ mil ã kə nuze õgje]
  ('Il y a quasi un mille ans que nous sommes anglais.')

Syntactic structures like these are not found in Standard English and are obviously based on a transference. Moreover, it seems realistic to assume that the syntactic pattern with [ja] has generally exerted an influence on *there is* in English. It should be remembered that [ja] is a very common syntactic structure in Norman French, as is *il y a* in Standard French. Therefore, it appears likely that a frequent and familiar syntactic pattern such as [ja] is generally translated by *there is* in English. One should also note the formal parallels between [ja] and *there is*. [ja] is singular in form, and remains unchanged even if the following subject is plural. The same is true of *there is* in English. The syntactic structure *there was* + plural subject can likewise be explained by transference, the source of influence here being the past tense form [javɛ] (*il y avait*).

One can conclude that there are two good explanations for the frequent use of *there is/was* + plural subject. On the one hand, the feature may have been adopted from other varieties of British English; on the other hand, an influence from Norman French may have contributed to the high frequency of this feature.[8] Evidently, the problem is how to measure the relative strength (or weakness) of an influence. But if there is more than one explanation for a particular feature, then they should not necessarily be regarded as mutually exclusive; rather, it is reasonable to assume that there is a convergence of different sources of influence, reinforcing and complementing each other.

---

[8] There is an interesting parallel case in the Gaelic-speaking area of Scotland where, according to Shuken (1984:155), sentences starting with *there is/was* are typical (e.g. *There's that many English people here now, it's English you talk mostly*). Shuken states that this particular syntactic structure is a transference from Gaelic. But here again one has to acknowledge that an influence from other, especially Scottish, varieties is possible, too.

Part II

The Celtic Languages

11   The history of the Celtic languages in the British Isles

Paul Russell

When in 55 BC the standard-bearer of the tenth legion leapt into the sea at Richborough and led Caesar's forces ashore onto British soil, not only did he bring permanent social and political change to Britain but also enormous linguistic change to the speakers of Celtic languages in the British Isles. Like all defining moments it is easy to make too much of them; for not only had contact between Britain and Rome been ongoing for many years before Caesar landed in Britain, but at this stage the Romans did not stay; they reappeared briefly in the following year and then it was not until AD 43 under Claudius that the Romans made their presence in Britain permanent. Nevertheless, it provides one of a number of useful staging points from which to survey the history of the Celtic languages in the British Isles. This one is, however, particularly significant as it is the point at which Britain entered the Roman world where it was to remain for the next five centuries; and the influence of Rome was to be much longer lasting than that.

This will be the format of the first part of this chapter: a tour of the British Isles pausing at key points both historical and geographical from which we may consider the development of the Celtic languages. The second part of the chapter then goes on to examine a number of features of the Celtic languages in greater detail. A language is defined as Celtic by reference to a number of diagnostic features which are shared by all Celtic languages. Among them certain phonological features are significant: the most important is probably the gradual loss of /p/ in all environments, e.g. Old Irish *athair* 'father', Gaulish *ater* < *pater, Old Irish *íasc* 'fish', Welsh *Wysg* (river name (English Usk)) < **eisko-* < **peisko-*, etc.; another important feature is the change of /g^w/ to /b/, e.g. Old Irish *bó* 'cow', Middle Welsh *bu* < **g^{w}ou-*, Old Irish *ben* 'woman', Welsh *ben(yw)*, Gaulish *bnanom* < **g^{w}en-*, etc. (for a full list, see McCone 1996:37–65, Russell 1995:10–14; the standard historical grammar remains Pedersen (1909–13) (abridged and translated into English as Lewis & Pedersen 1974); there are a number of volumes discussing the Celtic languages: Ball & Fife 1993, MacAulay 1992 and Russell 1995).

It may be appropriate, before we return to the standard-bearer of the tenth legion, to consider the overall range of the discussion. Celtic languages were originally spoken throughout the British Isles and their history is in one sense a narrative of westward retreat to the extent that by the seventeenth century a snapshot would show Celtic languages spoken in Cornwall (Cornish), Wales (Welsh), Isle of Man (Manx), western and northern Scotland (Scottish Gaelic) and Ireland (Irish). Since then, both Cornish and Manx have died out in terms of native speakers at least (both languages have strong revival movements). Before the seventeenth century Cumbric (spoken in Cumbria) and Pictish (if this is Celtic, spoken in Scotland) had already died out completely. To complete the picture, Breton is still spoken in Brittany; it is genetically related to Cornish and Welsh and its presence on the continent is due to southerly migration in the sixth and seventh centuries. In the classical period Celtic languages were spoken throughout western Europe, notably in Gaul, northern Italy and parts of Spain. The interrelationship of these languages has been subject to debate: geographically it is conventional to classify them as 'insular' languages (Irish, Scottish Gaelic, Manx, Welsh, Cornish, Breton, Cumbric) and 'continental' languages (Gaulish, Lepontic, Celtiberian), and this has been taken to reflect genetic origins as well. Within the insular group it is less controversial to make a distinction between Goidelic languages (Irish, Scottish Gaelic) and Brittonic languages (Welsh, Cornish, Breton, Cumbric; British is used here to refer to the language spoken in Britain at the time of the Roman occupation, the notional ancestor of the Brittonic languages). However, another relationship has been proposed whereby the Brittonic group is seen to be more closely related to Gaulish (the Gallo-Brittonic hypothesis: Koch 1992; cf. Schrijver 1995:463–5), though this need not imply a concomitant relation between Irish and Celtiberian as has sometimes been suggested (Schmidt 1988). Within Goidelic the separation of the dialects seems to have been a gradual and relatively late phenomenon; there is no evidence for differentiation between Scottish Gaelic and Irish before the twelfth century, though any differences may have been concealed by the use of a standard literary language. Within Brittonic, Cornish and Breton form a close group; further north the precise relationship between Welsh (perhaps northern Welsh), Cumbric and Pictish is uncertain (and the precise relationship of Pictish remains problematic).

One of Caesar's reasons for invading Britain was to safeguard control of Gaul; all too often he had found that the Gauls were receiving reinforcements from Britain and that when under pressure their leaders might take refuge in Britain (Caesar, *BG*, V.1, II.14). Some Gaulish kings also ruled in Britain (Caesar, *BG*, II.4) and Tacitus tells us that there was little difference between the languages of Britain and Gaul (Tacitus, *Agricola*, 11). The early history of the Celtic languages, then, is closely linked to the continent: not only were Celtic languages spoken in continental Europe as well as in Britain but also our first glimpses of the Celtic languages of the British Isles come through the eyes of the classical world. For it is precisely that contact which gave the speakers of Celtic languages the wherewithal to speak with their own voice and be heard; for contact with Greece (especially in the Greek colonies of southern Gaul) and Rome taught them to write. For the Britons, then, the arrival of the Romans marked a watershed in a number of respects of which, as Tacitus stresses, literacy was perhaps one of the most important. It would probably be many centuries before they applied those literary skills regularly to writing their own languages (it is possible that there are two inscriptions written in British found at Bath (Tomlin 1987, 1988)), but even writing in Latin they (and classical writers before them) had to devise ways of writing their own names and places. It is hardly surprising, therefore, that most of the evidence for the earliest stages of the Celtic languages in the British Isles is onomastic, e.g. personal names: *Boudicca, Caratacus, Mandubracius*; tribal names: *Catuvellauni, Brigantes*; placenames: *Camulodunum, Verulamium, Camboglanna*, all of which have been fitted into Latin declensional patterns. Placenames and tribal names are also supplied by the geographer Ptolemy writing in Greek at the end of the first century AD, who also provided the earliest information about Ireland (Parsons & Sims-Williams 2000). The evidence for Celtic in mainland Europe at this period is more substantial (Russell 1995:2–6). Longer exposure to Greek and Roman literacy had given rise to a vernacular literacy: Gaulish inscriptions written in Greek script are found in southern Gaul from the first and second centuries BC and in various types of Roman script further north in Gaul from the first century BC onwards (Lambert 2003). In Spain the area around modern Zaragoza (notably Botorrita) seems to have been inhabited by Celtiberians, speakers of a Celtic language; they produced inscriptions probably based on Roman models written in a local version of the Phoenician script of southern Spain. Northern Italy has produced perhaps the oldest extant Celtic inscriptions in Lepontic, possibly dating from as early as the sixth century BC; they are written in a script derived from the northern Etruscan script. Though this continental material is tangential to our prime purpose, it is important to note that for the early period the weight of evidence is firmly loaded towards the continent in contrast to the exiguous evidence from the British Isles. By contrast, with the increasing power of Rome, Celtic languages had begun to die out in continental Europe by the time of the disintegration of the Roman Empire (Breton being a later reimportation from south-west Britain).

It is far from clear how the linguistic situation in Roman Britain evolved during the period of the occupation (D. E. Evans 1983; also Schrijver 2002). The natives spoke British when the Romans arrived; the placename and personal name evidence is sufficient to show that. But it is less clear how effective Romanisation was in teaching Latin to the natives and eradicating British. It is in part a question of geography: south-east Britain was far more heavily Romanised than further west or north, though the decrease in Romanisation would not have been even; areas of heavy militarisation, such as Hadrian's Wall or around York and Chester, would have produced more highly Latinate areas. Similarly, towns would have been more Romanised than the countryside. Social gradience too would have been a factor: those aspiring to civic office and high status would have spoken Latin, but the question is whether, or until when, they continued to speak British at home. The evidence for the Brittonic languages shows that British survived in the west but precisely how far east and in what density it still extended by the fourth or fifth centuries is unclear. It is striking and well known that Old English contains very few Celtic loanwords, and it has been argued that the English settlers largely came into contact with speakers of Latin rather than of British. However, such a view may not do justice to an extremely complicated sociolinguistic situation in southern Britain. To judge from elsewhere in the Roman empire, and especially from Gaul, bilingualism seems to have been extremely common (Harris 1989:181–3; see also Adams 2003), and it is far more likely that the Romanised inhabitants of southern Britain spoke and were literate in Latin on formal occasions and continued to speak British at home or on the farm. The very low level of British loanwords in Old English may, therefore, have been a function of the source of the borrowings – they were borrowing words from the elite in contexts where Latin was being spoken – and may tell us less about the distribution of British at this period (on the Brittonic languages more generally (and especially their phonological development), see Jackson 1953 and Schrijver 1995; on the early epigraphic material from Britain, see Sims-Williams 2003).

At the period of the English invasions (fifth–sixth centuries), the western side of Britain was still largely British speaking. In addition, there were Irish-speaking settlements in Cornwall and in south and north Wales, and also in Scotland. Further north, the British-speaking continuum extended north of the Roman walls where it came into contact not only with the Irish settlers in the west of Scotland but also with speakers of Pictish. Pictish has remained something of an enigma, mostly because the linguistic remains are so thin that classification has been very difficult. Modern thinking has brought it very firmly back into the ambit of Celtic and Brittonic (Forsyth 1997).

The inexorable westwards movement of English speakers saw the gradual fragmentation of this continuum into the individual languages familiar to us today. The northern range, generally known as Cumbric, was spoken in southern Scotland, northern England in the three kingdoms of Strathclyde (south-west Scotland), Gododdin (south-east Scotland between the Forth and the Tyne) and in Rheged (the basin of the Solway and the Eden valley) (Price 2000). Apart from possible survivals in ways of counting sheep, it seems not to have survived beyond the twelfth century at the latest. Evidence for the language is preserved largely in placenames which indicate a Brittonic language, e.g. *Lanark* (cf. Welsh *llanerch* 'glade'), *Pencaitland* (Welsh *pen* 'head, top', *coedlan* 'copse'), *Melrose* (Welsh *moel* 'bald', *rhos* 'headland'), etc. In addition, there was a very strong literary tradition reflected in early Welsh literature in works by Aneirin and Taliesin which probably derive from the 'old north'.

Further south the survival rate of Brittonic languages was higher, in part at least because English settlers did not in the first instance push as far into the western peninsulas as they had done further north. One important stage in the English migrations westwards may have been when in the sixth century they reached the Severn and effectively broke the land route between Wales and the south-west. It is difficult though to gauge the linguistic impact of this separation; after all, it may have been as easy to sail across the Bristol channel as to wade through the mud of the Severn valley. While the process of settlement was gradual, the eventual effect was to create at least geographically a south-west group of speakers of a Brittonic language separate from those in Wales. The south-west Brittonic group was the ancestor of Cornish and Breton. The westward movement of the English may have in part been responsible for the migrations of south-west Brittonic speakers to Brittany, though it is possible that the incursions from Ireland may have also encouraged migration. It is clear that Cornish and Breton are more closely related to each other than either is to Welsh; see, for example, the following isoglosses: /ntl ntr/ > Welsh /θl θr/ only, e.g. Welsh *cethr* 'spike', Middle Cornish *centr* < Latin *centrum*, /iyá/ >Old Welsh /aia/, Cornish and Breton /oia/, e.g. Welsh *haearn* 'iron', Old Cornish *-hoern*, Breton *hoiarn* < **iyárno-* < **isarno-* (Russell 1995:129 for further examples). Distinctions between Cornish and Breton only arise later, such as the eleventh century Cornish assibilation of final -/d/ to -/z/ (usually spelt -*s* in Middle Cornish), e.g. Middle Cornish *cas*, Welsh *cad* 'battle' < **katu-*.

Cornish is less well attested than any other Brittonic language apart from Cumbric. There are a few glosses in Old Cornish and some personal names and saints' names from the tenth century. The earliest important source is the *Vocabularium Cornicum* (c 1100), a glossary of Old Cornish based on a Latin–Old English glossary. Any more detailed evidence for Cornish had to wait until the Middle and Late Cornish literary texts dating from the sixteenth and seventeenth centuries (Jackson 1953:59–62; the standard grammar is Lewis (1946) (German translation and updated in Zimmer 1990)). The placename evidence is an important source for the language and is especially helpful in tracing the erosion of the language through the county (Padel 1985).

By contrast Welsh is far better attested from an early period. Much of Old Welsh is in the form of single words, phrases or verses glossing Latin texts or as marginalia; the earliest Old Welsh is a series of memoranda in the *Lichfield Gospels*. The *Book of Llandaf*, a twelfth-century collection of charters, contains material dating from as early as the seventh century. Nevertheless, all in all Old Welsh is very thinly attested and we have to wait until Middle Welsh (1250 onwards) for the great outpouring of early Welsh literature which permits a full understanding of the language (the standard grammar is D. S. Evans (1964)). In linguistic terms, the phonological changes which mark out Middle Welsh from Old Welsh are relatively slight (perhaps because our knowledge of Old Welsh is so thin), and as much related to orthography as to anything more substantive. In terms of morphology, the verbal system probably innovated most in that there was a steady process of replacing synthetic forms with analytic ones; for example, the growth of a periphrastic present (originally probably continuous) to replace a synthetic form which was used as a future, e.g. Middle Welsh *daw* 'he comes' : Modern Welsh *y mae ef yn dod* 'he comes' beside *daw* 'he will come'.

One feature of Middle Welsh to receive attention recently is the evidence for dialectal variation in the medieval period (Thomas 1989, 1993). In broad terms, it is difficult to go beyond a basic north–south distinction with some greyer areas in between, but it does raise questions about how deeply embedded some dialectal features are. For it is possible that some features of southern Welsh are more closely related to features in Cornish and Breton; for example, the tendency for suffixes to contain /y/ between the stem and suffix (e.g. north Welsh *blewiach* : south Welsh *blewach*) seems to be a predominantly northern feature which is not shared by southern Welsh (nor by Cornish and Breton). While it might be going too far to suggest that southern Welsh should be grouped dialectically with south-west Brittonic (in arboreal terms), the evidence might be better explained by thinking in terms of a dialect continuum running from northern Britain to Cornwall (and onwards to Brittany), where different isoglosses group different areas together. Links between north Wales and further north are of course less easy to establish, given the paucity of evidence, though early literary traditions would speak for strong links. In these respects, as was observed earlier, the sea may have proved to be a less challenging obstacle than the mountains of mid-Wales or the Lake District.

Across the Irish Sea from Britain, Ireland had to a large extent remained outside the influence of Rome. Ptolemy included a section on the place-names and tribal names of Ireland mainly derived from merchants and traders. However, it is troubling that relatively few of them correspond to later names, for example, *Auteinoi* = *Úaithni*, *Bououinda* = *Bóind* (River Boyne). The last example is, nevertheless, sufficient to show that Celtic speakers were already present in Ireland in this period: *Bououinda* < **bou-* 'cow' (cf. Old Irish *bó*), *-ouinda* /winda/ 'white' (cf. Old Irish *find*, Welsh *gwyn*, Gaulish *Vindo-*). In both a geographical and cultural sense Ireland remained on the fringe: despite Agricola's belief in AD 82 that he could conquer Ireland with just one legion (Tacitus, *Agricola*, 24), it did not, unlike most of Britain, become part of the Roman empire, even though there is plentiful evidence for trading contacts which almost certainly brought with them the beginnings of Latinate culture and literacy. While a few loanwords of a military and commercial nature may have entered Irish in the next few centuries, e.g. *míl* < Latin *miles*, *long* < (*navis*) *longa*, *ór* < *aurum*, etc., it was the arrival of Christianity in Ireland which marked a significant increase in the level of contact with the Latinate world. From the fourth century onwards there had been Irish settlements in Wales and these may have been instrumental in the introduction of Christianity. Nevertheless, the important date is 431 when Palladius came to Ireland as bishop to minister to those Irish who believed in Christ; he was shortly followed by Patrick. At this period the literate culture was Latinate but, in addition to names in Latin texts, the vernacular language can be seen emerging on both sides of the Irish Sea in the *Ogham* inscriptions of the fifth and sixth centuries. The *Ogham* script involves for each letter a set of lines or notches cut in a particular direction in relation to a stem-line (McManus 1991). Despite appearances it is thought to be Latinate in origin, deriving from the classification of letters established by the Latin grammarians of the first to the fourth centuries AD (McManus 1991:19–27). The *Ogham* inscriptions are of prime importance for the linguist as they span the period of the fundamental changes in Irish which changed it from a language comparable in structure to Latin or Greek into a neo-Celtic language which has undergone loss of final sylla-bles and a fundamentally rearranged syllable structure (Koch 1995); for example, we may compare CVNORIX (Wroxeter) with its Old Irish descendant *Conrí*, or even more spectacularly, VEDDELLEMETTO (Thomastown, Co. Kilkenny) with Old Irish *Feidlimid* (early Modern Irish *Feidhlimidh*). In terms of morphology, however, the *Ogham* inscrip-tions are less informative; a funerary inscription usually contains names in the genitive and little more. A few lexical items are attested, e.g. MAQI 'son' (= Old Irish genitive singular *meic*), INIGENA 'daughter' (= Old Irish *ingen*), ANM 'name' (= Old Irish *ainm*), VELITAS 'poet' (Old Irish *fili*, genitive singular *filed*), but no verbs. For strings of Old Irish we have to wait until the seventh century, by which point most of the important phonological developments had already taken place. The *Ogham* inscriptions do show some development, and forms can be found to exemplify some of the changes during this period; for example, the ending of the genitive singular feminine originally *-/iyaːs/ developed to Old Irish -/e/, and many of the intermediate stages can be seen in *Ogham* (relevant segment in bold): -/iyaːs/ (e.g. MAQI ERCIAS) > -/iyas/ (shortening of unaccented long vowels) > -/e(y)as/ (raising, e.g. MAQI RITEAS) > -/e(y) ah/ > -/e(y)a/ (final -/s/ to -/h/ and resegmentation of /h/ to next word, e.g. MAQI ESEA) > -/e/ (loss of final syllable, e.g. MAQI RITE) (for full discussion, see McCone 1996:105–25).

The language of the period from 700 to 900 is generally called Old Irish, sometimes for convenience subdivided into early Old Irish (700–800) and classical Old Irish (800–900) (the standard grammar of Old Irish is Thurneysen 1946; on the Goidelic languages generally see the essays in McCone *et al.* 1994 (in Irish), Russell 2005; on phonology, see McCone 1996, Sims-Williams 2003:296–350). Evidence for this stage of the language from contemporary sources is relatively thin on the ground; it largely consists of glosses and short commentaries on Latin biblical and grammatical texts, some of it written on the continent by Irish monks and not in Ireland itself. In addition there are occasional Irish verses added in the margins of Latin texts. However, most of the material attributed to the Old Irish period is found in the great manuscript collections of the twelfth to the sixteenth centuries, such as *Lebor na hUidre* 'The Book of the Dun Cow', and the *Book of Leinster*, etc. Linguistically, the material can be problematic in that in the process of copying it has been subject to alteration and modernisation.

Two general and interrelated aspects of Old Irish are worthy of comment. The remains of the language, as it has come down to us, is remarkably free from dialectal variation. Though some features have been adduced to suggest regional variation, there is little which can unequivocally be put down to dialect variation (Ahlqvist 1988). In part this is because of the exiguous nature of the sources; but it is also in part due to our inability to localise much of our material. Yet given the fragmented nature of early Irish political structures and the way languages work, it would be extraordinary if there were not regional variation. As far as one can tell, the 'standard' Old Irish which has been preserved seems to represent the rise of one dialect rather than, for example, like classical

Modern Irish, a standard which admitted forms from different areas. It has been further suggested that the pre-eminent dialect was that of the northern Uí Néill who were prominent in the northern half of Ireland in the seventh and eighth centuries. It also seems to have been more than a *Schriftsprache*, a written standard; the orthographical variations suggest that it represented an elite register spoken as well as written. This view is supported by the fact that in some of the contemporary collections of glosses traces of lower registers can be detected, e.g. confusion of tense formants between weak and strong verbs and the interpretation of single verbs as compounds betraying an underlying understanding of the verbal system in which simple verbs are thought of as the basic structures (McCone 1985). Interestingly, many of the lower register features attested in the glosses are next found in Middle Irish, the stage of the language between 900 and 1200 (approximately between the arrival of the Vikings and the arrival of the Normans).

Taking the long historical view, Middle Irish has been characterised as the chaos between the order of Old Irish and Early Modern Irish, but that would probably be to misunderstand the linguistic developments in progress. There is no doubt that the Irish of this period seems much more diverse and less amenable to the imposition of tidy patterns. There may be practical reasons for this: there is vastly more evidence for Middle Irish and much of it remains unedited. There may also be historical reasons. We have seen how Old Irish largely belonged to an elite register with only occasional glimpses of the lower registers which were much closer to Middle Irish. It is possible that the emergence of Middle Irish is a consequence of the removal of that top register of elite language; to what extent this can be explained as the long-term impact of the arrival of the Vikings is debatable (Breatnach 1994:225–6). There are no significant linguistic changes which indelibly mark the shift into Middle Irish. Phonologically, even in Old Irish unaccented vowels had been moving towards an indistinct pronunciation /ə/; in Middle Irish that shift was completed but with consequences: for example, declensional patterns where distinctions were marked by variation in the quality of final vowels were gradually replaced by more distinct consonant stem markers – this was particularly the case in maintaining number distinctions in nominatives and accusatives. There were consequences too for the verbal system, where pretonic vowel distinctions were also lost, leading to a loss of distinction between infixed pronouns. In addition, the gradual loss of the neuter gender brought about a reassigning of gender to originally neuter nouns. In the verbal system there was a steady process of simplification with simple verbs (often deriving from the prototonic form of a compound (see below for further discussion)) replacing compounds; where in Old Irish compound verbs had been used to infix unaccented object pronouns, in Middle Irish and beyond simple verbs began to be used with independent accented object pronouns.

From the fifth century onwards Scotland was settled from Ireland (as indeed were Cornwall and Wales). Linguistically, the Irish spoken by these settlers remained indistinguishable from the Irish of Ireland until about the thirteenth century and to this day southern dialects of Scottish Gaelic have much in common with northern dialects of Irish, to the extent that it may make sense to talk of a dialect continuum. The earliest evidence for Scottish Gaelic is found in the Gaelic entries in the twelfth-century *Book of Deer* (associated with the abbey of Deer in Buchan). These entries are, apart from some orthographical differences, indistinguishable from Middle Irish. Furthermore, access to the spoken language of the period from the twelfth to the seventeenth century remains difficult as most of it is written in a standardised form of Early Modern Irish. One exception is the early sixteenth-century *Book of the Dean of Lismore* which is written in an orthography which is in line with the conventions of contemporary Scots spelling, and allows us to see some of the changes which had affected Scottish Gaelic of this period, such as the regular loss of fricatives and the diphthongisation of the flanking vowels, e.g. *breour* 'powerful' (= early Modern Irish *brioghmhar*), *awir* 'material' (= *adhbhar*), *fai'w* 'looking' (= *feathamh*).

The earliest evidence for Manx is even later. John Phillips' translation of the Book of Common Prayer and his Bible translations appeared in the early seventeenth century though they were not printed until 1894. The precise linguistic relationship of Manx to Scottish Gaelic and Irish has been debated: it seems generally to be more closely related to Scottish Gaelic, though Norse influence has been canvassed as a possible explanation of the distinctive features of Manx (Williams 1994). One difficulty is its relative isolation; with the loss of the Irish dialects of Co. Down and the loss of Gaelic in Galloway, it is far less easy to locate it in its proper dialectal framework.

So much for the broad historical overview. It remains to consider a number of features of Celtic languages in the British Isles so as to bring the general comments into sharper relief. The features under discussion, stress accent, lenition and mutations, loss of final syllables, and aspects of the verbal system, are ones which are often highlighted as being in some sense peculiar to Celtic.

Stress accent

The workings of the accent in the Common Celtic period remain unclear (Salmons 1992, Schrijver 1995:16–22). The variation between the position of the accent in Goidelic and Brittonic along with the uncertainty about the continental Celtic evidence (de Bernardo-Stempel 1995) makes any reconstruction fraught with difficulty.

In Goidelic there was a stress accent on the initial syllable of a word, and its weakening effects on following syllables gave rise to many of the fundamental changes to affect early Irish. Modern Irish to a large extent has retained the initial stress accent, though in southern dialects the stress is often attracted to a later long syllable in the word (as also in Manx). In early Irish, the earliest effect of the stress was to reduce unaccented long vowels to short vowels, e.g. Old Irish *muilen* 'mill' < */ˈmolina/ < late Latin /molˈiːna/, with the result that only in initial syllables did original vowel quantity remain distinct. Secondary long vowels did develop subsequently from clusters of spirant and resonant, e.g. Old Irish *anál* 'breath' < */anaθlo/- < */anatlo/- (cf. Welsh *anadl*), the very common diminutive/ hypocoristic suffix *-án* < *-/agno/-. After the loss of final syllables the pressure of the initial stress accent brought about a wholesale syncope of unaccented vowels in the second (and in longer words fourth) syllable, thus rearranging the syllable structure of Irish, e.g. *cosmail* /ˈkosμəlʲ/ 'similar' < */ˈkosaμalʲ/, *teglach* 'household' /ˈtɣrləχ/ < */tegoslougo/-. The reduction in articulation of unaccented vowels was an ongoing process which did not eradicate all vowel quality in unaccented vowels until well into the Middle Irish period. Consonants were not exempt from its effects; thus, in early Old Irish /θ/, spelt *th*, and /ð/, spelt *d* (< */t/ and /d/ respectively), were distinct at the end of unaccented syllables, but by about 700 they had fallen together as /ð/, spelt *d*, e.g. the regular verbal noun ending: early Old Irish *-uth* (< *-/tu/-) > classical Old Irish *-ud, -ad*.

By contrast, in Brittonic (and perhaps Gaulish (de Bernardo-Stempel 1995)) the stress accent fell on the penultimate syllable. Syncope of a preceding short syllable was regular in polysyllables where an acceptable cluster resulted, e.g. (using Latin loanwords as examples because they give us a clear starting point) Welsh *cardod* 'charity' < Latin /kar(i)ˈtaːt/- (*caritas*), *esgob* < Latin /epˈiskopus/ (*episcopus*) (note the British stress pattern; Latin had /eˈpiskopus/). With the loss of final syllables (see below) the stressed syllable had now become the final syllable. Gradually over the next few centuries in all Brittonic languages (except the Vannetais dialect of Breton), the stress shifted back to the new penultimate syllable. In Welsh (but perhaps not in Cornish and Breton (Schrijver 1995:161–8)), there had been a similar reduction of vowel quality as in Irish, which affected pretonic vowels, e.g. Latin /ˈkupidus/ (*cupidus*) > /kuˈpidus/ (with Brittonic stress) > late Brittonic /kuˈbɨð/ > Old Welsh (pre-accent shift) /kəˈbɨð / > Old Welsh (post-accent shift) /ˈkəbɨð/ > Welsh *cybydd* 'miser'. The effect of the accent shift was to move the accent back onto a syllable the vowel quality of which had been reduced by its originally pretonic position. Similarly, after the accent shift there was a reduction in originally stressed diphthongs, e.g. the Middle Welsh suffix *-awc* /aug/ (< *-/aːko/-) which was reduced to *-og* -/ɔg/ after the accent shift.

Lenition and the grammaticalisation of the initial mutations

One of the striking features of all the Insular Celtic languages is the way in which the initial consonant of a word can be modified to mark grammatical categories, e.g. Old Irish *catt* 'cat': *mo chatt* /mə ˈχat/ 'my cat', Welsh *tad* 'father': *fy nhad* /və ˈnhad/ 'my father', Middle Cornish *den* 'man': *dew then* 'two men' (for details, see the chapters on individual languages). These patterns of mutations are deeply embedded in Celtic languages. While in surviving modern languages they are showing some signs of simplification and erosion, they still function as important grammatical markers of gender, case, number, etc. The Welsh particle *yn* /ən/ is a good example; it has three functions differentiated by mutation or its absence: (a) followed by a nasal mutation, the preposition 'in', e.g. *Bangor* : *ym mangor* 'in Bangor', *Caerdydd* 'Cardiff' : *yng Nghaerdydd* 'in Cardiff'; (b) followed by lenition (soft mutation), a predicate marker, e.g. *gwyn* 'white' : *mae'r ci yn wyn* 'the dog is white', *cyflym* 'quick' : *yn gyflym* 'quickly'; (c) no mutation, aspect marker, e.g. *canu* 'sing' : *mae Sara yn canu* 'Sara is singing'.

Historically, these changes affecting initial consonants are part of a more widespread set of changes involving all intervocalic consonants or consonants following /n/. The outcome was, however, slightly different in Goidelic and Brittonic. The changes affecting intervocalic consonants, known as lenition, were as follows: in Brittonic languages intervocalic /p t k b d g m/ developed to /b d g v ð ɣ μ/ respectively (i.e. voiceless stops were voiced and voiced stops developed into the corresponding fricative); in Goidelic voiced stops developed into the fricatives in the same way, thus /b d g m/ > /v ð ɣ μ/, but the voiceless stops likewise became fricatives, i.e. /p t k/ > /f θ χ/. For Brittonic, Latin loanwords provide a helpful corpus of examples to illustrate the above developments, since we know the starting point: Welsh *abostol* < Latin *apostolus*, *Addaf* /aðav/ < Adam, *ysblennydd* < *splendidus*, etc. Latin loanwords are a less useful quarry for evidence for Irish as many of them entered the language via speakers of British who then passed them on with a British accent (and a British spelling). For Irish we may compare Old Irish *suide* /suðʲə/ 'seat' < */sodyo/-, *tige* /tʲiɣʲə/ 'house' (genitive singular) < */tegesos/, *athair* /aθərʲ/ 'father' < */pater/. Double consonants underwent different changes: in Brittonic they were spirantised, e.g. Welsh *cath* < Latin *cattus*, *boch* 'cheek' < Latin *bucca*, but in Irish they simplified to the simple stop, e.g. *ruccae* /rukə/ 'redness' < */rukkiya/ < */rud-kiya/.

The pattern of initial mutations developed out of these phonetic changes. In the first place, the changes at word juncture were the same as occurred internally, that is, where a word ended in a vowel (often -/a/ in feminine nouns), the initial consonant of the next word was lenited as it would have been internally. Likewise, an initial consonant would be nasalised after a final -/n/ in the preceding word (as in an accusative singular or a genitive plural). The process would have remained at the phonetic level (as indeed it has done in English, e.g. *in Paris* [im'haris]) but the loss of final syllables removed the conditioning factors and at that point some of the grammatical load carried by the endings was carried over into the mutation; hence the tendency for feminine nouns to be followed by lenited adjective or genitive, and in Old Irish the accusative singular and genitive plural to be followed by nasalisation.

The origins of these consonantal changes is debated (McCone 1996:81–98). It has been seen as a fifth-century development in Insular Celtic or as a phonetic change which began deep in Proto-Celtic and can be traced in continental Celtic. Another issue is whether the changes involving unvoiced and voiced consonants are contemporary. Recent theories suggest that voiced stops may have moved towards a fricative pronunciation at a very early stage (there is perhaps evidence in Celtiberian for the change of /d/ > /z/ (presumably via /ð/ (see Isaac 2002 for discussion)) which may be relevant if it is to be interpreted as showing lenition in Celtiberian). Within Insular Celtic the different reflexes of the lenited form of voiceless consonants in Brittonic and Goidelic suggest that they are separate developments.

Loss of final syllables

The loss of final syllables occurred in both branches of Insular Celtic but with different outcomes. We know more about the process of loss in Irish than in Brittonic. It appears to have been a gradual erosion of distinctions, such as the loss of distinction between long and short vowels in final syllables, the loss of final lenited consonants, etc. The effect on noun classes was variable: -*o*-stems and -*a*-stems lost final syllables almost completely (vestiges were preserved in some cases), but -*yo*-stems and -*ya*-stems preserved a remnant of an ending throughout, namely -*e*, -*i* or -*u*. For Goidelic the upshot was that sufficient markers survived in any final surviving vowels and consonants together with lenition or nasalisation of a following initial consonant for declension to be preserved. Irish had also developed a set of palatal consonants beside the normal set which had arisen from environments where the consonant had originally been followed by a front vowel. Thus, for example, the singular of an -*a*-stem declension in Old Irish could maintain all the necessary distinctions (superscript [L] marks lenition of the following word, superscript [N] marks nasalisation): nominative singular *túath*[L] < */toːta/, accusative singular *túaith*[N] < */toːten/, genitive singular *túaithe* < */toːteyah/, dative singular *túaith*[L] < */toːti/. While a -*yo*-stem declension preserved sufficient markers in Old Irish, notably in terms of distinctions between final vowels, with the Middle Irish reduction of final vowels to /ə/ a process of remarking was needed. The striking feature about this stage was that the main preoccupation was to distinguish singular and plural rather than cases usually by the importation of case endings from consonant stem nouns.

We know far less about any stages by which final syllables were lost in British, nor is it clear whether there is any causal relation between that and the complete loss of declension in Brittonic languages. It is increasingly the view that loss of final syllables would not have been as catastrophic for the declensional system as had been thought, not least because it can be shown that a case system could have survived the loss of final syllables both for vowel and consonant stem nouns by the use of other markers (Hamp 1975–6, Russell 1995:123–4). However, that is not to say that it did survive the loss of final syllables; the few traces of case endings which have survived are too sparse to speak for the recent expiry of the declensional system. A more plausible account would argue that the case system was in steep decline well before the loss of the final syllables (Koch 1982–3). The evidence of late Latin inscriptions from Britain shows a general confusion of case endings and indicates that understanding of nominal morphology was at the very least shaky. Furthermore, as in Middle Irish, the main preoccupation seems to have been focussed on maintaining singular–plural distinctions, and this was achieved by the generalisation of certain consonant stem endings, in Welsh notably -(*i*)*on* < */(y)ones/ (*n*-stem) and Old Welsh -*ou*, Middle Welsh -*eu*, Modern Welsh -*au* < *-/owes/ (*u*-stem). Original vowel stem patterns, because they were dependent on final vowels, largely disappeared; the only one to show any productivity was the *o*-stem plural *-/i/ which caused vowel affection and thereby left behind a clear marker, e.g. *gwr* 'man' : *gwyr* 'men' < */wiros/ : /wiriː/; its productivity can be shown by its spread to, for example, *cestyll* 'castles' (: singular *castell*) which is derived from Latin *castellum* and therefore its original plural would have been *castella*.

Verbal system

A full discussion of the Celtic verbal system is not possible here. The intention is to focus on one particularly problematic area of the verbal system in early Celtic languages, namely the rise of a double inflection of the verb. We may take Old Irish *berid* 'he carries' as an example. When used in declarative statements, an 'absolute' set of endings is used, e.g. *berid* 'he carries', *berait* 'they carry', but a different set of 'conjunct' endings is used when a pretonic particle is required before the verb, for example a negative or interrogative particle, e.g. *ní·beir* /niː'bʲerʲ/ 'he does not carry', *in·beir?* /in'bʲerʲ/ 'does he carry?' Similarly, if a particle is required to carry an 'infixed' pronoun, then the conjunct form is used, e.g. *nom·beir* /nom'vʲerʲ/ 'he carries me' (in archaic Old Irish such pronouns were suffixed, e.g. *beirthium*). Compound verbs show a more extended version of this pattern: *do·beir* 'he brings, he gives', by virtue of having a pretonic preverb, has the expected 'conjunct' form of the basic verb. However, when that verb takes a negative or interrogative, the preverb moves into the accented position with important effects on the rest of the verb, e.g. *ní·tabair* /niː'tavʲərʲ/ 'he does not give'. Thus, while for a simple verb there are two forms of conjugation, 'absolute' and 'conjunct', for a compound verb there are two forms determined not by the form of the conjugation but by accent position, 'deuterotonic', e.g. *do·beir* /do'bʲerʲ/, and 'prototonic' -/'tavʲərʲ/.

The historical origins of this pattern are much debated and will not be discussed in detail here (for surveys, see Sims-Williams 1984, Russell 1995:49–54). The system is at its height in the Old Irish period and Middle Irish is witness to its gradual breakdown, though elements have survived better in Scottish Gaelic and Manx: e.g. Scottish Gaelic *gabhaidh* 'he takes' : *nach gabh* 'he does not take'. Sufficient traces of a similar pattern are preserved in the early stages of the Brittonic languages to indicate that the origins of this pattern of double inflection are to be found in Proto-Celtic, or at least in Insular Celtic. In Old and Middle Welsh the verbal conjugation shows a mixture of forms deriving from both the absolute and the conjunct inflections; thus, Welsh *archaf* < */arkami/ (absolute), but *eirch* < */erkiːt/ (conjunct). The system can still be seen in certain proverbial expressions in Middle Welsh (verbs in bold): e.g. **tyuit** (absolute) *maban, ni* **thyf** (conjunct) *y gadachan* 'an infant grows, his swaddling clothes do not'. Similarly, traces of the deuterotonic: prototonic patterns may be found in variant forms such as *gogel : gochel* 'hides' (< */wo-kel/-).

12 Gaelic

Kenneth MacKinnon

Gaelic, the original – and still surviving – language of the Scots

The origins of the Gaelic language, and the Kingdom of the Scots, are generally taken to lie in the movement of people from the north-east of Ireland in the fifth century AD and the relocation of the Kingdom of Dal Riata from present-day County Antrim into western Argyllshire in this period. Whether a Gaelic or closely related language was spoken in Scotland earlier than this is debatable. Such was the view of nineteenth-century writers such as Logan (1831, 1876, 1976:46–7), who certainly thought so – as also did Skene (1860–90, v1: 68 – cited in Watson 1926:45). Scholarship in the twentieth century (e.g. Bannerman 1974) regarded Gaelic as essentially arriving with the Dalriadan settlement, although the problem has been more recently debated (e.g. Forsyth 1997, Campbell 2001).

From the reign of Malcolm III 'Ceannmòr' (1054–96), Gaelic lost its pre-eminence at court and amongst the aristocracy to Norman French, and subsequently in the Lowlands through the establishment of English-speaking burghs in eastern and central Scotland to Scots. In the northern Highlands and Islands, Norse settlement brought the Norn language which survived through the Middle Ages in Caithness and the Northern Isles. By the eighteenth century Norn became extinct, but has influenced both the northern dialects and literary Scots, as well as Gaelic (Geipel 1971:74–5). In contrast to Norn, Gaelic continues as one of Scotland's living indigenous languages, and as an *Abstand* Celtic language, has been better able than has Scots to resist English influences in speech forms.

From the late fifteenth century into the eighteenth century a number of acts of the Scottish and British parliaments were aimed at promoting English literacy, first amongst the Gaelic aristocracy, and subsequently amongst the general population, the outlawing of native learned orders and finally the disarming of the clans and the prohibition of Highland dress and music. By the seventeenth century Gaelic had retreated into the Highlands, Hebrides and Clyde Islands, comprising the Scottish

Gaidhealtachd, or Gaelic-speaking area. Although there was a rapid loss of their political independence, Gaelic speakers retained a distinctive culture and social structure. The Scottish, and subsequent British state, both regarded these as inimical to its interests.

In the nineteenth century, the enforced movement of the crofting people during the notorious Highland Clearances removed many Gaelic speakers from the Highlands and Islands to settle overseas, e.g. in Nova Scotia. Many migrated to the industrial centres of Lowland Scotland. These latter movements have been studied in detail by Withers (1984, 1988a, b, 1991), and in more general and comparative terms by Durcacz (1983). Contemporaneously with these movements from the Gaidhealtachd during the earlier nineteenth century, a popular and successful voluntary Gaelic Schools system was established. This was superseded after legislation in 1872 by a national English-language schools system in which Gaelic had little if any place. Despite adult male suffrage from 1867, security for crofting from 1886 and the development of local government in the 1880s and 1890s, recognition for Gaelic was minimal. Gaelic thus survived as an oral rather than as a literary medium for the majority of its speakers. Within the Presbyterian churches, Gaelic literacy was promoted at Sunday schools, and Bible reading and psalm-singing were – and continue to be – practised both in congregational and home worship. Differences in literacy were still noticeable into the late twentieth century between Catholic and Protestant Gaelic communities (MacKinnon 1978:65–7).

Throughout the twentieth century there has been a general decline in the numbers of Gaelic speakers. At the end of the nineteenth century there were over a quarter of a million speakers: 254,415 enumerated in the 1891 census. This had decreased to 65,978 a century later in the 1991 census, and to 58,969 in 2001. As well as a reduction in numbers there has been a marked geographical redistribution. In 1891, 89% of all Gaelic speakers resided in the Highlands and Hebrides; a century later in 1991, this had reduced to 59%, and to 55% in 2001. Outward migration has greatly affected distribution patterns and the two world wars accelerated the process. In World War I there was great loss of life amongst the menfolk of the Highlands and Islands, and in the 1920s there was considerable emigration from the Hebrides. After World War II, increased educational and employment opportunities in the Lowlands drew many young people from the Gaelic areas.

Since 1975 there have been increasingly vigorous efforts to improve the position of Gaelic in education, the media and public life. Local government reorganisation in 1975 was followed by bilingual education schemes and in 1985 by the inception of Gaelic-medium schooling. In the mid-80s Gaelic on radio increased considerably, and on television from 1992.

A Minister for Gaelic was appointed in the new Labour government of 1997, and with Scottish devolution in 1999, task forces and reports on Gaelic recommended new initiatives in language planning (Milne 2000, Macpherson 2000, Meek 2002). At the same time the use of Gaelic was collapsing in its traditional domains: the family, neighbourhood life and the church (MacKinnon 1997a, b).

Linguistic characteristics of Scottish Gaelic and its dialects

Scottish Gaelic is a Celtic language, a member of the Goidelic or 'Q-Celtic' branch, closely related to Irish and Manx, with both of which it shares a large part of its lexicon and grammatical structure. It is more distantly related to Welsh, Cornish and Breton which comprise the Brythonic or 'P-Celtic' group. It is quite lexically distinct from these, although again there are many similarities of grammatical structure and idiom.

Scottish Gaelic is basically a VSO language: its typical sentence commencing with the verb, followed by the subject and then the rest of the predicate. Adjectives for the most part follow the nouns which they qualify. Adverbs are formed generally by prefixing *gu-* to the corresponding adjective. A distinctive feature which Scottish Gaelic shares with other Celtic languages is in the combination of prepositions and personal pronouns. Thus prepositions decline for persons rather like verbs in other Indo-European languages. Thus *do* 'to' combines with *mi* 'I, me' to form *dhomh* 'to me', and so forth: *dhuit* 'to thee, you', *dhà* 'to him, it', *dhí* 'to her, it', *dhuinn* 'to us', *dhuibh* 'to you', *dhaibh* 'to them'. Verbs do not however decline for person (except for first person subjunctive), and there are only ten irregular verbs.

There are two forms of the verb 'to be'. *Bidh!* is the basic form for straightforward statements. It conjugates fully for tense, and can combine with the present participle of other verbs to form continuous tenses, and past participles to form perfects (much as English does in contrast to other Germanic languages). The emphatic form of the verb 'to be' exists in only two forms: present-future *is*, and all past tenses *bu*. These two verbs together with prepositions, and prepositions combined with pronouns, enable a vast array of idioms to be formed. These enable actions in the 'real world' to be grammatically distinguished from abstract, mental, psychic and emotional states. A 'real' action may be conveyed by a simple verb-subject-object structure. For example, *phòg e a' bhoireannach* 'he kissed the woman'. This can be contrasted grammatically with *bha gaol aige oirre* 'he loved her'. This equates to, literally, '(there) was love at-him for-her'. Similarly *is urrainn dhomh* 'I can', literally '(there) is ability to-me'. Also, *tha fios agam air* 'I know it', literally, '(there) is knowledge at-me for-it'. These features present a very different way of handling meaning from the majority of other Indo-European languages.

There is of course a large number of loanwords borrowed from English into Scottish Gaelic throughout the period of language contact between them. Examples include: *ad* 'hat', *barant(as)* 'warrant', *breacaist* 'breakfast', *brot* 'broth, soup', *comhfhurtail* 'comfortable', *geata* 'gate', *mionaid* 'minute – of time', *paidhir* 'pair', *rathad* 'road', *stràid* 'street', *targaid* 'target'. Some of these English borrowings were via Latin, Middle French, and Scots. More direct borrowings from Latin include: *aingeal* 'angel', *airgiod* 'silver, money', *crois* 'cross', *eaglais* 'church', *Ifrinn* 'Hell', *feasgair* 'evening', *gineal* 'offspring', *manach* 'monk'. The influence of the religious domain in producing these is obvious. Substantial contact with Norse also led to a great many borrowings. These include: *faodhail* ('ford, crossing' – from Norse *vadhil*), *gocaman* ('lookout' – from Norse *gokman*, *gauksman*), *sgioba* ('crew' – from Norse *skip*), *sgalag* ('lackey' – from Norse *skalkr*), *uinneag* ('window' – from Norse *windauga*).

The pre-aspiration in present-day Scottish Gaelic dialects before the final vowels in words such as *mac* 'son', *sop* 'wisp' and *sloc* 'pit' is very typical of south-west Norwegian dialects and north-western Scottish Gaelic dialects (according to Marstrander, in Geipel 1971:83). Historically Scottish Gaelic dialects were very greatly contrasted between the north-west with its islands, and the east-central together with the eastern Highland areas. Today the dialects of the east are well-nigh extinct – as indeed all mainland dialects are moribund. Eastern dialects did not diphthongise the long /eː/ in words like *meud* 'measure', *beul* 'mouth', or intrude /s/ between final /r/ and /t/ in words like *tart* 'thirst', *neart* 'strength', etc. Similarly the northwestern dialects intrude /t/ between initial /s/ and /r/, as in *sruth* 'stream, current', *srath* 'strath, wide valley', *srian* 'reins, bridle' – again a likely Norse influence (Marstrander, in Geipel 1971:83). Today the dialects of the east are more or less extinct and only Gaelic 'pockets' remain on the north-west mainland, though it is a strong feature of the Western Isles, Inner Isles and Skye.

As with Irish, Scottish Gaelic observes the spelling convention of *caol ri caol is leathan ri leathan* 'narrow to narrow and broad to broad'. Where a narrow vowel /i/ or /e/ occurs before a consonant, that consonant must be followed by a narrow vowel. Where a broad vowel /a/, /o/ or /u/ occurs before a consonant, that consonant must again be followed by a broad vowel. Pronunciation of consonants is determined by the surrounding vowels, e.g. the consonants thus flanked by narrow or broad vowels are regarded as correspondingly 'narrow' or 'broad' and pronounced accordingly. Gaelic has only the letters <a b c d e f g i l m n o p r s t u>. The letter <h> is not regarded as a regular letter – no words commence with it, except the odd Norse-derived placename, such as *na Hearadh, Hearach* ('Harris', placename and 'Harris', adjective and person), and it never stands alone in spelling, except in the accidence of nouns and adjectives in prefixing the genitive case feminine singular of words commencing in vowels (e.g. *bun na h-aibhne* 'the foot of the river'), or in prefixing the nominative, accusative and dative cases plural both masculine and feminine where the word begins with a vowel (e.g. *na h-uighean* 'the eggs'). Yet /h/ commonly joins with the consonants /b k d f g m p s t/ to render distinctive phonemes, and also to indicate modification to an initial consonant by way of aspiration or lenition in grammatical change for tense, case or word combination.

The geographical distribution of Gaelic speakers[1]

One of the main problems facing the language and its speakers at the outset of the twenty-first century is how to strengthen Gaelic in the family. In 1991 only 29% of Gaelic speakers lived in a family in which all of the members were Gaelic speakers (1991 Census, Topic Monitor for Gaelic Language, Table 3). In the community only 27% lived in census output areas where Gaelic was the majority language, and only 17% in areas of over 75% incidence (Census 1991 Gaelic Report, Table 3, SAS Table 67S).

Of the 65,978 Gaelic speakers in 1991, the Western Isles was home to 19,546 (29.6%) of this total, the Highland Council area 14,713 (22.3%), and Argyll and Bute 4,583 (6.9%). These areas approximating to the traditional Gaidhealtachd contained 38,842 (59%) of Scotland's Gaelic speakers. The strongest Gaelic speech communities in 1991 were in the Western Isles, Skye and Tiree with 69%, 42% and 56% respectively of their populations speaking Gaelic. Rapid language shift has reduced these numbers over the ten years to the 2001 Census, which indicated a total number of 58,969 Gaelic speakers. The majority Gaelic areas thus contracted to Western Isles (59.8%) and Kilmuir parish in Skye (55.7%) (2001 Census, Tables T27, UV12). Within the traditional Gaidhealtachd defined above, smaller pockets of Gaelic speakers, chiefly of the older age groups, live in the other islands and western coastal areas of the Highland and Argyll and Bute council areas. At the outset of the twenty-first century, there were still some vestiges of native Gaelic in other Highland areas, including Highland Perthshire. In the past contacts between the Gaelic speech communities have thus been difficult. The Highlands and Islands are sparsely settled, with small populations separated by the sea and its indentations and a mountainous terrain. Townships are often isolated

---

[1] Permission to use census material and Small Area Statistics supplied by General Register Office (Scotland) is gratefully acknowledged (http://www.gro-scotland.gov.uk/statistics/index.html).

from one another – particularly as people in the Hebrides and west coast areas now travel by car rather than by boat. The development of Gaelic broadcasting on radio and television in recent decades has done something to overcome this.

Even in 2001, though, almost all parts of the traditional Gaidhealtachd still had a proportion of Gaelic speakers greater than the national rate. However, an important and growing proportion of all Gaelic speakers resides in Lowland Scotland: 55% in 2001, including over 15,000 persons with knowledge of Gaelic in the Greater Glasgow area. This trend emphasises the need to provide educational and cultural infrastructure for Gaelic nationwide. Demand for Gaelic-medium education for their children is increasing – especially among young, articulate Gaelic parents in city areas. This led to the inception of the first Gaelic-medium primary units – in Glasgow and Inverness in 1985 – and to the first dedicated all-Gaelic school – in Glasgow in 1999.

The dispersal of the Gaelic-speaking population provides an acute problem for the future of the language, and the roles of the communications media and of local administration are thus particularly important in overcoming these difficulties. The Western Isles Council was created in 1975 and made responsible for all local government services. It has developed a bilingual administrative policy, conducting its affairs and deliberations in both languages, introducing Gaelic on its public signs and notices, and enhancing its position in education. However in the school year 2003/4, only 23.3% of its primary pupils were educated through the medium of Gaelic – and even fewer (3.5%) at the secondary stage, although some 60.5% were taking Gaelic as a subject: 38.9% as learners and 21.6% as fluent speakers (Comhairle nan Eilean Siar 2004).

Four other local authorities formulated bilingual policies and set up Gaelic committees between 1975 and 1996: Highland Region, Skye and Lochalsh District, Ross and Cromarty District and Argyll and Bute District. Strathclyde Region nominated a councillor with responsibility for Gaelic. The situation since the local government reorganisation of 1996 has resulted in four of the 32 unitary authorities having Gaelic policies and dedicated staff: Western Isles (CNES), and the Highland, Argyll and Bute, and Perth and Kinross Councils in addition to staff in Gaelic education.

Language-maintenance and shift

Since the late nineteenth century the Gaelic speech community has rapidly contracted and likewise aged. There have been few ostensible increases. Between 1881 and 1891 the numbers of Gaelic speakers increased from 231,433 to 254,415, as a result of changing the census definition from 'habitual speaker' to 'can speak Gaelic' – although within the Gaidhealtachd numbers nevertheless declined. In 1921 a summer census date resulted in increases in some Gaelic areas – probably of returning Gaels on holiday. Between 1961 and 1971 total numbers again increased from 80,987 to 88,892, resulting from a change of question – the inclusion of questions on reading and writing, and numbers within the Gaidhealtachd continued to decline. However, in 1981 there were increases of speakers in Gaelic areas. These were amongst young people where Gaelic had been introduced into primary education, and in Skye and the Western Isles associated with oil-related developments (see Figures 12.1–12.3 and MacKinnon 1991a:122, 1987c, 1991b:527–9).

In subsequent censuses these encouraging developments received a set-back. However, the upturn amongst school-aged children did continue in areas such as the Highland Region, which had developed Gaelic-medium primary provision, but in the Western Isles in 1991, where Gaelic-medium provision was then slight, there was a considerable reduction of younger Gaelic speakers from over two-thirds of the 3–15 age group to under one-half. Over the period 1971–81–91–2001 numbers and percentages within the total age group of Gaelic speakers aged 3–15 increased in the Highland Region: 1,593–1,810–1,988–2,171 (4.2%–4.8%–5.6%–6.3%) compared with a decline in the Western Isles: 4,396–4,385–2,571–1,966 (67.6%–67.8%–49.5%–46.3%) (Census Small Area Statistics 1971: Table 40, 1981, 1991: Table 67S; Census 2001: Table S206, UV12). This was the principal factor in reducing the previous trend of increase of speakers in this age group nationally.

In 1981 there were local neighbourhoods within the Gaidhealtachd in which the proportion of young people aged 5–24 speaking Gaelic matched or exceeded the proportion in older age ranges. These areas, which were thus potentially viable Gaelic communities, comprised 30 of the 140 enumeration districts in the Western Isles (chiefly in western Lewis, southern Harris, the Uists and Barra), and 9 of the 50 enumeration districts in Skye (chiefly its northern and southern extremities). Comparison with 1991 is not possible (owing to replacement of enumeration districts by larger output areas) but a substantial contraction of areas where Gaelic was successfully maintained was apparent (Census 1981 Scotland Small Area Statistics, Table 40; 1991, Table 67S). Data from the 2001 Census at these levels are still awaited, but comparable data at census ward levels in the Western Isles indicate that these trends strongly continue.

There is some evidence that in the strongest Gaelic communities, sup-portive attitudes and usage of the language were less well represented amongst the younger women, as compared with other age and gender groups during this period. This could be accounted for by the differential

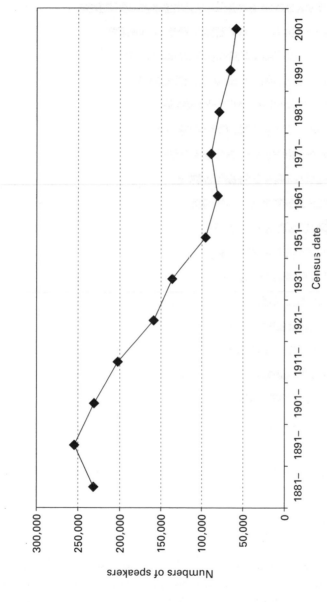

Figure 12.1 The decline in the number of Gaelic speakers: 1881–2001

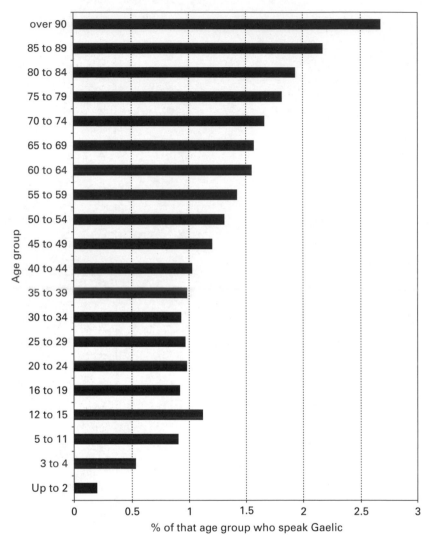

Figure 12.2 People who speak Gaelic as a percentage of the total age group in the 2001 Census

migration of younger women as compared with younger men from these areas (MacKinnon 1977, 1984a, 1986, MacDonald 1984). Within the occupational continuum of Gaelic communities, Gaelic appears to be best conserved within the semi-skilled agricultural group, which comprises the crofting 'core'. Young unmarried people may seek Gaelic-speaking

Figure 12.3 Proportions of Gaelic speakers in different areas of Scotland (1991)

partners, but often it will be a non-Gaelic-speaking spouse who is brought home, which means that the prospects for intergenerational transmission are diminished.

The social class distribution of Gaelic-speaking abilities is patterned by migration. The prospects for employment in professional, managerial, skilled non-manual and skilled manual occupations are limited within the Gaelic areas. Many of those who would take up 'leadership' roles, which tend socially to be associated with these occupational categories, have emigrated to Lowland Scotland and elsewhere. The skilled occupational categories – especially the non-manual group – have tended to be less supportive of Gaelic in usage and loyalty terms, perhaps because they were in a sense of the generation who were 'educated out' of using the language (MacKinnon 1985, 1991a). However, where new industry has attracted young, skilled and semi-skilled Gaelic speakers back to the home areas to work, this has increased both the incidence of Gaelic (MacKinnon 1991b) and its profile in the community (Prattis 1980).

Gaelic–English bilingualism has been studied in East Sutherland (Dorian 1981), Mull (Dorian 1980), Skye (MacKinnon 1988a, Macaulay 1998, Macdonald 1997), Harris (MacKinnon 1977), Barra (MacKinnon & MacDonald 1980, MacDonald 1984, MacKinnon 1985) and the Western Isles as a whole (MacKinnon 1998, Macaulay 1998). The general pattern emerging from these studies indicates that community and neighbourhood usage of Gaelic, particularly exchanges with older relations and friends, may often stand up better than family usage of the language. Children's usage of Gaelic, even within the home, is decreasing rapidly. In strongly Gaelic communities Gaelic predominates in most work domains – especially crofting. Local post offices and shops can be pivotal domains for community usage, and where these have been taken over by non-Gaelic-speaking incomers (as in southern Skye), Gaelic may rapidly retreat. Even within the religious domains Gaelic usage is weakening and may not function much longer as the bulwark it once was.

The demographic shifts in Gaelic speakers are mirrored by changes in the use of the language. Virtually all Gaelic speakers are today functionally bilingual. Gaelic monolingualism is restricted to a handful of the most socially isolated old people and to preschool infants. One of the chief influences of English upon Gaelic is in finding terminology to describe modern concepts. Code-switching and calquing are commonplace (MacAulay 1982). Various initiatives have been taken to create and develop the use of Gaelic neologisms, and many that are now common were first introduced in broadcasting. In 1987 a Gaelic terminology database was established at Sabhal Mòr Ostaig, the Gaelic College on Skye (Gorman 1993). The Scottish Parliament published a Gaelic dictionary in 2001 (McNeir 2001).

Broadcasting has also been a butt for controversies regarding Gaelic dialects and speech varieties. Listeners often state they find difficulty in understanding dialects other than their own. Paradoxically, survey informants frequently claim that 'the proper Gaelic' is not spoken in their home area. Such reactions result from lack of exposure to alternative speech varieties and perhaps to some image of 'pulpit Gaelic' or 'newsreaders' Gaelic' as in some way providing a standard variety. Both reactions probably result from deficiencies of the education system in insufficiently developing people's linguistic repertoire and awareness in Gaelic as compared with English.

Cultural infrastructure

The principal Gaelic language organisation was for many years *An Comunn Gaidhealach* ('The Highland Association'). It has been active in educational, publishing and cultural fields. With the appointment of a professional director in 1966, it involved itself in socioeconomic issues and put more active pressure on both central and local government. In the mid-1980s these roles in public life and education, together with youth work and media, were taken up by a new organisation *Comunn na Gàidhlig* (CNAG) originally funded by the Highlands and Islands Development Board (HIDB) and now by its successor Highlands and Islands Enterprise (HIE) and the Scottish Executive. In 1987 the Scottish Arts Council funded a National Gaelic Arts Project, *Pròiseact nan Ealan*, which has developed into an agency with a remit to develop new arts and cultural initiatives. In 1982 the HIDB assisted the newly established Gaelic playgroups organisation, *Comhairle nan Sgoiltean Àraich* (CNSA) and helped to establish a learners' organisation, *Comann an Luchd-Ionnsachaidh* (CLÌ Gàidhlig).

The Conservative government (1979–97) produced official statements concerning Gaelic in 1985 and 1987, which went little beyond unspecific general support. However, the then Scottish Office did establish a specific grants fund for Gaelic from 1986, and from 1992 an annual television fund of some £8–9 million. The succeeding Labour government on taking office in May 1977 appointed a Minister of State with responsibility for Gaelic, a function which has been taken over by a minister in the new Scottish Parliament from 1999. There is now provision for the use of Gaelic in parliamentary business and bilingual signage.

There is once again, after a considerable gap, a professional Gaelic theatre company, *Tosg*. Amateur drama is vigorous and popular. With aid from the National Gaelic Arts Project, a children's theatre group *Òrdag is Sgealbag* ('Thumb and Forefinger') commenced in the early 1990s. A Gaelic community film unit, Sùil, in the 1970s developed into the international Celtic Film and Television Festival. Training for young Gaels in professional film, television and video production in the late 1980s led to new Gaelic television companies. The establishment of the television fund administered by Comataidh Telebhisean Gàidhlig from 1992 (now since 2004, *Seirbhisean Meadhonan Gàidhlig*) has increased Gaelic output and stimulated a Gaelic television industry. However, there is as yet no dedicated Gaelic television or full-time radio station. Proposals for digitalisation may enable these to be established.

Within Scottish music there has been a revival of interest in the folk tradition, which has stimulated interest in Gaelic music. People throughout Scotland are learning the clarsach, pipes, fiddle, accordion and whistle, and playing Gaelic tunes. Bands such as Runrig, Capercaillie and Wolfstone have brought Gaelic music and song to national and international audiences. This interest has been encouraged by the *Fèisean* movement, a community-run organisation providing opportunities to learn Gaelic performance arts, such as song, storytelling, music and dance. By 1999 there were 32 fèisean, involving more than 3,000 participants, and subsequently a national festival, *Fèis Alba*.

The cultural heritage of the Gaidhealtachd has come more to the forefront with the establishment of heritage centres and local museums. As well as exhibitions, some are building up genealogical and historical archives. There are some 30 *Comannan Eachdraidh* throughout the Western Isles and beyond, and there are plans to digitalise the database of sound recordings of Gaelic and Scots tradition held by the BBC and the School of Scottish Studies in Edinburgh, and make them more accessible locally: *Tobar an Dualchais*/Kist o' Riches Project. In 1997 *Iomairt Chaluim Chille*, the Columba Initiative, was set up to forge links between the Gaelic communities of Scotland, Northern Ireland and the Irish Republic. The more vigorous branches of *An Comunn*, and self-help learners' groups, provide Gaelic-medium events in various places.

Education and the reproduction of language

Since 1882 it has been possible to take Gaelic as part of a university degree in Celtic, and the 1918 Education Act provided for Gaelic to be taught in 'Gaelic-speaking areas' – although these were never defined. The act was similarly unspecific as to whether instruction was to be through the medium of Gaelic – or merely of Gaelic as a specific subject.

Although there is no general provision for Gaelic in Scottish education as there is for Welsh in Wales, by the mid-twentieth century some provision for Gaelic had been made by Highland county education authorities. From 1958 Gaelic was used as an initial teaching medium in the early primary stages in Gaelic-speaking areas, and it could be studied as an examination subject in parity with other languages at the secondary stage. Since then, Gaelic in education has undergone increasingly rapid development (MacKinnon 1987c, 1992). By the mid-1970s schemes for the provision of Gaelic as a second language had been introduced in many Highland primary schools – and in Highland Perthshire. With the establishment of a unitary authority for the Western Isles in 1975, the Primary Bilingual Education Project was initiated, and subsequently extended supposedly to every school in the area. The Highland Region implemented a similar scheme in Skye a few years later. There followed an increasing demand for Gaelic-medium schooling, and in 1985 two units commenced in Glasgow and Inverness. By 2001/02 these had grown to 60 units, including a dedicated all-Gaelic school in Glasgow, with 1,859 pupils receiving their primary education through the medium of Gaelic. An evaluation of Gaelic education by the Lèirsinn Research Unit for Gaelic Affairs and the Scottish Centre for Language Teaching and Research, concluded that these pupils were in no way held back but in many cases were doing better than their counterparts in English-medium education (Johnstone, Harlen, MacNeil, Stradling & Thorpe 1999).

However, the rapid growth of the system had slackened off by 1997/98, chiefly owing to a shortage of qualified teachers. A further weakness has been that buoyant numbers in Gaelic preschool groups have not translated into the primary stage, and these have translated into even fewer numbers in the secondary stage. On five-year average figures up to 2001, 1,075 3-year-olds were entering preschool Gaelic groups, but only 292 were entering Gaelic-medium primary units, and even fewer – 104 – were entering secondary Gaelic streams. Clearly a preschool initiative with the potential to remedy overall language loss was being stalled by the lack of primary and secondary development. Developments at secondary level had been hindered by the failure of the Western Isles to extend the primary bilingual scheme to the secondary level in 1979, and by subsequent lack of support by the incoming Conservative government. Development was further hindered by a report of Her Majesty's Inspectorate, which declared Gaelic-medium secondary education to be 'neither desirable nor feasible', and that 'availability of teachers of quality ... will be a continuing obstacle' (Scottish Office 1994:3). More recent developments appear more supportive, with proposals for local and in-service training of Gaelic-medium teachers, and recognition by the General Teaching Council. This would certainly address the main problem for Gaelic-medium education, namely that of teacher supply.

By the late 1990s, facilities for adults to learn Gaelic to fluency were improved by the establishment of immersion courses in colleges of further education and at Sabhal Mòr Ostaig, the Gaelic college on Skye. By 2001/02 some 150 students were on such courses, including University of the Highlands and Islands courses in broadcasting, information technology, business studies, administration, social sciences and rural development through the medium of Gaelic, as well as taking advanced Gaelic immersion courses and Gaelic degrees.

Problems and possibilities

The crisis in teacher supply has greatly hindered meeting the increasing demand for Gaelic in education – and thus checking a most fruitful field for language conservation and enhancement. Gaelic education at the outset of the twenty-first century clearly still requires the co-ordination of career development opportunities, ease of teacher movement around the system and the extension of initial and in-service teacher training. Curriculum development has been greatly aided by the Specific Grants Scheme started in 1985 and by 2007/08 running at some £4.466 million annually. A national education resource centre has been established in Lewis. At Sabhal Mór Ostaig the Lèirsinn Research Unit for Gaelic Affairs was established in 1992, and has since undertaken a great deal of research, chiefly in educational and media fields.

By the late 1990s only BBC2 Scotland and on ITV only Grampian and Scottish Television were broadcasting Gaelic programmes (totalling some 500 hours annually). This of course was a very small proportion of the total broadcast time on terrestrial and satellite channels. Similarly on radio: BBC radio has seven UK-wide analogue and digital channels plus Radio Scotland. BBC Radio nan Gàidheal is essentially an opt-out from Radio Scotland on FM. It is not available in all areas and produces about 45 hours in Gaelic weekly. This is far from the dedicated full-time Gaelic radio channel which the BBC Gaelic department had half-promised 'when things improve' from 1985, and is now long overdue. The advent of digital broadcasting has provided a new opportunity for dedicated Gaelic television and radio channels. This has been recommended by a broadcasting task force set up in 1999, and which reported in 2000 (Milne 2000).

These developments and problems in education and the media are reminders that by the outset of the twenty-first century there were several initiatives which called for a coherent language policy for Gaelic in Scotland. The Macpherson Task Force was appointed in 1999, and reported in 2000, calling for both legislation and a national plan (Macpherson 2000). A Ministerial Advisory Group on Gaelic (MAGOG) was appointed to realise these objectives, and published its proposals in 2002 (Meek 2002). Two other initiatives on language in Scotland at this time were Scotlang, on language teaching in Scotland, and a parliamentary inquiry into Scotland's indigenous and ethnic minority languages and policies. The initial report on Scotlang (Lo Bianco 2001) was followed by various initiatives co-ordinated by the Scottish Centre for Information on Language Teaching and Research. However, the go-ahead for a major research study on Gaelic, to be funded by the Scottish Funding Council, was still awaited in December

2006. The parliamentary inquiry reported in November 2002, and the volume of evidence was published in February 2003 (McGugan 2002, 2003). The report drew attention to the specific needs of each language, was officially welcomed and has led to a new impetus for Gaelic in both public and academic life.

The most urgent need for the future of the Gaelic language may however lie in the domains of family and community life. The demographic processes which have weakened the language in these fields have been illustrated in recent research surveys. In the 1970s studies of Gaelic-speaking communities were undertaken in Harris and Barra with Social Science Research Council funding (MacKinnon 1977, MacKinnon & MacDonald 1980, MacDonald 1984). In the mid-1980s, the Economic and Social Research Council funded a survey in the Western Isles and Skye to investigate language maintenance and viability. This drew attention to the acute decline of intergenerational transmission and use of Gaelic in the home (MacKinnon 1988a, b, 1991b, 1994). Almost a decade later, in 1994/5, the EU Euromosaic Project funded the first national sample survey of Gaelic speakers throughout Scotland and their everyday use of Gaelic. With a similar methodology and questions to earlier surveys, and to surveys of other European minority languages, the results of this survey suggested that the continued weakness of intergenerational transmission of Gaelic was gathering momentum. Compared to the use of Gaelic to and between grandparents in previous generations, the use of Gaelic by parents to children was reducing sharply, and between children themselves was becoming minimal. These intergenerational changes are illustrated in Figure 12.4. In the community, the use of Gaelic, whilst standing up comparatively well amongst friends and neighbours, was declining quite considerably at church services and local social and cultural events, and quite drastically in shopping locally. These changes are illustrated in Figure 12.5 (Euromosaic 1995, MacKinnon 1997a, b, 2001a, b). The problem for language planners is how to reverse these declines.

Although the political climate is – as ever – one of economy, there is now both an urgency and a vitality about Gaelic issues and Gaelic culture in Scotland. Great strides have been made in creating infrastructure for the language in education, the media and the arts. Gaeldom has successfully seized and pressed home its opportunities.

The 2001 census results announced in February 2003 indicated a slowing down of intercensal decline and some growth resulting from Gaelic-medium education. In other respects it was a 'wake-up call' for those concerned with the language. The newly appointed Gaelic language board, *Bòrd na Gàidhlig*, and the Minister for Gaelic commenced work

Generation/Interlocutor

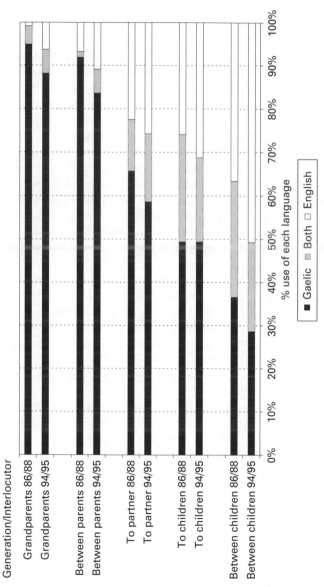

% use of each language

■ Gaelic   ▦ Both   □ English

Figure 12.4 Gaelic usage in the Western Isles by generation and interlocutor (1986–8 and 1994–5)

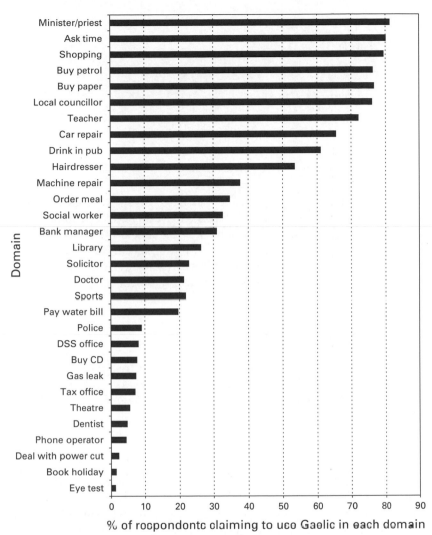

Figure 12.5 Gaelic use in the Western Isles: domain analysis based on the Euromosaic Survey 1994/5

on a National Plan for Gaelic, which was published in 2006, and a Gaelic language bill which received the royal assent in July 2005. This act took effect on 13 February 2006, gave official recognition to the language and constituted the Gaelic Language Board as a statutory public board. These and other measures may yet see the tide turn for the language.

13 Irish

Pádraig Ó Riagáin

Introduction

Until the thirteenth century speakers of Irish, together with the related languages Scottish Gaelic and Manx, formed a single speech community. Thereafter, socio-political developments fragmented the larger community and substantial morphological and phonological differences developed. These historical connections notwithstanding, in this chapter the primary focus concerns the Irish language, its history and current situation on the island of Ireland.

Linguistic history

Most scholars divide the historical development of Irish into four periods on the basis of socio-historical and/or linguistic evidence. These periods are, by convention, referred to as *Old Irish*, *Middle Irish*, *Early Modern* and *Modern Irish*.

Old Irish (500–900)

Irish appears to have been spoken in Ireland from at least the early centuries of the Christian era. While it is clear that the language was first brought to Ireland by Celtic groups migrating from continental Europe, a precise date for its introduction into the island has not been established.

The earliest written evidence of the language spoken in Ireland dates from the fifth and sixth centuries, when a form of writing known as *Ogham* was developed. This was based on the Latin alphabet and was written along the edges of stone monuments as a series of coded notches cut into the stone. The earliest written sources with continuous texts in Irish – glosses and commentaries on biblical texts – date from the seventh century. Later sources include a large number of lyric poems and epic tales. This was a fairly settled period during which the form of the written language was standardised by learned classes located in the monasteries.

From the beginning of the sixth century, Irish speakers began to colonise the western coasts of Scotland. From this base, they later expanded their territory eastwards. The colonisation process was reinforced by the activities of Irish monks who established a network of Christian monasteries throughout Scotland. Over the remainder of the first millennium, Irish became the common language of Scotland as well as Ireland.

Middle Irish (900–1200)

Both Ireland and Scotland were subjected to Viking incursions from the eighth century. By the tenth century, there were substantial settlements of Norse speakers in both countries. While their impact on the Irish language in Ireland was limited, it was more substantial among Irish speakers in Scotland. In this period a wide-ranging series of morphological changes also occurred, which by the end of the twelfth century left the language more or less in its modern form (Ó Murchú 1985), and Irish continued as the language of the learned classes in both Ireland and Scotland until the thirteenth century.

Early Modern Irish (1200–1600)

Norms in written Irish in this period were maintained by a professional class of literary scholars associated with secular schools of language and literature. While this served to ensure the standardisation of written Irish over the period, it also meant that no detailed data exist to show how the modern dialects – especially the major differentiation between Irish and Scottish Gaelic – developed (Ó Cuív 1976). The social and political circumstances which allowed this literary tradition to prosper were, however, about to decisively change.

At this time Irish was by far the dominant language spoken in Ireland. But by the sixteenth century the English kingdom, and as a consequence the English language, had established a foothold in the eastern region of Ireland.

Modern Irish

It was only a matter of time before the territorial ambitions of the English monarchy would stimulate an expansion westwards from its initial eastern base. By the early part of the seventeenth century the English system of land tenure had been successfully established and a series of plantations beginning at this time dispossessed many of the old Irish aristocratic families and introduced relatively large numbers of native-born English to form a new landlord class.

The upper classes among the native Irish had most to gain from complying with the new social and political order and, not surprisingly, it is among this class that language shift to English first occurred. Towards the end of the eighteenth and the beginning of the nineteenth centuries the upwardly mobile among the middle classes and especially the lower middle classes were also vulnerable to the social and economic pressures favouring language shift. The role of the towns, as the main locations of British military and administrative influence, were significant. Over the eighteenth century the shift to English spread through the urban network, diffusing into the rural hinterlands along a general east–west axis.

Just before the Great Famine (1846–48), 30% of the population were Irish speaking, mostly in western regions. However, in absolute terms, there were more Irish speakers alive at this time than at any other point in history. The population of Ireland in 1841 was close to eight million people, of whom some two and a half million were Irish speakers. By present-day European standards, this was a very sizeable minority. Because of the failure of food crops in the famine years, the population of Ireland declined by two and a half million due to starvation and emigration. These demographic changes were most severe in Irish-speaking areas. This not merely altered the demo-linguistic balance in Ireland, but the subsequent rise of large-scale emigration added a powerful new weight to the incentive to learn English.

There had been, since the end of the eighteenth century, a succession of learned societies concerned with the Irish language, but their interests inclined towards the scholarly investigation of medieval and early modern literature rather than contemporary issues (Ó hAilín 1969). After the Famine, however, a more active concern with the decline in the numbers of Irish speakers developed. This topic will be taken up later. However, before the discussion moves on to contemporary matters, a little should be said about the language itself.

Linguistic variation

By the end of the nineteenth century, there were three quite distinct dialect areas apparent in Ireland. These were located in scattered coastal communities to the south-west, west and north-west. They are commonly referred to as the dialects of Munster, Connacht and Ulster respectively. While it is clear that these variations had developed much earlier in history, a full reconstruction of the genesis of linguistic variation is no longer possible due to the absence of reliable data.

Present-day dialects differ at all linguistic levels. While the range of syntactic differences is small, variation in the realms of phonetics and phonology is quite large. There is clearly a continuum of dialects running from south to north, with substantial differences between northern and southern extremes. Word stress is an important phonological feature distinguishing northern dialects, which manifest a pattern of initial stress, from southern dialects, in which vowel length and stress are co-extensive (Ó Cuív 1951, Russell 1995).

However, while differences between the dialects are clearly in evidence, no one dialect had either the social or demographic weight to command respect as the standard. In addition, Irish hardly existed as a literary language in the nineteenth century. Both these features of the linguistic situation posed considerable problems for corpus planning in the twentieth century.

Phonology

As already noted, there is no agreed standard pronunciation, and this obviously makes it difficult to provide a straightforward phonological overview without simultaneously noting dialectal variations. Such detail cannot, for reasons of space, be supplied here.

The vowel system of Irish has seven short vowels, six long vowels and two diphthongs. The exact phonological character of diphthongs depends on the character of the adjacent consonants, that is, whether they are broad or slender. The consonantal system has two sets of consonants, palatal (slender) and non-palatal (broad), with considerable inter-dialectal variation.

The initial sounds of words in Irish undergo significant morphophonemic changes, called mutations, depending on how the word is being used. Perhaps the most fundamental change is lenition, a reduction in articulation affecting all single intervocalic consonants. Other initial mutations include nasalisation or eclipsis, together with minor mutations that prefix *h-* or *t-* to vowels or *t-* to initial *s-*.

The most significant features distinguishing Irish (and Scottish Gaelic) from other Insular Celtic languages (especially Welsh) are also primarily phonological. The features which mark out Irish in this context are: (a) the stress on the initial syllable – in Welsh the stress is on the penultimate syllable, and (b) the well-known difference based on the reflex of the proto-Celtic *kw*, which in the Irish and Scottish Gaelic languages loses its velar quality and becomes a voiceless labial stop, but in Welsh and the other cases retains the velar point of articulation (see Russell 1995, Ó Dochartaigh 1992, Ball & Fife 1993 and MacAulay 1992 for a fuller discussion).

Morphology

Irish is an Indo-European language, and many current and historic features of Irish are to be found in other languages within this family. For example, the verbal systems have a full range of tenses and moods, and the series of declensions of nouns also correspond to those found in other Indo-European languages. In a comparative context, Irish is partly distinguished by its particular combination of Indo-European features, and partly by some linguistic features which are unique to it.

Irish nouns are traditionally divided into masculine and feminine. While there is a tendency for masculine nouns to end in a broad consonant and feminine nouns in a slender one, overall predictability is not strong (Russell 1995). Nouns also vary with case (nominative/accusative, genitive, dative, vocative) and number (singular and plural). There has been some erosion of the case system, with the use of the genitive declining in some dialects. Plural forms are rather fluid in the spoken language, with a variety of plural endings derived from Indo-European stems.

Pronouns vary with person (first, second and third) and number (singular and plural). The third person singular distinguishes masculine and feminine. Adjectives vary only for number, and then only when used attributively. Adjectives have comparative forms. Verb forms vary with tense, person, number and mood. There is no infinitive. Each verb has instead an associated verbal noun, generally based on the same root, which is used to fill the functions of the infinitive.

Irish has two fully conjugated verbs 'to be', distinguished both in form and function. They are traditionally known as the substantive verb and the copula. The substantive is used to express position, time and condition, to predicate most adjectives, in a variety of structures and idioms. The copula is used to predicate nouns in statements of definition and identity.

A large system of prepositions effect morphophonemic changes on following nominal objects, and many of them also undergo changes in association with the article. They coalesce with pronouns to form a conjugated system of 'prepositional pronouns' (for a fuller discussion, see Ó Dochartaigh 1992, Russell 1995).

Syntax

The standard word order is verb + subject + object (i.e. VSO). Other elements, such as adverbs and prepositional phrases, tend to follow the VSO structure, although their order can be variable. While the verb is generally assumed to be initial, it is frequently preceded by unaccented particles marking tense or type of sentence (e.g. negative, interrogative, etc.).

Irish syntax has been subject to a number of detailed analyses in recent years. (Russell (1995) provides a brief overview, and more extended discussions can be found in Ó Dochartaigh (1992), Wigger (1972), McCloskey (1979, 1985), Stenson (1981) and Ó Siadhail (1989).)

Lexicon

The Irish lexicon is basically Celtic. Beginning in the sixth century, many loanwords were borrowed from Welsh, but follow the Irish rules for internal and final lenition. In later centuries Norse, (Norman) French and Old and Middle English contributed to the development of the Irish lexicon. The loans in each case tended to reflect the cultural elements introduced by the speakers, for example, maritime words from Norse and legal and architectural words from French.

Since the seventeenth century there has been much lexical borrowing from Modern English. At the present time, this goes so far as to displace many ordinary Irish words in everyday speech and to inhibit the language's capacity to extend its vocabulary from its own resources (see Mac Eoin (1993) for a fuller discussion).

Writing and orthography

The development of a writing system for Irish, using the letters of the Roman alphabet, appears to have been completed by the end of the sixth century. Most letters of the alphabet are utilised, the exceptions being <l k q x z>. The phonetic values of the Roman letters in Irish orthography appear to have been determined by the correspondence observed by Irish monks to obtain between Latin as spoken in Britain and traditional Latin orthography.

Over the following centuries, shortcomings and anomalies of the Old Irish spelling system were gradually rectified. Lenition was signalled by generally using <h> after the consonant. Eclipsis was expressed by prefixing the appropriate voiced consonant. The expression of the contrast between broad and slender consonants was developed and refined. All of these features had appeared in use by the beginning of the Early Modern period (1200–1600) and were further consolidated when books in Irish began to be printed in the sixteenth century. This more or less standardised system of orthography continued in use until well into the twentieth century. However, by then it was clear that the original orthography had become divorced from the phonology which had evolved in the meantime (Russell 1995, Ó Murchú 1985).

Language 'Revival'

As the linguistic shift to English entered an advanced phase, a movement for the preservation of Irish emerged (Hutchinson 1987, Grote 1994). Despite the well-established dynamic of decline and the unpromising contemporary pattern of bilingualism – no more than 18% of the population were Irish speakers – the newly independent Irish state in 1922 launched a comprehensive strategy to reverse the process of shift towards English and restore Irish as the national language (Ó Riagáin 1997).

There is a good deal of confusion about the exact character and objective of Ireland's language policy. This is in no small measure due to the enduring tendency, in popular and academic discourse alike, to refer to the policy as the 'Irish Language Revival'. This is misleading. The Irish language was not extinct at the time Ireland became independent, but was spoken by a minority of the population in western areas.

There are other confusions. The objective of the so-called 'Language Revival' policy has often been taken to mean the displacement of English by Irish among the national population (Ó Cuív 1969:130). Whatever may have been the views of individual politicians or spokespersons of the language movement, the constitutional and legislative provisions made for Irish in the 1920s and 1930s do not suggest that anything other than the establishment of a bilingual state was ever envisaged. The first Constitution of Ireland in 1922, and all subsequent revisions, pointedly recognised both English and Irish as official languages of the state.

However, despite the marked regional bias in the distribution of Irish speakers at the time towards western areas, the Irish state did not legislate for a bilingual policy organised on territorial lines. While an Irish-speaking region was defined (the *Gaeltacht*) and special measures were formulated to deal with it, Irish language policy applied to the state as a whole and not just a region of it. Of course, outside the Irish-speaking areas, Irish speakers formed negligible proportions of an almost entirely English-speaking population. In this region, the bilingual policy was not, therefore, one designed to meet the needs of an already existing bilingual community, but rather it sought to create one. It is only in that qualified sense that the policy can be described as a language revival type of policy.

Language policy

A series of policy developments over the 1920s and early 1930s gave legislative content to the constitutional provisions, and a broad three-pronged strategy emerged that in essence remains the framework of language policy to this day.

One element of this strategy was to maintain Irish as the spoken language in those areas where it was still the community language. As these areas (the Gaeltacht) were among the most impoverished and remote areas in the state, this dimension of the strategy quickly took on the character of a regional economic development programme. Included in what official documents refer to as 'Gaeltacht policy' are a range of policies dealing with industrial, agricultural, housing and physical development (Ó Riagáin 1992, 1997). Administratively, provision was made to ensure that, as far as possible, state services to the Gaeltacht should be provided through the medium of Irish. The areas to which these policies applied were defined on linguistic criteria in 1926, but a drastic rezoning occurred in 1956 which greatly reduced the areas regarded as Irish speaking for policy purposes.

Elsewhere the problem, and therefore the policies, were different. Here Irish speakers were only a tiny scattered proportion of an almost entirely English-speaking population. Accordingly, the state looked to the educational system for an increase in the numbers of Irish speakers in society. Because participation rates in post-primary schools were then very low, the primary schools carried the main weight of the policy until the 1970s. The objective of the policy, as originally formulated, was not simply to make the teaching of Irish compulsory for all children from English-speaking as well as Irish-speaking homes, but to have all subjects on the curriculum taught through Irish. The policy of gaelicising the schools was increasingly effective from the 1920s up to the 1950s, at which point just over half the state's primary schools were offering an immersion programme of a full or partial type (i.e. teaching all or part of the school programme through Irish to children whose mother tongue was English). This, however, proved to be the high point. Subsequently, the amount of bilingual or immersion education declined and nowadays Irish is taught primarily as a subject. There has, however, been a revived interest in immersion education since 1970, and there are over 100 such schools now in operation. Universities and third-level institutions (apart from teacher-training colleges) were, however, only marginally the target for Irish language policies although a qualification in Irish was, and is, necessary for entry to the National University of Ireland.

Overriding both these dimensions of the strategy a third was concerned with the provision of the necessary infrastructure or context for maintenance and revival dimensions alike. This large and varied package of policies included measures to: standardise and modernise the language; directly or indirectly promote publications in Irish; provide for radio (and later television) services in Irish; provide for public notices, street signs, official documents and forms in Irish or bilingual formats; establish procedures to recruit state servants with a good knowledge of Irish; and many others.

To list the headings of individual policies does not, of course give any indication of the vigour or efficiency with which they were implemented or the size of the target populations. That matter cannot be pursued here. Suffice it to say that the range of policies incorporated within the broad strategy was very wide, ambitious and demanding when viewed against the resources of a small state coping with the problems of independence. Nevertheless, although performance was by no means uniform either between or within different language policy sectors, the strategy was implemented with a good deal of determination, commitment and some limited success between 1925 and about 1970. Since then some key elements of the strategy have been greatly modified, while at the same time the state has tried to develop other policy initiatives.

Language standardisation

In the field of corpus planning, progress has been substantial and continuous. The policy of the state required the use of Irish in public administration, in law, in education and in the media. These were domains in which Irish had not been used for centuries. As already noted, the literary tradition itself had by the nineteenth century become almost defunct and many spelling and grammatical forms were archaic by comparison with the variants used in everyday speech.

The key body to undertake further work on language reform was the Parliamentary Translation Office. This office was set up in 1922 to service parliament and, in practice, government departments generally when English documents were required in Irish translation.

Innovations in the fields of orthography and grammar began quite early in the work of this office, but it was not until after 1945 that this work was codified and published. The official guide to a new standardised spelling system was published in 1947, and this was followed in 1958 by the publication of a guide to the standardised principles of Irish grammar (see *Gramadach na Gaeilge agus Litriú na Gaeilge* (Government Publications Office 1958)). Later, in 1959, an English–Irish dictionary, incorporating the principles of the new standard forms, was published, and in 1977 an Irish–English dictionary became available. Similarly, a Terminological Committee within the Department of Education issued a series of specialised dictionaries from the 1920s onwards (for a fuller discussion of language standardisation, see Ó Murchú 1977).

Changes in societal bilingualism

Although the population of the original Irish-speaking area has declined in both absolute and relative terms, there has been an increase in the proportions of Irish speakers elsewhere and the regional distribution has changed radically. As can be seen from the percentages in Table 13.1, there has been a gradual convergence in the pattern of regional variations.

Table 13.1. *Percentage of persons claiming the ability to speak Irish by region, 1851–2002 (selected years)*

Year	Leinster (east)	Munster (south)	Connacht (west)	Ulster (north-west)	State
	%	%	%	%	%
1851	3.5	43.9	50.8	17.0	29.1
1901	2.3	25.7	38.0	20.7	19.2
1946	15.1	22.0	33.2	26.0	21.2
1981	28.1	34.6	38.8	30.8	31.6
1991	30.5	36.3	40.1	32.0	32.5
1996	37.4	45.4	48.2	39.3	41.1
2002	38.2	46.8	48.5	39.4	41.9

Source: Central Statistics Office (2004:12).

(It should be noted that the census language question was changed in 1996 (see Ó Riagáin 2001), but this does not invalidate the conclusions drawn here.)

In the mid-nineteenth century, the regions in the south and west contained the most extensive Irish-speaking districts but these were, even then, contracting. Since 1926, there has been a gradual, but continual, revival in the ratios of Irish speakers, particularly among residents of the eastern region. As there has also been a shift in the regional distribution of population over the period towards the east (and to towns generally), the combined result of these two trends has been to move the spatial concentration of Irish speakers eastwards as well. About 50% of Irish speakers now reside in Leinster (including Dublin), compared with about 5% in 1851. Therefore, the overall trend has been for the proportion of Irish speakers in all regions to converge towards the national average.

Table 13.2, which presents the percentages of Irish speakers (as defined in census data) in each age group, allows the changes in patterns of language reproduction since 1926 to be broadly identified. The age-specific data show that the national increase in the proportion of Irish speakers was primarily caused by a continual improvement – since the 1920s – in the proportion of young adult cohorts claiming the ability to speak Irish.

The pattern for 1926 is bi-modal, peaking around the 10–20-year-old group and again among the over 65s. It is clear that, even then, two processes of language change were operating. The relatively higher percentages among the older age groups reflect the typical pattern found in communities where a language is in decline, while the higher percentages within younger age groups reflect the initial impact of revival strategies.

228   *Pádraig Ó Riagáin*

Table 13.2. *Percentage of persons with ability to speak Irish by age group (selected years 1926–2002)*

Age group	1926	1946	1981	2002
	%	%	%	%
3–4	4.6	4.1	4.9	10.3
5–9	19.8	21.6	27.8	51.3
10–14	39.2	47.5	50.8	68.7
15–19	27.6	43.4	51.0	66.3
20–24	15.8	32.2	40.0	51.2
25–34	13.2	20.8	32.8	39.1
35–44	11.9	11.2	30.0	35.5
45–54	13.7	10.0	28.3	38.5
55–64	16.9	9.5	22.9	34.6
65+	25.1	11.9	13.0	31.2
Total (over 3 years)	18.3	21.2	31.6	42.8

Source: Central Statistics Office (2004:26).

By 2002, the pattern revealed by the census data had become most unusual, if not unique, as compared to other minority language situations. The largest proportion of Irish speakers is to be found in the 10–19-year-old age groups, after which it consistently becomes smaller.

The census evidence (Ó Riagáin 1997) would strongly suggest that only 3% of the population of the state lived in Irish-speaking districts in 1926 and, at most, another 3% lived in bilingual districts (both referred to as Gaeltacht districts). There was a significant fall in population in all Gaeltacht districts between 1925 and 1970, and language shift in bilingual areas was not stabilised. Furthermore, after 1970, the original core areas themselves became unstable in linguistic terms. Social interaction systems shifted very considerably in the period since 1970, due to changes in demographic, occupational, educational, retailing and car ownership patterns. Until this point, social networks in Gaeltacht areas tended to be localised, and this worked in favour of language maintenance. Since 1970, social networks have become increasingly more extensive and differentiated. Nowadays, people may only reside in rural areas, but work, attend school and shop elsewhere. Migration into the small Irish-speaking districts is one of the main reasons for the substantial, but very recent changes in bilingual reproduction levels (Ó Riagáin 1992).

Nonetheless, in the post-1970 Gaeltacht districts the use of Irish as measured by language surveys is still very much higher than the national average. Census data would suggest that 40% of persons resident in these areas in 2002 speak Irish on a daily basis – compared to 9% nationally. However, the Gaeltacht accounts for only 2.3% of the national population, the districts are small and scattered and significant proportions of Gaeltacht residents are not Irish speakers.

But bilingual trends in these small western areas do not, of course, tell the whole story. The research evidence consistently indicates that the most significant achievement of the policy in other areas since the 1920s has been an increase in moderate bilingual abilities. In the 2002 Census of Population some 40% claimed the ability to speak Irish, and similar proportions in national surveys (42%) claim at least some ability to read Irish (Ó Riagáin 1997). However, the shift was mostly to levels of moderate ability (i.e. able to speak 'a few simple sentences' and 'parts of conversations'). This level of ability did not typically express itself in active use of Irish in conversation, but in passive, non-reciprocal activities. In 2001, about 10% of the population watched some Irish language programme on television weekly and up to 45% watched such programmes at least occasionally (Ó Riagáin, in press).

But only about 10% of national survey respondents claim levels of speaking ability in Irish that approach or reach real fluency in the language (Ó Riagáin 1997, Ó Riagáin in press). Even smaller proportions report extensive use of Irish in their homes, neighbourhood or at work. The proportion who use Irish as their first or main language is clearly no higher than, and probably under, 5%. Nonetheless, at this aggregated level, these figures, when taken in conjunction with those of the Gaeltacht, suggest an overall measure of stability compared to the position in the first quarter of the century.

However, if the spatial, demographic and social distribution of Irish speakers is taken into account, this tentative conclusion of stability becomes less plausible. Outside of the small Gaeltacht districts, Irish-speaking families are scattered throughout English-speaking areas. They do not form a fully-fledged community (i.e. capable of supporting a full range of social domains) at any non-Gaeltacht location. Not surprisingly, the ability of Irish-speaking networks to reproduce themselves is limited by their distribution, number and size. Overall, both within and outside the Gaeltacht, bilingual reproduction is extremely problematical. In fact, when census data are classified by age, it becomes clear that the national increase in the proportion of Irish speakers was primarily caused by a continual improvement – since the 1920s – in the proportion of young adult cohorts able to speak Irish. But in view of the small number of Irish-speaking homes, it is clear that the above average ratios of Irish speakers in young adult groups is generated by the schools rather than home or community bilingualism.

As all children in the first- and second-level education systems are obliged to follow courses in Irish, most children study prescribed courses in Irish from the age of four until they are about eighteen. Although over time the proportion of Irish speakers in older adult cohorts has improved and continues to improve, the improvement is much smaller than the ratio of Irish speakers in school-age cohorts would suggest. Replies to survey questions appear to indicate that social use of Irish – as distinct from its use in the school classroom – is also highest among school-going age groups. As these cohorts leave the education system, many stop speaking Irish. This pattern of slippage across the life cycle of bilingual individuals reflects the tenuous position of bilingualism in Ireland.

Furthermore, since 1980 only 10–15% of school-age cohorts opt for the higher-level courses in Irish in post-primary schools and, even after thirteen years' study of the subject, the speaking ability of the majority of the cohort is only moderate or, in the case of a growing minority, negligible (Advisory Planning Committee 1986). While the immersion sector is showing signs of a revival since 1970, it is still too small to greatly affect the national pattern.

Attitudes towards Irish

Throughout the nineteenth and early twentieth centuries the economic and political incorporation of Ireland into the wider British system intensified. Language shift occurred in circumstances that created very unfavourable views of the utility of Irish among the public and the clearly visible evidence of language shift reinforced these views. However, since the early part of this century the counter-process of a language revival movement and state intervention has cut across this process of decline contesting, but not eliminating, the earlier perspectives. Thus the relationship between the Irish language and ethnic identity on the one hand, and perceptions of its limited value as cultural capital on the other, form two opposing perspectives which determine attitudes towards policy. Support for Irish language is higher in many respects than the objective position of the Irish language in society would appear to justify, yet it is not high enough in regard to the strongly interventionist policy options which could significantly alter the linguistic picture.

Public support for Irish is shown to be very positive when attitudinal questions in surveys tap into the role the Irish language is perceived to have in defining and maintaining national cultural distinctiveness (CILAR 1975, Ó Riagáin 1997). While there is a weak relationship between this dimension of the attitudinal system and actual language use, it is positively and strongly related to levels of public support for language policies.

Successive surveys have shown that a majority of the public support policies to maintain Irish in the Gaeltacht, to provide Irish language services on the national television channels, to use Irish on public notices etc., to provide state services in Irish and officials who could speak Irish and to support the voluntary Irish language organisations. In all of these matters, there was an increase in public support between 1973 and 1993 (Ó Riagáin 1997). Thus, the general population is willing to accept a considerable commitment of state resources to ensuring its continuance and even to support the imposition of legal requirements to know or use Irish on certain groups within the society, such as teachers and civil servants.

For most people, it is within the educational system that they have the most direct contact with Irish language policy. Not surprisingly, given the relationship between educational achievements and the qualifications needed for entry into the largely English-speaking labour market, the public are not prepared to support policies which would discriminate strongly in favour of Irish in the school system. While the policy presently in operation is supported by a large majority, this policy does no more than ensure that Irish is kept on the curriculum of all recognised schools. It does not, by and large, produce large numbers of competent bilinguals and, on the other hand, the sanctions incorporated in the policy appear unable to prevent a steady growth in the proportion of pupils who either fail the subject in state examinations or do not present for the Irish paper at all (Advisory Planning Committee 1988). The attitudes to school Irish suggest that where policies directly affect respondents' own material opportunities, or those of their children, they lose majority support. However, although only about one-quarter of the public would support more intensive programmes, this is significantly larger than the percentages of pupils (about 5%) currently being accommodated in these types of programmes.

Therefore, although a majority of the Irish public would appear to espouse some form of bilingual objective, the evidence from surveys would suggest that many of this majority seek at best to simply maintain the status of Irish in the Gaeltacht, in artistic life and within the low levels of social bilingualism now pertaining. The survey evidence would indicate that this viewpoint is now the dominant consideration for those favouring a general bilingual objective (Ó Riagáin 1997, in press).

Economic development and language policy

The modernisation of Irish society, a process which developed slowly prior to 1960, exerted a powerful influence on language policy in subsequent years. With the rapid growth of economic prosperity since 1970 has come a widening of economic, political, demographic and cultural contacts and influences as Ireland became more comprehensively incorporated within the framework of international capitalism. These external influences, with their various and differentiated impacts on Irish society, have created severe problems for policies designed to maintain Irish as a minority language.

Irish language policy, particularly in the period 1922–60, succeeded to the extent it directly or indirectly changed the 'rules' of the social mobility process. It is the relationship between educational qualifications and the labour market – and not pedagogic factors per se – which is crucial to understanding the effectiveness of Irish language policies in the schools. The Irish economy before 1960 was dominated by family businesses – mostly in farming – and the self-employed (Breen, Hannan, Rottman & Whelan 1990). Job opportunities for those with cultural rather than economic capital were very limited. Therefore, participation rates in post-primary education were low. Yet research studies have consistently shown that the education system's capacity to produce competent bilinguals was closely related to the number of years an individual spent in school and, of course, the type of language programme followed.

The selective impact of language policy in the schools was reinforced by policies regulating entry to the professions (via third-level education) and the public service. As a consequence the percentages of Irish speakers in both sets of occupations increased after 1922 (Ó Riagáin 1997). But Irish language policy was relatively ineffectual in the case of those labour market sectors where entry depended on inheritance rather than educational qualifications. Thus the very limited degree of social mobility in Ireland in these early decades placed some severe limitations on the social impact of Irish language policy.

The new economic policy, which was elaborated in a series of economic development programmes between 1960 and the early 1970s, placed emphasis on export markets and foreign industrial investment. Education was primarily seen as a form of investment within the context of economic growth. In short, the modern industry targeted by the economic programmes required a well-educated labour force. A range of new policies led to huge increases in second-level participation rates, and simultaneously the number and range of third-level institutions was widened. Meanwhile, as a more direct consequence of the economic programmes, the range of employment opportunities outside the professions and the public sector expanded. Thus the relationship between education and the labour market was consolidated and extended, but the state was unable to adapt the scope of its language policies to regulate these new developments. In fact, it effectively gave up the struggle. In 1973, Irish ceased to be a compulsory subject for examinations or a requirement for entry to the public service. These societal trends thus severely reduced the institutional support for Irish and the reproduction of high levels of ability in certain key social groups (Advisory Planning Committee 1988).

However, some elements of the original policy continue to operate. Irish must still be included on the curriculum of schools in receipt of state support and it remains necessary for entry to the four colleges of the National University of Ireland. As post-primary education became more widely available, parents in the upper social classes increasingly sought third-level education for their children as a means of maintaining their class advantage. Thus, the Irish language requirement for entry to the universities maintained the class element in language reproduction, and with rising participation rates in both second- and third-level education the class base of Irish speakers has widened.

It is important to note that, while the Gaeltacht is located in peripheral rural areas, it too was directly affected by these changes in economic structures. As late as 1961 nearly three-quarters of males in these areas were working in agriculture, but by 1981 agriculture was employing less than half of the workforce, while other sectors had grown proportionately and in absolute terms (Ó Riagáin 1992).

Social reproduction and Irish-speaking networks

The significance of socioeconomic trends for language reproduction arises from their impact on Irish-speaking networks and communities. The available research evidence indicates that the small farm economy of Gaeltacht areas supported a pattern of social networks which were very localised and restricted in spatial scope in the first half of the twentieth century. The relative stability of these network boundaries was an important factor in sustaining Irish-speaking communities. As economic development began to percolate into rural areas in the post-1970 period, a major transformation of social network patterns occurred which served to intensify the frequency of interactions between Irish speakers and English speakers. As a consequence, the overall proportion of Irish-speaking families has been declining (Ó Riagáin 1992).

Outside Gaeltacht areas, the relationship between social class and Irish has been a significant factor in the formation of Irish-speaking networks in these English-language regions. The spatial distribution of bilinguals varies with the class character of residential areas and, therefore, spatial variations in the distribution of Irish speakers are apparent in large urban areas (Ó Riagáin 1997:242). The social concentration of high ability Irish speakers within the middle classes and, in particular, within the public sector, facilitated the formation and maintenance of Irish-speaking networks. The capacity of these networks to attract 'novice' or 'reluctant' bilinguals is evidence that Irish-speaking networks are capable, in these circumstances at least, of recruiting new members.

Irish in Northern Ireland

The preceding discussion relates the position of the Irish language in the Republic of Ireland. The history of the language in the north-eastern part of the island in the twentieth century has been different. Northern Ireland consists of the six north-eastern counties of the island of Ireland which remained part of the United Kingdom after 1922.

Northern Ireland, as a semi-autonomous region within the UK, was a contested entity from the outset, a site for tension and conflict between the two competing nationalisms present in early twentieth-century Ireland – one being an Irish nationalism and the other a British nationalism. Whereas in the island as a whole, adherents to a British nationalism were in a minority, in the new Northern Ireland they were in a majority and nearly entirely Protestant. Adherents to an Irish nationalism were mostly Catholics and in a minority. Since 1922, the positions taken up by Catholics and Protestants regarding the significance of the Irish language within politics and society has been sharply polarised.

Prior to the separation of the six counties from the rest of Ireland, Irish was recognised as an extra and optional school subject in all of Ireland, including Northern Ireland. Andrews (1991) has estimated that it was taught to about 8% of primary school pupils overall at this time, but this represented some 25% of Catholic, and practically no Protestant, pupils.

With a permanent Protestant majority in the Northern Ireland Parliament after 1922, Unionist values dominated educational policy, and in language policy the aim was assimilation. The result was a reduction in the number of pupils learning Irish. The situation then remained unchanged for almost forty years (Andrews 1991:95). Irish had no legal status in Northern Ireland throughout this period. In these decades, those wishing to learn Irish had to rely on the informal educational activities of the Gaelic League, together with some partial, and 'relatively limited development' within Catholic schools (Maguire 1991:46).

At the official level, this situation did not begin to significantly change until 1989, when Irish was recognised as a 'foreign language' on the same level as French, German or Spanish in post-primary schools. In the 2001 census, 19.3% of all 12–15-year-olds were returned as Irish speakers. Of these, 95.2% were Catholic and 4.8% were Protestant. However, while nearly all Irish speakers in this age group were Catholic, it should also be noted that they comprised only 23% of all Catholics in this age group.

In a survey of 1,000 adult respondents in 2000–2001, it was found that about 30% of Catholics claim high or partial levels of ability to speak Irish, while hardly any Protestants (5%) claim any level of ability whatsoever, even 'the odd word' is rarely claimed.

But Northern Ireland Catholics do not see Irish as a central element of Northern Irish identity, and a certain degree of polarisation is apparent in some of the survey findings, especially those dealing with education. This disagreement about basic policy options reflects internal divisions among Catholics, not only about the language issue in general, but also about identity.

Protestants generally speaking describe themselves as either indifferent or hostile to the Irish language. Nonetheless, they cannot be regarded in monolithic terms any more than Catholics can. While very few Protestants want their own children to learn Irish, a sizeable minority is prepared to see public resources made available so that others can do so (see Ó Riagáin, in press, for details).

Future directions

At the political level it is not surprising to find state agencies now speaking more of survival rather than revival. The principal realignment of policy over the past two decades has been a move towards the maintenance dimension of the original strategy and a consequent weakening emphasis on revival. The practical focus of policy is directed at the provision of certain basic state services in and through Irish, i.e. Irish-language schools, television and radio stations, sections of public offices, etc. Even from the perspective of maintenance, there are dangers in this development. A policy built around the provision of state services to Irish speakers may find that they do not exist in large enough numbers nor are they sufficiently concentrated to meet the operational thresholds required to make these services viable. But, as Tovey (1988) points out, the more policy singles out 'Irish speakers' as the target for language policies on the grounds of their rights as a minority group, the less plausible it becomes to sustain the residual policies to revive Irish.

In all of these respects, one feels that Irish language policy is now at a critical stage. To further complicate the issue, Irish language policy has emerged as a key element in the Northern Ireland peace process. Under the terms of the peace agreement concluded in April 1998 (the 'Good Friday' Agreement), a new all-Ireland language policy agency was established to oversee language policy in both the Republic and Northern Ireland. This will bring together, as part of one policy operation, two very different Irish-language situations. The Irish language is very much part of the nationalist programme in Northern Ireland, while the Republic has already moved into a post-nationalist phase. On the other hand, despite all the foregoing analysis of its weaknesses, the Irish language is considerably stronger in the Republic than it is in Northern Ireland. It remains to be seen whether the political impulse from the North will give language policy overall new energy, or whether the less intensive language policy in the North will become the norm towards which policy in the Republic will invariably drift.

14   Welsh

Martin Ball

Introduction

Welsh is a Celtic language, belonging to the Brythonic group along with Cornish (effectively extinct in the early nineteenth century, though spoken today by numbers of enthusiasts; see George 1993) and Breton (spoken in Brittany, see Stephens 1993, Humphreys 1993). Census figures (see National Statistics Online 2003)[1] confirm that Welsh is the liveliest of the modern Celtic languages, both in terms of actual numbers of speakers (575,168), and in terms of percentage of speakers within the political boundaries of the country (20.5%). We will be looking in more detail at issues of language maintenance and language planning later in this chapter.

Welsh has also been subject to more linguistic research than other Celtic languages. A flavour of the studies undertaken in book form can be given here, the large numbers of journal articles being impossible to refer to. The phonetics of the language is the subject of a recent publication (Ball & Williams 2001), but there is also the traditional transcription primer of Jones (1926). Welsh phonology was the focus of a collection published in 1984 (Ball & Jones), while there have been several studies in a variety of theoretical approaches to syntax (for example, Awbery 1976, Jones & Thomas 1977, Sadler 1987, Rouveret 1994). Fife (1990) investigated the semantics of the verb, and a traditional descriptive grammar appeared in 1996 (Thomas) (though see also King 1993 and Williams 1980), while the mutations of Welsh were the focus of a study by Ball & Müller (1992). Sociolinguistic studies have also appeared (Ball 1988), and those concentrating on regional dialects, for example Awbery (1986), Thomas & Thomas (1989) and G. Jones (2000).

---

[1] National Statistics Online at http://www.statistics.gov.uk/downloads/census2001/Report_on_the_Welsh_language.pdf

Language description

In this section we will provide a brief description of the phonology, morphology, mutations and syntax of the modern standard language, concentrating on the main characteristics of these areas.[2]

Phonology

Northern standard pronunciation of Welsh will form the basis of this section as the phonological system is larger than in southern varieties. Where these differ, this will be noted in the relevant places.

The consonant system comprises contrastive units in the plosive, nasal, fricative, affricate, trill and approximant categories. There are six plosive phonemes: /p b t d k g/, with fortis plosives strongly aspirated and the lenis subject to devoicing. One can also posit six contrastive nasal stops: /m̥ m n̥ n ŋ̊ ŋ/. However, as the so-called 'voiceless' nasals occur only as mutation reflexes of fortis plosives (see section 'Mutations' below), so it is normal to classify them as clusters of the nasal plus /h/.

Welsh has eight contrastive fricatives: fortis-lenis pairs at the labio-dental and dental positions, and voiceless fricatives at the alveolar, post-alveolar, velar/uvular and glottal places: /f v θ ð s ʃ x h/. A voiced alveolar fricative may be used in some loanwords from English, especially by southern speakers (e.g. *sŵ* /su/ ~ /zu/, 'zoo'). The lenis fricatives are usually subject to considerable devoicing. The glottal fricative is often omitted in casual speech in southern varieties.

Affricates at the postalveolar position (/tʃ dʒ/) are found in the language, but are the result of borrowings from English or are speech rate variants of clusters of /t/+/j/ or /d/+/j/.

Welsh has a series of four liquids: a voiced and a voiceless trill, a voiced lateral approximant and a voiceless lateral fricative (for the sake of symmetry we class the lateral fricative here with the lateral approximant; this is supported by morphosyntactic alternations between the two): /r r̥ʰ l ɬ/. The trills are alveolar, and the voiceless trill is normally followed by aspiration, but in southern varieties it is merged with its voiced counterpart.

Finally, the language has two central approximants, the labio-velar /w/ and the palatal /j/. Both approximants have fortis variants in certain morphosyntactic contexts (e.g. *iaith* [jaiθ] 'language' ~ *ei hiaith* [i hjaiθ] 'her language'; *wats* [watʃ] 'watch' ~ *ei hwats* [i hwatʃ] 'her watch'), but these are normally considered to be clusters of /h/ plus the approximant.

---

[2] For a fuller sketch of the language see Thomas (1992) or Watkins (1993).

The vowel system is large in northern varieties, with 13 monophthongs and 13 diphthongs. Southern varieties have smaller systems, however, with a formal register probably distinguishing 11 monophthongs and 8 diphthongs. Monophthongs are normally paired in descriptions of the language into phonologically long and short vowels.

The short vowels are /ɪ ɛ a ɔ ʊ ɨ/ and the long vowels are /i e ɑ o u ɨ/. There is also an unpaired mid-central vowel /ə/ which, unlike schwa in English, can appear in stressed syllables. It should be noted that generally only northern varieties of Welsh retain the high central vowels, in southern varieties they are merged with the short and long high front vowels.

The northern diphthong system has three glides moving towards the high front position, five glides moving towards a high back position, and five moving towards a high central position. These are /aɪ ɔɪ əɪ/, /ɪʊ ɛʊ aʊ əʊ ɨʊ/ and /aɨ ɑɨ ɔɨ ʊɨ əɨ/.

In southern varieties, the diphthongs with a close central element replace that with a close front one. This gives us two subsystems: four glides to a high front position and four to a high back position: /aɪ ɔɪ ʊɪ əɪ/ and /ɪʊ ɛʊ aʊ əʊ/.

One final aspect of segmental phonology we can consider is phonotactics. We do not have the space to go into this in any great detail (see Awbery 1984 for a thorough treatment), but Table 14.1 shows some possible consonant clusters (adapted from Ball & Williams 2001).

There are also constraints on phonologically long and short vowels and coda consonants, some of which differ between varieties (see Awbery 1984).

Table 14.1. *Some consonant clusters of Welsh*

Syllable type	Consonant type	Examples
CCV*	obstruent+obstruent	sb sd sg
	obstruent+sonorant	kn tr dr tl fr gl
VCCV	obstruent+obstruent	gv xg ɬd
	sonorant+sonorant	rm rl mn
	sonorant+obstruent	ŋg mð rd rθ
	obstruent+sonorant	dn br vn
VCC	obstruent+obstruent	sg ɬd
	sonorant+sonorant	rn rm
	sonorant+obstruent	mp rd rð lx
	obstruent+sonorant[†]	dr br vn
CCCV	/s/+stop+liquid	sdr sgl

* Excluding mutation reflexes (see 'Mutations' below).
† Except in very formal speech these clusters are normally separated by a copy epenthetic vowel in southern varieties.

Minimal pairs with these vowels are possible only in syllables closed with /m n ŋ l r/.

Suprasegmental aspects of Welsh phonology have not been studied to such an extent as segmental (though see Ball & Williams 2001 and references cited within). Word stress in Welsh is regularly on the penult with a small number of exceptions. Interestingly, however, major pitch movements of the intonation system take place on the final syllable of accented words and so pitch and stress are separated. Major pitches have been described by several authors (Thomas 1967, Pilch 1975, Rhys 1984, Ball & Williams 2001). The consensus view is that the language has four broad categories of pitch movement: fall, rise, rise-fall and level.

Morphology

Welsh has a rich system of derivational morphology; however, we do not have the space to describe this (see Williams 1980, Thomas 1996). Inflectional morphology is also of interest with, as with the other Celtic languages, the unusual features of inflected prepositions. We will look briefly at the main word classes displaying inflectional morphology.

Determiner Welsh has a single, definite, article. This has three forms: *yr* /ər/ before a vowel, *'r* after a vowel, and *y* /ə/ elsewhere.

Nouns A large variety of ways of forming plurals from singulars exist. They fall into two broad categories: those involving a vowel change to the singular form, and those involving the addition of a suffix (possibly with a vowel change as well). In addition we can note certain mass nouns where the base form is plural in meaning and singulars are formed by adding a singulative suffix. It should be noted that singular forms of nouns are used after numerals (e.g. *pum dafad* 'five sheep'), though an alternative construction is possible, especially with higher numbers: *cant o ddefaid*, 'hundred of sheep', 'a hundred sheep'.

Nouns are grouped into two genders: masculine and feminine. While there is no general morphological marker of gender, certain semantic classes, derivational classes and phonological shapes are more likely to belong to one gender than to the other. Gender is also shown in the choice of pronouns, demonstratives and the morphological form of some adjectives. Finally, noun gender has implications for consonant mutation, which we return to below. Examples are *y dyn bychan hwn* 'the man small this' 'this small man', vs. *yr wraig fechan hon* 'the woman small this' 'this small woman'.

Pronouns Personal pronouns do not distinguish subject and object forms. Nevertheless, a wide range of personal pronoun forms exist, including reduplicated (emphatic) forms (e.g. *myfi* 'I, me'), conjunctive forms (e.g. *minnau* 'and me'), possessives (e.g. *fy* 'my') and infixed forms used in certain verbal constructions (e.g. *'m* 'me, my'). The basic set, with colloquial spellings in parenthesis are as follows: *mi, fi* (i) 'I/me'; *ti, di* 'you' singular; *ef, fe, fo, (e, o)* 'he/him, it'; *hi* 'she/her, it'; *ni* 'we'; *chwi (chi)* 'you' plural; *hwy (nhw)* 'they/them'.

Adjectives and adverbs Certain adjectives inflect for number and for gender, although both plural and feminine forms are often replaced by the masculine singular forms in less formal varieties of the language (except for in some set phrases). Examples of masculine, feminine and plural forms are as follows: *bychan, bechan, bychain* 'small', *gwyrdd, gwerdd, gwyrddion* 'green', *trwm, trom, trymion* 'heavy'. Some adjectives have a plural form but no feminine form: *tlawd, tlodion* 'poor'.

Inflections are used to form the comparative, superlative and equative ('as x as') degrees. For example, *gwyn* 'white'; *gwynnach* 'whiter'; *gwynnaf* 'whitest'; *gwynned* '(as) white (as)'. It is usual for polysyllabic adjectives to be compared periphrastically.

Adverbs derived from adjectives are the same as them in form, and follow the verb after a predicative particle (*yn*). The example here uses *cyflym* 'fast, quick': *dyn cyflym* ~ *mae'r dyn yn cerdded yn gyflym*, 'a fast man' ~ 'the man is walking quickly'. (Note that the difference between the form *cyflym* and *gyflym* is due to the operation of consonant mutation discussed below.)

Numerals The numerals 2–4 inflect for gender, and while *un* 'one' does not, it does cause soft mutation to feminine nouns but not to masculine. The forms of 'two' are *dau* masc., *dwy* fem.; of 'three' are *tri* masc., *tair* fem.; and of 'four' are *pedwar* masc., *pedair* fem. The numbers 1–10 are: *un, dau, tri, pedwar, pump, chwech, saith, wyth, naw, deg*; 100 is *cant*, and 1,000 is *mil*.

The traditional numeral system of the literary language is based on several competing bases: a base-twenty (20: *ugain*, 40: *deugain*, 60: *trigain*, 80: *pedwar ugain*), a base-ten (11: *un ar ddeg*, 12: *deuddeg*, 13: *tri ar ddeg*, 14: *pedwar ar ddeg*, 15 *pymtheg*), a base-nine (18: *deunaw*), and a base-fifteen (15: *pymtheg*, 16: *un ar bymtheg*, 17: *dau ar bymtheg*, 19: *pedwar ar bymtheg*). In many local varieties speakers often shift to English numerals for higher numbers, especially when reckoning amounts of money. A decimal system has been used in schools for many years (e.g. 11: *un deg un*, 12: *un deg dau*, etc).

Verbs Verbs inflect for person in four tenses in the indicative mood (present/future, past, imperfect/conditional and pluperfect), two in the subjunctive (present and imperfect) and a single present tense in the imperative mood. There is no passive voice, but each tense has an impersonal form, and periphrastic constructions with passive semantics can also be used. Both phonologically and semantically there are many differences between the literary language and spoken varieties as regards the tense system. The verb 'to be' (*bod*) is highly irregular and manifests more tenses than regular verbs, but also morphological variants linked to definiteness of the subject and form of the sentence (e.g. positive vs. negative, question vs. statement).

Aspect is marked periphrastically by using forms of the verb *bod* with a variety of aspect markers that are derived from prepositions: *mae Dafydd yn mynd*, 'Dafydd is going' (progressive, *yn* 'in'); *mae Dafydd wedi mynd* 'Dafydd has gone' (perfective, *wedi* 'after'); *mae Dafydd am fynd* 'Dafydd wishes to go' (volitional, *am* 'for'); etc. Periphrastic forms of all tenses are increasingly commonly heard in the spoken language as alternatives to the inflected tenses. Note that the third person plural is used only with the third person plural pronoun; plural nouns take the third person singular: *canodd Ieuan, canodd y dynion, canan nhw*, 'Ieuan sang, the men sang, they sang'.

For regular and irregular verbal paradigms see Williams (1980), Watkins (1993) or Thomas (1996).

Prepositions A range of common prepositions are inflected for person. In the literary language these forms may drop the following personal pronoun, but in the spoken varieties the pronoun is normally retained. There are several different sets of endings, for example, *ar* 'on', *arnoch* 'on you'; *tros* 'over', *trosto*, 'over him'.

Mutations

Mutations are phonological changes to word-initial consonants that are triggered by a range of morphosyntactic contexts. A full account of mutations and the environments that trigger them is given in Ball & Müller (1992), but we can give a brief description here. There are three main sets of consonants changes: soft mutation (SM) or lenition, nasal mutation (NM) and aspirate mutations (AM) or spirantisation. Table 14.2 shows the changes in orthography and phonology.

Common triggering environments for these mutations are as follows:

SM: feminine singular noun after the article, after the numeral *un*; adjective following feminine singular noun; word following *ei* 'his', *dy* 'your' sing.; words following

Table 14.2. *Initial consonant mutations*

Radical		Soft mutation		Nasal mutation		Aspirate mutation	
p	p	b	b	mh	m^h	ph	f
t	t	d	d	nh	n^h	th	θ
c	k	g	g	ngh	$ŋ^h$	ch	x
b	b	f	v	m	m		
d	d	dd	ð	n	n		
g	g	deleted	–	ng	ŋ		
m	m	f	v				
ll	ɫ	l	l				
rh	$r̥^h$	r	r				

N.B. Unfilled cells mean that the mutation does not change the radical in these cases.

a range of common prepositions; verbs following a range of preverbal particles (e.g. marking questions, statements, negatives); items following a range of numeral forms (e.g. *dau/dwy* 'two', *ail* 'second'); adjectives following the complementiser *yn* (but not verbs); direct object of an inflected verb (but not of a periphrastic construction), and adverbials of time, among numerous others.
NM: words following *fy* 'my'; nouns following the preposition *yn* 'in'; various set expressions with numerals and time expressions.
AM: words following *ei* 'her'; words following a range of prepositions (*â, gyda* 'with', *tua* 'towards'); words following various negative particles; words following the numerals *tri* 'three' masc., *chwech* 'six', and the adverb *tra* 'very'.

A feature called prevocalic aspiration by Ball & Müller (1992) can also occur in some contexts, and here an /h/ is added to vowel-initial words, for example, following *ei, ein, eu* 'her, our, their'.

Syntax

Sentence The basic clause pattern in Welsh is VSO: *gwelodd Ieuan Iona*, 'saw Ieuan Iona', 'Ieuan saw Iona', though this order can be altered to achieve focus on specific items (e.g. *Iona a welodd Ieuan*, 'Iona that saw Ieuan', '(it was) Iona that Ieuan saw'). A set of preverbal particles is available that denote questions and negatives; some of these are generally omitted in the spoken language, while emphatic particles for positive statements are more common in the spoken than literary form.

EMPHATIC: *Fe/Mi welodd Ieuan Iona*, 'Ieuan *did* see Iona' (*fe* commoner in the south, *mi* commoner in the north)
NEGATIVE: *Ni welodd Ieuan Iona*, 'Ieuan did not see Iona'; colloquial: *(Ni) welodd Ieuan mo Iona* (*mo* is assumed to derive from *ddim o* 'nothing of'. With an indefinite object we get *(ni) welodd Ieuan ddim tai newydd yn y stryd*, 'Ieuan didn't see any new houses in the street').

INTERROGATIVE: *A welodd Ieuan Iona?* 'Did Ieuan see Iona?' In spoken varieties the *a* is often omitted with intonation and mutation alone carrying the question form.
NEGATIVE INTERROGATIVE: *Oni welodd Ieuan Iona?* 'Didn't Ieuan see Iona?' Colloquially this could appear as *Welodd Ieuan mo Iona?*
Question words precede the inflected verb: *pryd welodd Ieuan Iona?* 'when did Ieuan see Iona?'

Verb phrase In periphrastic and modal verbal constructions the inflected (or 'tensed') verb is in initial position, while the verb-noun (equivalent of the infinitive) is post-subject. For example: *fe fydd Ieuan yn gweld Iona*, 'part. will Ieuan see Iona', 'Ieuan will see Iona'; *gall Ieuan weld Iona*, 'can Ieuan see Iona', 'Ieuan can see Iona'. In these constructions, if the direct object is a personal pronoun, a possessive construction is found (see below for further details of possessives): *fe fydd Ieuan yn ei gweld hi*, 'part. will Ieuan part. her see she', 'Ieuan will see her'.

Subordinate clauses When subordinate clauses are taking an adverbial role, a tensed verb follows the subordinator: *rwy'n gwybod pwy oedd yn y tŷ*, 'am part. know who was in the house', 'I know who was in the house'. In instances where the subordinate clause has a subject, this can be expressed with a prepositional phrase: *cyn y cododd Ieuan, dechreuodd hi'n bwrw eira/cyn i Ieuan godi, dechreuodd hi'n bwrw eira*, 'before part. rose Ieuan began she part. throw snow/before to Ieuan rise, began she part. throw snow', 'before Ieuan rose it began to snow'.
Clauses taking roles other than adverbial are introduced with *y(r)/a/na(d)* for positive statement, negative, and interrogatives respectively. For example: *rwy'n gwybod y daw (e)/dwi ddim yn siwr a ddaw e/rwy'n siwr na ddaw e*, 'I know he will come/I'm not sure he will come/I'm sure he won't come'.

Noun phrase The order of elements in a noun phrase in Welsh is determiner+numeral+head-noun+adjectives after which follow any post-modifying prepositional phrases or clauses. For example: *Y tri dyn hyll yn y stryd a oedd yn canu* ... 'the three man ugly in the street who were part. sing', 'the three ugly men in the street who were singing ...'
Constructions with personal possessives can have a possessor before the noun, and a personal pronoun following. In the literary language the copy pronoun is often omitted, whereas in the spoken language the possessor is often omitted: *fy nhŷ (i)/'nhŷ i* 'my house'; *ei dŷ (ef)/'dŷ e* 'his house'; *ei thŷ (hi)/'thŷ hi* 'her house'; *ein tŷ (ni)/'tŷ ni* 'our house'.

Varieties of Welsh

In the previous section I often made reference to different varieties of the language, using terms like 'colloquial', 'formal', 'literary' and 'spoken'. In this section I will discuss different varieties of the language, and comment further on some of the linguistic differences between them.

Non-regional differences

As with any language, Welsh demonstrates sociolinguistic variation (see Ball 1988). However, in this subsection I am less interested in the microsociolinguistic variation that has been reported, rather in the macrosociolinguistic situation of the language. As Fife (1986, 1990) pointed out, Welsh has a strong differentiation between the literary language and various regionally differentiated colloquial forms (see also R. M. Jones 1993). These differences range over phonology, morphology, syntax and lexis to an extent almost reminiscent of the diglossic situations described for languages such as Arabic (Ferguson 1959). We can repeat Fife's (1990) example of the difference between literary and colloquial registers (colloquial here representing a northern variety) for the sentence 'you had not seen him':

Literary: *ni welsech ef* (lit: negative saw+past/2ndplur he)
Colloquial: *'do chi ddim wedi weld o* (lit: were you not see him)

The usage patterns of these varieties are not a straightforward distinction between written and spoken, however. Literary Welsh (sometimes referred to as standard Welsh, see Uned Iaith Genedlaethol Cymru 1978, D. G. Jones 1988, R. M. Jones 1993) is heard, for example, in formal speaking contexts, such as newsreading on the radio or television, or in formal speeches. In this spoken form, the phonology will be influenced by the regional background of the speaker.

Conversely, colloquial varieties can be written. There is a lively modern literature in Welsh, and colloquial forms of the language may be found written in novels, for example, in sections of direct speech, or in dialect literature where whole stories may be written in colloquial Welsh. Welsh orthography is particularly suited to portraying phonological variation, with its close phoneme–grapheme correspondences.

As we have implied, neither literary Welsh nor colloquial Welsh is a single variety, of course. Literary Welsh is a cline of variation from ultraformal styles based on the 1588 translation of the Bible, through to forms heavily influenced by spoken forms. At this less formal end, for example, there may be frequent use of periphrastic constructions, less pronoun drop with inflected verbs and inconsistent usage of preverbal particles. However, the phonology would be regional standard, localised lexis and syntactic patterns would be avoided and normally consonant mutation patterns would follow the rules of literary Welsh. Colloquial Welsh, on the other hand, has probably a still more complicated make-up. Apart from stylistic differences (i.e. colloquial influenced by literary through to most localised forms), there are of course regional varieties, and we return to these in the next subsection.

Somewhat complicating the matter is a variety called *Cymraeg Byw* (living Welsh, see Davies 1988, Coupland & Ball 1989), established in the 1960s as a variety for second language learners. This was based on a number of regional spoken varieties (at the more formal end of their ranges) to provide a regular (for example in terms of inflectional morphology and the numeral system) variety not totally divorced from literary Welsh, but well adapted to aid learners' transition to the local Welsh-speaking community. It suffered severe criticism from language purists, and was often sufficiently different from local varieties that its goal of aiding transition was not met as it was readily recognised as 'learner Welsh'. Today, most learners are taught varieties derived from *Cymraeg Byw*, but adapted more specifically for the region in which they live. Nevertheless, it seems that the effects of learners' varieties have impacted the language: both Hatton (1988) and Jones (1998), for example, report regional forms being displaced in children's Welsh by standard forms ultimately derived from learners' varieties. This is probably being accelerated through the use of such standardising forms of the language in Welsh-medium immersion education which we discuss later.

Regional differences

Traditionally, Welsh was divided into four broad dialect areas: Venedotian (north-west Wales), Powysian (north-east and mid-Wales), Demetian (south-west Wales) and Gwentian (south-east Wales) (see Morris Jones 1913). However, due to disproportionate percentage decline of Welsh speakers in different areas over the last 150 years, these dialect zones have to a large extent been fragmented, and the Gwentian dialect has been severely reduced. Thomas (1973) proposes a major division between southern varieties, midland varieties and northern varieties, with each of these areas subdivided into east and west. Further, he suggests that midland and northern varieties share certain features that allow an overarching grouping and division between south and north (as used in the section 'Language description' above).

There is a long history of dialect research into the language sponsored by the University of Wales in the form of research dissertations, starting in the

1930s and continuing to the present day (see the list in Ball & Williams 2001). Most of this work is unpublished, but a popular account of Welsh dialects appeared as Thomas & Thomas (1989), and more recently a detailed investigation of Breconshire Welsh was published by leading Welsh linguistic scholar Glyn Jones (2000). A large-scale linguistic geography of Wales (mainly lexical and phonological) was undertaken by Alan Thomas, with results published in 1973 and 1980, and a further detailed survey was undertaken in the 1990s (see Thomas 2000).

In the section 'Language description' above, we referred to several dialect differences at different linguistic levels. Here, we will add a few more important dialect characteristics, but cannot, of course, aim to do more than scratch the surface. In the area of phonetics and phonology, we can note the use of [æ] (representing [ɛ] or [a̧]) for standard /ɑ/ in mid-Wales and also in some syllabic contexts in south-eastern varieties as well. There is also the use of [we] for [ɔɪ] in Pembrokeshire Welsh which, like the previous example, is overtly stereotypical of the dialect for Welsh speakers. Pembrokeshire Welsh is also notable for the virtual loss of the central vowel /ə/, where it is replaced by one of the high vowels /i ɪ u ʊ/. Surprisingly, in the neighbouring south Cardiganshire dialect, schwa has an extended distribution, occurring in monosyllables spelt with *y*. Finally, we can note that in south-eastern varieties provection occurs intervocalically following a stressed syllable. Examples include *ebol* 'foal' /ˈebɔl/ → /ˈepɔl/, *agor* 'open' /ˈɑgɔr/ → /ˈɑkɔr/, *adnod* 'Bible verse' /ˈadnɔd/ → /ˈatnɔd/.

At the morphological level we can note the different forms of the third person singular, present/future tense in spoken varieties. For example, 'he sees' in southern colloquial is *(g)weliff e*, whereas apart from the south, the usual form would be *(g)welith o*. (The initial *g* is often mutated, even though a preverbal particle may not be pronounced.) For syntax we can consider the use of auxiliary verbs used in periphrastic constructions other than *bod* 'to be'. *Gwneud* 'to make, to do' can be used to form simple past and future constructions. As such it does not carry the extra emphatic connotation when used in English (i.e. 'I did read the book'). This gives us three ways to form 'I read the book': inflected: *darllenais i'r llyfr*; *bod*-periphrastic form: *bues i'n darllen y llyfr*; and *gwneud*- periphrastic form: *wnes i ddarllen y llyfr*; with the style moving from most to least formal. While *gwneud* forms can be found in all dialects, there is a specifically northern alternative: *ddaru* 'to happen'. This verb is uninflected and has a simple past meaning; our example sentence would then appear as: *(mi) ddaru mi ddarllen y llyfr*.

Finally, we can consider lexis. As is usual, the most visible differences between regional varieties are found in vocabulary. In Table 14.3 we list a few examples of common words which have different forms in the north

Table 14.3. *Some lexical differences between northern and southern varieties*

Item	Northern form	Southern form
milk	llefrith	llaeth
grandfather	taid	tad-cu
grandmother	nain	mam-gu
lad	hogyn	crwtyn
table	bwrdd	bord
key	agoriad	allwedd
finish	gorffen	cwpla
sweets	fferins	loshins
fox	llwynog	cadno
cattle	gwartheg	da

N.B. Other, more localised, forms may also be used for these examples.

from those in the south. Much fuller lists can be obtained from Thomas (1973, 2000).

The social context of the language

In this section we will look briefly at the history of the language in demographic terms, charting its numerical decline but also changing patterns of perceived status. We will conclude the section by looking at efforts in language maintenance and language planning, especially in the light of the recently established Welsh Assembly.

Language decline

Wales lost political independence in 1282, but the language in its literary form, which had been supported by the patronage of the princes, was still vigorous, as local nobility maintained the patronage system. However, the Act of Union between Wales and England in 1536 robbed the language of political and legal domains, and the poetic tradition went into a slow decline (Jones 1988). Such a loss of public domains can have a disastrous effect on a politically subordinate language (see, for example, the decline of Irish in Chapter 13). However, the Protestant reformation in England and Wales with its push to provide the scriptures and prayer books in vernacular languages, provided what might be thought of as a lifeline to Welsh. The translation of the Prayer Book and New Testament in 1567, and the complete Bible in 1588, not only provided a new official domain for the language (religion), but also helped provide a standardised form of the language and of the spelling. Indeed, the modern literary and standard forms of the language (see 'Varieties of Welsh' above) are derived to a large extent from biblical Welsh. Following the appearance of the Bible, other printed works in Welsh appeared (R. O. Jones (1993) notes 170 books between 1546 and 1695, 126 from 1695 to 1718 and 250 between 1718 and 1740). Periodicals also began to appear; R. O. Jones notes 32 period-icals and 25 newspapers in 1896. The language was supported by several religious revivals throughout the eighteenth and nineteenth centuries, and by the 'circulating schools' founded by Griffith Jones in the eighteenth century which taught the rudiments of Welsh literacy to aid reading of the scriptures. The dominance of non-conformist Christianity in Wales led, as R. O. Jones points out, to large numbers of Welsh speakers being exposed to formal, public registers through the sermons preached in Welsh-language chapels.

However, there were also powerful forces militating against the main-tenance of the language. Some of these were demographic, others part of an overt attempt by educational and other governmental agencies to suppress the language. The Industrial Revolution led in south Wales to the development of coal fields right across the south Wales valleys. In turn this led to an influx of workers from other areas of the United Kingdom. Up to 1850, most of the new workers came from other parts of Wales, but after this date most came from outside Wales (R. O. Jones 1993). To begin with, non-Welsh speakers learnt Welsh to communicate with their fellow workers. But, as the numbers of English speakers increased, the balance shifted, such that Welsh speakers switched to English to facilitate commu-nication. This was coupled with the fact that English was the language of the pit owners and professional classes. Further, a Royal Commission into education in Wales reported in 1847 and described the Welsh language as a drawback to progress and a barrier to the moral and commercial progress of the Welsh people. Elementary schools founded in the wake of this report taught only through English, and the use of Welsh by pupils was punished. Intermediate schooling was established in 1889 where again English was the only medium of education. As R. O. Jones (1993) notes, Welsh was restricted to the domains of home, chapel and *eisteddfod* (literary competition).

Estimates of the percentage of Welsh speakers in the total population of Wales prior to the first census of 1891 are: 1801, 80%; 1871, 66%; with the first census recording 54.5%. These figures show the beginning of the effect of industrialisation, as the 20% English-speaking figure of 1801 reflects long-standing anglicised areas such as Radnorshire, south Pembroke and Gower. It is probable that the education changes can be seen in the decline between 1871 and 1891. The figures in the twentieth century show further

Table 14.4. *Decline in Welsh speakers*

	1901	1911	1921	1931	1951	1961	1971	1981	1991
%	49.9	43.5	37.1	36.8	28.9	26.0	20.8	18.9	18.6
Numbers	928,824	977,366	922,092	909,261	714,686	656,002	542,425	503,549	508,098

rapid decline derived from the continuing low status of the language and in-migration of English speakers coupled with out-migration of Welsh speakers from depressed rural areas. Table 14.4 shows the figures from 1901 to 1991 (Price 1984); the really interesting figure is the increase in speaker numbers (and very slight percentage drop) between 1981 and 1991, possibly reflecting the previous thirty years of language activism (see more below).

This decline has been differentiated geographically. The effects of the Industrial Revolution were more marked in the south-east than elsewhere and led to anglicisation in that region before many others. More recently the development of seaside resorts encouraged in-migration of English speakers to run seaside businesses and to buy local property for retirement. Full details of the geographical distribution of Welsh can be found in Aitchison & Carter (2000), and their maps show the dramatic collapse of the Welsh heartland areas (over 80% Welsh speaking) between 1961 and 1991.

Language revitalisation

In 1962, Saunders Lewis delivered his radio broadcast *Tynged yr Iaith* ('Fate of the Language'), in which he pointed out that without action the Welsh language would be dead early in the twenty-first century. This broadcast prompted the foundation of *Cymdeithas yr Iaith Gymraeg* (The Welsh Language Society) that, over the next decades, organised a series of non-violent civil disobedience campaigns to gain equality for Welsh. These campaigns focussed on, for example, the provision of bilingual forms and publications by local and central government, bilingual road signs, the establishment of Welsh-language radio and television stations (*Radio Cymru*, run by the British Broadcasting Corporation, and *Sianel Pedwar Cymru* which received part of its material from the BBC and part from independent companies), and the provision of Welsh language policies by the Post Office, British Telecom, the universities, local government and private businesses. Broader campaigns to provide Welsh-medium education and legal status for the language in Acts of Parliament also followed. Many other long-established organisations (such as *Urdd*

Gobaith Cymru, the Welsh League of Youth, and *Merched y Wawr*, the Welsh Women's Organisation) have also played their part in maintaining and promoting the language. Of great importance has been the *Eisteddfod Genedlaethol* (the National Eisteddfod) that travels to different parts of Wales each year and, apart from organising competitions in the arts, provides a focus for all things Welsh in entertainment, merchandise and promoting adult learners of the language. It has an impact on the surrounding areas, at least for a time. Many smaller, local *eisteddfodau* also occur throughout the year.

Paralleling these popular campaigns (led mostly by highly committed young people) was the development of Welsh-medium education. While a few schools teaching partly or mainly through Welsh had been established in the 1930s, the sixties and seventies saw a great increase in parental demand for and subsequent establishment of Welsh-medium education at both the primary and secondary level. Kindergarten-level schools have been set up on a voluntary basis by *Mudiad Ysgolion Meithrin* (Welsh Nursery School Movement), which now receives governmental subsidy. Many of these schools exist in mainly anglicised areas, and operate there as an immersion system, with Welsh introduced at the nursery level. Many English-speaking parents choose Welsh-language education for their children due to its perceived advantages in academic development, employment potential and greater commitment of the teachers. The success of bilingual schooling was seen in the 1991 census, where figures for 3–15-year-olds showed an increase in Welsh speakers of 22.8%. The results from the 2001 census (see below) go some way to answering how many of these continued to use the language regularly after leaving school.

We should also note that throughout Wales there has been for many decades a large number of adult learners' classes catering for those who need Welsh as part of their employment and (mainly) those who are learning it for their own enjoyment. More efforts are being put into helping learners transfer into Welsh-speaking society, though in many parts of Wales such society may be maintained through social networks rather than geographical proximity.

Language maintenance

Apart from the many institutions just mentioned that help maintain the status and influence of the language, statutory bodies have, in recent years, been put in place by government which have language planning as part of their remit. Williams & Morris (2000) describe the recent legislative history of Welsh. In 1967 the first Welsh Language Act can be seen (as Williams & Morris note) as merely legitimising Welsh as a minority language within

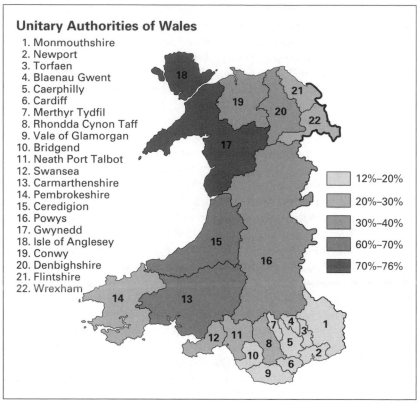

Unitary Authorities of Wales

1. Monmouthshire
2. Newport
3. Torfaen
4. Blaenau Gwent
5. Caerphilly
6. Cardiff
7. Merthyr Tydfil
8. Rhondda Cynon Taff
9. Vale of Glamorgan
10. Bridgend
11. Neath Port Talbot
12. Swansea
13. Carmarthenshire
14. Pembrokeshire
15. Ceredigion
16. Powys
17. Gwynedd
18. Isle of Anglesey
19. Conwy
20. Denbighshire
21. Flintshire
22. Wrexham

12%–20%
20%–30%
30%–40%
60%–70%
70%–76%

Figure 14.1 Map showing one or more skills in the Welsh language (2001 census) by unitary authority areas (National Statistics Online 2003)

Wales. In other words, it provided contexts wherein the language could be used officially, but had no mandate to help promote the language or widen these contexts. Pressure for wider-reaching legislation resulted in the Welsh Language Act of 1993, which among other provisions established the Welsh Language Board (*Bwrdd yr Iaith Gymraeg*). The Board aims to promote Welsh, especially in public and legal domains, to a status of equality with English. It has undertaken a great deal of work since its establishment; however, the private sector is excluded from its remit, and it can only issue recommendations that are put into practice if feasible. The British government minister responsible for Wales (the Secretary of State for Wales) vetted all the Board's plans. Williams & Morris provide a critique of the operations of the Board to date, but while there are obvious shortcomings we must recognise that this is the first governmentally organised language planning mechanism in the history of the language.

The other recent development that may well impact the language is the establishment in 1999 of the new National Assembly of Wales, as part of the devolution plans of the Labour government that came into power in 1997. The Assembly now has overall control of the Welsh Language Board, and there is a ministry that oversees 'the languages of Wales' among a broader cultural remit. Both the establishment of an Assembly and its overseeing of the Board may be positive moves, and it is pleasing that the debating chamber has simultaneous translation equipment, and that the language is frequently heard in debates.

Demographic results of this revitalisation effort appear to be reflected in recent figures. According to the 2001 census, Welsh is spoken by 575,168 people in Wales, representing 20.5% of the population over three years of age (National Statistics Online 2003). This percentage is an increase of around 2% since the 1991 census and is, in fact, the first increase in speakers (in percentage terms) since figures started to be collected in the late nineteenth century. In the capital city, Cardiff, the number of Welsh speakers has increased from 5.67% of the city's population in 1981 to 10.86% today. In fact, the percentage of the population who has one or more skills in Welsh is now around 25%, and the distribution of these speakers can be seen in Figure 14.1. Most encouraging is the increase in percentages of young people with skills in Welsh; for example, 42% of 10–15-year-olds can speak Welsh (a considerable increase on the 1981 figures), compared to about 15% in the age range 35–60.

The social context of the language has altered beyond recognition over the last fifty years. Much is being done to promote the language in education, the media and in official domains. Nevertheless, a minority language facing the might of the most powerful language currently spoken on the planet must still fear for its future.

Part III

The Other Languages of the British Isles

15 Multilingualism

Mark Gibson

Background

Multilingualism has been ever-present throughout the recorded history of the British Isles. Yet it is a phenomenon which only recently appears to be recognised, discussed and even celebrated in the UK and Ireland. An article published in early 2005 claims that London today hosts more linguistic, cultural and racial diversity than any other city on Earth or in history (Benedictus, *The Guardian* 21 January 2005).[1] This chapter provides an overview of the extent of multilingualism currently found in the British Isles. Multilingualism cannot be viewed in isolation. Rather, it is intimately linked with concepts such as identity, culture, ethnicity, religion and minority status in a UK context. To be a native speaker of a language other than English is often a marker of being culturally and ethnically 'different' from the mainstream population.

In addition, as with Anglo-Saxon and probably even the Celtic languages at an earlier time, new languages are introduced into the British Isles as a result of migration. This chapter places multilingualism within the context of such major demographic changes, particularly as experienced in the UK during the twentieth century. It then examines attitudes from government and mainstream society towards minority communities and their languages, using healthcare as an example, with particular emphasis on health information provision. It discusses how language, alongside factors such as socioeconomic status, lifestyle and culture, is often identified as a barrier to receiving quality healthcare, and which may contribute to widening health inequalities in the UK. Yet, while such inequalities are recognised, healthcare providers acknowledge that it is no simple task to provide information which would be beneficial to patients for whom language is a barrier. Initiatives that are launched in the UK are often

---

[1] Benedictus L, 'Every race, colour, nation and religion on earth': Parts 1, 2 and 3. *The Guardian*, 21 January 2005. [http://www.guardian.co.uk/g2/story/0,3604,1395269,00.html – last accessed 28 November 2006].

the efforts of fragmented professional or patient groups with limited resources and limited direction from central or local government.

Introduction

Multilingualism is a de facto norm in the British Isles. However, in step with other western European nations, the UK historically sought to deny this reality. From the dawn of the political union of the British Isles, English was favoured above French, or any other language, as the sole medium of public life and opportunity. Similar to Bonaparte's 'one nation – one language' doctrine, the myth of the monolingual nation became a dominant ideology in the British Isles. English became a foundation upon which British political authority would rest, reinforcing the notion of a truly *united* kingdom.

The monolingual myth has been effective in the UK context. Even today, the pre-eminent role of English in British public life as a vehicle for social mobility does not appear to be in question (Thompson, Fleming & Byram 1996:100). Yet, while there has not been any official written language policy, there have nonetheless been linguistic practices. Such practices, ranging from the *linguicidal* to the *linguicist* (Skutnabb-Kangas 1988:13),[2] have enabled English to triumph as the dominant language of the UK. This has been a contributory factor in the massive decline and, in the case of Manx and Cornish, the attrition, of the UK's indigenous Celtic languages. Today, Celtic language erosion has been such that most of their speakers lie in the outermost western peripheries of a speech area which once stretched from Ireland to the Caucasus. With speaker numbers dwindling, only recently has the British government accorded any special status to Welsh, Irish and Scottish Gaelic in public life (Thompson, Fleming & Byram 1996:106–8). The public use of Welsh and Scottish Gaelic has been further boosted with the recent devolution of political power in Wales and Scotland. Nonetheless, competence in English and notions of British 'citizenship' are closely linked and tougher immigration measures mean that proficiency in English is likely to become one of the prerequisites of entry for new settlers into the UK. Thus, to be British is to know English (Assinder, BBC News, 7 February 2005).[3]

---

[2] Here the term 'linguicism' is employed to describe a form of social prejudice in a linguistically diverse society, whereby speakers of one language (usually the majority) are seen to discriminate against the function and use of another language (usually the minority).

[3] Anonymous, 'Language tops Britishness poll', BBC News, 7 December 2004 [http://news.bbc.co.uk/1/hi/uk/4074801.stm – last accessed 28 November 2006]; Assinder, N. 'Immigration to be an election issue', BBC News, 7 February 2005 [http://news.bbc.co.uk/1/hi/uk_politics/4242451.stm – last accessed 28 November 2006].

The reality is that the majority of the UK population is monolingual. Before 1945, linguistic diversity in a Celtic context was for many people regarded as a curiosity of 'far off rural Wales', 'on the West coast of Ireland' or 'up in the Highlands and Islands of Scotland'. In other words, the distribution of Celtic language speakers in much of the British Isles was historically regarded as territorial (Rosen & Burgess 1980:6), although industrial areas such as the north-east of England attracted working-class migration from Celtic language speaking areas, particularly in the nineteenth century (Gibson 1996). After World War II, England, in particular, was to experience an unprecedented demographic change which would alter the sociolinguistic map of the UK forever. This change would come in the form of large-scale immigration during and after the post-war boom. Along with the cultures and religions of these new settlers, scores of new languages would be introduced into Britain, thus bringing the phenomenon of multilingualism to every region of the country.

In the face of such changes, official attitudes to diversity remained largely reactionary, as the needs of speakers of languages other than English were often ignored in areas such as healthcare, local government planning, education and the workplace. With the onset of post-war immigration, policy makers faced the fresh profile of UK multilingualism with a time-honoured weapon, the 'convenient fiction' of a monolingual Britain (Rosen & Burgess 1980:6). Speakers of other languages were expected to sink or swim, discard their 'difference' and fall in line and learn to speak the Queen's English as a platform for upward social mobility. Despite this, linguistic diversity became just as vibrant in cities such as Bradford or Leicester, as it was in Mumbai or Lahore. Consequently, the traditional notion of insular 'Britishness', based on one language and one culture, was becoming increasingly fictitious in view of the country's newer cosmopolitan reality (Rassool 2000:391).

The demo-linguistic composition of minority ethnic communities in the UK: immigration into the UK

The British Isles has experienced ongoing and sustained immigration throughout its recorded history. The presence of Romans, Anglo-Saxons, Normans and Vikings throughout the country not only enhanced linguistic diversity within the British Isles, but also played a considerable part in the lexical and grammatical development of the English language. From the Middle Ages, further waves of immigrants settled in different regions of Britain. The Huguenots of East London (seventeenth century), the Flemish weavers in East Anglia (sixteenth century), German and Arabic speakers in the north-east (nineteenth century), people from eastern and southern Europe settling in regions such as West Yorkshire (nineteenth century) and the Roma peoples (sixteenth century) formed sizeable communities throughout the Isles. However, the influx of pre-1945 immigrants was so relatively insignificant that they did not appear to pose any major problems with respect to their assimilation into mainstream society. By the early twentieth century, many of these communities, such as the Jewish, Greek, Italian and Arabic-speaking groups, had become well established and relatively well integrated into British life.[4]

Nevertheless, it was not until during and after the post-war boom that the majority of immigrant groups arrived in the UK. World War II had left much of Britain's infrastructure in ruins and this was coupled with a severe labour shortage amongst the indigenous population. In common with other western European nations, the UK found itself in desperate need of a cheap labour force and needed to import labour from abroad. The UK looked for assistance from the countries newly independent from, or still part of, a shrinking British Empire. In response, people mostly from the Caribbean and South Asia came into Britain in their thousands.

The UK was portrayed as a benevolent and welcoming metropolis of immense opportunity to these citizens of the Commonwealth and subjects of the British Crown. Many saw their chance to make a fresh start in what they regarded as their own mother country and came to the UK assured of higher standards of living in exchange for their labour. Soon after arriving, however, many found little improvement to their conditions and rapidly became ghettoised in inner-city Britain.

Throughout the latter part of the twentieth century, official treatment of these 'newcomers' ranged from an ebb of anglocentric parochialism to a flow of liberal tolerance. Whatever the official response, many of the settlers from the post-war boom, many of whom in time saw their status change from 'immigrant' to 'UK citizen', have contended with sustained racism and institutional discrimination in many aspects of British public and social life.

Immigration rose steadily between 1955 and 1970 (Linguistic Minorities Project 1985:55). During this time, many people from the white mainstream were becoming increasingly concerned with the number of non-White

---

[4] Unless it was a time of national crisis. See Linguistic Minorities Project (1985:55) to read about the treatment of Britons of Italian origin during World War II. Similarly, one may question the extent to which people from such communities were truly accepted by the mainstream society. Jewish people in the UK are periodically singled out for bouts of discrimination and scapegoating (e.g. the defacing of Jewish headstones) which are well known in history. Gibson (2002) offers an account of discrimination experienced by males from the small but centuries-old Jewish community in Sunderland attempting to break into the 1970s local football scene which was dominated by White Christian males.

minorities coming into Britain. According to widespread, albeit extremist, thinking, these settlers were coming into 'their' country and stealing 'their' opportunities. Never before had modern Britain witnessed such an influx of people settling into the country. Therefore, it became obvious that the sheer volume of newcomers would make their cultural and linguistic assimilation into British society virtually impossible. Visibly, such assimilation was inconceivable, as racial diversity became a serious challenge to preconceived notions of a White Britain. Indeed, this concern gained political momentum and culminated in the passing of the 1962 Immigration Act and was envisioned in former British Health Minister and Conservative politician Enoch Powell's 'rivers of blood' speech. The 1962 Act was further ratified in the 1971 Act which placed more draconian restrictions on immigration, especially from the Caribbean and South Asia.

In the 1990s and the first years of the new millennium, immigration in its traditional sense has been reduced to a relative trickle, limiting itself to an average of fifty thousand immigrants a year, half of which continue to come from the countries of the New Commonwealth (Office for National Statistics 1996:10). However, the past two decades have witnessed a sharp increase in people claiming asylum in the UK, introducing a whole new plethora of languages and cultures, such as Kurdish, Albanian and Somali, hitherto unrepresented in significant numbers in the UK. Once more, such a new influx of peoples is not without its controversy, as the asylum seeker issue took centre stage in the run-up to the 2005 UK general elections, especially in the electoral campaigns of right-leaning parties (Assinder, BBC News 7 February 2005).[5]

Minority ethnic communities in the UK

With reference to the figures provided in the 1991 Census, the UK composition of minority ethnic communities is shown in Table 15.1.

In England and Wales, Census 2001 revealed that the proportion of minority ethnic groups has increased from 6% in 1991 to 7.9% of the UK population, or 4.6 million people. Half of the total minority ethnic population were Asians of Indian, Pakistani, Bangladeshi or Other Asian origin. A quarter of minority ethnic people described themselves as Black, that is, Black Caribbean, Black African or Other Black. Fifteen percent of the minority ethnic population described their ethnic group as Mixed. About a third of this group were from White and Black Caribbean

[5] Assinder, N. 'Immigration to be an election issue', BBC News, 7 February 2005 [http://news.bbc.co.uk/1/hi/uk_politics/4242451.stm – last accessed 28 November 2006].

Table 15.1. *UK composition of minority ethnic communities (1991 Census)*

Indian	840 000	27.9%
Black Caribbean	500 000	16.6%
Pakistani	477 000	15.8%
Other non-Asian	290 000	9.6%
Black African	212 000	7.0%
Other Asian	198 000	6.6%
Black Other	178 000	5.9%
Bangladeshi	163 000	5.4%
Chinese	157 000	5.2%

Source: Ordnance Survey 'Statlas UK' (1995:23).

backgrounds. One reason for this increase is due to the inclusion of Mixed as an ethnic group in 2001, whereas this category was absent in previous censuses.[6]

The UK Census 2001 reveals the ethnic composition of England and Wales as shown in Table 15.2.

It is possible to see that Indians remain the largest minority group, followed by Pakistanis, those of Mixed ethnic backgrounds, then people of Black Caribbean, Black African and Bangladeshi origin. The remaining minority ethnic groups (such as 'Chinese' and 'Other') together accounted for a further 1.4% of the UK population (National Statistics Online 2003).[7]

Before Census 2001, the UK decennial census failed to include figures concerning people from minority ethnic groups who were born in the UK (Reid 1984:410). In 1995 it was estimated that 47% of people from minority ethnic backgrounds were born in the UK (Dorling 1995:40). In comparison to findings from earlier censuses, it is clear that the Black and Minority Ethnic (BME) population has increased by 1.9 million people since 1981. Between 1991 and 2001 the UK minority ethnic population grew by 53%, from 3.0 million in 1991 to 4.6 million in 2001.

Figures from Census 2001 show that White groups have an older age structure than other ethnic groups. Furthermore, given that the BME population has a younger age structure and a higher fertility pattern than the White population, the Runnymede Trust predicts that by the year 2020, the BME population will have doubled (Runnymede Trust

---

[6] National Statistics Online 13 February 2003 [www.statistics.gov.uk/census2001 – last accessed 28 November 2006]; [www.statistics.gov.uk/cci/nugget.asp?id = 273 – last accessed 28 November 2006].

[7] Table taken from National Statistics Online – Population Size: Ethnicity [http://www.statistics.gov.uk/cci/nugget.asp?id = 273 – last accessed 28 November 2006].

Table 15.2. *Population size of minority ethnic groups in the UK, April 2001
(7.9% of the UK population is from a minority ethnic group)*

Ethnic group	Total population count	Total population %	Minority ethnic population %
White	45 153 898	92.1	n/a
Mixed	677 117	1.2	14.6
Asian or Asian British:			
Indian	1 053 411	1.8	22.7
Pakistani	747 285	1.3	16.1
Bangladeshi	283 063	0.5	6.1
Other Asian	247 664	0.4	5.3
Black or Black British:			
Black Caribbean	575 876	1.0	12.2
Black African	485 227	0.8	10.5
Black Other	97 585	0.2	2.1
Chinese	247 403	0.4	5.3
Other	230 615	0.4	5.0
All minority ethnic population	4 635 296	7.9	100
All population	58 789 194	100	n/a

1994, cited in Gillborn and Gipps 1996:7), in a context where 10% of the
child population aged between 0 and 14 in England and Wales are non-
White (Balarajan 1995:82). In addition, it is claimed that the birth rate
amongst the BME population in the UK is increasing 15 times greater
than that of the mainstream White population (Carvel, *The Guardian*,
21 September 2001).[8]

Approximately two-thirds of all ethnic minority residents are reported
to live in the conurbations of the West Midlands, West Yorkshire, Greater
Manchester and London. In this sense, with over 300 languages spoken
across the city, over a third of schoolchildren speaking a language other
than English at home and with one in four residents having been born
outside the UK, it is evident that London is one of the most linguistically
diverse cities in the world (Baker & Eversley 2000:5; 71, Benedictus, *The
Guardian*, 21 January 2005).

In spite of these facts, however, there are no official figures available
concerning language use and diversity on a national level. For example, the
UK national Census neglects to include any questions regarding language,
even though efforts have been made to incorporate the languages question
in the census since 1920 (1991 Census of Great Britain: OPCS 1995:10).

---

[8] Carvel, J., 'Minority groups grow by 15%', *The Guardian*, 21 September 2001. [http://
www.guardian.co.uk/uk news/story/0,,555316,00.html – last accessed 28 November 2006].

However, the Office for National Statistics state that in future censuses, questions about language use and its relationship with ethnicity may be reintroduced (National Statistics Online 2003).[9]

This dearth of language-specific information is repeatedly bemoaned in the literature and it is recognised that there is no centralised initiative to collect data of macroscopic, national scope (Baker & Eversley 2000:5, Soni Raleigh & Balarajan 1995:82). However, there have been a number of smaller-scale localised initiatives which attempt to shed light on language diversity at a local level. For example, the Inner London Education Authority (ILEA) conducted biennial surveys between 1978 and 1988. Despite failing to elicit any information relating to the use of the numerous creoles spoken as a first language in London, these surveys serve to provide some of the few comprehensive language statistics for Inner London schools (Alladina 1993:58). However, the ILEA was abolished in 1989 and research into language diversity ceased to receive official support from the decentralised Local Education Authorities which replaced the ILEA. The results from the last ILEA survey, carried out in 1988, indicated that 184 languages were represented by children in Inner London schools, 16 of which had more than one thousand speakers.

However, these figures, now 18 years old, reflect little on the linguistic situation of Inner London today. With considerable demographic changes within London itself, languages supplant each other in terms of diffusion and speaker numbers. The London linguistic mosaic is constantly subject to change. For instance, before post-war immigration, Greek used to be the traditionally most dominant language in parts of the capital after English (Reid 1988:183). However, since the 1970s Panjabi and Bengali speakers significantly outnumber speakers of Greek in most parts of the city.

Baker & Mohieldeen (2000:5) claim that most LEAs in London regularly collect data relating to the languages spoken by pupils attending schools within that Authority. The 'Languages of London Project', conducted in the late 1990s, gives fresher data, provided by a number of Greater London LEAs, which may paint a more accurate picture of multilingualism in a London context. The study reveals that over 300 languages are spoken by schoolchildren at home throughout London. The ten most dominant of these languages are shown in Table 15.3.

However, while the information in Table 15.3 sheds interesting light on linguistic diversity amongst schoolchildren, it may still fail to reflect the multilingual situation amongst the wider London adult population.

---

[9] National Statistics Online 2003 [http://www.statistics.gov.uk/about/classifications/ns ethnic classification.asp – last accessed 28 November 2006].

Table 15.3. *Ten most dominant languages spoken at home by London schoolchildren*

Language	Speaker Number	Percentage
English	608,500	67.86
Bengali and Sylheti	40,400	4.51
Panjabi	29,800	3.32
Gujarati	28,600	3.19
Hindi/Urdu	26,000	2.91
Turkish	15,600	1.74
Arabic	11,000	1.23
English-based creoles	10,700	1.20
Yoruba	10,400	1.16
Somali	8,300	0.93

Source: Baker & Mohieldeen (2000:5).

Increasing numbers of refugees and asylum seekers from around the world, 63% of whom are adult males aged between 18 and 34 years of age without dependants, settle for an undetermined length of time in urban centres such as London (Grundy & Jameson 2002). As a matter of course, these applicants bring their languages with them and speakers of languages such as Kurdish, Yoruba and Somali are forming sizeable communities in their own right. Such rapid demographic upheaval is discussed by Rosen & Burgess, who state that 'change is in fact what is typical of London diversity now. New languages appear, settled languages change as the language X spoken in X-land becomes language X as spoken in Britain' (Rosen & Burgess 1980:25).

Nevertheless, the languages which asylum seekers speak are sometimes much harder to detect than their geographical origins and it is unclear how or if the Home Office elicits any information relating to an applicant's linguistic repertoire. For instance, while it may be relatively easy to find out that an applicant may come from Iraq or Afghanistan, it may be much more difficult to identify that person's immediate language needs without some knowledge of the language situation of the countries of origin, or without appreciating in which languages the applicant has become proficient since leaving his or her country of origin.

In addition, because a British citizen may tick the 'Pakistani' box in the ethnicity section of the 2001 UK Census, this does not mean that simple assumptions can be made about the languages such a person may speak. The reality may be anything from a monolingual English speaker, born in England to a family of Pakistani origin, having lived in Leeds since 1948 to a Mirpuri-Panjabi-Urdu-English quadrilingual who arrived in the UK eighteen months prior to taking part in the census. Therefore, on a national level, such is the paucity of official information on language usage in the UK that it may be problematic to place concrete figures on community language speaker numbers in the UK. Similarly, the profile of migrant workers from EU member states may not be apparent in Census 2001 figures, since they would be likely to tick the 'White' box on the census. Therefore, information about languages spoken in the UK by people from the EU member states is largely unknown.

However, in order to establish which community languages are spoken throughout the UK, the following classifications are proposed:[10]

NATIVE: These are languages which are considered native to the British Isles, such as English, Welsh, Scottish and Irish Gaelic.

TRADITIONAL: These are languages such as Panjabi, Hindi/Urdu, Bengali, Gujarati, Cantonese, Greek, Turkish and Arabic. With the exception of Bengali, these languages have been represented in the UK for a significant part of the twentieth century and earlier. Due to the population size of the respective communities, these languages are most likely to be spoken in numbers of over one hundred thousand people each.

RECENT: These are languages which have been introduced into Britain by relatively recent waves of settlers and asylum seekers, such as Kurdish, Farsi, Somali and Albanian or by people from the new EU member states, such as Polish and Czech. In the UK, we have but a very imprecise knowledge of speaker numbers of these languages, such as Somali and Kurdish.[11]

AUXILIARY: These are lingua francas on a global scale which are also represented in the UK, including Spanish, French, Portuguese, Russian and Hebrew.

It is conceded that many UK languages are difficult to pigeonhole in this way. For instance, Hindi and Urdu may be so-called 'traditional' languages according to the above framework, but Hindi particularly is used as an auxiliary language amongst many people of South Asian origin, both in the UK and the Indian subcontinent. Similarly, both Urdu and Bengali could be auxiliary languages amongst people of Pakistani and Bangladeshi origin respectively. Arabic has been represented in the UK for several

---

[10] These classifications were created in an attempt to inform policy makers within the Department of Health about the need to provide health information in dominant UK community languages (Purves & Wilson, Electronic Health Horizons, University of Newcastle/Department of Health, 2000).

[11] Based in London, The Home Office is responsible for everything which is not the responsibility of another government department. Among responsibilities which relate to the personal social services are the Probation Service in England and Wales, asylum seekers and inter-country adoption. Their website http://www.homeoffice.gov.uk/rds/immigration1.html (last accessed 28 November 2006) offers official figures about asylum applications and countries of origin of applicants and is updated every three months.

hundred years, yet is also a language brought into the country by recent waves of asylum seekers from countries such as Algeria and Iraq. Similarly, Romani/Angloromani are languages that have been spoken in Britain for several centuries, and dialects of Romani such as Sinte and Vlax particularly have been brought into the country by relatively smaller numbers of Roma asylum seekers from Eastern European countries.

Also of interest is British Sign Language (BSL), the preferred language of up to 70,000 people in Britain. Yet, up until 2003, the UK government did not recognise BSL as an official language. This lack of official recognition until recent years has had deep implications for the British Deaf Association (BDA), an organisation that has developed a 'Sign Language Policy Statement'. The statement claims that BSL users' 'vision is of a society in which the right of Deaf people to use British Sign Language is both recognised and actively promoted so that they can participate as equal citizens' (The Royal Deaf Organisation 2000).[12] Similarly, the Royal National Institute of the Blind (RNIB) estimates that there are up to 20,000 fluent readers of Braille in the UK (Raynor & Yerassimou 1997).

Multilingualism outside England

European Charters commit the EU to promote and respect the multilingualism of over 40 million of its citizens. Enshrined in the 1992 Council of Europe Charter for Regional or Minority Languages and then the 1995 Directorate General XXII, the European Union has implemented 'unprecedented measures to protect minority rights' (O'Driscoll 2001:475). The European Bureau for Lesser Used Languages (EBLUL), for example, celebrates over twenty years of actively promoting EU 'policy-making in favour of regional or minority languages' and defining the 'linguistic rights of the speakers of those languages' (EBLUL 2002).[13]

In line with this European framework, the UK government has made numerous steps to provide public services in certain community languages in addition to English. With increased devolution in Wales, for example, all public services, notices and documents must be rendered in both English and Welsh. This is an obligatory measure for which the National Assembly of Wales has been responsible since its inception in 1999. A recent policy review for the Welsh language estimates that approximately 18% of the population in Wales speaks Welsh. Figures from Census 2001 indicate that 20.8% of the population (582,368 people) claim to speak

---

[12] The Royal Deaf Organisation 2000 [http://www.signcommunity.org.uk/ – last accessed 25 January 2007].
[13] EBLUL 2002 [www.eblul.org – last accessed 28 November 2006].

Welsh and 26% of people in Wales under the age of 35 claim to be speakers, an increase of almost 9% on 1991 figures (Office for National Statistics, Census 2001. Report on the Welsh Language. HMSO, 2004).

In localities where Scottish Gaelic is represented in significant numbers, such as the Comhairle nan Eilean, the Western Isles Council, all public services are provided in both English and Gaelic. Furthermore, the Scottish Parliament has a Culture Minister with responsibility for Gaelic,[14] and the Scottish Executive has established a number of advisory groups, inquiries and surveys to suggest a path forward for the revitalisation of Gaelic.

The 1998 Good Friday Agreement, as well as organisations such as the Conradh na Gaelige, have resolved to promote and encourage the use of Irish Gaelic, as well as Ulster Scots, in public life in Northern Ireland (Craith 1999). The Agreement explicitly recognises Northern Ireland's linguistic diversity, by committing itself to recognising 'the importance of respect, understanding and tolerance in relation to linguistic diversity, including ... the Irish language, Ulster-Scots and the languages of the various ethnic minority communities, all of which are part of the cultural wealth of the island of Ireland'.[15] The mention of Ulster Scots in the Agreement is reported to have been a political concession to appease Unionists' distaste for the official recognition granted to Irish Gaelic in Northern Ireland. It is interesting to note that in the wording of the Agreement that word 'language' is not ascribed to Ulster Scots, perhaps reflecting its wide recognition as a dialect of Scots, rather than a 'language' per se.

Traditionally, Northern Ireland is described as 'a source of emigration rather than immigration' and thus has not experienced the same levels of immigration as England and Wales. However, within the 'ethnic minority communities' mentioned in the 1998 Good Friday Agreement are Chinese (8,000 people) speaking Cantonese, Mandarin and Hakka; people of South Asian origin (2,500 people) speaking Hindi, Urdu, Panjabi, as well as people of African origin (1,500 people) who speak Arabic, Swahili, Fulani and Xhosa.

Since gaining independence in 1921, the Republic of Ireland has followed a political and cultural destiny that is separate from the UK. However, like the UK, Ireland offers its own multicultural and multilingual richness. Since the emergence of the Irish Free State, Irish Gaelic has been accorded an official role in Irish public life and education, and is an essential symbol of

[14] Scottish Parliament [www.scottish.parliament.uk – last accessed 28 November 2006].
[15] McKendry, E., 'Community Languages in Northern Ireland', July 2002 [http://www.cilt. org.uk/comlangs/cl_ni.rff – last accessed 5 December 2006].

Irish identity. In reality, the majority of Irish Gaelic speakers are found along the western coasts of Ireland, an area known as the Gaeltacht. The Irish Census of 2002 indicated that 1.57 million people claimed to be able to speak Irish, an increase when compared to figures from 1996 (1.43 million). However, there is a difference between knowing Gaelic and using it, as there has been a slight decline of Irish speakers in percentage terms throughout the Gaeltacht areas, with the exception of Meath. Over 25% of the Gaeltacht population reported speaking Irish frequently and 7.4% claimed to never speak the language (Central Statistics Office 2003).[16] *The Irish Times* reports that over 90 languages, in addition to Gaelic and English, are spoken in Dublin (Coigligh, *The Irish Times*, 24 April 2002).[17]

Anarchy in the UK: the provision of healthcare information in dominant community languages

In the UK, there is no coherent nationwide strategy to provide public information in community languages and whatever initiatives there are often vary from region to region. This is particularly the case for healthcare information. Since the 1990s, local authorities have commissioned, via the Department of Health and patient associations, disease-specific patient information in languages such as Hindi, Urdu, Panjabi and Bengali. Since then, the provision of multilingual public information has been assigned increasing importance by healthcare planners, since it has been well documented that there are issues of epidemiology, inequality and social exclusion which affect particular BME groups in the UK. Bennett, Qutub & Bellis (1998:15) describe these issues clearly by reporting that 'individuals from Black and Ethnic Minority communities have shorter life expectancies and poorer physical ... health. They must often struggle with a health service which is not adequately equipped to deal with or adequately sensitive to their particular language, cultural and religious needs'.

In 2000 the Department of Health Information Policy Unit published 'Electronic Health Horizons', a report which examined how IT is shaping the future of UK healthcare. The document recognises that today's problems of accessing public services are certain to be exacerbated in tomorrow's 'Information Society' if not systematically addressed now (Purves, Wilson & Gibson 2000:60). Much of the research published in this domain indicates that primary care services represent one area which

[16] Central Statistics Office 2003, Information Section, 19 June 2003 [www.cso.ie – last accessed 5 February 2005].

[17] Coigligh, Cn, 'Multilingualism in Ireland', *The Irish Times*, 24 April 2002 [http://www.asu.edu/educ/epsl/LPRU/newsarchive/art174.txt – last accessed 28 November 2006].

people with a limited knowledge of English find difficult to access. This is not to assume of course that, amongst the more dominant linguistic groups at least, individuals from these communities do not visit their GPs. Evidence suggests that members of the African-Caribbean, Indian, Pakistani and Bangladeshi communities have more consultations with their GPs on an annual average basis than the general population (Bennett *et al.* 1998:15).

In terms of socioeconomics, people from Black and Ethnic Minority groups are twice as likely to be found amongst the poorest one-fifth of the UK population. Henley & Schott (1999:41) relate that half of Pakistani and Bangladeshi households in the UK have no income from employment. Perceived and sustained racial discrimination from mainstream society is believed to have a direct link to the high incidences of clinical depression and other mental health conditions amongst members of Black and Ethnic Minority communities (p. 42). Hawthorne (1994:453) reports South Asian patients with ischaemic heart disease frequently wait longer for referrals in cardiology clinics in Leicester in comparison with White patients. Moreover, while over a quarter of Leicester's population is of South Asian origin, Rashid & Jagger (1992) state that South Asian patients experience more problems accessing their GPs than non-Asian patients.

Henley & Schott (1999:268) explain that patients who have limited competence in English are frequently provided with less information relating to their needs from their GPs and are often offered fewer treatment choices. Moreover, because there are no real feedback mechanisms in place for speakers of languages other than English, these patients often find themselves 'out of the loop' of, and not included in, UK healthcare planning outcomes (p. 269). This could be particularly the case for recent settlers in the UK such as refugees and asylum seekers (Hargreaves, Holmes & Friedland 2000:531). What is more, the cost of clinical mismanagement of the diverse patient needs in the UK inevitably leads to poorly treated conditions, increased mortality and morbidity and wasted time and money (Henley & Schott 1999:22). It is ironic to note that the chronic marginalisation of patients for whom language is a chief barrier to receiving quality healthcare occurs while current health policy, largely imported from the US, paints a picture of UK patients being empowered and informed, expert in their own care, working in partnership with healthcare professionals, managing their own health and making their own decisions about their treatment (Department of Health 1998, 2001).

However, there are practicalities of providing patient information in community languages which merit consideration. With over three hundred languages represented in the UK, a key question when examining this issue is which languages would be eligible for translation. Demand for translation appears to be recognised in terms of speaker numbers. Clearly, it is relatively easy to address the former by means of identifying those community languages which are more numerically dominant. Ideally, these would include languages such as Urdu, Panjabi, Hindi, Cantonese and so on.

However, identifying speaker numbers is all well and good, but pinpointing community need is more difficult. For instance, Somali, Kurdish, Pashto and Romani groups may be in more urgent need of patient information to help bolster primary care provision for people currently seeking asylum in Britain, even though they have fewer members than more established language communities, who may also have relatively more community resources (family members, people in the community) to draw upon (Hargreaves, Holmes & Friedland 2000, Lehti & Mattson 2001).

Many speakers of other languages in the UK have ancestral links with regions such as South Asia which are culturally and linguistically complex. This is reflected in speakers' linguistic repertoires in the UK. The question of which language should be addressed becomes relevant. To target the Bangladeshi community, should health information be rendered in Sylheti or Bengali? Opting for the former would mean that the information should be in audio/audiovisual format, since Sylheti does not have a written form. On the other hand, producing information in Bengali would assume that Bengali speakers are able to read text in Bengali. A sizeable section of the Pakistani community in the UK speak both Panjabi and Urdu, yet read only Urdu, as Panjabi from Pakistan is not normally written. Many citizens of Indian origin speak Gujarati or Panjabi rather than Hindi, yet Hindi may be a more practical language for health information translation owing to its status as a South Asian and British Asian lingua franca.

Wilson et al. (1997) recommend that English language patient information leaflets should be aimed at an 'understandability' level of 12 years old in order to achieve maximum and effective dissemination of the message. However, it is difficult to ascertain the literacy competences of speakers of community languages. To complicate matters further, it should not be assumed that speakers are literate in their respective languages. Hawthorne (1994:455) reports that in Blackburn 11% of Gujarati speakers and 26% of Panjabi speakers could not read or write their respective languages. Similarly, some languages are written using more than one script. For example, Kurdish is written in three alphabets, a Romanised script mostly used by Kurds in Turkey and Armenia, an Arabic script in widespread use amongst Kurds from Iran, Iraq and Syria and a Cyrillic script used by smaller communities of Kurds scattered throughout the Central Asian republics of the former USSR. In the UK, a large amount of public health information in Kurdish is produced in the Arabic script, yet this may exclude Kurds with limited English who can only read the Romanised script.[18]

Furthermore, information translated into community languages ought to be relevant and easy to understand and access. Hawthorne (1994:455) claims that many translated leaflets are direct translations from English and relate to an 'English' way of life, and the content itself is often replete with grammatical and spelling errors. To counter this, www.mypil.com was an initiative set up by GPs in Lancashire between 2001 and 2006 to address directly community language health information needs. The website emphasised effective communication rather than the pursuit of literary 'purity'. Much of their patient information in Urdu, Hindi and Bengali involved code-mixing with English to explain certain issues in order to enable maximum understandability of the message. Nevertheless, the use of this resource presupposes that patients will be able to access and use the Internet, or rely on the GP to find this information on their behalf (Gibson 2003a). Paramedics in the Bristol area are supplied with a 31-language phrasebook covering basic phrases, such as 'Does it hurt here? Yes/No'. The resource has been used to assist the preliminary diagnosis and on-the-scene emergency care involving patients whose first language is not English. However, this assumes the patient is able to read the language in question (BBC News 1 March 2003).[19]

Another interesting method of providing health information for people with limited knowledge of English or basic skills is to render this information in pictogram form. The use of pictograms has been pioneered in South Africa and Canada with the specific aim of providing basic information about health and medicine use, such as 'take this medicine three times a day', amongst linguistically diverse groups (Mansoor & Drowse 2003). However, one challenge with pictograms is to create images which are universally recognisable and culturally appropriate. For example, would an image depicting a fork, knife and plate to denote 'meal' or 'mealtime' be instantly recognised by people from a non-Western cultural background, such as speakers of Somali?

Furthermore, as a means of reducing potential costs it is becoming increasingly apparent that the Internet is an ideal vehicle for the deployment of public, multilingual information. At the click of a mouse, it is possible to render the contents of the National Assembly for Wales and the Scottish

[18] See the Norfolk and Norwich University Hospital patient information section of its website for examples of this [http://www.nnuh.nhs.uk/leaflet.asp?f = %7CHealth%7C – last accessed 28 November 2006].

[19] Anonymous, BBC News, 'Patients' phrasebook aids 999 crews', 1 March 2003 [http://news.bbc.co.uk/1/hi/england/2810713.stm – last accessed 28 November 2006].

Parliament websites in Welsh and Scottish Gaelic, respectively. Similarly, a resource such as mypil.com has the potential of providing free information in as many languages as possible and on as many healthcare and lifestyle topics as demand dictates.

Key electronic resources include (Gibson 2003a):

- www.patient.co.uk. This website offers over 500 evidence-based leaflets on healthcare and lifestyle issues which GPs can print out for patients. The resource offers a wide and increasing range of condition-specific information in dominant community languages;
- www.multikulti.org.uk is a Lottery-funded London Advice Services Alliance project which provides culturally appropriate and translated health information in 11 dominant UK languages;
- The Minority Ethnic Health Awareness Project UK is a Department of Health funded initiative and provides information in South Asian and Middle Eastern languages in book, CD-ROM and video formats;
- The Health for Asylum Seekers and Refugees Portal (HARP) at www. harpweb.org.uk is a large resource which offers multilingual health information and appointment cards. HARP links much of its inform- ation to the New South Wales Multicultural Health Communication Service at www.mhcs.health.nsw.gov.au. This resource provides inform- ation for a wide range of conditions in 46 languages, many of which are relatively under-resourced in the UK, such as Kurdish and Somali.

While resources such as these are available, healthcare providers in the UK face more fundamental issues with multilingual patients. For example, how does the GP ascertain who speaks which language? One way to record this information would be to include this in the patient's Electronic Patient Record (EPR), which in the future is likely to be linked to pharmacies and hospital departments (Gibson 2003c). While the technological capabilities are in existence, and recording language-specific information merely entails adding a simple field in a database, this is not done in practice. Moreover, while hospital and GP interpreting services are a growing industry in the UK, healthcare professionals often report problems access- ing interpreters for patient consultations or in an emergency, as many have to be booked some time in advance (Gibson 2003a).

The Internet is a valuable resource for the provision of multilingual information. An example to follow could be the BBC online news service which offers key news items in 43 languages. However, while over two- thirds of the UK population are regular users of the Internet (BBC News 20 August 2001),[20] the digital divide between the IT 'haves' and 'have-nots'

---

[20] Anonymous, 'UK Internet usage surges', BBC News, 20 August 2001 [http://news. bbc.co.uk/1/hi/business/1500668.stm – last accessed 28 November 2006].

is nonetheless perceptible. For example, whereas the speed and accessibility of Internet services through cable broadband and digital TV are theoretically available to every home in the UK, the start-up costs of getting connected may still be prohibitive for many UK households. Cost, inclination, lack of skills and vision problems could act as barriers to older people, in particular, accessing a technology such as the Internet. To address this issue, public service planners need to consider multiple public access points, such as a library or day centre, in order to maximise the access to relevant multilingual health information services (Purves, Wilson & Gibson 2000).

Finally, even when access to the Internet is possible and multilingual information about health is sought, there are two major issues that come into play. Firstly, how does the lay user distinguish between 'good' and 'bad' health information (Gibson 2003b, Purves *et al.* 2000)? Secondly, it is a fact that not everyone understands technical medical information, which often forms much of the content of patient information (Raynor & Knapp 2000). So, even native speakers of English face their own language problems when accessing health information, whether verbal or written, as the 'voice of the life world' (everyday language) comes into contact with the 'voice of medicine' (a high-register, domain-specific language) (Mishler 1984). In both cases, it is clear that all patients, regardless of first language, require a healthcare professional such as a GP to act as 'broker' of this information, to advise on the validity of information that the patient has found and provide additional information from other medical sources. Whatever the solution, the fact remains that, in general, the healthcare needs of patients who speak a language other than English are poorly met by UK healthcare providers. This represents an area which requires urgent attention if inequalities of health that are potentially caused by language difficulties are to be improved.

Summary

Multilingualism is the rule rather than the exception in the British Isles today. Over the last five decades, linguistic and cultural diversity has been such that demographic trends in the United Kingdom have been altered irreversibly. In 2005, the BME population accounted for 8% of the population and these communities represent an impressive spectrum of cultural, religious, racial and linguistic backgrounds (National Statistics Online 2003). However, it is recognised that the full extent of multilingualism in the UK remains largely unknown. Therefore, current initiatives to provide public information in community languages may not be entirely well-informed in the sense that listening to groups with the loudest voice may not correspond to those groups who have the greatest demand to receive public service information in the requisite languages, such as may be the case with asylum seekers in the UK.

Yet, with a younger age structure, the BME population is expected to double in number by the year 2020. Therefore, members of these communities are likely to become relatively powerful forces in the country's political arena and public life and are likely to become increasingly important in British policy making. A central consideration of this is the role that community languages will play in the British Isles of tomorrow.

16 Caribbean creoles and Black English

Mark Sebba

The origins of Caribbean creoles in Britain and British Black English

There have been Caribbeans living in Britain for several centuries, and cities such as London, Bristol, Cardiff and Liverpool have long-established Caribbean communities dating back to the era of slavery. However, the present-day African-Caribbean community dates mainly from the period following World War II. From 1948 onwards, to compensate for labour shortages in Britain, workers were recruited in the former British Empire in the West Indies. According to census returns, in 1951 there were 15,000 persons born in the West Indies living in England and Wales. By the end of 1958, an estimated 117,000 West Indians had entered Britain (Wood 1960). However, by 1962, the labour shortage over, legislation had been passed with a view to limiting immigration from the New Commonwealth, and migration from the West Indies began to decline.

The fact that migration from the Caribbean area was regulated, by employment opportunities on the one hand and by immigration laws on the other, means that the first, second and subsequent generations of African-Caribbeans are relatively easy to distinguish by age. Thus typical first-generation members will have been born by about 1950, and members of the second generation from 1960 onwards, probably with a peak in the 1970s. A third generation is reaching maturity.

The language situation in the Commonwealth Caribbean

Standard English is the language of administration and education in all of the Caribbean territories which were formerly part of the British Empire. However, the vernacular in these countries is generally a creole language: English-lexicon (i.e. an 'English-based Creole') in the majority, French-lexicon in a few, such as St Lucia and Dominica. The Caribbean English-lexicon creoles are often divided into those of the Eastern Caribbean (Lesser

Antilles, Trinidad and Guyana) and the Western Caribbean (most importantly Jamaican Creole, but also the English-lexicon creoles of Central America (Belize, Costa Rica and Nicaragua) and the Colombian islands of Providencia and San Andrés). In practice each Caribbean territory has its own vernacular, the result of specific conditions of language contact and development, and distinguishable from all others by some combination of phonology, lexis and grammar. For a few of these language varieties, detailed linguistic descriptions exist: for example, for Jamaican (e.g. Bailey 1966, Cassidy & Le Page 1967/1980, Patrick 1999); Guyanese (e.g. Bickerton 1975, Rickford 1987); Belizean (e.g. Young 1973). Wells (1982) has phonological descriptions of some of these. Descriptions are also available for some non-geographical varieties, e.g. the language of Rastafarians (Pollard 1994). For the rest, information is less readily available or available only for some part of the grammar (e.g. phonology).

In those parts of the Caribbean where an English-lexicon creole vernacular is in contact with Standard English in its role as the official language, the majority of the population speak neither the one nor the other consistently. Instead, a wide range of intermediate varieties is found. De Camp (1961) was the first to describe the Jamaican situation as a *dialect continuum* linking the broadest creole (known in this model as the *basilect*, and nowadays possibly more a theoretical construct than a reality) with the local form of Standard English, called the *acrolect*. The term *mesolect* is used for all the varieties in between.

The continuum model has become the dominant one in the study of language variation in Caribbean creoles, though speakers themselves continue to perceive the situation as one where two discrete languages or codes are in use (Mühleisen 2002). The continuum model is taken to reflect both the *social hierarchy*, with Standard English speakers at the top, and a *historical process*, whereby creole speakers gradually and differentially gained more access to education (see De Camp 1971, Alleyne 1980).

The exact linguistic nature of the hypothesised continuum remains a subject for debate (see Rickford (1983) for a discussion). According to one line of argument, Standard English *forms* may appear in mesolectal speech without necessarily having the *function* of similar items in Standard English. Thus the basilectal copula /a/ in (1) is replaced by the Standard English form <iz> in the more mesolectal version (2); however, /iz/ for speakers who use it in this way is not necessarily a conjugated form of the Standard English verb *to be*, but could be an invariant verbal form, as shown in (3), which might be uttered by the same hypothetical speaker who uttered (2).

(1)   \<mista juonz a di tiicha\> 'Mister Jones is the teacher'

(2)   \<mista juonz iz di tiicha\>

(3)   \<mi iz di tiicha\> 'I am the teacher'

So for mesolectal speakers, it is possible that basilectal creole forms are substituted by Standard English forms without fundamental grammatical changes in the direction of Standard English taking place. Where the grammar is changed, this is likely to happen at some stage *after* the adoption of the corresponding Standard English form.

Whether or not the continuum model is the best one for the observed data, it is a fact that the vernacular of the 'English-speaking' Caribbean territories is characterised by a very high degree of variability. Both 'Creole' and 'Standard English' forms may be found in the majority of everyday utterances, posing challenges to conventional sociolinguistic notions of dialectal variation and bilingualism.

Caribbean Creoles in Britain

Name of the language

In Britain, the term 'Creole' in its linguistic sense, though increasingly familiar to the general public, is used mainly by linguists. English-lexicon creole is most commonly called *patois* (also spelt *patwa*) by its users. Other terms are 'Black Talk', 'Nation Language' and 'Black Slang'. The term 'Dread Talk' usually refers to the particular variety used by Rastafarians. The terms *British Black English* (the title of David Sutcliffe's (1982) book, the first on the topic) and *London Jamaican* (probably first used in print by Rosen & Burgess (1980), later the title of Sebba's (1993) book) are not usually used by the speakers of these varieties, though they may be known to professionals, e.g. teachers.

The origins of 'British Black English'

Migrants to Britain came from all parts of the Caribbean region: even the smallest islands were represented. The first generation were thus linguistically diverse, to the extent that they were speakers of different, though related, vernaculars. Most will have been speakers of mesolectal varieties, and will have had some contact with Standard English through schooling.

In Britain, the first generation came into contact with local varieties of British English, for example London English, in addition to Standard English. Wells (1973) is a study of adaptations in pronunciation made by adult Jamaicans of this generation living in London, under the influence of local varieties of British English.

Given that the first generation of migrants retained most of the linguistic characteristics of their native varieties, it might have been expected that the second generation would, likewise, speak a range of 'mother tongues'. This is a common outcome of migration, where the second generation learn the migrant community's language mainly at home, and the majority language mainly outside the home. An alternative scenario – one which has been realised in some situations of migration – would have been for *koineisation* to have taken place. According to Trudgill (1986:126), koineisation 'comprises the process of levelling, which involves the loss of marked and/or minority variants; and the process of simplification [. . .] through which even forms and distinctions present in all the contributory dialects may be lost'. This might have meant the development of a new creole variety common to the whole second generation, with 'levelling' of features unique to individual Caribbean varieties. The result would have been a variety that was recognisably Caribbean in origin, but which was not identical with any previously existing variety.

The actual outcome was not either of these. What happened in reality was that Jamaican Creole emerged as the 'heritage language' used among the second generation, even those whose parents were *not* Jamaican Creole speakers. By the late 1970s or early 1980s, a number of commentators had observed that a variety of Jamaican Creole was being used in British schools, by children of Caribbean but not necessarily Jamaican extraction. With the studies of Sutcliffe (1982), Hewitt (1986) and Sebba (1993, based on research conducted by Sebba and Robert Le Page between 1981 and 1984) it became clear that in London, Jamaican Creole had spread well beyond the boundaries of the Jamaican community and was being used as a symbol of group identity by 'Black British' children and adolescents generally – as well as by some White adolescents in friendship groups with Black peers.

The emergence of a 'Black British' identity with its linguistic hallmark, the ability to code-switch between Creole ('Patwa') and a local non-standard form of English, is discussed by Paul Gilroy (1987). He attributes the loss of separate identities relating to the individual Caribbean territories, and their blending in a new 'Black British' identity, to the shared experiences of 'race' and social class which the first generation underwent. In Britain, their territorial origins and their previous social status became irrelevant: they were seen as 'West Indian' and working class. The consciousness of this in the second generation gave rise to the new identity, self-consciously both British and Black, lacking the strong links with specific Caribbean places which the first generation had felt.

The adoption of Jamaican Creole as a unifying 'heritage language' for the whole second-generation Caribbean community could be seen as the linguistic equivalent of the social process described in the last paragraph. The reasons for adopting Jamaican for this purpose, rather than some 'levelled' pan-Caribbean creole, are most likely the following: (a) the fact that Jamaicans were the largest single group, in the majority in some areas but not all; (b) the popularity among Caribbean youth of reggae music, which had its origins in Jamaica and whose single most influential exponent, Bob Marley, was a Jamaican; and (c) the popularity of the Rastafarian religious and cultural movement (closely linked to reggae music), which was also largely Jamaican.

Research into 'British Black English'

Discussions of 'Black English' or 'Creole' in London prior to 1980 are mostly anecdotal. The first systematic descriptions of the use of this variety appear in the work of Roger Hewitt (especially Hewitt 1986) on cross-ethnic adolescent friendships. Sebba (1993) is a detailed report of the only full-scale research project to date which has focussed specifically on the language of Caribbeans in London. The research was carried out between 1981 and 1984. Thereafter the next major study is Mühleisen (2002), based on fieldwork in South London in 1996–7.

Outside London, research has been unevenly distributed both in space and time. Substantial research projects have been carried out in Bedford/ Luton (Sutcliffe 1982); Dudley, West Midlands (Edwards 1986: the research was carried out by Edwards, Sutcliffe and associates) and PhD projects in Birmingham (Wright 1984) and Sheffield (Willis 1999). Smaller-scale studies have been undertaken in Bradford (Tate 1984) and Sheffield (Bottomley 1996). Obvious gaps are the lack of research in two of the oldest and largest African-Caribbean communities in the west of Britain – Cardiff and Bristol – and two others in the north of England – Liverpool and Manchester – as well as many smaller ones, which may be of special interest because their composition in terms of place of emigration and other socio-cultural factors may be different from the larger communities already studied.

The use of British Creole

Speakers of British Creole, from the second generation onwards, are users from an early age of a local variety of British English, and will make contact with Standard English at school, if not earlier. The language of the second (and possibly subsequent) generations is characterised by the use of code-switching under appropriate social circumstances. When the participants in an interaction are able to use both Creole and English, where the speakers know each other and where the setting is sufficiently informal or oriented towards a shared Caribbean culture, the speakers are likely to switch between Creole and English from time to time.

Research by Sebba (1993) showed that second-generation Caribbeans in London used a very high proportion of London English in everyday informal conversation. Nevertheless Creole was used in many conversations, often towards the end of a conversational sequence to highlight important points or a 'punch line'. Most code-switches were functional, i.e. motivated by some conversation-internal or conversation-external goal; the pattern of non-functional language alternation which occurs in some communities was not observed (Sebba 1993, Sebba & Wootton 1998).

Given that virtually all of these speakers have native fluency in British English, Creole has become for them almost unnecessary for purely communicative functions. Its use is largely symbolic – but its symbolism, especially as a marker of group identity, is powerful. Creole serves this identity-marking function even for those speakers who have limited fluency in it. Such speakers may rely on the use of *token* Creole features as an indication that Creole is one of the codes in use. Using small amounts of stereotypically Creole vocabulary, discourse markers, phonology and vocatives such as *man*, *guy* and *star*, may be enough to mark a conversation as a 'Creole event' or to have a particular utterance assigned to the 'Creole' code in contrast to the 'English' one. Seen in this way, Creole in the London context is a speech *style*, defined by the participants of an interaction in contrast with 'English', and marked by a selection of salient 'non-English' features. Put another way, Creole is a *performance*. This is different from the notion of Creole as a distinct language with its own norms of grammar, phonology, etc., which would be more appropriate to the Caribbean.

Linked to this symbolic use of Creole is the fact, observed by several researchers, that adolescent speakers of British Creole tend to focus on Creole forms which are maximally different from the corresponding Standard English ones. For example, Edwards (1986:104) comments on 'the preference for basilectal rather than mesolectal forms' in her speakers from the West Midlands – in other words, where a Creole form could be realised in any of several ways which are English-like to varying degrees, these speakers will choose the one which is least English-like. This is to be expected if the main value of Creole is symbolic, as such choices maximise the distance from English and emphasise that the code in use is Creole.

In spite of this preference for uncompromisingly Creole forms, many adolescent Creole users in Britain have less than native-speaker-like abilities in the language, judged relative to native speakers of Jamaican Creole *in Jamaica*. By this criterion, second-generation speakers vary greatly in their 'fluency'. Viv Edwards and David Sutcliffe found about one-third of their sample to be 'very fluent' but a quarter had only 'limited competence in Patois' (Edwards 1986:100). Edwards describes the behaviour of this group as 'highly reminiscent of that of second language learners'. Moreover, she notes the existence of an 'acquisitional hierarchy', with certain features systematically being acquired by some speakers but not others. Edwards concludes that these speakers are in fact *second language learners* of Creole. However, similar acquisitional hierarchies have been observed in *second dialect* learners (Trudgill 1986), who learn how to 'transform' their existing dialect to sound like a new one.

Clearly, some adolescent British Creole speakers cannot be 'native speakers' in the usual sense. Speakers who lack a Jamaican parent cannot have acquired this form of Jamaican Creole solely in the home. Even some Jamaican parents are known to have avoided using Creole with their children in the hope of helping them to learn English better.

Furthermore, we find a number of hybrid linguistic forms which can be explained *only* by speakers using a strategy of adapting British English forms to make them 'sound' Creole. For example, one adolescent speaker says:

You call dem law but dey break de law
[ju kɑːl dɛm luɔɹ bt dɛ brɛk̚ di luɔɹ]
'You call them law, but they break the law!' = 'They're police but they break the law!'

Here, the form [luɔɹ] *law* appears to be derived from British English by analogy with other words which rhyme with *law* in the London English of this speaker. He is aware that words like *poor* and *sore* ([pɔː] and [sɔː] for this speaker) have their Jamaican Creole equivalent pronounced with a postvocalic /r/: [puɔɹ] and [suɔɹ]. By analogy he produces a rhotic form [luɔɹ] for law, but the analogy is wrong: in Jamaican Creole (as in many North American varieties), *law* does not rhyme with *poor* and *sore*, since historically it lacks a postvocalic /r/. Instead it patterns with words like *thought*. The basilectal Jamaican pronunciation of *law* is thus [laː] and the more acrolectal pronunciation [lɔː]; [luɔɹ] is not a Jamaican pronunciation at all and could be viewed as a form of hypercorrection.

Other speakers are recorded as saying:

Did him give you what you a look for?
'Did he give you what you were looking for?'

What time did unu [you-plural] *reach home?*
'What time did you get home?'

These utterances, which are marked as Creole by pronunciation (throughout), pronoun forms (*him, unu*), and in the case of the first, grammar (use of the aspect marking *a* in *a look*), would not be uttered by a first-language speaker of Creole in Jamaica. Jamaican Creole has no subject–auxiliary inversion in questions (because in fact it has no auxiliary; tense and aspect markers such as *a* and *did* are invariant preverbal particles, not verbs), so the expected forms of these utterances in Jamaica would be:

Him did give you what you a look for?

and

What time unu [you-plural] *did* [or *en*, or Ø] *reach home?*

The forms actually produced by the second-generation adolescent speakers in London suggest a strategy of 'dressing up' a basically London English sentence (*Did he give you what you were looking for?* etc.) as Creole by adding Creole phonology, lexis and grammar. As in the case of the speaker who produced [luɔɹ] on an incorrect analogy, the strategy has not been entirely successful. The resulting sentences sound Creole enough to count as Creole for the purposes of the interaction, but would not be produced by a native speaker of Jamaican Creole.

The circumstances of the use of British Creole – in particular, the fact that it is used by second-generation adolescents who do not have a Jamaican background – indicate that it is acquired sequentially *after* the local vernacular by some people. Although this could mean that those speakers are actually second language learners of Creole, as Edwards (1986) proposes, the fact that some speakers seem to produce their Creole via a series of adaptations from British English suggests that they are best seen as 'second dialect' learners (Trudgill 1986), who are acquiring a new *variety* of a language they already speak.

The research which has been reported for the African-Caribbean communities outside London reveals largely similar trends to those in London. The findings of Edwards and Sutcliffe have already been mentioned. Willis (1999) found that her subjects in Sheffield 'used Creole almost exclusively in the context of code-switching, exhibiting a wide range of forms of Creole and English and demonstrating a shared understanding of the contexts and meaning of Creole usage in the in-group situation'.

Linguistic characteristics of British Creole

To a large extent, the linguistic features which distinguish British Creole from other varieties of English in Britain are exactly the same as those which distinguish Jamaican Creole from British English varieties. Detailed descriptions already exist for Jamaican Creole syntax (Bailey 1966), lexis (Cassidy & Le Page 1967/1980) and phonology (Wells 1982). These descriptions alone are not sufficient for British Creole because of its variability and the fact that local varieties of British English (e.g. London English) have influenced it in various ways and to different extents. There have also been some independent developments in British Creole, especially in the lexicon.

In this section I shall list only a selection of the most salient grammatical and phonological markers of British Creole and shall make only a few remarks about the lexicon.

Grammar

The pronoun system The Jamaican Creole (JC) 'basilectal' pronominal system has only seven terms, as follows:

	singular	plural
1	mi	wi
2	yu	unu
3	im (m/f)	dem
	i (n)	

More mesolectal varieties would differentiate *im* (masculine) and *shi* (feminine) in the third person. These forms are used in subject, object and possessive functions (although an alternative construction, *fi* + PRONOUN, e.g. *fi-mi*, is available for the possessive). In British Creole, there is some evidence of the loss of the strict distinction between *yu* (singular) and *unu* (plural), inasmuch as *yu* is sometimes used for plural, on analogy with Standard English.

Plural marking Basilectal JC does not mark the plural of nouns, except in the case of animate nouns, which may be followed by the suffix *-dem*. In mesolectal varieties the Standard English suffix *-s* may co-occur with the JC suffix *dem* and this is also commonly found in British Creole, with animate and sometimes also inanimate nouns:

Look how me make yuh dumplin's dem fresh and crispy (source: *Corpus of Written British Creole*; see Sebba 1998 and Sebba & Dray 2003).

Possessives In Basilectal JC, possession is expressed simply by juxtaposition, with the possessor preceding the possessed. The effect is that the ordering of nouns is as in Standard English, but there is no possessive marker *(')s: di bwai niem*, 'the boy's name'. This structure applies to common nouns but also to pronouns, so we find *mi buk* 'my book', *unu kyaa* 'your car', etc. In British Creole, the possessive *'s* of Standard English may appear variably.

Tense and aspect marking The tense/aspect system of JC is fundamentally unlike that of English. The exact details are complex (and have been studied more for Guyanese than for Jamaican, see Bickerton (1975), Gibson (1982)). However, there are obvious superficial differences in the way tense and aspect are marked. JC has two preverbal particles, *a and en*. Although these resemble the forms *are* and *been* of the English verb *to be*, which is used as a preverbal auxiliary, *a* and *en* are not verbs. They are simply invariant particles, and cannot stand alone in the way that English *to be* can. Furthermore, their function is wholly different. Bailey (1966:45–6) calls *en* a 'tense indicator' and *a* the 'aspect marker'. The following examples show the different tense and aspectual forms of the JC verb:
(a) Mi ron
     'I run (habitually); I ran'
(b) Mi a ron
     'I am running'
(c) Mi ena (en + a) ron
     'I was running'
(d) Mi en ron
     'I have run; I had run'
The tense marker which Bailey cites as *en* does not usually appear in that form in British Creole. It occasionally appears as *bin*, a form which is also used in Jamaica. Much more frequently it appears as *did*, which seems to fulfil exactly the same function. In terms of Creole linguistic structure, this should be analysed as an invariant particle rather than a verb; there is evidence, however, that some speakers treat it as an auxiliary (see 'The use of British Creole' above).

   Mesolectal varieties of JC may use a suffix /in/ (modelled on the Standard English *-ing* ending) as an alternative to the *a* + VERB form, thus: *mi ronin = mi a ron*. Other forms influenced by Standard English such as *mi iz ronin* are also possible.

   While JC has no morphologically marked past tense forms corresponding to English (cf. *looked, went, drove*), in some cases the base form of the JC verb derives historically from an English past tense. Examples are *brok* ('break/broke') and *lef* ('leave/left'). These forms are used in JC for both present and past.

   The copula In Standard English the verb *to be* is used in at least the following four ways:

(a) As an auxiliary verb: *I am writing*, etc.
(b) As an equative verb: *I am a teacher*, etc.
(c) As a locative verb: *We are in London*, etc.
(d) As a copular verb with an adjective: *This book is old*, etc.

Basilectal JC uses a different expression for each of these:

(a) Auxiliary verbs are not used to form tenses or aspects of the verb in
     Jamaican Creole (see above).
(b) The JC equative verb *a* 'regularly connects two nominals' (Bailey
     1966:32): *mi **a** di tiicha*.
(c) JC has a separate locative verb *de*: *Weh your pickney deh*? 'Where is
     your child?' (source: *Corpus of Written British Creole*)
(d) With true adjectives in JC, no copula is required: *Them old enough. Yuh
     so cantankerous and stubborn.* (source: *Corpus of Written British Creole*)

Mesolectal varieties, as noted above, may use <iz> as a substitute for *a*
and/or *de*, obscuring the grammatical differences between JC and
Standard English.

Negation The main JC negator is *no*, as in: *mi naa* [no + a] *ron* 'I'm
not running', *wi no de a London* 'We're not in London'. Other possible
negators are *neba* or *neva*, used only for the past (*mi neba nuo dat* 'I didn't
know that') and *duont*, used for habitual action and with psychic state
verbs (e.g. *think*) (Bailey 1966:54).

'Double negatives' are used with quantitatives in basilectal JC, and are
frequently found in British Creole, where their distribution is similar to
that in most non-standard British varieties of English:

Nothing don't seriously wrong wid him (source: *Corpus of Written British Creole*)

Infinitive marking The English infinitive marker *to* is most often
translated by *fi* in JC, although in some cases it is optional in Creole where
it is obligatory in English (cf. *im waant go a skuul/im waant fi go a skuul*). In
the Caribbean *fi* is considered to be a marker of extremely broad Creole;
many otherwise broad Creole speakers will use *tu* (English *to*) in preference. (See Bailey 1966:122ff. for a description of the use of *fi*.)

Word order in questions The process of subject–auxiliary verb
inversion which characterises some kinds of question in written and formal
Standard English is absent in basilectal JC, so the word order of a question
is the same as the order of the corresponding statement, e.g.:

So how Ethel's been doing? (source: *Corpus of Written British Creole*)

You heard about Fluxy? (source: *Corpus of Written British Creole*)

Note that British speakers of Creole may produce hybrid forms which appear to have subject–auxiliary inversion (see 'The use of British Creole' above).

Cleft and predicate cleft Cleft structures are common in JC, especially with questions.

*So, **is whe** me ah go stay?* (source: *Corpus of Written British Creole*)

Predicate cleft is a JC construction which involves fronting and repeating the main verb, e.g.:

*Work?! Where? Here? **Joke** you a **joke**, man!* (source: *Corpus of Written British Creole*)

Verb chaining Verbs in JC may be combined in ways which are not possible in English. One set of possibilities involves the motion verbs *go* and *come* immediately followed by another verb, e.g.:

*Prettyboy, **go bring** you gran'uncle something to drink* (source: *Corpus of Written British Creole*)

A second possibility is where the motion verb follows a main verb with lexical content, e.g.:

*Weh you ah **rush go** so?* (source: *Corpus of Written British Creole*)

Other combinations of verbs are sometimes found both in JC and in British Creole.

Phonology

Detailed descriptions of Jamaican Creole phonology are readily available elsewhere, for example in the introduction to Cassidy & Le Page (1967/1980), and in J.C. Wells (1973, 1982). Most of the characteristics of Jamaican Creole phonology are also to be found in British Creole, although variably so, and often affected by the phonology of local vernacular varieties of English.

This section will therefore merely summarise some of the most salient features of the phonology of British Creole, in contrast with indigenous British varieties of English. Much of the information here is derived from Wells (1982), Volume 3, which remains the most authoritative source on Caribbean pronunciations of English-lexicon creoles.

The vowels Table 16.1 summarises some of the salient contrasts between vowels of Jamaican Creole and vowels found in British English

Table 16.1. *Vowels*

Standard lexical set	Cassidy orthography	Basilectal Jamaican Creole	Acrolectal Jamaican Creole	RP equivalent	Comments
LOT	a	[ɒ]	[ɒ]	[ɒ]	is not distinguished from TRAP in the basilect
TRAP	a	[a]	[a]	[æ]	is not distinguished from HOT in the basilect
STRUT	o	[ɔ]	[ɔ]	[ʌ]	'back and rounded, between [ɔ] and [ɘ]' (Wells 1982:576)
NURSE	o(r)	[ɔ]	[ɔr] ~ [ɜ]	[ɜː]	rhotic forms are found in the mesolect and acrolect
THOUGHT	aa	[aː]	[ɔː]	[ɔ]	
FACE	ie	[ɪɛ]	[eː]	[ɛ]	a few JC monosyllables, e.g. *say, make, take,* have [ɛ], thus: [sɛ] *say*
GOAT	uo	[uɔ]	[oː]	[əʊ]	a few JC monosyllables, e.g. *go,* have [ɒ], thus: [ɡʊ] *go*
PRICE	ai	[aɪ]	[aɪ]	[aɪ]	is not distinguished from CHOICE in the basilect
CHOICE	ai	[aɪ]	[ɔɪ]	[ɔɪ]	is not distinguished from PRICE in the basilect
MOUTH	ou	[ɔʊ]	[ɔʊ]	[aʊ]	
START	aa(r)	[aː]	[aː(ɹ)]	[aː]	'sporadic preconsonantal rhoticity is characteristic of many mesolectal and some acrolectal speakers' (Wells 1982:577)
NORTH	aa(r)	[aː]	[aː(ɹ)]	[ɔː]	'In the lower mesolect, final /r/ is quite common in careful pronunciations of lettER words' (Wells 1982:577)
FORCE	uor	[oːɹ]	[oːɹ]	[ɔː]	
lettER	a	[ə]	[ə]	[ə]	

varieties (exemplified by RP). Standard lexical sets are used to refer to groups of words containing a particular vowel, e.g. the LOT vowel is the vowel of the word *lot*, found also in many other words.

The consonants There are relatively few differences between the Caribbean creole and British English consonant systems but those there are seem to be very salient for speakers.

RHOTICITY: Jamaican Creole has postvocalic /r/ in positions where it was found in earlier varieties of English, as usually reflected in the spelling. Basilectal Creole, however, lacks postvocalic /r/ 'in weak syllables' and 'before a consonant in the same morpheme' (Wells 1982:577); hence there is a contrast between basilectal JC /faːm/ and Jamaican English (acrolectal) /faːrm/ *farm*. Most of the British English varieties (whether high or low prestige) used by Caribbeans in Britain lack postvocalic /r/. Although no systematic research has been done on this, it may well be that in Britain, the pronunciations with postvocalic /r/ are interpreted as markers of Creoleness rather than as being more socially prestigious.

POSTVOCALIC /l/: The /l/ of *milk* and *bell* is a point where there is a clear division between Jamaican on the one hand and many British English varieties on the other. Jamaican /l/ is invariably 'clear' in all contexts, i.e. pronounced with the tongue forward in the mouth. In both RP and London English, as well as some other British varieties, when /l/ is postvocalic the tongue is retracted and the back of the tongue approaches the velum to produce a 'dark l' or even a [u] vowel.

THINK /θ/ AND BOTHER /ð/: In basilectal JC, these consonants are represented by the plosives /t/ and /d/: [tɪŋk] *think*, [wid] *with*. In many British English varieties, especially in London and the south-east, TH-fronting operates, causing these phonemes to be realised as [f] and [v] in some contexts: [fɪŋk], [wɪv]. These pronunciations are sometimes heard in stretches of speech of younger British Caribbeans which are otherwise marked as Creole. TH-fronting does not occur in Jamaica.

'H-DROPPING': The phoneme /h/ is subject to variation in many dialects of English. The variable loss of word initial /h/ is regarded as substandard by prescriptivists. H-dropping occurs in Jamaica as well. 'Alongside the frequent H-Dropping of [aːf] *half*, [uɔl] *hole-whole*, etc. there is the frequent use of [h] in words such as *egg*, *off*, *end*. This can be seen either as hypercorrection [...] or merely as an emphatic device used whenever a word beginning phonologically with a vowel is emphasised' (Wells 1982:568). In the context of London, according to Hewitt (1986:192) 'very emphatic initial glottal stops on words such as "appen" and "eart" are characteristic of creole-influenced LE'. There has been no systematic study of this phenomenon.

GLOTTALLING OF /t/: The glottalling of /t/ (e.g. [bʌʔə], RP [bʌtʰə]) is a very widespread feature of many British English varieties, though still regarded as substandard. However, /t/-glottalling is not a feature of Jamaican speech at any level of society. Wells (1973:31) observed a case of a first-generation Caribbean in London saying [boːʔ ə dɛm] *both of them*. This, he surmises, is the result of applying the London rule of /t/-glottalling to the creole form [boːt] *both*. The resulting pronunciation is 'characteristic neither of West Indians in the West Indies nor of Cockneys in London, but just of West Indians in Cockney London'. Since 'glottalled /t/' is pervasive in south-eastern British English for younger speakers, it could serve to differentiate 'Creole' from 'English' for speakers of those varieties, but evidence suggests it does not; glottalled pronunciations like [pʰaːʔi] *party* are fairly common in stretches of speech which are otherwise marked as Creole.

PALATAL AND LABIAL-VELAR GLIDES: After /k/ and /g/ and before an open vowel, /j/ (yod) tends to appear in Jamaican Creole: /kjat/ *cat*, /kjar/ *car*, /gjal/ *girl*. The /j/ does not appear if the vowel corresponds to the classes LOT, THOUGHT, NORTH: this maintains the distinction between *cot* /kat/ and *cat* /kjat/ (see Wells 1982:569). Similarly, /w/ may appear after /p b f v m/ before the vowels of NORTH, STRUT and CHOICE: /fwaːti/ *forty*, /mwɔni/ *money*, /bwaɪ/ *boy*. /w/ before /aɪ/ occurs in words from the lexical set of CHOICE but not PRICE: hence /pwaɪnt/ *point* but /paɪnt/ *pint*. All these typically Jamaican pronunciations may be found in British Creole but variants lacking the glides are also heard. The glides occur in common words and are often indicated in spellings like <bwoy>, <bwai>, <gyal>, <cyan>, suggesting that they are salient for speakers.

Lexicon

The lexicon of British Creole is different from that of Jamaican Creole in largely predictable ways. Words for traditional occupations and Caribbean species of flora and fauna are not much needed in Britain and therefore less likely to be known and used by the generations born here. The fact that British Creole is popular with adolescents and young adults favours particular areas of vocabulary, to do with music, recreation, sex and swearing; in these areas there is a rapid turnover of slang vocabulary, some of which is also current outside the Black community (see 'British Creole beyond the Black community' below).

Written Creole in Britain

The only written language supported across the curriculum in the English education system is Standard English, although studying non-standard varieties of English may form a small part of the curriculum. Thus British Caribbeans are usually monolingual in Standard English when it comes to writing.

In spite of this, there is a growing body of writing in Creole in Britain in a range of genres. Poetry in Creole or Creole-influenced varieties of English has been published in Britain and in the Caribbean for several decades. Some performance poets like Linton Kwesi Johnson, Jean Binta Breeze (both Caribbean-born but working in Britain) and Benjamin Zephaniah publish books of their poetry. The practice of printing the lyrics of songs and performance (e.g. 'dub') poetry on record sleeves or CD inserts has been common since the 1970s. There is also some non-commercial publishing of poems and fiction, sometimes with public subsidies.

Since the early 1990s a genre of inner-city crime fiction ('yardie' novels) has appeared in Britain, featuring Caribbean characters with characteristically Caribbean speech. While the narrative in these novels is usually in Standard English (with occasional exceptions), characters are often depicted as using Creole or mixtures of Creole and British English, as in the following extract from the novel *Yardie* (1992) by Victor Headley (Standard English stretches are in bold).

'Lord! D.. is you fe true?' **she exclaimed, stepping towards him, arms open. She hugged him, then, looking at him closely**: 'Wait, you a grow beard now,' **she quipped, passing her hand over the short stubble on his chin**. 'Is when you reach, man? So why you never write tell me seh you coming?' (Headley 1992:20)

Apart from poetry, the main use of British Creole *in print* is undoubtedly in dialogue in novels like the one above. However, there is an unknown but potentially large amount of Creole used in writing for private purposes such as letters between friends.

Like its spoken counterpart, written British Creole shows a high degree of variability, in grammar, lexis and orthography. This area remains little researched, though Sebba, Kedge & Dray (1999) have established an experimental *Corpus of Written British Creole* as a resource for researchers in this area (see Sebba 1998 and Sebba & Dray 2003).

British Creole beyond the Black community

A striking phenomenon in the period since the mid-1970s has been the adoption of Creole lexis and discourse forms by adolescents from outside the Caribbean community. Hewitt (1986) speaks of a 'local multi-racial vernacular' in London – London English which shows the influence of Creole in its vocabulary and some discourse marking. The popularisation of such speech styles through their association with cultural forms such as rapping and hip-hop has meant that they have become widely recognised (though less widely *used*) outside the Caribbean community, and even outside urban areas. The wide availability of crime fiction with a Caribbean gangster theme (see above) may have contributed to this as well: certainly not all the readers of these novels are Caribbeans.

Research by Rampton (1995a) identified a phenomenon of *crossing* among urban adolescents – the use of a language usually taken as 'owned' by an ethnic group different from that of the speaker. The use of Creole – usually in small amounts – by adolescents of White, African and South Asian ethnicity is widespread and was also noted by Hewitt (1986) and Sebba (1993).

The trend has since become even more marked. In 1999 the White comedian Sacha Baron Cohen popularised 'Black' speech patterns through his spoof chat-show host character 'Ali G', a young man of ambiguous ethnicity whose speciality is trapping politicians and celebrities into making foolish admissions in interviews. Relentlessly playing on ethnic stereotypes while at the same time subverting them, 'Ali G' started a craze for both spoken and written 'Creole' – the latter found mainly on the many Internet sites (bulletin boards, 'guest books', etc.) set up by Ali G or by devoted fans. The language of Ali G himself is characterised by a variable mixture of stigmatised Southern British English forms and salient Creole grammatical and phonological features. There is a limited amount of Creole vocabulary, with a high proportion of taboo and obscene words. The written 'Creole' used on the Ali G websites is not authentic – much of it is produced by individuals who have probably never even met a Creole speaker – but it reflects some of the most salient phonological features of actual British Creole, and incorporates some of the lexis made popular by Ali G. Although it is possible to dismiss Ali G's stage language as 'mock Creole', in fact, it is constructed using much the same strategy as the actual 'Creole' used by some adolescents of genuinely Caribbean heritage, i.e. by grafting salient features which have stereotypical or symbolic value as Creole on to a base which is essentially local British English (see Sebba 2003).

Though the Ali G fad may soon die out, its popularity demonstrates that Creole has made its mark on the consciousness of speakers of British English – and not just in urban areas where Caribbeans and non-Caribbeans are most likely to mingle. This suggests that even if Creole is largely relinquished as a main medium of communication in the Caribbean community in succeeding generations, it will continue to exist as a language of youth and adolescence, well beyond the confines of its original ethnic roots.

17 Indic languages

Mike Reynolds and Mahendra Verma

Introduction

At the beginning of the twenty-first century, Indic languages have established themselves as a very significant part of the linguistic mix of multicultural Britain. The number of Indic languages is, of course, great, but in the British context, there are five, with their varieties, that are most quantitatively significant: Bangla, Gujarati, Hindi, Panjabi and Urdu. The vast majority of South Asians in Britain speak one or another of these languages, which all belong to the Indo-Aryan branch of the Indo-European family of languages. Nonetheless, communities of speakers of other Indic languages must not be overlooked, in particular Tamil (a Dravidian language spoken in South India and Sri Lanka) and Pashto (one of the four main regional languages of Pakistan).

Background and history

Contact between Indic-language and English speakers has a long history, beginning with the arrival of the English in India at the end of the sixteenth century, continuing throughout the period of British colonialism in the Indian subcontinent, and since Independence through the migration of Indians, Pakistanis and Bangladeshis to Britain. Immigration, too, has a long history. There were Bangla migrations in the 1920s and 1930s, and Sikh peddlers were to be seen in many British cities (Agnihotri 1987:15–16, Mahandru 1991:117–18). But the major movements into Britain came in two waves: first in the 1950s and 1960s, from post-Independence India, West and East Pakistan (which later emerged as Bangladesh), and second in the late 1960s and 1970s from East Africa (Kenya and Uganda) when policies of Africanisation forced South Asians to uproot. Among this second wave were the majority of Gujarati-speaking immigrants (Dave 1991:90). There were important socioeconomic differences between the members of these two immigrant groups. The East African immigrants were often well educated and had professional and commercial

293

occupations. The earlier immigrants, especially from the Indian and Pakistani Panjab, and from what is now Bangladesh, were mainly from rural areas, and with basic education.

Demography and geography

The number of speakers of Indic languages in Britain is increasing quite substantially. However, the demographic and geographical situation is beset with uncertainties and inaccuracies. There are two main aspects of the problem, one deriving from the sociolinguistic complexity of the Indian subcontinent, the other only to some extent connected with this, in the shortcomings of data collection for official UK purposes. The Census only collects data on the basis of ethnicity, not home language, and this remains the statutory basis for the collection of educational statistics (at least for England and Wales). The relevant ethnic categories are 'Indian', 'Pakistani' and 'Bangladeshi'. This leaves the linguistic researcher with a lot of uncertain and even dubious inferencing to do, in all three categories.

The majority of Bangladeshis in Britain, for instance, come from the Sylhet province in the north-east of Bangladesh, and speak Sylheti as their home language, rather than standard Bangla. A very substantial number of Pakistani immigrants to Britain came from the Mirpur province and speak Mirpuri. Smaller numbers of Pakistanis have Pashto as their home language. Many Pakistanis, and Afghans too, also have Urdu as a language of literacy. Most difficult of all is how to assign membership of the 'Indian' ethnic group to a specific speech community. The London survey (Baker & Eversley 2000), for instance, lists up to 22 Indic languages spoken in the capital.

The Panjabis are the most interesting group in view of the complexities of their language choice, their choice of literacy and the role religion and politics have contributed to it. In the British context the ethnolinguistic group called the 'Panjabis' are subcategorised into Panjabi Sikhs, Panjabi Hindus and Panjabi Muslims based on their religious persuasions. The geographical area called the Panjab (East and West) is united by its common language – Panjabi, which forms a bond between the three groups divided by religion. Another interesting characteristic of their linguistic behaviour is the choice of language in education and government. The Panjabi Sikhs' mother tongue is Panjabi, and it is also their language in education and the language of literacy in Gurmukhi script. The Hindu and the Muslim Panjabis, on the whole, perceive Panjabi as a colloquial language, which as a marker of their cultural ethnicity is also the natural language of folk music, songs and dance on festive occasions. However, their language choice in education is not their primary mother tongue but their heritage language – Hindi and Urdu respectively. But it is also attested that some Sikh and Hindu Panjabis have both interest and competence in the two literacy traditions.

The problem of classifying languages and estimating accurately how many speakers there are is compounded by the way in which statistics are collected on the ethnicity and home languages/mother tongues of the children in the state school sector.[1] There is little or no uniformity, and local educational authority officers in charge of such statistics admit that their systems are inadequate and often inaccurate. One authority listed 'Panjabi-Pakistani' as a reported home language, along with 'Panjabi-Sikh', 'Panjabi-Hindi' and 'Panjabi-Mirpuri'. Another lists Mirpuri and Urdu: how many of the children in that area in fact speak both? A third has 'Panjabi (Urdu script)' and 'Urdu'. However, many LEAs with significant numbers of Indic home language speakers in their schools are now collecting detailed and reasonably interpretable statistics.

London has a tradition of collecting such statistics from the days of the old Inner London Education Authority's Research and Statistics Department. These surveys were discontinued with the disbanding of the ILEA, but in 2000 a comprehensive survey of the languages spoken by London's schoolchildren, *Multilingual Capital* (Baker & Eversley 2000) appeared. This project has used the detailed large-scale techniques of language mapping available through Geographical Information Systems (GIS). This survey shows that, of the top 40 languages used by children in London, Panjabi is second (after English), with between 143,600 and 155,700 speakers. Next comes Gujarati (138,000 to 149,600 speakers). Hindi/Urdu – controversially classified here as one language – is fourth, with a high estimate of 136,500 speakers, closely followed by Bangla-Sylheti, with somewhere between 120,000 and 136,300 speakers. Three other Indic languages figured in the 'top 40': Tamil (17th), Sinhala (37th) and Pashto (39th).

The number of speakers of Indic languages has grown more than four-fold in the thirty years between the 1971 and 2001 Censuses, from under half a million to over two million, of whom just over half are 'Indian'. Moreover, it is very possible that the Census under-reports the true figures. Since 1991 the South Asian population has continued to grow at a faster rate than that of the White majority. Of these totals, over half of the Pakistanis were born in Britain, and nearly half of all Indians and

---

[1] The authors wish to acknowledge the help given by education officers in the educational statistical departments and Ethnic Minority Achievement Services of many LEAs in England and Scotland who were consulted for the up-to-date figures of children of South Asian ethnicity and speakers of Indic languages.

Bangladeshis. They have settled principally in the larger conurbations of England. The largest concentrations are in Outer and Inner London, followed by the West Midlands, West Yorkshire, Greater Manchester and Lancashire. There are significant numbers in Bedfordshire and Berkshire, 'home counties' north of London, and in the smaller industrial towns of Warwickshire, to the south of Birmingham. In Scotland the main concentrations of Pakistanis and Indians live in Strathclyde, and above all Glasgow. In Wales, there are significant numbers of all three South Asian communities in Cardiff, but insignificant numbers elsewhere.

Panjabi speakers, of both Indian and Pakistani ethnicity taken together, represent easily the largest group of all the Indic language speakers in Britain. Panjabi (Gurmukhi) speakers are most numerous in the Inner London borough of Newham and in the Outer London boroughs of Hounslow, Ealing, Greenwich, Waltham Forest and Redbridge. Outside London, there are sizeable communities in Birmingham, Coventry and Wolverhampton in the West Midlands and Bradford and Leeds in West Yorkshire. There is also a community of nearly 7,000 in Gravesham in Kent.

The largest Bangla/Sylheti speech community lives in Tower Hamlets in London, with over 65,000 (2001 Census). After this in London there are over 12,000 living in Camden, and outside London, the largest communities are in Birmingham (nearly 21,000), Oldham in Greater Manchester (nearly 10,000), Luton in Bedfordshire (over 7,500) and Bradford (nearly 5,000).

The Pakistani Panjabis settled in much the same areas as their Indian brethren, in Inner and Outer London, in Birmingham (over 100,000), Bradford (just under 68,000) and in Greater Manchester – especially Manchester, Oldham and Rochdale – where the community is over 50,000 strong.

The Gujarati speech community is most prominent in Leicester. Other sizeable communities are found in Brent and Harrow in Outer London, Bolton and Blackburn in Lancashire and Kirklees in West Yorkshire.

The Hindi-speaking community is much the smallest of the main five. In London, the main areas are Newham, Brent, Ealing and Hounslow. Outside London, Verma (1991) reports communities in Peterborough, Bradford, Coventry and Leeds. Unlike other Indic language groups, the Hindi speech community is more middle class and less bottom-heavy in its demographic profile than the others, and perhaps more dispersed across the country.

The presence of Indic language speakers in Britain's schools is of growing importance, and great attention is given by national and local government to questions of ethnic minority achievement, albeit from a perspective of raising achievement in English rather than in home/community languages.

Indic language speakers came to over a quarter of the total state school population in Birmingham (2003 figures). In Leicester, in 2000, about 22% of the school population (over 11,300) were Gujarati speakers. Bradford had nearly 20,000 – again 22% – Urdu speakers in its schools. The proportion of Bangla/Sylheti speakers in Tower Hamlets and City of London was over 53% and over 56% respectively (Baker & Eversley 2000). Such figures demonstrate dramatically the significance of Indic language speakers in certain urban areas.

In the public examination system, it is noteworthy that Urdu has become the fourth most frequently taken foreign language exam at GCSE and A/S levels (after French, German and Spanish, and before Italian). Numbers have been rising gradually over the past decade, with a high point of over 6,900 in 2002. At A level it is in sixth place, with over 700 entrants in 2003. Urdu is the only Indic language offered at the new AS level in England and Wales; it is also the only such language on offer in Scotland, at Standard grade only, where there were 122 takers in 1998 and 124 the following year. On the debit side, however, Hindi has been dropped as an examination subject, except for the Cambridge International Examinations.

To conclude this section, it must be said that descriptions of the state of Indic languages in Britain are seriously hampered by the fragmentary and variable nature of the demographic and geographical information available. A comprehensive survey, along the lines undertaken by the Languages of London project (Baker & Eversley 2000) is badly needed for the whole country. The information collected needs to be standardised in terms of the naming of languages spoken, and then in the manner of its collection nationwide.

Educational status and issues

Language debates in the National Curriculum

Britain has had a long tradition for teaching the languages of the subcontinent. The expansion and consolidation of the Indian empire necessitated the training of its British civil servants and army personnel in the languages of colonial India. The setting up of 'oriental' studies at the universities of Cambridge, London and Oxford to offer courses in Hindi-Urdu-Hindustani, in particular, was, however, guided more by 'instrumental' than 'integrative' motivation. This nevertheless also resulted in pedagogic and linguistic/philologic research in Indic languages.

The sociolinguistic situation however has completely changed in Britain since the arrival of the immigrants in the post-colonial period. The arrival of a large number of immigrant children from the Indian subcontinent in the inner-city schools in Britain in the 1960s attracted a variety of rushed educational responses by the language policy planners in the LEAs, the DES and the Home Office. It generated language debates which veered away from linguistic diversity to 'English only' in the early education of these children. The linguistic and educational needs of these children were initially perceived as 'problems' – both linguistic and cultural. The parents were frequently so trapped in socioeconomic pressures and traumatic socio-cultural experiences that they were easily persuaded that their mother tongue/heritage languages would interfere with the children's acquisition of English as a foreign/second language. Their mother tongue was perceived as a 'handicap' and their lack of competence in English as a 'disadvantage'. The Plowden Report (1967:69) said that 'it was absolutely essential to overcome the language barrier'. During the period 1967–75 most of the discussions centred round the teaching of English with the conviction that it would help the children overcome the handicap and the disadvantage.

The Bullock Report (1975) was the first major positive assessment of the pedagogical and socio-cultural significance of the mother tongues of the ethnic minority children. It recognised these as 'an asset . . . to be nurtured' (1975:249) by schools. Despite its limitations the Report did act as a fillip to the mother tongue debate.

The European Council of Resolution on Education issued the Directive on 'The schooling of children of migrant workers' (77/486) for the maintenance of their language and culture in 1977. After some reservations the Department of Education and Science (1981) Circular 5/81 recommended to LEAs that '. . . they should explore ways in which mother tongue teaching might be provided, whether during or outside school hours, but not that they are required to give such tuition to all individuals as of right' (DES Circular 5/81:2). In a subtle way the DES absolved the LEAs of the obligation to implement a mother tongue teaching programme in the school curriculum.

The Directive was followed by several government-funded projects to research the depth and extent of linguistic diversity and mother tongue maintenance among ethnic adults and schoolchildren. The DES-sponsored Linguistic Minorities Project (1979–83) developed four survey instruments (Schools Language Survey, Secondary Pupils Survey, Adult Language Use Survey and Mother Tongue Teaching Directory). The only bilingual education (Panjabi and English) teaching research was the Mother Tongue and English Teaching (MOTET) project sponsored jointly by the DES and Bradford LEA (1978–80). The Project concluded that 'as far as Panjabi was concerned, the clear superiority in performance of the experimental group was accompanied by indications of a transfer of higher level ability to more complex tasks in English' (Fitzpatrick 1987:109).

The European Community-sponsored Mother Tongue and Culture Teaching Project (1976–80) in Bedford concluded that Panjabi children seem to have achieved a higher level of literacy in English than in Panjabi, but in oral skills they seem to be more fluent and accurate in Panjabi than in English (Tosi 1980:61). A second project, the Schools Council Mother Tongue Project (1981–85), developed a variety of resources to help teachers of primary age children learning Bangla in community and mainstream schools.

The arguments for and against including the heritage languages began to surface as polarised. The professional associations of teachers responded positively in favour of the heritage languages, putting forward pedagogical arguments for mainstreaming the teaching of ethnic minority languages in primary schools. The ethnic minority communities began to realise that their culture embedded in their languages was slowly disappearing from the repertoire of their children. Apart from setting up community language classes by the mid seventies, they became the catalyst in the formation of *The National Council for Mother Tongue Teaching* which spearheaded the sociolinguistic arguments for the promotion of minority mother tongues. This has had a positive effect on some LEAs. Tsow's (1984) survey of mother tongue provision in the LEAs (1980–82) found that some did offer tuition in a select number of minority languages, which included Indic languages. Tansley & Craft (1984) in their survey reported that 23 LEAs claimed to be offering primary school provision of heritage languages. Despite this positive thinking reflecting a multilingual ideology, the central government was not impressed by it, although it did admit the multicultural nature of Britain.

The Swann Report (1985), specially set up by the DES to inquire into the education of children from ethnic minority groups, ignored the arguments put forward by the community and the professionals. It rejected the arguments on two assumptions: (i) that mother tongue in the primary classroom would be a 'barrier' in the acquisition of English; and (ii) that mother tongue would become a foreign language by the time ethnic minority children will have entered secondary education.

Swann argued that if the heritage languages were 'truly the mother tongues' of the community the members of the community could organise language classes for their survival. State language planning policy was gradually taking shape in defranchising the ethnic children of their right to have either lessons in their heritage language alongside English or heritage language lessons as languages in mainstream education. Swann's recommendation to include the Indic languages in the modern foreign languages curriculum confirmed the 'English only' ideology current in the corridors of the DES.

Language planners in the National Curriculum for England and Wales (1988) found a natural ally in Swann and promoted a model of language planning ideal for non-preservation (Verma, Corrigan & Firth 2000:510). Unlike Welsh in Wales there was no separate curriculum for the teaching of heritage languages as mother tongues in either the primary or the secondary curriculum. Although the Kingman (1988) and Cox Reports (Department for Education and Science 1989) used a rhetoric of entitlement and rights to heritage languages, they endorsed Swann's recommendation. They even amalgamated language rights with territorial rights legitimising the curriculum for Welsh. The devising of a National Curriculum (DES 1989) promoted the rationale for a modern foreign language 'languages for all' policy in the secondary curriculum and produced a list of nineteen languages pigeonholed into two 'schedules': EU and ethnic minority languages. The ideology behind this division is reflected in the provision for these languages in mainstream schools. The absence of teacher training opportunities in higher educational institutions is glaring, and it is demotivating for any prospective graduate to study any of the Indic languages from this perspective. The Harris Report (Department for Education and Employment 1995) spells out the rationale, the programmes of study and attainment targets. The pedagogic arguments for a separate curriculum for the ethnic minority heritage languages similar to that for Welsh as a first language and as a second/foreign language were virtually lost.

Another important aspect has been the 'market' approach to the assessment of these languages adopted by the examination boards. The future of the GCSE and A level assessments in these languages is, in the eyes of the Examination Boards, dependent on their economic viability.

The teaching of the Indic languages continues to be determined on a local rather than national level, depending on the ethnolinguistic population of individual schools and LEAs, and also on the 'parent power' of individual groups. The current modes and provisions for teaching the Indic languages can be categorised into three: (i) voluntary community language classes managed entirely by the communities with minimal financial help from the local authorities; (ii) community language classes timetabled outside school hours on the school premises; and (iii) community language classes offered as part of the mainstream curriculum leading on to GCSE/A level examinations. Although the Royal Society of Arts' Diploma in Teaching Community Languages and the University of York Easter residential INSETS equipped a large number of teachers in modern professional language teaching methods, the lack of will to address the needs of these teachers on the part of the schools of education have orphaned this community enterprise in more ways than one. This includes the lack of professionally produced language teaching methods and materials. Irrespective of this, Indic language organisations, the ethnic media and the radio and television channels continue to foster and develop the motivation in some young learners to pursue their interests in their heritage languages.

Sociolinguistic issues: the state of languages – language maintenance and shift, attrition and endangerment, the mixed code

In his response to the linguistic diversity in British society, Cox (Department for Education and Science 1989) said that ethnic minority schoolchildren had the right to maintain their heritage language within the domains of their home and community. In the last section we examined how language planning policies in the school curriculum have transformed 'mother tongues' into 'foreign' languages, driven by an ideology not to foster or support bilingualism but to teach these languages for academic and commercial pursuits. In this section we shall look at the impact of these policies on the patterns of language use among the main Indic speech communities. This should unravel any signs of language maintenance and shift, and any variation and change in their use.

Romaine (1983), on patterns of language use among Panjabi schoolchildren in Birmingham, outlined 'a classic [pattern] in the conduct of contact bilingualism', that is, a gradual community-wide shift to English, with its locus in the pattern of interaction between siblings in the home. Let us apply this finding in the case of each of the five languages: Panjabi, Hindi, Urdu, Gujarati and Bangla.

Panjabi (Gurmukhi)

The first in-depth study was Agnihotri's (1979), on the speech repertoire of 10–16-year-old Panjabi Sikh children and their elders in Leeds. He found how conscious the older generation was about the intertwining of Panjabi, Sikhism and identity, and how it was very worried about the signs of language loss and shift from Panjabi to English in young schoolchildren.

Panjabi was secure (80%) in child–mother interactions. The signs of language shift were clear, however, among the siblings, with only 14% reporting using Panjabi (Agnihotri 1987:91). Although the Sikh children mostly used Panjabi with parents and other members of the extended family, some of them used English or the mixed code to communicate with their fathers. Through their own or their parents' motivation, 50% of the children attended Panjabi lessons at the gurdvara despite the lack of adequate teaching materials and of trained teachers. The symptoms of decline in the children's control over Panjabi increased with their length of stay and the extent of their contact with the host community. Agnihotri concluded that Sikh children rarely used 'unadulterated Panjabi' and 'mixed code' had become the medium of intra-group communication with English as the medium of inter-group contact (Agnihotri 1987:108).

The Linguistic Minorities Project (LMP 1985) showed that the use of Panjabi, both oral and literate, and knowledge of Panjabi was quite solid as far as maintenance of Panjabi was concerned among the adult population, but among 42% of the children English was becoming the dominant language. Mahandru (1991:118) analysed the ILEA figures on Panjabi (Language Census, 1981–87) and the LMP (1985) figures on English and Panjabi language skills, and confirmed the evidence of shift in the linguistic behaviour of second and subsequent generations from Panjabi to English. But there was also evidence of resistance to shift and stability of the language in families where English was rarely used.

Panjabi-Hindi

Saxena's (1995) study of the Panjabi Hindus in Southall found that the three main languages in the speech repertoire of this community had domain-specific role and function. Panjabi was predominantly associated with the family domain, Hindi with Hindu religion, Panjabi and English with community, and English with education and employment. In addition, the older generation from East Africa had knowledge of Swahili and Gujarati and the younger generation at school in the UK had competence in French and German.

According to Saxena's findings there appears to be a double overlapping diglossic situation in the Panjabi Hindu community. 'Hindi is the High language and Panjabi the Low at the community level; and English is the High language and both Panjabi and Hindi are the low languages at the wider societal level' (Saxena 1995:220). As to the future of Panjabi and Hindi and the signs of shift from Panjabi to Hindi to English, Saxena concluded that English had not encroached enough on the family domain to threaten the minority languages (Saxena 1995:225).

Panjabi-Urdu

The LMP (1985) survey of Muslim adults and the members in their families who speak Panjabi/Panjabi-Urdu but who choose Urdu as their language of literacy, came up with very similar findings to those for Panjabi (Gurmukhi). Understanding and speaking was almost universal; literacy competence was marginally lower. Language shift among the children, however, was appreciably less. The problem with these data is that they assume that most Muslim Panjabis have Panjabi as their only spoken Indic language. On the basis of personal observation in the Bradford community, it is clear that many adults have both Panjabi and Urdu as part of their repertoire.

In Khan's (1991) study Urdu emerged as 'having greater currency for first-generation than second-generation speakers' (Khan 1991:133). She found indications of a shift towards the use of English, in domains outside the home and in the case of interactions with parents and grandparents but particularly in conversation with siblings. The most interesting finding was that the English-dominated second generation reported lower incidence of Panjabi-Urdu or English-Panjabi code-switching.

Reynolds (2001), the most recent empirical study of Panjabi (Urdu), from Sheffield, concluded that the situation of the heritage languages in contact with English in the Mirpuri community was one of 'stable variability', at least in the home domain. Outside the home domain community language loss among the children was occurring. Their data suggested that language loss was gradual rather than rapid, with counter-evidence of language maintenance. They observed the use of 'mixed code' and claimed this phenomenon to be part of the evidence for maintenance.

Hindi

There is a real dearth of facts and figures on the use of Hindi and the learning and acquisition of Hindi as mother tongue (HMT) by children whose family originates from the Hindi-speaking states in India, and also on the use and acquisition of Hindi and/or its sister languages, such as Bhojpuri. HMT speakers form a community without any kind of neighbourhood network; it is a small professional group whose patterns of settlement are diffuse, but whose social network is strong. Most HMT speakers live in nuclear families and can call on the extended family but seldom on the village network. This has had obvious implications for mother tongue maintenance (Verma 1991:109). He found that in the 'family' and 'friendship' domains Hindi ceased to be the only language. Although Hindi appeared to be the dominant language in these domains among older male and female speakers, who could also speak Bhojpuri, English had become significant in the interaction among young people.

Gujarati

Wilding (1981) found that in Leicester both Gujarati and English were part of the repertoire of the community. The young Gujarati adults thought English was primarily important for getting good jobs. A large number of adults both felt it was important to maintain Gujarati and had positive attitudes towards English.

The LMP evidence from Coventry and Leicester also found a high level of competence in Gujarati in the adult population and a high incidence of actual use of Gujarati among family members. Once again, it was among the children that the trend of shift to English began to appear. Dave (1991) confirmed the signs of maintenance of Gujarati in the older generation but reported examples of a 'wide range of code-switching' in the speech of the younger members of the community, possibly indicating language shift.

Choudhry & Verma (1994) studied 109 adults and 141 children from the Gujarati community (Hindus and Muslims) in London, Leeds, Bradford and Leicester. The majority thought that ethnicity without mother tongue was not sustainable. Gujarati remained dominant cross-generationally in the home domain. However, the pattern of shift to English mixed code among the third and fourth generations was also in evidence. Despite this, the claim often made about the relationship between length of stay and language shift was not supported by their data.

Sneddon (2000) concluded that among Gujarati Muslim families strong family networks and the maintenance of close links with the region of origin had helped the sustenance of 'a high level of vitality' in the older generation. However the lack of literacy skills among children in Gujarati was striking.

The study of literacy practices in the Gujarati community (Bhatt & Martin-Jones 1994) demonstrates a clear difference between the older and younger generations. The former continue with their multiple literacy practices, while with the latter the case is often one of monoliteracy in English.

Bangla

Most of the research carried out in the UK on the Bangla speech community – largely Bangladeshi Muslims but some Hindus too, including those from West Bengal in India – has been on the Sylheti-speaking Bangladeshis whose language of literacy is standard Bangla.

Husain's (1991) analysis of the LMP data concluded that Sylheti/Bangla seemed quite secure in the community. A high percentage of the respondents and members in their households claimed to know the language 'fairly well' or 'very well'. Blackledge (2000), in his study of a school in Birmingham, stated that for Bangladeshi parents Bangla and Sylheti languages were their defining cultural features. The encroachment of English in the safe domain of households and family interactions was visible according to the parents. Sylheti was secure in children's interaction with elders, but English was the language among the siblings. Two-thirds of the eighteen Bangladeshi women interviewed claimed to have good control over literacy in Bangla. Gregory (1997) and Gregory & Williams (2000a) studied the literacy practices and literacy histories of Bangladeshi families and found that the children spent 'many hours' learning to read the Qur'an in Arabic, and learning to read and write in Bangla. The acquisition of literacy was very closely linked to their heritage as both Muslims and as Bangladeshis.

In Verma *et al.*'s (2001) pilot study of five Bangladeshi families in Leeds most respondents claimed Bangla as their mother tongues, with one claiming Sylheti, one Bangla and Sylheti, and one English/Bangla. Most of the younger school-going children (11) claimed to use English every day. Their competence in Bangla was difficult to assess because of their preference for English as the language for interaction with their age peers and even with the researchers. Only four of the respondents had good competence in literacy in Bangla. On reflection one cannot be sure whether the children had lost their competence in Sylheti or Bangla.

In conclusion, the overall pattern seems to be that the Indic speech communities are in a state of flux. The heritage languages are still in active use in the family and the community, but there are signs of English gradually making inroads into the home domain.

New developments: research and policy

Much needs to be done to ensure the status and the maintenance of the Indic languages in Britain in the areas of research and language policy, though there are currently some promising initiatives in this area.

Although *The Nuffield Languages Inquiry* (Nuffield Foundation 2000) and the national languages strategy documents for England and Scotland make reference to the linguistic diversity of the country as a resource, there is a wide gap between such expressions of support and actual practice. Educationally, an assimilationist concentration on English as an Additional Language ignores the contribution that bilingualism can make to literacy, or rather literacies. Literacy in the home/community language is a prerequisite of language maintenance, if it is to extend its currency beyond the home domain to public domains. Blackledge (2000) has shown how teachers are often reluctant to tap into the parental resource of oral literacy competence in the community language (see 'Bangla' above). Charmian Kenner, in her case study of a Gujarati child, similarly stresses the importance of a 'home–school discourse' 'open to children's everyday bilingual literacy experiences' (Kenner 1997:85).

Fortunately, biliteracy and multilingual literacies are now receiving the research attention they need (cf. Martin-Jones & Jones 2000, Hornberger 2003), and research generally into community languages in the UK is beginning to thrive. The British Association for Applied Linguistics is in the process of establishing a Special Interest Group (SIG) in this area. A study of complementary schools in Leicester,[2] focussing in particular on an ethnographic study of two Gujarati schools, has recently been published (Martin *et al.* 2004). It emphasises the important role of such schools, of which Kempadoo & Abdelrazak (2001) list nearly 500 for the 'big five' Indic languages, in the management of bilingualism, the enhancement of the children's languages and community language literacy and in their contribution to the children's development and appreciation of their multilingual selves and of a positive identity as successful learners.

However, many of these schools exist on a shoestring, and suffer from a number of problems. These are a lack of materials and textbooks suitable for youngsters who have been born and brought up not in South Asia but in urban Britain, a shortage of professionally qualified staff, traditional and grammar-centred teaching methods, and in many cases a resistance to parental pressure to attend (see Khan & Kabir 1999 and Martin & Stuart-Smith 1998). These have caused demotivation for many.

The need for properly qualified teachers of community languages is becoming one of urgency, especially in those mainstream schools where Indic languages are taught. The age profile for community language teachers is top-heavy and there will be a problem in replacing them in a few years' time. One difficulty has been that of getting qualified teacher status (QTS), but in the last three years the situation has improved. There are now six HE institutions putting on PGCE courses in Indic languages.[3] CILT – the National Centre for Languages – has established a 'Register of Specialists' for community language teachers and trainers, maintains a

---

[2] These are, alternatively, in some places called 'community language schools'. However, the Leicester denomination as 'complementary' deserves to establish itself as the standard, for the positive nuance it implies to the process of developing bilingualism in the characteristically multilingual and multiethnic social reality of Britain today.

[3] The six are: Edge Hill College (in Urdu) – the first one; then Goldsmiths' College, University of London (Panjabi and Urdu), University of East London (Bangla), Strathclyde University (Urdu) and London Metropolitan University, with a PGCE in KS2/3 'Languages in the community' which includes Indic languages. Sheffield's PGCE is in Urdu (CILT 2006:9).

Community Languages Network and website (www.cilt.org.uk/commlangs) and publishes a regular Community Languages Bulletin.

Continuing research is needed into sociolinguistic issues concerning Indic languages. Among these, of course, remains the issue of how much the languages are being maintained, into and beyond the third generation of speakers in Britain. The previous section has shown that they are being maintained in the home domain whilst being lost outside the home and family. An important resource for maintenance is TV and video: the Indian film industry is enormous, and very popular. Research is needed into the impact on younger viewers'/listeners' language maintenance of Zee TV, Laskhar TV, Bangla TV, BBC Asian and other ethnic channels.

Code-switching practices among Indic language speakers, and the allied phenomenon of 'mixed code' (Agnihotri 1979, 1987, Kachru 1978) need further attention. This should include further examination of 'fused lects' (Auer 1999) and 'crossing' (Rampton 1995a).

As far as educational policy concerning the state of Indic languages in Britain today is concerned, we would like to end with the following comments and suggestions.

1. There is no government support for including community languages in primary schooling, unlike the situation with Welsh and Scots Gaelic, in their respective territories.
2. Including Indic languages as modern foreign languages, which is the status they have been given in the National Curriculum, puts them on a foreign language basis for their L1 speakers.
3. There is a lack of clear co-ordination in the education sector between setting the curriculum and providing teachers (but see the efforts mentioned above by CILT and the Community Languages Network and working groups). What we do not want is a continuation of 'planning for non-preservation' (Verma, Corrigan & Firth 2000).
4. There is a need for both home and institutional support in order for language maintenance beyond the home to occur.

In short, therefore, we would recommend that non-indigenous community languages, such as the Indic languages, should be put on the same footing as the indigenous minority languages, Welsh and Scots Gaelic. It is encouraging here to note that they may be chosen as languages available at Key Stage 2 (ages 7–11) under the national languages strategy (DfES 2002b). It may be worth noting that speakers of the five main Indic languages in Britain outnumber speakers of the indigenous minority languages, and that their geographical densities are greater. Finally, it is of course the case that most of these suggestions apply equally to all community languages, not just those of South Asian origin.

18 Chinese

Li Wei

Sociolinguists have long argued that one cannot talk about language, any language, adequately and accurately without making reference to its speakers. While the ultimate aim of this chapter is to present an up-to-date picture of the Chinese language in the British Isles, a very large part of it will be devoted to the Chinese people in Britain.

The Chinese are one of the largest and longest-established ethnic minorities in the UK. They are a socially and linguistically highly diverse population. There are many issues concerning the Chinese in Britain – their cultural heritage, their beliefs and values and their social organisation – which are of interest and importance to sociolinguists. They would, however, require book-length studies to do them justice. I can only discuss briefly those aspects which are of direct and primary relevance to the current sociolinguistic situation of the British Chinese communities. The discussion will concentrate in turn on the history and demography of the Chinese population in the UK, the linguistic background of the various groups of Chinese people, and the current language use patterns in the Chinese communities.

The British Chinese communities: history and demography

Although the Chinese have always had a geographically large homeland, mass external migration has long been a regular part of Chinese history. Until the early twentieth century, overseas Chinese settlements had mainly been in South-East Asia. Apart from Hong Kong and Taiwan, where the Chinese make up over 99% of the indigenous populations, countries such as Singapore, Malaysia, Indonesia, Thailand and the Philippines all host very large Chinese communities.

I am grateful to the continuing support of the Chinese community in Tyneside. Some of the information given in this chapter comes from studies financed by the ESRC (R000232856; R000235869 and RES000231180). I am particularly grateful to David Britain and Zhu Hua for their insightful comments on earlier drafts of the chapter.

Chinese migration to regions outside Asia is a relatively recent pheno-menon. In the mid-nineteenth century, poor peasants and artisans plus a few small merchant traders went from south-eastern provinces of mainland China (mainly Cantonese, Hokkien and Hakka speaking areas) to North America and the Caribbean. This movement continued well into the twentieth century, with people fleeing the Japanese occupation and subsequent civil wars between the nationalists and the communists, although the size of migration has greatly reduced due to immigration restrictions of receiving countries.

Western Europe became a destination for sizeable Chinese settlements only after World War II. The bulk of the Chinese in this part of the world come from South-East Asia, partly as a result of the established colonial links between the two regions. They are sometimes called 'second-hand' overseas Chinese, because they migrated from China to South-East Asia generations ago and transferred to Europe in the last two centuries.

It is popularly believed that Britain hosts the largest Chinese population in western Europe, followed by France, the Netherlands and Germany. In the 2001 Census, the UK had a total of 247,403 Chinese residents, which was 0.4% of the national population. The Chinese settlement in the UK has gone through four distinct phases:

1. pre-war (WWI) arrivals;
2. post-war (WWII) arrivals (till mid-1960s);
3. reinforcement (till mid-1970s);
4. new arrivals (from 1980s).

Pre-World War I arrivals

The pre-World War I arrivals consisted mainly of seamen who had been recruited aboard European freighters from the south-eastern provinces of China including Hong Kong (under Chinese government at that time). With the expansion of trade with China following Britain's success in the two Opium Wars (1832–40 and 1858–60), employing Chinese seamen became a regular practice. By the 1880s, Chinese seamen could be found in most of the major port areas of Britain, such as Bristol, Cardiff, Liverpool and London. At the same time, members of the Chinese aristocracy began to come to Britain. But there could be no greater contrast between this small number of intellectual elite and the large groups of seamen and labourers. Contacts between them were extremely limited, if they existed at all.

During the inter-war years, the Chinese population in Britain declined considerably. Pre- and post-World War II demolition for urban redevelop-ment led to the dispersal of the two largest Chinese settlements in London and Liverpool away from the original dockland areas. Due to the imbalanced ratio of Chinese men and women in the UK at the time, many seamen subsequently married non-Chinese women and distanced themselves from other Chinese people. Thus, the pre-World War I Chinese had not been able to make their mark as a cohesive social group in Britain.

Post-World War II arrivals

The post-World War II arrivals which began in the 1950s have been attributed largely to decline in traditional agriculture in Hong Kong, then a British colony. Until after World War II, Hong Kong had been heavily dependent upon rice farming. Post-war changes in the international rice markets resulted in the undercutting of Hong Kong produce costs by Thai and other imports. Small-scale farmers who occupied the less fertile land were no longer able to make a profit. As they were qualified only for the most menial and low-paid industrial jobs, most of them were not prepared to work in the emerging urban Hong Kong.

It so happened that there was an economic boom in Britain in the late 1950s and early 1960s, and a change of eating habits away from traditional British cuisine. The displaced Chinese farmers were thus presented with a unique opportunity to leave Hong Kong and seek catering jobs in the UK. It is believed that over 90% of the Chinese who came to Britain during the decade between 1956 and 1965 were from the rural areas of Hong Kong, and have since engaged in some form of food trade.

Reinforcement

The growing popularity of Chinese cuisine in Britain called for expansion of trade and reinforcement of the workforce. Between the mid-1960s and the mid-1970s, there was a marked increase in the number of Chinese emigrating from Hong Kong to Britain. Unlike the previous phases, the arrivals during this period were highly organised.

The increasingly restrictive immigration laws of Britain required that admission into the UK should be at the invitation of a relative or a specific employer to a particular job. Kinship ties thus provided an important channel for immigration. More elaborate immigration networks based on common birthplace or shared dialect were also at work (Watson 1975, 1977). Usually, travel documents and work permits were arranged by the families in the UK; employment in Chinese eating establishments was promised; passage money was paid as an advance of wages. It seems somewhat ironic though that the British immigration laws which were imposed to restrict increases in the number of immigrants have in reality contributed to the delay in returning home of the first post-World War II arrivals in order that their relatives who wished to come to the UK could use their contacts.

New arrivals

Since the 1980s, the number of Chinese immigrants to the UK has been greatly reduced. The 1981 British Nationality Act made it difficult even for dependants to gain access to the UK. An unexpected addition to the Chinese population in Britain was the arrival of the refugees from Vietnam, or 'boat people'. The majority of them were ethnic Chinese who fled political and ethnic conflicts in Vietnam in the 1970s. Many of them stayed in refugee camps in Hong Kong before they were admitted into the UK. According to the statistics given in the Report of the 4th National Conference on the Chinese Community in Britain (National Children's Centre 1984) and in *The Sunday Times*, 3 April 1988, between 13,000 and 16,000 refugees from Vietnam were accepted by Britain in the late 1970s and early 1980s. Once they settled in the UK, the refugees from Vietnam had access to the same range of cultural and linguistic activities as other Chinese groups in the country and seem to be quite ready to be part of the Chinese community, especially in areas where there were large numbers of Chinese people and their own numbers were small (Wong 1992).

In the aftermath of the Tiananmen Incident in June 1989, concerns about the future of Hong Kong after the 1997 transition of sovereignty eventually forced the British government to pass the British Nationality (Hong Kong) Act of 1990, which offered UK citizenship to 50,000 Hong Kong heads of households and their families. There have been reports in the press that the take-up rate of the offer was low, as the majority of Hong Kong residents at the time preferred to emigrate to Canada or Australia. In any case, the families who were admitted into Britain under the 1990 Act had to satisfy stringent financial and educational criteria.

Throughout the history of Chinese settlement in Britain, there have always been the so-called professional transients from China and Chinese-speaking regions who came to the UK for educational purposes and usually without any family. They comprise academics, medical doctors, solicitors, architects, accountants, nurses, teachers and students. Some of them have obtained employment or married UK nationals and decided to stay. They are socially and linguistically a highly diverse group. Consequently, there are no official statistics as to how many such Chinese professionals are currently in the country. During the 1980s and 1990s, some 3,000 Chinese who were employed by public institutions (e.g. universities, hospitals, legal and financial organisations) were granted indefinite leave to remain in the UK. They interact with the other Chinese immigrants to some extent by providing various professional services. Since the 1990s, there has been a significant increase of non-legal migrants from southern provinces of China. For obvious reasons no reliable statistics are available.

Concentration in the catering trade

According to estimates by the Home Affairs Committee in their 1985 report, 90% of the Chinese in Britain were in catering-related trades. As many as 60% were believed to be in family-owned takeaways. Such overwhelming concentration in catering by the Chinese in Britain can be attributed to a number of factors. First of all, employment opportunities for immigrants in the UK have generally been restricted. Work permits for jobs in which they might be in direct competition with the 'indigenous' British population are known to be extremely difficult to obtain. For their part, the Chinese immigrants were usually aware of the potential consequences of appearing overambitious and competitive. Subsequently, they opted for family-based businesses and self-employment. Secondly, family-based, small-scale businesses served well the purpose of immigration which was to seek economic survival and eventually independence, and were in line with traditional Chinese cultural values which are centred round high levels of loyalty and commitment within a complex kinship system. Thirdly, the Chinese immigrants, especially those from the rural parts of Hong Kong and south-eastern China, were generally unskilled in professions other than farming and fishing and spoke little English. They could only go into occupations where no formal qualification was needed and where diligence alone could succeed. Fourthly, the Chinese have a traditional love of cuisine. They usually celebrate various folk festivals with an elaborate family dinner and home-made food is frequently given to each other as presents. Fifthly, the Chinese food trade met a growing need for diversification in the British catering industry, as tastes were becoming more catholic and society generally more affluent. A combination of these factors, and perhaps others, has resulted in the concentration of the Chinese in Britain in the catering trade.

The concentration in catering has significant implications for the settlement pattern and social life of the Chinese people in Britain. In order to provide services for the maximum number of potential customers, Chinese caterers do not live in identifiable settlements. The so-called Chinatowns in larger cities such as London, Liverpool, Manchester and Glasgow are established for business, and increasingly tourism, rather than residential purposes. The Chinese thus present a sharp contrast with other ethnic minority communities in Britain who tend to cluster in specifiable urban areas. Roper (1988) suggested that while London and the south-east of England had the highest concentration of Chinese residents, half of the Chinese in the UK lived outside metropolitan areas. It is often said that there is at least one Chinese takeaway in a place of 2,000 residents.

The emergence of a British-born generation

Apart from the above-mentioned new arrivals of refugees from Vietnam and educational and professional transients, the Chinese population in Britain has grown since the 1980s mainly by the emergence of a British-born generation. They are now estimated to constitute over a quarter of the Chinese population in the country.

While information about the Chinese communities in Britain is generally sketchy, that about the British-born Chinese is particularly scarce. Studies of the Chinese children and adolescents in Britain tend to focus on those who were born in the Far East, or the few who, for various reasons, have been sent to Hong Kong to receive part of their education. There has been a particular tendency to concentrate on the few who are judged to be low achievers in schools. The majority of the British-born Chinese, on the other hand, have been exposed to the British culture and the English language from a very young age. They are generally perceived as assimilated or at least 'better adjusted' to the British way of life and sharing similar characteristics with their British peers and thus are not perceived as presenting a problem to the mainstream society (Taylor 1987).

Significantly, however, the British-born generation is perceived by the Chinese communities themselves as a major cause of concern. They are seen as lacking respect for traditional culture (e.g. the authority structures of the family) which is often expressed through their anglicised social behaviour (e.g. speaking English) (e.g. Ng 1986, Li Wei 1993). Derogatory names such as 'banana kids', meaning 'yellow outside, white inside', have been used to refer to this generation (e.g. Macphedran 1989). Although reports of the communication difficulties between the British-born and previous generations of Chinese immigrants are becoming more numerous, there remains a serious gap in empirical and systematic research into this particular generation. Parker (1995) examined the emerging cultural identities of young Chinese in the city of Birmingham which showed new forms of political activity and cultural creativity being developed alongside a continuing interest in Hong Kong's contemporary youth culture.

Chinese immigrants as a 'community'

Given the diversity of background, socioeconomic status and geographical settlement, to what extent can we describe the Chinese in Britain as a 'community'? 'Community' as a sociological concept refers to 'a cohesive and self-conscious social group' (Cohen 1982). On the surface, it would appear rather difficult to apply such a concept in the case of the UK

Chinese population. The differences in place of origin, phase of immigration, occupation and settlement form a basis for group boundaries, which in turn inform the behaviour and attitude of their members. In a study of the Chinese in Liverpool, O'Neill (1972) finds that the first-generation immigrants saw the younger, later arrivals as 'flighty and unreliable and not showing due respect', while they themselves were perceived as 'old-fashioned'. The Liverpool-born Chinese, on the other hand, seemed to be more concerned with their relationships with the White English community, compared with the Hong Kong-born generations who were more aware of regional differences according to their birthplace. Ng (1986) and Pong (1991) reported their observations among the Chinese in the Tyneside area that the immigrants from the New Territories of Hong Kong were perceived by the Chinese students and professional groups as 'uneducated, uncivilised and lacking in intelligence', while the immigrants viewed the students and professionals as 'over-privileged, self-centred and lacking in respect for tradition'. Stereotypes such as these, coupled with the secular nature of the Chinese culture which lacks strong religious ties compared with, for example, communities of Indian or Pakistani origin, have undoubtedly contributed to the difficulty in viewing the Chinese as a single, united community.

Nevertheless, none of these internal differences can be compared to the dichotomy between the Chinese and the non-Chinese, a dichotomy established from the very beginning of the Chinese history and maintained by the Chinese people wherever they are. In his study of the Chinese in London, Watson (1977) claimed that while traditional group differences based on place of origin, socioeconomic status and dialects were clearly perceived as significant, the Chinese often found it to their advantage to unite themselves, or at least to appear to be united, against their common rival, which was the non-Chinese generally. Redding (1990) suggests that the majority of the Chinese people living overseas have not psychologically left China, or at least not left some ideal and perhaps romanticised notion of Chinese civilisation. Indeed, the name given to the immigrants by the Chinese themselves, *Huaqiao*, signifies a short-term visitor, a sojourner. The fact that many families have sojourned for centuries does not alter the expectation that they will eventually be returning to their homeland – China – even perhaps in their afterlife. The word *faan* (in Cantonese) or *hui* (in Putonghua), meaning *to return (to)*, is frequently used when the Chinese in Britain talk about going to Hong Kong and China, even amongst the British-born Chinese who have never spent any significant period of time outside the UK. The 'synthesising mind' (Bond 1991) of the Chinese people which has been kept alive by the legacy of China and the Chinese culture has been one of the most distinctive features of their ethnic identity.

What is particularly interesting, however, is that despite their deeply rooted sense of opposition between the Chinese and the non-Chinese, the Chinese appear to be the most acceptable ethnic minority in Britain. In the 1950s and 1960s when racial conflicts became a feature of British society, the Chinese managed to avoid overt discrimination. Watson (1977) reported that when English landlords posted 'No Coloureds' signs in their windows, Chinese students were generally exempt from that category.

The superficially harmonious relationship the Chinese have managed to maintain with others owes a great deal to their belief that everyone has a specific role in society and in order to have peace one must know one's precise social position and behave accordingly. Thus, while few of the immigrants have illusions about their socially defined role as caterers or waiters, they have made no specific efforts to change it. They tend to see themselves as living and working in someone else's country, even though many of them have decided to settle in the UK permanently.

The linguistic background of the Chinese in Britain

The Chinese language is an independent branch of the Sino-Tibetan family. It is spoken, in various forms, by over one billion people as a native language, and its written form has an unbroken history since 1500 BC. It may be useful first of all to make a distinction between the spoken and written forms of Chinese. Spoken Chinese comprises a large number of related varieties, known to the Chinese as *fangyan*, or regional speech. Traditionally, the Chinese *fangyan* are classified into eight groups in terms of geographical distribution and linguistic-structural affiliation. The eight *fangyan* groups are:

(1) *Beifang* (Northern), the native language of about 70% of the Chinese population.
(2) *Yue*, the majority of whose speakers are in Guangdong province, the southern-most mainland province of China, with the capital city of Guanzhou (Canton) as its centre. Large numbers can also be found amongst the overseas Chinese diaspora.
(3) *Kejia* (Hakka), whose speakers came from small agricultural areas and are now scattered throughout south-eastern China.
(4) *Min Bei* (Northern Min), spoken in the northern part of Fujian (Hokkien) province, the mainland province on the western side of the Taiwan Strait.
(5) *Min Nan* (Southern Min), spoken in the southern part of Fujian, as well as in Taiwan and the Hainan islands.
(6) *Wu*, spoken in the lower Changjiang (the Yangtze River) region, including urban metropolitan centres such as Shanghai.

(7) *Xiang*, mainly spoken in the south-central region.

(8) *Gan*, spoken chiefly in the south-eastern inland provinces.

Within each *fangyan* group, there are sub-varieties with their own distinctive features. For example, Cantonese, as it is known in the West, is a sub-variety within the Yue *fangyan* group; Shanghainese a sub-variety in Wu; and Hokkien in Min Nan. It is in this sense, i.e. being a sub-variety of a *fangyan* group, that the Chinese linguists talk about Cantonese, Shanghainese and Hokkien as 'dialects', an important point often misunderstood and misrepresented in the linguistics literature in the West.

One prominent feature of spoken Chinese is the unintelligibility between one *fangyan* and another. This unintelligibility is often regarded by the Chinese as a social group boundary marker distinguishing people of different origins and used by some linguists to argue that *fangyan* are in fact different 'languages'. Among the Hong Kong Chinese, for example, Cantonese is spoken by the Cantonese *Punti* (native) people as their native language; others speak Hakka, Chiuchow (or Chiuchou, Teochiu, Teochew, Chaozhou), Hokkien, Shanghainese and other dialects and sub-dialects.

In addition to these regional varieties, there is a spoken Chinese form known as *Guoyu* (literally 'national speech') which has evolved from *Guanhua*, a hybrid, standardised spoken form used during the Qing (also known as Manchu) Dynasty (1644–1911) and which has been officially endorsed and promoted as the lingua franca in China since the 1920s. It is now widely used, in modified forms, in mainland China where it is known as *Putonghua* (or common speech), in Taiwan where it is known as *Guoyu* (national language), and in Singapore where it is known as *Huayu* (the Chinese language).

Guoyu is better known in the English-speaking world as Mandarin. As the story goes, Mandarin is the transliteration of *Man daren*, or Manchu officials, who ruled China for nearly three hundred years. Thus, it was used to refer to both the people and their language, in the same way as English or French. Since the Manchu dynasty was overthrown by the republicans in 1911, the term has been used to refer to the official spoken language of China. As the official language of China is based on the structure and vocabulary of *Beifang fangyan*, Mandarin is also often used to refer to *Beifang* (Northern) varieties of Chinese.

The Chinese writing system is not alphabetic. Instead of letters, a system of written characters is used to represent words. The characters began as pictographs but evolved into complex symbols often combining semantic and phonetic radicals. The Chinese written characters were first standardised in about 200 BC. By about AD 200, the system of characters still in use today had taken shape.

It is important to point out that the same system of written characters is shared by all literate Chinese whatever *fangyan* they may speak. The

Chinese traditionally place great emphasis on the written language and see it as a major cultural symbol distinguishing the Chinese from all other peoples. Chinese schools at all levels devote a considerable amount of time to literacy – in the Chinese context, the reading and writing of written characters.

One reason for such emphasis seems to be due to the unique and complex relationship between the Chinese phonological system and the written script. Chinese is a monosyllabic and tonal language. Every written Chinese character represents a syllable with a tone. There are over 48,000 written characters in the standard Chinese dictionary *Zhonghua Da Zidian*. Yet according to Putonghua pronunciation, there are only 300-odd legal combinations of sounds, or syllables, with four different tones. Consequently, there are numerous homophones in Chinese, distinguishable primarily in written forms.

Since the 1950s, there has been a series of mass campaigns in mainland China and in Singapore to popularise the official forms of Chinese (Putonghua and *Huayu* respectively). The rationale behind these campaigns is to remedy communication difficulties caused by the differences in regional speech varieties, or *fangyan*. Two principal strategies have been used in the campaigns: simplification of some of the characters and the introduction of a phonetic spelling system. The latter is known as *pinyin*. It is designed to represent the written characters as they are pronounced in Putonghua, so that non-native-Chinese speakers or speakers of non-standard Chinese dialects could learn a standard pronunciation. There are as yet no agreed phonetic spelling systems for the other spoken varieties of Chinese, and given the popular perception among the Chinese that there is only one Chinese language, it seems unlikely that efforts will be made to design such systems. However, since 1997, the Linguistics Society of Hong Kong has developed a Cantonese romanisation scheme, known as *Jyut Ping* and is trying to promote it in the region.

With regard to the linguistic background of the Chinese in Britain, it is estimated that up to 70% of the Chinese in Britain speak Cantonese as their native language; some 25% speak Hakka; and the rest speak Hokkien and other varieties of Chinese *fangyan*. Today, Cantonese is used as the lingua franca of the Chinese communities, especially amongst the immigrant generations. Putonghua and Guoyu are used to a much lesser extent than Cantonese, but are increasingly taught in Chinese community schools.

Current patterns of language use in the Chinese communities in Britain

Like other immigrant communities in the country, the Chinese in Britain face the sociolinguistic dilemma of maintaining their ethnic language on

Table 18.1. *Polyglossia of the Chinese communities in Britain*

	Within the community	Beyond the community
High	*Cantonese* (for everyday communication) *Putonghua/Guoyu* (for political, symbolic purposes)	*English* (for socioeconomic/educational purposes) *Putonghua/Guoyu* (for political, symbolic purposes)
Low	Chinese *fangyan*	Regional varieties of English

the one hand and developing proficiency in English on the other. In terms of the status of the various languages involved, a complex pattern of *polyglossia* has emerged, with English as the socioeconomically High variety, Cantonese the community High variety, Putonghua or Guoyu the politically High variety within the community context, and all the other Chinese *fangyan* and some regional forms of English Low varieties (see Table 18.1).

In terms of language use, a three generational language shift has taken place, with the grandparent generation remaining Chinese monolingual, the parent generation using Chinese as their primary language of communication but having some English for specific purposes and the child generation becoming English dominant. This is caused largely by the Chinese communities' concentration in the catering trade and their dispersed settlement pattern.

Recall that the majority of the Chinese in Britain are engaged in catering-related businesses, which are family-based and form a close-knit network of ties. One would think that in such circumstances, the grandparents and parents would have plenty of opportunities to transmit their language to the younger generation. It is true that most Chinese families have been able to maintain some use of Chinese in everyday communication; in some cases their children have been brought up speaking fluent Cantonese, Hakka or Hokkien. Yet the fact that the catering business requires the adults to work very long hours, beginning exactly at the time when their children finish school and come home (between 3:00 and 4:00 in the afternoon), means that there are very few opportunities for the parents to be involved in any joint social activities with their children. In order to maximise business opportunities, the Chinese caterers tend to be scattered in different places. Very few Chinese households live close enough to allow the children to interact on a regular basis. Unlike other ethnic minorities children, the Chinese children rarely constitute more than 3% of the school population in any given area. Even in large metropolitan centres such as London and Manchester, where there are sizeable Chinese populations, the Chinese children never form a significant group for the local education authorities to provide any special support. The children spend most of their time with English speakers. Consequently, they use English as their primary language of communication. This is not to say that the Chinese children do not have any knowledge of the Chinese language at all. Most Chinese children in Britain do understand Chinese and can speak it with varying degrees of fluency. However, the Chinese spoken by the children shows clear signs of English language influence, and the literacy level in Chinese is extremely low in the British-born generation.

Cantonese in Britain

In a recent study of 34 British-born children of Cantonese-speaking parents in Tyneside, Li Wei & Lee (2001) found that where the typological differences between Cantonese and English are the greatest, for instance, the use of noun classifiers and quantifiers, the children's Cantonese speech is often influenced by English. Some of them would avoid the use of Cantonese altogether by code-switching to English. The following are some of the examples:

(1) Boy, aged 7:

ngo5	*used-to*	*fan3gaau3*	*hai5*	*dai6yi6 fong2*	*aa3* (gaan1)
I	used-to	sleep	in	second room	PRT

'I used to sleep in another room'

The classifier **gaan1**, which is normally used with nouns denoting buildings and rooms, should be placed before the noun.

(2) Girl, aged 5:

gan1zyu6	*baai2*	*seoi2*	*go2*	*dou3*
and then	put	water	that	place
		(**di1**)	(**hai5**)	

'and then (they) put some water over there'

The classifier for non-count nouns **di1** would normally be used before the noun 'water'. A locative element **hai5** should also be added.

In example (3), the boy was asked if he went swimming at all. In his response, a code-switch was made to English for the quantified phrase, which functions as an adverbial. It is placed clause-initially, preceding the verb phrase, which is a legitimate position in English and the only legitimate position in Cantonese. However, the clause-final position of the verb phrase following the prepositional phrase conforms to Cantonese word-order rules only. The preferred usage of quantification in Cantonese is given in parentheses below each example (3–6).

(3) Boy, aged 11:

    erm jau5 uhm, *every* Monday *tung4 ngo5 hok6haau6 heoi3 jau4seoi2*
    erm yes uhm, every Monday with   my   school   go   swimming
    'every Monday, (I) go swimming with my school'
    (...**mui5go3**   **lai5baai3jat1**   **dou1**   ...**heoi3**   **jau4seoi2**)
    (...each   CL   Monday 'dou1'   ...go   swimming)

In (4), the quantified phrase, together with a lexical item, is in English, while in examples (5) and (6) the only elements in English are the quantified phrase. In contrast to example (3) above, the children in examples (4) to (6) are not using the usual word order for Cantonese, since in every case their quantified expression follows rather than precedes the verb. This seems to suggest that the children are either using an underlying English word order, or in the case of examples (5) and (6), they might also be merely keeping to the default Cantonese (S)VO word order, not being aware of the need to move the verb phrase to clause-final position when expressing quantification.

(4) Boy, aged 11:

ngo5	*jau5*	*jat1*	*go3*	*homework*	*each*	*day*	*aa3*
I	have	one	CL	homework	each	day	PRT

    'I have one piece of homework each day'

(**ngo5**	**mui5**	**jat6**	**dou1**	**jau5**	**jat1**	**joeng6**	**gung1fo3**)
(I	each	day	'dou1'	have	one	CL	homework)

(5) Boy, aged 15:

jiu3	*duk6*	*everything*	*ge2*
need	study	everything	PRT

    '(you) need to study everything'

(**joeng6**	**joeng6**	**dou1**	**jiu3**	**duk6**	**ge2**)
(type	type	'dou1'	need	study	PRT)

(6) Boy, aged 5:

ngo5	*zung1ji3*	*both*
I	like	both

(**ngo5**	**loeng5**	**dou6**	**dou1**	**zung1ji3**)
(I	two	CL	'dou1'	like)

Findings such as these suggest that the structural characteristics of the Cantonese morphosyntax of the British-born Chinese children resemble patterns of Cantonese acquisition which are closer to those of L2 learners than those of L1 learners.

The Hakka speakers in Britain

Most of the existing studies of the Chinese communities in Britain focus on the Cantonese group, as they are by far the largest Chinese group in the country. In a small survey of the Hakka-speaking families in Tyneside, we have found that all of the 14 Hakka L1-speaking women have acquired Cantonese, the lingua franca of the Chinese community in Britain, and use it regularly in social interaction, but only 3 of them claimed to be able to speak English. However, only 3 out of the 9 Hakka L1-speaking men we studied have acquired Cantonese, yet all of them can speak English. Furthermore, all the children of the Hakka-speaking families that we studied have acquired Cantonese and English, although only 6 out of a total of 22 claimed to be able to speak Hakka (Li Wei 2000).

If we considered language shift in the Chinese communities in Britain as a change of habitual language use from Chinese to English, it might appear that the Chinese men are leading the shift. However, the women in the community have also significantly changed their language choice patterns, although it is not to English but to Cantonese, the community lingua franca. Language shift in this case is not simply a matter of making a linguistic choice, but part of a socio-cultural process of forming a community. The Hakka speakers see themselves first and foremost as part of the Chinese community and wish to acquire the appropriate language in order to function as members of the larger community. The Hakka women, who have taken on the role of bridging the family and the community, see Cantonese particularly useful for this purpose. The Hakka men, on the other hand, have more opportunities to interact with English speakers and fewer with other Chinese, due partly to the catering trade. They therefore regard English as more useful than Cantonese for their purposes.

Putonghua/Guoyu in Britain

As has been mentioned before, Putonghua and Guoyu have a relatively high socio-political and symbolic status in the Chinese communities in Britain. This is partly due to the fact that Putonghua and Guoyu are the official languages of mainland China and Taiwan respectively, to which the Chinese in Britain feel some sense of belonging. After the transition of sovereignty of Hong Kong from Britain to China, more and more Chinese people in the UK feel they should learn Putonghua. Putonghua is also being promoted by the British educational system, through formal examinations (GCSE and A level). There are secondary schools in England that offer Putonghua as a modern language subject alongside the usual European languages such as French, German and Spanish.

Although the number of Putonghua speakers from mainland China living in the UK is relatively small, their interaction with the other Chinese immigrants is increasing. Many of them are occupying important business, academic and professional positions and their voices will be heard more in the future.

Literacy in Chinese

By far the biggest challenge to the Chinese communities in Britain in their language maintenance efforts is the maintenance of literacy in Chinese – the reading and writing of Chinese characters – especially amongst the British-born children. In the existing literature on language maintenance and language shift in linguistic minority communities, bilingual speakers' ability to use written language(s) has not been subjected to the same vigorous and systematic examinations as their ability to use spoken language(s). Yet, bilinguals, especially young bilinguals, can very often speak two languages with similar degree of fluency while being literate in only one – usually the language they learn in school. More importantly perhaps, members of bilingual communities do seem to regard the ability to read and write as an indicator of a speaker's communicative competence. In communities such as the Chinese, where written language becomes a symbol of traditional culture, a reduction or loss of ability to read and write their ethnic language may take on particular social significance for members of those communities.

The Chinese communities in Britain have set up weekend language schools – some 120 of them across the country – specifically for the purpose of teaching the British-born children to read and write Chinese. Yet research evidence seems to suggest that there is little improvement in the literacy level of the Chinese children (Wong 1992, Li Wei 1993).

In the meantime, there are some elderly Chinese who do not read or write Chinese very well. The majority of the Chinese adults read and write in full characters as opposed to the simplified version used in mainland China and Singapore. Nevertheless, for the Chinese adults the literacy problem is with English not Chinese.

English spoken by the Chinese in Britain

It has been described earlier how the Chinese in Britain tend to live in geographically diverse parts of the country. They are usually surrounded by English speakers, although their interaction with them may be limited. The Chinese children are brought up in an English-dominant environment. The English language they are exposed to varies from highly localised vernacular forms, such as Geordie and Glaswegian, to standard British English through the media. There is no evidence of a Chinese English variety emerging from the community. Some of the adults speak

English non-fluently and with distinct accents, similar to the Hong Kong Chinese speakers of English. But these are signs of developing skills of the language rather than a new language variety.

Influences from Hong Kong, the media and ICT

As the majority of the Chinese in Britain can trace their origins to Hong Kong, the Hong Kong influence can be seen in every aspect of their social life including their language use. In the 1980s, a small number of words and phrases could be observed amongst the Cantonese speakers in the UK which seemed to suggest an emerging local variety of Cantonese. Most of them were obviously influenced by contact with English, for example, *bafong* (derived from *ba(th)*+*fong* 'room') as opposed to the Hong Kong Cantonese *saisanfong* 'bathroom', or *toijau* (literally 'table+wine') as opposed to *jau* 'wine'. Yet, in the late 1990s, such words and phrases seemed to have given way to the Hong Kong version. The Cantonese spoken by the majority of the Chinese in Britain is largely indistinguishable from that spoken in Hong Kong today.

One of the reasons for the diminution of a British variety of Chinese, or indeed a variety of English spoken by the Chinese in Britain, is the rapid expansion of information and communication technology (ICT). Communication with East Asia, especially China, Hong Kong and Taiwan, has never been easier and faster. Ownership of satellite television and home computers is widespread in the Chinese families in Britain. Whatever happens in East Asia is immediately known by the Chinese over here. New words and phrases, and special ways of speaking, which appear in China, Hong Kong and Taiwan soon become popularly used amongst the Chinese in Britain. For example, the following newly coined phrases are frequently heard in the Chinese communities in Britain today:

din yau	'e-mail'
baan cool	'pretend to be cool'
ngaam kii	'to get along well'
jaai talking	'talk only' (especially gay jargon)

Newspapers and magazines from China, Hong Kong and Taiwan are widely available in shops in Chinatowns, alongside the popular European Chinese newspaper *Sing Tao Daily*. Chinese language television can be received via satellite or cable. Public libraries in major cities such as London, Birmingham, Manchester and Newcastle have stocks of Chinese-language books published in China, Hong Kong and Taiwan.

The Hong Kong influence extends to the general attitudes towards language and language learning. Since 1997, there are growing numbers of Hong Kong-born Chinese learning Putonghua, in response to the political and social changes of the Special Administrative Region, the new status accorded to Hong Kong by the Chinese government. A similar trend is detectable in Britain, where the Chinese community schools have introduced Putonghua classes and teaching materials (textbooks and CD-ROMs) for the simplified characters from mainland China are being imported and used.

The Chinese in Britain are the third largest immigrant community in the country, after those of West Indian origin and from the Indian subcontinent. While it looks unlikely that there will be any sizeable Chinese immigration in the near future, the Chinese population in the UK will continue to grow with the British-born generations. To what extent the Chinese language can be maintained, and indeed which particular variety of Chinese will be maintained, remain interesting questions. The Chinese communities in Britain have certainly realised the importance of language maintenance and are trying to reverse the trend of language shift by setting up language schools where the British-born Chinese can learn their community languages. Nevertheless, the use of the Chinese language will be confined to specific domains (e.g. family and in-community communication). A Chinese-English bilingual community is emerging, which will play an increasingly significant role in the social, economic and cultural lives of Britain.

19 European immigrant languages

Penelope Gardner-Chloros

Introduction

The presence of a separate chapter on European immigrant languages in this volume should be seen as a measure of the ever-growing importance of Europe in Britain's affairs. In the absence, however, of any directly relevant Census information or comprehensive surveys on European languages in the UK, the brief to write a chapter on these languages posed several challenges. Two significant issues are, firstly, the use and significance of European languages among the existing population, and secondly the question of the – probably increasing – impact of languages of European immigration on the domestic picture in the future. In the last part of the chapter, I briefly discuss some linguistic aspects of the European immigrant groups and in particular of one of the largest groups, the Greek Cypriots, so as to give an idea of the sociolinguistic developments which can occur over several generations in an immigrant setting.

Which Europe?

The issues mentioned above beg the preliminary question as to which languages should be counted as European, and therefore of the appropriate definition of Europe. The broadest definition one might take would be the Member States of the Council of Europe, numbering forty-three and spanning the continent from the North Cape to Gibraltar and from Ireland to Vladivostok. Such a number would be to say the least unwieldy, especially taking into account the internal multilingualism of many of these states. A more practical definition is that of the European Union (EU). One of the main reasons for taking the EU as a unit of reference for the purposes of this chapter is that it embodies a set of rules among which

The author wishes to thank Efstratios Chatzidoukakis and Sylvain Jouhette of Eurostat, John Grinyer of the DfES, Siobhan Carey of the ONS and Paul Cheshire for their help with statistical sources. Any errors or misinterpretations are solely the author's responsibility.

is freedom of movement, and the right for member state nationals to settle and work in any of the EU countries. Beyond the economic inter-relationship, there is therefore a clear expectation that a certain number of nationals of the new member states will settle in the UK, which is bound to have some impact on the existing linguistic picture.

On 1 May 2004, the EU enlarged from fifteen to twenty-five member states, and a further two joined on 1 January 2007.[1] EU membership is not, of course, the only reason for people to move from one European country to another. Some of the eastern European states, for instance, have long-standing historic links with the UK, for example Poland, in spite of the fact that until the fall of the Iron Curtain, it gave its citizens the reverse of freedom of movement. Some 'excluded' groups, such as Kurds or Albanians, may also be present in relatively significant numbers, whether they are detained in the UK, asylum seekers or simply here illegally. To take a comparison, Turkish and Moroccan immigrants have had a significant impact on the linguistic picture in Germany and the Netherlands, although their presence is due to specific recruitment drives which were nothing to do with the EU (see the papers in Extra & Verhoeven 1993).

A referendum held in 2004 in Cyprus came down against the northern part of Cyprus, Turkish-speaking and illegally occupied since 1974 by Turkey, joining the EU as part of a single unit with the Greek-speaking south. Turkey had been anxious that an agreement should be reached that would allow this, as Turkey's own projected membership is tied up with this issue. Norway and Switzerland both decided by referendum against membership, and Iceland has never been a candidate. In the meantime, the current enlargement brings the number of official languages in the EU from eleven to twenty-two, with the prospect of Turkish following on soon. Fears have been expressed that there will also be a huge influx of illegal immigrants and asylum seekers entering the EU through those of the new member states which have borders with non-EU countries such as Albania or Russia.

Which language for Europe?

On one level, linguistic policy and the linguistic picture in the UK overall is less likely to be affected by the enlargement than that in other countries. For one thing, the UK is not home to any of the major EU institutions, and so

---

[1] In alphabetical order, the pre-2004 members were: Austria, Belgium, Denmark, Finland, France, Germany, Greece, Ireland, Italy, Luxembourg, the Netherlands, Portugal, Spain, Sweden and the United Kingdom. The new member states are Bulgaria, Cyprus, the Czech Republic, Estonia, Hungary, Latvia, Lithuania, Malta, Poland, Romania, Slovakia and Slovenia.

does not have to cope directly with the major institutional difficulties of translation and interpretation which the arrival of the new members entails.[2]

Secondly, it is well known that English is the most widely learned and spoken second language in the current EU, and this is likely to be the case in the enlarged Union as well. A 1998 survey by Eurostat, the EU statistical organisation, reported that 90% of pupils in the EU learn English as a second language (Hoffman 2000). A survey carried out in 2001 on 'Europeans and Languages' by the EU's Directorate General of Education and Culture (INRA (Europe) 2001) reported that 41% of the population of the EU claimed to speak English on top of their mother tongue – more than the next four languages (French, German, Spanish and Italian) combined. There was an inverse correlation between knowledge of English and age and a strong positive correlation with educational level (2001:10). An article in *The Times* (9 January 2004) cites a European Commission survey showing that seven out of ten EU citizens believe that everyone in the EU should be able to speak English – though one might wish to question the journalist's conclusion that achieving this would 'do wonders for cultural understanding' and 'inspire European unity'.

Although we do not yet have equivalent figures for the new member states, there is likely to be a similar trend. Since the break-up of the Soviet Union, the countries formerly under its domination have been systematically replacing the compulsory teaching of Russian in schools with that of English. This makes it more likely that any new arrivals following enlargement will be in a position to adapt relatively quickly to an English-speaking environment, although, as the Australian experience has shown, many other factors come into play as regards: (a) cultural assimilation and; (b) loss or attrition of the mother tongue (Clyne 1991). It has been pointed out that there appears to be a tendency for foreign groups in the UK to assimilate, rather than forming a 'hyphenated' identity (as in 'Italian-Americans', etc. in the US), which can help maintain ethnolinguistic vitality (Sherwood 1991). On the other hand, it is clearly economic and cultural influence from the US which is responsible for the strength of English in the first place (see the papers in Cenoz & Jessner 2000).

Surveys of European languages in the UK

Two main questions are relevant here: first, the question of the language skills of the existing population and the linguistic policies affecting them; and second, the question of existing community languages. The second is

---

[2] The number of translations between different EU languages required for EU documents has increased from 110 before the accession of new member states in 2004 and 2007 to over 420 now.

obviously part of the first, but will be discussed separately as the issues raised are quite different.

Language skills among the 'native' population

Educationalists and others have long deplored the UK's poor record in learning and speaking other languages. Research in second language acquisition suggests that attitudes and motivation are key factors in success. Comparisons with other European countries whose native languages are not widely spoken outside their borders suggest that the rest of the world's propensity to learn English has been a serious disincentive to the British as regards learning other languages. Recognising their inferior performance compared with other countries but not necessarily recognising its causes, it is a common stereotype among the White English population that they are intrinsically less gifted than other nationals at language learning. In a European Commission survey in 2001, 65.9 percent of UK respondents stated that they did not speak any language apart from their mother tongue – by far the highest proportion of the EU countries participating in the survey (Eurobarometer 2001).

The responsibility for this situation lies, historically, at least partly with unenlightened and unimaginative educational policies in this field. Two brief contrasts may be drawn. First, with Canada where, unlike in the UK, policy makers have taken account of research findings which show the advantages of bilingualism for pupils' linguistic and cognitive development (Hamers & Blanc 2000); the success of immersion schools has been particularly striking. Second, with the Netherlands, where in *gymnasia*, the more academic secondary schools, *three* modern foreign languages are taught on top of Latin and Greek, making up more than half the curriculum (Extra & Verhoeven 1993). In Britain, by contrast, parents of bilingual children continue to be misadvised by some teachers, speech therapists, etc. to the effect that it would be better for their children's development if they were only spoken to in English. In most schools, the only foreign language taught is French, regardless of the pupils' language skills, ethnic background or particular motivations. While it has often been pointed out that French is not the ideal choice for all pupils in the UK, for reasons too numerous – and partly too obvious – to go into here, there is now also a serious shortage of teachers who could teach any *other* language in mainstream schooling. As languages have been given such a low priority in schools over the last decades, a vicious circle has developed where fewer and fewer people are qualified to study languages at university and so numerous university language departments have shrunk or closed down entirely, thus producing fewer and fewer language teachers. Realising the seriousness of the situation, the government has recently brought out a 'national strategy for languages', which involves providing some additional funding (£115 million over three years) to provide support for foreign language teaching in primary schools in England (they are currently taught in only one in five primary schools) (DfES 2005). However it has also recently been made optional to take a language up to age 16, whereas it was compulsory before – so the overall trend is unlikely to improve in the foreseeable future. The government has recently announced (March 2007) that this policy will be maintained but that there will be some compulsory language teaching introduced gradually in primary schools. In Scotland, by contrast, 99% of participants in a recent survey of languages at secondary school were studying another language. For the majority (81%), this language was French, which had also been studied by 75% of respondents at primary school (Scotlang 2002).

A policy developed by the Department for Education and Skills (2002b), entitled *Languages for All: Languages for Life*, summarises the situation thus: 'The number of young people studying for language qualifications post-16 continues to decline, although numbers taking A levels and participating in higher education have increased. There were over 500,000 pupil entries for language GCSEs in 2002, but at A level this number reduced dramatically to under 30,000, equivalent to fewer than 5% of total entries. Numbers are declining at degree level too, with fewer than 3% of students in 2000/01 enrolled on first degree courses studying language subjects.' (2002b:11). Oddly, this situation does not reflect a lack of demand in the employment market, quite the reverse: 'Language graduates score highly on employability compared to graduates of other disciplines . . . Language skills audits commissioned by a number of Regional Development Agencies over 2000–2001 have indicated that 45% of international businesses surveyed experience language and cultural issues as barriers to international business . . . 30% of British companies have over 20% of their customer base outside the UK and . . . over 70% conduct some business in other countries' (2002b:13).

Census data on European language communities in the UK

There are no comprehensive sources of statistical data on speakers of European languages in the UK. Instead one has to rely on piecemeal, related evidence from various surveys and organisations. It would be extremely useful if future Censuses could include a question on language skills – since they do include questions on generally more sensitive issues such as ethnic group and religion, there seems no reason to continue omitting this important information.

The last Census, carried out in 2001, and applicable to England and Wales only, showed the following figures for place of birth (Census 2001):

Born in UK:	53,883,986
Born elsewhere in EU:	1,306,731
Born outside EU:	3,598,477
TOTAL:	58,789,194

The comparable figures for Scotland, Northern Ireland and for the Republic of Ireland are as follows:

Scotland (www.scrol.gov.uk)

Total population	5,062,011
Born elsewhere in EU	1.10%
Born outside EU	2.25%

Northern Ireland (www.nisra.gov.uk)

Total population	1,685,267
Born elsewhere in EU	0.6%
Born outside EU	1.2%

Republic of Ireland (www.cso.ie) (NB the Republic of Ireland Census was carried out in 2002)

Total population	3,917,203
Born elsewhere in EU	0.9%
Born outside EU	3.1%

Various guesses can be made as to how these figures relate to the number of people who speak another European language as a mother tongue or as a joint mother tongue with English:

- The most significant imponderable is how many of those born in these countries are of second or third generation migrant origin and therefore probably native or near-native speakers of other languages on top of English. To make a guess at this, one can make the following calculation: 87% of the population of England and 96% of that of Wales gave their ethnic origin as White British. If we reckon that, averaging these out, 91.5%[3] of those born in England and Wales are White British, that leaves 4,580,139 who are not. Most of these are made up of Indians (2%

---

[3] The average of the two percentages – a rough figure as it has not been weighted for the difference between the populations of England and Wales.

of the population of England and Wales), White Irish[4] (1.2%), Black Caribbeans[5] (1.1%), Africans (0.9%), Bangladeshis (0.5%), Chinese (0.4%) and Other Black groups (0.2%). Between them, these represent approximately 6.5% of the population (= 3,502,459). So this leaves a potential maximum of just over a million people born in England and Wales who are neither White British nor of one of the other ethnic groups, i.e. likely to be second or third generation 'Other-Whites'. A factor to take into account in relation to Northern Ireland is the almost total lack of net immigration; a situation which is gradually changing since the ceasefire and the Good Friday Agreement, though the most numerous groups of immigrants are non-European.

- A small number of those born elsewhere in the EU may be people of British parents who happened to be born abroad, but we can reasonably guess that most people born 'elsewhere in the EU' speak another EU language.

- A certain proportion of those born *outside* the EU would also be speakers of European languages: they might be either from European countries not in the EU, such as Norway or Switzerland, or from other continents but still speakers of EU languages (including English if they are American, Australian, etc.) or they might speak a European language as part of the repertoire of their multilingual country of origin (e.g. French speakers from Africa).

The sum of those born elsewhere in the EU and those likely to be second generation speakers of European languages is, on the basis of these figures, well under 2.5 million people.

Other surveys providing relevant data

Since the disbanding of the Inner London Education Authority (ILEA), which used to carry out Language Censuses (1981–87), and since the Linguistic Minorities Project (1985), which included a survey of Adult Language Use but is now over twenty years out of date, no large-scale survey of minority languages in London or the UK has been carried out. Community language provision was surveyed, however, in a European research project funded in this country by the Department for Further Education and Skills, and co-ordinated by CILT and Scottish CILT. The results were published in September 2005, to coincide with the European Day of Languages.[6] Further information about the current situation in

---

[4] Some of these are of course Gaelic speakers.

[5] Some of these would be French and/or Creole speakers. Africans may also be French speakers.

[6] See http://www.cilt.org.uk/key/trends2005/trends2005_community.pdf [last accessed 25 January 2007].

Scotland is provided in a publication by the Centre for Education and Racial Equality in Scotland (1999).

For the time being we can extract relevant information from various sources. These include:

- the EU's Labour Force Survey (2003), which shows the figures, in each EU member state, for employed nationals of that state, other EU nationals and non-EU nationals;
- the International Adult Literacy Survey (1996), which asked about 'conversational' languages spoken, and in which a sample of 3,184 respondents were given six chances to state which languages they could hold a conversation in (84 languages as options);
- the Skills for Life survey, carried out in 2003 for England only, among 460 people who speak English as a foreign language and 8,270 native English speakers;
- the National Literacy Trust's EAL survey (2000) of the most common mother tongues for children in London.

Relevant information provided by each of these is detailed below.

The EU Labour Force Survey (Eurostat 2003)

This shows that out of a total of 28,115,388 people employed in the UK in the second quarter of 2003, 886,403 were nationals of other EU states (roughly as many again were nationals of non-EU states). This is further broken down by nationality as follows:

German	40,531
Danish	11,535
Spanish	35,651
Finnish	10,216
French	63,626
Greek	10,056
Irish	185,828
Italian	56,139
Dutch	24,535
Portuguese	55,255
Swedish	13,896

(Figures for Austria, Belgium and Luxembourg were not reliable due to small sample size.)

The breakdown is significant as by far the greatest number of other EU nationals employed in the UK turn out to be the Irish, whose home language would, in almost all cases, be English.

The International Adult Literacy Survey (IALS)

The IALS (OECD 2000) was a survey conducted by the Organisation for Economic Co-operation and Development in Great Britain in 1996 about 'conversational' languages spoken (sample size 3,184). Respondents were given six chances to state in which languages they could hold a conversation. As the majority were native English speakers, this gives some idea of foreign language ability (98.4% claimed to speak English well enough to conduct a conversation).

Looking first at the EU member states' official languages:

- 0.1%[7] of those surveyed claimed to speak Danish (weighted up for the UK population this would represent 28,561 people).
- 0.2% claimed to speak Dutch (65,435 people) and roughly another 10,000 claimed to speak Flemish.
- 15% claimed to speak French (amounting to 5,431,688 people). Since this is the most significant percentage after English, a further check revealed that some 170,000 French nationals are registered with the French Embassy in London. The remainder therefore represent native speakers of English (or other languages) who speak French as an L2.
- 0.1% claimed to speak Czech (24,742 people).
- 6.1% claimed to speak German (2,202,426 people).
- 0.4% claimed to speak Greek (150,699 people).
- 0.1% claimed to speak Hungarian (25,167 people).
- 1.2% claimed to speak Italian (423,394 people).
- 0.2% claimed to speak Polish (73,880 people).
- 0.2% claimed to speak Portuguese (13,751 people).
- 2.4% claimed to speak Spanish (878,956 people).
- 0.1% claimed to speak Swedish (24,415 people).
- 6,926 people claimed to speak Finnish.

Since Czech, Hungarian and Polish speakers are now in the EU and can therefore settle without difficulty in the UK, the figures for these languages are presumably on the increase.

It would be interesting – but unfortunately beyond our scope here – to investigate the ethnolinguistic vitality of, say, German or Spanish – learned by a relatively large number of people in Britain as second languages – and languages such as Greek, for which the figure above represents almost exclusively native or second/third generation speakers. It would also be worthwhile to investigate the effect of having a second national language, in particular in the Republic of Ireland and Wales, on European language learning in schools in those countries.

[7] Percentage figures are rounded up here, but weightings are calculated from the full percentage. This explains why apparently the same percentage (e.g. 0.1%) in some cases corresponds to a different weighted figure.

The Skills for Life Survey (DfES 2003)

This survey took 8,270 native English speakers and 460 people who spoke English as a foreign language, aged 16–65 inclusive. Apart from being somewhat more recent and based on a larger sample, the main difference from the IALS Survey above is that the native English speakers are treated separately from those whose first language is not English.

(i) *Languages spoken well enough to have a conversation: respondents with English as first language*

   EU members' official languages

Czech	0.04%
Danish	0.04%
Dutch	0.33%
Flemish	0.01%
French	11.90%
German	4.27%
Greek	0.22%
Hungarian	0.01%
Italian	0.86%
Maltese	0.02%
Polish	0.08%
Portuguese	0.16%
Spanish	2.43%
Swedish	0.07%

(ii) *Respondents with English not as a first language*

   EU members' official languages

Czech	0.7%
Danish	1.1%
Dutch	2.0%
Finnish	0.9%
French	14.3%
German	7.6%
Greek	1.3%
Italian	6.5%
Maltese	1.5%
Polish	2.6%
Portuguese	2.6%
Spanish	6.7%
Swedish	1.1%

(NB there were presumably no native Hungarian speakers in this sample.)

The National Literacy Trust's EAL Survey

The National Literacy Trust's website[8] states that despite Britain's quarter century membership of the EU, only 2% of pupils in Britain are from 'Other-White backgrounds' (as compared with, for example, Asians from the Indian subcontinent who account for more than 7% of primary children and 6% of secondary). More than 300 languages are spoken by children in London's schools, and for more than a third English is not the language they speak at home. The figures for mother tongues of European language speaking children in London schools are given as follows (*Evening Standard*, 21 January 2000):

English	608,500
Greek	6,300
French	5,600
Spanish	5,500
Italian	2,500
Polish	1,500
German	800

The total excluding English is 22,200. The rank order compared with adults who speak these languages (see the other surveys) is, interestingly, quite different.

Overall, it can be seen that knowledge of European languages in the UK, with a population of almost 59 million, looking at both the native and non-native population, is both very low and fragmented. No language apart from French comes even close to being spoken by 10% or more of the population. Some 5 million people claim to be able to speak French and some 2 million German. Considering that everyone is taught one of these languages at school, that is not an impressive record. Nor is it the case that other languages spoken by millions worldwide are better represented – Spanish, for example, is spoken by well under a million. Major non-European languages such as Hindi/Panjabi/Urdu, Chinese, Arabic and Russian are spoken almost exclusively by those who use them as a first language (Alladina 1993).

Community usage

In order to put some flesh on these bones, one needs to turn to a small number of publications and assorted research projects which concern

[8] See http://www.literacytrust.org.uk/Database/stats/EALstats.html#2006 [last accessed 25 January 2006].

individual communities. After considering some general issues which emerge, notably from the relevant papers in Alladina & Edwards (1991), I will briefly discuss some of the linguistic aspects of community usage in relation to the largest group of European extraction, the Greek Cypriots.

Issues affecting community usage

Alladina & Edwards (1991) contains chapters by various authors on communities long established in the UK. Of these, three are long-standing EU members, i.e. the Italians, Spaniards and Portuguese. Other chapters concern the Greek and Turkish Cypriots whose EU position was discussed above, and three other newer members: Lithuanians, Poles and Hungarians.

Typically, these immigrant communities are made up of subgroups who came over in different waves in the twentieth century. Some of these came for economic reasons, such as the earliest Cypriots and Lithuanians. Such migrants were often peasants and illiterate, whereas later waves, which came for political reasons, were more socially varied, including many professionals such as doctors and teachers. Communities grouped together under a common language umbrella are therefore often extremely internally varied – contrast the wealthy middle-class mainland Greek expatriates with the working-class Greek Cypriots in Haringey.

The various communities also differ widely in size. Estimates suggest that the largest are the Italians and Cypriots (about 200,000 each), followed by the Poles (about 100,000), the Spaniards (50,000) and the Portuguese (40,000), with Hungarians and Lithuanians making up very small numbers and furthermore being less cohesive owing to being scattered. The make-up of the existing communities in the UK is likely to change considerably in those cases where the country of origin is now in the EU. The likely influx of nationals from Poland, Lithuania, etc. should have some positive impact on the ethnolinguistic vitality of the existing communities of speakers of those languages. At the same time, the new arrivals will find their passage to Britain eased by the existence of structures supporting their mother tongue and traditions.

Ethnolinguistic vitality depends partly on continued contact with the country of origin, and groups which were cut off from their country of origin by virtue of having left for political reasons have found it more difficult to maintain their identity (e.g. Hungarians or Lithuanians). At the same time there can be factionalism within the immigrant community, with divisions along social and political lines, and according to the social, regional and dialectal origins of particular migrant groups.

Mother tongue teaching is not always well-supported or organised. Britain's record of supporting community languages has not been impressive, and projects such as the Bedfordshire EEC Mother Tongue and Culture Project (1979–80) (Tosi 1984) and the European Commission Project on Community Language in the Secondary Curriculum (1984–87) (Community Language in the Secondary Curriculum Project 1987) have been few and far between. Even in the case of languages taught as foreign languages in Britain (e.g. Spanish or Italian) – whose communities are in a stronger position than those whose language is considered a minority language only – the different needs of young people learning their community language and others learning the same language as a foreign language are often not recognised. Some of the main initiatives for producing teaching materials in community languages are described in Edwards (2000); overall, the responsibility for doing this is left to the communities themselves. The country of origin may offer them teaching and/or support materials which are both culturally and linguistically inappropriate for children of the second and third generations of migrants. For example, the Greek government provides teachers who try and teach Standard mainland Greek in Saturday schools to children in the Cypriot community whose only contact with any type of Greek has been with the (spoken) Greek Cypriot dialect.

Particular attention has been drawn to the influence of economics in determining language use, maintenance and shift. As Edwards (1985) observes, the lack of economic advantage or pragmatic motivation attached to the use of a community language are among the most significant factors in its abandonment. A conflict may arise between the desire for maintenance of the language and culture of the country of origin, and a need to assimilate to the host society in order to have equal rights with the indigenous population and a better standard of living.

Linguistic aspects: the Greek Cypriot example

Even those communities which have been most successful in maintaining their language and identity eventually show signs of assimilation over two to three generations (Clyne 1991). Regardless of wide differences of culture and circumstances, similar linguistic and attitudinal changes occur in most immigrant communities over time. The 200,000-strong Greek Cypriot community in London has been mentioned as the largest group in Britain speaking a European language other than English (Anthias 1992, Christodoulou-Pipis 1991). Although Greek-speaking migrants are often among the best at maintaining their language and culture (Clyne 1991, Smolicz 1985), a recent study found that the younger generation of Cypriots do not consider the widespread use of English within the community to be a threat to the ethnic language to the same extent as their elders. Therefore, in spite of continuing to value their ethnic identity, the youngest generation report an overwhelming use of English, even in the private sphere and with other family members (Gardner-Chloros, MacEntee-Atalianis & Finnis 2005).

Linguistically speaking, the commonest phenomenon reported in many communities is borrowing and code-switching (i.e. the use of two languages within the same conversation or sentence). In the first generation, particularly where this consists of relatively uneducated people from rural backgrounds, there is typically an influx of borrowed words which are morphologically and phonologically integrated with the mother tongue and which principally concern cultural concepts and items which have acquired prominence in the new setting. Examples from Cypriot Greek include *paso* 'bus', *marketa* 'market', *kitʃi* 'kitchen', *taspin* 'dustbin' and *Xaspas* 'husband'. A comparable example from Italian migrants, quoted by Tosi (1984) is the sentence:

*Nun'ce stanna i **moni**, li sordi per le **olidei***
[There is no **money**, the money for the **holidays**.]

The second generation usually code-switches in a more varied manner depending on the topic of conversation, being generally equally fluent in English and the language of origin. This more linguistically complex and deliberate kind of mixing often constitutes the 'in-code' and even acquires a name (e.g. *BBC Gringlish*). In the following example, an aerobics teacher in North London gives her instructions to her pupils in a 'mixed code' (Gardner-Chloros, unpublished example):

Monon to hip **na kamni** *move*
[Only the]   [should be moved]
Cheria to the side, I want you **na stathite kai na kanete** *touch the ceiling*
[Hands]   [to stand up and to (do)]

Estebanez (1991) quotes the following, comparable example of Spanish–English code-switching:

*Me gusta la **Bibici** con el **frich ful** y la **jita on***
[I like the **BBC** with the **fridge full** and the **heater on**.]

As the younger, British-born generations create a mixed identity for themselves, so they elaborate new ways of speaking, using the resources of both languages and exploiting them for new purposes of their own. Notably, disapproval for code-switched speech is attenuated in each successive generation, and the possibility of alternating languages is increasingly appreciated as functional. In another study for instance, it was shown that young women switched to Greek in order to exploit the greater directness and positive politeness associated with Greek and to express themselves more openly and forcefully than they could have if they had stuck to English throughout (Gardner-Chloros & Finnis 2003). The following example illustrates this tactic:

(1) Speaker F(=female)1, after asking the same question in English twice and failing to get a response from speaker M(=male)1, switches to Greek to elicit a response. Having succeeded in doing so, she then switches back to English.

F1 Stop, how many days is the conference?
M1 Guys, I wanna finish at seven o'clock.
F1 I'm asking ! How many days is the conference?
M1 ??? It's half past six.
F1 *Kirie Meniko, poses imeres einai?*
    [Mr Meniko, how many days is it?]
M1 It will be around four days, I imagine.
F1 Ok, four days, good . . . and what time?

The potentially face-threatening act – an escalation of repeated questions – is carried off thanks to the switch to Greek, which not only allows greater directness but is also the 'we-code' and the language of humour. Thus code-switching provides a powerful toolkit for women in the community, who can get away with jokes, strong repartee, etc. without appearing aggressive or unfeminine. The possibilities offered by code-switching are – perhaps paradoxically – one reason for keeping the ethnic language alive, as is recognised in the next example, where young Greek Cypriots comment on the 'bonding' function of code-switching, as below, in relation to text messaging:

(2)

F1 English letters, but we do a little joke in – in you know, Greek but with the English letters . . . just text each other *'kalimera koubara, pos pai'*
                                            [good morning, friend, how's it going]
    just occasionally, you know . . . its just –
F2 Yeah, its a kind of bonding thing, isn't it?

Although such mixed modes of speech have, traditionally, been frowned upon by purists, within the educational system in particular, the evidence is clear that they arise in all immigrant contexts, European or otherwise. While they may have a limited long-term impact on the development of English, they represent an important phase of acculturation in the lives of such communities and are of growing interest to linguists, as they reveal many aspects of how languages change through contact (Thomason 2001).

Conclusions

Describing the use and presence of other European languages in the UK is like sewing a patchwork quilt with many very small patches.

First, it is clear that active knowledge of other European languages is restricted to a small proportion of the native population – mainly the educated elite. Only French, German and Spanish are taught to any substantial extent in schools, barring exceptions, and there appears to be a total lack of co-ordination between educational language policy and the nation's language needs from a trade or foreign relations perspective. This lack of vision applies equally – perhaps one should say *a fortiori* – to non-European languages, both those which have a substantial presence in the UK, such as Hindi and Urdu, and those which may be less widely spoken but have a huge importance in the world, such as Arabic or Chinese.

The presence of several substantial native European language speaking groups is a separate issue, with Greek and Italian speakers currently being the largest groups, though groups of Eastern and Baltic origin will acquire greater prominence as their nationals take advantage of their entitlement to settle in the UK, following the latest EU enlargement. Members of these groups gradually assimilate to their environment, over approximately three generations, linguistically as in other respects, and in the case of the UK this assimilation is likely to be expedited by the 'world popularity' of English. Along the way to assimilating, the younger generations of migrant origin often create new mixed forms of speech. Some, like creole, leave a mark on the local varieties (Sebba 1993, Rampton 1995a), though this has, so far, been less noticeable in the UK than in other comparable settings, such as North African influences in France or Italian influences in Switzerland.[9]

---

[9] Since completing this chapter, a new survey of language teaching at school in EU countries has been announced. See http://europa.eu/rapid/pressReleasesAction.do?reference=IP/07/496&format=HTML&aged=0&language=EN&guiLanguage=en

20   Sign languages

Bencie Woll and Rachel Sutton-Spence

There are two sign languages native to the British Isles. British Sign Language (BSL) is used by the Deaf community of England, Scotland, Wales and Protestant signers in Northern Ireland. Irish Sign Language (ISL) is used by members of the Deaf community in the Republic of Ireland (McDonnell 2004) and Catholic signers in Northern Ireland (Matthews 1996). The two sign languages are distinct, not believed to be genetically related, and mutually unintelligible. Both are natural, living community languages. Although the two sign languages are unrelated, there have been some mutual influences in relation to lexical borrowing; although they are both independent of the English language used by the hearing society surrounding them, both exist in a minority relationship with English and consequently show some evidence of English influence.

As the social and educational experiences of the British and Irish Deaf communities have been very different historically (and still are, to a certain extent), the social aspects of the two languages need to be described separately. However, the linguistic features of BSL and ISL, and, it should be noted, other European sign languages, are sufficiently similar for a single basic description of the grammar of BSL to be applicable to ISL, unless noted otherwise.

BSL and ISL differ from English in three main ways:
- they are visual-spatial languages (not sound-based like English);
- they are unwritten (not having the great literary tradition of English); and
- they are numerically minority languages, with users numbered in the thousands (ISL) or tens of thousands (BSL) (not the approximately 60 million British and Irish English users).

British Sign Language

There are no accurate figures for the number of users of BSL. Figures quoted range between 30,000 and 60,000. Although the language is

We would like to thank Lorraine Leeson at Trinity College, Dublin, for her advice on ISL.

341

primarily used by people who are born deaf or who become deaf at an early age, with profound prelingual deafness, there is no exact correlation between degree of deafness and BSL use (see Woll & Lawson 1982/1990 for a description of British Deaf community membership). It is also well attested that degree and age of onset of deafness do not map exactly onto language community membership (Wilcox 1989). Many deaf people are brought up orally, speaking English and using lip-reading and amplified residual hearing to understand the speech of others. Such individuals are often not members of the Deaf community, while others who have been deafened later in childhood or in adulthood have chosen to learn BSL and join the Deaf community. The hearing children of signing Deaf parents may also be fluent BSL users. In addition, because of the widespread uptake of further education classes in BSL (particularly over the last twenty years) there are more hearing people with some knowledge of BSL than there are Deaf signers (Woll 2001).

Despite worries by the eugenicists of the nineteenth and early twentieth centuries, deaf children are rarely born to deaf parents. (A widely quoted figure is 5–10% in Britain (Kyle & Woll 1985), although it varies around the world.) Most children born severely or profoundly deaf or who become deaf in childhood have hearing parents. This difference in hearing status leads to atypical language transmission between the generations, and hence to atypical language acquisition, since most hearing parents do not know BSL before their deaf children are born. In the past, and still in some parts of Britain today, hearing parents have been told not to sign to their children on the grounds that this impedes their acquisition of English and impairs their ability to socialise with other, hearing, children. Despite the long-term belief of educators that this is the case, there is really no reliable supporting evidence (Marschark 1993). Although an increasing number of hearing parents are learning BSL in order to communicate with their children, parental fluency in the language is rarely achieved and the language situation in most homes with a deaf child is very complex. The problem of the language environment becomes more acute when the language of the home is not English. Deaf children can find themselves surrounded by one spoken and written language (with an associated culture) at home and another spoken and written language at school. In addition, they need to find a place for BSL and the culture of the British Deaf community.

Deaf education and BSL

The education of deaf children has had a great impact on BSL. Due to the relatively low incidence of deafness, Deaf communities as we know them did not exist until the growth of cities during the Industrial Revolution, although there are many early accounts of Deaf friends and families (cf. Jackson 1990). However, the opening of deaf schools had probably the greatest impact on the development of sign languages and Deaf communities. When children were brought together in residential schools, signing communities were formed and the language developed and expanded (cf. Kegl, Senghas & Coppola 1999).

Policies of Deaf education have historically been dictated by hearing educators and philanthropists. The first schools for deaf children in Britain were established in the mid-eighteenth century, with BSL used as the language of instruction (Watson 1809). The signing was frequently referred to as 'natural signing' to distinguish it from 'methodical signing'. Methodical signing was developed by the founder of education for deaf children in France, the Abbé de l'Epée (de l'Epée 1784). This system used the basic sign vocabulary of the Parisian deaf community, adding new signs for French morphology in order to create a visual version of French grammar. This idea of replacing the visual, spatial and temporal grammar of the natural sign language with signs representing the grammar of another language is common in deaf education around the world; in English-speaking societies it is termed 'signed English'.

Although BSL enjoyed widespread use in British deaf schools throughout the nineteenth century, there were always educationalists who believed that the oral approach to education was preferable and that deaf children should use English rather than sign language. This philosophy gradually gained strength and by the early twentieth century all teachers were being trained in oral methods rather than signing (e.g. Fay 1881). Signing was frequently banned in schools and children punished for its use (Kyle & Woll 1985). In the 1970s, as oralism was found to have delivered poor literacy skills to deaf children (Conrad 1979), signing in the classroom was reintroduced. However, just when signing (most often signed English) became more accepted as an educational language in British schools, the movement towards integration in education resulted in the closure of special schools for deaf children, and deaf children were sent to mainstream schools. In the 1970s, most deaf children were educated in schools for the deaf, but by the end of the century, 85% of deaf children in the UK were in mainstream education. Although there may be many educational and social benefits in the closure of so many deaf schools, one important effect was to remove children's access to the community of signers and the linguistic and cultural role model that this community provided to young deaf children.

Deaf Associations and BSL

It is important not to overemphasise the importance of deaf schools in the maintenance of BSL, however. In the century in which signing was prohibited in schools, deaf children continued to sign and the language was transmitted to younger children. After leaving school, many deaf people joined the Deaf community (with the local Deaf club as a major feature of social life) where BSL was accepted and valued. The British Deaf and Dumb Association (now the British Deaf Association (BDA)) was founded in 1881 to protect sign language and the rights of the deaf community to use the language against the increasing influence of oralism in education. The 1880 Congress of Milan, at which oralist methods were internationally approved for deaf education, was the spur for the BDA's foundation. Other organisations such as the British Deaf Sports Council also promoted the use of BSL, Deaf culture and the Deaf community. In the 1970s, politically active members of the Deaf community, concerned by the dominance of hearing people over their lives, formed the National Union of the Deaf (NUD) to fight more strongly for the recognition and acceptance of BSL within the wider society. One major success for the NUD was the broadcasting of BSL on BBC television (Ladd 2003). Their pilot programme encouraged the BBC to broadcast a magazine programme for Deaf people in BSL. This programme has run weekly or fortnightly in some form since 1981 and has had a major impact on the status, use and public awareness of BSL.

Historical records of BSL

British Sign Language has no written form. Consequently, historical records of the language are rare. Of the few early recorded references to sign language use in Britain, most are in the form of descriptions in English by hearing writers (e.g. Bulwer 1648, Nevins 1895). We do know that deaf people have been using some form of signing in Britain since at least the sixteenth century. A description of the signs used by a deaf man to make his marriage vows in 1575 was recorded by the parish clerk of the church of St Martin's in Leicester.

The sayd Thomas, for the expression of his minde, instead of words of his owne accord used these signs: first he embraced her with his armes, and took her by the hande, putt a ring upon her finger and layde his hande upon her harte and held his handes towardes heaven; and to show his continuance to dwell with her to his lyves ende he did it by closing of his eyes with his handes and digginge out of the earthe with his foote, and pulling as though he would ring a bell with divers other signs approved.

Illustrations were costly to publish and few appeared: Bulwer (1648) contains drawings of signs; the earliest manual alphabet chart appeared in 1680 (Dalgarno). It is not until the late nineteenth century that substantial numbers of illustrations of signs were published (e.g. *The Dictionary of D & D Signs* 1895). (For a more detailed history of BSL, see Kyle & Woll, 1985.)

Regional dialects

Although BSL and ISL are distinct from each other and from other national sign languages, neither has a single, invariant form, with both BSL and ISL exhibiting dialect variation. For social and historical reasons, regional dialects are particularly significant in BSL, while gender differences have been more salient in ISL.

Woll (1991) identified considerable lexical variation in the BSL used in Glasgow, Newcastle, Manchester, London and Bristol. Regional differences were seen in culturally key signs (e.g. DEAF,[1] HEARING, INTERPRETER[2]), 'everyday' words (e.g. BRITISH, BUSINESS, THEATRE) and lexical items new to the deaf community (e.g. DISCRIMINATION, COMMUNITY). In some core semantic areas such as colour terms, days of the week and numerals, signs exhibit substantial regional variation. It was the case, however, that while there were substantial regional differences, there was usually one variant recognised and accepted across all regions, suggesting gradual development of a national standard.

BSL regional dialects were perpetuated in the past because deaf people were regionally isolated, with no written variety, no telephone access and no radio or television broadcasts in the language. With national broadcasting of BSL on television for more than twenty years, and greater mobility, regional dialect differences may be reducing. While this may explain current dialect levelling in BSL, it cannot account for the original development of BSL dialects.

There is a commonly held lay assumption that regional dialects are deviations from one original homogeneous language variety (Francis 1983). This does not apply to BSL since there is no evidence that there was once a single variant of BSL, which was spread from a central source and then became less homogeneous. The main source of dialect differences in BSL probably arose from the regional organisation of deaf education in large autonomous residential schools. Each school was independently run and there was no centralised training institution for signing teachers of the

---

[1] Following convention, sign glosses are given in capital letters.
[2] In the Deaf community, interpreters are an important part of interaction with the hearing world.

deaf (unlike in America where most teachers were taught either at the Hartford Asylum for the Deaf or by teachers who had trained there themselves).

Irish Sign Language

ISL is the second minority language of Ireland (after Irish). In the mid-1990s, the size of the Irish Deaf community was reported to be 3,526 (Matthews 1996). Although used predominantly in the Irish Republic, ISL is also used in Northern Ireland by the Catholic population, and in areas of mainland Britain where there are communities of signers from Ireland (i.e. Glasgow, Liverpool and London).

The first school for deaf children in Ireland was established in Dublin in 1816. The first headmaster of this school trained at Thomas Braidwood's academy in Edinburgh (the first deaf school in Britain, established in the 1780s) and must have known BSL. The Dublin school was the main school for deaf children in Ireland for thirty years and taught Protestant doctrine, even though most of the children were from Catholic families.

There are many signs used in ISL today that are similar or identical to BSL signs. Although some may be recent loans from BSL, others reflect the original BSL substrate from the early 1800s. For example, some elderly deaf people use the two-handed British manual alphabet, and the ISL sign GUINNESS is made using the two-handed manual letter -g-,[3] although this sign is not found in BSL.

A small Catholic school was established in Cork in 1822, and Roman Catholic clerics felt it was important to provide Catholic education for deaf children in Dublin to counteract the Protestant influence. Dominican nuns were sent to Caen in Normandy to learn the educational techniques used by the French deaf educators and returned to establish St Mary's School for Deaf Girls in Dublin in 1847.

The school used a version of the signed French system, adapted for English. One method of creating sign vocabulary was to use 'initialised signs' in which the handshape of the sign was replaced with a handshape representing the manual letter corresponding to the initial letter of the written word. Matthews (1996) gives examples of the closely related signs PRACTISE, WORK and BUSY, which differ only in handshape: PRACTISE has a .P. handshape, WORK has a .W. handshape and BUSY has a .B. handshape. Although the principle of initialised signs was borrowed from French, most

---

[3] Following convention, letters from the British two-handed manual alphabet are written in lower case, bounded by hyphens. Letters from one-handed alphabets are written in upper case, bounded by full stops.

examples in ISL were created using English words as the source for the initialisation. However, some ISL signs are clearly loans from French Sign Language. The ISL signs FRIDAY and LOOK-FOR are made with the .V. and .C. handshapes respectively (from *vendredi* and *chercher*).

The Christian Brothers established St Joseph's School for Deaf Boys in 1856, adopting the methods of St Mary's School. When children transferred from the Protestant to the Catholic schools they brought with them the BSL manual alphabet and some BSL signs, which became incorporated into the signing brought from France. Burns (1998) mentions that the Irish Vincentian priest who worked to bring the French system into the Dominican schools modified the signs for the two schools, making the signs for the girls at St Mary's 'soft and feminine' and the signs for the boys at St Joseph's 'bold and masculine'. Children from the two schools had little contact. Consequently the varieties of ISL used in the two schools diverged considerably so that by the 1960s there were two identifiable dialects of ISL – men's and women's. Le Master & Dwyer's study of ISL found that approximately 70% of male and female signs differed to some degree (Le Master & Dwyer 1991).

St Mary's introduced oral methods of education (banning ISL) in the 1950s, with St Joseph's following in the 1960s. Over that period, the boys' form of ISL had higher status and was adopted by some orally educated girls after leaving school. More recent relaxation of the rules of segregation of boys and girls and a decrease in the rolls of St Mary's and St Joseph's (with corresponding increases in mainstream education) have reduced the gender differences in ISL today.

The Irish Deaf community also has its own organisations, most importantly the Irish Deaf Society and the National Association for Deaf People. It also has its own social and sports clubs which are an important part of community life, such as the Dublin Deaf Association, with a membership of 1,000 (Burns 1998). Given that this is approximately one-third of the entire estimated national Deaf community, it is clear that Deaf clubs are an essential part of the language community. However, as in the British Deaf community, new technology is causing attendance at Deaf clubs to decline. Increased use of communication technology such as email and text telephone services has lessened dependence on face-to-face contact. Increased availability of subtitling on television and video has allowed alternative entertainment to the meetings of the Deaf clubs (Matthews 1996).

The structure of BSL and ISL

Although the social histories of the languages are different in many respects, their grammars are similar. Many of the superficial differences between ISL and BSL are a result of the influence of English grammar on ISL through the 'signed English' of the schools. However, the basic grammatical similarities of structure of BSL and ISL are sufficient for us to treat them together here.

BSL and ISL are structurally different from English and other European languages. Hearing educators have often compared sign languages to spoken (European) languages unfavourably, noting that sign languages frequently 'lack' certain features seen in European spoken languages, such as tense, gender or determiners, and conclude that sign languages are in some way 'deficient'. In fact BSL and ISL share many features with other language groups. For example, BSL and ISL share some features with the 'active type' languages of Micronesia (Nichols 1992). These include lack of a copula, adjectives operating as intransitive verbs and a distinction between inclusive and exclusive pronouns (e.g. 'we' may include or exclude the addressee). Verbs in this language type often use classifiers (based on shape or animacy, for example), show direct object incorporation, have rich inflection including aspect and show little opposition of active and passive voice.

The grammars of BSL and ISL also can be compared to European languages other than English. For example, in common with Irish and Finnish respectively, most dialects of BSL have no general signs for 'yes' and 'no' (although ISL does) and neither BSL nor the ISL of most signers makes a distinction between 'he' and 'she' in its pronouns. This is not the case for all sign languages, though: Taiwanese and Japanese Sign Languages have pronoun signs HE and SHE. In fact, even ISL does make use of gender-specific pronouns in some variants, although they were originally 'artificial' constructions from signed English. They are used primarily by older signers who deliberately wish to use more 'English-like' constructions. HE is signed with an .L. handshape, moving from the contralateral side of the chest to the ipsilateral side. SHE is signed with an .S. handshape (a closed fist) and follows the same pattern of movement.

Although BSL and ISL grammatical features are frequently similar to those in spoken languages, use of the visual-spatial modality provides a different range of structural possibilities from those available to spoken languages. Spoken languages utilise forms based on the physical possibilities created by using the vocal apparatus and signed languages use forms based on the physical possibilities of articulation using the hands, body, face and head. Visual imagery, space and movement, and multiple articulators are not so readily available in spoken languages.

Different types of visually motivated signs

Spoken languages are capable of incorporating the auditory features of referents into the language (as in onomatopoeia). BSL and ISL, as visually perceived languages, are well suited to representing the visual features of referents. In common with all sign languages, they have signs that are visually isomorphic with their referents to some degree (Taub 2001). They may reflect the visual form of the referent, or some way that they move or are located. Visual motivation as the basis for a sign is not an indication of a deficiency when compared to the more arbitrary symbols used in spoken languages, but an exploitation of the modality. Significantly, signers use these signs without considering their motivation (Klima & Bellugi 1979). It should be noted that not all signs (for example, WANT, WHO, GREEN and SISTER in BSL) bear a clear visual motivation. In ISL, visual motivation may appear to be less, because of the process of 'initialisation', mentioned earlier.

All signs consist of a specified handshape, articulated at a specified location with a specified movement. Only one or two of these three parameters may be visually motivated. For example, in ISL the movement and location of a sign may be visually motivated while the handshape is not. This is because ISL signs have often adopted the handshape from the manual alphabet corresponding to the first letter of the English translation of the sign. Thus, the ISL signs HAPPY, HEARING and HOUR may all be made with the handshape of the Irish manual letter .H. However in other ways the signs show visual motivation. HAPPY is made at the chest, a location with a visually motivated metaphorical association with emotions, HEARING is located at the ear and the movement of HOUR is circular, reflecting the circular movement of a clock hand. (We should note, however, that there are other non-initialised ISL sign synonyms for these signs.)

Whether or not a sign is visually motivated, all signs exhibit a conventionalised relationship between the form and the referent. A sign can be visually motivated but the particular aspect of the referent that is represented is arbitrary. For example, the BSL sign COFFEE reflects the action of 'drinking' while the ISL sign reflects the act of 'grinding'.

Use of space

Signs can be placed in different locations, and the placement and movement of signs within a linguistically determined area of space around the signer are a central feature of BSL and ISL.

Location of the hands functions at various levels of linguistic structure in sign languages. The location of signs can reflect visual motivation in a variety of ways. For example CEILING, SHELF and FLOOR are made in different areas of 'neutral space' corresponding to the relative heights of the referents. The BSL signs HAT, COUGH, SERGEANT and RESPONSIBLE are located respectively at the head, the chest, the upper arm (where a sergeant's stripes are found) and the shoulder (where one 'shoulders' a

BROTHER INDEX left.................. ....INDEX right OLDER INDEX
THAT SISTER (brother)

Figure 20.1 'The brother is older than his sister'

responsibility). These locations are also found in the corresponding ISL signs, based on the same visual motivation.

However, placement and movement of signs in space also have considerable grammatical functions, and this has been a topic of interest within sign linguistics. Two major uses of space have been identified: topographic and non-topographic. This is particularly evident in the realisation of verbs. In all known sign languages, the movement of verbs between points in space is used for grammatical purposes. For example, the BSL sentence 'The brother is older than the sister' can be represented as in Figure 20.1.

Points in space are marked indexically in sign languages, so that the meaning of 'locating signs' may be directly related to points in real space, rather than having an arbitrary relationship between form and meaning, as we would expect in spoken languages (where words such as *here*, *there*, *this*, *you* and *me* express essentially spatial ideas). Sign language verbs may also move between these points in space, so that in a verb meaning 'put it there', the location of the sign reflects the location where the object is being put (see Liddell 2003). Despite this, most sign linguists regard these signs as abstract linguistic representations, reflecting arbitrary spatial relations between referents at the conceptual level. Space is also used *referentially*, to differentiate semantic roles and grammatical classes (subjects and agents, patients and objects of actions), without any implication of a spatially constrained relationship.

Signed language can also convey spatial relations more directly: sentences can be constructed *topographically*. In this case the space within which signs are articulated is used to describe the position and orientation of objects or people. The spatial relations among signs correspond in a topographic manner to actual relations among objects described. The linguistic conventions used in this spatial mapping specify the position of objects in a highly geometric and non-arbitrary fashion by situating certain sign forms (e.g. classifiers) in space such that they maintain the topographic relations of the world-space being described (Emmorey, Corina & Bellugi 1995:44).

In a BSL sentence such as 'The man put on the hat from the top shelf' (Figure 20.2), the shape of the hand in the verb represents handling a flat 3D object (the hat brim), the orientation of the hand represents the orientation of the hat on the shelf, and the movement path represents the path from the shelf to the man's head. All these features are simultaneously specified by the grammar and characterised by features of the world derived from spatial images (characteristics of the referent, orientation and trajectory of actions). Within these structures, the handshapes in verbs of motion and location in topographic sentences represent object features or classes (how objects are handled, their size and shape, or their function).

HIGH-SHELF   HAT   INDEX   MAN   BRING-   PUT-ON-
                       (hat location)   DOWN-HAT   HEAD

Figure 20.2 'The man put on the hat from the top shelf'

These have been termed 'classifiers' (Supalla 1986, Engberg-Pedersen 1993).

Sign languages thus appear to differ from spoken languages, not only because space is obligatorily recruited for language, but additionally in that certain linguistic structures use spatial characteristics of semantic roles (classifiers) and spatial locations topographically. Such sentences map a number of spatial and image characteristics, both globally in terms of the relative locations of referents and the action paths that link them, and at a relatively fine grain, capturing local relationships (Sutton-Spence & Woll 1999).

Simultaneous signs

Both spoken and signed languages articulate lexical items sequentially. However, some linguistic information can also be given simultaneously (as in, for example, tone languages), and general prosody gives further grammatical and affective information to the lexemes uttered. Essentially, though, humans have only one vocal apparatus so spoken languages must use sequential structures. The availability of two hands, head and face provides BSL, ISL and other sign languages with the possibility of using simultaneously articulated structures.

This simultaneous use of articulators allows the signer to place referents in space and represent their relative locations. Signs may also move in space. Two different referents may be presented at the same time in different locations in sign space, creating an image of a spatial array of referents and their relative movements. The timing of production of simultaneous signs indicates the temporal and spatial relationships between the referents in the real world. BSL can directly represent the timing of two events relative to each other, by showing the two events using two different articulating 'channels'. In representing, for example, a person reaching for a book while holding a pen, English conjoins clauses using *while* or *as* to indicate two events happening simultaneously. In BSL and ISL, 'holding the pen' can be signed on one hand, while 'reaching for the book' can be signed on the other. English uses prepositions such as *next to* or *behind* to represent relative locations, whereas sign languages can simply place the two signs in the relative locations of the two referents.

It should be noted, however, that simultaneity is an option exercised differently by BSL and ISL. In a comparison of sentences generated from the same picture materials in ISL and BSL, ISL signers used simultaneous signs in 20% of their utterances and BSL used them in 80% (Saeed, Sutton-Spence & Leeson 2000).

Figure 20.3 'Three of us doze', showing a dog, a bird and a human sleeping simultaneously

Simultaneity is extended for aesthetic effect in art signing, such as elevated storytelling and poetry. In a well-known BSL poem by Dorothy Miles, 'Trio', the poet, a dog and a bird all doze together after a good lunch. This is signed by using three articulators simultaneously, using one hand to refer to the dog, one hand to refer to the bird, and the head to refer to the poet (Figure 20.3).

BSL and ISL as minority languages

From the description of the structure of BSL and ISL, it should be clear that they are fully independent of English, both lexically and grammatically. There is no doubt however that English has influenced BSL, and to a greater extent, ISL. This influence is to be expected when any powerful majority language surrounds a minority language. It is possible that the BSL and ISL of many signers has been so influenced by English that it would be considerably impoverished were all the influences of English to be removed. This is not the same, however, as saying that BSL or ISL are not independent languages. Given that the sign languages of the British Isles and English have been in such close proximity for many generations, the former have come to use certain forms derived from English.

We would expect both sign languages to borrow from English for new terminology, and we see this occurring, especially through the use of fingerspelling,[4] but also through loan translation (Sutton-Spence 2000). Signers can also borrow from any written language using fingerspelling.

Using English loanwords for core vocabulary items is not some sort of linguistic inadequacy of BSL but simply the natural result of linguistic and social closeness, strengthened by an education system in which English is the dominant language. Family terms, calendar vocabulary items and signs for units of measurement of time and space in BSL are frequently of English origin, although many BSL loan signs have synonyms unrelated to English. Other sign languages do not make use of loans from their co-geographical spoken languages for these terms. Although BSL and ISL both have the signs MOTHER and FATHER derived from the manual alphabet, American Sign Language (ASL) does not rely on English for these, so loans from English are clearly not a linguistic necessity.

BSL also reflects the influence of English in its use of mouth patterns derived from spoken English ('mouthings'). BSL uses mouthings in a wide variety of ways (Sutton-Spence & Day 2001) and in conjunction with other mouth patterns unrelated to English ('mouth gestures'). The use of mouthings varies with the age and social and linguistic background of the signer, as well as with the situational variety. The influence of spoken languages on the mouth patterns of sign languages are not all the same. Anecdotal evidence and comments from ISL signers familiar with BSL suggest that BSL uses many more mouthings than ISL. Comparative research on a range of European sign languages, as well as other sign languages, including ASL and Indo-Pakistani sign language, shows that mouthings feature in all languages, and function in similar ways (Boyes-Braem & Sutton-Spence 2001). However, the amount of use and the exact functions of the spoken components vary. ASL uses considerably fewer spoken

---

[4] Fingerspelling allows a signer to represent orthography, using handshapes from the manual alphabet. The manual alphabets used in BSL and ISL are different. The BSL manual alphabet is two-handed; the ISL manual alphabet is one-handed. Both, however, have 26 letters.

components than BSL, and German Sign Language uses considerably more (Ebbinghaus & Hessmann 2001).

The use of the manual alphabet is also an example of influence from English. This, again, can be understood in the context of other sign languages and the general relationship between minority sign languages and majority spoken (and written) languages. Fingerspelling may have originated among hearing people but it now influences many sign languages (Sutton-Spence 1994).

While BSL is a minority language with respect to English and borrows from English, it also acts as a donor to other sign languages. The higher social position of BSL in relation to ISL has led ISL to borrow signs from BSL (Burns 1998). In Northern Ireland, anecdotal evidence suggests that the two languages are frequently extensively mixed.

Sign languages as unwritten languages

There are many unwritten languages around the world, both spoken and signed. Of the 6,000 languages in current use, only 78 have enough recorded writing to have a 'literature' (Ong 1982). BSL and ISL are among the many languages not among the 78. A signer who writes a message must do it in another language, such as English. BSL and ISL can both be written phonetically and there are several systems that have been designed or adapted for writing (e.g. SignWriting (Sutton 1999), HamNoSys (Prillwitz, Leven, Zienert, Hanke & Henning 1989 etc.)). It is possible that BSL and ISL will be written regularly in the future, but at present, sign language communities are not literate in their own sign languages. This has considerable implications for the structure and function of the sign languages, and comparison of the features of unwritten spoken languages and the uses of language in non-literate communities indicates that BSL and ISL, while different from a literate language like English, have some similarities to many of the majority of the world's non-literate languages.

Ong has written extensively on unwritten languages and the influences of literacy on language structure and use (Ong 1982). Branson, Miller & Gede Marsaja (1996) have applied his ideas to sign languages. A language that is unwritten is used only face to face. This means that the language is used only in the 'here and now'. Most of the time English is unwritten and used only in the 'here and now', too. However, all speakers of British English are influenced by the fact that English can be used to transmit information across space and time. Technology and literacy have made English very different from unwritten languages such as BSL and ISL.

The existence of a writing system leads to the development of a grap olect. It cuts across the regional dialects of a language, while also sometimes incorporating certain of their features. Its lexicon and grammar are considered to represent the 'standard' form of the language. The dictionaries of the English grapholect contain over 500,000 words, according to Ong. Unwritten languages have only a few thousand words and the semantic history of these words is frequently unknown. Since vocabulary size is usually calculated according to dictionary headwords or from surveys of written language, language communities which do not have the resources for dictionary creation, nor a written corpus for lexicographers to draw on, will appear to have relatively small vocabulary counts.

BSL and ISL are unwritten languages and so, by definition, do not have a grapholect. Because of this, BSL would not be expected to have a vocabulary of the size of English. The Dictionary of British Sign Language/English (Brien 1992) suggests that BSL has an active vocabulary of somewhere between 5,000 and 10,000 signs. Although the size of the BSL vocabulary may appear to compare unfavourably with that of English, we should remember that it is comparable in size to the vocabulary of many unwritten languages.

el Island French

Jones

The Channel Islands form a small archipelago lying at the entrance to the gulf of St Malo, some 80 miles off the southern coast of England. The eight islands, in descending order of size, are Jersey, Guernsey, Alderney, Sark, Herm, Jethou, Lihou and Brecqhou (see Figure 21.1). A variety of Romance has been spoken on the islands for over two thousand years and, despite the fact that the archipelago has been united politically with Great Britain since 1204, until relatively recently the majority of the inhabitants were francophone. Although the dialect of Alderney became extinct in the 1950s, before any systematic analysis could be undertaken,[1] the surviving dialects of the Channel Islands all contain what Joret (1883) considered to be the defining features of Norman (see also Lepelley 1999) and, according to Fleury (1886:4), they show greatest linguistic affinity with the varieties of mainland Norman spoken in and around La Hague.[2]

Despite the large number of features that they undoubtedly share, it would, however, be mistaken to consider the varieties spoken in the Norman zone – or even on the Channel Islands – as homogeneous. Even though Sark Norman French (Sercquiais) developed from a western form of Jersey Norman French (Jèrriais) after the island was colonised from Jersey in 1565 (Spence 1993:53), there is no longer any striking resemblance between these two varieties (Brasseur 1978b:302) and, although it is claimed that the inhabitants of Sark understand the variety spoken in the west of Jersey, speakers of Jèrriais do not understand Sercquiais very well (Brasseur 1977:100). Furthermore, despite the geographical proximity of

---

[1] The anglicisation of Alderney began when large numbers of Irish and other English-speaking labourers were brought to the island between 1845 and 1864 for the construction of naval and military installations (Price 1984:211). It was probably encouraged by the permanent presence of a large English-speaking garrison on the island. For information on Alderney Norman French (Auregnais), see Emanuelli (1906, 1907), Le Maistre (1982) and point 396 of the Atlas Linguistique de la France.

[2] The phonological similarities between the dialects of Jersey, Guernsey, Sark and Magneville (the latter is on the Norman mainland) are described in Brasseur (1978a). Note, however, that in his study Brasseur examined only one variety of mainland Norman. It is possible that a different variety may have yielded a slightly different result.

358

Figure 21.1 A map of the Channel Islands

their respective islands, neither speakers of Sercquiais nor Guernsey Norman French (Guernesiais) can readily understand one another. Some degree of mutual comprehension is possible between Jèrriais and Guernesiais but, in my experience, this often varies from one speaker to the next. Brasseur claims that of all the varieties of Insular Norman, the most difficult for a speaker of mainland Norman to understand is the Guernesiais of the south-west of Guernsey (1977:100).[3]

Brasseur has calculated that, of the four extant varieties of Norman, it is Sercquiais which diverges most from Standard French (1978b:302). His

---

[3] Details of the phonology of the extant dialects may be obtained from Spence (1957, 1985, 1987, 1988), Mari C. Jones (2001) (Jersey), Lewis (1895), Sjögren (1964) and Tomlinson (1981) (Guernsey) and Liddicoat (1989, 1991) (Sark).

survey highlighted 43 differences between these two varieties compared with 37 between mainland Norman and Standard French, 36 between Guernesiais and Standard French and 34 between Jèrriais and Standard French. Although greater linguistic proximity was therefore found to exist between Jèrriais and Standard French than between Standard French and any other variety of Norman, it is clear that the differences between the varieties themselves remain so salient that it is impossible to suggest that any one variety of insular Norman has any particular affinity with another.

As well as differing between themselves, the dialects of the Channel Islands also display considerable internal variation. Even though Jersey and Guernsey measure only some 45 and 30 square miles respectively, marked regional variation is still plainly visible on both islands. In the case of Jersey, the sub-varieties are usually divided into two main groups – East and West – with the Eastern varieties differing most from Standard French, mainly due to secondary developments in the vowel system (Spence 1993:20; Mari C. Jones (2001:30–38); see also Le Maistre 1979a–d, 1993). On Guernsey, the main regional differences are between the varieties spoken in the north and south of the island (De Garis 1982:xi; Mari C. Jones (forthcoming)). However, on both islands, even more localised variation than this is readily observable and most native speakers can pinpoint geographically the speech of a fellow islander with a remarkable degree of exactitude, although Le Maistre (1947) and De Garis (1982:xxii) both lament the fact that some so-called linguistic pockets are fast disappearing. Even Sercquiais, spoken on an island of less than two square miles, was purported to show some degree of variation in times gone by. Little Sark, to which Sark is joined by a causeway, apparently once had its own distinct variety.[4] However by today, Sercquiais is relatively homogeneous.

Estimating speaker numbers with any great degree of accuracy for any time before the immediate present is a difficult task. To date, this information has only ever been gathered officially for Jersey twice (in the 1989 and 2001 Censuses) and for Guernsey once (in the 2001 Census). A comparison of the Jersey results from the two Censuses provides us with a clear indication of the decline of the dialect in recent years. In 1989, there were 5,720 speakers of Jèrriais, representing 6.9% of the total resident population. By 2001, this had gone down to 2,874 speakers, or 3.2% of the total resident population, with some two-thirds of these speakers aged over 60. The 2001 Census also recorded that only 113 speakers declared Jèrriais

[4] Brasseur (1998:146) claims that the differences between the dialects of Sark and Little Sark were primarily lexical in nature.

to be their usual everyday language (http://www.gov.je/Statistics/census/). On Guernsey, the number of people able to speak Guernesiais fluently in 2001 was 1,327, or 2.2% of the total resident population, with nearly 70% of these speakers aged over 64 (http://www.gov.gg/ccm/navigation/ government/facts---figures/census/). Numbers for Sark are harder to guess. In 1998, Brasseur speculated that fewer than 20 out of the 600 permanent inhabitants (roughly 3.5% of the population) were still able to speak Sercquiais (1998:152).[5]

As well as being few in number, speakers of Norman French are distributed unevenly throughout Jersey and Guernsey (Sark has only one village). On both islands, the highest concentration of dialect speakers tends to be found in the parishes furthest removed from their respective capitals, St Helier (Jersey) and St Peter Port (Guernsey) which have, for centuries, represented focal points of anglicisation. This means that, on Jersey, Norman French is most likely to be heard in northern and western parishes (States of Jersey 1990:16) whereas on Guernsey its stronghold lies in the west and south-west of the island (Sjögren 1964:xviii–xix). However, even in their last refuges, the dialects are no longer spoken by any children and probably by no more than a handful of adults under the age of fifty.

The reasons behind the anglicisation of the Channel Islands are many and complex and will only be outlined here.[6] English has been present on Jersey and Guernsey since the Middle Ages, when garrisons were established to defend the islands against the French. However, the dialects remained as the everyday variety of the majority of islanders until well into the nineteenth century – although from this time on increasing trade links and more regular transport services, which also precipitated the start of the islands' tourist industry, led to ever more frequent contact between the Channel Islands and the British mainland. Indeed, by 1840, there were some 15,000 English residents on Jersey (Uttley 1966:174), representing some 32% of the total resident population. Mass evacuation of the islanders to the British mainland in the days preceding the German occupation of the Channel Islands during World War II also had severe linguistic repercussions as a considerable proportion of the child population of each island therefore spent the next five years (1940–45) cut off from their native tongue and immersed in the very language with which the latter was in competition.[7] On their return, many had either forgotten their

[5] No Census return has been made for Sark since 1971.
[6] For more detailed accounts, see Ramisch (1989), Domaille (1996), Syvret & Stephens (1998), Lemprière (1974) and Jones (2001:7–17).
[7] Tomlinson (1981:14) claims that all schoolchildren were evacuated from Guernsey (cf. Bunting 1996:23–4).

Channel Island French or chose to continue using English, which they saw as a means to prosperity and social advancement. The events of the war strengthened existing doubts within the indigenous speech communities as to the utility of the dialects. They could not offer the rewards of English and became increasingly stigmatised as the hallmarks of country bumpkins, with parents no longer passing them on to their offspring. This state of affairs was, of course, exacerbated by the large-scale immigration to Jersey and Guernsey from the British mainland that occurred in the second half of the twentieth century, most notably with the establishment of the offshore banking industry that currently represents the main generator of income on both islands. Needless to say, the immigrants saw no need to learn the local dialect.

The situation on Sark was somewhat different. This island was later to anglicise than Jersey and Guernsey due to the fact that it was only rarely visited by Englishmen before the nineteenth century. Indeed, in 1787, one of John Wesley's missionaries who had been visiting Sark reported that, at that time, not a single family understood English (Ewen & De Carteret 1969:105). It seems likely that the anglicisation of this island stems from the arrival of English-speaking miners who, in 1835, were brought to work in a tin mine on Little Sark. The development of the island's tourist industry shortly afterwards must also have been a contributory factor. As only 129 of the 600-strong population left Sark during World War II, it seems likely that the war had less of an anglicising influence here than on the other Channel Islands.

The fact that, today, every speaker of the three extant dialects of Channel Island French is also fluent in English has had far-reaching linguistic consequences which have served to further differentiate insular and mainland Norman. The most immediately noticeable effect is in the lexis, where English borrowings abound in many everyday domains (see Spence 1993:23–9 and Mari C. Jones 2001:118–28, 140–55 for Jèrriais, Tomlinson 1981:Part 2 for Guernesiais and Liddicoat 1994:298–300 for Sercquiais). However, the use of a borrowing in one insular variety does not necessarily imply that it is also used in another: for example, in Jèrriais, the borrowing *ticl'ye* is used to denote a kettle (< English *teakettle*), whereas in Guernesiais the indigenous *caudjère* is used; similarly, in Sercquiais, the borrowing /skrɛ̃/ (from English *screen*) is used for 'grain riddle',[8] whereas in Jèrriais, *cribl'ye* is used. In most cases, the borrowings are modified phonetically or at least orthographically. However, in many 'modern' domains such as technology, words are often taken into the

---

[8] As no writing system has ever been devised for Sercquiais, I follow Liddicoat in using phonetic script to transcribe the dialect.

dialects 'wholesale'. Mari C. Jones (2001:140–55) also found that, on Jersey, many common terms were being forgotten or only partially recalled, a sign perhaps that lack of opportunity to use the dialect is making speakers 'rusty' in their native variety.

The structural effect of English on Jèrriais and Guernesiais is examined in detail in Mari C. Jones (2000a, 2000c, 2001:97–128, 2002:148–59, 2005a, 2005b and forthcoming) and Liddicoat (1990). Reasons of space preclude a detailed discussion here but it should be noted that the changes found fall broadly into two categories. The first of these involves an increase in frequency of syntactic constructions more isomorphic with the structure of English (Mari C. Jones 2001:97–118, 2002:148–59, 2005b).

Whereas English and French both have just one form to convey all functions of the preposition 'with' (*avec* in standard French), the Channel Island dialects traditionally have different prepositions, each of which has a distinct function. The unmarked form, which also tends to be used when the referent is animate, is *auve* (Jèrriais), *dauve* (Guernesiais), /ov/ (Sercquiais), hence:

(1) *J'voulais palair **dauve** son frère*
     'I wanted to speak to her brother' (Guernesiais)

However, when the instrumental function is being conveyed, or when the object is inanimate, then another preposition is used, namely *atout* (Jèrriais), *atou* (Guernesiais), /atu/ (Sercquiais):

(2) /nuz ɛrɛ d la pɛ̃ a marʃi dã lɛː rγː **atu** tuo ʃɛː mɒutœ kɑː/
     'We would have trouble walking on the roads with all those motor cars' (Sercquiais) (Liddicoat 1994:280)

In Jèrriais, a third preposition, *acanté*, is traditionally used to convey a comitative meaning:

(3) *Je m'en vais **acanté** lyi*
     'I am going along with her' (Birt 1985:166)

A cognate form, *à quànté*, is cited for Guernesiais by De Garis (1982:214).

In the modern dialects, however, this threefold (Jersey, Guernsey) (Birt 1985:165–7, De Garis 1982:214, Mari C. Jones 2001:99–100, 103–4, 2002:157, 2005b:166–7, 169 and forthcoming) or twofold (Sark) (Liddicoat 1994:279–80) opposition is being progressively eliminated by the unmarked form taking over all of these functions, along the lines of the English construction. On Jersey and Sark, these prepositions are often replaced by the French loanword *avec*.

As is discussed in Mari C. Jones (2000a, 2001, 2005b), the motivation behind the prolific amounts of change currently being witnessed is not always straightforward and, in cases such as the above, it is arguable that simplification may also be a contributory factor, although there do exist cases where influence from English is unambiguous (Mari C. Jones 2001:118–28, 2002:149–54).

The second type of change found in Jèrriais and Guernesiais involves syntactic calquing from English (Mari C. Jones 2001:122–7, 2002:149–54 and forthcoming), where a direct translation of an English construction may be used, thereby introducing a hitherto unattested pattern of usage into the dialects, for example:

(4)   *J'fallais aller en cours*
      'I had to go to the lesson' (Jèrriais)

Historically, *faller* is a defective verb which is only used in the third person (Birt 1985:262).

(5)   *La langue va*
      'The language is going', i.e. 'disappearing' (Guernesiais)

As in Standard French, *allaïr* ('to go') cannot historically be used without a complement.

(6)   /par l sɛ tu tɛ fɪnɪ/
      'By evening everything was finished' (Sercquiais) (Liddicoat 1994:276)

The preposition *par* followed by a specified time is not used in mainland French to express the point in time or the period by which an event occurs and it is likely that its use in the insular dialects is attributable to the influence of the English preposition *by*.

In addition, the formal similarity that may exist between semantically distinct verbs of English and Jèrriais/Guernesiais often leads to the meaning and connotations of the English verb being adopted in the respective dialects.

(7)   *I' sont bein supportés*
      'They are well supported' (Jèrriais)

Supporter traditionally means 'to bear' and not 'to support'.

(8)   *Not' desnaïr fut attendu par 230 persaonnes*
      'Our dinner was attended by 230 people' (Guernesiais)

Attendre traditionally means 'to wait for' and not 'to attend'.

Realisation that the local dialect is declining rapidly in terms of speaker numbers has prompted the establishment of a number of language planning measures, which aim to maintain and strengthen the use of these varieties. These receive very little official backing and have been left to a group of enthusiasts with no real linguistic training (Mari C. Jones 2000b, 2001:70–96).

The earliest language planning initiative on both islands was the establishment of a society for dialect speakers (*L'Assembliée d'Jèrriais*, founded in 1951 (Jersey) and its sister society *L'Assembllaïe d'Guernesiais*, founded in 1956 (Guernsey)). Both of these publish regular bulletins and organise social events which allow members frequent access to contexts in which the local dialect is, for once, seen as primary. 1995 saw (coincidentally) the establishment of a new society on each island. On Jersey, the *Section de la Langue* of the well-established *Société Jersiaise* was founded, with the aim of presenting the dialect on a wider stage. It has, among other things, campaigned successfully for the presence of bilingual signs at the airport and harbour, launched Jèrriais on the World Wide Web (http://www.societe-jersiaise.org/geraint/jerriais.html) and plays an active role in modernising the dialect's vocabulary (see, for example, *Société Jersiaise* 2000). On Guernsey, the creation of *Les Ravigoteurs* ('The Revivalists') stemmed from a desire to encourage younger people to take an interest in the dialect. As part of Guernsey's millennium celebrations, it published the first children's book ever to appear in Guernesiais. Jèrriais and Guernesiais are also promoted in the *eisteddfodau*[9] of the respective islands. On Sark, there is less public interest in the fate of the dialect. However, a *Société Sercquiaise* was founded in 1975.

Unlike many dialects of the French mainland, both Jèrriais and Guernesiais have been codified. This has been done chiefly via the publication of dictionaries (Le Maistre 1966, De Garis 1982) and, on Jersey, standardisation has been carried further by the publication of *Le Jèrriais Pour Tous* (Birt 1985), a work doubling as both a grammar of Jèrriais and a textbook for beginners.[10] No grammar of Guernesiais has yet been published and, to date, the only grammatical surveys undertaken of the dialect are De Garis (1983) and Tomlinson (1981). As mentioned in footnote 8, there is no agreed written form of Sercquiais. For the grammar of this dialect, see Liddicoat (1994), although this contains several errors (see Morin 1996).

Although the twelfth-century author Wace is known to have hailed from Jersey, no literary writings in Channel Island French exist until the nineteenth century. The first published work in any of the dialects was by Georges Métivier (1790–1881), whose *Rimes Guernesiaises* date from 1831. The first author to use Jèrriais as a medium for his work was Matthieu Le

---

[9] An annual cultural festival which includes competitions in music, poetry and theatre plays.

[10] To date, more works have been published on Jèrriais than on Guernesiais, possibly due to the establishment on Jersey of the Don Balleine Trust. This was created from a substantial legacy left, in 1943, for the publication of works in Jèrriais. It has published, among other things, Le Feuvre (1976) and (1983), the only two substantial volumes of prose ever to have appeared in the dialect.

Geyt (1777–1849). Much of his work is to be found in the volume *Rimes et Poësies Jersiaises* (1865). Although both islands produced several poets and writers during the course of the nineteenth and twentieth centuries, their work is not easily accessible due to the fact that instead of producing complete books, they tended to publish in newspapers, almanacs and in the form of short pamphlets. For details of individual authors and their work see, for example, Lebarbenchon (1988), Lepelley (1999:123–51), Mari C. Jones (2003, forthcoming) and Price (1984: 209).[11] Two short texts in Sercquiais (transcribed phonetically) – a description of life on Sark and the 'Parable of the Sower' – may be found in Liddicoat (1989:700–701).

Since the standard language of all the Channel Islands has been French and never the indigenous dialects, their presence in 'official' domains has been virtually non-existent. Standard French (and now English) has been the language of religion and legislation and English has always been dominant in the education system. Since the 1970s, Jèrriais and Guernesiais have been allocated a few minutes each week in terms of radio broadcasts (this has recently been slightly increased on Jersey) and, at present, they also appear in print in the local newspaper in the form of a monthly (Guernsey) or fortnightly (Jersey) column. In terms of television broadcasting, both dialects are given one hour of air time every two years (see Mari C. Jones 2000b, 2001). Sercquiais has no presence in any form of media.

Norman French evening classes have been held on Jersey since 1967 and on Guernsey since the mid-1980s. However, numbers are not high and those who enrol tend to be adults. In an attempt to increase interest among the younger generation, September 1999 saw the establishment of a two-year pilot programme on Jersey to teach Jèrriais on a voluntary, extra-curricular basis for thirty minutes per week to pupils in their last two years of state-run primary education. This has recently been extended for a further five years and it is intended to extend the classes to secondary education. Since January 2004, Guernesiais has been taught as part of the curriculum in three of Guernsey's primary schools.

The results of two extensive surveys I carried out on Jersey and Guernsey revealed that 90% and 96.5% respectively of the dialect speakers questioned on each island would back the implementation of increased language planning measures (see Mari C. Jones 2001:62–7 for the Jersey figures). However, despite such overwhelming support, it seems extremely

[11] The *Section de la Langue* of the *Société Jersiaise* is planning to publish an anthology of Jèrriais writings in the near future. This will include pieces from each of the most important Jèrriais authors, as well as other texts to show the variety of written Jèrriais through the centuries both in terms of social and literary function and dialectal variation.

doubtful that any variety of insular Norman will succeed in ousting English as the dominant language of the Channel Islands. Indeed, unless extensive and immediate action is forthcoming, the dialects of Jersey, Guernsey and Sark will soon be as dead as that of Alderney.

Although insular Norman may therefore be destined to disappear over the next few decades, the toponymy and patronymics of the Channel Islands will remain as ubiquitous legacies of their francophone heritage. Moreover, the last vestiges of the dialects will undoubtedly be preserved for some time after their extinction as vernaculars in the form of the substrate imprint that they have left on the distinctive variety of English spoken in the islands (Ramisch 1989, Barbé 1994, Mari C. Jones 2001:167–74).[12] Nevertheless, as Ramisch found that some of the Norman substrate features in Guernsey English were far more frequent in the speech of Guernesiais speakers than in that of younger monolingual speakers of English who were indigenous to Guernsey and who had lived on the island all their lives (1989:97–8, 123, 139, 150–2, 152–3), at present it would appear that any form of reprieve that the dialects might enjoy in this guise is likely to be short-lived.

---

[12] Although the varieties of English spoken on Jersey and Guernsey reveal a common substrate influence, further research is needed to establish the degree of similarity that exists between them.

22   Angloromani

Peter Bakker and Donald Kenrick

Introduction

In 1547 Andrew Borde published some sentences in a strange language, learned from people in a tavern who clearly had come from far away, under the heading 'Egipt speche'. The sentences are still understandable today to the majority of Gypsies (from 'Egyptians') or Roma in the world. It is the oldest specimen of the Romani language that has been written down (Borde's text is reproduced in Hancock (1978) and Acton & Kenrick (1984:118)).

Romani is the language spoken by the people called 'Gypsies' by outsiders. Most speakers call themselves 'Rom', plural 'Roma', which means 'human, man, husband'. The speakers call their language *Romanes*, an adverb meaning 'in the manner of a Rom', or *Romani čhib*, 'Rom tongue'. In western Europe, all Gypsies use the term *Romanes*, but not all use the term 'Roma' for their group. In Britain two names have been documented. *Kalo* was used by the Gypsies in Wales, whose language became extinct in the twentieth century, and *Romanichal* is still being used in England.

The first Roma had arrived in south-eastern Europe around the year 1200. In the following centuries they spread over Europe. By the sixteenth century virtually all countries had a population of Roma, including Great Britain. Romani finds its origins in India. Linguistic evidence suggests that the ancestors of the Romani speakers must have left India around the year 1000. They travelled as one community through Asia to south-eastern Europe, from where they spread. Most of the basic vocabulary is Indic, and so are many function words (lower numerals, prepositions, demonstratives), virtually all of the morphology (almost all of its eight case endings, person and tense marking on the verb, etc.), as well as some sounds and semantic distinctions.

The indigenous British variety of Romani with Indic grammar is now extinct in Great Britain. It was longest preserved in Wales, where it died out in the second half of the twentieth century (see Tipler 1957). It has been magnificently documented by the Liverpool librarian John Sampson

(1926). In the twentieth century immigrants from the continent have brought similar forms of Romani to Britain, such as coppersmiths speaking the Kalderash variety of Romani before World War II, and most recently immigrants from Poland, the Czech Republic and the former Soviet Union to Britain, all in all several thousand speakers.

The indigenous variety, however, does survive, but in a rather different form, called Angloromani here. It no longer uses the indigenous grammatical system but the system of local colloquial forms of English, in which Romani and some other words are embedded. The everyday language of Romanichals in England and Wales is that of the majority rural or urban community in which they live and work, i.e. English. In addition they possess a special lexis of between 200 and 1,000 words which they can use to replace the English lexemes when they want to. It no longer functions as a language of everyday communication, but it is used as a means of identification (an oral passport), and as a secret language to bypass outsiders who are listening. It is not spoken by parents to their children from birth but learnt as older children take on the work and household roles of adults.

Counting Gypsies is notoriously difficult: using a linguistic definition (Romani speakers and their descendants) or a definition based on a supposedly typical cultural trait (nomadism) will lead to widely diverging figures. It has been estimated that some 30,000 to 50,000 people lived in caravans in 2000. There are no official census data in the UK, and many Gypsies avoid discrimination by hiding their identity. There may be as many as 150,000 Travellers in the UK, more than half of them Romanichals. Romanichals fare worse in health, educational and employment statistics than the general population.

Knowledge of the Angloromani vocabulary differs from individual to individual. The language is known under several names. Speakers call it *Romnis* (= Romanes; attested in eighteenth-century Britain), *Romani*, *Pogadi Chib* (literally 'broken language'), *posh-ta-posh* 'half-and-half' or pejoratively *Pikey talk* (meaning 'tramps' talk'). Outsiders call it *Gypsy*, *Romany/Romani*, *Angloromani* (Hancock 1971), *Romani English* (Kenrick 1979) or *English Romani/Romanes*. The terms *Deep Romani* and *Puri Jib* (literally 'old language') refer to varieties with mainly non-English words/lexemes.

One could describe the language as a mixed language combining Romani vocabulary with the grammatical system of English. This type of language is not common, but it is also found among some Gypsy groups in other parts of Europe. Linguists have coined the terms 'Para-Romani' (Cortiade 1991), 'Romani mixed dialects' (Boretzky & Igla 1994) and 'intertwined Romani' (Bakker & Mous 1994) for this type of language.

Nature of the language

Angloromani is a combination of two languages that can be combined to different extents, with a range of lexical choices. When talking to a house dweller, Romanichals have only one way of expressing themselves – English, e.g. (1) *The TV is broken*. If they are talking to other Gypsies they have two additional choices: (2) the TV is *poggerdi*; (3) the *dikkin' mokta* is *poggerdi*. Whichever one uses, the Gypsy hearer will understand, so the choice of the language or register depends on the social setting.

The English component differs from Standard English. English dialect words or obsolete forms are used. For example *I was found panj bar*, which in rural Kent dialect would be 'I was found five pound' and in Standard English 'I was fined five pounds'.

The phonology, morphology and syntax are close to rural English dialects, whereas the vocabulary is non-English. There are a few exceptions, in that some speakers preserve the Romani phoneme /x/, and some pronouns, prepositions and demonstratives from Romani are used, as well as a few bound morphemes (see Hancock 1978, 1984a).

Rather typical for Angloromani and other Romani varieties of western Europe is the formation of new words using the original genitive suffixes which agree with the following noun (the item possessed): singular in *-eskro* (masc.) or *-eskri* (fem.), e.g. *thagareskri chai* 'King's daughter'. In Angloromani these suffixes are used to create new nouns. For example *muskro* 'policeman' from *mui* 'mouth' and *rukasamengri* 'squirrel' from *rukh* 'tree'.

Trawling through books and articles one might find two to three thousand distinct words recorded in all, but the average vocabulary of a middle-aged Romanichal would be in the region of 300. The two vocabularies which Tom Wilson compiled for his children contain some 500 words, but they include some loans from Welsh, and others which clearly came from a book. It was the source for the vocabulary in Acton & Kenrick (1984).

Most of the words in Angloromani are of Indian origin through Romani, like *mush* 'man', *chavvi* 'boy', *rakli* 'girl', *thud* 'milk', *pani* 'water'. Some words come from Persian, Greek and the other shared Asian borrowings of Romani. In addition there are Romani words from European languages, for instance from Slavic languages, e.g. *pushka* 'shotgun'. Most of those are also found in other western European Romani varieties. A few words from Gammon, the language of the Irish Travellers, are used, e.g. *lemmish* 'sugar'. There are also words from the slang used by those living on the edge of society in earlier centuries, such as *kenner* 'house' (other Romani varieties have *kher*) and *kennik* 'housedweller'.

The sociologist Thomas Acton (in Acton & Kenrick 1984) has pointed out it is not just a case of replacing Romani English words by Romani words in an English sentence. There are many other ethnolectal differences in intonation and type of English involved.

Origin and history

Gypsies have been present in Britain at least since 1505. Until very recently the Romanichals have generally not been interested in putting their language on paper. Scientific interest in Britain and elsewhere dates from the late eighteenth century (Rüdiger and Grellmann in Germany, Marsden and Bryant in Britain), and that is when written records start to appear. Except for Borde in 1547, there are no publications in or on British Romani until the 1780s. A recently discovered manuscript of 1616 fills a gap. Bakker (2002) shows that already at the time that this word list was compiled, the original Romani grammatical system had been replaced by an English system. Three books on Angloromani (with some Indic Romani) appeared in the 1870s: Borrow (1874), Smart & Crofton (1875) and the controversial Leland (1874). The Gypsy Lore Society was founded in 1888. Its members collected a considerable number of vocabularies, sentences and texts in Britain and published them in their journal. These, combined with Sampson's grammar, texts and dictionary (1926) make the varieties of British Romani among the best documented of the world.

Linguists have been discussing the origin of Angloromani since the 1970s, when it was first debated at a conference in Oxford. Ian Hancock believed that the language was a conscious creation, agreed upon by representatives of English-speaking vagrants and Romani-speaking Romanichals, and he pointed to early documents describing such events. Donald Kenrick believed the language was the result of gradual disappearance of the original Indic inflection and its replacement with the English system, presumably in the nineteenth century. The nineteenth-century sources usually show more traces of Indic grammar, he argued, and he pointed to similar processes currently going on in Finland. Later Boretzky (1985) suggested that Angloromani and similar languages were formed when young people no longer had access to the full system of the language, and were only able to insert the most conspicuous elements (words) from the language of their parents or grandparents into the local language (English) that had become their mother tongue. This seems to be an idea that is shared by several others now, even though there is still disagreement. For discussion, see the papers in Acton & Kenrick (1984) and Bakker (2000) for the British situation, and Bakker & Cortiade (1991),

Boretzky & Igla (1994), Bakker & Mous (1994), Matras (1998) and Matras & Bakker (2003) for comparative perspectives.

Even though Angloromani has been compared with pidgins and creoles (e.g. Hancock 1970, 1976, Acton 1989), neither the social circumstances nor the structural properties of Angloromani justify this.

It is difficult to date the transition from Indic Romani to English Romani in Britain. This is partly due to lack of adequate documentation and partly due to regional variation, as most families travel only in certain regions and they may not be in contact with other families. The supposition that Indic Romani became English Romani in the eighteenth or nineteenth century is motivated by the fact that some of the speakers that Smart and Crofton worked with were able to speak both Indic and English Romani. In addition, a few rare sentences from the late 1800s (quoted in Matras (2000), who thinks they witness the transition) show both Indic and English inflections. The discovery of an early seventeenth-century document (McGowan 1996), however, shows that English Romani was already spoken in 1619, a century after the arrival of the Romanichals in Britain.

Language use

In a sense Angloromani today has the function of a register of English rather than a language acquired from birth (although it may have been a mother tongue in the past; Bakker 1998). We enumerate some of the circumstances in which it is used today in preference to English.

TRADING A small number of Romani words are used in a few trades such as horse-dealing where the professionals understand them but not the casual customer. Market traders use an exotic vocabulary which contains items derived from both Romani and Yiddish. An example is: *It's a maazel it didn't pani* 'It's lucky it didn't rain', where *maazel* 'luck' is from Yiddish and *pani* 'water' from Romani.

TEST OF IDENTITY/SELF IDENTIFICATION To say to a stranger 'I am a Romany, are you?' may get a negative or even aggressive reaction. If a Gypsy is in a café or at a car auction and wonders whether someone who looks like a Romanichal is one, then the best way to check is to slip a Romani word into the conversation. The same method can be used to test whether a stranger is likely to be friendly or hostile. Most people who mix with Romanichals have picked up a few words of the lexicon. A common word like *chavvi* 'boy' can be slipped into the conversation and the effect monitored.

The use of a Romani word can be taken a step further to mean: 'You are a Gorgio [a non-Gypsy] but I know you are friendly to Gypsies'. A caravan dwelling Romanichal recently said to one of the present authors: *I was in a kenner but it didn't jel*, meaning: 'I was in a house but it didn't work (lit. go)'. Most likely the speaker's use of Angloromani was merely an expression of closeness and acknowledgement or recognition that the Gorgio was likely to know some basic words.

SECRECY Angloromani is not a criminal slang, although it does have the necessary words, e.g. *chor* 'to steal' and *gavver* 'policeman'. However, the vocabulary contains words – unique to Angloromani and not found in continental Romani – such as *rukasamengri* 'squirrel' or *bori bila-vangusta* 'elephant'. One cannot imagine any circumstances in which a Romanichal might want to talk secretly about either squirrels or elephants. Yet these are comparatively recent formations, not inherited from the Indian stock.

Nevertheless, some families have developed code usages of some words. Individual families use special counting systems which are different from other Gypsy families. This is especially useful when trading within the community. Possibly the word *vonger* 'money' (lit. 'coals') began as a secret word within one family, which then spread and replaced the earlier *luvva*. It is now common in English slang, like some other Romani words.

OATHS AND THREATS For example, *I'll more you* 'I'll beat you'.

SONGS There are a fair number of songs in Romany English (see Coughlain 2001), many of which are still known by Romanichals who otherwise have lost the language. This is in contrast to Gammon (see below) and Scottish Highland Travellers' Cant, which are not commonly used in songs.

WORD GAMES The use of the language as a word game is rare now. Romanichals challenge others to come up with Romani words for items not normally discussed in the language, e.g. Parliament, telephone or a signpost. For the latter, the most common answer is *pukering kosh* 'talking wood'.

EMOTION Thomas Acton (in Acton & Kenrick 1984) has reported that at wakes and wedding parties, there seemed to be a greater use of Angloromani than in normal everyday life. This is due to the emotional circumstance when members of the same family come together, so that there is again a time for Angloromani to take a foremost place.

Other forms of Traveller speech

Apart from the Pogadi Chib of the Romanichals, there are at least four other exotic vocabularies used by nomadic groups in the UK. *Gammon* is the home language of Irish Travellers (Kirk & Ó Baoill 2002). This differs in use from Angloromani in that it is used from birth with the youngest children. In the past the vocabulary was used in an Irish Gaelic framework but now it is only used in an English framework, as few Travellers even in the Republic speak Irish fluently, if at all (Hancock 1984b). The vocabulary is partly disguised Irish, partly of unknown origin. Further there is *Lowland Cant*, used in a framework of Scots English by Scottish Travellers, and *Highland Cant*, used in a framework of Gaelic. Polari is an Italian lexicon used by circus people, and nowadays also in gay circles (Hancock 1984b, Baker 2002). Only two of these have the status of a distinct language for their speakers, Gammon and Angloromani.[1]

---

[1] The University of Manchester has started a documentation project on Angloromani. Some speech samples can be found on the following website: http://www.llc.manchester.ac.uk/Research/Projects/romani/files/21_angloromani.shtml

Part IV

Applied Sociolinguistic Issues

23 Language policy and planning

Dennis Ager

Unfettered freedom to do what we like with our words

There has long been a naive and romantic belief that in Britain language, like culture, is a simple reflection of a mysterious social consensus nonetheless based on a robust, democratic, individualism which rejects outside influences. 'We've ruled ourselves and allowed the natural forces of change to be curbed only loosely by general dogma and prejudice' (John Simpson in *The Guardian*, 27 December 1995); 'It is that unfettered freedom to do what we damn well like with our words that is the glory of English' (Elmes 2000:106). Taken to the extreme, it is suggested that British English has a life independent of British society. It is my belief that such reification of language is dubious; that, as in most countries, there has long been control and management of language and particularly of language behaviour; and that language control by authority, much of it connected to the state, continues. This chapter will briefly discuss a dozen examples of language policy and planning (henceforth LPP) occurring mainly over the 25 years from 1975 to 2000 in the British Isles, or in the United Kingdom unless Ireland is specified.

Everybody agrees with Saussure (1916) that language change, and language behaviour more generally, are directly affected by society. Ever since Labov's (1966) studies of covariation in New York City, and Trudgill's (1974) work on Norwich, sociolinguistic studies have tracked covariation between dependent linguistic variables (such as h-dropping) and independent social variables (such as class). Economic forces, too, affect language use, as Coulmas (1992:30) has shown in the case of the growth in the market in printed books which led to the Reformation, the need for language codification and the use of vernaculars rather than Latin. Few could deny that Britain's industrialisation and consequential economic need for a literate workforce led to the Education Acts of the 1880s and to increasing use of Standard English. But only rarely, and recently, have political ideologies, parties and personalities been invoked to explain or understand changes in language behaviour. 'Language becomes a crucial focus of tension and debate at critical historical moments, serving as the site upon which political positions are contested' (Crowley 1989:258).

Language planning and language policy

Language planning and policy is both a practical activity and an area of study and research (Ricento 2000). ' "Language planning" is an activity ... intended to promote systematic language change in some community of speakers ... Language policy (promulgated by government or other authoritative body or person) is a body of ideas, laws, regulations, rules and practices intended to achieve the planned language change' (Kaplan & Baldauf 1997:xi). LPP research investigates such deliberate attempts to influence language, firstly from a linguistic (language-internal) point of view, where research tracks the ways in which LPP affects the forms of a language through linguistic processes like codification (standardisation) and elaboration (terminological expansion). Secondly, from a sociological (language-external) standpoint, research investigates influence on the status in society of particular languages or language varieties as manifested in social processes such as the selection of these and the acceptance of norms. Research also discusses the acquisition (teaching and learning) of language(s) and language varieties. These three widely recognised areas of application (technically known in LPP as corpus, status and acquisition) are sometimes complemented by a fourth, concerned with what might be called symbolic or prestige policy, attempts to manipulate the image of a language its users, or others, hold towards it. So corpus policy may bring about a spelling reform, as with dictionary entries; a particular language may be allowed to enter parliamentary use in order to improve its status, as with Scottish Gaelic; textbooks may be written to enable or encourage its acquisition, as with Cornish; and the prestige of a language may be raised by making it more visible, erecting new road signs in Welsh.

LPP practice is seen by some as a mechanism mainly concerned with deciding who in society should have access to power and economic resources. The ideology of language planners is often cited as though it were itself a social variable, determining language use, in the same way that social class correlates with speech variables. Thus for Tollefson (1991:16–17) 'there is a close association between language, power, and privilege'. For Rahman (2002:289) 'power should be the focal analytical category ... in the US ... freedom of linguistic choice is denied in practice, and non-English speakers learn English ... or remain powerless ... in Australia, nationalist (language policy) ... was supported by powerful elite groups.' An account of language planning and policy in a particular context hence needs to identify, not solely what is proposed, what behavioural prescriptions are put forward, but 'what actors attempt to influence what behaviours of which people for what ends under what conditions by what means through what decision-making processes with what effect?' (Cooper 1989:98). We could also ask 'why?' What motivates planners? A range of social actors try to influence language: authoritative individuals; groups, categories and communities which often lack direct political power but do exert collective pressure; and the politically powerful government and state, on whom we shall concentrate here. Dr Johnson and Shakespeare have both left their mark on English; the British elite, particularly, has had a major role in influencing how every member of British society speaks and writes Standard English. Our question, here, is how, and how far, British governments and public authorities have influenced and do influence language and language behaviour.

Language communities and language attitudes in Britain

In a country of nearly 60 million people, attitudes towards language are bound to vary. The English-speaking indigenous population of England seems to lack generally accepted symbols of its national identity, and the English language does not constitute 'an effective symbol of Englishness' (Barbour 2000:29–30). Contemporary widely shared attitudes towards English may reflect a desire for linguistic control, through a 'tradition of complaint' identified by Milroy & Milroy (1985:37) about correctness (*them houses*) and morality (of attempts to confuse). Shared attitudes towards English could also include the following, based on Bailey (1991:267–87) and Cameron (1995). Note that terms in quote marks themselves reflect some of these attitudes:

- some minor doubts about the spelling system, 'irregular' grammar and 'unrestrained' vocabulary but also about 'inbuilt racism, gender bias and a history of linguistic oppression' both within the British Isles and abroad;
- greater prestige for middle-class ('standard') forms ('U' – *napkin*) than for lower-class vocabulary and syntax ('non-standard') ('non-U' – *serviette*, ain't, *I don't want none*);
- greater prestige for Received Pronunciation (RP) and for southern English accents than for northern ones;
- while some regional dialects and accents please (Somerset, Scottish), others don't (Cockney, Birmingham);
- a belief that 'Standard English' is 'correct', 'neutral' and 'unmarked', is substantially uniform and is used by 'educated people' everywhere in Great Britain;
- a feeling that Anglo-Saxon terms are 'real' English while Romance/ Latinate vocabulary is a 'difficult', superimposed layer;

- pride in cultural and literary history, with a particular belief that Shakespeare is the greatest literary figure of all times and countries;
- pride in a simple grammar, a large lexicon and the ability to borrow words easily from foreign languages;
- pride in the ease with which English can be learnt, an associated pride in the worldwide role of the language, and tolerance towards non-British forms including 'foreigner talk';
- pride in the 'modernity' of the language, enabling it to be used in all domains, particularly prestigious ones like science and technology.

Even so, attitudes towards Standard English vary from the positive ('a sensible means of communication or as a useful resource for all', as with Honey (1997)) to the negative ('the symbol of an oppressive, authoritarian and class-based minority', as with Bex (1999)). Purist attitudes, too, can be recognised in a British liking for archaic, elitist or reformist criticism of how people, particularly newspapers, use their own language (see Thomas 1991).

When we come to consider the English regions, or social communities such as a particular class, the other countries of the UK (Wales, Scotland and Northern Ireland) or the non-territorial language communities (recent immigrants), variation in attitudes becomes more marked. The prestige of Standard English is strong, although often resented as 'elitist'. Regional feeling itself is strong in only a few areas such as Yorkshire or Cornwall, where dislike of Standard 'southern' English and support for a dialect or for a regional language can sometimes be fierce. In some English regions, and certainly in some countries other than England, attitudes have often been close to despair:

English is a killer ... It is English that has killed off Cumbric, Cornish, Norn, and Manx. It is English that has now totally replaced Irish as a first language in Northern Ireland. And it is English that constitutes such a major threat to Welsh and to Scottish Gaelic, and to French in the Channel Islands, that their long-term future must be considered to be very greatly at risk. (Price 1984:170)

Insofar as the non-territorial languages are concerned, support for language maintenance has been strong in some cases (Urdu), less so in others (Chinese), although such attitudes may simply reflect the strength of demand for official support in education. In some cases, too, support for a language/dialect may reflect a religious motive (Arabic, Hebrew) or a desire to establish or re-establish feelings of identity (British Black English).

Social, political and economic aims

LPP by the state for English can be said to have started with King Alfred's political decision to make translations into Anglo-Saxon in AD 880. It continued with the replacement of the language among the aristocracy for three centuries after 1066. The 1362 Statute of Pleading, 'rediscovering' English and instituting it as the language of the courts, rejected both Latin and French as official languages. Similar socio-political aims were involved as English was codified up to 1800. Educational aims (Mulcaster in the 1580s) and religious ones (the King James Bible in 1611), both semi-official in that both required royal support, gave way to social and more elitist aims in the following century. Dr Samuel Johnson's work on English reinforced the usage of the 'best authorities', rejected 'mere native English' and the casual and mutable 'fugitive cant' of the 'laborious and mercantile part of the people'. The result of his work, if not its intention, was to strengthen the role of the London elite over what was accepted as correct English. Dr Johnson's role as language 'Dictator', beating France's forty immortals at their own game of standardisation and codification, was confirmed by the award of an official pension after his *Dictionary* of 1762, perhaps compensating for the politically inspired rejection of an official language Academy in 1714. In the nineteenth century, the planning of social behaviour, including language behaviour, became the responsibility of the public schools, acting on behalf of the elite as gatekeeper to social advancement, using knowledge of the classical languages as the key and hence ensuring the reproduction of the controlling social category and its hold on power. Outside England, language planning was more directly political. Conquest had already imposed English as the language of Wales, Scotland and Ireland, and continued this political solution by the spread of the language abroad to colonies, to the Empire and to Dominions. This mix of political and social aims and methods for status and corpus language planning and policy, although hardly democratic, remained dominant until economic purposes became more important through the nineteenth century. Language planning now increasingly targeted the working class through acquisition policy as Education Acts took over from the churches and as education, literacy and an increased role for the standard language became the means for ensuring that the workforce could read, understand instructions and accept the social norms of a stratified society. The process may not have been deliberately political, but widening access to (the standard) language and to the education and hence social advancement available through it closely accompanied widening access to political argument and to political control.

Governments in Britain have rarely seen language as a major direct target for policy decisions. Language policy, until the twentieth century, accompanied or was a by-product of social or economic policy. It is in the twentieth century that increasingly overt, increasingly organised and increasingly political attempts to influence language use have seen the institution of language legislation. Many individuals, societies and groups have thus seen their work on language supported, and sometimes taken over, by official action. Reformers like Sir James Pitman and his initial teaching alphabet (ita) saw their work adopted by many teachers; spelling reformers like Mont Follick nearly managed to force the Department of Education to adopt their work. George Orwell's advocacy of a 'plain and transparent style' led him to satirise political discourse in *Animal Farm* and *Nineteen Eighty-Four*. These books became set requirements in education for generations of British schoolchildren, and were for decades weapons in the ideological struggle against what was later called the 'evil empire' of Communism. Organised groups such as the Queen's English Society followed, in the 1980s, in the tracks of Lord Bridges' Society for Pure English (1913–45), aiming to raise public awareness of language corruption and decay and proposing a purer English.

Authoritative and governmental LPP decisions are sometimes regarded as according or refusing rights to use or acquire a language variety or language; as developing the resources a society has or wishes to develop among its citizens; or as offering solutions to the problems which confront a state or government (Ruiz 1984). Many decisions fall neatly into such categories, although there remain plenty which do not or which combine them in different ways. The dozen examples of British language policy and planning which follow have been organised in this way.

Language rights

a.   Sexism

Both the French and American Revolutions introduced ideas of human rights. These have been defined and redefined in international organisations (United Nations, European Union) and although they only formally entered British law with the Human Rights Act of 1998, discriminatory language use was starting to be controlled well before.

In Britain, the feminist movement early noted the 1850 Act for shortening the language used in statutes, ruling that 'masculine gender should be taken to include females', a practice which continues even, remarkably, in the Human Rights Act: 'No one shall be deprived of his life . . . his liberty . . . in a language which he understands . . . his civil rights'. Feminists started by pointing to sexist language ('generic he and man and titles that mark women's marital status') and sexist language use ('the ways in which women are denied the right or the opportunity to express themselves freely'), particularly in the media and publishing. The idea that women suffered from linguistic deficit (lack of assertiveness) soon gave way to the notion that male use of language represented both dominance and difference, bred into the sexes by early upbringing and social conventions, and which should be corrected by performing gender differently in the hope of changing not merely language but also recurrent unequal pay, sexual harassment, rape and domestic violence (see Cameron 1998). The association between language use and social customs became more and more important: 'In 1982, when I first considered writing a book about gender differences in language, the topic was perceived as being of interest only to a specialist minority … the book has been reprinted many times since it was first published in 1986' (Coates 1993:ii). Official policy responses tackled the issue of discrimination in employment, with the Equal Pay Act of 1970 and the Sex Discrimination Act of 1975, which outlawed discrimination on the grounds of sex or marriage and saw language as epitomising it. Discriminatory advertisements are banned. The Equal Opportunities Commission, set up by the 1975 Act, issues such guides to language use as the Sex Discrimination Code, making the use of words like *waiter*, *salesgirl* or *stewardess* in an advertisement 'an intention to commit an unlawful discriminatory act' unless the advertisement specifically states that the job is open to men and women. Advertisements must be worded to avoid presenting men and women in stereotyped roles. The language legislation has reflected, or perhaps provoked, a significant change in society:

Our use of language should reflect not only changes in society but also the newspaper's values. Phrases such as career girl or career woman, for example, are outdated (more women have careers than men) and patronising (there is no male equivalent): never use them. (Marsh & Marshall 2000)

b.   Racism

The topic broadened to include official proscription of all types of discrimination, particularly racist language use, in Britain during the mid-1970s. Again, the movement has been worldwide. Official British anti-racial-discrimination legislation started with the Race Relations Act of 1976. This Act also set up a monitoring organisation, the Commission for Racial Equality. In 1986 the Public Order Act Part III made it an offence 'to use threatening, insulting or abusive words or behaviour with the intention of stirring up racial hatred'. The MacPherson Report into the murder of Stephen Lawrence, published in 1999, coined the phrase 'institutional racism', widened the concept of racial discrimination still further, and a number of high-profile legal cases in the late 1990s and later have also served to keep the concepts and words of racial discrimination in the forefront of public awareness. There is little doubt that attitudes towards rights, exemplified in the cases of sexism, racism and indeed disability, have changed drastically during the twenty-five years since 1975: 'One of the most striking differences, qualitatively, . . . was an increased awareness and sensitivity towards other people . . . This was most notable in terms of racial abuse, but other groups were also mentioned: people with disabilities, those from different religious faiths, homosexual men and women, and also national minorities' (Millwood-Hargrave 2000). Legislation seems to have closely accompanied if not preceded this attitudinal change. Official language policy in favour of antidiscrimination rights seems to have worked: by 2001 journalism, publishing and public speeches carefully avoided provocative language use. The 'rights agenda' is a political bone of contention. Conservative governments in power in the UK between 1979 and 1997, while not repealing earlier antidiscrimination legislation and indeed occasionally promoting it as in the case of disability, generally treated such planning as a product of the 'loony Left'. Antidiscrimination language planning, which has continued since the advent to power of the Labour Party in 1997, has not always been favourably received by the wider public. The Report of the Commission on the Future of Multiethnic Britain, set up by the Home Secretary to advise the Labour government, received a less than favourable public reception for its contention that 'the word "British" will never do on its own . . . Britishness, as much as Englishness, has systematic, largely unspoken, racial connotations . . . Britishness is racially coded' (Parekh 2000:38). This latter phrase was deliberately recast by some newspapers as '"British" is a racist term'.

c.   *The maintenance of non-indigenous languages*

Parliamentarians, like civil servants, are well aware of the multicultural and indeed multilingual nature of modern British society. Official documents are sometimes produced in languages other than English. Which languages are chosen varies from case to case, as in the versions of the Small Claims leaflets, available through the Lord Chancellor's department only in Welsh and English up to 1998 and in these plus Arabic, Bengali, Chinese, Gujarati, Hindi, Panjabi and Urdu thereafter; the National Health Service Plan Summary of 2000 (Arabic, Bengali, Chinese, Greek, Gujarati, Hindi, Panjabi, Somali, Turkish, Vietnamese, Urdu); or the information leaflets and questions for the 2001 Census in England, available also in Albanian/Kosovan, Croatian, Farsi/Persian, French, Italian, Japanese, Polish, Portuguese, Russian, Serbian, Spanish, Swahili and thus in 24 languages. Policy seems to be rather ad hoc.

Acquisition policy became important after the issue of the European Economic Community's Directive 4861 of July 1977 (Thompson, Fleming & Byram 1996). This required member states to 'promote the teaching of the mother tongue and culture (of the children of migrant workers) in accordance with normal education'. DES Circular 5/81 made it clear that although at that time the curriculum was not under central control, 'For the local education authorities in this country, [the EEC directive] implies that they should explore ways in which mother-tongue teaching might be provided, whether during or outside school hours, but not that they are required to give such tuition to all individuals as of right'. The Department for Education and Science then funded a major investigation of the 'other' languages of England in the Linguistic Minorities Project (1985). This strongly advocated greater recognition for minority languages. Her Majesty's Inspectorate of Schools, at that time the only body able to put curriculum recommendations to schools from the central government, agreed in 1984, 'It is educationally desirable that bilingual children in primary schools should be given the chance to read and write their mother-tongues and to extend their skills in these languages' (DES, 1984). But by 1985, with the appearance of the Swann Report, the government had concluded that schools were not the place for teaching minority languages; rather, 'the first priority in language learning ... must be given to the learning of English' (p. 426). The English language needs of bilingual children should be met within mainstream education, and communities, rather than central or local authorities, should be responsible for the maintenance of their own language(s).

This is the approach that has been officially followed since, despite much work by Local Education Authorities, faced with large numbers of non-English-speaking children beginning school. The most common response has been the employment of bilingual assistants in schools, whose task is to act as interpreters and helpers for children who have no English, in order to help them to enter mainstream education as rapidly as possible.

Language as a resource for the citizen

d.   Adult literacy

One recurring issue, requiring both corpus policy and acquisition policy, is the linguistic competence of citizens, and particularly the level of literacy in society. Literacy has been at the top of UNESCO's agenda since the 1950s. European governments, not just Britain, at first had to be persuaded that such issues should matter to them, since they were the first to introduce mass education at the beginning of the twentieth century and a hundred years of education had, they often thought, meant that their populations were now literate. In 1974, however, the UK government founded an Adult Literacy and Basic Skills Unit (ALBSU). Provision was made for teaching English and improving literacy for adults, mainly through the further education system. After 1979, with the election of the Conservative government which was to remain in power for 18 years, there began a series of radical policy initiatives. Such changes were not cosmetic: they signalled a degree of distrust of the education 'mafia' and its 'trendy, progressive' ideas developed through the 'permissive' 1960s; they made clear that the function of education was to provide what society wanted, not what it thought society needed; and they made clear that the government would decide not merely the funding but also the curriculum, previously the preserve of the institutions themselves. The government's basic ideological stance was that adults were, or should be, responsible for their own education, while training was, or should be, the responsibility of employers. Nonetheless the Family Literacy and Numeracy Project, managed by ALBSU, was introduced in 1994 and by 2000 was helping more than 50,000 parents and children every year.

UNESCO's International Adult Literacy Survey of 1996 showed continuing poor scores in Britain. The New Labour government of 1997 was still faced by a functional illiteracy rate of 20% of adults, just as in 1974. It tackled the literacy problem through the White Paper *Skills for Life* (DEE 2000b). The plans involved a major restructuring and reorganisational effort aimed at bringing together education and training: they are a good example of constituent or agency planning, restructuring the machinery of language policy as much as changing the 'sharp end'. The policy outlined in *Skills for Life* was modest. It aimed 'to reduce the number of adults in England with literacy and numeracy difficulties to that of our main competitors' – from one in five to one in ten or better. Above all, the policy would follow New Labour procedures used elsewhere by setting targets and steering funding to achieve them. So, 'by 2004, our strategy will improve the literacy and numeracy skills of 750,000 adults in England', and the detail specifies provision for 130,000 job seekers, 10,000 public sector employees, 50,000 refugees and speakers of other languages, and 50,000 people who live in disadvantaged communities.

e.   Language in the civil service

A widespread complaint is that civil servants seem unable to write clearly and simply but use 'gobbledygook' and 'officialese'. The Treasury's invitation to Sir Ernest Gowers to produce guidance, originally for internal civil service documents, led to *The Complete Plain Words* in 1954, constantly updated and widely available since to the public at large after its publication by Penguin.

But by the 1980s a whole culture change was in process in the civil service, and the aim of 'effectiveness' in conveying government policy became as important as 'efficiency' (Ager 1996:109–113). Prime Minister Thatcher wrote in 1988 that 'Plain English must be the aim of all who work in Government', introducing a short pamphlet on the topic, itself prepared by the Plain English Campaign (PEC) in 1983 (Central Office of Information, *Making it Plain* 1988). The PEC, founded in 1974 by Chrissie Maher and Martin Cutts with the intention of ensuring benefits claimants in Liverpool could understand official forms and leaflets, was seized on by Margaret Thatcher as a method of training the civil service to adopt competitive approaches and business ethos. After the PEC's open-ing stunt of shredding government forms in Parliament Square in 1979, a series of 'Inside Write' competitions was established with government support, with prestigious prizes for clarity and the reduction of officialese, accompanied by Golden Bull awards for the most convoluted and unin-formative use of language. These awards continue, implementing govern-ment's language policy with a mixture of rewards and punishment.

John Major's governments of 1990 to 1997, introducing Citizens' Charters, strengthened even more the 'businesslike', less inward-looking official style which adopted much of the rapidity and immediate style of the private sector's work in publicity. Departments (no longer Ministries) developed a new style and vocabulary for civil service language, with the result that traditional neutrality and objectivity has been replaced by discoursal features such as 'spin' (subtle interpretative discourse), 'style without substance' (a deliberate search for a striking form of expres-sion, adopted for any initiative or even lack of it), 'business-speak' (a delight in adopting the latest buzz-words of the management gurus) and love of 'soundbites' (short, sharp phrases of a sentence or less which make impressive-sounding quotations for replay during television news).

f.   *Political discourse*

The rhetoric of radical Thatcherism and of 'third way' Blairism reveals a subtler form of language planning, aiming at changing the way political debate is structured by changing the language practice in which politics is discussed. Thatcherian discourse, revealing and shaping Thatcherian poli-tics, was based on such phrases as *value for money*, *choice* and *standards* and on casting the concepts of monetarism in terms of the family budget (Phillips 1998). The discourse combined three, somewhat contradictory, strands of right-wing thinking: traditional authoritarianism, political and economic individualism, and a populist appeal to the ordinary person, particularly, as in many of the prime minister's own speeches, to the housewife. Populism meant the use of everyday vocabulary, even within a context of international finance or trade, so Margaret Thatcher's comparison of the national budget and the housekeeping requirement to squirrel away tins of groceries in reserve gave a new slant to the need to reduce public expenditure and taxes. Under Prime Minister John Major from 1990 to 1997, Citizens' Charters aimed at empowering the citizen as consumer. New Labour has built on Thatcherian discourse after 1997, adopting its populism and its themes of national renewal, responsibility, competition and governmental limitation, but replacing its inbuilt polemical need to define and if necessary create an adversary by a consensual, all-inclusive process of going beyond and transcending the Left–Right divide, combining responsibilities and enterprise with rights and attacking poverty (Fairclough 1999). Of course, neither Thatcher nor Blair invented political discourse or spin doctors. Language in use necessarily incorporates a point of view, noticed most when it is one the listener or reader does not share. The language use of advertising and public relations is just as devious, and similarly locked in a specific universe of discourse. Whether political or commercial discourse changes add to citizens' abilities in language use is doubtful: certainly, nonetheless, such changes affect the way language is used throughout society, and hence the linguistic resources available to citizens. The corpus of the language is changed, in the sense that new meanings are developed and old ones lost or changed.

g.   *The Better English Campaign*

Quite apart from such matters is the issue of 'Better English', the title of a short-lived semi-political campaign initially funded by the Department for Education and Employment from 1994. The issue was first raised after David Pascall, a senior oil company executive who became head of the Curriculum Council, professed his belief that 'accurate English' was essential in education, and that 'understanding dialects and accents was not a central purpose of the national curriculum' (*The Guardian*, 14 October 1994). Pascall's confusion between Standard English and accurate English was mirrored by Gillian Shephard, Secretary of State for Education, who was outspoken in a newspaper interview as she condemned 'expression by grunt', the 'accelerated erosion' of the language and the spread of Estuary English. To counter the degradation of the language by television presenters, disc jockeys and pop musicians, Gillian Shephard launched a Better English Campaign, associating it with the 'final' version of the National

Curriculum. Corpus policy became important in an attempt to influence the way people spoke and indeed wrote.

This semi-political campaign claimed to support the use and teaching of Standard English as a resource for all: 'For too long we have been too slack in the treatment of English and we have impoverished our children in the process'. The heady mixture of attacks on 'sloppy English', insistence on stricter teaching of grammar, spelling and punctuation, and encouragement of a vital skill without which young people did not get jobs, was designed to raise support for Conservative party educational policy on the National Curriculum by appealing to prejudice, but the Campaign soon realised it would gain support only from purists for such an approach. Trevor McDonald, a Black newsreader who told how he had taught himself Standard English, changed the tone and stressed delight in the 'good' use of English as well as the 'hard economic case for better English'. Prince Charles, too, helped the Campaign along, as, eventually, did early opponents like the National Association of Teachers of English. This grass-roots approach to the Campaign, which was uncannily close to the uproar in France which led to the 1994 Toubon Law 'defending' French against Americanisms, should have ensured it a long life and a continuing importance, but it does not seem to have survived into the 2000s.

Language resources for the state

h.   *English language teaching*

English is a major international language (Crystal 1997, Graddol 1997). Why should English be so widespread? Some commentators, Graddol among them, allege that English has certain characteristics which make it intrinsically an excellent choice: it is a hybrid and permeable language, made up of a mixture of Germanic and Latin roots in both vocabulary and grammar; it can transform elements from other languages, which it borrows with ease; it is easy to learn, so the cost of acquiring it is low; and it is now a valuable addition to economic capital for individuals as well as states, simply because of its use in many domains from diplomacy to science. Finally, whatever may be the truth of such beliefs – and since many of them are subjective they are not amenable to factual discussion and even less to proof – the facts remain that English is the language of the world's largest and most powerful economy (the USA) and of another one in the top five (the UK); and that it is widely used by the world's second largest (Japan). It cannot be avoided; there is no alternative.

Since English is so widespread, British language industries make considerable money, about five billion pounds in the year 2000, much of which is derived from the export of English Language Teaching (ELT). ELT is conducted by both private providers, of whom there are many, and by the British Council, a non-departmental public body nominally an independent organisation, which has long been extensively funded through the Foreign Office and the Ministry for Overseas Development. British government policy towards it, and hence towards the role of English as an international language, has varied from the time in 1934 when the Council was set up at arm's length from government and today. Under Margaret Thatcher, the British Council's ELT had to be self-financing. This was an apparent rejection of any role for the state in the global language situation. It took ten years, until the (new) Prime Minister was 'told off by the Mayor of Shanghai for failing to promote English abroad' (*The Guardian*, 29 October 2000), for the government to get the message and provide extra money. By 2000, half the Council's income (i.e. about £170 million) was derived from selling ELT and other services.

There is a further political dimension to ELT. The British Council, and ELT generally when provided by Western countries, has been heavily criticised by some for a 'colonialist and imperialist' language teaching programme and methods which support 'the totalitarian tendencies – of local nationalist groups and Western multinational agencies – through uniformity of thought and communication', and prevent 'the struggle of communities for empowerment' (Canagarajah 1999:197). Such attacks are hotly rejected (Crystal 2000), but may account for the way British Council, and UK, policy towards cultural diplomacy and towards ELT stresses both the ethical dimension in their undertakings and their partnership with other countries.

i.   Teaching foreign languages

For many years after World War II, teachers and planners alike considered that foreign language learning should be restricted to children of higher ability, yet also claimed considerable advantages for this element of the curriculum: it 'enhanced career possibilities, cultural enrichment, linguistic understanding and character development' (Hornsey 1983:1). Such national policy as there was was made in a devolved system by two non-governmental groups: commercial publishers and the Examination Boards. The publishers catered for a market where purchasing decisions were made by each school in pursuance of its own decisions on curriculum and methods. The Examination Boards, run by some universities, were all-powerful, since they competed with each other, and responded less to planning than to the needs of individual large schools.

Changes in this situation were to come about as a result of membership of the European Union, and the educational rationalisation and reform of the 1980s under the Conservative government of the time. The process took ten years to bring about a shift from the devolved 'secret garden' of the curriculum to the centralised National Curriculum with its precision, its detail and its testing processes. An early change followed the publication of *Primary French in the Balance* in 1974 (Burstall *et al.*), a research report which questioned the value of early foreign language teaching, enabling Local Education Authorities to save money by closing much of this provision. It took until 2002 before the Secretary of State for Education proposed that primary schools again teach foreign languages. In the National Curriculum of 1994 a foreign language became compulsory for all to age 14, causing a massive increase in numbers taking languages in secondary schools.

The Nuffield Report of 2000 (McDonald & Boyd 2000), following a large-scale survey of the position, detailed a decline in the numbers studying languages, particularly at A level, and the low esteem in which a knowledge of foreign languages was held in the country. It savagely criticised the lack of a coherent national strategy for the use and promotion of foreign languages, particularly in education but also in working life. The Report's fifteen recommendations were ambitious, and led to a governmental policy document *Agenda for Languages*, published in 2001 (King & Johnstone). This proposed measures to teach more foreign languages, while being aware of different requirements in each of the four constituent countries of the United Kingdom, of the need to promote social inclusion as well as economic advancement, of the need to promote non-indigenous languages of British communities and of the need to involve many groups and organisations as well as the government. This is policy by consultation rather than by fiat. Nonetheless, a parallel decision in 2002 to stop the obligation to teach languages to age 14 seems to run counter to a policy for the expansion of foreign language teaching.

Language as a problem

j.   Standard English and the National Curriculum

The mainstream teaching of English in Britain had been the subject of innumerable British government reports prior to the introduction of the National Curriculum, among them the Newbolt Report of 1921, the Bullock Report of 1975, the Swann Report of 1985, and the Kingman Report of 1988. The National Curriculum, introduced by the Education Reform Act of 1988, brought with it the establishment of national learning and achievement targets, and national assessment of schools, as opposed to local control of education. For the first time, national programmes and national standards of achievement were set up for four Key Stages of education: ages 5–7, 8–11, 12–14 and 15–16 with tests at the end of each stage. Most importantly, there would be a national curriculum of subjects to be taught, and centrally determined syllabuses for each. The English syllabus was developed by a committee working with Professor Brian Cox of Manchester University. The background to his Report was a strong, politically coloured debate on the nature and role of Standard English. A widespread view among educators was that the linguistic differences between language varieties, as in Bernstein's 'restricted' (working-class) and 'elaborated' (middle-class) codes, made them markers of social difference; that it was no part of the purpose of education to denigrate working-class children because of their accent or dialect; and that thus social and regional dialects should be encouraged and valued in the school (see e.g. Bernstein 1971, Halliday *et al.* 1964). Among significant contributors from the opposite point of view were Dr Rae, headmaster of Westminster School, and Dr John Honey who in 1983 wrote *The Language Trap*, into which working-class children dropped through not being obliged to learn Standard English. Professor Cox was left in little doubt about the political nature of his task:

The left argued that children who speak dialect at home could not be expected to speak standard English, which they regarded as middle class, and that it was improper to make this an essential attainment target in a national curriculum. The right thought that we were too soft on primary school children, who should be expected to speak and write standard English as soon as they arrive in the classroom. (Cox 1991:26)

Language became the site of major political controversy as the New Right social engineering agenda was driven through. A particularly influential contribution was Marenbon's *English, our English*, a pamphlet produced by the Conservative think-tank, the Centre for Policy Studies, in 1987, and which, with *The Language Trap*, may have been the impetus for the change from implicit to explicit language policy in the UK.

How pernicious, then, was this Conservative party LPP, which is reflected in our examples (g) (The Better English Campaign), (j) (Standard English and the National Curriculum) and, below, (k) (Multiculturalism)? The issue has been much discussed and analysed (see for example Cox 1991, Crowley 1989, Cameron 1995:78–115, Thompson *et al.* 1996:102–6, Honey 1997, Bex & Watts 1999, Holborow 1999, Milroy 2001). Generally, the majority of language experts and educationalists tend to regard LPP of this time as misguided and excessive, founded on a poor understanding of both linguistics and education. By contrast, the government and its supporters claimed that both common sense and the need to remove left-wing politics from the classroom required firm support for 'the mainstream view'. There is of course no objective way of deciding whether the policy was 'right' or 'wrong'. The government was consistent throughout the debate; its credibility and legitimacy among the general population were absolute, as shown by the re-election of the Conservative party, by large majorities, between 1979 and 1992. There is hence absolutely no doubt that this policy did not offend the British public in this period, nor that the Conservative party was (politically) fully justified in pursuing it. The issue symbolised the contrast between the macro policies of what was thus the ideologically consistent, credible and perfectly legitimate government and the micro policies, generally ideologically opposed to Conservatives, of authority figures in the classroom and particularly of their professional associations and leading thinkers.

One of the most interesting aspects of the 'great grammar crusade' is the extent to which professional linguists were involved and to which what had previously been basic assumptions in (socio)linguistics were put on public trial, particularly that all languages and dialects are equally good and that 'correctness' is a social, not a linguistic, fact (see Milroy 2001). To this extent, the process followed the pattern of Thatcherite 'handbagging' of established interest groups and professionals, and was by no means an unusual exercise in that context. History teachers, and indeed economists, are other professional groups that suffered much the same fate.

k.   *Multiculturalism*

The Standard English problem was closely related to the issue of multiculturalism in schools and in society generally, again a bone of contention between political Left and Right (Tomlinson 1993). The underlying political issue is the debate between the primacy of civil society with its different and sometimes competing groups and that of the overarching state: between pluralism and assimilation. How acceptable is cultural diversity? In language terms, should the state language, English, be a requirement for citizenship, or should the state accept that citizens may use any of many languages? As with the standard language issue, these approaches are not 'right' or 'wrong'; they are political choices.

Insistence on teaching Standard English in schools was seen in the 1980s by the multicultural Left as symbolising a rejection of the languages, varieties, accents and cultures not merely of traditional dialect areas but of ethnic groups including those speaking English-based creoles, and hence as a rejection of such social groups themselves. But even during this period there existed at least a 'remedial' policy of making provision for some of the obvious problems facing immigrants and the offspring of former immigrants. One of the main vehicles for this has been through 'Section 11 Grant', a fund which was set up in 1966 by the Local Government Act, providing 50% funding for local authorities, schools and further education colleges 'to help members of ethnic communities to overcome barriers of language or culture, and thereby to play a full part in the social, economic and political life of the country'. The largest single use of the grant was to employ teachers or bilingual assistants to teach English as a second language in schools.

The 1997 Labour government was based, among other things, on ideas of multiculturalism and communitarianism which received their probably most outspoken presentation in the speech by Prime Minister Tony Blair to the Labour Party Conference of October 2001. It was believed that minority ethnic communities suffered a double disadvantage: while they were concentrated in deprived areas and thus suffered from the problems that affect everyone in such areas, they also suffered 'overt and inadvertent racial discrimination; an inadequate recognition and understanding of the complexities of minority ethnic groups, and hence services that failed to reach them and their needs; and additional barriers like language, cultural and religious differences'. Language, and ability in English, was seen by different groups in two distinct and conflicting ways in this situation: as positive, a means of accessing the labour market and a necessary help to assimilation and economic advance; or as negative, a cultural imposition, indicative of a patronising approach and potentially racist. Language became the symbol of the policy battle. The multicultural policy of New Labour has been somewhat modified by increases in social tension, by the high prominence of 'asylum seeking' and by terrorism in the early 2000s. The issues have come together in the larger, ideological one of 'belonging': citizenship, employment and communication are closely related. Four reports on the race riots of 2001 in Oldham, Bradford and Burnley decided that 'single-race ghettos' had been created, and that separate development had not served immigrant communities well. Home Secretary David Blunkett has urged new migrants to take part in British society, and in particular to follow programmes in which they are taught English language. Indeed, he was moved to urge ethnic minority communities to 'abide by British norms of acceptability', and accept that social cohesion was a 'two-way street'. David Blunkett was attacked for such 'racist' views by many political friends (reported in *The Times*, 10 December 2001):

Children born and brought up here feel themselves to be British, are proud to be British and I don't think they need any lessons from anybody about their patriotism and Britishness. (Mohammed Sarwar, Labour MP for Glasgow)

Nonetheless Trevor Phillips of the Commission for Racial Equality declared in April 2004 that the stress on division and separation, rather than on the 'core of Britishness' that unites citizens, meant that the term 'multiculturalism' was no longer helpful. Even Lord Parekh pointed out (*The Guardian* Letters, 16 April 2004) that the Report of the Commission on the Future of Multi-ethnic Britain (Parekh 2000) 'unambiguously rejects segregationist multiculturalism'. Professor Bernard Crick, also a member of the Commission, supported the policy consequences the Home Secretary had already announced: a citizenship curriculum for schools, a language and civics test for naturalisation and improved opportunities for English language learning.

l. *The territorial languages and the European Charter for Regional or Minority Languages*

Wales was formally united with England in 1536; Scotland in 1707 and Ireland in 1800, in each case after a history of battle and settlement dating from shortly after the Norman Conquest. All four countries have a closely entwined history, their economies can barely be disentangled, and their cultures have influenced each other. Yet sufficient of the former separate political identity has remained in cultural differences, including to a certain extent language, to ensure that political devolution could be strengthened in 1998 with the passage of Acts that effectively transferred responsibility for many matters to the Scottish Parliament, the Welsh Assembly and the Northern Ireland Assembly.

Until very recently, the UK's formal acceptance of documents like the European Charter for Regional or Minority Languages represented a major political problem for the Westminster executive. It was not until the IRA ceasefire, eventually followed by the British–Irish Agreement, that 'normal' politics could start to address the question. The same type of difficulty had affected Wales although to a much lesser degree, and Scotland even less strongly. Generally speaking, the Conservative party had supported ideas of cohesiveness and unity, while the Labour party had given support for greater local and regional control of affairs and argued for less domination from London.

Formal devolution in all three countries occurred shortly after the Labour election victory of 1997. Soon after, the UK government signed the European Charter for Regional or Minority Languages, and ratified it as a Convention in March 2001. Each devolved authority – Parliament or Assembly – is now responsible for implementing the Convention, and substantially for its own language policy, so that the actual format adopted in each of the three countries is different, both in the specific language(s) referred to and in other ways. Cornish, a language that had died in the nineteenth century and has since been revived by activists, was added as the sixth official language of the United Kingdom in 2002 (the others are English, Welsh, Scottish Gaelic, Ulster Scots and Irish).

For the first time, a language question ('Can you understand spoken Gaelic (in Scotland), Welsh (in Wales), Irish (in Northern Ireland), speak, read or write it?') appeared in the 2001 Census forms, themselves separate for each country. The forms for England blandly stated that 'this question is not applicable in England'.

There had been other language legislation before the ratification of the Convention. The 1942 Welsh Courts Act allowing Welsh to be used in legal proceedings had followed the trial of two activists in which they refused to testify in English. A broadcast in 1962, following the 1961 Census results showing further decline in Welsh speaking, was followed by the creation of the Welsh Language Society, a campaign of demonstrations and disobedience, an official report and the 1967 Welsh Language Act, passed just two years before Prince Charles was inaugurated as Prince of Wales in Caernarvon. This Act proposed the principle of 'equal validity' for English and Welsh in Wales. Its 1993 successor formalised this and set up a Welsh Language Board, decried by language activists at the time as falling far short of the powerful body they felt would be necessary to bring about the state of 'natural bilingualism' they wanted. Indeed, the main method proposed to support Welsh was for the Board to require public bodies to set up Welsh Language Schemes, rather than to impose its own. This legislation was the result, partly, of intense pressure group activity and of the decline of the Conservative Party in Wales: at General Elections Conservative Party seats declined from 14 in 1983 to 6 in 1992. The statistics on Welsh language speakers between the 1991 and 2001 Censuses actually show a slight increase, from 19% to 21% of the population over three years old. Previously, there had been a consistent decline since 1921, when 37.1% of the population spoke Welsh. LPP in Wales has concentrated on status and image planning, particularly on promotion to ensure that the language is used in the higher-level domains and that it becomes more visible in public places. Despite fairly constant calls for corpus work, for example in complaints on the 'degradation' of the language by borrowing from English, the Welsh Language Board has only moved to consider corpus planning as a whole in 2001. The topic is sensitive: cultural nationalists aim to preserve the language untouched, particularly by English, but the wish to help young learners underlines the need to develop new vocabulary and to represent the modern world.

In Scotland the creation of the Scottish Parliament and added funding for Gaelic means that the language should have a better chance of surviving and of being more used than before. Official language support before devolution was already quite strong: Gaelic versions of important documents were regularly produced, particularly if they specifically affected the language, such as the 5–14 curriculum guidelines and the 1994 Inspectorate report on Gaelic education. The Education (Scotland) Act of 1980 had required Gaelic to be taught in Gaelic-speaking areas, as indeed had the 1918 Act; specific grants for Gaelic organisations and education had been made since 1986; Gaelic road signs had been authorised since 1981; and the Broadcasting Acts of 1990 and 1996 required support for Gaelic-language broadcasts. Gaelic has been used since devolution as a debating medium in the Scottish Parliament, subject only to the approval of the Presiding Officer, notably in the debate on the future of Gaelic on 2 March 2000, although its use remains rare. Nonetheless the 1991 Census statistics indicated that Gaelic was spoken by 65,978 people, a mere 1.4% of the Scottish population; in 2001, the figures were 1.2% and 58,969 speakers. The Gaelic-speaking areas are the Western Isles, the Highlands and Argyll, with an urban concentration in Glasgow. There is general agreement that the use of Gaelic is continuing its decline, since there had been 210,677 speakers in 1901 (5.2% of the population). The general analysis is that although things have improved on the planning and policy front since 1980, 'it is a tribute to its tenacity, if not a miracle, that Gaelic has survived thus far' (Macpherson 2000).

The Government of Ireland Act 1920, followed by the creation of the Irish Free State in 1922 and the Republic in 1948, meant the restoration of an Ireland independent from the British Crown after a long and bitter struggle crowned by the 1916 uprising. The Irish language had been an important symbol in this process. In 1922, Article 4 of the Constitution of the Free State declared Irish to be the National Language, also recognising English as co-official. The language is treated by the state not as a minority language but as the 'real' native language of Irish citizens, and it hence enjoys the highest status. By the 1920s it had fallen out of use in elite circles, and had to be recreated by corpus policy from the rural dialect of the socioeconomically disadvantaged. To this extent it is an artificial language.

Surprisingly, there is no general Language Law, although one was being prepared in 2001 (see Ó hIfearnáin 2000:94–7). Knowledge of Irish was, and indeed still is, required of civil servants in the Republic, and all children had and have compulsory lessons, so the language is now strongest in the urban middle-income bracket, although the Irish-speaking communities in the Gaeltacht, from whose dialect the language had been recreated, are still rural and still poor. As a result of nearly a century of language planning, the 1991 Census gave a figure of 32.5% of the population as Irish speakers. Despite the high status, despite the favourable policy and language planning, Irish remains, not merely a minority language, but indeed in an endangered state for a number of reasons, and 'state agencies in the 1980s and 1990s (were) speaking more of survival than revival' (Ó Riagáin 2001:209).

Northern Ireland, formally part of the United Kingdom, is a different case. Language has long been a symbol of the religious and political differences between the two main communities there (Crowley 1999). The aim of devolution after 1997, insofar as it affects language in Northern Ireland, was to institute closer ties between the Republic of Ireland and Ulster, and the main result has been to create cross-border bodies and councils to oversee practical ways of working together. The North–South Ministerial Council thus enables political ministers and administrative civil servants from both the Republic and Northern Ireland to meet, discuss their area of expertise and align policy if this seems appropriate. In the case of language, a North/South Language Body was set up following Article 2 of the British–Irish Agreement to support Irish, Ulster Scots and Ullans 'across the island of Ireland'. The North/South Language Body has two parts, one for Irish and one for Ulster Scots. It is intended to provide advice for both administrations. The two separate Agencies, working for this controlling Body, are the active components, and while the Irish Language Agency absorbs the functions of the Irish government bodies the *Bord na Gaeilge* (Board for Gaelic), *An Gum* (publishing) and *An Coiste Téarmaíochta* (Terminology Development), the Ulster Scots Agency (Tha Boord o Ulstèr-Scotch) was newly formed and has allocated its operations and resources in four areas: linguistic development, culture, education and public awareness and promotion.

The 1991 Census question on Irish produced a figure of 45,338 people claiming to speak Irish of a total population aged over three years of 1,502,835 (3%) in Northern Ireland (quoted in Northover & Donnelly 1996:47). Identity politics are at the heart of the support for both Irish and for Ulster Scots in the province; language choice has become a badge of differentiation. Motivation for language support in Northern Ireland had become a matter of political ideology, and language policy and planning has in effect recognised this by associating the Republic with the Province in the support of Irish, and by allocating support for Ulster Scots for the first time.

British language planning and policy in perspective

There are possibly three ways in which a country's LPP can be evaluated: by international comparisons; by examining issues of power and control;

and by investigating planners' motives (Ager 2003). Here we shall concentrate on a comparison with France, the country with the most obviously different language policy (Ager 1996, 1999). It has a long history of official support for the standard language going back to the 1539 Royal declaration that French should be used in drafting and administering the law, even though the British equivalent dates from 1362. The French Revolution of 1789 consecrated French as the language of Reason, of Liberty and of the Rights of Man, and started the process by which French has come to be seen as the embodiment not of Frenchness alone but, at the same time, of universal human rights, of democracy and justice: the 'Republican Values'. Politicians and most French citizens, of Right and Left alike, see the language as a vital part of French identity, and its protection as a duty for all democrats and indeed for humankind. French was formally declared to be the language of the Republic in a Constitutional amendment in 1992. French is now protected by the Toubon Law of 1994, particularly against Americanisms. There is an extensive mechanism of Terminology Committees in each ministry, and neologisms must be approved by the French Academy, a state-supported body originally formed in 1634, a century before Swift's abortive attempt in Britain. The Academy's decisions are legally binding on the civil service. The Academy's technical work is also carried out in the Culture Ministry by the Délégation Générale aux Langues de France (DGLF), for which there is also no British equivalent, and whose predecessor was set up by de Gaulle in 1966. The Délégation, with a co-ordinating role in France covering both corpus and status issues affecting French, the regional languages and 'immigrant languages', has teeth: it provides an annual report to Parliament, has a large budget and, significantly, the ability to conduct or support court cases aimed at enforcing the Toubon Law. It is because of the philosophical and political pedestal on which French was and is placed that the battle for regional language rights has been much fiercer in France than Britain and much more central to politics: regionalists have been accused since the eighteenth century not merely of trying to fragment or 'balkanise' the state, but of attacking the very idea of democracy and with it, of cultural advancement and intellectual worth. Like Britain, France signed the European Charter for Regional or Minority Languages in 1998, but immediately found that the Constitutional clause protecting French prevented its ratification. The clause is still invoked, for example to outlaw state support for the Breton private bilingual schools.

The main contrast with Britain is that French LPP has been consistent for centuries in protecting French as the language of both state and nation. Since the 1960s it has been given more significant resources, and contravention now leads to significant fines. It is the continuing responsibility of the state rather than of successive governments. Because of the centrality of language and culture to French political life, there is wide awareness of, and generally widespread public support for French LPP. The most important point however is that France is convinced there is only one major problem, which must be countered: the (bad) effects of (American) English on French.

So what is specific about British language policy? Top-down and political management of language behaviour has occurred in the past and is present in the UK today. There is language legislation, which reflects the political ideology, beliefs and issues of its time: the Welsh Language Act; the ratification of the European Charter for Regional or Minority Languages and the subsidiary legislation associated with it; anti-discrimination legislation on gender, race, disability, with more to come; legislation on language and citizenship; some media regulation; and the National Curriculum specifications of language(s) to be taught, how they will be taught, and how they will be tested. Public language use is managed through such mechanisms as the control of public discourse and the mixture of reward and punishment in bureaucratic English. Both status and acquisition policy can thus easily be exemplified. There is some limited corpus policy. But there is no single Language Law, no one piece of legislation called Control of, or Defence of, English, no grand symbolic gesture, no official declaration that English alone may be used as the medium of education, no legislation outlawing borrowings from other languages, no legislation requiring that the media broadcast songs in English, no law declaring that asylum seekers will only be addressed in English and must make their demands in English (although they must show a knowledge of one of the ipso facto official languages of the country if they wish to obtain naturalisation). In England, there is no specific governmental machinery for implementing language policy, although major administrations like the Foreign Office and the Department for Education and Skills are involved. Interestingly, the Department for Culture, Media and Sport is involved simply in issues of media regulation. In Scotland, Wales and Northern Ireland, however, specific governmental machinery implements present and advises on future language policy, with remits to investigate and promote languages other than English.

British language policy demonstrates the fallacy of the idea of the 'unfettered freedom' of language users to 'do what they damn well like' with 'their' language. The 'natural forces of (linguistic) change' are natural only if social change is 'natural', or if political opinions are implemented in 'natural' legislation. Language ideologies and the consequent policies affecting language use are a component part of British cultural life.

24   Non-standard English and education

Ann Williams

Introduction

The twenty years since the first edition of *Language in the British Isles* have seen far-reaching changes in many spheres of life in Britain. One of the most fundamental has been the introduction, for the first time in Britain, of a National Curriculum to be followed by all children in state schools. The motivation for the initiative has been attributed variously to the need to improve educational standards, to promote equality of opportunity, to impose cultural unity on an increasingly diverse nation or to attempt to return to the values and traditions of the past (see Cameron & Bourne 1988 for full discussion). The core subject of the new curriculum as conceived by the Conservative government of the time, was to be the English language, and in particular Standard English.

Standard English (SE) is a social dialect, generally defined as 'a set of grammatical and lexical forms typically used in speech and writing by educated native speakers' (Trudgill 1984b:32). While there are no linguistic grounds for maintaining that it is superior to other dialects of English (Trudgill passim), it is nevertheless the 'prestige' variety, widely used in education, in the media and in almost all forms of writing (although in recent years Scottish and Caribbean writers have started to publish works in non-standard vernaculars[1]). In spite of its high status, research suggests that Standard English is the home dialect of approximately 15% of the population of the UK (Trudgill 1999b). It is estimated that between 9% and 12% of the population speak Standard English with a regional accent, while RP (Received Pronunciation), the prestigious accent associated with the aristocracy and those who have received a public school[2] education, is the native accent of only 3% of the UK population (Trudgill & Cheshire 1989).

---

[1] For example, James Kelman and Irvine Welsh.
[2] In Britain, 'public school' is the term used for one of the prestigious, long-established private schools.

These figures would suggest that the majority of English speakers in Britain grow up speaking some form of a non-standard (NS) dialect with a regional accent. Numerous studies carried out since the 1970s (Macaulay 1977, Trudgill 1974) have shown a clear correlation between the number and variety of NS features a speaker uses and social class, with speakers at the lower end of the socioeconomic scale using a higher proportion of NS regional features. Most working-class children therefore start school speaking a dialect other than Standard English. In spite of the efforts of linguists to educate the public about the regular, rule-governed nature of NS dialects, the view that such dialects are inferior and full of errors, 'bad' or 'incorrect' English still prevails, even among some speakers themselves. The role that Standard English has traditionally played in education, in literature and in the media on the other hand, means that it is often considered to be a linguistically superior variety and that speakers of SE speak 'good' or 'correct' English. It is this conflict between the populist view of dialects on the one hand and expertise based on linguistic analysis on the other, that has characterised the curriculum debates on English for more than 15 years.

In the next section we will trace the position of NS dialects in the successive versions of the National Curriculum and then we will consider the educational implications for children who speak a NS dialect at home and in their community.

Non-standard varieties in the National Curriculum

Background

The relationship between Standard English, non-standard dialects and education has never been straightforward. With the introduction of universal elementary education in Britain in the 1870s, the variety of English required and rewarded in British schools was Standard British English. Non-standard dialects had no place in the education system as the following statements from early publications on the teaching of English so emphatically stated:

It is the business of the elementary school to teach all its pupils who either speak a definite dialect or whose speech is disfigured by vulgarisms, to speak standard English and to speak it clearly and with expression. (Newbolt Report 1921:6)

Boys from bad homes come to school with their speech in a state of disease, and we must be unwearied in the task of purification. (Sampson 1924, cited in Crowley 2003)

Attitudes such as these remained virtually unchallenged until the 1960s, when a number of factors which included the switch from selective to comprehensive secondary schooling, the arrival in schools of children who spoke dialects of English originating outside the UK or whose mother tongue was not English, combined with a move towards a child-centred approach to teaching, brought about changes in educational thinking. Freed from the shackles of a rigidly prescribed eleven plus examination syllabus,[3] primary teachers were free to experiment. Creative writing became an important part of the syllabus and children were encouraged to write in an imaginative and uninhibited manner. The teaching of formal, traditional grammar (and in some cases spelling) was dropped in the belief that it might induce boredom and damage creativity and still be unsuccessful. Contemporary educationists such as David Holbrook believed that 'civilisation begins anew in every child' and the culture, skills and language that each child brought to school were considered to be at the heart of all teaching and learning. The use of languages and dialects other than SE in school was sanctioned by the Bullock Report, *A Language for Life*, in the much quoted words '*no child should be expected to cast off the language and culture of the home as he crosses the school threshold*' (DES 1975).

For some years the status of NS dialects in the education system was unclear. Although the use of NS varieties in speech and writing was promoted by some educationists (Richmond 1979) and strongly supported by linguists such as Trudgill (1975), Cheshire (1982b) and Edwards (1983), educational guidelines on the subject were somewhat inconsistent and what happened in practice was not clear. For example, there appeared to be no consensus on how to deal with NS dialects in school work. In a study of teachers in Reading, Williams (1994b) found considerable inter-teacher variation in the 'correction' of NS dialect forms in writing, with the percentage of corrections ranging from 9.7% to 64% per teacher. Studdert & Wiles (1982) drew attention to the lack of clear policies:

Some schools may accept, even encourage the use of dialect in speech but have a school language policy which urges the use of standard English in writing. It is not unknown for state schools to state that they will not display writing in dialect on the classroom walls. Other schools may even encourage the use of dialect in writing particularly for dialogue or perhaps poetry. What teachers find less acceptable is the combination of the two perhaps because it is difficult to respond to: Is it right or wrong? (cited in Edwards 1983:121)

---

[3] Public selective examination taken at age 11. Thirty percent of children gained places at grammar schools.

The National Curriculum: Kingman and Cox

This 'softening' of attitudes was to come to an abrupt halt however with the 1988 Education Reform Act, 'widely regarded as the most radical shift in policy and practice enacted by a British government since the Second World War' (Cameron 1995:80). The Conservative government, by then in its third term of office, sought to limit the power of local authorities, many of whom it saw as left-wing and permissive, by bringing education under more centralised control. Among other measures, the Act introduced a National Curriculum which all pupils aged between 5 and 16 in state schools in England and Wales were required to follow. Detailed programmes of study and attainment targets were to be laid down for the core subjects and all children in the state sector were to take compulsory national tests (SATs[4]) at ages 7, 11 and 14 with the results published in the national press. English was to be 'at the heart of the National Curriculum' (Department for Education and Science 1993:71).

The responsibility for recommending the model of spoken and written English to be taught in schools was assigned to a committee appointed by Kenneth Baker, Secretary of State for Education, and made up of academic linguists, HMIs,[5] members of the teaching profession, journalists and broadcasters, novelists and poets, under the chairmanship of Sir John Kingman FRS, a professor of mathematics. The committee took evidence from a number of bodies and individuals, including many linguists, and produced a model with four interdependent sections:

Part 1: The forms of the English Language
Part 2: Communication and comprehension
Part 3: Acquisition and development
Part 4: Historical and geographical variation (Kingman 1988:17)

NS varieties of English were given prominence in Part 4, which listed dialect-related topics which would enable pupils 'to comment illuminatingly upon the process of language change and the history of English' (p. 30). Subjects for discussion included 'the systematic ways in which the grammar of some dialects differs from the grammar of SE', 'the retention of forms in some dialects which have disappeared from SE' and 'the reasons why there is more and greater dialect variation in the British Isles than in Australia' (p. 30). The recommendation was that pupils should be introduced to a

---

[4] Standard Attainment Tests. Key Stage 1: from age 5–7; Key Stage 2: 7–11; Key Stage 3: 11–14. The tests are taken at the end of each Key Stage, i.e. at ages 7, 11 and 14.
[5] HMI: Her Majesty's Inspector of Schools.

descriptive grammar of English based on linguistic analyses of both standard and NS varieties. In contrast, the teaching of *prescriptive* grammar (i.e. 'traditional' grammar based on Latin 'rules') was not recommended. '[We do not] see it as part of our task to plead for a return to old-fashioned grammar teaching and learning by rote' (p. 3). The rejection of traditional grammar teaching meant that the report was not received with full approval by the government when the proposals were presented to them in April 1988.

In spite of reservations, the government appointed a National Curriculum English Working Group to draw up attainment targets, programmes of study and associated assessment arrangements for English. It was to be chaired by Brian Cox, Professor of English Literature at Manchester University and formerly a member of the Kingman Committee. Two linguists, Katherine Perera and Michael Stubbs, were among the nine members of the working group. The Cox Report was published in June 1989. The overriding aim of the new English curriculum was 'to enable all pupils to develop to the full their ability to use and understand English ... and the fullest possible development of [their] capabilities in speaking, listening, reading and writing' (DES 1989:2.13). As in the Kingman Report, the emphasis was on descriptive rather than prescriptive grammar.

Although the Cox Report stressed the entitlement of all children to Standard English, since 'if pupils do not have access to Standard English, many opportunities are closed to them in cultural activities, in further and higher education and in industry, commerce and the professions' (DES 1989:4), it was clearly stated that SE is a social dialect 'which has particular uses' and should not be confused with 'good English' (4.11). Moreover, it stressed that SE should be taught 'in ways that do not denigrate the NS dialects spoken by many pupils' (4.42). Knowledge about language was to be addressed in all sections of the English curriculum: teachers should encourage an interest in both rural and urban NS dialects; the grammar of both SE and NS dialects should be discussed and contrasted 'using the pupils as the linguistic experts' on the latter. The ages at which proficiency in SE might be expected were clearly specified: all children should realistically be expected to be able to use SE in speech by the age of 16; 'there should be explicit teaching about the nature of SE in the top years of primary school' and 'there should be the beginnings of the expectation of SE in written work *where appropriate* by the age of 11' (4.38).

The Report was not well received. 'Mr Baker, Secretary of State for Education, "very much disliked" it' (Cox 1991:11), believing that it did not place enough emphasis on grammar, spelling and punctuation.

'Mrs Rumbold, then Minister of State for Education, found the Report "distasteful" ... and from her radio and television appearances it seemed she found repugnant [the] insistence that a child's dialect is not inaccurate in its use of grammar and should be respected' (Cox 1991:11). The Prime Minister, Margaret Thatcher, was the final arbiter. She 'agreed to allow the Report to go out for consultation provided that, in the Attainment Targets for Writing where [it] stated, "Use Standard English where appropriate" the phrase *"where appropriate"* was deleted'. Professor Cox changed the text to 'Use Standard English, except in contexts where non-standard forms are necessary for literary purposes, e.g. in a dialogue or a playscript' (Cox 1991:12).

English and the politicians

The English language had by now ceased to be merely part of the school curriculum. It had become 'a crucial focus of tension and debate . . . serving as a site upon which political positions [were] argued' (Crowley 1989:258). Kingman and Cox had not produced the model of English the government required. Cox subsequently reflected, 'Many politicians and journalists were ignorant about the problems in the teaching of grammar and the status of Standard English and simply desired to reinstate the disciplines of study typical of the 1930s' (Cox 1991:4). More in tune with Conservative sentiments was John Marenbon, a medieval historian and member of the Centre for Policy Studies, whose pamphlet *English, our English* exhorted politicians to 'keep strong in their common sense, distrustful of experts and chaste towards fashion . . . for in the future of its language there lies the future of a nation' (Marenbon 1987:40). In the succeeding revisions of the National Curriculum, expert linguistic advice was eschewed in favour of 'common sense' or folk linguistic views of language.

An immediate casualty was the LINC (Language in the National Curriculum) project, a post-Kingman, government-funded initiative established in April 1989 to produce in-service training materials to support teachers' implementation of English in the National Curriculum (see Carter 1995). Basing their work on the Kingman and Cox recommendations, the LINC team produced a set of materials for teachers which 'stressed above all the richness and variety of the English language', concentrating on language in social and cultural contexts. Traditional grammar in the form of decontextualised classroom analysis of language was not included. The materials were never published. After two years in preparation, publication was blocked by Mr Tim Eggar, Minister of State for Education, on the grounds that 'the materials could be misused'. According to *The Times Educational Supplement*, Mr Eggar '[wanted] a simple set of traditional grammatical exercises which teachers [could] use in schools instead of ... a 500 page document which argued that language should be placed in a social context'. The sections which ministers found most objectionable were predictably those which dealt with accents and dialects, language in its social context (language and gender, language and power) and multilingualism. The 'common sense' view of language had prevailed. Mr Eggar's decision to block the report received enthusiastic support in some sections of the press:

Mr Tim Eggar, as education minister refuses to waste £120,000 on the publication of a report by educational theorists which recommends among other things that dialects should have equal status with the Queen's English in Britain's schools. It is deplorable that 25 so-called experts after five years of alleged research and the expenditure of £21 million should have come up with such an absurd report full of badly written 1960s social science gobbledygook as the following: 'The speech situation is almost always a shared one and the writing situation is usually an isolated one'. Mr Eggar says the report is banal and theoretical and fails to give children the basic grammar they need to speak and write the English that can be understood throughout these islands. It is as though 'the experts' were determined to destroy the concept of correctness in language and literature ... (*Evening Standard* editorial, 26 June 1991)

In spite of the setbacks, schools began to work with the 1989 Cox curriculum, following the programmes of study and attainment targets set out therein. Although teachers were happy with the new curriculum (Cox, cited in the *Sunday Times*, 4 April 1993), the government were not satisfied, and in July 1992 the National Curriculum Council, under the chairmanship of David Pascall, a chemical engineer, put forward *The Case for Revising the Order*, the objection being that, in the Cox curriculum, there was insufficient emphasis on Standard English, 'the grammatically correct language used in formal communication throughout the world' (NCC 1992:4). Pascall drew attention to the fact that in the Cox Curriculum children were not required to *speak* Standard English until late in secondary school. He argued that children should be required to speak Standard English from the earliest years in school, both in the classroom and in the playground. His proposal to revise the Cox curriculum was accepted and a new curriculum was drafted.

In the new proposals 'English for ages 5 – 16 (1993)', the first paragraph which stated 'Pupils should be taught the importance of clarity and audibility ... they should be taught to speak Standard English' set the tone for the whole document. NS dialects received one brief reference: 'The requirement to speak standard English does not undermine the integrity of either regional accents or dialects although clear diction is important to enhance communication' (p. 9). Common NS forms are cited as examples of 'incorrect English'. Thus at Key Stage 2 children are required to 'speak using the basic vocabulary and grammar of Standard English' using 'correct plurals: *three miles not three mile*'; 'correct use of adjectives and pronouns: *pass me those* (not *them*) *books*'; and 'negative forms avoiding double negatives: *we haven't seen anybody* (not *nobody*)'. The English Orders now conveyed to teachers exactly the populist, folk-linguistic views on language that Cox and his team had worked so hard to combat when they wrote: 'Non-standard usages should be treated as objects of interest and value, and not ridiculed . . . the aim is to add Standard English to the repertoire, not to replace other dialects and languages' (DES 1989:4.42).

In spite of widespread criticism from linguists and educationists however, the final form of a drastically slimmed down English curriculum was published in January 1995. Virtually every trace of linguistic expertise had been eradicated from the curriculum.

The National Literacy Strategy

With a change of government in 1997 came a shift in emphasis. The immediate concern of the new Labour government whose election slogan was 'Raising Standards' was not Standard English but standards in English literacy. The question was no longer 'what kind of English should we teach?' but 'how can we improve literacy standards?' A Literacy Task Force had been set up in 1996 while the Labour Party was in opposition and when the party came to power in 1997, the National Literacy Strategy (NLS) was put in place. The keystone of the new strategy is the Literacy Hour, a daily hour of closely prescribed literacy teaching, compulsory in every class in all state primary schools in England and Wales.[6] The programmes for primary level are set out in the 1998 document *The National Literacy Strategy* (DfEE 1998).

Implicit throughout the document is that SE is the required variety. The first reference comes at the end of Year 3 when 'pupils should be taught: to ensure grammatical agreement in speech and writing of pronouns and verbs eg *I am, we are* in Standard English'. In Year 5, 'pupils should be taught to understand the basic conventions of Standard English and consider why Standard English is used in the following: agreement between nouns and verbs; consistency of tense and subject; avoidance of double negatives, avoidance of non-standard dialect words' (DfEE 1998:44). There is little opportunity in this curriculum for pupils and

---

[6] Unless the school can demonstrate through its action plan, schemes of work and test performance that its own approach is at least as effective.

teachers to discuss language in its social context, the regional and social distribution of dialects or to use their own expertise to compare varieties. No details of the morphology, distribution or use of NS forms are given in the document with the exception of the double negative which is surprisingly defined, not as a widely used NS dialect form, but as 'the use of two negative forms which effectively cancel each other out, as in "*I never took nothing*". Often used by children for emphasis' (DfEE 1998:78).

Subsequent publications for teachers dealing with the grammars of written and spoken language (DfEE 2000a, 2001c, QCA 2004) provide little information on regional variation in English: 'the description of some important grammatical characteristics of spoken English is not related to discussions about "non-standard" or "standard" spoken English' (QCA 2004:14). Thus while the NLS remains true to the spirit of the original Cox curriculum in that it supports the entitlement of all children to SE, the NS varieties spoken outside school by many of these children and their families are firmly relegated to the margins. The effect this marginalisation has on speakers of NS varieties as they progress through the education system will be considered next.

Educational implications

Attitudes to NS varieties

One of the problems inherent in the teaching of English, as apparent in the curriculum debates outlined above, is that it is difficult for speakers other than linguists to disengage from the affective associations that standard and NS dialects carry with them. Despite the substantial efforts linguists have made over the past 30 years to inform the public about the nature of language variation (see Trudgill 1975, Bauer & Trudgill 1998), prejudices against NS varieties are difficult to eradicate (Milroy & Milroy 1995). Unless there is adequate training, teachers and other members of the educational establishment are just as likely to hold uninformed views as any other member of the public and it has been shown that such prejudices can have a deleterious effect on children's educational achievement (Williams 1989). The following views of the language of working-class children, for example, are uncannily similar:

1. *... many children, when they come to school, can scarcely talk at all. Sometimes, a witness told us, they cannot even remember their eyes, ears, toes and so forth.*

2. *A generation of young teachers has gone into schools recently, convinced that working class parents never talk to their children ... that the language they do possess is lacking many essential features.*

3. Teacher: *And in fact in Reception,*[7] *you notice it there ... just in the lack
of language ... the number of children that are just not speaking.*
   AW: *What do you attribute this to then?*
   Teacher: *Nobody talks to them.*

The above quotations depressingly span 80 years: the first was written in
1921,[8] the second in the 1970s[9] and the third was recorded in 2001 in an
interview with a special educational needs teacher in a working-class area
in the affluent south of England.[10] Nor are pupils themselves unaware of
the negative evaluations teachers make of NS speech, as working-class
teenagers in Hull stated in 1996: 'Miss C corrects all our language. She
says, "You're not on the street now, you know." She takes us for estate
kids. Estate kids are meant to be real bad – druggies and everything'
(Kerswill & Williams 1997:165). It is hard to believe that even in the
twenty-first century children who speak NS dialects do not start school
at a considerable disadvantage.

More serious possibly, is the handicap NS speakers may face when they
sit the SATs tests. Standard English is the variety required in writing by
Key Stage 2 and script markers may be both prejudiced and ignorant of
dialect variation. One examiner, writing in the *Telegraph,* described
14-year-olds as 'displaying blatantly inadequate levels of literacy' for
using expressions such as 'the words *what* they use', 'me and my dad *was
living* in N., but we *was made* to move', and 'I *come* here last year' (*The Daily
Telegraph,* 5 July 1995). The morphological features the writer objected to
are all common NS dialect forms. It is perhaps not surprising that schools
in areas where NS dialects are widely spoken tend to appear in the lower
sections of the league tables of test results. While entitlement to SE is intended
to promote equality of opportunity, linguistic prejudice and compulsory
testing may further disadvantage the very children it seeks to benefit.

Reading

It is precisely such negative attitudes to dialects rather than problems
inherent in reading or the language itself that may give rise to difficulties
when speakers of NS dialects learn to read. Although there has been very
little research on NS dialect speakers and reading, scholars tend to agree

---

[7] The first year of school in UK. The children are aged between 4 and 5.
[8] Newbolt Report (Newbolt 1921:68 cited in Crowley 1989:241).
[9] Rosen & Rosen (1973) cited in Cheshire (1982b).
[10] *Literacy Practices at Home and at School: Community Contexts and Interpretations.* Brian
     Street, Dave Baker, Eve Gregory and Ann Williams. Leverhulme funded project:
     2000–2003.

that it is teachers' attitudes to regional varieties rather than reading per se that can cause problems. Dr Rhona Stainthorpe (personal communication) states that in order to have the necessary data to map letter–sound correspondences, children need to develop phonemic awareness. But being aware of phonemes she maintains 'has nothing to do with accent'. Teaching children to read 'is more a matter of teacher knowledge, expertise and sensitivity. Teachers need to be aware of the phonemic system of the accent children are using in order to help them map the letter–sound correspondences of that accent.' Similar views are expressed by Goodman & Goodman who, in a longitudinal study carried out in the USA, found that 'it was not dialect differences that lead to problems, but dialect rejection' (cited in Cheshire 2005c). 'Given appropriate opportunities and experiences with a range of content and texts', they maintain, 'all readers are capable of using their language flexibly to become literate members of their communities' (Goodman & Goodman 1978:434). The consensus among reading experts appears to be that it is preferable to encourage dialect speakers to read SE texts in their own dialect rather than be taught using specific dialect materials.

Speaking

It is the teaching and testing of spoken SE that has proved to be the most controversial element in the National Curriculum debates. There is ample sociolinguistic evidence that most speakers adjust their speech, using more or fewer NS features, depending on the status of their interlocutors and the formality of the context. The age at which children learn to style-shift in this way, however, has been disputed, and it is questionable whether it is realistic or even desirable for children to be required to speak SE in school at all. In a quantitative analysis of eleven NS morphosyntactic variables in the speech of eight working-class boys aged between 11 and 14, Cheshire (1982a) found clear evidence of style-shifting. The boys were recorded talking to their friends in adventure playgrounds in Reading and to their teachers in school. Most features, including NS present tense suffix -*s* (*they likes sweets*), NS *was* (*we was waiting*), negative concord (*I didn't do nothing*) and demonstrative *them* (*pass me them pens*) occurred less frequently in classroom interactions than in the playgrounds. Other NS features however, including *ain't* (*I ain't got it*) and the past tense forms *come* and *done* were invariant, occurring 100% of the time in both contexts. As the data were collected before the introduction of the National Curriculum and the boys had not discussed the differences between the grammar of their local dialect and that of SE, their style-shifting could be seen as a conscious adjustment to the norms of school. The shift to SE was not total however, and even in conversations with teachers, pupils continued to use a majority of NS forms.

Hudson & Holmes (1995) also found a variety of NS forms in their analysis of the spoken English of 350 children 'recorded [in schools] in situations [where they would be] likely to use the standard rather than NS English'. The data, which were collected as part of a national survey in four different regions of England, consisted of children aged 11 and 15, carrying out specific spoken language tasks and speaking in the presence of an unfamiliar adult whom they knew to be a teacher. The results indicated that even in conversations with unknown teachers, 68% of the children in this random sample used NS forms in their speech. A cluster of the most commonly used NS forms occurred in all four regions. These included: *there is* with a plural notional subject; *she come*; *out the window* and *them books*. Interestingly, many speakers who used NS forms also used the SE equivalents, suggesting that by secondary school age many children have both NS and SE forms in their repertoires. Hudson & Holmes' results would suggest that many children are not ignorant of SE forms but that they are not always able to distinguish between NS and SE variants. The study also suggested that there is a core of features, including some past tense verb forms such as *come* and *done*, which are so widely used that pupils are unaware of their NS status. This phenomenon has also been reported by Harris (1995), who recounts a lesson in which he asked students to translate a fellow pupil's sentence *Me and my mate was walking home* into SE. The final 'SE' version produced by the class was *My friend and I was walking home*. Harris comments, 'the students could see nothing wrong with this version. As far as they were concerned it was accurate SE' (Harris 1995:127).

Writing

The expectation that all children will learn to use SE in writing is less controversial and research suggests that most speakers of NS dialects acquire some control over Standard written English by the end of secondary school. Learning to write is a complex process in which children have to master the mechanics of handwriting, spelling, punctuation, sentence formation, text organisation and readers' reactions among other things. Children who start school speaking a NS dialect however, also have to master a new set of morphosyntactic forms already present in the speech of SE-speaking children, a process not unlike learning a second language (Kress 1982). In the initial stages, the writing of all children closely resembles 'talk written down' (Kroll & Vann 1981) and young children can be expected to incorporate many features of speech, including NS features, in their written work. Research carried out in Reading has shown that working-class children do include NS forms in their school writing but that the incidence decreases as children move up through secondary school. Williams (1989, 1994a, 1994b) quantified the occurrence of twelve categories of NS syntactic and morphosyntactic features, including verb forms, relative pronouns, negative constructions, demonstrative pronouns and prepositions in approximately 1,000 written texts collected from 120 schoolchildren aged between nine and fourteen in Reading. The results indicated that by age nine, children who spoke Reading English were beginning to shift to SE in their writing although not all SE features were acquired simultaneously. *Ain't* for example, widely used by all working-class participants in recorded conversations, was clearly identified as a spoken form and not present in any of the written texts. Similarly, the NS present tense suffix -*s* (used throughout the paradigm in Reading English) occurred in the spoken texts of 89% of the working-class children but in the written texts of only 38% of the same group. The following excerpt from an interview with three nine-year-old girls shows how frequently the NS Reading present tense form was used in speech:

MH: I writes to my pen-pal Miss. Well not my pen-pal, I writes to my uncle in Australia.

KH: I writes letters to myself.

MH: She writes letters to her friend... to herself from Dawn.

AW: Where do you put them then?

KH: In my pocket and I sends them.

DM: I keeps them. I puts them in a envelope and <u>put</u> Miss D M and I leaves them on a shelf and opens them the next day.

MH: She's a nutter!

Written texts produced by the girls in the same term indicated that the standard form was also present in their repertoires and recognised as the required written form:

DM: ... after that we went to see some lambs the were sucking on these red things and milk comes out. When they are older their tails <u>come</u> off.

MH: When I got dressed and half an hour later when I was at school we was doing Oxford Junior English and I <u>hate</u> that.

KH: If I had three wishes I would wish for a little baby sister cos I have all brothers but I <u>like</u> boys as well.

Other SE forms such as relative pronouns and negative constructions appeared to be acquired later. In the written texts of the nine-year-old working-class cohort, negative concord was the preferred construction in

65% of negative contexts. It was still used in 27% of negative contexts in the work of the fourteen-year-old working-class students.

There were no examples of negative concord in the writing of the teenage boys Cheshire recorded in adventure playgrounds in her study of adolescents' speech in Reading (Cheshire 1982a), although such constructions were near categorical in speech. This suggests that by their mid-teens these adolescents were able to switch to standard forms in their school writing.

Similar findings were reported by Williamson & Hardman (1997a, 1997b) who carried out two studies in Newcastle Upon Tyne in which they compared the school writing of sixteen- and eleven-year-olds. Although grammatical errors accounted for approximately 10% of all errors, only a small proportion of those could be attributed to the Tyneside dialect. Interestingly the proportion of NS dialect forms was consistent for the two age groups. The authors concluded that although NS dialect forms appear to be a relatively minor problem in writing, there is nevertheless a core of persistent forms that children have difficulty in identifying as NS, possibly because they are such an integral part of their speech patterns.

Spelling

Certain accent features appear to be similarly impervious to conscious modification. English orthography is a notoriously mixed system that involves correspondences not only between graphemes and phonemes, but between graphemes and morphological and lexical elements at a more abstract level (Stubbs 1986). As such, it is proposed, it reflects no particular dialect and all learners are equally disadvantaged (Perera 1984). Certain regional accents however, permit phoneme–grapheme correspondences that can result in mis-spellings. In Reading, as in many NS dialects, word initial *h* is frequently omitted in stressed positions. Williams (1994a) found that this resulted in spellings such as *The ingese (hinges) need oiling* and *It it (hit) one of are* [sic] *men*. The fronting of TH to [f] and [v] in words such as *think* and *mother* respectively, an increasingly widespread NS feature in speech (Williams & Kerswill 1999), resulted in spelling errors such as '*I fort she was a pig; It's not breving*. L-vocalisation also gave rise to errors such as *The dow* (bell) *went and we was alowd to go home*. In all, Williams found that spellings influenced by such features of the Reading accent accounted for 8.28% of spelling mistakes in the working-class children's written texts but for only 0.84% of the spelling mistakes in the middle-class children's work. Such errors were less common in the work of children in secondary school when the reliance on phonic cues, characteristic of very young writers, is diminishing.

Hypercorrection

The complex, developmental relationship between speech and writing has been described as passing through four stages: preparation, consolidation, differentiation and integration (Kroll & Vann 1981). Few writers, it is suggested, reach the final stage, 'in which speech and writing are appropriately differentiated and systematically integrated', and in fact many high-school graduates remain suspended between the two modes. As we saw earlier, differentiation between spoken and written can be particularly problematic for children who have both standard and NS variants in their repertoires. Anxiety to write the 'correct' form often leads to hypercorrection as the following spellings taken from Reading children's texts demonstrate:

The sound was <u>deatherning</u>
He had a <u>knithe</u> in his hand
I ran <u>other</u> there
My face has eyes, noues, <u>melf</u>(mouth), *ears, cheeks and eyebrows.* (Williams 1989)

Further, it is questionable whether teacher intervention at an early age helps children to distinguish clearly between SE and NS forms. The following sentences were collected over a six-month period in the work of nine-year-old Jackie. (In Jackie's dialect the past tense of DO is *done*):

1. *We down the housework*
2. *We don done our homework*
3. *My brother <u>dond</u> done ^{did} a jigsaw*   (teacher's correction)
4. *We <u>don</u> ^{did} a bit more dancing*   (Jackie's correction)
5. *When we had <u>done</u> ^{did} some work*   (Jackie's correction) (Williams 1994b)

Examples such as these might suggest that insistence on SE in the early stages of writing puts NS-speaking children at a disadvantage. As Shaughnessy wrote, 'When learners move into uncertain territory, they tend to play by the rules even when the rules lead them to produce forms that sound completely wrong. Their intuitions have proved them wrong in so many instances that they may even conclude that sounding wrong is a sign of being right' (1977:99).

Conclusion

The past two decades have shown the relationship between NS dialects and education to be strongly influenced by politicians. Very high on the present Labour government's agenda is social inclusion and equality of opportunity. While such egalitarian intentions are to be welcomed, insistence on Standard English in all sections of the English syllabus may not result in equal outcomes for all students. Concerns of linguists focus on the marginalisation of regional dialects in the NLS which largely ignores the richness and variety of regional English. The few opportunities provided for children to explore the dialects spoken in their communities and to act as linguistic experts themselves, can do little to advance social inclusion and dispel the kind of linguistic prejudice referred to above. Indeed, the lack of attention paid to local dialects could be interpreted by both teachers and pupils as a tacit acknowledgement that regional speech is 'substandard' or not worthy of consideration. By concentrating almost exclusively on SE, the NLS neatly evades the problem of how to reconcile valuing and encouraging the use of regional dialects, both urban and rural, with the entitlement of every child to proficiency in Standard English.

On social justice grounds it might be argued the government has been short-sighted in assuming that equal accountability in high stakes tests equates with equality of opportunity. Speakers of NS dialects do not start on an equal footing with SE-speaking children, particularly in the primary level tests, unless they have teachers who are sensitive and linguistically informed and as yet there is little expectation that teachers should be experts in the local variety of the area in which they teach. However, we have also suggested that many speakers of NS varieties do acquire Standard written English as they proceed through secondary school. What is lacking is adequate provision to assure children learning to write or speak Standard English, that the NS dialects spoken by their families, neighbours and friends are not 'inferior, incorrect or bad' English but essential elements in an immensely rich, multi-faceted and constantly changing language.

25 Education and speakers of languages other than English

Ben Rampton, Roxy Harris and Constant Leung

This chapter charts deteriorating state school provision for speakers of languages other than English in the years between 1984, when the first edition of *Language in the British Isles* was published, and 2002.[1] It focusses primarily on England and it addresses the teaching of English as a second/additional language (ESL/EAL) as well as the teaching of minority ethnic languages. It begins with a brief characterisation of the approach to multilingualism epitomised in the 1985 Swann Report, and it then points to how this was altered by the processes associated with globalisation. The education system's involvement in these processes is outlined, particularly in terms of the impact on pupils with a family knowledge of other languages, and there is a critical discussion of the role that linguistic research played in these shifts. Government showed little interest in research on language diversity in the 1990s, but this did not deter researchers, and if government rediscovers multilingualism, it will be able to connect with a substantial knowledge base.

Education, language and ethnicity c.1970–85: The 'Swann Report'

Education for All – 'the Swann Report' (DES 1985) – was the last major government report on linguistic and ethnic diversity in education, and it illustrates the discourses and political arrangements that were central to education policy in England at the time of the first edition of *Language in the British Isles*.

Power in educational policy making was distributed very differently from how it is today. Central government had no direct powers over the curriculum, and curriculum decision-making lay in the hands of teachers

---

[1] We are unable to assess developments beyond 2002 – the aftermath of 9/11, increasingly hostile media commentary about asylum seekers, refugees and economic migrants, and the setting-up of prescriptive norms with an English language requirement for British citizenship (Blunkett 2002).

417

and individual schools, who were usually provided with strong guidance by their Local Education Authorities (LEAs) (DES 1985:221, 334). Central government provided specific funds for the substantial numbers of EAL teachers and multicultural curriculum advisers who either worked peripatetically from an LEA base or were stationed in particular schools, but for the most part, control over education spending was delegated from central government to LEAs (Bourne 1989).[2] LEA services came under the auspices of local government – the metropolitan, county and borough councils – and accountability to the local electorate encouraged dialogue about education with the representatives of ethnic minorities in areas where they constituted a significant proportion of the local vote. These groups were themselves often vocal in the expression of their educational concerns and expectations: many were relatively well established in the industrial workforce, were sympathetic to the labour movement (Goulbourne 1998:84, Ramdin 1987:362) and could draw on discourses of equality and rights that had been successful in relatively recent struggles for colonial independence. Political arrangements such as these made education policy development a matter of persuasion and dispute, and spurred on by the urban riots of 1981, one of the Swann Report's central objectives was to generate a view of ethnic pluralism with which central and local government, teaching unions and minority communities could all concur.

What kind of view was this? Swann offered a vision of nested communities within the framework of the nation-state: Britain as a community of communities, engaged in the process of reconciling itself to the legacy of its imperial past. For the most part, the Report conceptualised its ethnic minorities as well known, well defined, settled and stable, and it made light of any connections that they might seek to maintain with other parts of the world. It focussed primarily on people of Caribbean and South Asian descent (DES 1985:649), drawing on specially commissioned reviews of the substantial research on these groups (Taylor 1981, Taylor & Hegarty 1985). It dismissed a European Directive on the teaching of minority languages on the grounds that these groups were British and here to stay; it described their thoughts of living in other countries as the '*myth* of an alternative' and the '*myth* of return' (DES 1985:20–1); and it was in local social services rather than in world markets that minority language proficiency was envisaged as being useful (DES 1985:409–10). Similarly, the Report's discussion of the mass media, TV and press looked no further than the British nation-state (DES 1985:16ff. & 38–44).

---

[2] In 1970, there were just under 150 LEAs in England.

The educational strategy that the Swann Committee proposed consisted of three basic elements. First, any linguistic and cultural disadvantage that minorities were suffering should be overcome, e.g. through the teaching of English as a second language. Second, *all* children, minority *and* majority, should be encouraged to respect the richness of minority cultures. Third and most consequentially for the teaching of languages other than English, there should be no ethnic segregation within the public schooling system. Not only should all EAL teaching take place in the mainstream classroom there could also be no provision through the medium of languages other than English, since 'both bilingual education and mother tongue maintenance can only be of relevance to mother tongue speakers of languages other than English, i.e. to pupils from certain ethnic minority groups' (1985:406–7). Schools and LEAs were encouraged to provide resources to assist the mother-tongue classes organised by local communities after hours and at weekends, but within the state school system itself, sustained bilingual provision risked social fragmentation. To help 'overcome the trauma... of entering an English speaking environment', some transitional bilingual support could be provided for very young pupils entering school for the first time (pp. 406–7), and in the final years of schooling minority languages could form a part of the exam curriculum in modern foreign languages (1985:412–13). Even so, in infant classes, bilingual support staff should serve as a resource for everyone, and exam classes in minority languages should be open to all. The role of state schools was to eliminate segregation and disadvantage, and to ensure that everyone shared in whatever benefits minority students brought with them. Rather than cultivating any specialised cultural or linguistic resources that ethnic minorities might have, the Swann Report sought in effect to *nationalise* them (*Education for* All).

The Swann Report was written against a background of considerable contestation over ethnicity and race, and was published during the ascendance of Thatcherism, not long after the war in the Falklands/Malvinas and a landslide Conservative general election victory in 1983. In certain respects – in the frontal engagement with racism and the insistence that minorities belonged – it stands out as an important liberal text. In other respects, it said much less than it might, and the refusal to countenance any sustained bilingual education in the state school system was widely criticised by those involved in the teaching of ethnic minority languages (NCMTT 1985). Here, however, we are less concerned with its strengths and weaknesses than with the glimpse it gives of the educational and political landscape just prior to the transformations associated with globalisation and neo-liberal market capitalism. It is to these transformations that we should now turn.

Globalisation

In the Swann Report, the nation-state was the supreme political entity, but this is now challenged by the processes associated with globalisation. Flows of people, finance, technologies and communications media criss-cross national borders (Appadurai 1990), and it is increasingly hard for the state to exercise effective authority within its traditional territory (Abercrombie & Warde *et al.* 2000:15). Instead, it comes under increasing pressure to act as the hopeful host to transnational business, seeking to attract inward invest-ment by offering a secure and stable environment, an abundance of skilled low-wage labour, and limited state regulation (Bauman 1998).

There have also been major changes in the nature of migrant labour. Particularly in the 1950s, 1960s and 1970s, Britain encouraged the inward flow and settlement of new peoples who were needed to work in the manufacturing, transport and health sectors where the recruitment of indigenous labour was proving difficult (Rose *et al.* 1969), and this led to the emergence of the relatively stable, vocal, working-class ethnic com-munities that Swann was primarily concerned with. More recently in the 1990s, however, massive political upheavals, including the collapse of the Soviet Union and the 'Eastern Bloc', have produced a dramatic growth of unofficial immigration, both in Britain and across Europe and Asia (Papastergiadis 2000:48). In the UK, there has been a very large increase in people seeking asylum,[3] and there are also very substantial numbers without work and residence permits: 'in practice, such people either exist in limbo, outside state benefits and employment, or else are eventually granted some status due to the passage of time' (Fiddick 1999:13). They also tend to be politically voiceless: 'there is a strong incentive for those who are here illegally to keep as low a profile as possible, and avoid unnecessary contact with Government agencies' (Grabiner 2000:17). At the same time, global capitalism has altered the conditions for more established minority ethnic groups. For people who migrated during the 1950s, 1960s and 1970s, jobs in the UK might have been low paid, but initially anyway, they were reasonably secure, and the prohibitive costs of international travel encouraged them to build a congenial milieu in their local vicinities. In recent years, however, global market capitalism has changed this, so that 'after transferring location, people are able to main-tain instantaneous links with their point of origin through media and

---

[3] Asylum applications in UK from 1985–88 averaged about 4,000 a year, whereas in 1998 there were 46,000 applications (Watson & McGregor 1999). In 1998, the British Home Office estimated that it had an outstanding backlog of 93,000 asylum seeker cases (Fiddick 1999:10).

communications systems, strengthening the capacity of migrants to manage their own diasporic identities while resisting full assimilation into the new nation' (Marginson 1999:2).

In Swann's conception, 'minority' status was historically linked, either in actuality or in public perception, to forms of disadvantage that could be best remedied by migrants' full participation in the nation-state. In an age of global flows, however, there can be distinct benefits to diaspora membership, and social identity can become much more 'deterritorialised':

Members of diaspora are almost by definition more mobile than people who are rooted in national spaces... In the age of globalisation, their language skills, familiarity with other cultures and contacts in other countries make many members of diasporas highly competitive in the international labour, service and capital markets... What nineteenth-century nationalists wanted was a 'space' for each 'race', a territorialising of each social identity. What they have got instead is a chain of cosmopolitan cities and an increasing proliferation of subnational and transnational identities that cannot easily be contained in the nation-state system. (Cohen 1997:168–98, 175)

The cosmopolitan or 'global' cities mentioned by Cohen serve as centres of finance, transport and communications, and as such, they are inhabited by populations that are both highly diverse and highly stratified, as can be seen in major regional variations in England. In the late 1990s in the north-east of England, 2.6 percent of pupils in maintained primary schools were described as belonging to ethnic minorities, and in the south-west, the figure was 2.7 percent. In contrast, the figures for Inner London were 56.5 percent, Outer London 31.2 percent, and the West Midlands 15.9 percent (DfEE 1999). The linguistic consequences for schools are shown in a recent survey of the languages of London's schoolchildren (Baker & Eversley 2000:5), which states that in Greater London the range of home languages spans more than 350 language names, with English dominant amongst 67.86 percent of the 850,000 schoolchildren surveyed. At the same time, wealth and income differentials are also sharper in London than anywhere else in the UK (Abercrombie, Warde et al. 2000:126). On the one hand, it is a home for cosmopolitan elites, professionals and business people, while on the other, there are large numbers of people working in low-skilled, low-paid jobs, often in a substantial hidden economy[4] (see also Hannerz 1996:129–31, Cohen 1997:167–9).

---

[4] See Grabiner (2000): 'It would be impractical to arrive at a precise and meaningful figure as to the scale [of the hidden economy]. For the purposes of this report, I have assumed that the hidden economy... involv[es] billions of pounds, and in view of what I have learned in conducting this review, I am quite sure this assumption is a reasonable one... Typically, businesses in the informal economy tend to be low-wage and labour-intensive, often with a

World cities of this kind aren't merely 'nodes in networks' however. They are also places in themselves, settings for the juxtaposition and mixing of different cultural traditions in a range of different and distinctive combinations. Ethnic and cultural differences are highly salient, and subculturally specific resources – food, dress, music, speech – can be aestheticised and/or commodified, used in artistic production or sold commercially to a wide range of different consumers and not just to tourists and the transnational elite. As a point where a plurality of different transnational and diaspora flows intersect, this is an environment that generates high levels of local meta-cultural learning and awareness (cf. Hannerz 1996:135–7, Portes 1997), and although there will be different combinations and processes in different locations, this produces a post-colonial experience 'defined, not by essence or purity, but by the recognition of a necessary heterogeneity and diversity; by a conception of "identity" which lives with and through, not despite, difference; by *hybridity*' (Hall 1990:235–6).[5] Hall goes on to quote the cultural critic Kobena Mercer:

The subversive force of this hybridizing tendency is most apparent at the level of language itself where creoles, patois and Black English decenter, destabilize and carnivalize the linguistic domination of 'English' – the nation-language of master-discourse – through strategic inflections, reaccentuations and other performative moves in semantic, syntactic and lexical codes. (1988:57)

We will return to the linguistic dimension of these processes in due course. But before that, we need to consider the ways in which state education has participated in these shifts.

Changes in language education policy and provision since 1985

Three years after the publication of Swann, the Conservative government embarked on a major programme of educational reform, bringing in the Education Reform Act (ERA) in 1988. The policy initiated in ERA can be summarised as neo-liberal market economics combined with cultural authoritarianism, and overall, it had a negative impact on the language education of multilingual pupils.

The 'Local Management of Schools' – 'LMS' – was one of the corner-stones of the new policy, and it paved the way for a major shift of power

seasonal or irregular element to their work. Examples include: domestic service, household building, taxis and mini-cabs, market trading, tourism, hotels and catering, agriculture and fishing, fashion and clothing manufacture' (2000:3, 4).

[5] See, for example, Qureshi & Moores (1999) on Glasgow, Sansone (1995) on Amsterdam, Auer & Dirim (2003) on Hamburg, Heller (1999) on Toronto. On processes within the UK, closely connected to Hall's (1988) 'new ethnicities' framework, see also Mercer (1994) and Gilroy (1987, 1993).

away from Local Education Authorities to individual schools, with the result that by the year 2000, 82% of the money spent on schools was controlled by head teachers and school governors, compared with around 5% in 1990 (Audit Commission 2000). As part of this process, the responsibility for spending on pupils in need of support with EAL shifted from LEAs to local schools, so that rather than being able to call on an LEA service that was provided free of charge, schools had to plan for EAL support in their own budgets and to pay the LEA to provide them with specialist teachers. EAL provision wasn't mandatory, and with a lot of other competing financial priorities, there were inevitable pressures on schools to reduce EAL expenditure.

At the same time as market principles like this were introduced to the way specialist resources were distributed, creating a competitive 'internal market' among schools and LEAs within state education, responsibility for the design and specification of the curriculum for 5- to 16-year-olds was centralised. Individual teachers and schools were no longer the principal curriculum decision-makers, and the processes of persuasion and debate that the Swann Report had been tuned to were replaced by legislative coercion. A series of national working parties were set up for the 'core' curriculum areas of English, Maths and Science, as well as for a range of other subjects (though not EAL), and by the mid-1990s, a legally binding National Curriculum for 80% or more of the school day had been established, together with a system of national tests for 7-, 11- and 14-year-olds. These tests meant that the performance of children at different schools could be compared, and their publication in league tables was initiated and justified on the grounds that this was essential 'consumer information' for another new element in education policy, 'parental choice'. Prior to the 1988 ERA, children in the public education system had been allocated to a particular school by their LEA, but parental choice now gave parents the right to choose which school their child went to, with state funding following the child. In this way, a complex combination of marketisation and central control was developed. In order to survive, schools needed to attract parents, and they could vary their spending priorities in order to increase their competitiveness. But at the same time, central government dictated curriculum input and standardised the measurement of output (see Henry et al. 1999:89, Bernstein 1999:252).

These processes had an inevitable effect on schools' attitudes to pupils who were learning English as a second language. The league tables on school performance published raw data, and made no allowance for major differences between schools in their student intake. In this context, pupils from homes where English speaking was limited were increasingly seen as a threat to a school's public performance profile, depressing its published test scores, undermining its appeal to parents, and ultimately endangering its funding base. Whereas the Swann Report had called for inclusiveness, with the new market principles it was no longer in a school's interest to welcome refugee children and other newcomers to England.

These structural changes undermined the position articulated by Swann and they were accompanied by a number of major changes in the terms of debate. We describe some of these in the next section, but here it is worth noting that one of the factors widely judged to have helped the Conservatives win the 1987 general election was the so-called 'loony London effect', a perception that the Labour Party was dominated by London-based radicals who were committed to a dogmatic multiculturalism and who were antipathetic to the traditional values of Englishness. In other words, (what others later came to call) the 'global city' was deemed a political liability, and in its place, the hearts and minds of 'Middle England' became the main target of competition between the major political parties. At the same time, as the replacement of the phrase 'middle class' with 'Middle England' itself reflects, social class also became less and less of a reference point in public discourse.

This decline in the usability and salience of traditional notions of social class was partly the product of the economic restructuring attendant on globalisation.[6] But the disappearance of class from public discourse also fitted with the ascendance of two newer ideologies. On the one hand, the traditional association of class with collective solidarity, worker identities and the critique of capitalism was ill-suited to the new emphasis on individualism, consumption and the market. On the other, notions of long-standing class conflict and division were at odds with an increasingly influential strand of opinion which emphasised (high) national culture as a central unifying element in the new National Curriculum (e.g. Tate 1996). In practical terms, this meant that when particular groups continued to underachieve at school, the blame was shifted away from political economy – in which everyone was implicated, including the government – to culture, which laid responsibility with the underachievers themselves. In this way, the relatively poor performance of working-class boys became a problem of masculinity, while the disaffection of working-class boys of Caribbean descent was put down to ethnicity. Whereas the Swann Report made an effort to address the ways in which school achievement was influenced by both class and ethnicity together (DES 1985:71–6), Gillborn & Gipps'

---

[6] More specifically: the decline of area-based manufacturing industries like mining, steel and shipbuilding; the growth of the service sector; and with women and Black people almost 50% of all manual labour, a major shift in the demographic composition of the workforce (Abercrombie & Warde *et al.* 2000:167, Gilroy 1987:19, Reay 1998).

review of research noted in 1996 that 'data on social class is often absent from research ... [and] it is exceptional to find studies of achievement by ethnic minority pupils that give full attention to *both* these factors' (1996:16, Gillborn 1997:377–80, Gillborn & Mirza 2000).

In 1997, the Conservative government finally lost power after 17 years in which free market economics had been extended progressively further into the public sector. They were replaced by a 'New Labour' party that came to office determined to tackle social exclusion and to eradicate the 'long "tail" of underachievement in Britain, and [the] relatively poor performance from lower ability students' (Barber 1997:10). For the most part, however, this was not a return to class analysis,[7] and free market philosophies continued to dominate education policy. The state school system, it was said, had much to learn from private schools,[8] the 'discipline of the market' still played a major part in the relationship between LEAs, schools and parents, and indeed schools and LEAs deemed 'failing' were privatised and taken over by educational and other management companies.[9]

The technological dimensions of globalisation were given some recognition, and as part of the attempt to build a 'knowledge-driven society ... to succeed in this digital age' (Gordon Brown 16 February 2000), the New Labour government began to invest £1 billion over three years up to 2002 in the 'National Grid for Learning', a programme to equip every school with computer technology connected to the web. At the same time, however, a National Literacy Strategy (NLS) was instituted first in primary and then in secondary schools, and in many ways this seemed to intensify their predecessors' rejection of the cultural dynamics of globalisation. The new digital communications systems embrace a huge plurality of expressive forms, values, interests and imaginings, and many commentators – including the Prime Minister – have suggested that this new power presents a considerable challenge to the traditional authority of parents and teachers (see e.g. Castells 1996:374–5, Sefton-Green 1998:12, Holmes & Russell 1999). The NLS looked designed to reassert the kinds of authority that now felt threatened. The centrepiece of the NLS was the 'Literacy Hour' – an hour a day that all schools in England were pressured to dedicate to reading and writing (DfEE 1998) – and this not only dictated what to teach but also how, prescribing a minute-by-minute programme in which whole-class teaching – with pupils' eyes and ears tuned to the teacher – formed the main part

---

[7] See e.g. Barber: 'Whilst general societal factors (such as the status given to school learning or the prevalence of television viewing amongst adolescents) may be responsible for some of the poor British performance, most are agreed that the educational system bears the main responsibility' (1997:10).

[8] Cf. Estelle Morris, *Times Educational Supplement*, 6 October 2000.

[9] For example Hackney and Islington LEAs in London.

(two-thirds). In terms of content, the Literacy Hour assumed native English speaker knowledge of spoken language and cultural meaning. Pupils' attention was focussed on the basics of print literacy and Standard English grammar, and both the multi-modality of integrated communications systems and the heteroglossia and multilingualism of the global city were overwhelmingly ignored. It was confidently asserted that the NLS would 'facilitate [bilingual pupils'] acquisition of literacy' (DfEE 1997:34), but there was little evidence to support this claim, and subsequently it was tacitly accepted that pupils who spoke languages other than English might need more differentiated attention (DfES 2002a, Cameron 2003).

In the period after Swann, then, there were a number of major structural changes which substantially weakened the provision for teaching English as a second language. Through LMS and the delegation of specific purpose funds to schools, the market-inspired creation of a competitive environment led to the disbanding of specialist LEA language support teams in most local authorities, leaving EAL provision at the discretion of head teachers. League tables led to the stigmatisation of pupils with limited English, and EAL remained on the margins of the National Curriculum (Barwell 2004).

What of languages other than English? As already noted, the Swann Report rejected the idea of sustained educational provision through the medium of any other languages in England, and this rejection was reiterated in subsequent National Curriculum texts (e.g. DES 1989: para 10.1). Admittedly, there was legal provision for teaching of minority ethnic languages within the modern foreign language (MFL) curriculum in the last few years at secondary school, but the scope and success of this were inhibited: (a) by curriculum specifications which assumed a monolingual English starting point (Department for Education and Employment 1995:6–9); (b) by the absence of support for the development of pedagogies capable of responding to groups of pupils with mixed levels of proficiency; and (c) by the realities of local and national resourcing (see Stubbs 1991 [1994], Brumfit 1995a: Ch 8). Indeed, more generally, modern foreign language learning has tended to languish in the state school sector, and in 2000 an independent inquiry into the UK's future needs in MFL concluded that government had no coherent approach to modern language education; there was no planning for children to start other language learning early; almost all children stopped other language learning at the earliest opportunity; and that there was a desperate shortage of language teachers (Nuffield Foundation 2000).[10]

---

[10] Since this paper was written, government has decided that modern foreign languages should no longer be a compulsory element of the National Curriculum for pupils aged 14 and older.

Overall, then, since 1985, it is difficult to report any positive developments in state school provision for the needs and potentialities associated with multilingualism. *Outside* the mainstream sector, however, there has been a very tenacious voluntary commitment to the teaching of community languages amongst the minority communities themselves. Given the dearth of research in this field, it is difficult to be very specific about patterns of co-ordination, growth or decline in language teaching provision in the voluntary sector, but the most comprehensive database to date reveals at least 2,000 supplementary and mother-tongue projects across England, with the largest concentration in London (Kempadoo & Abdelrazak 2001). In fact, the Swann Report recommended that Local Education Authorities 'should offer support for community based language provision' (DES 1985:772), and in recent years, official interest in the sector appears to have increased (cf. e.g. Centre for Language Teaching and Research 1999:2, 2000:13). Many of the projects reported in this national database are in receipt of state funds, often channelled through LEAs, and the organisation producing this information, the Resource Unit for Supplementary and Mother-tongue Schools, has itself received funding from (among other sources) the DfES and the National Lottery Charities Board. The Resource Unit came into existence in the late 1990s and it points to a significant growth in the institutionalisation of the sector (Abdelrazak 2001),[11] although there is still a dearth of research on curriculum and pedagogy within these voluntary schools. But whatever the vicissitudes of state support and funding, there is clearly very substantial commitment to teaching minority/diaspora languages outside the state school system.

Otherwise, though, since the first edition of *Language in the British Isles*, there has been a deterioration in educational provision for pupils with a

---

[11] The Resource Unit singles out a number of LEAs (Tower Hamlets, Lewisham, Waltham Forest, Islington, Camden, Manchester and Birmingham) as being 'particularly impressive in that they had good support systems for and accurate information about the supplementary and mother-tongue schools in their areas' (Abdelrazak 2001: viii). Indeed, as well as a mother-tongue policy, the London Borough of Tower Hamlets has a Mother Tongue Unit which employs three full-time and one part-time staff, and from its location in the LBTH Education Directorate, the Unit manages the mother-tongue provision in the borough in partnership with both schools and community voluntary organisations. At least 100 part-time tutors are employed on permanent contracts to teach Bengali, Cantonese, Somali, Urdu and Vietnamese; some 3,000 children aged 5–16 attend these classes (Tower Hamlets Education nd.); and in the year 2001–2002 this provision spanned 54 Tutor Funded and Grant Aided Mother Tongue Projects (Mother Tongue Service 2001). Tower Hamlets LEA has also been involved in producing a Curriculum Framework for Mother Tongue Teaching in Bengali (Ali & McLagan 1998), and the local Further Education College now runs a 35-hour part-time accredited course, the Certificate in Teaching Community Languages (Tower Hamlets College 2001).

family knowledge of other languages in England, and in a spirit of reflexivity, it is worth asking what part linguistics played in this. In her 1984 paper on roughly the same subject, Martin-Jones certainly wasn't overoptimistic about the future, noting that 'the overall picture of provision within the [English] mainstream education system is discouraging' (p. 436). Even so, she was able to report a flurry of official interest and government-funded research that far exceeds anything that has been witnessed since. So we need to ask: where did research on language stand during the decline we have charted? How come the research on multilingualism lost so much ground?

The role of linguistic research in the ideological debates about language education

During the educational restructuring described above, both language and language education were major political issues, providing the focus for intense dispute between (a) a broadly liberal coalition of teachers, local government, teaching unions, researchers and academics, and (b) back-to-basics conservatives (central government, its policy advisers, and much of the national media) calling for grammar, standards and a return to traditional teaching methods.[12] With the benefit of hindsight, there seem to be at least two major flaws in research on multilingualism during the 1980s which weakened its value as a resource for resisting the pressure to return to monolingual basics.

First – like much research elsewhere in sociolinguistics and the social sciences (Gilroy 1987, Rampton 1998, 1999) – research on multilingualism during the late 1970s and 1980s tended to assume (i) that a person's ethnolinguistic identity was fixed in place during their early years at home and in their local community, and (ii) that this home-based ethnicity was likely to be the most important aspect of their identity. 'Ethnic absolutism' of this kind underlay the Swann Report, and it was generally tied to a vision of multilingualism in which languages, cultures and communities were seen as clearly bounded, relatively homogeneous and principally preoccupied either with maintaining or losing their ethnic distinctiveness (cf. 'Education, language and ethnicity' above; Rampton 1995a: Ch 13, 1998, 1999, Harris 1997, 1999). Unfortunately, an idiom like this is limited in the purchase it provides on the cultural and demographic processes associated with globalisation, and it is very difficult to make

---

[12] The division into two camps somewhat simplifies the lines of argument and allegiance over this period, but space prevents a fuller account. But see Bernstein (1996: Chapter 3) and e.g. Cameron and Bourne (1988), Stubbs (1991 [1994]), Cox (1995), Brumfit (1995b), Cameron (1995: Chapter 3), Rampton, Leung & Harris (1997), Brumfit (2001:65–78).

sense of flows and mixing, diaspora and deterritorialisation if notions like 'community' and 'authenticity' serve as the conceptual lodestars (Harris & Rampton 2002). Essentialism like this made it very hard for educationalists to recognise the emergence of new ethnicities and hybridised sociolinguistic varieties identified by Hall & Mercer (see 'Globalisation' above), and they were not helped to do so by the fact that during this period, language research overwhelmingly relied on surveys and self-report (Martin-Jones 1984:431, Rosen & Burgess 1980:43, LMP 1985, Alladina & Edwards 1991:11). Describing one's own multilingualism is not necessarily easy, and spontaneous interaction can often involve subtle mixings and renegotiations of identity that can be hard to reflect on explicitly, that one may want not to admit to, and that short descriptive labels inevitably reify and treat simplistically (cf. Hewitt 1986:7–8). Research on the data of spoken interaction can be crucial in moderating these oversimplifications, and its scarcity and absence from public discussion meant that later on in the late 1980s and early 1990s, the prevailing ideas about ethnicity were ill-equipped to challenge the cultural essentialism that legitimated the policy of Welsh being promoted by the Welsh state, English by the English state, and minority languages being largely left to the minority communities.[13]

Second, the capacity of language education research to contest deteriorating provision for bilingual pupils was limited by the absence of adequate tools for the assessment of proficiency in English. Due to a long-standing lack of both standardisation and validity in ESL/EAL assessment (combined with an absence of central support) (CRE 1986, OFSTED 1994, Leung 1995), there was – and still is – a major scarcity of any research which used robust methods – methods capable of persuading the sceptical outsider – to test the levels of the linguistic proficiency produced by different pedagogies and forms of provision. Classroom processes were certainly investigated in a number of local and national language curriculum development projects in the 1980s,[14] but as with a great deal of action

[13] In research on young people of Caribbean descent, actual language use *was* analysed, and this did draw attention to diaspora language forms and to new mixed urban cultures that challenged the very basis of official ethnic classification. But the impact of this work was inhibited by a marked tendency to separate issues related to Caribbean language from other minority languages (e.g. DES 1989: Ch 10; see Rampton 1983, 1988, 1995a for critiques). This differentiation of African-Caribbean from other minority pupils obscured the new alignments developing in the complex interaction of locality, class, generation, gender and ethnicity in English cities, and in the official view, other minorities continued to be viewed as politely treated but rather peripheral strangers until the time that they assimilated.

[14] These often entailed teacher action research with a strong interest in multilingualism (cf. Bourne 1989:113). Through first-hand experience, they enabled participants to assess the value of different kinds of language pedagogy; they were the form of educational innovation most likely to have an immediate impact on pupils; they moved towards an

research, they did not produce claims supported by a body of evidence – a body of publicly recognisable 'facts' – that was capable of withstanding the scrutiny of unsympathetic outsiders, and beyond their articulation within the broad tenets of 'good practice',[15] they were not elaborated into a theoretical framework capable of systematic comparative examination (Brumfit 1995b:39). All of this meant that when EAL provision was radically affected by the structural shifts brought in by the 1988 Education Reform Act, there was no basis in research for arguing against – or indeed in favour of – these changes.

Those, then, are two major weaknesses specific to research on multilingualism which might help to explain why it became increasingly peripheral to the main currents of educational change after the first edition of *Language in the British Isles*. But analysis of worsening provision for bilingual pupils also needs to reckon with a more profound and more extensive shift in the notions of language that education-oriented researchers worked with.

The research and curriculum development work reported by Martin-Jones in 1984 generally emphasised the intimate relationship between language and identity, and it aspired to a curriculum that would be hospitable to a plurality of home languages, developing pupils' abilities by building organically on the minority ethnic languages that they brought to school. As in the debates about linguistic deficit and non-standard English that slightly pre-dated this growth of interest in minority languages (e.g. Trudgill 1975), researchers adopted a stance that tuned with the 1975 Bullock Report:

No child should be expected to cast off the language and culture of the home as he crosses the school threshold ... Every school with pupils whose original language is not English should adopt a positive attitude to their bilingualism and wherever possible help maintain and deepen their knowledge of their mother-tongue. (DES 1975: para 20.5, 20.17) (cited in Martin-Jones 1984:428)

In the period that followed, however, there was a distinct movement away from approaches which privileged the ties between language, home culture and identity, towards a perspective which treated language as a determinate object, as an autonomous code, that could be defined, broken down into parts, and imparted to everyone in the mainstream curriculum.

ideal of flexible multilingual pedagogy hospitable to the diversity of pupils' language backgrounds and proficiencies (Bourne 1989:63–4); and the reports they provided could be persuasive for colleagues.

[15] Notions of 'good practice' loosely drew in ideas from first language acquisition, process writing, communicative methodology and collaborative teaching (CRE 1986: Appendix 7, Bourne 1989:63–4, Blair & Bourne 1998).

'Mother tongue' was a key term in the 1970s and early to mid-1980s,[16] but from the late 1980s onwards, 'Standard English' became the central emblem. The first sign of this shift away from 'hospitality to diversity' came with the Kingman Committee, which was set up in 1987 to 'recommend a model of the English language as a basis for teacher training and professional discussion, and to consider how far and in what ways that model should be made explicit to pupils at various stages of education' (DES 1988:1). And over time, grammar, text and discourse came to be seen as the dimensions of linguistic knowledge most relevant for teachers, downgrading sociolinguistic variability and the links between language, culture and social group identity.[17]

What could account for this change? At least three influences can be identified. First, this movement synchronised with the much wider cultural shift in education that Bernstein has identified. The last 10 to 15 years have seen a major shift away from what Bernstein identifies as 'competence' theories towards what he calls 'performance' models (perhaps a little confusingly). From the 1960s until relatively recently, 'competence' theories were influential in education, in sociolinguistics and in the social sciences more generally, and in varying degrees, they involved a belief in:

1. a universal democracy of acquisition. All are inherently competent. There is no deficit;
2. the individual as *active* and *creative* in the construction of a *valid* world of meaning and practice . . .;
3. a celebration of everyday, oral language use and a suspicion of specialised languages;
4. official socialisers are suspect, for acquisition is a tacit, invisible act, not subject to public regulation or, perhaps, not primarily acquired through such regulation;
5. a critique of hierarchical relations, where domination is replaced by facilitation and imposition by accommodation (Bernstein 1996:150; see Rampton 1999 and Leung 2001 for elaborations).

These assumptions tuned with the dominance at the time of liberal child-centred pedagogy; they coincided with the respect for home languages enunciated by Bullock; and in the Swann Report, their influence could be seen both in the rejection of segregated EAL teaching, and in the importance attached to valuing – if not actually teaching – ethnic minority

---

[16] On problems with 'mother tongue' and 'native speaker', see Rampton (1995a:336–44) and Leung, Harris & Rampton (1997).

[17] This can be seen in a comparison of, for example, Stubbs (1983) and Carter (1992) (cf. Rampton 1995b:236–7).

languages. During the late 1980s and 1990s, however, there was a shift towards 'performance' models in education, with an emphasis on product rather than process, on carefully graded inputs from the teacher, on the specific texts and skills the learner was expected to produce and acquire, and on the extent to which the learner matched these (in performance models, evaluation focusses on what's missing and deviance is highly visible). Crucially, Bernstein argues for a profound compatibility between performance models and the requirements of a market economy. Where competence models favoured tacit socialisation and privileged the collective affiliations and the inherited social identities that students bring to school, performance models easily lend themselves to instrumental training, and are inclined to see the acquisition of target knowledge as a matter of individual ability and choice. In sum, this has been a shift in pedagogy that has moved in step with the wider market transformation of the education system, and Standard English has provided a far more tractable linguistic base for this than community languages.

Second, there were a number of more specific factors within the linguistics academy that contributed to this change in the working notions of language. During the 1980s, there had been an explosion of research interest in discourse analysis, and this overtook the study of dialect variation as a major focus of interest in British sociolinguistics. Beyond that, the linguistic background of socio- and applied linguists was itself no doubt a factor. Most linguists had much richer sociolinguistic intuitions – visceral instincts, indeed – about Standard English than they did about, say, Panjabi or Turkish, and among linguists as in the general public, Standard English served as a potent, condensed and multivalent symbol during the late 1980s and 1990s, eliciting intense interest from conservatives, liberals and radicals alike, either as the unifying core of national identity, as the carrier of a great national tradition, as the prerequisite for national economic efficiency, as the starting base for social mobility, equality of opportunity and democratic participation, or as the hegemonic tool of the social elite (see Stubbs 1986:64–97, DES 1989: 4.32). In addition, growing emphasis on grammar and linguistic structure consolidated the shift of interest from minority languages to English. When language education theory stressed the communicative significance of audience and purpose, diaspora languages might be accommodated in the curriculum by focussing on e.g. code-switching, but as soon as the focus turned to the more detailed structural features of language code, English inevitably moved into the foreground, since the overwhelming majority of researchers, teachers and pupils in England could neither speak nor write in British minority languages, and there was no mainstream educational provision to encourage or to teach them to do so.

Third, government influence and action also played a crucial part in the shift in emphasis from 'identity' to 'structure' in language. In the late 1980s and early 1990s, the Conservative government evidently found grammar, text and discourse more digestible as foci within language study than ethnolinguistic-diversity-&-social-group-identity, the former being much more easily accommodated within its mixed ideological commitment to back-to-basics fundamentalism, meritocratic individualism and the needs of industry (see above). And ultimately, whenever disputes developed between government and academic linguists, government had legislative force in the new centralised education system at its disposal, and it didn't hesitate to redraft or indeed finally to censor the expert advice that it commissioned. Direct intervention took its most spectacular form in 1991 when the government refused to allow the publication of training materials developed by the LINC Project, objecting, among other things, to a chapter on multilingualism (Abrams 1991), and asking, in the words of the minister of state: 'Why . . . so much prominence [is] given to exceptions rather than the norm – to dialects rather than standard English, for example . . . Of course, language is a living force, but our central concern must be the business of teaching children how to use their language correctly' (Eggar 1991).

Admittedly, there were some elements in the curriculum that eventually emerged that linguistics researchers could approve and indeed take some pride in. But it is hard to see how these changes benefited pupils who knew languages other than English. Plainly, there was nothing in any of these changes which boosted their opportunities to develop oral and literate proficiency in diaspora/minority languages, but neither was there very much to benefit students who were in the relatively early stages of learning English. The *mainstream* curriculum for English might have drawn on linguistic analyses that treated grammar and discourse as relatively alien objects – as structures and codes that needed to be explicitly taught, and that students could not be expected to acquire 'by osmosis' – but throughout the 1990s, there was no centrally co-ordinated attempt to produce an explicit language curriculum that was systematically tuned to the needs of early or intermediate learners.[18] Britain is still only at an incipient stage of debate about the contribution that functional grammar and genre analysis might make to the 'good practice' approach to teaching English as an additional language that dominated the 1980s, with its emphasis on pupils participating in the mainstream, on classroom organisation, and on very general communicative processes (Barrs 1991/92, Leung 1996, 1997,

---

[18] Contrast the much more sustained and elaborate approach developed in Australia (Mohan, Leung & Davison 2001).

Leung & Franson 1991, DfEE 2001b). There is still no reliable educational assessment specifically concerned with the performance and abilities of pupils learning English as an additional language (SCAA 1996:30–1); EAL lacks recognised subject discipline status; and there is no systematic initial teacher education in EAL as a main subject. Instead, in spite of constituting a student group which really could gain from some explicit instruction in the linguistic and discursive structures of English, learners of EAL have been rather left to languish in an enfeebled afterglow from the Swann Report (Leung 2001).

Conclusion

In England in the 20 years after 1985, the landscape described by the Swann Report was transformed by globalisation and by a period of massive educational restructuring. Globalisation profoundly affected the contours of multilingualism in ways that we are still struggling to comprehend, but the restructuring involved a substantial reduction in the levels of educational support for multilinguals. Applied and socio-linguistic research concerned with linguistic diversity had little effect as a counterweight to this deterioration in state educational provision, and mother-tongue was replaced by Standard English as the main linguistic idea in official thinking.

But growing official indifference to multilingualism did not put a stop to linguistic research in this area. Generally speaking, there was a move *away* from the increasingly constrained and ill-funded arena of central government-sponsored policy research (Pettigrew 1992) *towards* a more congenial involvement with local, regional and professional groups/organisations where an active commitment to multilingualism still remained.[19] Substantively, the 1990s saw a major increase in the description of everyday interaction, and much more attention was given to the linguistic and cultural knowledge-and-practices operating in multilingual social networks, and to the ideologies of the dominant institutional theories, policies or practices that multilinguals regularly engaged with.[20] Space limitations

---

[19] See, for example, the contributions to professional journals like *English in Education, Language Matters, Language Issues, The English and Media Magazine, NALDIC News,* as well as e.g. Verma *et al.* (1995), Clegg (1996), and the special edition of *Language Issues* 8.1 1996 – 'Sheffield the Multilingual City'.

[20] Although there were still some very impressive multilingualism surveys (e.g. Alladina & Edwards 1991, Baker & Eversley 2000, Kempadoo & Abdelrazak 2001), this general shift from surveys to more fine-grained ethnographic and discourse analytic research was also principled, motivated both by a sense of the explanatory limits of the surveys that dominated the 1980s (Nicholas 1994, Martin-Jones 1991), and by a desire to find out what actually happened inside multilingual settings (Martin-Jones 1995:90).

prevent a detailed listing (though see Rampton, Leung & Harris 1997, Rampton, Harris & Leung 2002), but there are now significant bodies of work focussing on:

- *interactional styles*, in work and bureaucratic settings, in pupil–teacher interaction and in literacy acquisition (e.g. Bremer, Roberts, Vasseur, Simonot & Broeder 1996, Creese 2000, Gregory & Williams 2000a);
- *multilingual literacies* (e.g. Martin-Jones & Jones 2000);
- *code-switching*, in infant school, family and informal adolescent settings (e.g. Martin-Jones & Saxena 1996, Li Wei 1994, Sebba 1993);
- *language crossing* (the use of diaspora/minority languages by ethnic outgroups – e.g. Hewitt 1986, Rampton 1995a);
- *language awareness* (Harris *et al.* 1990, Bhatt & Martin-Jones 1992);
- *EAL assessment* (Teasdale & Leung 2000, Rea-Dickins 2001).

Admittedly, as yet, there is comparatively little detailed observational research on:

- multilingualism in the later years of compulsory education (ages 11–16), when the tension between the values and priorities of formal education and vernacular culture is sharpest;
- the new multiethnic urban vernaculars,
- developmental trajectories in EAL;
- diaspora language teaching in community classes outside the state sector, and the reproduction of language traditions within minority communities more generally.

Indeed, even though the people studied are often at the front line of globalisation and contemporary culture, operating every day at the intersection of neighbourhood and nation-state, diaspora and global markets, there is still a great deal of work to be done in linking empirical research on multilingualism to wider debates about late modernity in the humanities and social sciences (see Hewitt 1995, Harris, Leung & Rampton 2001, Harris & Rampton 2002). Nevertheless, our knowledge of multilingualism in England is far deeper and more extensive than it was when the first edition of this volume was published, and if/when/as state education opens up to multilingualism, it will find a substantial body of research to engage with, as well as some clear and purposeful policy principles to think with, addressing language in the round (Brumfit 1995a:9–15, 2001:78–84).

References

Abdelrazak, M. (2001). *Towards More Effective Supplementary and Mother-tongue Schools (in England) (2nd edn)*. London: Resource Unit for Supplementary & Mother-tongue Schools.

Abercrombie, D. (1967). *Elements of General Phonetics*. Edinburgh: Edinburgh University Press.

Abercrombie, N. & A. Warde, with R. Deem, S. Penna, K. Soothill, J. Urry, A. Sayer & S. Walby. (2000). *Contemporary British Society (3rd edn)*. Oxford: Polity.

Abrams, F. (1991). Accents and dialects still unmentionable subjects. *Times Educational Supplement*, 14 June.

Acton, T. A. (1989). The value of 'creolized' dialects of Romanes. In S. Bali et al. (eds.) *Jezik i Kultura Roma*. Sarajevo. Inst. za Proučavanje Nacionalnih Odnosa. 169–80.

Acton, T. A. & D. Kenrick. (1984). *Romani Rokkeripen To Divvus. The English Romani Dialect and its Contemporary Social, Educational and Linguistic Standing*. London: Romanestan Publications.

Adams, G. B. (1965). Materials for a language map of 17th century Ireland. *Ulster Dialect Archive Bulletin* 4: 15–30.

(1981). The voiceless velar fricative in northern Hiberno-English. In M. V. Barry (ed.) *Aspects of English Dialects in Ireland, Volume 1. Papers Arising from the Tape-Recorded Survey of Hiberno-English Speech*. Belfast: Institute of Irish Studies, Queen's University of Belfast. 106–17.

(1986a). Common [consonantal] features in Ulster Irish and Ulster English. In G. B. Adams (ed.) *The English Dialects of Ulster*. Cultra: Ulster Folk and Transport Museum. 105–12.

(1986b). Phonological notes on the English of south Donegal. In G. B. Adams (ed.) *The English Dialects of Ulster*. Cultra: Ulster Folk and Transport Museum. 97–104.

Adams, G. B., M. V. Barry & P. M. Tilling. (1985). The tape-recorded survey of Hiberno-English speech: a reappraisal of the techniques of traditional dialect geography. In J. M. Kirk, S. Sanderson & J. D. A. Widdowson (eds.) *Studies in Linguistic Geography. The Dialects of English in Britain and Ireland*. London: Croom Helm. 67–80.

Adams, J. N. (2003). *Bilingualism and the Latin Language*. Cambridge: Cambridge University Press.

Adger, D. & J. Smith. (2005). Variation and the minimalist program. In L. Cornips & K. Corrigan (eds.) *Syntax and Variation: Reconciling the Biological and the Social*. Amsterdam: John Benjamins. 149–78.

Advisory Planning Committee. (1986). *Irish and the Education System: An Analysis of Examination Results*. Dublin: Bord na Gaeilge.

(1988). *The Irish Language in a Changing Society: Shaping the Future*. Dublin: Bord na Gaeilge.

Ager, D. E. (1996). *Language Policy in Britain and France: The Processes of Policy*. London: Cassell Academic.

(1999). *Identity, Insecurity and Image: France and Language*. Clevedon: Multilingual Matters.

(2003). *Ideology and Image: Britain and Language*. Clevedon: Multilingual Matters.

Agnihotri, R. K. (1979). *Processes of assimilation: a sociolinguistic study of Sikh children in Leeds*. Unpublished PhD dissertation. York: University of York.

(1987). *Crisis of Identity: The Sikhs in England*. New Delhi: Bahri Publications.

Agutter, A. (1988). The not-so-Scottish Vowel Length Rule. In J. Anderson & N. Macleod (eds.) *Edinburgh Studies in the English Language*. Edinburgh: John Donald, 120–32.

Agutter, A & I. N. Cowan (1981). Changes in the vocabulary of Lowland Scots dialects. *Scottish Literary Journal Supplement* 14: 49–62.

Ahlqvist, A. (1988). Remarks on the question of dialects in Old Irish. In J. Fisiak (ed.) *Historical Dialectology: Regional and Social*. Berlin: de Gruyter. 23–38.

(2002). Cleft sentences in Irish and other languages. In M. Filppula, J. Klemola & H. Pitkänen (eds.) *The Celtic Roots of English*. Joensuu: University of Joensuu, Faculty of Humanities. 271–81.

Aitchison, J. & H. Carter. (2000). *Language, Economy and Society*. Cardiff: University of Wales Press.

Aitken, A. J. (1984a). Scottish accents and dialects. In P. Trudgill (ed.) *Language in the British Isles*. Cambridge: Cambridge University Press. 94–114.

(1984b). Scots and English in Scotland. In P. Trudgill (ed.) *Language in the British Isles*. Cambridge: Cambridge University Press. 517–32.

Ali, A. & P. McLagan. (1998). *Curriculum Framework for Mother Tongue Teaching in Bengali*. London: CILT/Tower Hamlets Education.

Alinei, M. (1997). *Atlas Linguarum Europae. Perspectives Nouvelles en Géolinguistique*. Roma: Istituto Poligrafico.

Alladina, S. (1993). South Asian Languages in Britain. In G. Extra & L. Verhoeven (eds.) *Immigrant Languages in Europe*. Clevedon: Multilingual Matters. 55–66.

Alladina, S. & V. Edwards. (1991). *Multilingualism in the British Isles. Two Volumes*. London: Longman.

Alleyne, M. (1980). *Comparative Afro-American*. Ann Arbor: Karoma Press.

Altendorf, U. (2003). *Estuary English: Levelling at the Interface of RP and South-Eastern British English*. Tübingen: Narr.

Ammon, U. (1998). Measuring the broadness of dialectal speech. *Sociolinguistica* 12: 194–207.

Andersen, G. (2001). *Pragmatic Markers and Sociolinguistic Variation: A Relevance-theoretic Approach to the Language of Adolescents.* Amsterdam: John Benjamins.

Anderwald, L. (2001). Was/were variation in non-standard British English today. *English World-Wide* 22 (1): 1–21.

　(2002). *Negation in Non-standard British English: Gaps, Regularizations, Asymmetries.* London: Routledge.

　(2003). Non-standard English and typological principles: the case of negation. In G. Rohdenburg & B. Mondorf (eds.) *Determinants of Grammatical Variation in English.* Berlin: Mouton de Gruyter. 508–529.

　(2004a). Local markedness as a heuristic tool in dialectology: the case of 'amn't'. In B. Kortmann (ed.) *Dialectology Meets Typology: Dialect Grammar from a Cross-linguistic Perspective.* Berlin: Mouton de Gruyter. 47–67.

　(2004b). The varieties of English spoken in the Southeast of England: morphology and syntax. In B. Kortmann, K. Burridge, R. Mesthrie, E. Schneider & C. Upton (eds.) *A Handbook of Varieties of English: Morphology and Syntax.* Berlin: Mouton de Gruyter. 175–95.

Andrews, L. S. (1991). The Irish language in the education system of Northern Ireland: some political and cultural perspectives. In R. M. Pritchard (ed.) *Motivating the Majority: Modern Languages in Northern Ireland.* Coleraine: Northern Ireland CILT. 89–106.

Anthias, F. (1992). *Ethnicity, Class, Gender and Migration: Greek Cypriots in Britain.* Aldershot: Avebury.

Appadurai, A. (1990). Disjuncture and difference in the global cultural economy. *Public Culture* 2: 1–24.

Ash, S. (2002). Social class. In J. Chambers, P. Trudgill & N. Schilling-Estes (eds.) *The Handbook of Language Variation and Change.* Oxford: Blackwell. 402–422.

Assinder N. (2005). Immigration to be an election issue. BBC News: 7 February. [http://news.bbc.co.uk/1/hi/uk_politics/4242451.stm – last accessed 11 February 2005].

Audit Commission. (2000). *Money Matters: School Funding and Resource Management.* London: Audit Office.

Auer, P. (1999). From codeswitching via language mixing to fused lects: toward a dynamic typology of bilingual speech. *International Journal of Bilingualism* 3: 309–332.

Auer, P. & I. Dirim. (2003). Socio-cultural orientation, urban youth styles and the spontaneous acquisition of Turkish by non-Turkish adolescents in Germany. In J. Androutsopoulos & A. Georgakopoulou (eds.) *Discourse Constructions of Youth Identities.* Amsterdam: John Benjamins. 223–46.

Awbery, G. (1976). *The Syntax of Welsh: A Transformational Study of the Passive.* Cambridge: Cambridge University Press.

　(1984). Phonotactic constraints in Welsh. In M. Ball & G. E. Jones (eds.) *Welsh Phonology.* Cardiff: University of Wales Press. 65–104.

　(1986). *Pembrokeshire Welsh.* Cardiff: National Museum of Wales.

Ayto, J. (1995). *The Oxford School A–Z of English.* Oxford: Oxford University Press.

Bailey, B. L. (1966). *Jamaican Creole Syntax: A Transformational Approach.* Cambridge: Cambridge University Press.

Bailey, C.-J. (1996). *Essays on Time-based Linguistic Analysis*. Oxford: Clarendon Press.

Bailey, R. W. (1991). *Images of English: A Cultural History of the Language*. Cambridge: Cambridge University Press.

Baker, H. D. R. (1968). *A Chinese Lineage Village*. Stanford: Stanford University Press.

(1979). *Chinese Family and Kinship*. New York: Columbia University Press.

Baker, J. P. (2002). *Polari: The Lost Language of Gay Men*. London: Routledge.

Baker, P. & J. Eversley (eds.) (2000). *Multilingual Capital: The Languages of London's Schoolchildren and their Relevance to Economic, Social and Educational Policies*. London: Battlebridge Publications.

Baker, P. & Y. Mohieldeen. (2000). The languages of London's schoolchildren. In P. Baker & J. Eversley (eds.) *Multilingual Capital: The Languages of London's Schoolchildren and their Relevance to Economic, Social and Educational Policies*. London: Battlebridge Publications. 5–60.

Bakker, P. (1998). Para-Romani languages versus secret languages: differences in origin, structure and use. In Y. Matras (ed.) *The Romani Element in Non-Standard Speech*. Wiesbaden: Harrassowitz Verlag. 69–96.

(2000). The genesis of Angloromani. In T. Acton (ed.) *Scholarship and the Gypsy Struggle: Commitment in Romani Studies: A Collection of Papers and Poems to Celebrate Donald Kenrick's Seventieth Year*. Hatfield: University of Hertfordshire Press. 14–31.

(2002). An early vocabulary of British Romani (1616): a linguistic analysis. *Romani Studies* 12 (2): 75–101.

Bakker, P. & M. Cortiade (eds.) (1991). *In the Margin of Romani: Gypsy Languages in Contact*. Amsterdam: Instituut voor Algemene Taalwetenschap.

Bakker, P. & M. Mous (eds.) (1994). *Mixed Languages. 15 Case Studies in Language Intertwining*. Amsterdam: IFOTT.

Balarajan, R. (1995). Ethnicity and variations in the nation's health. *Health Trends* 27: 114–19.

Balarajan, R., P. Yuen, V. Soni Raleigh. (1989). Ethnic differences in general practitioner consultations. *British Medical Journal* 299: 14 October.

Ball, M. J. (ed.) (1988). *The Use of Welsh*. Clevedon: Multilingual Matters.

Ball, M. J. & J. Fife. (eds.) (1993). *The Celtic Languages*. London: Routledge.

Ball, M. J. & G. E. Jones. (1984). *Welsh Phonology*. Cardiff: University of Wales Press.

Ball, M. J. & N. Müller. (1992). *Mutations in Welsh*. London: Routledge.

Ball, M. J. & B. Williams. (2001). *Welsh Phonetics*. Lewiston: Edwin Mellen Press.

Bannerman, J. (1974). *Studies in the History of Dalriada*. Edinburgh: Scottish Academic Press.

Barbé, P. (1994). Guernsey English: my mother tongue. *Report and Transactions of La Société Guernesiaise* 23/4: 700–23.

(1995). Guernsey English: a syntax exile? *English World-Wide* 16: 1–36.

Barber, C. (1964). *Linguistic Change in Present-day English*. Edinburgh and London: Oliver and Boyd.

Barber, M. (1997). *A Reading Revolution: How We can Teach Every Child to Read Well*. London: Institute of Education.

Barbour, S. (2000). Britain and Ireland: the varying significance of language for nationalism. In S. Barbour & C. Carmichael (eds.) *Language and Nationalism in Europe*. Oxford: Oxford University Press. 18–43.

Barbour, S. & C. Carmichael (eds.) (2000). *Language and Nationalism in Europe*. Oxford: Oxford University Press.

Barrs, M. (1991/92). Genre theory: what's it all about? *Language Matters* 1: 9–16.

Barry, M. V. (1981). The southern boundaries of Northern Hiberno-English speech. In M. V. Barry (ed.) *Aspects of English Dialects in Ireland, Volume 1. Papers Arising from the Tape-Recorded Survey of Hiberno-English Speech*. Belfast: Institute of Irish Studies, Queen's University of Belfast. 52–95.

(1982). The English language in Ireland. In R. W. Bailey & M. Görlach (eds.) *English as a World Language*. Ann Arbor: University of Michigan Press. 84–133.

(1984). Manx English. In P. Trudgill (ed.) *Language in the British Isles*. Cambridge: Cambridge University Press. 167–77.

Barwell, R. (2004). *Teaching Learners of English as an Additional Language: A Review of Official Guidance*. Watford: National Association for Language Development in the Curriculum.

Bathurst, B. (1996). A cute accent? *The Observer Review*, 24 March.

Bauer, L. & P. Trudgill. (1998). *Language Myths*. London: Penguin.

Baugh, A. C. & T. Cable. (1978). *A History of the English Language*. Boston: Routledge.

Bauman, Z. (1998). *Globalisation: The Human Consequences*. Oxford: Polity.

Beal, J. (1993). The grammar of Tyneside and Northumbrian English. In J. Milroy & L. Milroy (eds.) *Real English: The Grammar of English Dialects in the British Isles*. London: Longman. 187–213.

(1997). Syntax and morphology. In C. Jones (ed.) *The Edinburgh History of the Scots Language*. Edinburgh: Edinburgh University Press. 335–77.

(2004a). English dialects in the North of England: morphology and syntax. In B. Kortmann, K. Burridge, R. Mesthrie, E. Schneider & C. Upton (eds.) *A Handbook of Varieties of English: Morphology and Syntax*. Berlin: Mouton de Gruyter. 114–41.

(2004b). *English in Modern Times*. London: Arnold.

Beal, J. & K. Corrigan. (2002). Relatives in Tyneside and Northumbrian English. In P. Poussa (ed.) *Relativisation on the North Sea Littoral*. Munich: Lincom Europa. 125–34.

(2005). 'No, nay, never': negation in Tyneside English. In Y. Iyeiri (ed.) *Aspects of Negation in English*. Kyoto: University of Kyoto Press. 139–57.

Bell, A. (1984). Language style as audience design. *Language in Society* 13: 145–204.

Benedictus, L. (2005). Every race, colour, nation and religion on earth. *The Guardian*, 21 January. [http://www.guardian.co.uk/g2/story/0,3604,1395269,00.html – last accessed 10 February 2005].

Bennett, J. & G. Smithers. (1966). *Early Middle English Verse and Prose*. Oxford: Oxford University Press.

Bennett, L., S. Qutub & M. Bellis. (1998). *Improving the Health of Black and Ethnic Minority Communities: A North West of England Perspective*. Liverpool: University of Liverpool.

Bergin, O. (1943). Bróg 'shoe'. *Éigse* 3: 237–9.

Bernstein, B. (1971). *Class, Codes and Control, Volume 1: Theoretical Studies towards a Sociology of Language.* London: Routledge & Kegan Paul.

(1996). *Pedagogy, Symbolic Control and Identity: Theory, Research, Critique.* London: Taylor & Francis.

(1999). Official knowledge and pedagogic identities. In F. Christie (ed.) *Pedagogy and the Shaping of Consciousness.* London: Continuum. 246–61.

Bex, T. (1999). Representations of English in twentieth-century Britain: Fowler, Gowers and Partridge. In T. Bex & R. J. Watts (eds.) *Standard English: The Widening Debate.* London: Routledge. 89–109.

Bex, T. & R. J. Watts (eds.) (1999). *Standard English: The Widening Debate.* London: Routledge.

Bhatt, A. & M. Martin-Jones. (1992). Whose resource? Minority languages, bilingual learners and language awareness. In N. Fairclough (ed.) *Critical Language Awareness.* London: Longman. 285–302.

(1994). Gujarati literacies in East Africa and Leicester: changes in social identities and multilingual practices. *University of Lancaster, Centre for Language in Social Life, Working Paper Series* 56.

Bickerton, D. (1975). *Dynamics of a Creole System.* Cambridge: Cambridge University Press.

Bilton, L. (1982). A note on Hull intonation. *Journal of the International Phonetic Association* 12: 30–35.

Birt, P. (1985). *Lé Jèrriais Pour Tous. A Complete Course on the Jersey Language.* Jersey: Don Balleine.

Blackledge, A. (2000). Power relations and the social construction of 'literacy' and 'illiteracy'. In M. Martin-Jones & K. Jones (eds.) *Multilingual Literacies.* Amsterdam: John Benjamins. 55–69.

Blair, M. & J. Bourne. (1998). *Making a Difference: Teaching and Learning Strategies in Successful Multi-ethnic Schools.* Norwich: Department for Education and Employment.

Bliss, A. J. (1972). Languages in contact. Some problems of Hiberno-English. *Proceedings of the Royal Irish Academy.* Section C 72: 63–82.

(1976). The English language in early modern Ireland. In T. W. Moody, F. Martin and F. J. Byrne (eds.) *A New History of Ireland.* Oxford: Oxford University Press. 546–60.

(1977). The emergence of modern English dialects in Ireland. In D. Ó Muirithe (ed.) *The English Language in Ireland.* Cork: Mercier.

(1979). *Spoken English in Ireland 1600–1740. Twenty-seven Representative Texts Assembled and Analysed.* Dublin: Cadenus Press.

(1984). English in the south of Ireland. In P. Trudgill (ed.) *Language in the British Isles.* Cambridge: Cambridge University Press. 135–51.

Blunkett, D. (2002). Integration with diversity: globalisation and the renewal of democracy and civil society. In P. Griffith & M. Leonard (eds.) *Reclaiming Britishness.* London: The Foreign Policy Centre. 65–77.

Bond, M. (1991). *Beyond the Chinese Face.* Hong Kong: Oxford University Press.

Boretzky, N. (1985). Sind Zigeunersprachen Kreols? In N. Boretzky, W. Enninger & T. Stolz (eds.) *Akten des 1. Essener Kolloquiums über Kreolsprachen und Sprachkontakt.* Bochum: Brockmeyer. 43–70.

Boretzky, N. & B. Igla. (1994). Romani mixed dialects. In P. Bakker & M. Mous (eds.) *Mixed Languages. 15 Case Studies in Language Intertwining*. Amsterdam: IFOTT. 35–68.

Börjars, K. & C. Chapman. (1998). Agreement and pro-drop in some dialects of English. *Linguistics* 36: 71–98.

Borrow, G. (1874). *Romano lavo-lil. Word-Book of the Romany; or, English Gypsy Language*. London: John Murray.

Bottomley, K. (1996). *An evaluation of language policies relating to the use of Creole in the classroom*. Unpublished BSc dissertation. Huddersfield: Department of Geographical and Environmental Sciences, University of Huddersfield.

Bourne, J. (1989). *Moving into the Mainstream*. Windsor: NFER-Nelson.

Boyes-Braem, P. & R. Sutton-Spence (eds.) (2001). *The Hands are the Head of the Mouth: The Role of the Mouth in Sign Languages*. Hamburg: Signum Press.

Bradbury, M. (1996). It's goodbye Memsahib, hello Sheila. *Daily Mail*, 20 March.

Bradford Education. (1996). *Manningham in Context*. Bradford: Bradford Education Policy and Information Unit.

Branson, J., D. Miller & I. Gede Marsaja. (1996). Everyone here speaks sign language too – a deaf village in Bali, Indonesia. In C. Lucas (ed.) *Multicultural Aspects of Sociolinguistics in Deaf Communities*. Washington, DC: Gallaudet Press. 39–57.

Brasseur, P. (1977). Le Français dans les îles anglo-normandes. *Travaux de Linguistique et de Littérature* 16: 97–104.

(1978a). Les principales caractéristiques phonétiques des parlers normands de Jersey, Sercq, Guernesey et Magneville (canton de Bricquebec, Manche): Première partie. *Annales de Normandie* 25 (1): 49–64.

(1978b). Les principales caractéristiques phonétiques des parlers normands de Jersey, Sercq, Guernesey et Magneville (canton de Bricquebec, Manche): Deuxième partie. *Annales de Normandie* 25 (3): 275–306.

(1980–84). *Atlas Linguistique et Ethnographique Normand*. Paris: Editions du CNRS.

(1998). La survie du dialecte normand et du français dans les îles anglo-normandes: remarques sociolinguistique. *Plurilinguismes* 15: 133–70.

Breatnach, L. (1994). An Mheán-Ghaeilge. In K. R. McCone, D. McManus, C. Ó Háinle, N. Willams & L. Breatnach (eds.) *Stair na Gaeilge in ómós do Pádraig Ó Fiannachta*. Maynooth: Department of Old and Middle Irish, St Patrick's College. 221–333.

Breen, R., D. Hannan, D. Rottman & C. Whelan. (1990). *Understanding Contemporary Ireland: State, Class and Development in the Republic of Ireland*. Dublin: Gill & Macmillan.

Bremer, K., C. Roberts, M.-T. Vasseur, M. Simonot & P. Broeder. (1996). *Achieving Understanding: Discourse in Intercultural Encounters*. London: Longman.

Bresnan, J. & A. Deo. (2001). *Grammatical constraints on variation: 'Be' in the Survey of English Dialects and (Stochastic) Optimality Theory*. Manuscript. (http://www.lfg.stanford.edu/bresnan/be-final.pdf – last accessed 21 March 2006).

Brien, D. (ed.) (1992). *Dictionary of British Sign Language/English*. London: Faber.

Brinton, L. (1994). The differentiation of statives and perfects in Early Modern English. In D. Stein & I. Tieken-Boon (eds.) *Towards a Standard English*. Berlin: Mouton. 135–70.

Britain, D. (1997a). Dialect contact and phonological reallocation: 'Canadian Raising' in the English Fens. *Language in Society* 26: 15–46.

(1997b). Dialect contact, focusing and phonological rule complexity: the koineization of Fenland English. *University of Pennsylvania Working Papers in Linguistics 4. A Selection of Papers from NWAVE* 25: 141–70.

(2001). Welcome to East Anglia!: two major dialect 'boundaries' in the Fens. In J. Fisiak & P. Trudgill (eds.) *East Anglian English*. Woodbridge: Boydell & Brewer. 217–42.

(2002a). Space and spatial diffusion. In J. Chambers, P. Trudgill & N. Schilling-Estes (eds.) *The Handbook of Language Variation and Change*. Oxford: Blackwell. 603–637.

(2002b). Phoenix from the ashes?: The death, contact and birth of dialects in England. *Essex Research Reports in Linguistics* 41: 42–73.

(2002c). Diffusion, levelling, simplification and reallocation in past tense BE in the English Fens. *Journal of Sociolinguistics* 6 (1): 16–43.

(2003). Exploring the importance of the outlier in sociolinguistic dialectology. In D. Britain & J. Cheshire (eds.) *Social Dialectology*. Amsterdam: John Benjamins. 191–208.

(2005a). Dialect and accent. In U. Ammon, N. Dittmar, K. Mattheier & P. Trudgill (eds.) *Sociolinguistics: An International Handbook of the Science of Language and Society (2nd edn)*. Berlin: Walter de Gruyter. 267–73.

(2005b). Innovation diffusion, 'Estuary English' and local dialect differentiation: the survival of Fenland Englishes. *Linguistics* 43 (5): 995–1022.

(in press). One foot in the grave?: Dialect death, dialect contact and dialect birth in England. *International Journal of the Sociology of Language*.

Britain, D., L. Rupp, M. Bray, S. Fox, S. Baker & J. Spurling (2007). Explaining the East Anglian subject rule. *Essex Research Reports in Linguistics*.

Britain, D. & S. Simpson. (2007). Dialect Levelling in Telford New Town. *Essex Research Reports in Linguistics*.

Britain, D. & P. Trudgill. (2005). New dialect formation and contact-induced reallocation: three case studies from the Fens. *International Journal of English Studies* 5 (1): 183–209.

Britton, D. (1991). On Middle English *she, sho*: a Scots solution to an English problem. *North-western European Language Evolution* 17: 3–51.

Brown, G. (2000). *Britain and the Knowledge Economy*. Speech given to the Smith Institute, London, 16 February.

Brumfit, C. (1995a). Teacher professionalism and research. In G. Cook & B. Seidlhofer (eds.) *Principle and Practice in Applied Linguistics*. Oxford: Oxford University Press. 27–42.

(ed.) (1995b). *Language Education in the National Curriculum*. Oxford: Blackwell.

(2001). *Individual Freedom in Language Teaching*. Oxford: Oxford University Press.

Buchstaller, I. (2004). *The sociolinguistic constraints on the quotative system – British English and US English compared*. Unpublished PhD dissertation. Edinburgh: University of Edinburgh.

(2005). Putting perception to the reality test: the case of *go* and *like*. *University of Pennsylvania Working Papers in Linguistics. Papers from NWAVE* 32. 10 (2): 61–76.

(2006). Diagnostics of age-graded linguistic behaviour: the case of the quotative system. *Journal of Sociolinguistics* 10 (1): 3–30.

Bullock, A. (1975). *A Language for Life: Report of the Committee of Inquiry under the Chairmanship of Sir Alan Bullock*. London: Her Majesty's Stationery Office.

Bulwer, J. B. (1648). *Philocophus: or the deafe and dumbe man's friend*. London: Humphrey Moseley.

Bunting, M. (1996). *The Model Occupation*. London: Harper Collins.

Burns, S. (1998). Irish Sign Language: Ireland's second minority language. In C. Lucas (ed.) *Pinky Extension and Eye Gaze: Language Use in Deaf Communities*. Washington, DC: Gallaudet University Press. 233–73.

Burstall, C., M. Jamieson, S. Cohen & M. Hargreaves. (1974). *Primary French in the Balance*. London: National Foundation for Educational Research.

Cameron, D. (1995). *Verbal Hygiene*. London: Routledge.

(1998). *The Feminist Critique of Language. A Reader (2nd Edn)*. London: Routledge.

Cameron, D. & J. Bourne. (1988). No common ground: Kingman, grammar and the nation. *Language and Education* 2 (3): 147–60.

Cameron, L. (2003). *Writing in English as an Additional Language at Key Stage 4 and post-16*. London: Office for Standards in Education.

Campbell, E. (2001). Were the Scots Irish? *Antiquity* 75: 285–92.

Canagarajah, A. S. (1999). *Resisting Linguistic Imperialism in English Language Teaching*. Oxford: Oxford University Press.

Carter, P. (2003). Extrinsic phonetic interpretation: spectral variation in English liquids. In J. K. Local, R. A. Ogden & R. A. M. Temple (eds.) *Phonetic Interpretation. Papers in Laboratory Phonology VI*. Cambridge: Cambridge University Press. 237–52.

Carter, R. (ed.) (1990). *Knowledge about Language and the Curriculum*. London: Hodder & Stoughton.

(1992). LINC: the final chapter? *BAAL Newsletter* 35: 10–16.

(1995). *Keywords in language and literacy*. London: Routledge.

Carvel, J. (2001). Minority groups grow by 15%. *The Guardian*, 21 September. [http://www.guardian.co.uk/uk_news/story/0,555316,00.html – last accessed 11 February 2005].

Cassidy, F. G. & R. B. Le Page. (1967/1980). *Dictionary of Jamaican English*. Cambridge: Cambridge University Press.

Castells, M. (1996). *The Rise of the Network Society*. Oxford: Blackwell.

Cave, A. (2001). *Language variety and communicative style as local and subcultural identity in a South Yorkshire coalmining community*. Unpublished PhD dissertation. Sheffield: University of Sheffield.

Cenoz, J. & U. Jessner (eds.) (2000). *English in Europe: The Acquisition of a Third Language*. Clevedon: Multilingual Matters.

'Censor' (n.d.). *Don't. A Manual of Mistakes and Improprieties More or Less Prevalent in Conduct and Speech*. London: Field and Tuer. [Reprinted by Pryor Publications, 1982].

Census 1891. (1891). *Islands in the British Seas. Isle of Man, Jersey, Guernsey and Adjacent Islands*. London: Her Majesty's Stationery Office.

Census 1971. (1971). *Scotland: Reformatted Small Area Statistics: Table 40*. Edinburgh: General Register Office, Census Customer Services.

Census 1981. (1981). *Scotland: Small Area Statistics: Table 40*. Edinburgh: General Register Office.

Census 1991. (1991). *Scotland: Local Base Statistics: Table 67S*. Edinburgh: General Register Office.

Census 1991. (1993). *Ethnic Group and Country of Birth. Great Britain, Volumes I and II*. London: Government Statistical Service, HMSO Publications Centre.

Census 1991. (1993). *Report for Great Britain, Part I*. London: Government Statistical Service, HMSO Publications Centre.

Census of Jersey. (2001). *Report on the 2001 Census*. Jersey: States of Jersey.

Central Office of Information (1988). *Making it Plain: A Plea for Plain English in the Civil Service*. London: Cabinet Office.

Central Statistics Office. (2003). *Information Section*: 19 June. [www.cso.ie – last accessed 5 February 2005].

(2004). *2002 Census of Population, Volume 11: Irish Language*. Dublin: Government Publications Office.

Centre for Education and Racial Equality in Scotland (CERES). (1999). *Bilingualism, Community Languages and Scottish Education*. Edinburgh: CERES.

Centre for Language Teaching and Research. (1999). *Community Languages Bulletin* 5 (Autumn). London: CILT.

(2000). *Community Languages Bulletin* 6 (Spring). London: CILT.

Chambers, J.K. (1998). TV makes people sound the same. In L. Bauer & P. Trudgill (eds.) *Language Myths*. London: Penguin. 123–31.

(2003). *Sociolinguistic Theory (2nd Edn)*. Oxford: Blackwell.

(2004). Dynamic typology and vernacular universals. In B. Kortmann (ed.) *Dialectology Meets Typology: Dialect Grammar from a Cross-linguistic Perspective*. Berlin: Mouton de Gruyter. 127–45.

Chambers, J.K. & P. Trudgill. (1998). *Dialectology (2nd edn)*. Cambridge: Cambridge University Press.

Chapman, C. (1998). A subject-verb hierarchy: evidence from analogical change in modern English dialects. In R. Hogg & L. Van Bergen (eds.) *Current Issues in Linguistic Theory: Historical Linguistics 1995: Volume 2*. Amsterdam: Benjamins. 35–44.

Cheshire, J. (1981). Variation in the use of *ain't* in an urban British dialect. *Language in Society* 10 (3): 365–81.

(1982a). *Variation in an English Dialect*. Cambridge: Cambridge University Press.

(1982b). Dialect features and educational conflict in schools. *Educational Review* 34 (1): 53–67.

(1989). Addressee-oriented features in spoken discourse. *York Papers in Linguistics* 3: 49–63.

(1998a). English negation from an interactional perspective. In P. Trudgill & J. Cheshire (eds.) *The Sociolinguistics Reader, Volume 1: Multilingualism and Variation*. London: Arnold. 127–44.

(1998b). Taming the vernacular: some repercussions for the study of syntactic variation and spoken grammar. *Te Reo: Journal of the Linguistic Society of New Zealand* 41: 6–27.

(1999a). Taming the vernacular: some repercussions for the study of syntactic variation and spoken grammar. In J. C. Conde Silvestre & J. M. Hernández-Campoy (eds.) *Variation and Linguistic Change in English*. Murcia: University of Murcia. 59–80.

(1999b). Spoken standard English. In T. Bex & R. J. Watts (eds.) *Standard English. The Widening Debate*. London: Routledge. 129–48.

(2003). Social dimensions of syntactic variation: the case of 'when' clauses. In D. Britain & J. Cheshire (eds.) *Social Dialectology*. Amsterdam: John Benjamins. 245–62.

(2005a). Syntactic variation and spoken language. In L. Cornips & K. Corrigan (eds.) *Syntax and Variation: Reconciling the Biological and the Social*. Amsterdam: John Benjamins. 81–106.

(2005b). Syntactic variation and beyond: gender and social class variation in the use of discourse-new markers. *Journal of Sociolinguistics* 9 (4): 479–508.

(2005c). Sociolinguistics and mother-tongue education. In U. Ammon, N. Dittmar, K. J. Mattheier & P. Trudgill (eds.) *Sociolinguistics: An International Handbook of the Science of Language and Society (2nd Edn)*. Berlin: Mouton de Gruyter. 2341–50.

Cheshire, J., V. Edwards & P. Whittle. (1989). Urban British dialect grammar: the question of dialect levelling. *English World-Wide* 10: 185–225.

(1993). Non-standard English and dialect levelling. In J. Milroy & L. Milroy (eds.) *Real English: The Grammar of English Dialects in the British Isles*. London: Longman. 53–96.

Cheshire, J., P. Kerswill & A. Williams. (2005). Phonology, grammar and discourse in dialect convergence. In P. Auer, F. Hinskens & P. Kerswill (eds.) *Dialect Change: Convergence and Divergence in European Languages*. Cambridge: Cambridge University Press. 135–70.

Cheshire, J. & J. Ouhalla. (1997). *Grammatical constraints on variation*. Paper presented at UKLVC1, University of Reading.

Cheshire, J. & D. Stein. (1997). The syntax of spoken language. In J. Cheshire & D. Stein (eds.) *Taming the Vernacular: From Written Dialect to Written Standard Language*. London: Longman. 1–12.

Cheshire, J. & P. Trudgill. (1989). Dialect and education in the UK. In J. Cheshire, V. Edwards, H. Münstermann & B. Welten (eds.) *Dialect and Education: Some European Perspectives*. Clevedon: Multilingual Matters. 94–109.

Choudhry, A. & M. Verma. (1994). *The Gujaratis in England: language maintenance and shift*. Paper presented at Sociolinguistics Symposium 10, Lancaster University.

Christodoulou-Pipis, I. (1991). *Greek Outside Greece III. Research Findings: Language use by Greek-Cypriots in Britain*. Nicosia: Diaspora Books.

CILT: The National Centre for Languages. (2006). Qualify to teach community languages. *Community Languages Bulletin* 18: 8–9.

Clarke, S. (1997). On establishing historical relationships between new and old world varieties: habitual aspect and Newfoundland Vernacular English. In

E. Schneider (ed.) *Englishes around the World: Studies in Honour of Manfred Görlach*. Amsterdam: John Benjamins. 277–93.

(1999). The search for origins: habitual aspect and Newfoundland Vernacular English. *Journal of English Linguistics* 27: 328–40.

(2004). Newfoundland English: morphology and syntax. In B. Kortmann, K. Burridge, R. Mesthrie, E. Schneider & C. Upton (eds.) *A Handbook of Varieties of English: Morphology and Syntax*. Berlin: Mouton de Gruyter. 303–318.

Claxton, A. (1968). *The Suffolk Dialect of the 20th Century*. Ipswich: Adlard.

Clegg, J. (ed.) (1996). *Mainstreaming ESL*. Clevedon: Multilingual Matters.

Clyne, M. (1975). *Forschungsbericht Sprachkontakt*. Kronberg (Taunus): Scriptor Verlag.

(1991). *Community Languages: the Australian Experience*. Cambridge: Cambridge University Press.

Coates, J. (1993). *Women, Men and Language (2nd Edn)*. London: Longman.

Cohen, A. P. (ed.) (1982). *Belonging*. Manchester: Manchester University Press.

Cohen, R. (1997). *Global Diasporas: An Introduction*. London: University College London Press.

Coigligh, C. (2002). Multilingualism in Ireland. *The Irish Times*, 24 April [http://www.asu.edu/educ/epsl/LPRU/newsarchive/art174.txt – last accessed 5 February 2005].

Collins, B. & I. M. Mees. (1989). The phonetics of Cardiff English. In N. Coupland & A. R. Thomas (eds.) *English in Wales: Diversity, Conflict and Change*. Clevedon: Multilingual Matters. 87–103.

(1996). Spreading everywhere? How recent a phenomenon is glottalisation in Received Pronunciation? *English World-Wide* 17: 175–87.

Comhairle nan Eilean Siar. (2004). *Education and Leisure Service – School Rolls from 1975 Forward*. Stornoway: CNES.

Commission of the European Communities. (2001). Europeans and Languages. *Eurobarometer* 54.

Commission for Racial Equality (CRE). (1986). *Teaching English as a Second Language: Report of a Formal Investigation in Calderdale Local Education Authority*. London: Commission for Racial Equality.

Committee on Irish Language Attitudes Research (CILAR). (1975). *Report*. Dublin: The Stationery Office.

Community Language in the Secondary Curriculum Project. (1987). *EC Pilot Project: Community Language in the Secondary Curriculum. Report 1984–87*. London: Centre for Multicultural Education, Institute of Education, University of London.

Connolly, J. H. (1989). Port Talbot English. In N. Coupland & A. R. Thomas (eds.) *English in Wales: Diversity, Conflict and Change*. Clevedon: Multilingual Matters. 121–9.

Conrad, R. (1979). *The Deaf School Child: Language and Cognitive Function*. London: Harper & Row.

Cooper, R. (1989). *Language Planning and Social Change*. Cambridge: Cambridge University Press.

Cornips, L. & K. Corrigan (eds.) (2005a). *Syntax and Variation: Reconciling the Biological and the Social*. Amsterdam: John Benjamins.

(2005b). Toward an integrated approach to syntactic variation: a retrospective and prospective analysis. In L. Cornips & K. Corrigan (eds.) *Syntax and Variation: Reconciling the Biological and the Social*. Amsterdam: John Benjamins. 1–27.

(2005c). Convergence and divergence in grammar. In P. Auer, F. Hinskens & P. Kerswill (eds.) *Dialect change: Convergence and Divergence in European Languages*. Cambridge: Cambridge University Press. 96–134.

Corrigan, K. P. (1990). Northern Hiberno-English: the state of the art. *Irish University Review* 20: 91–119.

(1993). Hiberno-English syntax: nature vs nurture in a creole context. *Newcastle and Durham Working Papers in Linguistics* 1: 95–131.

(2000a). What bees to be maun be: aspects of deontic and epistemic modality in a northern dialect of Irish English. *English World-Wide* 21: 25–62.

(2000b). What are 'small clauses' doing in South Armagh English, Irish and Planter English? In H. L. C. Tristram (ed.) *The Celtic Englishes II*. Heidelberg: C. Winter. 75–96.

(2003). For-to infinitives and beyond: interdisciplinary approaches to non-finite complementation in a rural Celtic English. In H. L. C. Tristram (ed.) *The Celtic Englishes III*. Heidelberg: C. Winter. 318–38.

(2007). *Parametric Variation Within a Socially Realistic Linguistics: Syntactic Variation and Change in South Armagh English*. Oxford: Blackwell.

Cortiade, M. (1991). Romani versus Para-Romani. In P. Bakker & M. Cortiade (eds.) *In the Margin of Romani: Gypsy Languages in Contact*. Amsterdam: Instituut voor Algemene Taalwetenschap. 1–15.

Coughlain, T. (2001). *Now shoon the Romani gillie. Traditional Verse in the High and Low Speech of the Gypsies of Britain*. Cardiff: University of Wales Press.

Coulmas, F. (1992). *Language and Economy*. Oxford: Blackwell.

Coupland, N. & M. J. Ball. (1989). Welsh and English in contemporary Wales: sociolinguistic issues. *Contemporary Wales* 3: 7–40.

Coupland, N. & A. R. Thomas (eds.) (1989). *English in Wales: Diversity, Conflict and Change*. Clevedon: Multilingual Matters.

Cox, B. (1991). *Cox on Cox: An English Curriculum for the 1990s*. London: Hodder and Stoughton.

(1995). *Cox on the Battle for the English Curriculum*. London: Hodder and Stoughton.

Craith, N. (1999). Irish speakers in Northern Ireland, and the Good Friday Agreement. *Journal of Multilingual and Multicultural Development* 20 (6): 494–507.

Creese, A. (2000). The role of language specialists in disciplinary teaching: in search of a subject? *Journal of Multilingual and Multicultural Development*. 21 (6): 451–70.

Crinson, J. & J. Williamson. (2004). Non-standard dialect in the formal speech of 15-year-olds on Tyneside. *Language and Education* 18 (3): 207–19.

Crowley, T. (1989). *The Politics of Discourse*. London: Macmillan.

(ed.) (1999). *Language and Politics in Ireland. A Critical Reader: 1366–1922*. London: Routledge.

(2003). *Standard English and the politics of language (2nd edn)*. Basingstoke, Palgrave Macmillan.

Cruttenden, A. (1995). Rises in English. In J. W. Lewis (ed.) *Studies in General and English Phonetics. Essays in Honour of Professor J. D. O'Connor.* London: Routledge. 155–73.

(1997). *Intonation (2nd edn).* Cambridge: Cambridge University Press.

(2001a). Mancunian intonation and intonational representation. *Phonetica* 58: 53–80.

(2001b). *Gimson's Pronunciation of English (6th edn).* London: Arnold.

Crystal, D. (1995). *The Cambridge Encyclopedia of the English Language.* Cambridge: Cambridge University Press.

(1997). *English as a Global Language.* Cambridge: Cambridge University Press.

(2000). On trying to be Crystal-clear: a response to Phillipson. *Applied Linguistics* 21 (1): 415–23.

Dalgarno, G. (1680). *Didascalocophus, or the deaf and dumb man's tutor.* London: J. Hayes.

Dalphinis, M. (1991). The Afro-English creole speech community. In S. Alladina & V. Edwards (eds.) *Multilingualism in the British Isles Volume 2: Africa, the Middle East and Asia.* London: Longman. 42–56.

Daly, M. (1990). Literacy and language change in the late nineteenth and early twentieth centuries. In M. Daly & D. Dickson (eds.) *The Origins of Popular Literacy in Ireland: Language Change and Educational Development 1700–1920.* Dublin: Anna Livia. 153–66.

Daly, M. & D. Dickson. (eds.) 1990. *The Origins of Popular Literacy in Ireland: Language Change and Educational Development 1700–1920.* Dublin: Anna Livia.

Dave, J. (1991). The Gujarati speech community. In S. Alladina & V. Edwards (eds.) *Multilingualism in the British Isles, Volume 2: Africa, the Middle East and Asia.* London: Longman. 88–102.

Davies, C. (1988). *Cymraeg Byw.* In M. J. Ball (ed.) *The Use of Welsh.* Clevedon: Multilingual Matters. 200–10.

Davies, J. (2000). Welsh. In G. Price (ed.) *Languages in Britain & Ireland.* Oxford: Blackwell. 78–108.

de Bernardo-Stempel, P. (1995). Gaulish accentuation. Results and outlook. In J. Eska, R. G. Gruffydd & N. Jacobs (eds.) *Hispano-Gallo-Brittonica. Essays in Honour of Professor D. Ellis Evans on the Occasion of his Sixty-fifth Birthday.* Cardiff: University of Wales Press. 16–32.

De Camp, D. (1961). Social and geographical factors in Jamaican dialects. In R. B. Le Page (ed.) *Creole Studies II: Proceedings of the Conference on Creole Language Studies.* London: Macmillan. 61–84.

(1971). Towards a generative analysis of a post-creole speech continuum. In D. Hymes (ed.) *Pidginization and Creolization of Languages.* Cambridge: Cambridge University Press. 349–70.

De Garis, M. (1982). *Dictiounnaire Angllais – Guernesiais.* Chichester: Phillimore.

(1983). Guernesiais: a grammatical survey. *Report and Transactions of La Société Guernesiaise* 21: 319–53.

De l'Epée, C. M. (1784). *La Veritable Manière D'instruire les Sourds et Muets, Confirmée par une Longue Experience.* Paris: Nyon.

Dennison, D. (1998). Syntax. In S. Romaine (ed.) *Cambridge History of the English Language: Volume IV: 1776–1997.* Cambridge: Cambridge University Press. 92–329.

Dent, R. W. (1994). *Colloquial Language in Ulysses. A Reference Tool.* Newark: University of Delaware Press.

Department for Education and Employment. (1995). *The Harris Report: Modern Foreign Languages in the National Curriculum.* London: Department for Education and Employment.

(1997). *Excellence in Schools.* London: HMSO.

(1998). *The National Literacy Strategy.* London: Department for Education and Employment.

(1999). *Minority Ethnic Pupils in Maintained Schools by Local Education Authority Area in England.* London: Department for Education and Employment.

(2000a). *Grammar for Writing,* London: Department for Education and Employment.

(2000b). *Skills for Life: The National Strategy for Improving Adult Literacy and Numeracy Skills.* London: Department for Education and Employment.

(2001a). *Literacy Across the Curriculum.* London: Department for Education and Employment.

(2001b). *Key Stage 3 National Strategy: Framework for Teaching English: Years 7. 8 and 9.* Suffolk: DfEE Publications.

(2001c). *The National Literacy Strategy: Developing Early Writing.* London, Department for Education and Employment.

(1975). *A Language for Life.* London: HMSO.

(1981). *West Indian Children in our Schools: Interim Report of the Committee of Inquiry into the Education of Children from Ethnic Minority Groups.* London: HMSO.

(1984). *Mother Tongue Teaching in School and Community.* London: HMSO.

(1985). *Education for All: The Report of the Committee of Inquiry into the Education of Children from Ethnic Minority Groups.* London: HMSO.

(1988). *Report of the Committee of Inquiry into the Teaching of English Language.* London: HMSO.

(1989). *English for Ages 5 to 16: The Cox Report.* London: HMSO.

(1990). *Modern Foreign Languages for Ages 11 to 16.* London: HMSO.

(1993). *English for Ages 5–16.* London: HMSO.

Department for Education and Skills. (2001). *Raising Aspects of Ethnic Minority Achievement: With Special Reference to Learning English as an Additional Language.* London: Department for Education and Skills.

(2002a). *Key Stage 3 National Strategy – Grammar for Writing: Supporting Pupils Learning EAL.* London: Department for Education and Skills.

(2002b). *Languages for All: Languages for Life.* London: Department for Education and Skills.

(2003). *Skills for Life Survey.* Nottingham: DfES Publications.

(2005). The National Languages Strategy: Press Notice 0034. www.dfes.gov.uk/languages/DSP_nationallanguages.cfm [last checked 28th February 2006].

Department of Health. (1998). *Information for Health.* London: HMSO.

(2001). *Building the Information Core: Implementing the NHS Plan.* London: HMSO.

Deterding, D. (1997). The formants of monophthong vowels in Standard Southern British English pronunciation. *Journal of the International Phonetic Association* 27: 47–55.

Devitt, A. (1989). *Standardizing Written English: Diffusion in the Case of Scotland 1520–1659*. Cambridge: Cambridge University Press.

Dickins, B. & R. M. Wilson. (1951). *Early Middle English Texts*. London: Bowes and Bowes.

Dictionary of D & D Signs. (1895). *Our Monthly Church Messenger to the Deaf* 2: 77, 131.

Dieth, E. (1932). *A Grammar of the Buchan Dialect*. Cambridge: Cambridge University Press.

Dobson, E. J. (1968). *English Pronunciation: 1500–1700 (2nd Edn)*. Oxford: Clarendon.

Docherty, G. J. (1992). *The Timing of Voicing in British English Obstruents*. Berlin: Foris.

Docherty, G. J. & P. Foulkes. (1999). Newcastle upon Tyne and Derby: instrumental phonetics and variationist studies. In P. Foulkes & G. J. Docherty (eds.) *Urban Voices: Accent Studies in the British Isles*. London: Edward Arnold. 47–71.

(2001). Variability in (r) production: instrumental perspectives. In H. Van de Velde & R. van Hout (eds.) *'r-atics: Sociolinguistic, Phonetic and Phonological Characteristics of /r/*. Brussels: ILVP. 173–84.

(2005). Glottal variants of /t/ in the Tyneside variety of English. In W. Hardcastle & J. Mackenzie Beck (eds.) *A Figure of Speech: A Festschrift for John Laver*. London: Lawrence Erlbaum. 173–99.

Docherty, G. J., P. Foulkes, J. Milroy, L. Milroy & D. Walshaw. (1997). Descriptive adequacy in phonology: a variationist perspective. *Journal of Linguistics* 33: 275–310.

Docherty, G. J., P. Foulkes, J. Tillotson & D. J. L. Watt. (2006). On the scope of phonological learning: issues arising from socially structured variation. In L. Goldstein, C. T. Best & D. H. Whalen (eds.) *Laboratory Phonology 8*. Berlin: Mouton de Gruyter. 393–422.

Dolan, T. P. (ed.) (1990). The English of the Irish. *Irish University Review* 20 (1).

(2005 [1998]). *A Dictionary of Hiberno-English. The Irish Use of English*. Dublin: Gill and Macmillan.

Domaille, D. R. F. (1996). *Analyse sociolinguistique du Guernesiais*. Unpublished PhD thesis. Bristol: University of Bristol.

Dorian, N. (1980). The valuation of Gaelic by different mother tongue groups in a Highland village. *Scottish Gaelic Studies* 13 (2): 169–82.

(1981). *Language Death – The Life Cycle of a Scottish Gaelic Dialect*. Philadelphia: University of Philadelphia Press.

Dorling, D. (1995). *A New Social Atlas of Britain*. Chichester: John Wiley & Sons.

Douglas, E. E. (1975). A sociolinguistic study of Articlave, Co. Londonderry: a preliminary report. *Ulster Folklife* 21: 55–67.

Douglas-Cowie, E. (1978). Linguistic code-switching in a Northern Irish village: social interaction and social ambition. In P. Trudgill (ed.) *Sociolinguistic Patterns in British English*. London: Edward Arnold. 37–51.

Douglas-Cowie, E. & R. Cowie. (1999). Prosodic style-shifting in a Northern Irish village. In J. Ohala, Y. Hasegawa, M. Ohala, D. Granville & A. Bailey (eds.) *Proceedings of the International Congress of Phonetic Sciences, 1–7 August, San Francisco*, Berkeley: Department of Linguistics, University of California at Berkeley. 137–40.

Dowling, P. J. (1968 [1935]). *The Hedge Schools of Ireland*. London: Longman.

Duncan, A. M. (1975). *Scotland: The Making of the Kingdom*. Edinburgh: Oliver & Boyd.

Durcacz, V. E. (1983). *The Decline of the Celtic Languages*. Edinbugh: John Donald.

Dyer, J. A. (2002). 'We all speak the same round here.' Dialect levelling in a Scottish English community. *Journal of Sociolinguistics* 6: 99–116.

Ebbinghaus, H. & J. Hessmann. (2001). Sign language as multidimensional communication – Or: why manual signs, mouthings, and mouth gestures are three different things. In P. Boyes-Braem and R. Sutton-Spence (eds.) *The Hands are the Head of the Mouth: The Role of the Mouth in Sign Languages*, Hamburg: Signum Press. 133–51.

Eckert, P. (1989). The whole woman: sex and gender differences in variation. *Language Variation and Change* 1: 245–67.

  (1997). Age as a sociolinguistic variable. In F. Coulmas (ed.) *Handbook of Sociolinguistics*. Oxford: Blackwell. 151–67.

  (2000). *Linguistic Variation as Social Practice*. Oxford: Blackwell.

Edwards, J. (1985). *Language, Society and Identity*. Oxford: Basil Blackwell.

Edwards, V. (1983). *Language in Multi-cultural Classrooms*. London: Batsford Academic.

  (1986). *Language in a Black Community*. Clevedon: Multilingual Matters.

  (1993). The grammar of Southern British English. In J. Milroy & L. Milroy (eds.) *Real English: The Grammar of English Dialects in the British Isles*. London: Longman. 214–38.

  (2000). Community languages in the United Kingdom. In G. Price (ed.) *Languages in Britain and Ireland*. Oxford: Blackwell. 213–29.

Edwards, V., P. Trudgill & B. Weltens. (1984). *The Grammar of English Dialect: a Survey of Research: A Report to the ESRC Education and Human Development Committee*. London: ESRC.

Eggar, T. (1991). Correct use of English is essential. *Times Educational Supplement* 28 June.

Ellis, A. J. (1869). *On Early English Pronunciation*. London: Early English Text Society.

Elmes, S. (2000). *The Routes of English*. London: BBC.

Emanuelli, F. (1906). Le parler populaire de l'île anglo-normande d'Aurigny. *Revue de Philologie Française* 20: 136–42.

  (1907). Le parler populaire de l'île anglo-normande d'Aurigny (suite). *Revue de Philologie Française* 21: 44–53.

Emmorey, K., D. Corina & U. Bellugi. (1995). Differential processing of topographic and referential functions of space. In K. Emmorey & J. Reilly (eds.) *Language, Gesture and Space*. Hillsdale, NJ: Lawrence Erlbaum Associates. 43–62.

Engberg-Pedersen, E. (1993). *Space in Danish Sign Language*. Hamburg: Signum Press.

Esling, J. H. (1978). The identification of features of voice quality in social groups. *Journal of the International Phonetic Association* 7: 18–23.

Estebanez, S. (1991). The Spanish speech community. In S. Alladina & V. Edwards (eds.) *Multilingualism in the British Isles. Vol. 1: The Older Mother Tongues and Europe*. Harlow: Longman. 241–53.

Etat Civil Committee. (2002). *Report on the 2001 Census: Jersey*. St Helier: States of Jersey.

Eurobarometer. (2001). *Europeans and Languages: Eurobarometer Report 54.* Brussels: European Commission.

Euromosaic Project. (1995). *Gaelic Language Use Survey.* European Bureau for Lesser Known Languages [www.eblul.org – last accessed 11 February 2005].

Eurostat. (2003). *EU Labour Force Survey.* Luxembourg: Eurostat.

Evans, D. E. (1983). Language contact in pre-Roman and Roman Britain. In H. Temporini & W. Haase (eds.) *Aufstieg und Niedergang der römischen Welt, Volume II.* Berlin: De Gruyter. 949–87.

Evans, D. S. (1964). *A Grammar of Middle Welsh.* Dublin: DIAS.

Ewen, A. & A. De Carteret. (1969). *The Fief of Sark.* Guernsey: Guernsey Press.

Extra, G. & L. Verhoeven. (1993). Introduction: immigrant groups and immigrant languages in Europe. In G. Extra & L. Verhoeven (eds.) *Immigrant Languages in Europe.* Clevedon: Multilingual Matters. 3–21.

Fabricius, A. H. (2000). *T-glottalling between stigma and prestige: a sociolinguistic study of modern RP.* Unpublished PhD dissertation. Copenhagen: Copenhagen Business School.

    (2002a). Ongoing change in modern RP: evidence for the disappearing stigma of t-glottaling. *English World-Wide* 23: 115–36.

    (2002b). Weak vowels in modern RP: an acoustic study of happY-tensing and KIT/schwa shift. *Language Variation and Change* 14: 211–37.

Fairclough, N. (1999). *New Labour, New Language?* London: Routledge.

Fay, E. (1881). The methods of the British schools. *American Annals of the Deaf and Dumb*, 26: 187–92.

Fenton, J. (2001 [1995]). *The Hamely Tongue. A Personal Record of Ulster-Scots in County Antrim.* Newtownards: Ulster-Scots Academic Press.

Ferguson, C. (1959). Diglossia. *Word* 15: 325–40.

Fiddick, J. (1999). *Immigration and Asylum.* London: House of Commons Library.

Fieß, A. (2000). Age-group differentiation in the spoken language of rural east Galway. In H. L. C. Tristram (ed.) *The Celtic Englishes II.* Heidelberg: C. Winter. 188–209.

Fife, J. (1986). Literary vs colloquial Welsh: problems of definition. *Word*, 37: 141–51.

    (1990). *The Semantics of the Welsh Verb.* Cardiff: University of Wales Press.

Filppula, M. (1991). Subordinating 'and' in Hiberno-English: Irish or English origin? In P. S. Ureland & G. Broderick (eds.) *Language Contact in the British Isles.* Tübingen: Max Niemeyer. 617–31.

    (1999). *The Grammar of Irish English. Language in Hibernian Style.* London: Routledge.

Finlay, C. (1994). Syntactic variation in Belfast English. *Belfast Working Papers in Language and Linguistics* 12: 69–97.

Finlay, C. & M. F. McTear. (1986). Syntactic variation in the speech of Belfast school children. In J. Harris, D. Little & D. Singleton (eds.) *Perspectives on the English Language in Ireland.* Dublin: Centre for Language and Communication Studies, Trinity College Dublin. 175–86.

Fischer, O. & F. van der Leek. (1983). The demise of the Old English impersonal construction. *Journal of Linguistics* 19: 337–68.

Fishman, J. (ed.) (2001). *Can Threatened Languages be Saved?* Clevedon: Multilingual Matters.

Fisiak, J. (1968). *A Short Grammar of Middle English.* Warsaw: Polish Scientific Publishers.

(ed.) (1995). *Language Contact under Contact Conditions.* Berlin: Mouton de Gruyter.

Fitzpatrick, B. (1987). *The Open Door.* Clevedon: Multilingual Matters.

Fletcher, J., E. Grabe & P. Warren. (2005). Intonational variation in four dialects of English: the high rising tune. In S.-A. Jun (ed.) *Prosodic Typology. The Phonology of Intonation and Phrasing.* Oxford: Oxford University Press.

Fleury, J. (1886). *Essai sur le patois normand de la Hague.* Paris: Maisonneuve et Leclerc.

Forsyth, K. (1997). *Language in Pictland: The Case Against Non-Indo-European Pictish.* Utrecht: de Keltische Draak.

Foulkes, P. (1997). Rule inversion in a British English dialect – a sociolinguistic investigation of [r]-sandhi in Newcastle upon Tyne. *University of Pennsylvania Working Papers in Linguistics 4. A Selection of Papers from NWAVE 25.* 259–70.

Foulkes, P. & G. J. Docherty. (1999). *Urban Voices: Accent Studies in the British Isles.* London: Arnold.

(2000). Another chapter in the story of /r/: 'labiodental' variants in British English. *Journal of Sociolinguistics* 4: 30–59.

Foulkes, P., G. J. Docherty & D. J. L. Watt. (2001). The emergence of structured variation. *University of Pennsylvania Working Papers in Linguistics 7. Selected Papers from NWAV 29.* 67–84.

Fox, S. (2007). *The demise of 'Cockneys'?: language change in London's 'traditional' East End.* Unpublished PhD dissertation. Colchester: University of Essex.

Francis, W. (1983). *Dialectology.* Harlow: Longman.

Francis, W. N. (1985). *Amn't I*, or the hole in the pattern. In W. Viereck (ed.) *Focus on England and Wales.* Amsterdam: John Benjamins. 141–52.

Fudge, E. C. (1984). *English Word-Stress.* London: Allen and Unwin.

Gardener, D. & H. Connolly. (2005). *Who are the 'Other' Ethnic Groups?* London: Office for National Statistics.

Gardner-Chloros, P. & K. Finnis. (2003). How code-switching mediates politeness: gender-related speech among London Greek-Cypriots. *Estudios de Socio-linguistica* 4 (2): 505–33.

Gardner-Chloros, P., L. MacEntee-Atalianis & K. Finnis. (2005). Language attitudes and use in a transplanted setting: Greek Cypriots in London. *Journal of Multilingualism* 2 (1): 52–80.

Geipel, J. (1971). *The Viking Legacy – The Scandinavian Influences on the English and Gaelic Languages.* Newton Abbot: David & Charles.

George, K. (1993). Cornish. In M. J. Ball (ed.) *The Celtic Languages.* London: Routledge. 410–68.

Gibson, K. A. (1982). *Tense and aspect in Guyanese Creole: a syntatic, semantic and pragmatic analysis.* Unpublished PhD dissertation. York: University of York.

Gibson, M. (2003a). Languages at a single click. *GP Newspaper*, 20 January.

(2003b). Informed patients require a broker. *GP Newspaper*, 27 January.

(2003c). Sharing electronic records. *GP Newspaper*, May 2003.

Gibson, P. (1996). *Southwick-on-Wear: Volume 4.* Southwick Publications.

(2002). *Football in Sunderland.* Sunderland: The People's History Ltd.

Giddens, A. (1984). *The Constitution of Society: Outline of the Theory of Structuration.* Cambridge: Polity Press.

(1989). A reply to my critics. In D. Held & J. Thompson (eds.) *Social Theory of Modern Societies: Anthony Giddens and his Critics.* Cambridge: Cambridge University Press. 249–301.

Giles, H. & N. Coupland. (1991). *Language: Contexts and Consequences.* Buckingham: Open University Press.

Gillborn, D. (1997). Ethnicity and educational performance in the United Kingdom: racism, ethnicity, and variability in achievement. *Anthropology and Education Quarterly* 28 (3): 375–93.

Gillborn, D. & C. Gipps. (1996). *Recent Research on the Achievement of Ethnic Minority Pupils.* London: OFSTED.

Gillborn, D. & H. Mirza. (2000). *Educational Inequality: Mapping Race, Class and Gender: A Synthesis of Research Evidence.* London: OFSTED.

Gilliéron, J. & E. Edmont. (1902–10). *Atlas Linguistique de la France.* Paris: Honoré Champion.

Gilroy, P. (1987). *There Ain't No Black in the Union Jack.* London: Hutchinson.

(1993). *The Black Atlantic: Modernity and Double Consciousness.* London: Verso.

Gimson, A. C. (1970). *An Introduction to the Pronunciation of English* (2nd Edn). London: Arnold.

(1980) *An Introduction to the Pronunciation of English* (3rd edn). London: Arnold.

(1984). The RP accent. In P. Trudgill (ed.) *Language in the British Isles.* Cambridge: Cambridge University Press. 45–54.

Godfrey, E. & S. Tagliamonte. (1999). Another piece of the verbal –s story: evidence from Devon in Southwest England. *Language Variation and Change* 11: 87–121.

Goodman, K. & Y. Goodman. (1978). *Reading of American children whose language is a stable rural dialect of English or a language other than English.* (NIE-C-00-3-0087). Washington, DC: US Department of Health, Education and Welfare.

Gorman, R. (ed.) (1993). *An Stor-Data Briathrachas Gaidhlig – The Gaelic Terminology Database.* Sleat, Skye: Clo Ostaig.

Goulbourne, H. (1998). *Race Relations in Britain since 1945.* London: Macmillan.

Government Publications Office. (1958). *Gramadach na Gaeilge agus Litriú na Gaeilge, An Caighdeán Oifigiúil.* Dublin: Government Publications Office.

Gowers, E. (1954). *The Complete Plain Words.* London: HMSO.

Grabe, E. (2004). Intonational variation in urban dialects of English spoken in the British Isles. In P. Gilles & J. Peters (eds.) *Regional Variation in Intonation.* Tübingen: Niemeyer. 9–31.

Grabe, E. & E. L. Low. (2002). Durational variability in speech and the rhythm class hypothesis. In C. Gussenhoven & N. Warner (eds.) *Laboratory Phonology 7.* The Hague: Mouton. 515–46.

Grabe, E., B. Post, F. Nolan & K. Farrar. (2000). Pitch accent realization in four varieties of British English. *Journal of Phonetics* 28: 161–86.

Grabiner, L. (2000). *The Informal Economy.* London: HMSO.

Graddol, D. (1997). *The Future of English? A Guide to Forecasting the Popularity of English in the 21st Century.* London: Glenton Press.

Graham, G. F. (1869). *A Book about Words.* London.

Grant, W. & J. M. Dixon. (1921). *Manual of Modern Scots.* Cambridge: Cambridge University Press.

Grant, William, *et al.* (eds.) (1931–75). *The Scottish National Dictionary (10 Volumes)*. Edinburgh: Chambers.

Greene, D. (1979). Perfects and perfectives in modern Irish. *Ériu* 30: 122–41.

Gregg, R. J. (1958). Notes on the phonology of a County Antrim Scotch-Irish dialect. *Orbis* 7: 392–406.

(1959). Notes on the phonology of a County Antrim Scotch-Irish dialect. Part II: Historical phonology (I). *Orbis* 8: 400–24.

(1964). Scotch-Irish urban speech in Ulster. In G. Adams, J. Braidwood & R. Gregg (eds.) *Ulster Dialects: An Introductory Symposium*. Belfast: Ulster Folk Museum. 163–92.

(1972). The Scotch-Irish dialect boundaries in Ulster. In M. F. Wakelin (ed.) *Patterns in the Folk Speech of the British Isles*. London: Athlone Press. 109–39.

(1985). *The Scotch-Irish Dialect Boundaries in the Province of Ulster*. Port Credit, Ontario: Canadian Federation for the Humanities.

Gregory, E. (1997). *One Child, Many Worlds: Early Learning in Multicultural Communities*. London: David Fulton.

Gregory, E. & A. Williams. (2000a). *City Literacies: Learning to Read across Generations and Cultures*. London: Routledge.

(2000b). Work or play? 'Unofficial' literacies in the lives of two East London communities. In M. Martin-Jones & K. Jones (eds.) *Multilingual Literacies*. Amsterdam: John Benjamins. 37–54.

Grice, M. & W. Barry. (1991). Problems of transcription and labelling in the specification of segmental and prosodic structure. *Proceedings of the XIIth International Congress of Phonetic Sciences* 5: 66–9.

Grote, G. (1994). *Torn between Politics and Culture: The Gaelic League 1893–1993*. Münster: Waxmann.

Grundy S. & L. Jameson. (2002). *Demography: 18–24 year olds in the population. UK Socio Demographic Profile of 18 to 24 year olds. Orientations of young men and women to citizenship and European identity*. [http://www.sociology.ed.ac.uk/youth/docs/UK_sociodem.pdf – last accessed 11 February 2005].

Guillot, C. (1975). *Les Iles Anglo-Normandes*. Paris: Presses Universitaires de France.

Guy, G. (1980). Variation in the group and individual: the case of final stop deletion. In W. Labov (ed.) *Locating Language in Time and Space*. New York: Academic Press. 1–36.

Guy, G. & J. Vonwiller. (1984). The meaning of an intonation in Australian English. *Australian Journal of Linguistics* 4: 1–17.

Haenni, R. (1999). *The case of Estuary English: supposed evidence and a perceptual approach*. Unpublished PhD dissertation. Basel: University of Basel.

Hall, S. (1988). New ethnicities. *ICA Documents* 7: 27–31.

(1990). Cultural identity and diaspora. In J. Rutherford (ed.) *Identity: Community, Culture, Difference*. London: Lawrence & Wishart. 222–37.

Halliday, M. A. K., A. McIntosh & P. Strevens. (1964). *The Linguistic Sciences and Language Teaching*. London: Longman.

Hamers, J. & M. Blanc. (2000). *Bilinguality and Bilingualism (2nd Edn)*. Cambridge: Cambridge University Press.

Hamp, E. P. (1975–6). Miscellanea Celtica. *Studia Celtica* 10–11: 54–73.

Hancock, I. F. (1970). Is Anglo-Romanes a creole? *Journal of the Gypsy Lore Society* 49: 41–4.

(1971). Comment on Kenrick. In T. Acton (ed.) *Proceedings of the Research and Policy Conference of the National Gypsy Education Council*. Oxford: National Gypsy Education Council. 15–18.

(1976). The pidginization of Angloromani. In G. Cave (ed.) *New Directions in Creole Studies*. Georgetown: University of Guyana. 1–23.

(1978). The social and linguistic development of Angloromani. *Working Papers in Sociolinguistics 38*. Austin: Southwest Educational Development Laboratory.

(1984a). Romani and Angloromani. In P. Trudgill (ed.) *Language in the British Isles*. Cambridge: Cambridge University Press. 367–83.

(1984b). Shelta and Polari. In P. Trudgill (ed.) *Language in the British Isles*. Cambridge: Cambridge University Press. 384–403.

Hannerz, U. (1996). *Transnational Connections*. London: Routledge.

Hardcastle, W. & W. Barry. (1989). Articulatory and perceptual factors in /l/ vocalisation in English. *Journal of the International Phonetic Association* 15: 3–17.

Hardie, A. & T. McEnery. (2003). The were-subjunctive in British rural dialects: marrying corpus and questionnaire data. *Computers and the Humanities* 37: 205–28.

Hargreaves S., A. Holmes & J. Friedland. (2000). Refugees, asylum seekers, and general practice: room for improvement? *British Journal of General Practice* 50: 531–2.

Harrington, J., S. Palethorpe & C. I. Watson. (2005). Deepening or lessening the divide between diphthongs: an analysis of the Queen's annual Christmas broadcasts. In W. Hardcastle & J. Mackenzie Beck (eds.) *A Figure of Speech: A Festschrift for John Laver*. London: Lawrence Erlbaum. 227–61.

Harris, J. (1984a). English in the north of Ireland. In P. Trudgill (ed.) *Language in the British Isles*. Cambridge: Cambridge University Press. 115–34.

(1984b). Syntactic variation and dialect divergence. *Journal of Linguistics* 20: 303–27.

(1985a). *Phonological Variation and Change. Studies in Hiberno-English*. Cambridge: Cambridge University Press.

(1985b). The Hiberno-English 'I've it eaten' construction: what is it and where does it come from? In D. P. Ó Baoill (ed.) *Papers on Irish English*. Dublin: Irish Association for Applied Linguistics. 36–52.

(1986). Expanding the superstrate: habitual aspect markers in Atlantic Englishes. *English World-Wide* 7: 171–99.

(1987). On doing comparative reconstruction with genetically unrelated languages. In A. G. Ramat, O. Carruba & G. Bernini (eds.) *Papers from the VIIth International Conference on Historical Linguistics*. Amsterdam: John Benjamins. 267–82.

(1990). More on Brogues and Creoles: What's been happening to English short u? *Irish University Review* 20 (1): 73–90.

(1991). Conservatism versus substratal transfer in Irish English. In P. Trudgill & J. K. Chambers (eds.) *Dialects of English. Studies in Grammatical Variation*. London: Longman. 191–212.

(1993). The grammar of Irish English. In J. Milroy & L. Milroy (eds.) *Real English. The Grammar of English Dialects in the British Isles*. London: Longman. 139–86.

(1996). On the trail of short *u*. *English World-Wide* 17: 1–42.

(1997). Phonological systems in collision in the north of Ireland. In H. L. C. Tristram (ed.) *The Celtic Englishes*. Heidelberg: C. Winter. 201–24.

Harris, M. (1967). *The phonology and grammar of the dialect of South Zeal, Devonshire*. Unpublished PhD dissertation. London: SOAS.

(1991). Demonstrative adjectives and pronouns in a Devonshire dialect. In P. Trudgill & J. K. Chambers (eds.) *Dialects of English: Studies in Grammatical Variation*. London: Longman. 20–28.

Harris, R. (1995). Disappearing language: fragments and fractures between speech and writing. In J. Mace (ed.) *Language, Literacy and Community Publishing*. Clevedon: Multilingual Matters. 118–44.

(1997). Romantic bilingualism: time for a change? In C. Leung & C. Cable (eds.) *English as an Additional Language: Changing Perspectives*. Watford: NALDIC. 14–27.

(1999). Rethinking the bilingual learner. In A. Tosi & C. Leung (eds.) *Rethinking Language Education*. London: CILT. 70–83.

Harris, R., C. Leung & B. Rampton. (2001). Globalisation, diaspora and language education in England. In D. Block & D. Cameron (eds.) *Globalisation and Language Teaching*. London: Routledge. 29–46.

Harris, R. & B. Rampton. (2002). Creole metaphors in cultural analysis: on the limits and possibilities of (socio-)linguistics. *Critique of Anthropology* 22 (1): 31–51.

Harris, R., I. Schwab, L. Whitman *et al.* (1990). *Language and Power*. London: Harper Collins.

Harris, W. V. (1989). *Ancient Literacy*. Cambridge: Harvard University Press.

Hatton, L. (1988). The development of the nasal mutation in the speech of school-children. In M. J. Ball (ed.) *The Use of Welsh*. Clevedon: Multilingual Matters. 239–57.

Haugen, E. (1966). Dialect, language, nation. *American Anthropologist* 68: 922–35.

Hawkins, S. (2003). Roles and representations of systematic fine phonetic detail in speech understanding. *Journal of Phonetics* 31: 373–405.

Hawkins, S. & J. Midgley. (2005). Formant frequencies of RP monophthongs in four age groups of speakers. *Journal of the International Phonetic Association* 35 (2): 183–99.

Hawkins, S. & R. Smith. (2001). Polysp: A polysystemic, phonetically-rich approach to speech understanding. *Rivista di Linguistica* 13: 99–188.

Hawthorne, K. (1994). Accessibility and use of health care services in the British Asian community. *Family Practice* 11 (4): 453–9.

Headley, V. (1992). *Yardie*. London: X Press.

Heath, C. D. (1980). *The Pronunciation of English in Cannock, Staffordshire*. Oxford: Blackwell.

Heller, M. (1999). *Linguistic Minorities and Modernity*. London: Longman.

Henley, A. & J. Schott. (1999). *Culture, Religion and Patient Care in a Multi-ethnic Society*. London: Age Concern England.

Henry, A. (1992). Infinitives in a *for-to* dialect. *Natural Language and Linguistic Theory* 10: 279–301.

(1994). Singular concord in Belfast English. *Belfast Working Papers in Language and Linguistics* 12: 134–76.

(1995). *Belfast English and Standard English. Dialect Variation and Parameter Setting*. Oxford: Oxford University Press.

(1996). Indirect questions in Belfast English and the analysis of embedded verb-second. *Belfast Working Papers in Language and Linguistics* 13: 161–72.

(1997). The syntax of Belfast English. In J. Kallen (ed.) *Focus on Ireland*. Amsterdam: John Benjamins. 89–108.

(2002). Variation and syntactic theory. In J.K. Chambers, P. Trudgill & N. Schilling-Estes (eds.) *The Handbook of Language Variation and Change*. Oxford: Basil Blackwell. 267–82.

(2005). Idiolectal variation and syntactic theory. In L. Cornips & K. Corrigan (eds.) *Syntax and Variation: Reconciling the Biological and the Social*. Amsterdam: John Benjamins. 109–22.

Henry, M., B. Lingard, F. Rizvi & S. Taylor. (1999). Working with/against globalization in education. *Journal of Education Policy* 14 (1): 85–97.

Henry, P.L. (1958). A linguistic survey of Ireland: preliminary report. In A. Lochlann (ed.) *Review of Celtic Studies, Volume 1. [Norsk Tidsskrift for Sprogvidenskap*, Suppl. Bind V]. 49–208.

(1964). Anglo-Irish word-charts. In G. Adams, J. Braidwood & R. Gregg (eds.) *Ulster Dialects: An Introductory Symposium*. Belfast: Ulster Folk Museum. 147–61.

(1985). Linguistic atlases and vocabulary: the linguistic survey of Anglo-Irish. In J.M. Kirk, S. Sanderson & J.D.A. Widdowson (eds.) *Studies in Linguistic Geography. The Dialects of English in Britain and Ireland*. London: Croom Helm. 157–71.

Henton, C. (1983). Changes in the vowels of Received Pronunciation. *Journal of Phonetics* 11: 353–71.

Henton, C. & A. Bladon. (1988). Creak as a sociophonetic marker. In L.M. Hyman & C.N. Li (eds.) *Language, Speech and Mind: Studies in Honor of Victoria A. Fromkin*. London: Routledge. 3–29.

Herriman, M. & B. Burnaby. (eds.) (1996). *Language Policies in English-dominant Countries*. Clevedon: Multilingual Matters.

Herrmann, T. (2003). *Relative clauses in dialects of English: a typological approach*. Unpublished PhD dissertation. Freiburg: Albert-Ludwigs-Universität.

(2005). Relative clauses in English dialects of the British Isles. In B. Kortmann, T. Herrmann, L. Pietsch & S. Wagner (eds.) *A Comparative Grammar of English Dialects: Agreement, Gender, Relative Clauses*. Berlin: Mouton de Gruyter. 21–123.

Heselwood, B. & L. McChrystal. (1999). The effect of age-group and place of L1 acquisition on the realisation of Panjabi stop consonants in Bradford: an acoustic sociophonetic study. *Leeds Working Papers in Linguistics and Phonetics* 7: 49–68.

(2000). Gender, accent features and voicing in Panjabi-English bilingual children. *Leeds Working Papers in Linguistics and Phonetics* 8: 45–70.

Heuser, W. (1904). *Die Kildare-Gedichte. Die ältesten mittelenglischen Denkmäler in anglo-irischer Überlieferung*. Bonn: Hanstein.

Hewitt, R. (1986). *White Talk, Black Talk*. Cambridge: Cambridge University Press.

(1995). The umbrella and the sewing machine: transculturalism and the definition of surrealism. In A. Ålund and R. Granqvist (eds.) *Negotiating Identities*. Rodopi: Amsterdam. 91–104.

Hickey, R. (1993). The beginnings of Irish English. *Folia Linguistica Historica* 14: 213–38.

(1995). An assessment of language contact in the development of Irish English. In J. Fisiak (ed.) *Language Contact under Contact Conditions*. Berlin: Mouton de Gruyter. 109–30.

(1997). Arguments for creolisation in Irish English. In R. Hickey & S. Puppel (eds.) *Language History and Linguistic Modelling: A Festschrift for Jacek Fisiak on his 60th Birthday*. Berlin: Mouton de Gruyter. 969–1038.

(1999a). Ireland as a linguistic area. In J. P. Mallory (ed.) *Language in Ulster*. Cultra: Ulster Folk and Transport Museum. 36–53.

(1999b). Dublin English: current changes and their motivation. In P. Foulkes & G. Docherty (eds.) *Urban Voices: Accent Studies in the British Isles*. London: Arnold. 265–81.

(2000a). Models for describing aspect in Irish English. In H. Tristram (ed.) *Celtic Englishes II. Proceedings of the Second Potsdam Colloquium on Celtic Englishes, 28–30 September 1995*. Heidelberg: Winter. 97–116.

(2000b). Dissociation as a form of language change. *European Journal of English Studies* 4 (3): 303–15.

(2001). The South-East of Ireland. A neglected region of dialect study. In J. Kirk and Ó Baoill (eds.) *Language Links: The Languages of Scotland and Ireland*. Belfast: Queen's University of Belfast. 1–22.

(2002). *A Source Book for Irish English*. Amsterdam: John Benjamins.

(2003a). A corpus of Irish English. In R. Hickey (ed.) *Corpus Presenter. Software for Language Analysis*. Amsterdam: John Benjamins.

(2003b). How and why supraregional varieties arise. In M. Dossena & C. Jones (eds.) *Insights into Late Modern English*. Frankfurt: Peter Lang, 351–73.

(2003c). Rectifying a standard deficiency: pronominal distinctions in varieties of English. In I. Taavitsainen & A. H. Jucker (eds.) *Diachronic Perspectives on Address Term Systems*. Amsterdam: John Benjamins. 345–74.

(2003d). What's cool in Irish English? Linguistic change in contemporary Ireland. In H. Tristram (ed.) *Celtic Englishes III. Proceedings of the Third Potsdam Colloquium on Celtic Englishes, 19–23 September 2001*. Heidelberg: Winter. 357–73.

(ed.) (2004a). *Legacies of Colonial English. Studies in Transported Dialects*. Cambridge: Cambridge University Press.

(2004b). English dialect input to the Caribbean. In R. Hickey (ed.) *Legacies of Colonial English. Studies in Transported Dialects*. Cambridge: Cambridge University Press. 326–359.

(2004c). Development and diffusion of Irish English. In R. Hickey (ed.) *Legacies of Colonial English. Studies in Transported Dialects*. Cambridge: Cambridge University Press. 82–120.

(2004d). *A Sound Atlas of Irish English*. Berlin: Mouton de Gruyter.

(2007). *Irish English. Its History and Present-day Forms.* Cambridge: Cambridge University Press.

Hickey, R. & S. Puppel (eds.) (1997). *Language History and Linguistic Modelling. A Festschrift for Jacek Fisiak on his 60th Birthday.* Berlin: Mouton de Gruyter.

Hodge, R. & G. Kress. (1993). *Language as Ideology (2nd edn).* London: Routledge.

Hoffman, C. (2000). The spread of English and the growth of multilingualism with English in Europe. In J. Cenoz & U. Jessner (eds.) *English in Europe: The Acquisition of a Third Language.* Clevedon: Multilingual Matters. 1–22.

Holborow, M. (1999). *The Politics of English: A Marxist View of Language.* London: Sage.

Holmes, D. & G. Russell. (1999). Adolescent CIT use: paradigm shifts for educational and cultural practices? *British Journal of the Sociology of Education* 20 (1): 69–78.

Home Affairs Committee, House of Commons. (1985). *Chinese Community in Britain (2nd Report).* London: HMSO.

Honey, J. (1983). *The Language Trap: Race, Class and the Standard English Issue in British Schools.* Middlesex: National Council for Educational Standards.

(1989). *Does Accent Matter?* London: Faber.

(1997). *Language is Power: The Story of Standard English and its Enemies.* London: Faber.

Honeybone, P. (2001). Lenition inhibition in Liverpool English. *English Language and Linguistics* 5: 213–49.

Honikman, B. (1964). Articulatory settings. In D. Abercrombie, D. Fry, P. MacCarthy, N. Scott & J. Trim (eds.) *In Honour of Daniel Jones.* London: Longman. 73–84.

Hope, J. (1994). *The Authorship of Shakespeare's Plays: A Sociolinguistic Study.* Cambridge: Cambridge University Press.

Hornberger, N. H. (ed.) (2003). *Continua of Biliteracy.* Clevedon: Multilingual Matters.

Hornsey, A. W. (1983). Aims and objectives in foreign language teaching. In G. Richardson (ed.) *Teaching Modern Languages.* London: Croom Helm. 1–18.

Hudson, R. (1999). Subject-verb agreement in English. *English Language and Linguistics* 3: 173–207.

(2000a). *I amn't. Language* 76: 297–323.

(2000b). The language teacher and descriptive versus prescriptive norms: the educational context. Lecture presented to a workshop in Paris on prescriptivism and foreign-language teaching, 17 March 2000. (http://www.phon.ucl.ac.uk/home/dick/standard.htm [last accessed 3 March 2006]).

Hudson, R. & J. Holmes. (1995). *Children's Use of Spoken Standard English.* London: School Curriculum and Assessment Authority.

Hughes, A. & P. Trudgill. (1979). *English Accents and Dialects: An Introduction to Social and Regional Varieties of English in the British Isles.* London: Arnold.

(1996). *English Accents and Dialects: An Introduction to Social and Regional Varieties of British English.* London: Arnold.

Hughes, A., P. Trudgill & D. Watt. (2005). *English Accents and Dialects: An Introduction to Social and Regional Varieties of English in the British Isles.* London: Hodder Arnold.

Hulme, H. M. (1941). Derbyshire dialect in the seventeenth century: from the Bakewell parish records. *Journal of the Derbyshire Archæological and Natural History Society* 62: 88–103.

Humphreys, H. (1993). The Breton language: its present position and historical background. In M. J. Ball (ed.) *The Celtic Languages.* London: Routledge. 606–43.

Husain, J. (1991). The Bengali speech community. In S. Alladina & V. Edwards (eds.) *Multilingualism in the British Isles, Volume 2: Africa, the Middle East and Asia.* London: Longman. 75–87.

Hutchinson, J. (1987). *The Dynamics of Cultural Nationalism: The Gaelic Revival and the Creation of the Irish Nation State.* London: Allen and Unwin.

Ihalainen, O. (1976). Periphrastic *do* in affirmative sentences in the dialect of East Somerset. *Neuphilologische Mitteilungen* 77 (4): 608–22.

(1980). Relative clauses in the dialect of Somerset. *Neuphilologische Mitteilungen.* 81: 187–96.

(1984). 'He took the bottle and put 'n in his pocket': the object pronoun 'it' in present-day Somerset. In W. Viereck (ed.) *Focus On: England and Wales.* Amsterdam: John Benjamins. 153–61.

(1985). Synchronic variation and linguistic change: evidence from British English dialects. In R. Eaton, O. Fischer, W. Koopman & F. Van der Leek (eds.) *Papers from the 4th International Conference on English Historical Linguistics.* Amsterdam: John Benjamins. 61–72.

(1991a). Periphrastic do in affirmative sentences in the dialect of East Somerset. In P. Trudgill & J. K. Chambers (eds.) *Dialects of English: Studies in Grammatical Variation.* London: Longman. 148–60.

(1991b). On grammatical diffusion in Somerset folk speech. In P. Trudgill & J. K. Chambers (eds.) *Dialects of English: Studies in Grammatical Variation.* London: Longman. 104–19.

(1994). The dialects of England since 1776. In R. Burchfield (ed.) *The Cambridge History of the English Language: Volume 5, English in Britain and Overseas: Origins and Development.* Cambridge: Cambridge University Press. 197–274.

Inglis, H. (1844). *The Channel Islands (4th edn).* London: Whittaker & Co.

Inner London Education Authority (ILEA). (1981, 1983, 1985, 1987). *Language Census.* London: ILEA Research and Statistics.

INRA (International Research Associates). (2001). *Les Européens et les Langues.* Eurobarometer 54 Special Report drafted for the Directorate General of Education and Culture. (English Summary available on: http://europa.eu. int/comm/public_opinion/archives/ebs/ebs_147_summ_en.pdf [last accessed 3 March 2006]).

Isaac, G. R. (2002). The Celtiberian alphabetic signs San and Sigma and the ablative singular. *Studia Celtica* 36: 1–20.

Isle of Man Government. (2002). *Isle of Man Census Report 2001* (2 Volumes). Douglas: Isle of Man Government Treasury.

Ito, R. & S. Tagliamonte. (2003). Well weird, right dodgy, very strange, really cool: layering and recycling in English intensifiers. *Language in Society* 32: 257–79.

Jackson, K. H. (1953). *Language and History in Early Britain*. Edinburgh: Edinburgh University Press.

Jackson, P. (1990). *Britain's Deaf Heritage*. Haddington: Pentland Press.

Jameson, F. (2000). Globalization and political strategy. *New Left Review* 4 (July/ August): 49–68.

Jarman, E. & A. Cruttenden. (1976). Belfast intonation and the myth of the fall. *Journal of the International Phonetic Association* 6: 4–12.

Johnson, A. L. (2001). *An auditory analysis of /l/ vocalisation in Derby English*. Unpublished undergraduate dissertation. York: University of York.

Johnston, P. A. (1979). *A synchronic and historical study of Border Area bimoric vowel systems*. Unpublished PhD dissertation. Edinburgh: University of Edinburgh.

  (1983). *A sociolinguistic investigation of Edinburgh speech*. Social Science Research Council End of Grant Report C/00/23/0023/1.

  (1984). Variation in the Standard Scottish English of Morningside. *English World-Wide* 4 (2): 133–85.

  (1985a). The rise and fall of the Morningside/Kelvinside accent. In M. Görlach (ed.) *Focus On: Scotland*. Amsterdam: Benjamins. 37–56.

  (1985b). *Worksheets on Scots dialects*. Based on material collected under a grant by the Nuffield Foundation, 1983–84. Unpublished handouts. Glasgow: University of Glasgow.

  (1997a). Older Scots phonology and its regional variation. In C. Jones (ed.) *The Edinburgh History of the Scots Language*. Edinburgh: Edinburgh University Press. 47–111.

  (1997b). Regional variation. In C. Jones (ed.) *The Edinburgh History of the Scots Language*. Edinburgh: Edinburgh University Press. 443–513.

Johnstone, R., W. Harlen, M. MacNeil, B. Stradling & G. Thorpe. (1999). *The Attainments of Pupils Receiving Gaelic Medium Education in Scotland*. Stirling: Scottish CILT.

Jones, C. (1996). *A Language Suppressed. The Pronunciation of the Scots Language in the 18th Century*. Edinburgh: John Donald.

  (ed.) (1997). *The Edinburgh History of the Scots Language*. Edinburgh: Edinburgh University Press.

Jones, D. G. (1988). Literary Welsh. In M. J. Ball (ed.) *The Use of Welsh*. Clevedon: Multilingual Matters. 125–71.

Jones, G. E. (1984). The distinctive vowels and consonants of Welsh. In M. J. Ball & G. E. Jones (eds.) *Welsh Phonology: Selected Readings*. Cardiff: University of Wales Press. 40–64.

  (2000). *Iaith Lafar Brycheiniog*. Caerdydd: Gwasg Prifysgol Cymru.

Jones, H. (2005). *A Longitudinal Study: Welsh in the Census*. Cardiff: Bwrdd yr Iaith Gymraeg.

Jones, Mari C. (1998). *Language Obsolescence and Revitalization*. Oxford: Oxford University Press.

  (2000a). Ambiguity and unpredictability: linguistic change in modern Jerriais. *Verbum* 22 (2): 203–22.

(2000b). Swimming against the tide: language planning on Jersey. *Language Problems and Language Planning* 24 (2): 167–96.

(2000c). The subjunctive in Guernsey Norman French. *Journal of French Language Studies* 10 (2): 177–203.

(2001). *Jersey Norman French: A Sociolinguistic Study of an Obsolescent Dialect.* Oxford: Blackwell.

(2002). Mette a haout dauve la grippe des angllaïs: convergence on the island of Guernsey. In M. C. Jones & E. Esch (eds.) *Language Change: The Interplay of Internal, External and Extra-linguistic Factors.* Berlin: Mouton de Gruyter. 143–68.

(2003). *Jèrriais: Jersey's Native Tongue.* Jersey: Don Balleine Trust.

(2005a). Some structural and social correlates of single word intrasentential codeswitching in Jersey Norman French. *Journal of French Language Studies* 15 (1): 1–23.

(2005b). Transfer and changing linguistic norms in Jersey Norman French. *Bilingualism: Language and Cognition* 8 (2): 159–75.

(forthcoming). *The Martin Manuscripts: An unexplored corpus of Guernsey Norman French.* Leuven and Paris: Peeters.

Jones, Mark. (1999). The phonology of definite article reduction. In C. Upton & K. Wales (eds.) *Dialectal Variation in English. Special Issue of Leeds Studies in English* 30: 103–21.

(2002). The origin of definite article reduction in northern English dialects: evidence from dialect allomorphy. *English Language and Linguistics* 6: 325–45.

Jones, Megan. (2002). 'You do get queer, see. She do get queer': Non-standard periphrastic DO in Somerset English. *University of Pennsylvania Working Papers in Linguistics* 8 (3): 117–32.

Jones, Megan & S. Tagliamonte. (2004). From Somerset to Samaná: preverbal 'did' in the voyage of English. *Language Variation and Change* 16 (2): 93–126.

Jones, R. F. (1953). *The Triumph of the English Language.* Stanford: Stanford University.

Jones, R. M. (1993). *Ar Lafar ac ar Bapur.* Aberystwyth: Astudiaethau Addysg Aberystwyth.

(1999). *The Welsh Answering System.* Berlin: Mouton de Gruyter.

Jones, R. M. & A. R. Thomas. (1977). *The Welsh Language: Studies in its Syntax and Semantics.* Cardiff: University of Wales Press.

Jones, R. O. (1993). The sociolinguistics of Welsh. In M. J. Ball (ed.) *The Celtic Languages.* London: Routledge. 536–605.

Jones, S. (1926). *A Welsh Phonetic Reader.* London: University of London Press.

Jones, T. (1993). *Britain's Ethnic Minorities.* London: Policy Studies Institute.

Jones, V. (1985). Tyneside syntax: a presentation of some data from the Tyneside Linguistic Survey. In W. Viereck (ed.) *Focus on: England and Wales.* Amsterdam: John Benjamins. 163–77.

Joret, C. (1883). *Des Caractères et de L'extension du Patois Normand.* Paris: Vieweg.

Kachru, B. (1978). Towards structuring code-mixing: an Indian perspective. *International Journal of the Sociology of Language* 16: 27–47.

Kallen, J. (1986). The co-occurrence of DO and BE in Hiberno-English. In J. Harris, D. Little & D. Singleton (eds.) *Perspectives on the English*

Language in Ireland. Dublin: Centre for Language and Communication Studies, Trinity College Dublin. 133–48.

(1989). Tense and aspect categories in Irish English. *English World-Wide* 10: 1–39.

(1990). The Hiberno-English perfect: grammaticalisation revisited. *Irish University Review* 20 (1): 120–36.

(1991). Sociolinguistic variation and methodology: *After* as a Dublin variable. In J. Cheshire (ed.) *English Around the World: Sociolinguistic Perspectives* Cambridge: Cambridge University Press. 61–74.

(1994). English in Ireland. In R. W. Burchfield (ed.) *The Cambridge History of the English Language: Volume 5*. Cambridge: Cambridge University Press. 148–96.

(1996). Entering lexical fields in Irish English. In J. Klemola, M. Kytö & M. Rissanen (eds.) *Speech Past and Present: Studies in English Dialectology in Memory of Ossi Ihalainen*. Frankfurt am Main: Peter Lang. 101–129.

(2000). Two languages, two borders, one island: some linguistic and political borders in Ireland. *International Journal of the Sociology of Language* 145: 29–63.

Kaplan, R. B. & R. B. Baldauf. (1997). *Language Planning: From Practice to Theory*. Clevedon: Multilingual Matters.

Kegl, J., A. Senghas & M. Coppola. (1999). Creation through contact: sign language emergence and sign language change in Nicaragua. In M. DeGraff (ed.) *Language Creation and Language Change: Creolization, Diachrony, and Development*. Cambridge, MA: MIT Press. 179–237.

Kekäläinen, K. (1985). Relative clauses in the dialect of Suffolk. *Neuphilologische Mitteilungen* 86: 353–7.

Kelly, J. (1995). Consonant-associated resonance in three varieties of English. In J. Windsor Lewis (ed.) *Studies in General and English Phonetics: Essays in Honour of Professor J. D. O'Connor*. London: Routledge. 335–349.

Kempadoo, M. & M. Abdelrazak (eds.) (2001). *Directory of Supplementary & Mother-tongue Classes (2nd edn)*. London: Resource Unit for Supplementary & Mother-tongue Schools.

Kennedy, D. (1996). Soap opera Australian-speak raises the tone. *The Times*, 19 March.

Kenner, C. (1997). A child writes from her everyday world: using home texts to develop biliteracy at school. In E. Gregory (ed.) *One Child, Many Worlds: Early Learning in Multicultural Communities*. London, David Fulton. 75–86.

Kenrick, D. S. (1971). The sociolinguistics of the development of British Romani. In T. Acton (ed.) *Proceedings of the Research and Policy Conference of the National Gypsy Education Council*. Oxford: National Gypsy Education Council. 5–14.

(1979). Romani English. *International Journal of the Sociology of Language* 19: 111–20.

Kerswill, P. (1984). Social and linguistic aspects of Durham (e:). *Journal of the International Phonetic Association* 14: 13–34.

(1987). Levels of linguistic variation in Durham. *Journal of Linguistics* 23: 25–49.

(1996a). Children, adolescents and language change. *Language Variation and Change* 8: 177–202.

(1996b). Milton Keynes and dialect levelling in south-eastern British English. In D. Graddol, J. Swann & D. Leith (eds.) *English: History, Diversity and Change*. London: Routledge. 292–300.

(2001). Mobility, meritocracy and dialect levelling: the fading (and phasing) out of Received Pronunciation. In P. Rajamäe & K. Vogelberg (eds.) *British Studies in the New Millennium: The Challenge of the Grassroots*. Tartu: University of Tartu. 45–58.

(2003). Dialect levelling and geographical diffusion in British English. In D. Britain & J. Cheshire (eds.) *Social Dialectology. In Honour of Peter Trudgill*. Amsterdam: John Benjamins. 223–43.

Kerswill, P. & A. Williams. (1997). Investigating social and linguistic identity in three British schools. In U. Kotsinas, A.-B. Stenström & A. M. Karlsson (eds.) *Ungdomssprak i Norden*. Stockholm: University of Stockholm Press. 159–76.

(2000). Creating a new town koine: children and language change in Milton Keynes. *Language in Society* 29: 65–115.

(2005). New towns and koineisation: linguistic and social correlates. *Linguistics* 43 (5): 1023–48.

Kerswill, P. & S. Wright. (1990). On the limits of auditory transcription: a socio-phonetic perspective. *Language Variation and Change* 2: 255–75.

Khan, A. (2007) *A sociolinguistic study of Birmingham English: language variation and change in a multiethnic British community*. Unpublished PhD dissertation. Lancaster: University of Lancaster.

Khan, F. (1991). The Urdu speech community. In S. Alladina & V. Edwards (eds.) *Multilingualism in the British Isles, Volume 2: Africa, the Middle East and Asia*. London, Longman. 128–40.

Khan, N. & M. A. Kabir. (1999). Mother-tongue education among Bangladeshi children in Swansea: an exploration. *Language Learning Journal* 20: 20–26.

Khattab, G. (2002a). VOT in English and Arabic bilingual and monolingual children. In D. Parkinson & E. Benmamoun (eds.) *Perspectives on Arabic Linguistics XIII-XIV. Papers from the Thirteenth and Fourteenth Annual Symposia on Arabic Linguistics*. Amsterdam: John Benjamins. 1–38.

(2002b). /l/ production in English-Arabic bilingual speakers. *International Journal of Bilingualism* 6: 335–53.

King, A. & M. Reiss (eds.) (1993). *The Multicultural Dimension of the National Curriculum*. London: Falmer Press.

King, G. (1993). *Modern Welsh: A Comprehensive Grammar*. London: Routledge.

King, L. & R. Johnstone. (2001). *An Agenda for Languages*. London: Centre for Information on Language Teaching and Research.

Kingman, J. (1988). *Report of the Committee of Inquiry into the Teaching of the English Language*. London: Her Majesty's Stationery Office.

Kingsmore, R. (1995). *Ulster Scots Speech: A Sociolinguistic Study*. Tuscaloosa: University of Alabama Press.

(1996). Status, stigma and sex in Ulster Scots speech. *Belfast Working Papers in Language and Linguistics* 13: 223–37.

Kingston, M. (2000). *Dialects in danger: rural dialect attrition in the East Anglian county of Suffolk*. Unpublished MA dissertation. Colchester: University of Essex.

Kirk, J. (1985). Linguistic atlases and grammar: the investigation and description of regional variation in English syntax. In J. Kirk, S. Sanderson & J. Widdowson (eds.) *Studies in Linguistic Geography*. London: Croom Helm. 130–56.

(1997a). Ulster English: the state of the art. In H. Tristram (ed.) *The Celtic Englishes I*. Heidelberg: C. Winter. 135–79.

(1997b). Ethnolinguistic differences in Northern Ireland. In A. R. Thomas (ed.) *Issues and Methods in Dialectology*. Bangor: Department of Linguistics, University of Wales, Bangor. 55–68.

(2003). Archipelagic glotto-politics: the Scotstacht. In H. Tristram (ed.) *The Celtic Englishes III*. Heidelberg: C. Winter. 339–56.

Kirk, J. & G. Millar. (1998). Verbal aspect in the Scots and English of Ulster. *Scottish Language* 17: 82–107.

Kirk, J. & D. Ó Baoill (eds.) (2001). *Language Links: The Languages of Scotland and Ireland*. Belfast: Queen's University of Belfast.

(eds.) (2002). *Travellers and their Language*. Belfast: Queen's University of Belfast.

Klemola, J. (1994). Periphrastic DO in south-western dialects of British English: a reassessment. *Dialectologia et geolinguistica* 2: 33–51.

(1996). *Non-standard periphrastic 'do': a study in variation and change*. Unpublished PhD dissertation. Colchester: University of Essex.

(2002). Periphrastic DO: dialectal distribution and origins. In M. Filppula, J. Klemola & H. Pitkänen (eds.) *The Celtic Roots of English*. Joensuu: Faculty of Humanities, University of Joensuu. 199–210.

Klemola, J. & M. J. Jones. (1999). The Leeds corpus of English dialects project. *Leeds Studies in English* 30: 17–30.

Klima, E. & U. Bellugi. (1979). *The Signs of Language*. London: Harvard University Press.

Knowles, G. O. (1973). *Scouse: the urban dialect of Liverpool*. Unpublished PhD dissertation. Leeds: University of Leeds.

(1978). The nature of phonological variables in Scouse. In P. Trudgill (ed.) *Sociolinguistic Patterns in British English*. London: Arnold. 80–90.

Koch, J. T. (1982–3). The loss of final syllables and loss of declension in Brittonic. *Bulletin of the Board of Celtic Studies* 30: 201–33.

(1992). 'Gallo-Brittonic' vs 'Insular Celtic': the inter-relationships of the Celtic languages reconsidered. In G. Le Menn & J.-Y. Le Moing (eds.) *Bretagne et pays celtique. Langues, histoire, civilisation. Mélanges offerts à la memoire de Léon Fleuriot*. Rennes: Saint Brieuc. 471–95.

(1995). The conversion and the transition from Primitive to Old Irish. *Emania* 13: 39–50.

Kortmann, B. (2002). New prospects for the study of English dialect syntax: impetus from syntactic theory and language typology. In S. Barbiers, L. Cornips & S. van der Kleij (eds.) *Syntactic Microvariation*. Amsterdam: Meertens Institute Electronic Publications in Linguistics. 185–213.

Kress, G. (1982). *Learning to Write*. London: Routledge Kegan Paul.

Kroll, B. & R. Vann. (1981). *Exploring Speaking and Writing Relationships: Connections and Contrasts*. Urbana: NATE.

Kyle, J. & B. Woll. (1985). *Sign Language: The Study of Deaf People and their Language*. Cambridge: Cambridge University Press.

Labov, W. (1966). *The Social Stratification of English in New York City.* Washington, DC: Center for Applied Linguistics.

(1972). *Sociolinguistic Patterns.* Oxford: Blackwell.

(1990). The intersection of sex and social class in the course of linguistic change. *Language Variation and Change* 2: 205–54.

(1994). *Principles of Linguistic Change, Volume 1: Internal Factors.* Oxford: Blackwell.

(2001). *Principles of Linguistic Change, Volume 2: Social Factors.* Oxford: Blackwell.

Labov, W., M. Yaeger & R. Steiner. (1972). *A Quantitative Study of Sound Change in Progress. Report on National Science Foundation Project no. GS-3287 (2 Volumes).* Philadelphia: US Regional Survey.

Ladd, P. (2003). *Understanding Deaf Culture: In search of Deafhood.* Clevedon: Multilingual Matters.

Ladefoged, P. (2003). *Phonetic Data Analysis.* Oxford: Blackwell.

Lambert, P.-Y. (2003). *La langue gauloise (2nd edn).* Paris: Editions Errance.

Lass, R. (1990). Early mainland residues in Southern Hiberno-English. *Irish University Review* 20 (1): 137–48.

(1999). Phonology and morphology. In R. Lass (ed.) *Cambridge History of the English Language: Volume III: 1476–1776.* Cambridge: Cambridge University Press. 56–186.

Laver, J. (1980). *The Phonetic Description of Voice Quality.* Cambridge: Cambridge University Press.

(1994). *Principles of Phonetics.* Cambridge: Cambridge University Press.

Lawson, E. & J. Stuart-Smith. (1999). A sociophonetic investigation of the 'Scottish' consonants (/x/ and /ʍ/) in the speech of Glaswegian children. *Proceedings of the 14th International Congress of Phonetic Sciences.* 2541–4.

Lawson, M. (1998). TV is the perp. *The Guardian*, 21 March.

Le Feuvre, G. F. (1976). *Histouaithes et Gens d'Jèrri.* Jersey: Don Balleine.

(1983). *Jèrri Jadis.* Jersey: Don Balleine.

Le Maistre, F. (1947). *The Jersey language in its present state. The passing of a Norman heritage.* Paper presented to the Jersey Society, London, 8 July 1947. London: The Jersey Society.

(1966). *Dictionnaire Jersiais-Français.* Jersey: Don Balleine Trust.

(1979a). *The Jersey Language (Booklet and Cassette 2).* Jersey: Don Balleine Trust.

(1979b). *The Jersey Language (Booklet and Cassette 3).* Jersey: Don Balleine Trust.

(1979c). *The Jersey Language (Booklet and Cassette 4).* Jersey: Don Balleine Trust.

(1979d). *The Jersey Language (Booklet and Cassette 5).* Jersey: Don Balleine Trust.

(1982). *The Language of Auregny: La langue normande d'Auregny.* Jersey: Don Balleine Trust & Alderney: Alderney Society and Museum.

(1993). *The Jersey Language (Booklet and Cassette 1).* Jersey: Don Balleine Trust.

Le Master, B. & J. Dwyer. (1991). Knowing and using female and male signs in Dublin. *Sign Language Studies* 73: 361–96.

Le Patourel, J. (1937). *The Medieval Administration of the Channel Islands 1199–1399*. London: Oxford University Press.

Lebarbenchon, R. J. (1988). *La Grève de Lecq. Littératures et cultures populaires de Normandie, Volume 1*. Cherbourg: Isoète.

Lehti, A. & B. Mattson. (2001). Health, attitude to care and pattern of attendance among gypsy women – a general practice perspective. *Family Practice* 18 (4): 445–8.

Leith, D. (1983). *A Social History of English*. London: Routledge.

Leland, C. (1874). *The English Gypsies and their Language*. London: Trubner.

Lemprière, R. (1974). *History of the Channel Islands*. London: Robert Hale.

Lepelley, R. (1999). *La Normandie dialectale: Petite encyclopédie des langages et mots régionaux de la province de Normandie et des Iles anglo-normandes*. Caen: Office Universitaire d'Etudes Normandes, Université de Caen.

Leung, C. (1995). *English as an Additional/Second Language (EAL/ESL) Stages/ Levels*. Consultant Report to Schools Curriculum and Assessment Authority, London.

(1996). Content, context and language. In T. Cline & N. Frederickson (eds.) *Curriculum Related Assessment, Cummins and Bilingual Children*. Clevedon: Multilingual Matters. 26–40.

(1997). Language content and learning process in curriculum tasks. In C. Leung & C. Cable (eds.) *English as an Additional Language: Changing Perspectives*. Watford: National Association for Language Development in the Curriculum. 28–39.

(2001). English as an additional language: distinctive language focus or diffused curriculum concerns? *Language and Education* 15 (1): 33–55.

Leung, C. & C. Cable. (eds.) (1997). *English as an Additional Language: Changing Perspectives*. Watford: NALDIC.

Leung, C. & C. Franson. (1991). English as a second language in the National Curriculum. In P. Meara & A. Ryan (eds.) *Language and Nation*. Clevedon: British Association for Applied Linguistics/Multilingual Matters. 117–25.

Leung, C., R. Harris & B. Rampton. (1997). The idealised native speaker, reified ethnicities and classroom realities. *TESOL Quarterly* 31 (3): 543–60.

Levey, S. (2005). *Variation in past BE in an urban vernacular: perspectives from adolescence*. Manuscript. London: Department of Linguistics, Queen Mary University of London.

(2006). Visiting London relatives. *English World-Wide* 27 (1): 45–70.

Lewis, E. S. (1895). Guernsey: its people and dialect. *Publications of the Modern Language Association* 10: 1–82.

Lewis, H. (1946). *Llawlyfr Cernyweg Canol (2nd edn)*. Cardiff: University of Wales Press.

Lewis, H. & H. Pedersen. (1974). *A Concise Comparative Celtic Grammar (3rd edn)*. Göttingen: Vandenhoeck & Ruprecht.

Lewis, J. W. (1989). Syntax and lexis in Glamorgan English. In N. Coupland & A. R. Thomas (eds.) *English in Wales: Diversity, Conflict and Change*. Clevedon: Multilingual Matters. 109–20.

Li Wei. (1993). Mother tongue maintenance in a Chinese community school in Newcastle-upon-Tyne. *Language and Education* 7 (3): 199–215.

(1994). *Three Generations Two Languages One Family: Language Choice and Language Shift in a Chinese Community in Britain.* Clevedon: Multilingual Matters.

(2000). Towards a critical evaluation of language maintenance and language shift. *Sociolinguistica* 14: 142–7.

Li Wei & S. Lee. (2001). L1 development in an L2 environment: The use of Cantonese classifiers and quantifiers by young British-born Chinese in Tyneside. *International Journal of Bilingual Education and Bilingualism* 4 (6): 359–82.

Liddell, S. K. (2003). *Grammar, Gesture and Meaning in American Sign Language.* Cambridge: Cambridge University Press.

Liddicoat, A. J. (1989). A brief survey of the dialect of Sark. *Report and Transactions of La Société Guernesiaise* 22 (4): 689–704.

(1990). Some structural features of language obsolescence in the dialect of Jersey. *Language Sciences* 12 (2–3): 197–208.

(1991). Le traitement de l'r intervocalique dans le dialecte de Sercq. *Revue de Linguistique Romane* 55: 119–24.

(1994). *A Grammar of the Norman French of the Channel Islands: The Dialects of Jersey and Sark.* Berlin: Mouton de Gruyter.

Lindblom, B. (1986). On the origin and purpose of discreteness and invariance in sound patterns. In J. Perkell & D. Klatt (eds.) *Invariance and Variability in Speech Processes.* Hillsdale: Lawrence Erlbaum Associates. 493–510.

(1990). Explaining phonetic variation: a sketch of the H & H theory. In W. J. Hardcastle & A. Marchal (eds.) *Speech Production and Speech Modelling.* Amsterdam: Kluwer. 403–439.

Linguistic Minorities Project. (1985). *The Other Languages of England.* London: Routledge & Kegan Paul.

Lippi-Green, R. (1997). *English with an Accent.* London: Routledge.

Llamas, C. (1999). A new methodology: data elicitation for social and regional language variation studies. *Leeds Working Papers in Linguistics and Phonetics* 7: 95–118.

Lo Bianco, J. (2001). *Language and Literacy Policy in Scotland.* Stirling: Scottish CILT/University of Stirling.

Local, J. (1990). Some rhythm, resonance and quality variations in urban Tyneside speech. In S. Ramsaran (ed.) *Studies in the Pronunciation of English: A Commemorative Volume in Honour of A. C. Gimson.* London: Routledge. 286–92.

(2003). Variable domains and variable relevance: interpreting phonetic exponents. *Journal of Phonetics* 31: 321–39.

Local, J., J. Kelly & W. Wells. (1986). Towards a phonology of conversation: turntaking in Tyneside. *Journal of Linguistics* 22: 411–37.

Local, J., W. Wells & M. Sebba. (1985). Phonology for conversation. Phonetic aspects of turn delimitation in London Jamaican. *Journal of Pragmatics* 9: 309–30.

Lodge, K. R. (1966). The Stockport dialect. *Le Maître Phonétique* 126: 26–30.

(1978). A Stockport teenager. *Journal of the International Phonetic Association* 8: 56–71.

Logan, J. (1831, reprinted 1876, 1976). *The Scottish Gael (2 Volumes).* Edinburgh: John Donald.

Lowry, O. (2002). The stylistic variation of nuclear patterns in Belfast English. *Journal of the International Phonetic Association* 32: 33–42.

Lowth, R. (1762). *A Short Introduction to English Grammar*. London.

Lucas, A. (ed.) (1995). *Anglo-Irish poems of the Middle Ages*. Dublin: Columba Press.

Mac Eoin, G. (1993). Irish. In M. Ball (ed.) *The Celtic Languages*. London: Routledge. 101–144.

Macafee, C. (1983). *Varieties of English around the World: Glasgow*. Amsterdam: Benjamins.

(1985). Nationalism and the Scots renaissance now. In M. Görlach (ed.) *Focus On: Scotland*. Amsterdam: Benjamins. 7–18.

(1994). *Traditional Dialect in the Modern World: A Glasgow Case Study*. Frankfurt: Peter Lang.

(ed.) (1996). *Concise Ulster Dictionary*. Oxford: Oxford University Press.

(1997). Ongoing change in Modern Scots: the social dimension. In C. Jones (ed.) *The Edinburgh History of the Scots Language*. Edinburgh: Edinburgh University Press. 514–50.

Macaulay, C. (1998). *Gaelic: a study of language maintenance and shift in the Scottish Gaidhealtachd*. Unpublished PhD dissertation. Hatfield: University of Hertfordshire.

MacAulay, D. (1982). Borrow, calque and switch: the law of the English frontier. In J. Anderson (ed.) *Language Form and Linguistic Variation*. Amsterdam: Benjamins.

(ed.) (1992). *The Celtic Languages*. Cambridge: Cambridge University Press.

Macaulay, R. (1977). *Language, Social Class and Education: A Glasgow Study*. Edinburgh: Edinburgh University Press.

(1991). *Locating Dialect in Discourse*. Oxford: Oxford University Press.

(1997). RP R. I. P. In R. Macaulay (ed.) *Standards and Variation in Urban Speech*. Amsterdam: John Benjamins. 35–44.

Macaulay, R. & G. D. Trevelyan. (1977). *Language, Social Class and Education: A Glasgow Study*. Edinburgh: Edinburgh University Press.

MacDonald, M. (1984). *Gaelic language and cultural maintenance in the Scottish Hebridean islands of Barra and Harris*. Unpublished PhD dissertation. Hatfield: University of Hertfordshire.

Macdonald, S. (1997). *Reimagining Culture: Histories, Identities and the Gaelic Renaissance*. Oxford: Berg.

MacKinnon, K. (1977). *Language, Education and Social Processes in a Gaelic Community*. London: Routledge.

(1978). *Gaelic in Scotland 1971: Some Sociological and Demographic Considerations of the Census Report for Gaelic*. Hatfield: Hertis Publications.

(1984a). Scottish Gaelic and English in the Highlands. In P. Trudgill (ed.) *Language in the British Isles*. Cambridge: Cambridge University Press. 499–516.

(1984b). *Gaelic in Highland Region – The 1981 Census*. Inverness: An Comunn Gaidhealach.

(1985). The Scottish Gaelic speech-community – some social perspectives. *Scottish Language* 5: 65–88.

(1986). Gender, occupational and educational factors in Gaelic language-shift and regeneration. In G. Mac Eoin, A. Ahlqvist & D. Ó hAodha (eds.) *Third International Conference on Minority Languages: Celtic Papers*. Clevedon: Multilingual Matters. 47–71.

(1987a). *Language-maintenance and viability in contemporary Gaelic-speaking communities: Skye and the Western Isles today (from census data)*. Paper presented to the Eighth International Congress of Celtic Studies, Swansea, 19–24 July 1987.

(1987b). *Occupation, Migration and Language-Maintenance in Gaelic Communities*. Hatfield: Hertis Publications.

(1987c). *The Present Position of Gaelic in Scottish Primary Education*. Leeuwarden: Fryske Akademy.

(1988a). *Gaelic Language-Maintenance and Viability in the Isle of Skye*. Hatfield: Hatfield Polytechnic.

(1988b). *Language Maintenance and Viability in Contemporary Gaelic Communities*. Report to Economic and Social Research Council, Swindon.

(1991a). Language retreat and regeneration in the present-day Scottish Gaidhealtachd. In C. Williams (ed.) *Linguistic Minorities, Society and Territory*. Clevedon: Multilingual Matters. 121–49.

(1991b). Language-maintenance and viability in contemporary Gaelic communities: Skye and the Western Isles today. In P. Ureland & G. Broderick (eds.) *Language Contact in the British Isles*. Tübingen: Niemeyer. 495–534.

(1992). *An Aghaidh nan Ceag: Despite Adversity – Gaeldom's Twentieth Century Survival and Potential*. Inverness: Comunn na Gaidhlig.

(1994). Gaelic language in the Western Isles. In A. Fenton & D. MacDonald (eds.) *Studies in Scots and Gaelic*. Edinburgh: Canongate. 123–37.

(1997a). *Gaelic as an endangered language – problems and prospects*. Paper presented to Workshop on Endangered Languages, University of York 26–27 July 1997.

(1997b). Gaelic in Family, Work and Community Domains: Euromosaic Project 1994–5. *Scottish Language* 17: 55–69.

(1998). Gaelic in family, work and community domains: Euromosaic Project 1994–95. In J. McClure (ed.) *A selection of papers presented at the Fifth International Conference on the Languages of Scotland and Ulster, Aberdeen, 1–5 August 1997*. Aberdeen: Association for Scottish Literary Studies. 55–69.

(2001a). *Gaelic at its 11th Hour*. Inverness: Comunn na Gaidhlig.

(2001b) Fàs no Bàs (Prosper or Perish) – prospects for survival. In J. Kirk & D. Ó Baoill (eds.) *Linguistic Politics – Language Policies for Northern Ireland, the Republic of Ireland, and Scotland*. Belfast: Queen's University Press. 255–8.

MacKinnon, K. & M. MacDonald. (1980). *Ethnic Communities: The Transmission of Language and Culture in Harris and Barra*. Report to Economic and Social Research Council, Swindon.

Macphedran, G. (1989). Banana split. *The Listener*, 28 September.

Macpherson, J. A. (2000). *Revitalising Gaelic – A National Asset*. Edinburgh: Scottish Executive.

MacPherson, W. (1999). *The Stephen Lawrence Inquiry*. London: Home Office.

Maguire, G. (1991). *Our Own Language: An Irish Initiative*. Clevedon: Multilingual Matters.

Mahandru, V. K. (1991). The Panjabi speech community. In S. Alladina & V. Edwards (eds.) *Multilingualism in the British Isles, Volume 2: Africa, the Middle East and Asia*. London: Longman. 115–27.

Mansoor, L. & R. Drowse. (2003). Effect of pictograms on readability of patient information materials. *Annals of Pharmacotherapy* 37 (7–8): 1003–9.

Marenbon, J. (1987). *English, our English: The New Orthodoxy Examined*. London: Centre for Policy Studies.

Marginson, S. (1999). After globalization: emerging politics of education. *Journal of Education Policy* 14 (1): 19–31.

Marschark, M. (1993). *Psychological Development of Deaf Children*. Oxford: Oxford University Press.

Marsh, D. & N. Marshall. (2000). *The Guardian Style Guide*. London: *The Guardian*.

Martin, D. & J. Stuart-Smith. (1998). Exploring bilingual children's perceptions of being bilingual and biliterate: implications for educational provision. *British Journal of Sociology of Education* 19: 237–54.

Martin, P., A. Creese, A. Bhatt & N. Bhojani. (2004). *Complementary Schools and their Communities in Leicester: A Final Report*. Leicester: School of Education, University of Leicester.

Martin-Jones, M. (1984). The newer minorities: literacy and educational issues. In P. Trudgill (ed.) *Language in the British Isles*. Cambridge: Cambridge University Press. 425–48.

  (1991). Sociolinguistic surveys as a source of evidence in the study of bilingualism: A critical assessment of survey work conducted among linguistic minorities in three British cities. *International Journal of the Sociology of Language* 90: 37–55.

  (1995). Codeswitching in the classroom: two decades of research. In L. Milroy and P. Muysken (eds.) *One Speaker, Two Languages*. Cambridge: Cambridge University Press. 90–111.

Martin-Jones, M. & K. Jones. (eds.) (2000). *Multilingual Literacies*. Amsterdam: John Benjamins.

Martin-Jones, M. & M. Saxena. (1996). Turn-taking, power asymmetries, and the positioning of bilingual participants in classroom discourse. *Linguistics and Education* 8: 105–123.

Mather, J. Y. & H.-H. Speitel. (1975, 1977, 1986). *The Linguistic Atlas of Scotland (3 Volumes)*. London: Croom Helm.

Mathisen, A. G. (1999). Sandwell, West Midlands: ambiguous perspectives on gender patterns and models of change. In P. Foulkes & G. J. Docherty (eds.) *Urban Voices*. London: Arnold. 107–123.

Matras, Y. (ed.) (1998). *The Romani Element in Non Standard Speech*. Wiesbaden: Harrassowitz Verlag.

  (2000). Mixed languages: a functional-communicative approach. *Bilingualism: Language and Cognition* 3: 79–99.

Matras, Y. & P. Bakker (eds.) (2003). *The Mixed Language Debate*. Berlin: Mouton de Gruyter.

Matthews, P. (1996). *The Irish Deaf Community (Volume 1)*. Dublin: The Linguistics Institute of Ireland.

McArthur, T. (1992). *The Oxford Companion to the English Language*. Oxford: Oxford University Press.

McCafferty, K. (1998a). Shared accents, divided speech community? Change in Northern Ireland English. *Language Variation and Change* 10: 97–121.

(1998b). Barriers to change: ethnic division and phonological innovation in Northern Hiberno-English. *English World-Wide* 19: 7–35.

(1999). (London)Derry: between Ulster and local speech – class, ethnicity and language change. In P. Foulkes & G. J. Docherty (eds.) *Urban Voices*. London: Arnold. 246–64.

(2001). *Ethnicity and Language Change. English in (London)Derry, Northern Ireland*. Amsterdam: John Benjamins.

(2003a). Language contact in Early Modern Ireland: the case of *be after V-ing* as a future gram. In C. Tschichold (ed.) *English Core Linguistics. Essays in Honour of D. J. Allerton*. Bern: Peter Lang. 323–41.

(2003b). I'll bee after telling dee de raison . . .: *be after V-ing* as a future gram in Irish English, 1601–1750. In H. Tristram (ed.) *The Celtic Englishes III*. Heidelberg: C. Winter. 298–317.

(2003c). Plural verbal *-s* in nineteenth-century Ulster: Scots and English influence on Ulster dialects. *Ulster Folklife* 48: 62–86.

(2003d). The Northern Subject Rule in Ulster: how Scots, how English? *Language Variation and Change* 15: 105–39.

(2004a). Innovation in language contact. *Be after V-ing* as a future gram in Irish English, 1670 to the present. *Diachronica* 21: 113–60.

(2004b). [T]hunder storms is verry dangese in this countrey they come in less than a minnits notice. . .: the Northern Subject Rule in Southern Irish English. *English World-Wide* 25: 51–79.

(2005a). William Carleton between Irish and English. What can literary dialect reveal about language contact and change? *Language and Literature* 14: 197–220.

(2005b). His letters is as short as ever they were: the Northern Subject Rule in nineteenth-century Ireland. In K. McCafferty, T. Bull & K. Killie (eds.) *Contexts – Historical, Social, Linguistic. Studies in Celebration of Toril Swan*. Bern: Peter Lang. 187–201.

(2005c). Future, perfect – and past? Changing uses of *be after V-ing* in Irish English. In G. Alhaug, E. Mørck & A. -K. Pedersen (eds.) *Festschrift for Tove Bull*. Oslo: Novus.

(2006). *Be after V-ing* on the past grammaticalisation path: how far is it after coming? In H. Tristram (ed.) *The Celtic Englishes IV*. Potsdam: Potsdamer Universitätsverlag.

McCloskey, J. (1979). *Transformational Syntax and Model-Theoretic Semantics: A Case Study in Modern Irish*. Dordrecht and Boston: D. Reidel.

(1985). The Modern Irish double relative and syntactic binding. *Ériu* 36: 45–84.

McClure, J. D. (1988). *Why Scots Matters*. Tillicoultry: The Saltire Society.

McClure, J. D., A. J. Aitken & J. Low. (1980). *The Scots Language: Planning for Modern Usage*. Edinburgh: Ramsay Head.

McCone, K. R. (1985). The Würzburg and Milan Glosses: our earliest source of 'Middle Irish'. *Ériu* 36: 85–106.

(1996). *Towards a Relative Chronology of Ancient and Medieval Celtic Sound Change*. Maynooth: Department of Old and Middle Irish, St Patrick's College.

McCone, K. R., D. McManus, C. Ó Háinle, N. Willams & L. Breatnach (eds.) (1994). *Stair na Gaeilge in ómós do Pádraig Ó Fiannachta*. Maynooth: Department of Old and Middle Irish, St Patrick's College.

McDonald, C. & J. Beal. (1987). Modal verbs in Tyneside English. *Journal of the Atlantic Provinces Linguistic Association* 9: 43–55.

McDonald, T. & J. Boyd. (2000). *Languages: The Next Generation. Report of the Nuffield Inquiry into Languages*. London: The English Company.

McDonnell, P. (ed.) (2004). *Deaf Studies in Ireland: an introduction*. Coleford: Douglas McLean.

McElholm, D. D. (1986). Intonation in Derry English. In H. Kirkwood (ed.) *Studies in Intonation*. Coleraine: University of Ulster. 1–58.

McGowan, A. (1996). *The Winchester Confessions 1615–1616. Depositions of Travellers, Gypsies, Fraudsters, and Makers of Counterfeit Documents, Including a Vocabulary of the Romany Language*. South Chailley, East Sussex: Romany and Traveller Family History Society.

McGugan, I. (ed.) (2002). *Report into the Role of Educational and Cultural Policy in Supporting and Developing Gaelic, Scots and Minority Languages in Scotland. Volume 1*. [The McGugan Report, Vol. 1] Edinburgh: The Stationery Office (SP Paper 778).

 (ed.) (2003). *Report into the Role of Educational and Cultural Policy in Supporting and Developing Gaelic, Scots and Minority Languages in Scotland. Volume 2 Evidence*. [The McGugan Report, Vol. 2] Edinburgh: The Stationery Office (SP Paper 778).

McIntosh, A. & M. Samuels. (1968). Prolegomena to a study of mediæval Anglo-Irish. *Medium Aevum* 37: 1–11.

McManus, D. (1991). *A Guide to Ogam*. Maynooth: An Sagart.

McNeir, C. L. (ed.) (2001). *Faclair na Parlamaid – Dictionary of Terms*. Edinburgh: The Scottish Parliament.

Meechan, M. & M. Foley. (1994). On resolving disagreement: linguistic theory and variation – 'there's bridges'. *Language Variation and Change* 6: 63–85.

Meek, D. (2002). *A Fresh Start for Gaelic*. Edinburgh: Scottish Executive.

Mees, I. M. & B. Collins. (1999). Cardiff: a real-time study of glottalisation. In P. Foulkes & G. J. Docherty (eds.) *Urban Voices*. London: Arnold. 185–202.

Melchers, G. (1985). 'Knappin', 'Proper English', 'Modified Scottish.' Some language attitudes in the Shetland Isles. In M. Görlach (ed.) *Focus On: Scotland*. Amsterdam: Benjamins. 87–100.

 (1992). Du's no heard da last o'dis – on the use of 'be' as a perfective auxiliary in Shetland dialect. In M. Rissanen, O. Ihalainen, T. Nevalainen & I. Taavitsainen (eds.) *History of Englishes: New Methods and Interpretations in Historical Linguistics*. Berlin: Mouton de Gruyter. 602–10.

Mercer, K. (1988). Diaspora culture and the dialogic imagination. In M. Cham & C. Andrade-Watkins (eds.) *Blackframes: Critical Perspectives on Black Independent Cinema*. Boston: MIT Press. 50–61.

 (1994). *Welcome to the Jungle*. London: Routledge.

Meurman-Solin, A. (1992). On the morphology of verbs in Middle Scots: present and present perfect indicative. In M. Rissanen, O. Ihalainen, T. Nevalainen &

I. Taavitsainen (eds.) *History of Englishes. New Methods and Interpretations in Historical Linguistics*. Berlin: Mouton de Gruyter. 611–23.

Meyerhoff, M. & N. Niedzielski. (2003). The globalization of vernacular variation. *Journal of Sociolinguistics* 7: 534–55.

Miller, J. (1993). The grammar of Scottish English. In J. Milroy and L. Milroy (eds.) *Real English:The Grammar of English Dialects in the British Isles*. Harlow: Longman. 99–138.

Millwood-Hargrave, A. (2000). *Delete Expletives?* London: Broadcasting Standards Commission.

Milne, A. (2000). *Gaelic Broadcasting Task Force Report*. Edinburgh: Scottish Executive.

Milroy, J. (1981). *Regional Accents of English: Belfast*. Belfast: Blackstaff Press.

(1992). *Linguistic Variation and Change*. Oxford: Blackwell.

(1995). Investigating the Scottish Vowel Length Rule in a Northumbrian dialect. *Newcastle and Durham Working Papers in Linguistics* 3: 187–96.

(1996). A current change in British English: variation in (th) in Derby. *Newcastle and Durham Working Papers in Linguistics* 4: 213–22.

(1997). Internal vs external motivations for linguistic change. *Multilingua* 16 (4): 311–23.

(2000). Historical description and the ideology of the standard language. In L. Wright (ed.) *The Development of Standard English, 1300–1800: Theories, Description, Conflicts*. Cambridge: Cambridge University Press. 11–28.

(2001). Language ideologies and the consequences of standardization. *Journal of Sociolinguistics* 5 (4): 530–55.

Milroy, J. & L. Milroy. (1985). Linguistic change, social network and speaker innovation. *Journal of Linguistics* 21: 339–84.

(1991). *Authority in Language: Investigating Language Prescription and Standardisation (2nd edn)*. London: Routledge.

(eds.) (1993). *Real English: The Grammar of English Dialects in the British Isles*. London: Longman.

(1995). *Authority in Language (3rd edn)*. London: Routledge.

Milroy, J., L. Milroy & S. Hartley. (1994). Local and supra-local change in British English: the case of glottalisation. *English World-Wide* 15: 1–33.

Milroy, L. (1987). *Language and Social Networks (2nd edn)*. Oxford: Blackwell.

(1999). Standard English and language ideology in Britain and the United States. In T. Bex & R. Watts (eds.) *Standard English: The Widening Debate*. London: Routledge. 173–206.

Milroy, L. & M. Gordon. (2003). *Sociolinguistics: Method and Interpretation*. Oxford: Blackwell.

Ministerial Advisory Group on Gaelic. (2002). *A Fresh Start for Gaelic*. Edinburgh: Scottish Executive.

Mishler, E. (1984). *The Discourse of Medicine: Dialectics of Medical Interviews*. New Jersey: Ablex.

Mohan, B., C. Leung & C. Davison. (2001). *English as a Second Language in the Mainstream: Teaching, Learning and Identity*. London: Longman.

Montgomery, M. B. (1994). The evolution of verb concord in Scots. In A. Fenton & A. MacDonald (eds.) *Studies in Scots and Gaelic*. Edinburgh: Canongate Academic. 81–95.

(1995). The linguistic value of Ulster emigrant letters. *Ulster Folklife* 41: 26–41.

(1997a). Making transatlantic connections between varieties of English: the case of plural verbal –s. *Journal of English Linguistics* 25: 122–41.

(1997b). A tale of two Georges: the language of Irish Indian traders in colonial North America. In J. Kallen (ed.) *Focus On Ireland*. Amsterdam: John Benjamins. 227–54.

(2001). British and Irish antecedents. In J. Algeo (ed.) *The Cambridge History of the English Language: Volume 6. American English*. Cambridge: Cambridge University Press. 86–153.

Montgomery, M. B. & R. J. Gregg. (1997). The Scots language in Ulster. In C. Jones (ed.) *The Edinburgh History of the Scots Language*. Edinburgh: Edinburgh University Press. 569–622.

Montgomery, M. B. & J. M. Kirk. (1996). The origin of the habitual verb *be* in American Black English: Irish or English or what? *Belfast Working Papers in Language and Linguistics* 13: 308–34.

(2001). My mother, whenever she passed away, she had pneumonia: the history and functions of 'whenever'. *Journal of English Linguistics* 29: 234–49.

Montgomery, M. B. & P. Robinson. (1996). Ulster English as Janus: language contact across the North Atlantic and across the Irish Sea. In P. S. Ureland & I. Clarkson (eds.) *Language Contact across the North Atlantic*. Tübingen: Max Niemeyer. 411–26.

Moore, E. (2003). *Learning style and identity: a sociolinguistic analysis of a Bolton high school*. Unpublished PhD dissertation. Manchester: University of Manchester.

Morgan, E. (1983). Glasgow speech in recent Scottish literature. In J. D. McClure (ed.) *Scotland and the Lowland Tongue: Studies in the Language and Literature of Lowland Scotland in Honour of David D. Murison*. Aberdeen: Aberdeen University Press. 195–208.

Morin, Y. C. (1996). Review of A. J. Liddicoat. (1994). A Grammar of the Norman French of the Channel Islands: The Dialects of Jersey and Sark. *Canadian Journal of Linguistics* 41 (2): 177–184.

Morris Jones, J. (1913). *A Welsh Grammar: Historical and Comparative*. Oxford: Clarendon Press.

Mother Tongue Service (Tower Hamlets). (2001). *Mother Tongue Service Directory*. London: Mother Tongue Service, Tower Hamlets.

Moylan, S. (1996). *The Language of Kilkenny*. Dublin: Geography Publications.

Mugglestone, L. (1995). *'Talking Proper'. The Rise of Accent as Social Symbol*. Oxford: Clarendon Press.

Mühleisen, S. (2002). *Creole Discourse: Exploring Prestige Formation and Change across Caribbean English-lexicon Creoles*. Amsterdam: John Benjamins.

Murison, D. (1977). *The Guid Scots Tongue*. Edinburgh: Blackwood.

Murphy, G. (1943). English 'brogue' meaning Irish accent. *Éigse* 3: 231–6.

Murray, J. (1873). *The Dialect of the Southern Counties of Scotland*. London: Philological Society.

National Children's Centre. (1984). *The Silent Minority: Report on the 4th National Conference on Chinese Children in Britain*. Huddersfield: National Children's Centre.

National Council for Mother Tongue Teaching. (1985). The Swann Report: Education for All? *Journal of Multilingual and Multicultural Development.* 6 (6): 497–508.

National Curriculum Council. (1992). *The Case for Revising the Order.* London: National Curriculum Council.

National Literacy Trust. (2003). English is second tongue for one tenth of pupils. *Times Educational Supplement,* 4 July.

Nevalainen, T. & R. Aulanko. (1996). Stressed vowels in East Somerset: an acoustic-phonetic case study. In J. Klemola, M. Kytö & M. Rissanen (eds.) *Speech Past and Present: Studies in English Dialectology in Memory of Ossi Ihalainen.* Frankfurt: Peter Lang. 236–64.

Nevalainen, T. & H. Raumolin-Brunberg. (1994). *Its* strength and the beauty *of it*: the standardization of the third person neuter possessive in Early Modern English. In D. Stein & I. Tieken-Boon (eds.) *Towards a Standard English: 1600–1800.* Berlin: Mouton de Gruyter. 171–216.

(eds.) (1996). *Sociolinguistics and Language History.* Amsterdam: Rodopi.

Nevins, J. B. (1895). *The Sign Language of the Deaf and Dumb.* Liverpool: Literary and Philosophical Society of Liverpool.

Newbolt, H. (1921). *The Teaching of English in England.* London: HMSO.

Newbrook, M. (1999). West Wirral: norms, self-reports and usage. In P. Foulkes & G. J. Docherty (eds.) *Urban Voices.* London: Arnold. 90–106.

Ng, R. C. Y. (1986). My people: the Chinese community in the North-East. *Multicultural Teaching* 4: 30–3.

Nicholas, J. (1994). *Language Diversity Surveys as Agents of Change.* Clevedon: Multilingual Matters.

Nichols, J. (1992). *Linguistic Diversity in Space and Time.* Chicago: University of Chicago Press.

Nicolaisen, W. (1977). *The Place-names of Scotland.* London: Batsford.

Nicolle, E. T. (ed.) (1893). *The Channel Islands (3rd edn).* London: Allen & Co.

Nielsen, H. (1998). *The Continental Backgrounds of English and its Insular Development until 1154.* Odense: Odense University Press.

Niven, L. & R. Jackson (eds.) (1998). *The Scots Language: Its Place in Education.* Newton Stewart: Watergaw.

Nolan, F. J. (1983). *The Phonetic Bases of Speaker Recognition.* Cambridge: Cambridge University Press.

(2002). Intonation in speaker identification: an experiment on pitch alignment features. *Forensic Linguistics* 9: 1–21.

Nolan, F. J. & P. E. Kerswill. (1990). The description of connected speech processes. In S. Ramsaran (ed.) *Studies in the Pronunciation of English: A Commemorative Volume in Honour of A. C. Gimson.* London: Routledge. 295–316.

Norman, P. (2001). What *would* 'Enry 'Iggins make of our Slop English? *Daily Mail,* 2 March.

Northover, M. & S. Donnelly. (1996). A future for English/Irish bilingualism in Northern Ireland? *Journal of Multilingual and Multicultural Development* 17 (1): 33–48.

Nuffield Foundation. (2000). *Languages: The Next Generation – The Nuffield Languages Inquiry.* London: The Nuffield Foundation.

Ó Baoill, C. (1997). The Scots-Gaelic interface. In C. Jones (ed.) *The Edinburgh History of the Scots Language*. Edinburgh: Edinburgh University Press. 551–68.

Ó Baoill, D. P. (1991). Contact phenomena in the phonology of Irish and English in Ireland. In P. S. Ureland & G. Broderick (eds.) *Language Contact in the British Isles*. Tübingen: Max Niemeyer. 581–95.

(1997). The emerging Irish phonological substratum in Irish English. In J. Kallen (ed.) *Focus on Ireland*. Amsterdam: John Benjamins. 73–87.

(eds.) (2001). *Linguistic Politics*. Belfast: Cló Oillscoil na Banríona. 255–8.

Ó Cuív, B. (1951). *Irish Dialects and Irish-speaking Districts*. Dublin: Institute of Advanced Studies.

(ed.) (1969). *A View of the Irish Language*. Dublin: Dublin Stationery Office.

(1976). The Irish Language in the early modern period. In T. Moody, F. Martin & F. Byrne (eds.) *A New History of Ireland, Volume 3: Early Modern Ireland 1534–1691*. Oxford: Clarendon Press. 509–45.

(1986). Irish language and literature 1691–1845. In T. Moody & W. Vaughan (eds.) *A New History of Ireland, Volume 4: Eighteenth-century Ireland 1691–1800*. Oxford: Clarendon Press. 374–423.

Ó Dochartaigh, C. (1992). The Irish language. In D. MacAulay (ed.) *The Celtic Languages*. Cambridge: Cambridge University Press. 11–99.

Ó hAilín, T. (1969). Irish revival movements. In B. Ó Cuív (ed.) *A View of the Irish Language*. Dublin: Stationery Office.

Ó hIfearnáin, T. (2000). Irish language broadcast media. *Current Issues in Language and Society* 7 (2): 92–116.

Ó Muirithe, D. (ed.) (1977). *The English Language in Ireland*. Cork: Mercier.

(1996). *Dictionary of Anglo-Irish. Words and Phrases from Irish*. Dublin: Four Courts Press.

Ó Murchú, M. (1977). Successes and failures in the modernisation of Irish. In J. Fishman (ed.) *Advances in the Creation and Revision of Writing Systems*. The Hague: Mouton.

(1985). *The Irish Language*. Dublin: Government Publications Office.

Ó Riagáin, P. (1992). *Language Maintenance and Language Shift as Strategies of Social Reproduction: Irish in the Corca Dhuibhne Gaeltacht 1926–86*. Dublin: Institiúid Teangeolaíochta Éireann.

(1997). *Language Policy and Social Reproduction: Ireland 1893–1993*. Oxford: Oxford University Press.

(2001). Irish language production and reproduction 1981–1996. In J. Fishman (ed.) *Can Threatened Languages be Saved?* Clevedon: Multilingual Matters. 195–214.

(in press). Relationships between attitudes to Irish, social class, religion and national identity in the Republic of Ireland and Northern Ireland. *The International Journal of Bilingual Education and Bilingualism*.

Ó Sé, D. (1992). The perfect in Modern Irish. *Ériu* 43: 39–67.

(2004). The 'after' perfect and related constructions in Gaelic dialects. *Ériu* 54: 179–248.

Ó Siadhail, M. (1989). *Modern Irish: Grammatical Structure and Dialect Variation*. Cambridge: Cambridge University Press.

O'Connor, J. D. (1973). *Phonetics*. London: Penguin.

O'Connor, J. D. & G. F. Arnold. (1973). *Intonation of Colloquial English (2nd edn)*. London: Longman.

O'Driscoll, J. (2001). Hiding your difference: how non-global languages are being marginalized in everyday interaction. *Journal of Multilingual and Multicultural Development* 22 (6): 475–90.

O'Hehir, B. (1967). *A Gaelic Lexicon for 'Finnegans Wake' and Glossary for Joyce's Other Works*. Berkeley & Los Angeles: University of California Press.

O'Neill, J. A. (1972). *The role of family and community in the social adjustment of the Chinese in Liverpool*. Unpublished MA dissertation. Liverpool: University of Liverpool.

Odlin, T. (1991). Irish English idioms and language transfer. *English World-Wide* 12 (2): 175–93.

OECD. (2000). *Literacy in the Information Age: Final Report of the International Adult Literacy Survey*. Paris: OECD.

Office for National Statistics. (1996). *Social Focus on Ethnic Minorities*. London: HMSO.

(2004). *Census 2001. Report on the Welsh Language*. London: HMSO.

Office of Population Censuses and Surveys [OPCS]. (1995). *1991 Census: General Report (Great Britain)*. London: Her Majesty's Stationery Office.

Office for Standards in Education. (1994). *Educational Support for Minority Ethnic Communities*. London: Office for Standards in Education.

(1998). *Report of Inspection of City of Leicester Local Education Authority*. London: Office of Her Majesty's Chief Inspector of Schools/Audit Commission.

Ogura, K. (1990). *Dynamic Dialectology*. Tokyo: Kenkyusha.

Ojanen, A.-L. (1982). *A syntax of the Cambridgeshire dialect*. Unpublished Licentiate dissertation. Helsinki: University of Helsinki.

Ong, W. (1982). *Orality and Literacy: the Technologizing of the Word*. London: Routledge.

Ordnance Survey. (1995). *Statatlas UK: A Statistical Atlas of the United Kingdom*. London: Ordnance Survey and HMSO.

Orton, H. *et al.* (1962–71). *Survey of English Dialects: The Basic Material*. Leeds: E. J. Arnold.

Owen, D. (1992). *Ethnic Minorities in Great Britain: Settlement Patterns*. Warwick: Centre for Research in Ethnic Relations, University of Warwick.

(1993). *Ethnic Minorities in Great Britain: Age and Gender Structure*. Warwick: Centre for Research in Ethnic Relations, University of Warwick.

Owens, E. A. (1977). *Distribution of /l/ in Belfast vernacular speech*. Unpublished MA dissertation. Belfast: Queen's University of Belfast.

Paddock, H. (1991). The actuation problem for gender change in Wessex versus Newfoundland. In P. Trudgill & J. K. Chambers (eds.) *Dialects of English: Studies in Grammatical Variation*. London: Longman. 29–46.

Padel, O. J. (1985). *Cornish Place-name Elements*. Nottingham: English Place Name Society.

Palmer, P. (2000). *Language and Conquest in Early Modern Ireland*. Cambridge: Cambridge University Press.

Papastergiadis, N. (2000). *The Turbulence of Migration: Globalization, Deterritorialization and Hybridity*. Cambridge: Polity Press.

Parekh, B. (2000). *The Future of Multi-ethnic Britain: Report of the Commission into the Future of Multi-ethnic Britain*. London: Profile Books.

Pargman, S. (2004). Gullah 'duh' and periphrastic 'do' in English dialects: another look at the evidence. *American Speech* 79: 3–32.

Parker, D. (1995). *Through Different Eyes: The Cultural Identities of Young Chinese People in Britain*. Aldershot: Avebury.

Parry, D. (ed.) (1977, 1979). *The Survey of Anglo-Welsh Dialects: Volume 1: The South-East, Volume 2: The South-West*. Swansea: privately published.

(ed.) (1999). *A Grammar and Glossary of the Conservative Anglo-Welsh Dialects of Rural Wales*. Sheffield: National Centre for English Cultural Tradition.

(2003). The conservative rural Anglo-Welsh dialects. In M. Jones (ed.) *Essays in Lore and Language: Presented to John Widdowson on the Occasion of his Retirement*. Sheffield: National Centre for English Cultural Tradition. 148–74.

Parsons, D. N. & P. Sims-Williams (eds.) (2000). *Ptolemy. Towards a Linguistic Atlas of the Earliest Celtic Place-names of Europe*. Aberystwyth: CMCS.

Patrick, P. (1999). *Urban Jamaican Creole: Variation in the Mesolect*. Amsterdam: John Benjamins.

Pavlenko, A. (1996). On the use of 'be' as a perfective auxiliary in modern Shetland dialect: hybridization and syntactic change. In P. Sture Ureland & I. Clarkson (eds.) *Language Contact Across the North Atlantic*. Tübingen: Max Niemeyer Verlag. 75–82.

Peach, C. (1996). Introduction. In C. Peach (ed.) *Ethnicity in the 1991 Census: Volume 2*. London: HMSO.

Pedersen, H. (1909–13). *Vergleichende Grammatik der keltischen Sprachen (2 Volumes)*. Göttingen: Vandenhoeck and Ruprecht.

Pegge, S. (1896). *Two Collections of Derbicisms*. London: English Dialect Society.

Peitsara, K. (1988). On existential sentences in the dialect of Suffolk. *Neuphilologische Mitteilungen* 89: 72–89.

(1996). Studies on the structure of the Suffolk dialect. In J. Klemola, M. Kytö & M. Rissanen (eds.) *Speech Past and Present: Studies in English Dialectology in Memory of Ossi Ihalainen*. Frankfurt: Peter Lang. 284–307.

(2002a). Relativizers in the Suffolk dialect. In P. Poussa (ed.) *Relativisation on the North Sea Littoral*. Munich: Lincom Europa. 167–80.

(2002b). Verbal -*s* in Devonshire – the *Helsinki Dialect Corpus* evidence. In H. Raumolin-Brunberg, M. Nevala, A. Nurmi & M. Rissanen (eds.) *Variation Past and Present. VARIENG Studies on English for Terttu Nevalainen*. Helsinki: Société Néophilologique. 211–30.

Peitsara, K. & A.-L. Vasko. (2002). The *Helsinki Dialect Corpus*: characteristics of speech and aspects of variation. *Helsinki English Studies: the Electronic Journal of the Department of English at the University of Helsinki* 2.

Penhallurick, R. J. (1991).*The Anglo-Welsh Dialects of North Wales: A Survey of Conservative Rural Spoken English in the Counties of Gwynedd and Clwyd*. Frankfurt am Main: Peter Lang.

(1993). Welsh English: a national language? *Dialectologia et Geolinguistica* 1: 28–46.

(1994). *Gowerland and its Language: A History of the English Speech of the Gower Peninsula, South Wales.* Frankfurt am Main: Peter Lang.

(1996). The grammar of Northern Welsh English: progressive verb phrases. In J. Klemola, M. Kytö & M. Rissanen (eds.) *Speech Past and Present: Studies in English Dialectology in Memory of Ossi Ihalainen.* Frankfurt am Main: Peter Lang. 308–42.

(2004a). Welsh English: phonology. In E. W. Schneider, K. Burridge, B. Kortmann, R. Mesthrie & C. Upton (eds.) *A Handbook of Varieties of English, Volume 1: Phonology.* Berlin: Mouton de Gruyter. 98–112.

(2004b). Welsh English: morphology and syntax. In B. Kortmann, K. Burridge, R. Mesthrie, E. W. Schneider & C. Upton (eds.) *A Handbook of Varieties of English, Volume 2: Morphology & Syntax.* Berlin: Mouton de Gruyter. 102–13.

Perera, K. (1984). *Children's Writing and Reading: Analysing Classroom Language.* Oxford: Blackwell.

Pettigrew, M. (1992). Government regulation of applied research: Contracts and conditions. *BAAL Newsletter* 42: 4–7.

Petyt, K. (1980). *The Study of Dialect.* London: Deutsch.

(1985). *Dialect and Accent in Industrial West Yorkshire.* Amsterdam: John Benjamins.

Phillips, L. (1998). Hegemony and political discourse: the lasting impact of Thatcherism. *Sociology* 32 (4): 847–67.

Phythian, B. A. (1993). *A Concise Dictionary of Correct English.* London: Hodder & Stoughton.

Pichler, H. & D. Watt. (2006). *We're all Scottish really: investigating the tension between claimed identity and linguistic behaviour in Berwick-upon-Tweed.* Manuscript. http://www.abdn.ac.uk/langling/resources/Berwick.ppt (last accessed March 2006).

Pierrehumbert, J. & J. Hirschberg. (1990). The meaning of intonational contours in the interpretation of discourse. In P. R. Cohen, J. Morgan & M. E. Pollack (eds.) *Intentions in Communication.* Cambridge, MA: MIT Press. 271–311.

Pietsch, L. (2003). *Subject-verb agreement in northern dialects of English.* Unpublished PhD dissertation. Freiburg-im-Breisgau: Albert-Ludwigs-Universität.

(2005a). *Variable Grammars: Verbal Agreement in Northern Dialects of English.* Tübingen: Niemeyer.

(2005b). 'Some do and some doesn't': verbal concord variation in the north of the British Isles. In B. Kortmann, T. Herrmann, L. Pietsch & S. Wagner (eds.) *A Comparative Grammar of English Dialects: Agreement, Gender, Relative Clauses.* Berlin: Mouton de Gruyter. 125–209.

Pilch, H. (1975). Advanced Welsh phonemics. *Zeitschrift für Celtische Philologie.* 34: 60–102.

Pitkänen, H. (2003). Non-standard uses of the progressive form in Welsh English: an apparent time study. In H. Tristram (ed.) *The Celtic Englishes III.* Heidelberg: Winter. 111–28.

Pitts, A. H. (1982). *Urban influence in Northern Irish English. A comparison of variation in two communities.* Unpublished PhD dissertation. Ann Arbor: University of Michigan.

(1985). Urban influence on phonological variation in a Northern Irish speech community. *English World-Wide* 6: 59–85.

(1986). Differing prestige values for the (ky) variable in Lurgan. In J. Harris, D. Little & D. Singleton (eds.) *Perspectives on the English Language in Ireland*. Dublin: Centre for Language and Communication Studies, Trinity College. 209–21.

(1989). Is urban influence varb-able? In R. W. Fasold & D. Schiffrin (eds.) *Language Change and Variation*. Amsterdam: John Benjamins. 95–106.

Plowden, Bridget. (1967). *Children and their Primary Schools: Report of the Central Advisory Council for Education (England)* [The Plowden Report]. London: HMSO.

Policansky, L. (1982). Grammatical variation in Belfast English. *Belfast Working Papers in Language and Linguistics* 6: 37–66.

Pollard, V. (1994). *Dread Talk*. Kingston: Canoe Press.

Pollner, C. (1985). *Englisch in Livingston. Ausgewählte sprachliche Erscheinungen in einer schottischen New Town*. Frankfurt: Peter Lang.

Pong, Sin Ching. (1991). *Intergenerational variation in language choice patterns in a Chinese community in Britain*. Unpublished MPhil thesis. Newcastle: University of Newcastle-upon-Tyne.

Poplack, S. (ed.) (2000). *The English History of African American English*. Oxford: Blackwell.

Poplack, S. & S. Tagliamonte. (2001). *African American English in the Diaspora*. Oxford: Blackwell.

Portes, A. (1997). *Globalization from Below: The Rise of Transnational Communities*. Oxford: Transnational Communities Programme.

Poussa, P. (1982). The evolution of early standard English: the creolization hypothesis. *Studia Anglica Posnaniensia* 14: 69–86.

(1994). Norfolk relatives (Broadland). In W. Viereck (ed.) *Regionalsprachliche Variation, Umgangs- und Standardsprachen: Verhandlungen des Internationalen Dialektologenkongresses: Band 3*. Stuttgart: Franz Steiner Verlag. 418–26.

(2001). Syntactic change in north-west Norfolk. In J. Fisiak & P. Trudgill (eds.) *East Anglian English*. Woodbridge: Brewer. 243–60.

Prattis, J. L. (1980). Industrialisation and minority-language loyalty: the example of Lewis. In E. Haugen, J. D. McClure & D. Thomson (eds.) *Minority Languages Today*. Edinburgh: Edinburgh University Press. 21–31.

Price, G. (1984). *The Languages of Britain*. London: Edward Arnold.

(2000). Cumbric. In G. Price (ed.) *Languages in Britain and Ireland*. Oxford: Blackwell. 120–6.

Prillwitz, S., R. Leven, H. Zienert, T. Hanke & J. Henning. (1989). *HamNoSys: Version 2: Hamburg Notation System for Sign Languages: An Introductory Guide*. Hamburg: Signum Press.

Przedlacka, J. (2002). *Estuary English? A Sociophonetic Study of Teenage Speech in the Home Counties*. Bern: Peter Lang.

Purves I., R. Wilson & M. Gibson. (2000). *Electronic Health Horizons*. Newcastle: SCHIN, University of Newcastle upon Tyne.

Puttenham, G. (1936 [1589]). *The Arte of English Poesie*. Cambridge: Cambridge University Press.

Qualifications and Curriculum Authority. (2000). *A Language in Common: Assessing English as an Additional Language*. London: QCA.
  (2004). *Introducing the Grammar of Talk*. London: QCA.
Quirk, R. (1957). Relative clauses in educated spoken English. *English Studies* 38: 97–109.
Quirk, R., S. Greenbaum, G. Leech & J. Svartvik. (1985). *A Comprehensive Grammar of the English Language*. London: Longman.
Qureshi, K & S. Moores. (1999). Identity remix: tradition and translation in the lives of young Pakistani Scots. *European Journal of Cultural Studies* 2(3): 311–30.
Rahilly, J. (1997). Aspects of prosody in Hiberno-English: the case of Belfast. In J. Kallen (ed.) *Focus on Ireland*. Amsterdam: John Benjamins. 109–32.
Rahman, T. (2002). Review of Ricento, T. (ed.) Ideology, politics and language policies. *Language in Society* 31 (2): 288–90.
Ramdin, R. (1987). *The Making of the Black Working Class in Britain*. Aldershot: Gower.
Ramisch, H. (1989). *The Variation of English in Guernsey, Channel Islands*. Frankfurt am Main: Peter Lang.
  (1994). English in Jersey. In W. Viereck (ed.) *Proceedings of the International Congress of Dialectologists*. Stuttgart: Steiner. 452–62.
  (2004). Channel Island English: phonology. In B. Kortmann, E. Schneider, K. Burridge, R. Mesthrie & C. Upton (eds.) *A Handbook of Varieties of English Volume 1: Phonology*. Berlin: Mouton de Gruyter. 204–16.
Rampton, B. (1983). Some flaws in educational discussion of the English of Asian schoolchildren in Britain. *Journal of Multilingual and Multicultural Development* 4 (1): 15–28.
  (1988). A non-educational view of ESL in Britain. *Journal of Multilingual and Multicultural Development* 9 (6): 503–29.
  (1995a). *Crossing: Language and Ethnicity among Adolescents*. London: Longman.
  (1995b). Politics and change in research in applied linguistics. *Applied Linguistics* 16 (2): 233–56.
  (1998). Speech community. In J. Verschueren, J.-O. Östman, J. Blommaert & C. Blommaert (eds.) *Handbook of Pragmatics*. Amsterdam: John Benjamins.
  (1999). *Deutsch* in inner London and the animation of a foreign language. *Journal of Sociolinguistics* 3 (4): 480–504.
Rampton, B., R. Harris & C. Leung. (2002). Education and speakers of languages other than English. *Working Papers in Urban Language and Literacies* 18: 1–30.
Rampton, B., C. Leung & R. Harris. (1997). Multilingualism in England. *Annual Review of Applied Linguistics* 17: 224–41.
Rashid, A. & C. Jagger. (1992). Attitudes to and perceived use of healthcare services among Asian and non-Asian patients in Leicester. *British Journal of General Practice* 42: 197–201.
Rassool, N. (2000). Contested and contesting identities: conceptualising linguistic minority rights within the global cultural economy. *Journal of Multilingual and Multicultural Development* 21 (5): 386–98.
Raynor, D. K. & P. Knapp. (2000). Do patients see, read and retain the new mandatory medicines information leaflets? *The Pharmaceutical Journal* 264 (7083): 268–70.

Raynor, D. K. & N. Yerassimou. (1997). Medicines information – leaving blind people behind? *British Medical Journal* 315: 268.

Rea-Dickins, P. (2001). Mirror, mirror on the wall: identifying processes of classroom assessment. *Language Testing* 18 (4): 429–62.

Reay, D. (1998). Rethinking social class: qualitative perspectives on class and gender. *Sociology* 32 (2): 259–75.

Redding, G. (1990). *The Spirit of Chinese Capitalism.* Berlin: Mouton de Gruyter.

Registrar General for Scotland. (2005). *Scotland's Census 2001: Gaelic Report.* Edinburgh: General Register Office for Scotland.

Reid, E. (1978). Social and stylistic variation in the speech of children: some evidence from Edinburgh. In P. Trudgill (ed.) *Sociolinguistic Patterns in British English.* London: Edward Arnold. 158–72.

  (1984). The newer minorities: spoken languages and varieties. In P. Trudgill (ed.) *Language in the British Isles.* Cambridge: Cambridge University Press. 408–424.

  (1988). Linguistic minorities and language education – the English experience. *Journal of Multilingual and Multicultural Development* 9 (1–2): 181–91.

Reynolds, M. (2001). Panjabi/Urdu in Sheffield: a case study of language maintenance and language loss. In J. Cotterill & A. Ife (eds.) *Language Across Boundaries.* London: BAAL/Continuum. 99–118.

Rhys, M. (1984). Intonation and the discourse. In M. Ball & G. Jones (eds.) *Welsh Phonology.* Cardiff: University of Wales Press. 125–55.

Ricento, T. (2000). Historical and theoretical perspectives in language policy and planning. *Journal of Sociolinguistics* 4 (2): 196–213.

Richardson, G. (ed.) (1983). *Teaching Modern Languages.* London: Croom Helm.

Richmond, J. (1979). Dialect features in mainstream school writing. *New Approaches to Multi-racial Education* 8: 10–15.

Rickford, J. (1983). What happens in decreolization. In R. Andersen (ed.) *Pidginization and Creolization as Language Acquisition.* Rowley, MA: Newbury House. 298–319.

  (1987). *Dimensions of a Creole Continuum: History, Texts and Linguistic Analysis of Guyanese Creole.* Palo Alto: Stanford University Press.

Rissanen, M. (1999). Syntax. In R. Lass (ed.) *Cambridge History of the English Language: Volume III: 1476–1776.* Cambridge: Cambridge University Press. 187–331.

Roberts, J. (2002). Child language variation. In J. Chambers, P. Trudgill & N. Schilling-Estes (eds.) *The Handbook of Language Variation and Change.* Oxford: Blackwell. 333–48.

Romaine, S. (1978). Postvocalic /r/ in Scottish English: sound change in progress? In P. Trudgill (ed.) *Sociolinguistic Patterns in British English.* London: Edward Arnold. 144–57.

  (1979). The language of Edinburgh schoolchildren: the acquisition of sociolinguistic competence. *Scottish Literary Journal. Supplement* 9: 54–60.

  (1983). Problems in the sociolinguistic description of communicative repertoires among linguistic minorities. In L. Dabène, M. Flasquier & J. Lyons (eds.) *Status of Migrants' Mother Tongues.* Strasbourg: European Scientific Foundation. 119–29.

(1989). *Bilingualism*. Oxford: Blackwell.

Roper, S. (1988). The needs and means for action. In Commission for Racial Equality (ed.) *The Needs of the Chinese Community in Scotland and the North-East of England*. London: CRE. 2–6.

Rose, E. and associates. (1969). *Colour and Citizenship: A Report on British Race Relations*. London: Oxford University Press.

Rosen, C. & H. Rosen. (1973). *The Language of Primary School Children*. Harmondsworth: Penguin.

Rosen, H. & T. Burgess. (1980). *Languages and Dialects of London School Children*. London: Ward Lock Educational.

Rosewarne, D. (1984). Estuary English. *Times Educational Supplement* 42, 19 October.

(1994). Estuary English: Tomorrow's RP? *English Today* 10(1): 3–8.

Rouveret, A. (1994). *Syntaxe du Gallois*. Paris: CNRS Editions.

Rowe, C. (2007). *He divn't gan tiv a college ti di that, man*! A study of *do* (and *to*) in Tyneside English. *Language Sciences*.

Ruiz, R. (1984). Orientations in language planning. *National Association for Bilingual Education Journal* 8: 15–34.

Runnymede Trust. (1994). *Multi-Ethnic Britain: Facts and Trends*. London: Runnymede Trust.

Rupp, L. (2005). Constraints on non-standard *-s* in expletive *there* sentences: a generative-variationist perspective. *English Language and Linguistics* 9: 225–88.

Rupp, L. & D. Britain. (forthcoming). *Concord Variation: A Generative-Sociolinguistic Perspective*. Basingstoke: Palgrave.

Rupp, L. & J. Page-Verhoeff. (2005). Pragmatic and historical aspects of Definite Article Reduction in northern English dialects. *English World-Wide* 26: 325–46.

Russell, P. (1995). *An Introduction to the Celtic Languages*. London: Longman.

(2005). 'What was best of every language': the early history of the Irish language. In D. Ó Cróinín (ed.) *The New History of Ireland. Volume I*. Oxford: Oxford University Press. 433–78.

Sadler, L. (1987). *Welsh Syntax: A Government-Binding Approach*. London: Croom Helm.

Saeed, J., R. Sutton-Spence & L. Leeson. (2000). *Constituent structure in declarative sentences in Irish Sign Language and British Sign Language – A preliminary examination*. Poster presented at the 7th International Conference on Theoretical Issues in Sign Language Research. 23–27 July 2000, Amsterdam.

Salmons, J. (1992). *Accentual Change and Language Contact*. London: Routledge.

Sampson, G. (1924). *The problem of grammar*. English Association Pamphlet 56. London: English Association.

Sampson, J. (1926). *The Dialect of the Gypsies of Wales*. Oxford: Clarendon Press.

Samuels, M. (1963). Some applications of Middle English dialectology. *English Studies* 44: 81–94.

Sangster, C. (2001). Lenition of alveolar stops in Liverpool English. *Journal of Sociolinguistics* 5: 401–12.

Sankoff, D. & S. Laberge. (1978). The linguistic market and the statistical explanation of variability. In D. Sankoff (ed.) *Linguistic Variation: Models and Methods*. New York: Academic Press. 239–50.

Sansone, L. (1995). The making of black youth culture: lower-class young men of Surinamese origin in Amsterdam. In V. Amit-Talai & H. Wulff (eds.) *Youth Cultures: A Cross-cultural Perspective*. London: Routledge. 114–43.

Saussure, F. de. (1916). *Cours de Linguistique Générale*. Paris: Payot.

Saxena, M. (1994). Literacies among the Panjabis in Southall. In M. Hamilton, D. Barton & R. Ivanic (eds.) *Worlds of Literacy*. Clevedon: Multilingual Matters. 195–214.

(1995). *A sociolinguistic study of Panjabi Hindus in Southall: language maintenance and shift*. Unpublished PhD dissertation. York: University of York.

Sayers, D. (2005). *Standardising diversity – the language revival paradox: can the Cornish language be revived without inhibiting its diversity?* Unpublished MPhil dissertation. Cambridge: Cambridge University.

Schilling-Estes, N. & W. Wolfram. (1994). Convergent explanation and alternative regularization: *were/weren't* levelling in a vernacular English variety. *Language Variation and Change* 6: 273–302.

Schmidt, K. H. (1988). On the Reconstruction of Proto-Celtic. In G. W. Maclennan (ed.) *Proceedings of the First North American Congress of Celtic Studies, Ottawa 1986*. Ottawa: Chair of Celtic Studies. 231–48.

School Curriculum and Assessment Authority. (1996). *Teaching and Learning English as an Additional Language: New Perspectives*. London: SCAA.

Schreier, D. (2003). *Isolation and Language Change: Contemporary and Sociohistorical Evidence from Tristan da Cunha English*. London: Palgrave.

Schrijver, P. (1995). *Studies in British Celtic Historical Phonology*. Amsterdam: Rodopi.

(2002). The rise and fall of British Latin: evidence from English and Brittonic. In M. Filppula, J. Klemola & H. Pitkänen (eds.) *The Celtic Roots of English*. Joensuu: Faculty of Humanities, University of Joensuu. 87–110.

Scobbie, J. (2006). Flexibility in the face of incompatible English VOT systems. In L. Goldstein, C. T. Best & D. H. Whalen (eds.) *Laboratory Phonology 8*. Berlin: Mouton de Gruyter. 367–92.

Scobbie, J., N. Hewlett & A. Turk. (1999). Standard English in Edinburgh and Glasgow: the Scottish Vowel Length Rule revealed. In P. Foulkes & G. J. Docherty (eds.) *Urban Voices*. London: Arnold. 230–45.

Scotlang. (2002). *Mapping the Languages of Edinburgh*. Edinburgh: Scottish CILT.

Scottish Office. (1994). *Provision for Gaelic Education in Scotland*. Edinburgh: Scottish Office Education Department.

Sealey, A. (1999). *Theories about Language in the National Literacy Strategy*. Centre for Research in Elementary and Primary Education, University of Warwick: Occasional Paper 12.

Sebba, M. (1987). Black English in Britain. In S. Abudarham (ed.) *Bilingualism and the Bilingual*. Windsor: NFER-Nelson. 46–65.

(1993) *London Jamaican: Language Systems in Interaction*. London: Longman.

(1998). Phonology meets ideology: the meaning of orthographic practices in British Creole. *Language Problems and Language Planning* 22 (1): 19–47.

(2003). Will the real impersonator please stand up? Language and identity in the Ali G websites. *Arbeiten aus Anglistik und Amerikanistik* 28 (2): 279–304.

Sebba, M. & S. Dray. (2003). Is it Creole, is it English, is it valid? Developing and using a corpus of unstandardised written language. In A. Wilson, P. Rayson & A. McEnery (eds.) *Corpus Linguistics by the Lune: A Festschrift for Geoffrey Leech.* Frankfurt am Main: Peter Lang. 223–39.

Sebba, M., S. Kedge & S. Dray. (1999). *The Corpus of Written British Creole: A User's Guide.* http://www.ling.lancs.ac.uk/staff/mark/cwbc/cwbcman.htm (last accessed 10 March 2006).

Sebba, M. & A. J. Wootton. (1998). We, they and identity: sequential vs identity-related explanation in code-switching. In P. Auer (ed.) *Code-switching in Conversation.* London: Routledge. 262–89.

Sefton-Green, J. (ed.) (1998). *Digital Diversions: Youth Culture in the Age of Multimedia.* London: University College London Press.

Share, B. (2003 [1997]). *Slanguage – A Dictionary of Slang and Colloquial English in Ireland.* Dublin: Gill and Macmillan.

Shaughnessy, M. (1977). *Errors and Expectations.* Oxford: Oxford University Press.

Sheard, J. A. (1954). *The Words we Use.* London: Andre Deutsch.

Sheridan, T. (1781). *A Rhetorical Grammar of the English Language Calculated Solely for the Purpose of Teaching Propriety of Pronunciation and Justness of Delivery, in that Tongue.* Dublin: Price.

(1999 [1762]). A course of lectures on elocution. In T. Crowley (ed.) *Proper English? Readings in Language, History and Cultural Identity.* London: Routledge. 63–72.

Sherwood, M. (1991). The Hungarian speech community. In S. Alladina & V. Edwards (eds.) *Multilingualism in the British Isles, Volume 1: The Older Mother Tongues and Europe.* Harlow: Longman. 129–35.

Shorrocks, G. (1990). Infinitive phrases in the urban dialects of the Bolton and Wigan areas (Greater Manchester County, formerly Lancashire). *Zeitschrift für Dialektologie und Linguistik* 57 (1): 28–41.

(1991). The definite article in the dialect of Farnworth and District (Greater Manchester County, Formerly Lancashire). *Orbis: Bulletin international de documentation linguistique* 34: 173–86.

(1998). *A Grammar of the Dialect of the Bolton Area. Part I: Introduction, Phonology.* Frankfurt am Main: Peter Lang.

(1999). *A Grammar of the Dialect of the Bolton Area. Part II: Morphology and Syntax.* Frankfurt am Main: Peter Lang.

Shuken, C. (1984). Highland and Island English. In P. Trudgill (ed.) *Language in the British Isles.* Cambridge: Cambridge University Press. 152–66.

(1985). Variation in Hebridean English. In M. Görlach (ed.) *Focus On: Scotland.* Amsterdam: John Benjamins. 145–58.

(1986). Vowel systems in Hebridean English. *Scottish Language* 5: 131–139.

Sims-Williams, P. (1984). The double system of verbal inflexion in Old Irish. *Transactions of the Philological Society* 82: 138–201.

(2003). *The Celtic Inscriptions of Britain.* Oxford: Blackwell.

Sjögren, A. (1964). *Les Parlers Bas-Normands de l'Ile de Guernesey. I: Lexique Français-Guernesiais.* Paris: Klincksieck.

Skene, W. F. (1860–90). *Celtic Scotland (3 Volumes)*. Edinburgh: David Douglas.

Skutnabb-Kangas, T. (1988). Multilingualism in the education of minority children. In T. Skutnabb-Kangas & J. Cummins (eds.) *Minority Education: From Shame to Struggle*. Clevedon: Multilingual Matters.

Smart, B. C. & H. T. Crofton. (1875). *The Dialect of the English Gypsies*. London: Asher & Co.

Smith, J. J. (1996). *An Historical Study of English*. London: Routledge.

Smolicz, J. J. (1985). Greek-Australians: a question of survival in multicultural Australia. *Journal of Multilingual and Multicultural Development* 6 (1): 17–29.

Sneddon, R. (2000). Language and literacy practices in Gujarati Muslim families. In M. Martin-Jones & K. Jones (eds.) *Multilingual Literacies*. Amsterdam: John Benjamins. 103–25.

Société Jersiaise. (2000). *Les Preumié Mille Mots*. Jersey: Société Jersiaise.

Soni Raleigh, V. & R. Balarajan. (1995). The health of infants and children among ethnic minorities. In B. Botting (ed.) *The Health of Our Children: Decennial Supplement. OPCS Series DS No 11*. London: HMSO. 82–94.

Spence, N. C. W. (1957). L'assibilation de l'r intervocalique dans les parlers jersiais. *Revue de Linguistique Romane* 21: 270–88.

 (1985). Phonologie descriptive des parlers jersiais: I: Les voyelles. *Revue de Linguistique Romane* 49: 151–65.

 (1987). Phonologie descriptive des parlers jersiais: II: Les consonnes. *Revue de Linguistique Romane* 51: 119–33.

 (1988). R aboutissement de latérale + consonne en jersiais. *Revue de Linguistique Romane* 52: 365–70.

 (1993). *A Brief History of Jèrriais*. Jersey: Don Balleine Trust.

Spurling, J. (2004). *Traditional feature loss in Ipswich: dialect attrition in the East Anglian county of Suffolk*. Unpublished BA dissertation. Colchester: University of Essex.

States of Jersey. (1990). *Report of the Census for 1989*. Jersey: States of Jersey.

Stenson, N. (1981). *Studies in Irish Syntax*. Tübingen: Gunter Narr Verlag.

Stenström, A.-B. & G. Andersen. (1996). More trends in teenage talk: a corpus-based investigation of the discourse items *cos* and *innit*. In C. Percy, C. Meyer & I. Lancashire (eds.) *Synchronic Corpus Linguistics*. Amsterdam: Rodopi. 189–203.

Stenström, A.-B., G. Andersen & I. Hasund. (2002). *Trends in Teenage Talk: Corpus Compilation, Analysis and Findings*. Amsterdam: John Benjamins.

Stephens, J. (1993). Breton. In M. Ball (ed.) *The Celtic Languages*. London: Routledge. 349–409.

Stockwell, R. & D. Minkova. (1997). On drifts and shifts. *Studia Anglica Posnaniensia* 31: 283–303.

Stoddart, J., C. Upton & J. Widdowson. (1999). Sheffield dialect in the 1990s: revisiting the concept of NORMs. In P. Foulkes & G. J. Docherty (eds.) *Urban Voices*. London: Arnold. 72–89.

Storkey, M. (2000). Using the schools language data to estimate the total number of speakers of London's top 40 languages. In P. Baker & J. Eversley (eds.) *Multilingual Capital: The Languages of London's Schoolchildren and their*

Relevance to Economic, Social and Educational Policies. London: Battle-bridge Publications. 63–6.

Stowell, B. & D. Ó Breasláin. (1996). *A Short History of the Manx Language.* Belfast: An Clochán.

Strand, E. (1999). Uncovering the role of gender stereotypes in speech perception. *Journal of Language and Social Psychology* 18: 86–99.

Stuart-Smith, J. (1999). Glasgow: accent and voice quality. In P. Foulkes & G. J. Docherty (eds.) *Urban Voices.* London: Arnold. 203–22.

Stuart-Smith, J. & F. Tweedie. (2000). *Accent Change in Glaswegian: A Sociophonetic Investigation.* Final Report to the Leverhulme Trust (Grant no. F/179/AX).

Stubbs, M. (1983). Understanding language and language diversity: what teachers should know about educational linguistics. In M. Stubbs & W. Hillier (eds.) *Readings on Language, Schools and Classroom.* London: Methuen. 11–38.

(1986). *Educational Linguistics.* London: Blackwell.

(1991 [1994]). Educational language planning in England and Wales: multicultural rhetoric and assimilationist assumptions. In F. Coulmas (ed.) *Language Policy for the European Community: Prospects and Quandaries.* Berlin: Mouton de Gruyter. 215–39.

Studdert, J. & S. Wiles. (1982). Children's writing in the multilingual classroom. *Centre for Urban Educational Studies Occasional Papers.*

Sullivan, A. E. (1992). *Sound Change in Progress.* Exeter: University of Exeter Press.

Sullivan, J. P. (1980). The validity of literary dialect: evidence from the theatrical portrayal of Hiberno-English. *Language and Society* 9: 195–219.

Sundby, B., A. Bjørge & K. Haugland. (1991). *Dictionary of English Normative Grammar 1700–1800.* Amsterdam: Benjamins.

Supalla, T. (1986). The classifier system in American Sign Language. In C. Craig (ed.) *Noun Classes and Categorization.* Amsterdam: Benjamins. 181–214.

Sutcliffe, D. (1982). *British Black English.* Oxford: Blackwell.

Sutton, V. (1999). http://www.SignWriting.org

Sutton-Spence, R. (1994). *The role of the manual alphabet and fingerspelling in British Sign Language.* Unpublished PhD dissertation. Bristol: University of Bristol.

(2000). The Influence of English on British Sign Language. *International Journal of Bilingualism* 3: 363–94.

Sutton-Spence, R. & L. Day. (2001). The role of the mouth in British Sign Language. In P. Boyes-Braem & R. Sutton-Spence (eds.) *The Hands are the Head of the Mouth: The Role of the Mouth in Sign Languages.* Hamburg: Signum Press. 69–85.

Sutton-Spence, R. & B. Woll. (1999). *The Linguistics of British Sign Language: An Introduction.* Cambridge: Cambridge University Press.

Swann, M. (1985). *Education for All. Report of the Committee of Inquiry into the Education of Children from Ethnic Minority Groups.* London: HMSO.

Syvret, M. & J. Stevens. (1998). *Balleine's History of Jersey.* West Sussex: Phillimore.

Tagliamonte, S. (1998). Was/were variation across the generations: view from the city of York. *Language Variation and Change* 10 (2): 153–92.

(2001). Come/Came variation in English dialects. *American Speech* 76: 42–61.

(2002a). Comparative sociolinguistics. In J.K. Chambers, P. Trudgill & N. Schilling-Estes (eds.) *The Handbook of Language Variation and Change*. Oxford: Blackwell. 729–63.

(2002b). Variation and change in the British relative marker system. In P. Poussa (ed.) *Relativisation on the North Sea Littoral*. Munich: Lincom Europa. 147–65.

(2003). Every place has a different toll: determinants of grammatical variation in cross-variety perspective. In G. Rohdenburg & B. Mondorf (eds.) *Determinants of Grammatical Variation in English*. Berlin: Mouton de Gruyter. 531–54.

(2004). Somethi[ŋ]'s goi[n] on! In B.-L. Gunnarsson, L. Bergström, G. Eklund, S. Fridell, L. H. Hansen, A. Karstadt, B. Nordberg, E. Sundgren & M. Thelander (eds.) *Language Variation in Europe*. Uppsala: Uppsala University Press. 390–403.

Tagliamonte, S. & R. Hudson. (1999). Be like et al beyond America: the quotative system in British and Canadian youth. *Journal of Sociolinguistics* 3 (2): 147–72.

Tagliamonte, S. & R. Ito. (2002). Think really different: continuity and specialization in the English dual form adverbs. *Journal of Sociolinguistics* 6 (2): 236–66.

Tagliamonte, S. & J. Smith. (2002). Either it isn't or it's not: NEG/AUX contraction in British dialects. *English World-Wide* 23: 251–81.

Tagliamonte, S., J. Smith & H. Lawrence. (2005). No taming the vernacular! Insights from the relatives in northern Britain. *Language Variation and Change* 17 (1): 75–112.

Tagliamonte, S. & R. Temple. (2005). New perspectives on an ol' variable: (t, d) in British English. *Language Variation and Change* 17 (3): 281–302.

Tandberg, A. (1996). *Innit from a grammatical and pragmatic point of view*. Unpublished MA dissertation. Bergen: University of Bergen.

Tansley, P. & A. Craft. (1984). Mother tongue teaching and support: a Schools Council inquiry. *Journal of Multilingual and Multicultural Development* 5 (5): 367–84.

Tate, N. (1996). *Cultural values and identity*. Paper presented to the SCAA Conference on Curriculum, Culture & Society, 7 February 1996.

Tate, S. (1984). *Jamaican Creole approximation by second-generation Dominicans?: the use of agreement tokens*. Unpublished MA dissertation. York: Department of Language and Linguistic Science, University of York.

Taub, S. F. (2001). *Language from the Body: Iconicity and Metaphor in American Sign Language*. Cambridge: Cambridge University Press.

Taylor, M. (1981). *Caught Between: A Review of Research into the Education of Pupils of West Indian Origin*. Windsor: NFER-Nelson.

(1987). *Chinese Pupils in Britain: A Review of Research into the Education of Pupils of Chinese Origin*. Windsor: NFER-Nelson.

Taylor, M. & S. Hegarty. (1985). *The Best of Both Worlds? A Review of Research into the Education of Pupils of South Asian Origin*. Windsor: NFER-Nelson.

Teasdale, A. & C. Leung. (2000). Teacher assessment and psychometric theory: A case of paradigm crossing? *Language Testing* 17 (2): 163–84.

Tench, P. (1989). The pronunciation of English in Abercrave. In N. Coupland & A. R. Thomas (eds.) *English in Wales: Diversity, Conflict and Change*. Clevedon: Multilingual Matters. 130–41.

Thomas, A. R. (1973). *The Linguistic Geography of Wales*. Cardiff: University of Wales Press.

(1980). *Areal Analysis of Dialect Data by Computer: A Welsh Example*. Cardiff: University of Wales Press.

(1984). Welsh English. In P. Trudgill (ed.) *Language in the British Isles*. Cambridge: Cambridge University Press. 178–94.

(1985). Welsh English: a grammatical conspectus. In W. Viereck (ed.) *Focus On: England and Wales*. Amsterdam: John Benjamins. 213–21.

(1992). The Welsh language. In D. MacAulay (ed.) *The Celtic Languages*. Cambridge: Cambridge University Press. 251–345.

(ed.) (2000). *The Welsh Dialect Survey*. Cardiff: University of Wales Press.

Thomas, B. & P. Thomas. (1989). *Cymraeg, Cymrâg, Cymrêg ... Cyflwyno'r Tafodieithoedd*. Cardiff: Gwasg Taf.

Thomas, C. H. (1967). Welsh intonation – a preliminary study. *Studia Celtica* 2: 8–28.

Thomas, G. (1991). *Linguistic Purism*. London: Longman.

Thomas, P. W. (1989). In search of Middle Welsh dialects. In C. J. Byrne, M. Henry & P. Ó Siadhail (eds.) *Celtic Languages and Celtic Peoples. Proceedings of the Second North American Congress of Celtic Studies*. Halifax: St Mary's University. 287–303.

(1993). Middle Welsh dialects: problems and perspectives. *Bulletin of the Board of Celtic Studies* 40: 17–50.

(1996). *Gramadeg y Gymraeg*. Cardiff: Gwasg Prifysgol Cymru.

Thomason, S. G. (2001). *Language Contact: An Introduction*. Edinburgh: Edinburgh University Press.

Thomason, S. & T. Kaufman. (1988). *Language Contact, Creolization, and Genetic Linguistics*. Berkeley: University of California Press.

Thompson, L., M. Fleming & M. Byram. (1996). Languages and language policy in Britain. In M. Herriman & B. Burnaby (eds.) *Language Policies in English-dominant Countries*. Clevedon: Multilingual Matters. 99–121.

Thurneysen, R. (1946). *A Grammar of Old Irish* (2nd edn, revised and translated by D. A. Binchy & O. J. Bergin). Dublin: DIAS.

Tipler, D. (1957). Specimens of modern Welsh Romani. *Journal of the Gypsy Lore Society* 36: 9–24.

Todd, L. (1984). By their tongue divided: towards an analysis of speech communities in Northern Ireland. *English World-Wide* 5: 159–80.

(1989). Cultures in conflict. Varieties of English in Northern Ireland. In O. Garcia & R. Otheguy (eds.) *English across Cultures, Cultures across English: A Reader in Cross-Cultural Communication*. Berlin: Mouton de Gruyter. 335–55.

(1990). *Words Apart: A Dictionary of Northern Irish English*. Gerrards Cross: Colin Smythe.

Tollefson, J. (1991). *Planning Language, Planning Inequality*. London: Longman.

Tollfree, L. F. (1999). South-east London English: discrete versus continuous modelling of consonantal reduction. In P. Foulkes & G. J. Docherty (eds.) *Urban Voices*. London: Arnold. 163–84.

Tomlin, R. S. O. (1987). Was Ancient British Celtic ever a written language? Two texts from Roman Bath. *Bulletin of the Board of Celtic Studies* 34: 18–25.

(1988). *Tabellae Sulis: Roman Inscribed Tablets on Tin and Lead from the Sacred Spring at Bath*. Oxford: Oxford University Committee for Archaeology.

Tomlinson, H. (1981). *Le Guernesiais – étude grammaticale et lexicale du parler normand de l'île de Guernesey*. Unpublished PhD dissertation. Edinburgh: University of Edinburgh.

Tomlinson, S. (1993). The multicultural task group: the group that never was. In A. King & M. Reiss (eds.) *The Multicultural Dimension of the National Curriculum*. London: Falmer Press. 21–9.

Torgersen, E. & P. Kerswill. (2004). Internal and external motivation in phonetic change: Dialect levelling outcomes for an English vowel shift. *Journal of Sociolinguistics* 8: 23–53.

Tosi, A. (1980). The EEC/Bedfordshire Mother Tongue Pilot Project. In CRE/Bradford College Mother Tongue Teaching Report.

(1984). *Immigration and Bilingual Education: A Case-study of Movement of Population, Language Change and Education within the EEC*. Oxford: Pergamon Press.

Tosi, A. & C. Leung (eds.) (1999). *Rethinking Language Education*. London: CILT.

Tovey, H. (1988). The state and the Irish language – the role of Bord na Gaeilge. *International Journal of the Sociology of Language* 70: 53–68.

Tower Hamlets College. (2001). *Student Handbook for Certificate in Teaching Community Languages*. London: Tower Hamlets College.

Tower Hamlets Education. (n.d.). *Mother Tongue Tutors' Handbook*. London: London Borough of Tower Hamlets Mother Tongue Service.

Trask, L. (1997). *A Student's Dictionary of Language and Linguistics*. London: Arnold.

Traugott, E. (1972). *A History of English Syntax*. New York: Holt, Rinehart & Winston.

Traynor, M. (1953). *The English Dialect of Donegal. A Glossary. Incorporating the collections of H. C. Hart 1847–1908*. Dublin: Royal Irish Academy.

Tristram, H. L. C. (ed.) (2000). *Celtic Englishes II. Proceedings of the Second Potsdam Colloquium on Celtic Englishes, 28–30 September 1995*. Heidelberg: Winter.

(2002). The politics of language: links between Modern Welsh and English. In K. Lenz & R. Möhlig (eds.) *Of Dyuersitie & Chaunge of Langage: Essays Presented to Manfred Görlach on the Occasion of his 65th Birthday*. Heidelberg: C. Winter. 257–75.

(ed.) (2003). *Celtic Englishes III. Proceedings of the Third Potsdam Colloquium on Celtic Englishes, 19–23 September 2001*. Heidelberg: Winter.

Trousdale, G. (2003). Simplification and redistribution: an account of modal verb usage in Tyneside English. *English World-Wide* 24: 271–84.

Trudgill, P. (1974). *The Social Differentiation of English in Norwich*. Cambridge: Cambridge University Press.

(1975). *Accent, Dialect and the School*. London: Arnold.

(ed.) (1984a). *Language in the British Isles*. Cambridge: Cambridge University Press.

(1984b). Standard English in England. In P. Trudgill (ed.) *Language in the British Isles*. Cambridge: Cambridge University Press. 32–44.

(1986). *Dialects in Contact*. Oxford: Blackwell.

(1995). Grammaticalisation and social structure: non-standard conjunction formation in East Anglian English. In F. Palmer (ed.) *Grammar and Semantics*. Cambridge: Cambridge University Press. 136–47.

(1996). Language contact and inherent variability: the absence of hypercorrection in East Anglian present-tense verb forms. In J. Klemola, M. Kytö & M. Rissanen (eds.) *Speech Past and Present: Studies in English Dialectology in Memory of Ossi Ihalainen*. Frankfurt: Peter Lang. 412–25.

(1997). British vernacular dialects in the formation of American English: the case of East Anglian 'do'. In R. Hickey & S. Puppel (eds.) *Language History and Linguistic Modelling: A Festschrift for Jacek Fisiak on his 60th Birthday, Volume II: Linguistic Modelling*. Berlin: Mouton de Gruyter. 749–58.

(1998). Third person singular zero: African American vernacular English, East Anglian dialects and Spanish persecution in the Low Countries. *Folia Linguistica Historica* 18: 139–48.

(1999a). *The Dialects of England* (2nd edn). Oxford: Blackwell.

(1999b). Standard English: What it isn't. In T. Bex & R. Watts (eds.) *Standard English: The Widening Debate*. London: Routledge. 117–28.

(1999c). Norwich: endogenous and exogenous change. In P. Foulkes & G. J. Docherty (eds.) *Urban Voices*. London: Arnold. 124–40.

(2000). *Sociolinguistics. An Introduction to Language and Society (4th Edn)*. Harmondsworth: Penguin.

(ed.) (2002a). *Sociolinguistic Variation and Change*. Edinburgh: Edinburgh University Press.

(2002b). The sociolinguistics of modern RP. In P. Trudgill (ed.) *Sociolinguistic Variation and Change*. Edinburgh: Edinburgh University Press. 171–80.

(2003). *The Norfolk Dialect*. Cromer: Poppyland.

(2004). The dialect of East Anglia: morphology and syntax. In B. Kortmann, K. Burridge, R. Mesthrie, E. Schneider & C. Upton (eds.) *A Handbook of Varieties of English: Morphology and Syntax*. Berlin: Mouton de Gruyter. 142–53.

Trudgill, P. & J. Cheshire. (1989). Dialect and education in the United Kingdom. In J. Cheshire, V. Edwards, H. Münstermann & B. Weltens (eds.) *Dialect and Education*. Clevedon: Multilingual Matters. 200–18.

Tsow, M. (1984). *Mother Tongue Maintenance: A Survey of Chinese Language Classes*. London: Commission for Racial Equality.

Tupper, F. B. (1876). *The History of Guernsey and its Bailiwick (2nd Edn)*. London: Simpkin, Marshall & Co.

Uned Iaith Genedlaethol Cymru. (1978). *Cyflwyno'r Iaith Lenyddol*. Y Bontfaen: D. Brown a'i Feibion.

Upton, C. & J. D. A. Widdowson. (1996). *An Atlas of English Dialects*. Oxford: Oxford University Press.

Ureland, P. & G. Broderick (eds.) (1991). *Language Contact in the British Isles. Proceedings of the Eighth International Symposium on Language Contact in Europe*. Tübingen: Niemeyer.

Uttley, J. (1966). *The Story of the Channel Islands*. London: Faber and Faber.

Vallancey, C. (1788). Memoir of the language, manners, and customs of an Anglo-Saxon colony settled in the baronies of Forth and Bargie, in the County of Wexford, Ireland, in 1167, 1168, 1169. *Transactions of the Royal Irish Academy* 2: 19–41.

Van den Eynden, N. (1996). Aspects of preposition placement in English. In J. Klemola, M. Kytö & M. Rissanen (eds.) *Speech Past and Present: Studies in English Dialectology in Memory of Ossi Ihalainen*. Frankfurt: Peter Lang. 426–46.

Van den Eynden Morpeth, N. (2002). Relativisers in the southwest of England. In P. Poussa (ed.) *Relativisation on the North Sea Littoral*. Munich: Lincom Europa. 181–94.

Vasko, A.-L. (2005). *Up Cambridge: Prepositional Locative Expressions in Dialect Speech: A Corpus-based Study of the Cambridgeshire Dialect*. Helsinki: Société Néophilologique.

Vennemann gen. Nierfeld, T. (2000). English as a 'Celtic' language. In H. Tristram (ed.) *Celtic Englishes II: Proceedings of the Second Potsdam Colloquium on Celtic Englishes, 28–30 September 1995*. Heidelberg: Winter. 399–406.

Verma, M. (1991). The Hindi speech community. In S. Alladina & V. Edwards (eds.) *Multilingualism in the British Isles, volume 2: Africa, the Middle East and Asia*. London: Longman. 103–14.

Verma, M., K. Corrigan & S. Firth, (eds.) (1995). *Working with Bilingual Children*. Clevedon: Multilingual Matters.

(2000). Minority children's heritage language: planning for non-preservation? In P. Wynn Thomas & J. Mathias (eds.) *Developing Minority Languages: Proceedings of the 5th International Conference on Minority Languages*. Llandysul: Gwasg Gomer. 506–28.

Verma, M., A. Mukherjee, A. Khanna & R. K. Agnihotri. (2001). The Sylhetis in Leeds: an attempt at a sociolinguistic profile. *The Journal of Social Issues* 91: 38–58.

Viereck, W. (1985). On the interrelationship of British and American English: morphological evidence. In W. Viereck (ed.) *Focus on: England and Wales*. Amsterdam: John Benjamins. 247–300.

(1988). The Channel Islands: an anglicist's no man's land. In J. Klegraf and D. Nehls (eds.) *Essays on the English Language and Applied Linguistics on the Occasion of Gerhard Nickel's 60th Birthday*. Heidelberg: Julius Groos Verlag. 468–78.

(1997). On negation in dialectal English. In R. Hickey & S. Puppel (eds.) *Language History and Linguistic Modelling: A Festschrift for Jacek Fisiak on his 60th Birthday, Volume II: Linguistic Modelling*. Berlin: Mouton de Gruyter. 759–67.

Vivian, L. (2000). /r/ in Accrington: an analysis of rhoticity and hyperdialectal /r/ in East Lancashire. Unpublished BA dissertation. Colchester: University of Essex.

Wagner, H. (1959). *Das Verbum in den Sprachen der britischen Inseln*. Tübingen: Niemeyer.

Wagner, S. (2003). *Gender in English pronouns: myth and reality*. Unpublished PhD dissertation. Freiburg: Albert-Ludwigs-Universität.

(2004). English dialects in the Southwest: morphology and syntax. In B. Kortmann, K. Burridge, R. Mesthrie, E. Schneider & C. Upton (eds.) *A Handbook of Varieties of English: Morphology and Syntax*. Berlin: Mouton de Gruyter. 154–74.

(2005). Gender in English pronouns: Southwest England. In B. Kortmann, T. Herrmann, L. Pietsch & S. Wagner (eds.) *A Comparative Grammar of English Dialects: Agreement, Gender, Relative Clauses*. Berlin: Mouton de Gruyter. 211–367.

Wakelin, M. F. (1972). *English Dialects: An Introduction (revised edition)*. London: Athlone.

(1986). *The Southwest of England*. Amsterdam: John Benjamins.

Walker, J. (1791). *A Critical Pronouncing Dictionary and Expositor of the English Language*. London.

Wall, R. (1995). *A Dictionary and Glossary for the Irish Literary Revival*. Gerrards Cross: Colin Smythe.

Walsh, J. J. (1926). Shakespeare's pronunciation of the Irish brogue. In J. Walsh (ed.) *The World's Debt to the Irish*. Boston: The Stratford Company. 297–327.

Walters, J. R. (1999). *A study of the segmental and suprasegmental phonology of Rhondda Valleys*. Unpublished PhD dissertation. Pontypridd: University of Glamorgan.

(2003). Celtic English: influences on a South Wales valleys accent. *English World-Wide* 24 (1): 63–87.

Wang, W. (1969). Competing changes as a cause of residue. *Language* 45: 9–25.

Wardhaugh, R. (1999). *Proper English. Myths and Misunderstandings about Language*. Oxford: Blackwell.

Warren, P. & D. Britain. (1999). Intonation and prosody in New Zealand English. In A. Bell & K. Kuiper (eds.) *New Zealand English*. Amsterdam: John Benjamins. 146–72.

Watkins, T. A. (1993). Welsh. In M. Ball (ed.) *The Celtic Languages*. London: Routledge. 289–348.

Watson, J. (1809). *Instruction of the Deaf and Dumb*. London: Darton and Harvey.

Watson, J. L. (1975). *Emigration and the Chinese Lineage: The Mans in Hong Kong and London*. Berkeley: University of California Press.

(1977). The Chinese: Hong Kong villagers in the British catering trade. In J. L. Watson (ed.) *Between Two Cultures: Migrants and Minorities in Britain*. Oxford: Blackwell. 181–213.

Watson, K. (2002). The realisation of final /t/ in Liverpool English. *Durham Working Papers in Linguistics* 8: 195–205.

Watson, M. & R. McGregor. (1999). *Asylum Statistics United Kingdom 1998*. London: Home Office.

Watson, W. J. (1926). *The History of the Celtic Place-names of Scotland*. Edinburgh and London: Blackwood.

Watt, D. (2000). Phonetic parallels between the close-mid vowels of Tyneside English: Are they internally or externally motivated? *Language Variation and Change* 12: 69–101.

(2002). 'I don't speak with a Geordie accent, I speak, like, the Northern accent': contact-induced levelling in the Tyneside vowel system. *Journal of Sociolinguistics* 6: 44–63.

Watt, D. & C. Ingham. (2000). Durational evidence of the Scottish Vowel Length Rule in Berwick English. *Leeds Working Papers in Linguistics and Phonetics* 8: 205–28.

Watt, D. & L. Milroy. (1999). Patterns of variation and change in three Tyneside vowels: Is this dialect levelling? In P. Foulkes & G. J. Docherty (eds.) *Urban Voices*. London: Arnold. 25–46.

Watt, D. & J. Tillotson. (2001). A spectrographic analysis of vowel fronting in Bradford English. *English World-Wide* 21: 269–302.

Watts, E. (2006). *Mobility-induced dialect contact: a sociolinguistic investigation of speech variation in Wilmslow, Cheshire*. Unpublished PhD dissertation. Colchester: University of Essex.

Wells, J. (1973). *Jamaican Pronunciation in London*. Oxford: Blackwell.

    (1982). *Accents of English (3 Volumes)*. Cambridge: Cambridge University Press.

    (1994a). Transcribing Estuary English: a discussion document. *Speech Hearing and Language: UCL Work in Progress* 8: 259–67.

    (1994b). *Recommendations for standardized phonetics of Estuary English*. Notes from a lecture given in Heidelberg, November 1994 (http://www. phon.ucl. ac.uk/home/estuary/estu-rec.htm).

    (1995). Age grading in English pronunciation preferences. *Proceedings of the 13th International Congress of Phonetic Sciences* 3: 696–9.

    (1997). Whatever happened to Received Pronunciation? In C. Medina Casado & C. Soto Palomo (eds.) *II Jornadas de Estudios Ingleses*. Jaén: University of Jaén. 19–28.

Weston, W. J. (n.d.). *A Refresher Course in English*. London: George Newnes.

Wigger, A. (1972). Preliminaries to a generative morphology of the modern Irish verb. *Ériu* 23: 162–213.

Wilcox, S. (1989). *American Deaf Culture*. Silver Spring, MD: Linstok Press.

Wilding, J. (1981). *Ethnic Minority Languages in the Classroom? A Survey of Asian Parents in Leicester*. Leicester: Leicester Council for Community Relations.

Williams, A. (1989). *The influence of a non-standard dialect on children's school writing*. Unpublished PhD dissertation. London: Birkbeck College.

    (1994a). Talk written down: the sociolinguistics of school writing. In S. Cmejrkova & F. Danes (eds.) *Writing vs Speaking*. Tübingen: Gunter Narr Verlag. 283–92.

    (1994b). Writing in Reading: syntactic variation in children's school writing. In G. Melchers & N. Johannesson (eds.) *Non-standard Varieties of Language*. Stockholm: Almqvist & Wiksell. 206–19.

Williams, A. & P. Kerswill. (1999). Dialect levelling: change and continuity in Milton Keynes, Reading & Hull. In P. Foulkes & G. Docherty (eds.) *Urban Voices*. London: Arnold. 141–62.

Williams, B. (1985). Pitch and duration in Welsh stress perception: the implications for intonation. *Journal of Phonetics* 13: 381–406.

Williams, G. & D. Morris. (2000). *Language Planning and Language Use: Welsh in a Global Age*. Cardiff: University of Wales Press.

Williams, M. (2000). The pragmatics of predicate fronting in Welsh English. In H. L. C. Tristram (ed.) *The Celtic Englishes II*. Heidelberg: C. Winter. 210–30.

Williams, N. J. A. (1994). An Mhanainnis. In K. R. McCone, D. McManus, C. Ó Háinle, N. Willams & L. Breatnach (eds.) *Stair na Gaeilge in ómós do Pádraig Ó Fiannachta*. Maynooth: Department of Old and Middle Irish, St Patrick's College. 703–44.

Williams, S. (1980). *A Welsh Grammar*. Cardiff: University of Wales Press.

Williamson, J. & F. Hardman. (1997a). To purify the dialect of the tribe: children's use of non-standard dialect grammar. *Educational Studies* 23 (2): 157–68.

 (1997b). Those terrible marks of the beast: non-standard dialect and children's writing. *Language and Education* 11: 287–99.

Willis, L. (1999). *Bilingualism in African-Caribbean young people in Sheffield: a micro-level study of bilingual interaction in friendship groups*. Unpublished PhD dissertation. Sheffield: University of Sheffield.

Wilson, J. & A. Henry. (1998). Parameter setting within a socially realistic linguistics. *Language in Society* 27: 1–21.

Wilson, R. T. Kenny, J. Clark, D. Moseley, L. Newton, D. Newton & I. Purves. (1997). *PILs Project Report: Ensuring the Readability, Understandability and Efficacy of the Phase 2 Prodigy Non-Drug Advice Leaflets*. Newcastle: The Sowerby Centre for Health Informatics, University of Newcastle.

Withers, C. W. J. (1984). *Gaelic in Scotland 1698–1981: The Geographical History of a Language*. Edinburgh: John Donald.

 (1988a). The geographical history of Gaelic in Scotland. In C. Williams (ed.) *Language in Geographical Context*. Clevedon: Multilingual Matters. 136–66.

 (1988b). *Gaelic Scotland – The Transformation of a Culture Region*. London: Routledge.

 (1991). An essay in historical geolinguistics: Gaelic speaking in urban Lowland Scotland in 1891. In C. H. Williams (ed.) *Linguistic Minorities, Society and Territory*. Clevedon: Multilingual Matters. 150–72.

Wolfram, W. & N. Schilling-Estes. (2003). Parallel development and alternative restructuring: the case of *weren't* intensification. In D. Britain and J. Cheshire (eds.) *Social Dialectology: In Honour of Peter Trudgill*. Amsterdam: John Benjamins. 131–54.

Woll, B. (1991). *Variation and Change in British Sign Language*. Swindon: Final report to the Economic and Social Research Council.

 (2001). Exploring language, culture and identity: insights from sign language and the deaf community. In J. Cotterill & I. Ife (eds.) *Language across Boundaries*: London: British Association for Applied Linguistics, in association with Continuum. 65–80.

Woll, B. & L. Lawson. (1982, revised edition 1990). British Sign Language. In E. Haugen, J. D. McClure & D. Thomson (eds.) *Minority Languages Today*. Edinburgh: Edinburgh University Press. 218–34.

Wong, L. Y. -F. (1992). *Education of Chinese Children in Britain and the USA*. Clevedon: Multilingual Matters.

Wood, D. (1960). A general survey. In J. Griffith, J. Henderson & D. Wood (eds.) *Coloured Immigrants in Britain*. Oxford: Institute of Race Relations & Oxford University Press.

Wright, F. J. (1984). *A sociolinguistic study of passivization amongst black adolescents in Britain*. Unpublished PhD dissertation. Birmingham: University of Birmingham.

Wright, J. (1905). *The English Dialect Grammar*. Oxford: Henry Frowde.

Wright, L. (1996). *Sources of London English*. Oxford: Clarendon Press.

Wright, S. (1989). The effects of style and speaking rate on /l/-vocalisation in local Cambridge English. *York Papers in Linguistics* 13: 355–65.

Wyld, H. C. (1934). The best English. *Proceedings of the Society for Pure English* 4 (Tract 39): 603–21.

(1936). *History of Modern Colloquial English (3rd edn)*. Oxford: Blackwell.

Young, C. N. (1973). *Belize creole: a study of the creolized English spoken in the city of Belize in its cultural and social setting*. Unpublished PhD dissertation. York: University of York.

Zai, R. (1942). *The Phonology of the Morebattle Dialect*. Lucerne: Raeber.

Zhang, Z., S. Boyce, C. Espy-Wilson & M. Tiede. (2003). Acoustic strategies for production of American English 'retroflex' /r/. In M. Solé, R. Recasens & J. Romero (eds.) *Proceedings of the 15th International Congress of Phonetic Sciences*. Barcelona: Universitat Autònoma de Barcelona. 1125–8.

Zimmer, S. (1990). *Handbuch des Mittelkornischen*. Innsbruck: Institut für Sprachwissenchaft der Universität Innsbruck.

Index

Abercrave 163
Aberdeen 106
ablaut 11
accent 38–42
accommodation 18, 54, 411
Accrington (*see also* north-west of
  England) 65
acoustic analysis 60–1
Acton, Thomas 371, 373
adjectives 12, 26, 202, 222, 241, 348, 408
adolescence 56–7
adult literacy and Basic Skills Unit 386
adverbs 43, 78, 93–5, 202, 241
affricates (*see also* consonants) 238
African American Vernacular English
  (AAVE) 79
age 56–7
Agnihotri, Rama 301
ain't (*see also* negation) 78, 84–5
Aitken/Johnston vowel class system (*see also*
  lexical sets (John Wells)) 113–17
Aitken's Law (*see* Scottish Vowel Length
  Rule)
Albanian 261, 266
Ali G 292
American Sign Language (ASL) 355
Anderwald, Lieselotte 83, 84, 85, 90
Anglicisation 137, 152, 153, 170, 189, 249,
  250, 358, 361–2
Anglo-Norman 18, 135, 137
Angloromani (*see also* Romanichal) 3, 267,
  368–74
Anglo-Saxon 9, 10, 30, 32, 257
approximants (*see also* consonants) 60, 238
Arabic 265, 266, 268, 335
Armagh 128, 130–1, 132
articles, definite and indefinite 26, 62, 103–4,
  119, 179, 240
aspiration 203, 243
asylum 261, 265, 267, 271, 273, 275, 326, 394,
  400, 417, 420, 424
audience design 58

auxiliaries (*see also* verbs) 83, 145, 147,
  148, 247
Awbery, Gwen 239
Ayto, John 45

Baker, Phillip 264, 294, 295, 421
Bakker, Peter 372
Ball, Martin 239, 240, 242, 243, 245
Bangla (*see* Bengali/Sylheti)
Bangladesh (*see also* Bengali/Sylheti) 261,
  262, 263, 266, 270, 271, 293, 294, 331
Beal, Joan 83, 89, 96, 100, 101
Bedford 280, 299
Belfast 123, 126, 127, 131, 132, 133–4, 142
Bengali/Sylheti 264, 265, 266, 269, 271,
  272, 293, 294, 295, 296, 297, 299,
  304–5, 427
Bernstein, Basil 431–2
Berwick 59, 68, 84
Better English Campaign 388–9, 392
bilingual education 201, 206, 213, 225, 231,
  232, 251, 298, 419, 430
Birmingham (*see also* Midlands;
  Sandwell) 72, 280, 296, 297, 301, 305,
  313, 379
Blackburn (*see also* north-west of England)
  65, 271, 296
Blackledge, Adrian 305
Blair, Tony (*see* Labour Government
  1997–2007)
Bliss, Alan 137, 139
Blunkett, David 394
Bolton (*see also* north-west of England) 65,
  77, 95
Borde, Andrew 368
Boretzky, Norbert 371
borrowing 14, 19, 29–32, 141, 188, 196,
  203, 223, 338, 341, 346, 355, 356, 362,
  380, 389
Bradford 60, 62, 65, 68, 70, 280,
  296, 297, 304
braille 267